MCSA 70-410 Cert Guide: Installing and Configuring Windows Server 2012 R2

Don Poulton
David Camardella

800 East 96th Street
Indianapolis, Indiana 46240 USA

MCSA 70-410 Cert Guide:
Installing and Configuring Windows Server 2012 R2

Don Poulton

David Camardella

ISBN-13: 978-0-7897-4880-5

ISBN-10: 0-7897-4880-0

Library of Congress Control Number: 2014944428

Printed in the United States of America

Fifth Printing: September 2015

Trademarks

All terms mentioned in this book that are known to be trademarks or service marks have been appropriately capitalized. Pearson IT Certification cannot attest to the accuracy of this information. Use of a term in this book should not be regarded as affecting the validity of any trademark or service mark.

Warning and Disclaimer

Every effort has been made to make this book as complete and as accurate as possible, but no warranty or fitness is implied. The information provided is on an "as is" basis. The authors and the publisher shall have neither liability nor responsibility to any person or entity with respect to any loss or damages arising from the information contained in this book or from the use of the CD or programs accompanying it.

Special Sales

For information about buying this title in bulk quantities, or for special sales opportunities (which may include electronic versions; custom cover designs; and content particular to your business, training goals, marketing focus, or branding interests), please contact our corporate sales department at corpsales@pearsoned.com or (800) 382-3419.

For government sales inquiries, please contact governmentsales@pearsoned.com.

For questions about sales outside the U.S., please contact international@pearsoned.com.m

Associate Publisher
Dave Dusthimer

Acquisitions Editor
Betsy Brown

Development Editors
Christopher Cleveland,
Ellie Bru

Managing Editor
Sandra Schroeder

Project Editor
Seth Kerney

Copy Editor
Megan Wade-Taxter

Indexer
Cheryl Lenser

Proofreader
Jess DeGabriele

Technical Editor
Chris Crayton

Editorial Assistant
Vanessa Evans

Multimedia Developer
Lisa Matthews

Book Designer
Gary Adair

Page Layout
Bumpy Design

Contents at a Glance

Table of Contents

About the Authors

Don Poulton (A+, Network+, Security+, MCSA, MCSE) is an independent consultant who has been involved with computers since the days of 80-column punch cards. After more than 20 years in environmental science, Don switched careers and trained as a Windows NT 4.0 MCSE. He has been involved in consulting with a couple of small training providers as a technical writer, during which time he wrote training and exam prep materials for Windows NT 4.0, Windows 2000, and Windows XP. Don has written or contributed to several titles, including *Security+ Lab Manual* (Que, 2004); *MCSA/MCSE 70-299 Exam Cram 2: Implementing and Administering Security in a Windows 2003 Network* (Exam Cram 2) (Que, 2004); *MCSE 70-294 Exam Prep: Planning, Implementing, and Maintaining a Microsoft Windows Server 2003 Active Directory Infrastructure* (Que, 2006); *MCTS 70-620 Exam Prep: Microsoft Windows Vista, Configuring* (Que, 2008); *MCTS 70-680 Cert Guide: Microsoft Windows 7, Configuring* (Que, 2011); *MCTS 70-640 Cert Guide: Windows Server 2008 Active Directory, Configuring* (Que, 2011); *MCTS 70-642 Cert Guide: Windows Server 2008 Network Infrastructure, Configuring* (Que, 2012); and *MCSA 70-687 Cert Guide: Configuring Microsoft Windows 8.1* (Que, 2014).

In addition, he has worked on programming projects, both in his days as an environmental scientist and more recently with Visual Basic to update an older statistical package used for multivariate analysis of sediment contaminants.

When not working on computers, Don is an avid amateur photographer who has had his photos displayed in international competitions and published in magazines such as *Michigan Natural Resources Magazine* and *National Geographic Traveler*. Don also enjoys traveling and keeping fit.

Don lives in Burlington, Ontario, with his wife, Terry.

David G. Camardella has more than 14 years of experience as a systems architect, network engineer, and IT manager. Throughout his career, David has used his technical and leadership skills to successfully support infrastructures from small to large organizations.

David's experience includes managing a North American datacenter, branch office server rooms, LAN/WLAN/WAN infrastructures, Active Directory/Messaging infrastructures, private clouds, and client computing systems.

Over the years, David has performed technical editing for several Microsoft and Cisco books. He holds a bachelor of science in business management as well as several levels of IT certifications, including MCSE.

In his spare time, David enjoys spending time with his family and engaging in outdoor activities and home brewing.

Dedication

I would like to dedicate this book to my wife Terry, who has stood by my side and encouraged me throughout the days spent writing this book. This project would not have been possible without her love and support.
—Don Poulton

I would like to dedicate this book to my family. I give thanks to my parents for instilling core values in me, to my wife for her continued love and support, and to my children who inspire me to succeed.
—Dave Camardella

Acknowledgments

I would like to thank all the staff at Pearson IT Certification and in particular Betsy Brown for making this project possible. My sincere thanks goes out to Chris Crayton for his helpful technical suggestions, as well as development editors Chris Cleveland and Ellie Bru for their improvements to the manuscript. Thanks especially to Dave Camardella for his contributions, without which this entire project would never have been possible. Thank you all.

—Don Poulton

I want to send a special thanks to Betsy Brown for providing me with the opportunity to write for Pearson IT Certification. I would also like to thank Don Poulton for guiding me through this journey. Additional thanks goes out to Chris Crayton for his technical feedback, Chris Cleveland, and all of the Pearson IT Certification staff for your guidance, feedback, and suggestions. Thank you.

—Dave Camardella

We Want to Hear from You!

As the reader of this book, *you* are our most important critic and commentator. We value your opinion and want to know what we're doing right, what we could do better, what areas you'd like to see us publish in, and any other words of wisdom you're willing to pass our way.

We welcome your comments. You can email or write to let us know what you did or didn't like about this book—as well as what we can do to make our books better.

Please note that we cannot help you with technical problems related to the topic of this book.

When you write, please be sure to include this book's title and authors as well as your name, email address, and phone number. We will carefully review your comments and share them with the authors and editors who worked on the book.

Email: feedback@pearsonitcertification.com

Mail: ATTN: Reader Feedback
            Pearson IT Certification
            800 East 96th Street
            Indianapolis, IN 46240 USA

Reader Services

Visit our website and register this book at www.pearsonitcertification.com/register for convenient access to any updates, downloads, or errata that might be available for this book.

Introduction

The *MCSA Installing and Configuring Windows Server 2012 Cert Guide* (Exam 70-410) is designed for individuals responsible for designing, implementing, configuring, or administering Windows Desktop/Server infrastructures. The *Cert Guide* contains materials needed to install and configure Windows Server 2012 R2. It is structured to prepare those pursuing the Microsoft Certified Solutions Associate (MCSA) or Microsoft Certified Solutions Expert (MCSE) certification for Windows Server 2012 R2.

This book covers the "Installing and Configuring Windows Server 2012" exam (70-410), the first of three exams under the MCSA certification track. For those working toward the MCSE certification, the 70-410 exam is the first of five exams required. The exam is designed to measure your skill and ability to install and configure Windows Server 2012 R2, roles and features, Hyper-V, Active Directory, Group Policy, DNS, and other core network services. Microsoft not only tests you on your knowledge of the server operating system, but also has purposefully developed questions on the exam that force you to solve problems in the same way you would when presented with scenarios or issues supporting an organization. Passing this exam demonstrates your competency to install and configure all editions of Windows Server 2012 R2.

This book covers all the objectives that Microsoft has established for exam 70-410. It doesn't offer end-to-end coverage of the Windows Server 2012 R2 operating system; rather, it helps you develop the specific core competencies you need to master as an administrator or engineer.

Goals and Methods

The number-one goal of this book is a simple one: to help you pass the 70-410 Certification Exam and thereby earn the first requirement toward the MCSA or MCSE certification. Because Microsoft certification exams stress problem-solving abilities and reasoning more than memorization of terms and facts, our goal is to help you master and understand the required objectives for the 70-410 exam.

To aid you in mastering and understanding the MCTS certification objectives, this book uses the following methods:

- **Opening Topics List:** This defines the topics to be covered in the chapter.
- **Do I Know This Already? Quizzes:** At the beginning of each chapter is a quiz. The quizzes, and answers/explanations (found in Appendix A), are meant to gauge your knowledge of the subjects. If the answers to the questions don't come readily to you, be sure to read the entire chapter.

- **Foundation Topics:** The heart of the chapter. Explains the topics from a hands-on and a theory-based standpoint. This includes in-depth descriptions, tables, and figures geared to build your knowledge so that you can pass the exam. The chapters are broken down into several topics each.

- **Key Topics:** The key topics indicate important figures, tables, and lists of information that you should know for the exam. They are interspersed throughout the chapter and are listed in table form at the end of the chapter.

- **Memory Tables:** These can be found on the CD-ROM within Appendix B, "Memory Tables." Use them to help memorize important information.

- **Key Terms:** Key terms without definitions are listed at the end of each chapter. Write down the definition of each term and check your work against the complete key terms in the glossary.

Study and Exam Preparation Tips

It's a rush of adrenaline during the final day before an exam. If you've scheduled the exam on a workday, or following a workday, you will find yourself cursing the tasks you normally cheerfully perform because the back of your mind is telling you to read just a bit more, study another scenario, practice another skill so that you will be able to get this exam out of the way successfully.

Learning Styles

To best understand the nature of preparation for the test, it is important to understand learning as a process. You are probably aware of how you best learn new material. You might find that outlining works best for you, or, as a visual learner, you might need to "see" things. Or, as a person who studies kinesthetically, the hands-on approach serves you best. Whether you might need models or examples, or maybe you just like exploring the interface, or whatever your learning style, solid test preparation works best when it takes place over time. Obviously, you shouldn't start studying for a certification exam the night before you take it; it is very important to understand that learning is a developmental process. Understanding learning as a process helps you focus on what you know and what you have yet to learn.

People study in a combination of different ways: by doing, by seeing, and by hearing and writing. This book's design fulfills all three of these study methods. For the kinesthetic, there are key topics scattered throughout each chapter. You will also discover step-by-step procedural instructions that walk you through the skills you need to master in Windows Server 2012 R2. The visual learner can find plenty of screen shots explaining the concepts described in the text. The auditory learner can reinforce skills by reading out loud and copying down key concepts and exam tips scattered throughout the book. You can also practice writing down the meaning of the key terms defined in each chapter, and in completing the memory tables for most chapters found on the accompanying CD-ROM. While reading this book, you will realize that it stands the test of time. You will be able to turn to it over and over again.

Thinking about how you learn should help you recognize that learning takes place when you are able to match new information to old. You have some previous experience with computers and networking. Now you are preparing for this certification exam. Using this book, software, and supplementary materials will not just add incrementally to what you know; as you study, the organization of your knowledge actually restructures as you integrate new information into your existing knowledge base. This leads you to a more comprehensive understanding of the tasks and concepts outlined in the objectives and of computing in general. Again, this happens as a result of a repetitive process rather than a singular event. If you keep this model of learning in mind as you prepare for the exam, you will make better decisions concerning what to study and how much more studying you need to do.

Study Tips

There are many ways to approach studying, just as there are many different types of material to study. However, the tips that follow should work well for the type of material covered on Microsoft certification exams.

Study Strategies

Although individuals vary in the ways they learn information, some basic principles of learning apply to everyone. You should adopt some study strategies that take advantage of these principles. One of these principles is that learning can be broken into various depths. Recognition (of terms, for example) exemplifies a rather surface level of learning in which you rely on a prompt of some sort to elicit recall. Comprehension or understanding (of the concepts behind the terms, for example) represents a deeper level of learning than recognition. The ability to analyze a concept and apply your understanding of it in a new way represents further depth of learning.

Your learning strategy should enable you to know the material at a level or two deeper than mere recognition. This will help you perform well on the exams. You will know the material so thoroughly that you can go beyond the recognition-level types of questions commonly used in fact-based multiple-choice testing. You will be able to apply your knowledge to solve new problems.

Macro and Micro Study Strategies

One strategy that can lead to deep learning includes preparing an outline that covers all the objectives and subobjectives for the particular exam you are planning to take. You should delve a bit further into the material and include a level or two of detail beyond the stated objectives and subobjectives for the exam. Then you should expand the outline by coming up with a statement of definition or a summary for each point in the outline.

An outline provides two approaches to studying. First, you can study the outline by focusing on the organization of the material. You can work your way through the points and subpoints of your outline, with the goal of learning how they relate to one another. For example, you should be sure you understand how each of the main objective areas for Exam 70-410 is similar to and different from one another. Then you should do the same thing with the subobjectives; you should be sure you know which subobjectives pertain to each objective area and how they relate to one another.

Next, you can work through the outline, focusing on learning the details. You should memorize and understand terms and their definitions, facts, rules and tactics, advantages and disadvantages, and so on. In this pass through the outline, you should attempt to learn detail rather than the big picture (that is, the organizational information that you worked on in the first pass through the outline).

Research has shown that attempting to assimilate both types of information at the same time interferes with the overall learning process. If you separate your studying into these two approaches, you will perform better on the exam.

Active Study Strategies

The process of writing down and defining objectives, subobjectives, terms, facts, and definitions promotes a more active learning strategy than merely reading the material does. In human information-processing terms, writing forces you to engage in more active encoding of the information. Simply reading over the information leads to more passive processing. Using this study strategy, you should focus on writing down the items highlighted in the book: bulleted or numbered lists, key topics, notes, cautions, and review sections, for example.

You need to determine whether you can apply the information you have learned by attempting to create examples and scenarios on your own. You should think about how or where you could apply the concepts you are learning. Again, you should write down this information to process the facts and concepts in an active fashion.

Best Practice Strategies

You should follow best practices when studying: You should study when you are alert, reduce or eliminate distractions, and take breaks when you become fatigued.

Pretesting Yourself

Pretesting enables you to assess how well you are learning. One of the most important aspects of learning is what has been called *meta-learning*. Meta-learning has to do with realizing when you know something well or when you need to study some more. In other words, you recognize how well or how poorly you have learned the material you are studying.

For most people, this can be difficult to assess. Memory tables, practice questions, and practice tests are useful in that they reveal objectively what you have learned and what you have not learned. You should use this information to guide review and further studying. Developmental learning takes place as you cycle through studying, assessing how well you have learned, reviewing, and assessing again until you feel you are ready to take the exam.

You might have noticed the practice exam included in this book. You should use it as part of the learning process. The Pearson IT Certification Practice Exam test-simulation software included on this book's CD-ROM also provides you with an excellent opportunity to assess your knowledge.

You should set a goal for your pretesting. A reasonable goal would be to score consistently in the 90% range.

Exam Prep Tips

After you have mastered the subject matter, the final preparatory step is to understand how the exam will be presented. Make no mistake: A Microsoft Certified Solutions Associate (MCSA) or Microsoft Certified Solutions Expert (MCSE) exam challenges both your knowledge and your test-taking skills. Preparing for the 70-410 exam is a bit different from preparing for those old Microsoft exams. The following is a list of things that you should consider doing:

- **Combine Your Skill Sets into Solutions:** In the past, exams would test whether you knew to select the right letter of a multiple-choice answer. Today, you need to know how to resolve a problem that might involve different aspects of the material covered. For example, on exam 70-410, you could be presented with a problem that requires you to understand how to install and configure the Hyper-V role, as well as identify symptoms caused by improperly configured virtual machine settings. Being able to zero in on what caused the problem and then resolve it for a specific situation is what you need to demonstrate. In fact, you should not only be able to select one answer, but also multiple parts of a total solution.

- **Delve into Excruciating Details:** The exam questions incorporate a great deal of information in the scenarios. Some of the information is ancillary: It will help you rule out possible issues, but not necessarily resolve the answer. Some of the information simply provides you with a greater picture, as you would have in real life. Some information is key to your solution.

- **TCP/IP Troubleshooting Is Built Right In:** Because TCP/IP is a core technology to the Windows 2012 R2 operating system, you are expected to know the fundamentals of Subnetting, DHCP, how to recognize IP conflicts, and how to use the TCP/IP tools to troubleshoot the problem. Furthermore, Microsoft expects you to know how to work with the new version 6 of TCP/IP along with the traditional version 4 that has been used for many years. You should also be able to discern between an IP problem and something wrong with the OS or hardware, or even some combination that involves IP along with some other element.

- **It's a GUI Test:** You should be able to recognize each dialog box, properties sheet, options, and defaults. You will be tested on recognizing specific configurations given a dialog box or screenshot of one or more consoles or MMC snap-ins. Be prepared to be presented with scenario-based questions that you must answer given an image or dialog of an existing configuration. Microsoft may present a multi part solution where multiple answers representing each step must be selected. For example, you could be given a question asking you to configure a storage pool containing the maximum usable storage. You could be presented with an image showing the existing server disk configuration as shown in disk management.

- **Practice with a Time Limit:** The tests have always been time restricted, but it takes more time to read and understand the scenarios now and time is a whole lot tighter. To get used to the time limits, test yourself with a timer. Know how long it takes you to read scenarios and select answers.

Microsoft 70-410 Exam Topics

The following list outlines the 70-410 exam objectives and weight each section carries:

Install and configure servers (15%–20%)

- **Install servers:** Plan for a server installation, plan for server roles, plan for a server upgrade, install Server Core, optimize resource utilization by using Features on Demand, migrate roles from previous versions of Windows Server

- **Configure servers:** Configure Server Core, delegate administration, add and remove features in offline images, deploy roles on remote servers, convert Server Core to/from full GUI, configure services, configure NIC teaming, install and configure Windows PowerShell Desired State Configuration (DSC)

- **Configure local storage:** Design storage spaces, configure basic and dynamic disks, configure master boot record (MBR) and GUID partition table (GPT) disks, manage volumes, create and mount virtual hard disks (VHDs), configure storage pools and disk pools, create storage pools by using disk enclosures

Configure server roles and features (15%–20%)

- **Configure file and share access:** Create and configure shares, configure share permissions, configure offline files, configure NTFS permissions, configure access-based enumeration (ABE), configure Volume Shadow Copy Service (VSS), configure NTFS quotas, create and configure Work Folders

- **Configure print and document services:** Configure the Easy Print print driver, configure Enterprise Print Management, configure drivers, configure printer pooling, configure print priorities, configure printer permissions

- **Configure servers for remote management:** Configure WinRM, configure down-level server management, configure servers for day-to-day management tasks, configure multiserver management, configure Server Core, configure Windows Firewall, manage non-domain joined servers

Configure Hyper-V (15%–20%)

- **Create and configure virtual machine settings:** Configure dynamic memory, configure smart paging, configure Resource Metering, configure guest integration services, create and configure Generation 1 and 2 virtual machines, configure and use enhanced session mode, configure RemoteFX

- **Create and configure virtual machine storage:** Create VHDs and VHDX, configure differencing drives, modify VHDs, configure pass-through disks, manage checkpoints, implement a virtual Fibre Channel adapter, configure storage Quality of Service

- **Create and configure virtual networks:** Configure Hyper-V virtual switches, optimize network performance, configure MAC addresses, configure network isolation, configure synthetic and legacy virtual network adapters, configure NIC teaming in virtual machines

Deploy and configure core network services (15%–20%)

- **Configure IPv4 and IPv6 addressing:** Configure IP address options, configure IPv4 or IPv6 subnetting, configure supernetting, configure interoperability between IPv4 and IPv6, configure Intra-site Automatic Tunnel Addressing Protocol (ISATAP), configure Teredo

- **Deploy and configure Dynamic Host Configuration Protocol (DHCP) service:** Create and configure scopes, configure a DHCP reservation, configure DHCP options, configure client and server for PXE boot, configure DHCP relay agent, authorize DHCP server

- **Deploy and configure DNS service:** Configure Active Directory integration of primary zones, configure forwarders, configure Root Hints, manage DNS cache, create A and PTR resource records

Install and administer Active Directory (15%–20%)

- **Install domain controllers:** Add or remove a domain controller from a domain, upgrade a domain controller, install Active Directory Domain Services (AD DS) on a Server Core installation, install a domain controller from Install from Media (IFM), resolve DNS SRV record registration issues, configure a global catalog server, deploy Active Directory infrastructure as a service (IaaS) in Microsoft Azure

- **Create and manage Active Directory users and computers:** Automate the creation of Active Directory accounts; create, copy, configure, and delete users and computers; configure templates; perform bulk Active Directory operations; configure user rights; offline domain join; manage inactive and disabled accounts

- **Create and manage Active Directory groups and organizational units (OUs):** Configure group nesting; convert groups, including security, distribution, universal, domain local, and domain global; manage group membership using Group Policy; enumerate group membership; delegate the creation and management of Active Directory objects; manage default Active Directory containers; create, copy, configure, and delete groups and OUs

Create and manage Group Policy (15%–20%)

- **Create Group Policy objects (GPOs):** Configure a Central Store, manage starter GPOs, configure GPO links, configure multiple local Group Policies

- **Configure security policies:** Configure User Rights Assignment, configure Security Options settings, configure Security templates, configure Audit Policy, configure Local Users and Groups, configure User Account Control (UAC)

- **Configure application restriction policies:** Configure rule enforcement, configure AppLocker rules, configure Software Restriction Policies
- **Configure Windows Firewall:** Configure rules for multiple profiles using Group Policy; configure connection security rules; configure Windows Firewall to allow or deny applications, scopes, ports, and users; configure authenticated firewall exceptions; import and export settings

Table I-1 lists the book chapters in which each exam topic is covered.

Table I-1 Microsoft 70-410 Exam Topics

Chapter	Title	70-410 Exam Topics Covered	70-410 Exam Topic Details
Chapter 1	Introducing Windows Server 2012 R2	Install servers	Plan for a server installation, plan for server roles, plan for a server upgrade, optimize resource utilization by using Features on Demand, migrate roles from previous versions of Windows Server
		Configure servers	Convert Server Core to/from full GUI
Chapter 2	Installing and Configuring Windows Server 2012 R2	Install servers	Install Server Core
		Configure servers	Configure Server Core, delegate administration, add and remove features in offline images, deploy roles on remote servers, configure services, configure NIC teaming, install and configure Windows PowerShell Desired State Configuration (DSC)
Chapter 3	Configuring Windows Server 2012 R2 Local Storage	Configure local storage	Design storage spaces, configure basic and dynamic disks, configure master boot record (MBR) and GUID partition table (GPT) disks, manage volumes, create and mount virtual hard disks (VHDs), configure storage pools and disk pools, create storage pools by using disk enclosures

Chapter 4	Configuring Access to Files and Shares	Configure file and share access	Create and configure shares, configure share permissions, configure offline files, configure NTFS permissions, configure access-based enumeration (ABE), configure Volume Shadow Copy Service (VSS), configure NTFS quotas, create and configure Work Folders
Chapter 5	Configuring and Monitoring Print and Document Services	Configure print and document services	Configure the Easy Print print driver, configure Enterprise Print Management, configure drivers, configure printer pooling, configure print priorities, configure printer permissions
Chapter 6	Configuring Remote Management of Servers	Configure servers for remote management	Configure WinRM, configure down-level server management, configure servers for day-to-day management tasks, configure multiserver management, configure Server Core, configure Windows Firewall, manage non-domain joined servers
Chapter 7	Configuring Hyper-V	Create and configure virtual machine settings	Configure dynamic memory, configure smart paging, configure Resource Metering, configure guest integration services, create and configure Generation 1 and 2 virtual machines, configure and use enhanced session mode, configure RemoteFX
Chapter 8	Creating and Configuring Virtual Machine Storage	Create and configure virtual machine storage	Create VHDs and VHDX, configure differencing drives, modify VHDs, configure pass-through disks, manage checkpoints, implement a virtual Fibre Channel adapter, configure storage Quality of Service
Chapter 9	Creating and Configuring Virtual Networks	Create and configure virtual networks	Configure Hyper-V virtual switches, optimize network performance, configure MAC addresses, configure network isolation, configure synthetic and legacy virtual network adapters, configure NIC teaming in virtual machines

Chapter 10	Configuring IPv4 and IPv6 Addressing	Configure IPv4 and IPv6 addressing	Configure IP address options, configure IPv4 or IPv6 subnetting, configure supernetting, configure interoperability between IPv4 and IPv6, configure Intra-site Automatic Tunnel Addressing Protocol (ISATAP), configure Teredo
Chapter 11	Configuring Dynamic Host Configuration Protocol (DHCP)	Deploy and configure Dynamic Host Configuration Protocol (DHCP) service	Create and configure scopes, configure a DHCP reservation, configure DHCP options, configure client and server for PXE boot, configure DHCP relay agent, authorize DHCP server
Chapter 12	Deploying and Configuring Domain Name System (DNS)	Deploy and configure DNS service	Configure Active Directory integration of primary zones, configure forwarders, configure Root Hints, manage DNS cache, create A and PTR resource records
Chapter 13	Installing Domain Controllers	Install domain controllers	Add or remove a domain controller from a domain, upgrade a domain controller, install Active Directory Domain Services (AD DS) on a Server Core installation, install a domain controller from Install from Media (IFM), resolve DNS SRV record registration issues, configure a global catalog server, deploy Active Directory infrastructure as a service (IaaS) in Microsoft Azure
Chapter 14	Active Directory User and Computer Accounts	Create and manage Active Directory users and computers	Automate the creation of Active Directory accounts; create, copy, configure, and delete users and computers; configure templates; perform bulk Active Directory operations; configure user rights; offline domain join; manage inactive and disabled accounts

Chapter 15	Active Directory Groups and Organizational Units (OUs)	Create and manage Active Directory groups and organizational units (OUs)	Configure group nesting; convert groups, including security, distribution, universal, domain local, and domain global; manage group membership using Group Policy; enumerate group membership; delegate the creation and management of Active Directory objects; manage default Active Directory containers; create, copy, configure, and delete groups and OUs
Chapter 16	Creating and Applying Group Policy Objects	Create Group Policy objects (GPOs)	Configure a Central Store, manage starter GPOs, configure GPO links, configure multiple local Group Policies
Chapter 17	Configuring Security Policies	Configure security policies	Configure User Rights Assignment, configure Security Options settings, configure Security templates, configure Audit Policy, configure Local Users and Groups, configure User Account Control (UAC)
Chapter 18	Configuring Application Restriction Policies	Configure application restriction policies	Configure rule enforcement, configure AppLocker rules, configure Software Restriction Policies
Chapter 19	Configuring Windows Firewall	Configure Windows Firewall	Configure rules for multiple profiles using Group Policy; configure connection security rules; configure Windows Firewall to allow or deny applications, scopes, ports, and users; configure authenticated firewall exceptions; import and export settings

How This Book Is Organized

Although this book could be read cover-to-cover, it is designed to be flexible and enable you to easily move between chapters and sections of chapters to cover just the material you need more work with. If you do intend to read all the chapters, the order in the book is an excellent sequence to use.

- Chapter 1, "Introducing Windows Server 2012 R2," is an introductory chapter that is designed to ease readers new to Server 2012 R2 into this book.

It provides a broad description of the components of the Windows Server 2012 R2 operating system, including the major items that are new or recently updated and the Windows interface. It provides an overview for those planning to install or upgrade to Windows Server 2012 R2 and introduces Server Roles and Features on Demand.

- Chapter 2, "Installing and Configuring Windows Server 2012 R2," identifies hardware requirements for Windows Server 2012 R2 and covers the process to install Windows Server 2012 R2 using GUI or Server Core options. This chapter also provides you with an overview and the process to delegate administrative activities, configure offline images, configure remote server roles, and configure and manage services and NIC Teaming.

- Chapter 3, "Configuring Windows Server 2012 R2 Local Storage," reviews basic disk fundamentals and advanced disk configurations. It covers the concepts and usage of virtual hard disks and provides a framework for you to identify the appropriate storage strategy for your servers.

- Chapter 4, "Configuring Access to Files and Shares," provides information on how you can share data with computers across the network and most importantly how to control who is able to access and/or modify this data. This chapter provides you with the resources and tools to administer and protect files and folders on your Windows Server 2012 R2 network.

- Chapter 5, "Configuring and Monitoring Print and Document Services," introduces the core components and fundamentals of printing within a Windows Server 2012 R2 environment. It covers the management and troubleshooting of printers and printer drivers as well as the installation, configuration, and sharing of printers.

- Chapter 6, "Configuring Remote Management of Servers," focuses on the various remote access methods, how to use daily management tools, how to prepare your server installations for remote access, and how to leverage Server Manager for management of multiple servers.

- Chapter 7, "Configuring Hyper-V," begins with an introduction to Hyper-V and the new functions available with the release of Windows Server 2012 R2. It continues to describe the processes of creating and configuring virtual machines; managing virtual machine settings; and configuring dynamic memory, smart paging, resource metering, and integration services.

- Chapter 8, "Creating and Configuring Virtual Machine Storage," focuses on the specifics on how to create, configure, and manage virtual machine storage for different scenarios for your Hyper-V infrastructure. It covers the processes to create and configure various types of virtual hard disks and virtual fibre channel adapters and how to create and manage checkpoints.

- Chapter 9, "Creating and Configuring Virtual Networks," provides you with a foundation for Hyper-V network virtualization. It discusses how to configure virtual network adapters, including optimizing virtual network performance, and how to configure virtual MAC addresses and implement network isolation. After reading this chapter, you will have an understanding of the key concepts for creating and configuring virtual networks.

- Chapter 10, "Configuring IPv4 and IPv6 Addressing," discusses versions 4 and 6 of the TCP/IP protocol together with setting up network connections and name resolution. It also discusses network connectivity problems.

- Chapter 11, "Configuring Dynamic Host Configuration Protocol," introduces the concept of DHCP and describes how the four-stage DHCP process works with IPv4. The chapter also describes the important new features of DHCPv6 and provides content on DHCP server configuration and how to leverage DHCP with the PXE boot process.

- Chapter 12, "Deploying and Configuring Domain Name System," provides you with background knowledge by introducing you to the fundamentals under which DNS is built. It then shows you how DNS works to resolve computer names to IP addresses in various situations you might encounter. The chapter continues to describe the process to install and configure DNS servers, server properties, and zones and how to manage resource records.

- Chapter 13, "Installing Domain Controllers," introduces you to the foundations of Active Directory. It provides guidance on how to plan for an Active Directory namespace. It concludes with material on how to create forests and domains; add and remove domain controllers, including the install from media option; and leverage Active Directory services in Windows Azure.

- Chapter 14, "Active Directory User and Computer Accounts," turns its attention to the nuts and bolts of Active Directory that enable all these activities to take place in a controlled manner. It shows you how to create user accounts for all these various employees and manage them in terms of groups. It then takes you through all the account management tasks.

- Chapter 15, "Active Directory Groups and Organizational Units," provides a framework for creating and managing group accounts and organizational units and how to effectively delegate Active Directory object management.

- Chapter 16, "Creating and Applying Group Policy Objects," provides an overview of Group Policy. After reading this chapter, you will be able to create, filter, and apply group policy objects; manage links; and interoperate with local group policies.

- Chapter 17, "Configuring Security Policies," provides you with the fundamentals to configure user rights, security options, and user account control. You will also learn how to leverage the auditing functionality of Active Directory services.

- Chapter 18, "Configuring Application Restriction Policies," discusses the tools that Microsoft provides to limit user access to software programs that can either damage computers and network access or distract users from important work objectives; it is important that you are able to configure these tools to maximize user productivity. This chapter introduces you to rule enforcement and provides you with information to configure software restriction policies and AppLocker rules.

- Chapter 19, "Configuring Windows Firewall," teaches you how to configure the Windows Firewall and how to successfully apply it using basic or advanced configurations.

In addition to these 19 chapters, this book includes tools to help you verify that you are prepared to take the exam. The CD-ROM includes the glossary, practice tests, and memory tables you can work through to verify your knowledge of the subject matter.

This chapter covers the following subjects:

- **What's New in Windows Server 2012:** This section introduces the most significant new and improved features that Microsoft has introduced in Windows Server 2012 and Windows Server 2012 R2.

- **Windows Server 2012 R2 User Interface:** This section describes the major features of the Windows Server 2012 R2 user interface, including the Start screen, charms, and the improved Server Manager utility. It also introduces and compares the user interface installation options available in Windows Server 2012 R2.

- **Planning for Server Installation and Upgrades:** This section outlines strategies for installing Windows Server 2012 R2 and identifies supported upgrade paths.

- **Server Roles and Role Migration:** This section provides an overview of the various roles and new capabilities available within Windows Server 2012 R2. It also outlines the process for migrating roles from previous installations.

- **Features on Demand:** This section describes Microsoft's new concept of features on demand and the ability to add and remove features with ease.

CHAPTER 1

Introducing Windows Server 2012 R2

Ever since the days of Windows NT, Microsoft has introduced new server versions of its flagship Windows operating system in parallel with the popular home and office Windows client computer systems. Microsoft continued this trend by introducing Windows 8 and Windows Server 2012. And in parallel with the introduction of Windows 8.1 in late 2013, Windows Server 2012 R2 is the latest entry into the server computing field. As with previous iterations of Windows Server, Microsoft has brought forth a new series of certification exams; however, Microsoft has departed from the recently used concept of separate exams for networking, Active Directory, applications infrastructure, and so on, replacing this series with a set of five exams that gradually delve into increasingly advanced topics of server administration. The 70-410 exam represents the first of these five exams required of individuals wanting to obtain the new Microsoft Certified Solutions Expert (MCSE) certification in Server Infrastructure. Passing the first three of these exams earns you the Microsoft Certified Solutions Associate (MCSA) certification.

In Windows Server 2012 and Windows Server 2012 R2, Microsoft has taken the capabilities of Windows Server 2008 many steps further, bringing out a server platform tailored to the twenty-first–century datacenter and cloud-based storage systems that many companies are migrating to. Using Windows Server 2012 R2, you can set up file services, applications, and websites in either your local network or on the cloud, all of which function seamlessly to provide users with the data and applications that they need to get their jobs done, all at the right time and place. At the same time, Windows Server 2012 R2 provides the tools you need to manage your network and maintain its security and audit compliance. Not forgotten in this enterprise push are small businesses that need just one or two servers; they can easily take advantage of all the features Windows Server 2012 R2 has to offer.

"Do I Know This Already?" Quiz

The "Do I Know This Already?" quiz enables you to assess whether you should read this entire chapter or simply jump to the "Exam Preparation Tasks" section for review. If you are in doubt, read the entire chapter. Table 1-1 outlines the major headings in this chapter and the corresponding "Do I Know This Already?" quiz questions. You can find the answers in Appendix A, "Answers to the 'Do I Know This Already?' Quizzes."

Table 1-1   "Do I Know This Already?" Foundation Topics Section-to-Question Mapping

Foundations Topics Section	Questions Covered in This Section
What's New in Windows Server 2012	1
Windows Server 2012 R2 User Interface	2–4
Planning for Server Installation and Upgrades	5
Server Roles and Role Migration	6–8
Features on Demand	9–10

1. You are a consultant charged with the responsibility of deploying a computer network to a new dental office. The dentist would like you to install a Windows Server 2012 R2 computer to store data for the office network, which is not expected to grow beyond a maximum of 10 computers including the server. The dentist wants to keep deployment costs as low as possible. Which edition of Windows Server 2012 R2 should you recommend?

   a. Windows Server 2012 R2 Foundation

   b. Windows Server 2012 R2 Essentials

   c. Windows Server 2012 R2 Standard

   d. Windows Server 2012 R2 Datacenter

2. You have been asked by the head manager of a development group to install a Windows Server 2012 R2 computer in his office. This manager would like to have the Windows 8.1 shell and access to the Windows Store available from this computer. Which installation option is required?

   a. Server Core

   b. Minimal Server Interface

   c. Server with a GUI

   d. Desktop Experience

3. You have been working with a Windows 8 Pro computer for several months now and find the charms feature very useful. You are planning to install a Windows Server 2012 R2 computer and would like to use this feature on the server. Which of the following installation options should you select? (Choose all that apply.)

   a. Server Core

   b. Minimal Server Interface

   c. Server with a GUI

   d. Desktop Experience

4. Which of the following actions can you perform by using Server Manager on a Windows Server 2012 R2 computer? (Choose all that apply.)

   a. Add or remove roles, role services, and server features

   b. Create a report that describes any issues on your server and provides recommendations for resolving them

   c. Display a subset of events from the Event Viewer System log and filter these events and perform queries to locate desired events

   d. Display a simple Performance Monitor graph and configure alerts that alert you to unusual performance situations such as high processor usage

   e. Create a server group

5. You are an administrator for your organization. You are currently administering three Server 2003 Standard Edition file servers. You have been tasked with upgrading these servers to Server 2012 R2. How can you accomplish this with the least amount of administrative effort?

   a. Perform a GUI in place upgrade to Server 2012 R2 Standard Edition

   b. Perform clean installations for new servers and use the Windows Server Migration Tools to migrate the shares and data

   c. Perform in place upgrades to Server 2008 Standard then upgrade to Server 2012 R2 Standard

   d. Boot with the Server 2012 R2 installation media and choose the Upgrade option from within the Setup

6. You have just installed a new server and are planning to use it to create, manage, and distribute operating system images. Which role should you install?

  a. Active Directory Domain Services

  b. Windows Fax Services

  c. Windows Imaging Services

  d. Windows Software Update Services

  e. Windows Deployment Services

7. Which of the following roles provides the ability to deliver virtual machines to your organization?

  a. Virtual Server Manager

  b. Hyper-V

  c. Virtual-V

  d. Virtualization Services

8. Which of the following roles enables the creation and management of an Active Directory database?

  a. Active Directory Data Services

  b. Domain Manager

  c. Group Policy

  d. Active Directory Domain Services

9. You have decided to remove a recently installed feature. Which methods can you use to remove this feature? (Choose all that apply.)

  a. Insert the Windows Server installation media and select the option to add/remove features.

  b. Launch Server Manager and click Remove Roles and Features from the manage menu.

  c. Run PowerShell as Administrator and execute the cmdlet to uninstall the appropriate feature.

  d. Launch Server Manager and click Add Roles and Features.

10. What is the command used to remove the feature for graphical management tools and infrastructure?

    a. `Uninstall WindowsFeature -Server Gui -Remove`

    b. `Uninstall-WindowsFeature Server-Gui-Mgmt-Infra -Remove`

    c. `Install -WindowsFeature /R Server-Gui-Mgmt-Infra`

    d. `Install -Remove Gui-Mgmt-Infra`

Foundation Topics

What's New in Windows Server 2012 and Windows Server 2012 R2

As with each previous version of Windows Server, Microsoft has introduced several new components and enhanced many other components to improve the functionality and manageability of Windows Server 2012 and Windows Server 2012 R2. This section briefly summarizes these components, many of which you will learn about later in this book, and others that you will learn about as you progress to the Cert Guides that deal with the other MCSA/MCSE exams on Windows Server 2012. Immediately following this list is a summary of new features specific to Windows Server 2012 R2.

- **New and improved features in Windows PowerShell:** Windows PowerShell 3.0 in Windows Server 2012 provides many new significant features that enable you to use its capabilities in many additional situations. The control and management of Windows-based environments from Windows PowerShell 3.0 is easier and more comprehensive than what was formerly possible in PowerShell 2.0; at the same time, all cmdlets and other capabilities of PowerShell 2.0 work in PowerShell 3.0 without the need for changes. We mention several areas of enhanced PowerShell management within this list.

- **Improved networking capabilities:** Windows Server 2012 enables you to manage the entire network from a single server. You can have the reliability and scalability of multiple servers at a lower cost. Downtime of file services availability is minimized by means of data redundancy and automatic rerouting of traffic around points of failure, so that users can always access required files and folders. For 802.1X authenticated wired and wireless access using the Extensible Authentication Protocol (EAP), support for the new EAP-Tunneled Transport Layer Security (EAP-TTLS) authentication type has been added.

- **Improvements to BranchCache:** BranchCache now copies content from the head office or hosted cloud content servers and caches this content at branch office locations. This enables branch office client computers to access this content locally and reduces the need for connections across the WAN.

- **Improvements to Dynamic Host Configuration Protocol (DHCP):** DHCP in Windows Server 2012 enables you to set up two servers to supply IP addressing information on the same scope for improved availability of DHCP services to client computers. The two servers replicate lease information between them to allow for load balancing and failover capabilities and ensure that duplicate IP addresses are never leased. You can also specify policies that govern IP address assignment and option configuration at the scope level or on a server-wide basis. Improved PowerShell cmdlets are also available for scripted management purposes. Also included is a new technology called IP Address Management (IPAM), which discovers, monitors, audits, manages, and reports on the IP address space used on a corporate network.

- **Improvements to Network Policy and Access Services:** Microsoft has enhanced the role services of Network Policy Server (NPS), Health Registration Authority (HRA), and Host Credential Authorization Protocol (HCAP) role services for remote authentication and authorization of Remote Authentication Dial-In User Service (RADIUS) servers and clients. Also included is the use of PowerShell to automate the installation and configuration of NPS servers.

- **System Center 2012 SP1:** Works with Windows Server 2012 to define a software-based networking solution that connects across cloud implementations of various sizes.

- **Enhanced cloud computing capabilities:** Microsoft has built a platform that it calls "the Cloud OD," which integrates Windows Server 2012 into modern datacenters by providing an infrastructure that goes beyond virtualization to maximize the deliverance of cloud services. Multiple servers can be managed and made continuously available with high levels of efficiency. In addition, Hyper-V network virtualization now employs a policy-based, software-controlled basis, reducing the overhead involved in managing cloud-based server virtualization. Additional new and improved capabilities to Hyper-V are too numerous to mention here; for more information, refer to Chapter 9, "Creating and Configuring Virtual Networks."

- **Integration with new applications:** Users can access every app on any cloud through the flexibility of solutions offered by Windows Server 2012. Users can access data and applications from almost anywhere on various devices; a rich user experience with total security is provided at all times.

- **Virtual Desktop Infrastructure (VDI):** VDI enables users to access data from virtually anywhere on popular mobile devices. Supported devices can provide a rich Windows 8-based desktop experience. At the same time, security of data and compliance requirements are ensured. Microsoft includes three flexible VDI deployment options: Pooled Desktops, Personal Desktops, and Remote Desktop Sessions. Remote Desktop Services provides enhanced support for VDI deployments; Session Virtualization deployments; centralized resource publishing; and a new, enriched user experience for users connecting to the server with Remote Desktop Protocol (RDP).

- **Remote FX:** This is a new set of features that enables you to provide a full, rich computing experience to users across wide-area network (WAN) connections. Included is the detection of end-to-end network bandwidth and techniques that help to circumvent network connection. Users can also connect USB devices such as flash drives and portable hard drives and see their contents within their VDI desktop.

- **User Profile Disk:** A feature that enables a consistent user VDI desktop experience. User productivity is enhanced by the maintenance of personalization and application data access across logons to different devices.

- **Enhanced flexible storage capabilities:** Improved functionality for failover clustering in Windows Server 2012 helps to ensure the continuous availability of data to users on the network. Clusters scale up to as many as 64 nodes and 8,000 virtual machines per cluster, and improvements in cluster shared volumes enhance the security, performance, and availability of data to users on the network.

- **Improvements to Active Directory Domain Services (AD DS):** AD DS in Windows Server 2012 improves support for cloud-based networking with virtualization-safe technologies and the ability to use cloning for deployment of virtual domain controllers. The domain controller installation wizard is integrated with Server Manager and can be scripted using Windows Power-Shell. You can even install AD DS on a remotely located server. Using the Active Directory Administrative Center, you can perform graphical tasks that automatically generate Windows PowerShell commands that you can include in a script for automating repetitive administrative tasks.

- **Improvements to Domain Name System (DNS):** Microsoft has enhanced support for DNS Security Extensions (DNSSEC) to include online signing and automated key management. Improvements to PowerShell cmdlets enhance the configuration and management of your DNS setup.

- **Improvements to Group Policy:** Microsoft has added several new functionalities to Group Policy and improved many others. New to Group Policy are capabilities for remote policy update; display of the status of Active Directory and SYSVOL replication as related to all Group Policy objects (GPOs) or a single GPO; local Group Policy support for new Windows RT devices; new Starter GPOs; and new Group Policy settings and preferences for Internet Explorer 10 and 11. Enhanced functionalities include updated reporting of Group Policy Results reports; improved application of GPOs at startup and shutdown as well as optimization of GPO processing during logons over slow WAN links; a new `Invoke-GPUpdate` PowerShell cmdlet that automates the updating of GPOs applied to remotely located computers; and an increased maximum `Registry.pol` size that enhances the application of Group Policy processing when a GPO contains a large number of Administrative Template settings. In addition, the Group Policy Client service will sleep when the Group Policy service is idle for longer than 10 minutes, providing improved performance for client computers.

- **Improvements to BitLocker:** You can now deploy Windows 8.1 and Windows Server 2012 R2 in an encrypted state during installation. Also new is the option to encrypt only the used space on a disk volume for a much faster encryption. BitLocker enables a standard user to change the BitLocker PIN or password on operating system volumes and data volumes as well as the capability for automatically unlocking the system volume during boot. These features reduce the help desk call volumes for lost PINs.

- **Improvements to File Server Resource Manager (FSRM):** New to FSRM is Dynamic Access Control, which helps you to control and audit access to data on a file server, the capability for manually classifying files and folders without the need to create automatic classification rules, and the capability to customize the `Access denied` error message to Windows 8/8.1 clients attempting to access resources for which the user has no permission. Updates have also been provided for automatic classification of data and file management tasks.

- **Security enhancements:** With improvements in data access that allow users to work from almost anywhere, there comes the need to ensure data security and compliance at all times and places. Microsoft has kept data security up-to-date with centralized security and compliance controls at the infrastructure and application services layers. Included are controls that factor in the roles and locations of users accessing data on the network as well as the use of security measures such as multifactor authentication and data encryption. Introduced in Windows Server 2012 is Dynamic Access Control (DAC), which is a new feature that helps to enhance data security and maintain compliance by factoring in user identity and device security access factors in granting access to data. You can enable users' roaming profiles and redirected folders immediately available when they log on from any device and remove sensitive data availability when they log off. Security auditing has also been enhanced with new expression-based audit policies and the capability to audit new types of securable objects as well as data located on removable storage devices. Additional information, including new audit events, is also now available for the auditing of file and folder access and user logons.

What's New in Windows Server 2012 R2

Microsoft has added or improved the following capabilities in Windows Server 2012 R2:

- **Windows PowerShell improvements:** Windows Server 2012 R2 introduces Windows PowerShell 4.0, which continues to extend the capabilities and functionality of earlier Windows PowerShell versions. In particular, Windows PowerShell Desired State Configuration (DSC) extends the capabilities of managing configuration data for software services and the environments in which they run. Many additional cmdlets and parameters have also been added, as well as scripting capabilities for managing additional server roles such as Windows Deployment Services (WDS).

- **Improved networking technologies:** Windows Server 2012 R2 adds new features and capabilities to 802.1X authenticated wired and wireless access. Other new features and capabilities have also been added to DHCP, DNS, Hyper-V Network Virtualization, Hyper-V Virtual Switch, Internet Protocol Address Management, and Remote Access. New to Windows Server 2012 R2 is Virtual Receive-side Scaling, which enables network adapters to distribute processing load across multiple virtual processors in multicore virtual machines, and Windows Server Gateway, which is a virtual machine-based software router that enhances the capability of routing network traffic among physical and virtual networks regardless of the initial source of the network traffic.

- **Improvements to AD DS:** Microsoft has enabled the integration capabilities with personal devices including smartphones, laptops, and tablets to enhance the availability and security of personal and corporate data. Devices can be associated with AD DS and used as a seamless second factor authentication, including the capacity for single sign-on (SSO) to the domain. New strategies of multifactor authentication and access control enable you to manage the risk of users accessing protected data from their devices and working from any location.

- **Improvements to Group Policy:** Windows Server 2012 R2 adds enhanced support for IPv6 and event logging. Further, a new feature called Policy Caching enables the latest versions of policies to be cached locally after being downloaded from a domain controller. You can control caching behavior by configuring the new Configure Group Policy Caching policy.

- **Improvements to BitLocker:** Support for device encryption has been added for computers with a TPM that supports connected standby.

- **Improvements to Remote Access:** Several new features have been added in Windows Server 2012 R2 and Windows 8.1, including multitenant site-to-site VPN gateway, multitenant remote access VPN gateway, the Web Application Proxy role service, and support for Border Gateway Protocol (BGP). Users of Windows 8.1 machines can create and edit their VPN profiles from the PC settings app.

- **New and improved data storage technologies:** Windows Server 2012 R2 introduces the concept of storage pools, which are groupings of physical disks that form a pool of resources from which you can create a form of storage virtualization. In addition, Windows Server 2012 R2 includes a new Work Folders role service, which enables users to access work data on personal computers and mobile devices.

- **Enhancements to virtual servers and virtual machine storage:** Hyper-V in Windows Server 2012 R2 enables you to create two types of virtual machines: Generation 1 virtual machines are similar to those used in older Hyper-V versions, while Generation 2 virtual machines provide additional features such as secure boot, the ability to boot from a SCSI virtual hard disk or virtual DVD, PXE boot from a standard network adapter, and UEFI firmware support. Storage Quality of Service (QoS) is an enhancement to Hyper-V that provides the ability to set certain QoS parameters for storage on virtual machines. This provides storage performance isolation in a multiuser environment and informs you if certain performance thresholds are not being met.

NOTE   This list is not intended to be exhaustive and introduces only the major new and improved technologies in Windows Server 2012 R2. For more information on improvements in Windows Server 2012 R2, refer to "What's New in Windows Server 2012 R2" and links contained therein at http://technet.microsoft.com/en-us/library/dn250019.aspx. In addition, for a list of older server features and functionalities that have been removed or planned for removal in Windows Server 2012 and Windows Server 2012 R2, refer to "Features Removed or Deprecated in Windows Server 2012 R2" at http://technet.microsoft.com/en-us/library/dn303411.aspx.

NOTE   As this Cert Guide was in the final stages of preparation, Microsoft introduced Windows Server 2012 R2 Update, which is made available to all server
users via Windows Update. As well as a cumulative roll-up of all security updates
and bug fixes, Windows Server 2012 R2 Update provides a series of user enhancements, including the following:

- **Enterprise Mode for Internet Explorer (EMIE):** Improves compatibility
  with server line of business applications.

- **Active Directory fix for Office 365:** Enables users to sign-on using an
  Office 365 email address, and provides a user experience parallel to that of
  Windows 8.1 Update.

- **User interface improvements:** On an installation using the full GUI, a
  search and power button have been added to the Start screen.

Enhancements and improvements introduced with Windows Server 2012 R2
Update are not discussed elsewhere in this Cert Guide. For more information on
Windows Server 2012 R2 Update, refer to "Windows Server 2012 R2 Update
is now available to subscribers" at http://blogs.technet.com/b/windowsserver/
archive/2014/04/02/windows-server-2012-r2-update-is-now-available-to-
subscribers.aspx.

Windows Server 2012 R2 Editions

Windows Server 2012 R2 is available in the following editions:

- **Windows Server 2012 R2 Foundation:** Enables a Windows Server experience for a small office network of up to 15 users. No virtualization rights are
  included. For more information on the capabilities and limitations of Windows Server 2012 Foundation, refer to "Introduction to Windows Server 2012
  Foundation" at http://technet.microsoft.com/en-us/library/jj679892.aspx.

- **Windows Server 2012 R2 Essentials:** A step up from the Foundation edition, this edition works well on small networks of up to 25 users and 50
  devices. This version provides preconfigured connectivity to cloud-based
  services, but no virtualization rights are included. Windows Server 2012 R2
  Essentials adds many new and enhanced features, including improved capabilities for server deployment, client deployment, user and group management,
  storage management, data protection, BranchCache, integration with Office
  365, management of mobile devices, restoration of client computers, management of remote web access, and integration with Microsoft online services.
  For more information, refer to "What's New in Windows Server Essentials"
  at http://technet.microsoft.com/en-us/library/dn303448.aspx.

- **Windows Server 2012 R2 Standard:** A robust, ideal platform for medium-sized offices that are designed upon a physical or minimally virtualized environment. Two virtual instances are included.

- **Windows Server 2012 R2 Datacenter:** The most robust edition of Windows Server 2012, this edition provides all the capabilities for running a highly virtualized, cloud-accessible networking environment.

Windows Server 2012 R2 User Interface

Microsoft has provided several options for setting up the user interface that, in part, reflect the new interface features of the Windows 8 and Windows 8.1 client operating system. When you install Windows Server 2012 R2 (as we will discuss in Chapter 2, "Installing and Configuring Windows Server 2012 R2"), you can choose between **Server Core Installation** and **Server with a GUI**.

First introduced in Windows Server 2008, *Server Core* is a stripped-down version of Windows Server 2012 R2 that does not contain any GUI, taskbar, or Start menu. After logging on, you are presented with a command prompt window, from which you perform all administrative actions. A Server Core computer uses less hardware and memory resources than a normal server but is able to perform most (but not all) of the roles that a normal server performs. Furthermore, a Server Core computer is more secure because it presents a smaller attack footprint than a normal server. In fact a Server Core installation uses about 4 GB less hard drive space for the operating system files compared to the same installation in the Server with a GUI mode. You can use the command line, Windows PowerShell, or remote methods to administer a server running in Server Core mode. You can also administer a Server Core computer from another server that is configured with the Server with a GUI option or from a Windows 8.1 computer with the Remote Server Administration Tools installed. Note that you must use the Windows 8.1 version of these tools; those that are included with previous versions of Windows don't work with Windows Server 2012 R2.

Key Topic

NOTE   For more information on Remote Server Administration Tools, refer to "Deploy Remote Server Administration Tools" at http://technet.microsoft.com/en-us/library/hh831501.aspx.

The Server with a GUI option in Windows Server 2012 R2 is equivalent to the Full Installation option in Windows Server 2008 R2. If you choose this option, you have the following choices that reflect the appearance and functionality of the base server option:

- **Server with a GUI:** This provides the standard GUI that includes the new Start screen based on the Windows 8.1 shell, but not the default apps that come with Windows 8.1 or the access to Windows Store. All server roles and features can be installed, and the Server Manager tool and Microsoft Management Console (MMC) snap-ins are fully functional. We provide more information on server roles and features later in this chapter.

- **Minimal Server Interface:** Windows Server 2012 R2 enables you to remove the Server Graphical Shell. In this option, the Start screen, File Explorer, Internet Explorer 11, and the desktop are not installed. This option includes MMC snap-ins, Server Manager, and a subset of Control Panel applets. This mode requires about 300 MB less disk space than the complete Server with a GUI option.

- **Full Desktop Experience:** This option adds support for the Windows Store and Windows Store apps included with the Windows 8.1 Shell to the Server with a GUI option.

NOTE   For more information on the available server installation options, refer to "Windows Server Installation Options" at http://technet.microsoft.com/en-us/library/hh831786.aspx.

The Windows Server 2012 R2 Start Screen and Charms

When you install Windows Server 2012 R2 with the GUI option, the installation includes the new Start screen similar to that of Windows 8.1. As shown in Figure 1-1, this screen includes tiles for the most used server management tools. It replaces the Start button and menu found in previous Windows versions dating back to Windows 95 and Windows NT 4.0. As in Windows 8.1, tiles are added to the Start screen when you install many applications on the server. You can access the Start screen from the desktop by hovering your mouse over the bottom left corner of the screen and clicking, or by pressing the Windows key.

Figure 1-1   The new Windows Server 2012 R2 Start screen, as it appears in a default GUI installation.

Also included is a set of three (server with a GUI option) or five (full desktop experience option) charms, which lie along the right side of your screen. You can access these charms by hovering your mouse pointer over the upper-right corner of the screen. These enable you to perform several common tasks, as follows:

- **Search:** Enables you to search for files, folders, or programs on your computer. You can even look up items on the Internet.

- **Share:** Enables you to share files and folders with other users or send data to another program without leaving the program you're running. You can also email photos to others, update your Facebook page, or send links to other programs. Available with the Full Desktop Experience installation option only.

- **Start:** Enables you to jump to the Start screen. If you're on the Start screen, you can return to the last app you were working with.

- **Devices:** Enables you to work with all peripheral devices on the computer. For example, you can print files, sync data with a smartphone, or stream a home movie to your TV. Available with the Full Desktop Experience installation option only.

■ **Settings:** Enables you to access the Control Panel and modify settings for the computer and its apps. You can also shut down or restart your computer from the Power icon accessed via this charm.

Server Manager

Is Server Manager a throwback to Windows NT 4.0? Not at all. It is true in name only. Introduced in Windows Server 2008 and completely redesigned in Windows Server 2012 and Windows Server 2012 R2, Server Manager is a Microsoft Management Console (MMC) utility that replaces the Computer Management console found in previous Windows Server versions and adds considerable new management functionality. In particular, it includes the management tools formerly part of the Manage Your Server, Configure Your Server, and Add or Remove Windows Components applications in Windows Server 2003. Because this book deals with Server Manager considerably throughout, a brief introduction of its capabilities is provided here.

When you first log on to a Windows Server 2012 R2 computer with the GUI installed, Server Manager opens by default. If Server Manager is not open, you can open it by selecting its tile on the new Start screen. This opens the Server Manager console to the Dashboard screen, as shown in Figure 1-2.

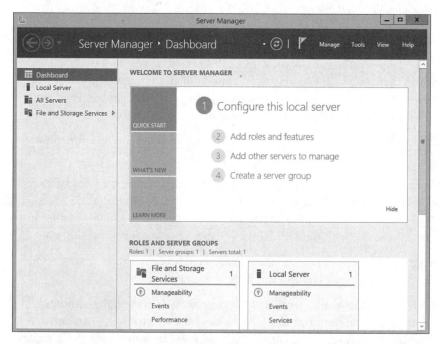

Figure 1-2   Server Manager, showing the default options in a new Windows Server 2012 R2 installation.

Several of the more significant administrative actions you can perform from Server Manager are as follows:

- Add or remove roles, role services, and server features

- View, manage, and modify the configuration of installed roles and features

- Perform general management tasks such as configuring local user accounts and groups, disk management, and service management

- Connect to remote servers to perform management tasks

- Verify server status, identify critical errors and other events, and troubleshoot configuration problems or server failures

From the Server Manager dashboard, you can perform the following tasks:

- **Configure the local server:** When you select this option, Server Manager displays the screen shown in Figure 1-3. Scroll down to obtain the following sections:

  - **Properties:** Enables you to view and configure many server properties. Click the values displayed in blue to display dialog boxes for this purpose.

  - **Events:** Displays a subset of events from the Event Viewer System log and enables you to filter these events and perform queries to locate desired events.

  - **Services:** Displays information about services running or stopped on the computer and enables you to start or stop services. You can also filter this list and perform queries.

  - **Best Practices Analyzer:** Enables you to create a report describing any issues on your server (including those with server roles and features that you have installed) and providing recommendations for resolving them.

  - **Performance:** Displays a simple Performance Monitor graph and enables you to configure alerts that inform you of unusual performance situations such as high processor usage.

  - **Roles and Features:** Lists roles, role services, and features installed on this computer and enables you to filter the list and remove roles or features.

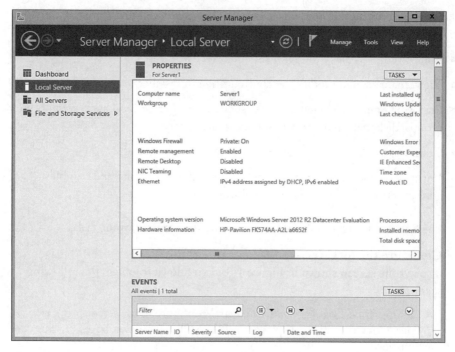

Figure 1-3   Server Manager enables you to view and configure basic server properties.

- **Add roles and features:** Starts the Add Roles and Features Wizard, as described in the next section.

- **Add other servers to manage:** On a domain controller or domain member server, it enables you to search for other servers using Active Directory Domain Services (AD DS). You can then perform various server management tasks on these computers.

- **Create a server group:** As shown in Figure 1-4, you can name a server group and add servers on the network to this group.

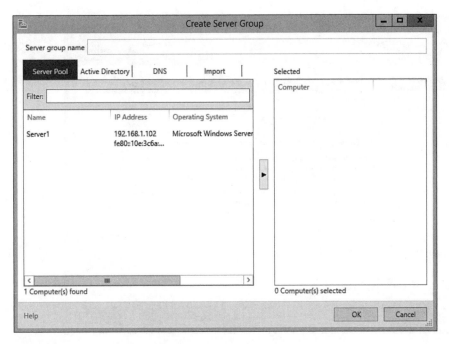

Figure 1-4   Using Server Manager to create a server group.

Adding Roles and Features

By selecting the **Add roles and features** option from the Server Manager dashboard, you can add roles and features. This starts the Add Roles and Features Wizard, as shown in Figure 1-5. The opening pages of this wizard enable you to select role services for VDI and choose servers or virtual hard disks on which to install roles and features. Figure 1-6 shows the roles you can add to the server using this wizard. Simply follow the instructions provided by the wizard and reboot the server if requested.

Many uses of Server Manager are discussed throughout this book. For further information on other uses of Server Manager, refer to *Cert Guide* books for exams 70-411, 70-412, 70-413, and 70-414.

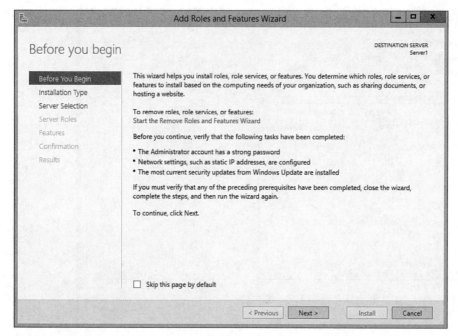

Figure 1-5 The Add Roles and Features Wizard starts with an initial page that reminds you of initial tasks you should perform before proceeding.

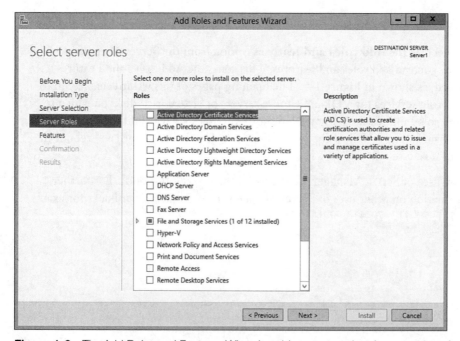

Figure 1-6 The Add Roles and Features Wizard enables you to select from a series of roles that you can add to your server.

Planning for Server Installation and Upgrades

As with previous implementations, planning remains an important step of a successful Server 2012 R2 deployment. Committing adequate time to plan up front will save countless hours in the future. Planning for a server installation includes the following tasks:

- Identifying hardware requirements

- Choosing an install method

- Considering upgrades

Identifying Hardware Requirements

As with any operating system, Server 2012 R2 has a minimum set of hardware requirements. Depending on the function of your server, additional resources may be required. Hardware requirements are covered in more detail in Chapter 2.

Choosing an Install Method

One of the first tasks during an install is selecting the appropriate install method. As you learned previously, Server 2012 R2 includes options for a Server Core Installation or Server with a GUI. There are several considerations to make when selecting the appropriate installation method:

- **Server Core:** Server Core is the default install option and is recommended by Microsoft. Server Core installs only those services, roles, and features required for your server. Roles are discussed further in the next section, but for now understand that fewer services and roles creates a smaller footprint. This ultimately reduces administrative overhead and server overhead so demands for RAM and disk space are less, and from a security standpoint there are fewer things for an attacker to exploit.

- Server Core can be installed to contain the following server roles:

    - Active Directory Certificate Services

    - Active Directory Domain Services

    - Active Directory Lightweight Directory Services

    - Active Directory Rights Management Server

    - DHCP Server

    - DNS Server

- File and Storage Services (Including File Server Resource Manager)

- Hyper-V

- Print and Document Services

- Remote Access (Including Routing) Services

- Streaming Media Services

- Web Server (IIS)

- Windows Server Update Services

- **Server with a GUI:** When requiring additional roles beyond those available under Server Core, or if you require GUI-based applications to be installed, consider the Server with a GUI install method. Similarly, if a smaller footprint is not a concern or if you just prefer a more traditional desktop user experience, choose the Server with a GUI install method. Server with a GUI enables you to easily access Server Manager, MMC snap-ins, Control Panel, and so on using either a Minimal or Full Desktop user interface as opposed to a command-line interface.

So what if you change your mind? Unlike Windows Server 2008 R2, Windows Server 2012 R2 allows you to change between Server Core, Server with a GUI, and vice versa by simply issuing a PowerShell command. Converting between installation methods is possible because the GUI has been introduced as a feature of Server 2012 R2 as opposed to a built-in interface as part of the installation. Features on Demand are discussed further the proceeding sections.

Considering Upgrades

After hardware requirements have been met and you have selected the install method, the next step is to determine how to make the move to Server 2012 R2. Server 2012 R2 can be deployed using the following methods:

- **Clean Install:** Used for new installations where the previous operating system will be deleted. Also required when changing from 32- to 64-bit architectures, when converting between different languages, and when converting from previous builds such as Release Candidates or pre-release versions. Clean installations are accomplished through the use of a bootable installation media.

- **Upgrade:** Upgrades are used when you need to replace your current operating system with a newer release using the same hardware. This may include upgrading from Windows Server 2008 R2 to Windows Server 2012 R2, from Windows Server 2012 to 2012 R2, from an evaluation version to a retail version, and so on. Upgrade Options are described in Table 1-2.

- **License Conversion:** Supported by recent operating systems, you can use the DISM command-line tool along with a valid license key to perform an in-place license conversion, that is, Windows Server 2012 R2 Standard to Windows 2012 R2 Datacenter edition. We cover DISM in Chapter 2.

- **Migration:** Provides the ability to transfer roles or features from one computer to another with a completely different hardware profile. Role migration is reviewed later in this chapter.

Table 1-2   Upgrade Options

Current Operating System	Upgrade Option
Windows Server 2003 Standard/Enterprise with SP2	Direct upgrade is not possible. Must upgrade to Server 2008 before upgrading to 2012. Can only upgrade to Windows Server 2012.
Windows Server 2008 Standard with SP2 or Windows Server 2008 Enterprise with SP2	Windows Server 2012 Standard, Windows Server 2012 Datacenter.
Windows Server 2008 Datacenter with SP2	Windows Server 2012 Datacenter.
Windows Web Server 2008	Windows Server 2012 Standard.
Windows Server 2008 R2 Datacenter with SP1	Windows Server 2012/R2 Datacenter.
Windows Server 2008 R2 Enterprise with SP1	Windows Server 2012/R2 Standard or Windows Server 2012/R2 Datacenter.
Windows Server 2008 R2 Standard with SP1	Windows Server 2012/R2 Standard or Windows Server 2012/R2 Datacenter.
Windows Web Server 2008 R2 with SP1	Windows Server 2012/R2 Standard.
Windows Server 2012 Datacenter	Windows Server 2012 R2 Datacenter.
Windows Server 2012 Standard	Windows Server 2012 R2 Standard or Datacenter.
Windows Server 2012 Foundation	Upgrades are not supported.
Windows Server 2012 Essentials	Upgrades are not supported.

NOTE   For more information on the available upgrade paths, including information on upgrading roles, refer to "Evaluation Versions and Upgrade Options for Windows Server 2012" at http://technet.microsoft.com/en-us/library/jj574204.aspx and "Upgrade Options for Windows Server 2012 R2" at http://technet.microsoft.com/en-us/library/dn303416.aspx.

Server Roles and Role Migration

Introduced with Server 2008, Microsoft has retained both roles and features in Server 2012 R2, but also included some enhancements. As a recap, a *role* is a specific function that a server can perform on the network, including file services, terminal services, and certificate services. Active Directory Domain Services (AD DS) is the server role that encompasses all domain control functions. In some cases roles are made up of smaller components that provide a specific function for the parent role. These smaller components are known as *role services*. A *feature* is an optional component that adds a specific function such as the .NET Framework 4.5, BitLocker Drive Encryption, Network Load Balancing, and so on. Certain roles require that specific features be installed, and these are automatically installed when you add a specific role.

Windows Server 2012 R2 Server Roles

Although many roles will be discussed in more detail later, Table 1-3 provides an introductory overview of server roles and outlines the new capabilities for Server 2012 R2.

Table 1-3   Server Roles

Role	Description
Active Directory Certificate Services	Server role responsible for public key infrastructure (PKI). This role is used if you need to deploy and manage digital certificates. New capabilities for 2012 R2 include integration with Server Manager, PowerShell management, server core support, support for auto renewal of certificate for computers unjoined to the domain, and so on.
Active Directory Domain Services	The Active Directory Domain Services (AD DS) role is responsible for the creation and management of an active directory database. It allows for the organization of resources, management of authentication, and integration with other services such as Microsoft Exchange. Enhancements to AD DS include virtual domain controller deployment options, improved domain controller promotion tools, new management procedures, and enhancements to the Kerberos protocol.

Role	Description
Active Directory Federation Services	Previously included as an additional download, Server 2012 R2 now includes Active Directory Federation Services (AD FS) as a role available under Server Manager. It provides a seamless secure method for single sign on (SSO). It enables internal and external user authentication to multiple resources without the hassle of remembering multiple logons. Additional new features include integration with dynamic access control and additional PowerShell cmdlet tools.
Active Directory Lightweight Directory Services	Active Directory Lightweight Directory Services (AD LDS) is a lighter version of AD DS. This role is used in scenarios where standalone servers with limited directory services are required.
Active Directory Rights Management Server	Active Directory Rights Management Services (AD RMS) is the role responsible for managing and controlling embedded file-level policies for encryption and access to data. Changes in 2012 R2 revolve around new requirements for SQL server integration, additional steps for PowerShell deployments, a new process for installation through server manager, server core support, and so on.
Application Server	The application server role is used in conjunction with custom-developed applications used by a business. It is typically associated with web servers.
DHCP Server	The dynamic Host Configuration Protocol (DHCP) server role is responsible for managing and configuring the automated configuration of IP addresses on clients. New to Server 2012 R2 is a DHCP failover option allowing two servers to share DHCP configurations for the purpose of redundancy. Secondly, Server 2012 R2 provides support for policy-based DHCP configurations. Clients can be assigned specific IP address ranges based on criteria such as client vendor type. Additional PowerShell options are also available for managing DHCP in 2012 R2.
DNS Server	The domain Name Server (DNS) role is responsible for name resolution for the internal network as well as Internet resources. DNS is a critical component for AD DS and other applications or services integrated with the domain.
Fax Server	The fax server role provides services for sending and receiving faxes.

Role	Description
File and Storage Services (Including File Server Resource Manager)	File and Storage Services provides a central point for storage management for file servers in your organization. File Server Resource Manager provides additional resources to control and manage access to files and resources shared on your server.
	Windows Server 2012 R2 includes Work Folders. This feature provides a consistent method for users to access their files from different devices. Additional enhancements for 2012 R2 include data deduplication, iSCSI integration, storage virtualization, improved remote management, and additional support for PowerShell cmdlets.
Hyper-V	The Hyper-V role is responsible for managing and supporting server virtualization in your organization.
	There have been several enhancements and new features incorporated into the 2012 R2 platform. Some of these include a new set of PowerShell cmdlets, a new virtual machine replication feature, resource monitoring, the ability to support SMB3.0, the ability to share virtual hard disks, Storage Quality of Service, virtual machine generation, and so on.
Network Policy and Access Services	The network policy and access services roles provide network access protection (NAP), 802.1X authentication, and central policy management using RADIUS.
	Unlike Windows Server 2008 R2, Server 2012 R2 includes PowerShell support for this role.
Print and Document Services	The print and document services role provides the ability to share and manage printers on the network.
	New functionality for 2012 R2 include the ability to support direct printing to branch offices, secure printing, high availability printing, and so on.
Remote Access (Including Routing)	The remote access role provides the ability for DirectAccess and RRAS. DirectAccess provides a seamless remote access method without requiring a virtual private network (VPN). The remote access server role allows for centralized administration, configuration, and monitoring of DirectAccess and any VPN-based services.
	Some differences in 2012 R2 include support for multiple domains, load balancing, support for Server Core and PowerShell, and so on.

Role	Description
Remote Desktop Services	Remote Desktop Services provide mobile support and the ability for users to connect to desktops and applications from virtually anywhere.
	Several improvements have been made to this service since Windows Server 2008. Some of these include a simple virtual desktop infrastructure (VDI), centralized publishing of resources, improved USB device support through the virtual session, multitouch/gestures, smoother audio/video playback, and so on. Enhancements in Windows Server 2012 R2 include the ability to monitor and control sessions, improved performance accessing common data, improved reconnection capabilities, reduced requirements for network bandwidth, increased support for additional remote desktop clients such as handheld/mobile devices, and so on.
Streaming Media Services	Provides support and management for the delivery of digital media to many clients over a web browser.
Volume Activation Services	Enables the automation and management of volume licenses for your organization. Key management services (KMS) as well as Active Directory–based activation further simplify the management of license activations across the organization.
Web Server (IIS)	Provides the ability to create and manage websites. In this new release of Internet Information Services (IIS), now at version 8.5, Microsoft has provided the ability for centralized SSL certificates for your web server farm, the ability to restrict connections based on IP addresses, FTP logon restrictions, CPU and bandwidth throttling, plus many more.
Windows Deployment Services	The Windows Deployment Services (WDS) role enables you to configure, manage, and deploy images for Windows operating systems over the network. WDS uses the preboot execution environment (PXE) function of network adapters.
	In the new release, Microsoft has included support for the latest operating systems, including Windows 8.1 and Server 2012 R2. Also included is improved support for virtual images, multicasting, driver provisioning, PowerShell scripting support, and so on.
Windows Server Update Services	The Windows Server Update Services (WSUS) role provides a centralized tool to manage and deploy the latest Microsoft product updates, security updates, and patches for your organization.
	In previous releases, WSUS was available via download. In 2012 R2 Microsoft has included this as an optional role available using Server Manager. New functionality for 2012 R2 includes PowerShell support, additional security including a SHA256 hash capability, and the separation of client and server using different versions of the windows update agent (WUA).

> **NOTE**   For more information on server roles and new capabilities for 2012 R2, refer to "Server Roles and Technologies in Windows Server 2012R2 and Windows Server 2012" at http://technet.microsoft.com/en-us/library/hh831669.aspx.

Role Migration

You probably have an existing server implementation but are looking to make the move to Server 2012 R2, or perhaps you have physical 2003 servers and are looking to implement a virtual presence. In many cases this can be a tedious task to say the least. How do you successfully move your services from one installation to another without the headache and with as little downtime as possible? By using the Windows Server Migration Tool and doing some planning, an administrator can migrate roles, features, operating system settings, user data, and shares from a previous installation to Windows Server 2012 R2.

As shown in Figure 1-7, the Windows Server Migration Tools are available as an installable feature using Server Manager. It can also be installed via PowerShell using the command `Install-WindowsFeature Migration -ComputerName`.

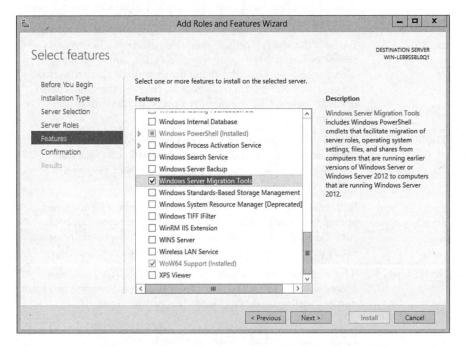

Figure 1-7   Add Roles and Features Wizard: Windows Server Migration Tools.

Once installed, the migration tools are accessible to those with administrator privileges via the Start screen or through a PowerShell session. When using the Windows Server Migration Tools, it is important to understand the following points:

- You should be familiar with using PowerShell and Server Manager.

- Features must be installed on both source and destination computers.

- Source operating system must be at least Windows Server 2003 (x86 or x64).

- Server Core 2008 R2 is supported as a source operating system.

- The destination will support Server 2012 R2 full and Core (x64) installation options.

- Supports migrations between subnets.

- Supports both physical and virtual servers.

- Migration between different language installations is not supported.

> **NOTE**   For detailed steps on how to migrate server roles, refer to "Migrate Roles and Features to Windows Server" at http://technet.microsoft.com/en-us/library/jj134039.aspx and "Windows Server Role Upgrade and Migration Matrix" at http://technet.microsoft.com/en-us/windowsserver/dn527660.

Features on Demand

Features on Demand was a new concept for Windows 8 and Server 2012 and is continued in Windows 8.1 and Windows Server 2012 R2. The primary function of this component is to allow you to remove roles and features, including files, from the operating system. This not only enables you to maintain a smaller footprint by reducing disk space, but also enables you to store content centrally, which is useful to support remote installations. In the event you need to reinstall a feature, Windows will prompt for the location of these files. The source location can be a network share, a specific path configured through Group Policy, Windows Update, or the original installation media. Installation source files are located under the \Sources\SxS folder on the original Windows Server 2012 R2 installation media.

Installed features can be removed using Server Manager or via running PowerShell as an Administrator and issuing the command `Uninstall-WindowsFeature <feature name> -Remove`. To produce a list of features installed, issue the command Get-WindowsFeature.

So for example if you have a full server installation and are looking to remove the Explorer shell and the full GUI, issue the `Uninstall-WindowsFeature Server-Gui-Shell -Remove` command as illustrated in Figure 1-8.

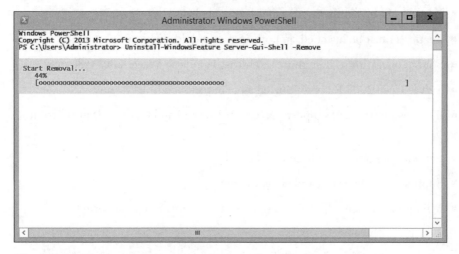

Figure 1-8   Features on Demand via Windows PowerShell.

Exam Preparation Tasks

Review All the Key Topics

Review the most important topics in the chapter, noted with the key topics icon in the outer margin of the page. Table 1-4 lists a reference of these key topics and the page numbers on which each is found.

Table 1-4   Key Topics for Chapter 1

Key Topic Element	Description	Page Number
Paragraph	Describes the features available in the Server Core version of Windows Server 2012 R2	15
Figure 1-1	Shows the Start screen as it appears in the Server with a GUI version of Windows Server 2012 R2	17
List	Summarizes the capabilities of Server Manager in Windows Server 2012 R2	19

Key Topic Element	Description	Page Number
Table 1-2	Lists the possible upgrade options for Windows Server 2012 R2	25
Table 1-3	Summarizes Roles and new capabilities in Windows Server 2012 R2	26
Paragraph	Describes Features on Demand and the removal of installed features	31

Complete the Tables and Lists from Memory

Print a copy of Appendix B, "Memory Tables" (found on the CD), or at least the section for this chapter, and complete the tables and lists from memory. Appendix C, "Memory Tables Answer Key," is also on the CD and includes completed tables and lists to check your work.

Definitions of Key Terms

Define the following key terms from this chapter, and check your answers in the glossary.

Remote Server Administration Tools, Server Core, Server Manager, Features on Demand, Role, Role Service, Feature

This chapter covers the following subjects:

- **Windows Server 2012 R2 Hardware Requirements:** Computers onto which you want to install Windows Server 2012 R2 must meet minimum hardware requirements. This section presents these requirements and describes several tasks you should perform before installing the server.

- **Installing Windows Server 2012 R2:** This section shows you how to install Windows Server 2012 R2 as either Server Core or Server with a GUI. It also shows you how to interconvert your server between Server Core and Server with a GUI, as well as the Minimal Server Interface and Full Desktop Experience options of Server with a GUI.

- **Delegation of Server Administration:** This covers best practices for delegating Server Administration and outlines some of the common tools used by delegates.

- **Configuring Offline Server Images:** This section shows you how to configure and update Offline Server images.

- **Configuring Remote Server Roles:** There are several methods for configuring server roles. This section shows you how to use the GUI and command line to configure roles on remote servers.

- **Configuring Windows Server 2012 R2 Services:** This section provides an overview of Windows Services, how they are configured, and how you can use the GUI and command line to modify Service properties.

- **Configuring NIC Teaming:** This section provides an overview of NIC Teaming and how it works with Server 2012 R2. It covers the installation and configuring of NIC Teams and how to configure the teams for different scenarios.

Installing and Configuring Windows Server 2012 R2

The Microsoft 70-410 exam assesses your ability to install, configure, and administer Windows Server 2012 R2 in business environments from small offices to large enterprises. This chapter focuses on installing Windows Server 2012 R2 in its basic configurations and introduces you to basic server configuration actions that you should be familiar with before you undertake any advanced actions.

"Do I Know This Already?" Quiz

The "Do I Know This Already?" quiz enables you to assess whether you should read this entire chapter or simply jump to the "Exam Preparation Tasks" section for review. If you are in doubt, read the entire chapter. Table 2-1 outlines the major headings in this chapter and the corresponding "Do I Know This Already?" quiz questions. You can find the answers in Appendix A, "Answers to the 'Do I Know This Already?' Quizzes."

Table 2-1 "Do I Know This Already?" Foundation Topics Section-to-Question Mapping

Foundations Topics Section	Questions Covered in This Section
Windows Server 2012 R2 Hardware Requirements	1–2
Installing Windows Server 2012 R2	3–4
Delegation of Server Administration	5–7
Configuring Offline Server Images	8
Configuring Remote Server Roles	9
Configuring Windows Server 2012 R2 Services	10
Configuring NIC Teaming	11

1. You have an older computer on which you want to install an evaluation copy of Windows Server 2012 R2 so that you can prepare for your MCSE exams. The server has a 1 GHz processor, 1 GB RAM, 50 GB hard drive space, and a 1024x768 monitor. After inserting the Windows Server 2012 R2 DVD-ROM, the computer copies the initial files and then displays an error message informing you that it is unable to install Windows Server 2012 R2. Which of the following problems is preventing you from proceeding?

   a. A processor that is too slow

   b. Insufficient RAM

   c. Insufficient hard drive space

   d. An inadequate monitor

2. You are preparing to install Windows Server 2012 R2 on your Windows 8.1 computer in a dual-boot manner. You have created a separate partition on which you plan to install Windows Server 2012 R2. Which of the following should you perform before beginning the installation? (Choose all that apply.)

   a. Disconnect uninterruptible power supply (UPS) devices

   b. Disconnect universal serial bus (USB) devices

   c. Disable antivirus software

   d. Run the Windows Memory Diagnostic tool

   e. Back up data

   f. Provide mass storage drivers if needed

3. You need to confirm which server roles and features are present on a computer running the Server Core version of Windows Server 2012 R2. What command should you run?

   a. `oclist`

   b. `Get-WindowsFeature`

   c. `ServerManagerCmd`

   d. `sconfig.cmd`

4. You are using a Windows Server 2012 R2 computer that is configured with the full GUI interface. However, you find working with the Start screen distracting and would like to simplify the user interface by removing this screen. You still want to have access to Server Manager in GUI mode. Which of the following commands should you run?

   a. `Remove-WindowsFeature Desktop-Experience`

   b. `Remove-WindowsFeature Server-Gui-Shell`

   c. `Uninstall-WindowsFeature Desktop-Experience`

   d. `Uninstall-WindowsFeature Server-Gui-Shell`

5. The organization is expanding, and administrative overhead is increasing. What should you to do help manage the workload?

   a. Install Server Manager on all workstations in the organization.

   b. Add additional servers containing the AD DS role

   c. Delegate Administrative responsibilities

   d. Switch to Server Core

6. Your company has recently hired a new helpdesk technician. You would like to provide the technician with the ability to monitor performance counters on your servers. You want to grant the technician this ability but provide him with the least amount of administrative access. How should you accomplish this?

   a. Add the technician's user account to the server's local administrator group

   b. Add the technician's user account to the Performance Monitor Users group

   c. Add the technician's user account to the Performance Log Users group

   d. Add the technician's user account to the Remote Desktop Users group

7. You are the system administrator for Pearson.com. You've been tasked with adding web services on 50 servers using a standard, company-approved IIS configuration. How can you accomplish this without altering any other applications on the servers (the solution must use the least amount of administrative effort)?

   a. Create a configuration checklist and execute it against all new web servers

   b. Configure one server, create a capture image, and deploy the image to all remaining servers

   c. Create a custom DSC configuration and deploy it against all servers in scope

   d. Reinstall Windows Server 2012 R2 and import an existing XML configuration for the web services

8. What can be done through servicing of an offline image? (Choose all that apply.)

   a. Enable or disable Windows features

   b. Enable Remote Install Services

   c. Upgrade to a higher edition of Windows

   d. Add or remove drivers

   e. Add or remove Remote Desktop Services

   f. Scan and remove active virus threats

9. What methods are available to add servers to Server Manager for remote management? (Choose all that apply.)

   a. Active Directory Search

   b. DNS Lookup

   c. Text file import

   d. Scan Subnet

   e. MMC

   f. RDP

10. Which of the following are methods used to manage services on a local or remote server? (Choose all that apply.)

    a. Services Manager for Windows

    b. `sc config`

    c. Remote Desktop Services

    d. `Services.msc`

11. You decide to reconfigure a server as a Hyper-V server. You want to use NIC Teaming with all available network cards. Which command do you use to establish the NIC Team?

    a. Reinstall the Operating System

    b. `Remove-NetLbfoTeam`

    c. `New-NetLbfoTeam`

    d. `New-NICTeam`

Foundation Topics

Windows Server 2012 R2 Hardware Requirements

As with previous Windows versions, your hardware must meet certain requirements for Windows Server 2012 R2 to function properly. First of all, Windows Server 2012 R2 requires a 64-bit processor; Microsoft has discontinued 32-bit software with this release of Windows Server. Table 2-2 outlines the minimum and recommended hardware requirements for Windows Server 2012 R2 as provided by Microsoft:

Table 2-2   Windows Server 2012 R2 Hardware Requirements

Component	Minimum Requirement	Microsoft Recommended
Processor	1.4 GHz	2 GHz or faster
Memory	512 MB RAM	2 GB RAM or greater
Available Disk Space	32 GB	40 GB or greater
Optical Drive	DVD-ROM drive	DVD-ROM drive
Display	Super VGA (800x600) monitor	XGA (1024x768) monitor

In addition, you must have the usual I/O peripherals, including a keyboard and mouse or compatible pointing device and a wired or wireless network interface card (NIC). If you can connect to a network location on which you have copied the contents of the Windows Server 2012 R2 DVD-ROM, you are not required to have a DVD-ROM drive on your computer. As with any other operating system installation, you will receive improved performance if you have a faster processor and additional memory on your system.

Computers with more than 16 GB RAM require additional disk space for paging, hibernation, and dump files. With disk space at an all-time minimum cost, it is easy to acquire a high-capacity hard disk. You will certainly need plenty of disk space on a server that will be a domain controller in a large domain.

NOTE   Support for Itanium processors ended with Server 2008 R2. Microsoft has removed support for Itanium processors under Windows Server 2012 and 2012 R2. https://technet.microsoft.com/en-us/library/cc772344(v=ws.10).aspx.

Microsoft recommends that you also perform the following actions before installing Windows Server 2012 R2:

- **Disconnect uninterruptible power supply (UPS) devices:** If you are using a UPS, disconnect its serial or USB cable before installing Windows Server 2012 R2. However, note that you do not need to disconnect other USB devices such as external hard drives, printers, and so on.

- **Back up data:** Perform a complete backup of configuration information for your servers, especially network infrastructure servers such as DHCP servers. The backup should include the boot and system partitions as well as the system state data.

- **Disable antivirus software:** Antivirus software can interfere with operating system installation.

- **Run the Windows Memory Diagnostic tool:** This tool tests your computer's RAM. For more information, refer to "Utility Spotlight: Windows Memory Diagnostic" at http://technet.microsoft.com/en-us/magazine/2008.09.utilityspotlight.aspx?pr=blog.

- **Provide mass storage drivers if needed:** Save the driver file to appropriate media so that you can provide it during setup.

- **Note that Windows Firewall is on by default:** Server applications that require inbound connections will fail until you create inbound firewall rules that allow these connections. For more information, refer to "Windows Firewall with Advanced Security Overview" at http://technet.microsoft.com/en-us/library/hh831365.aspx.

- **Prepare your Active Directory environment for Windows Server 2012 R2:** Before adding a Windows Server 2012 R2 domain controller or updating an existing domain controller to Windows Server 2012 R2, prepare the domain and forest by running Adprep.exe. We discuss this tool in Chapter 13, "Installing Domain Controllers."

Installing Windows Server 2012 R2

As already introduced in Chapter 1, "Introducing Windows Server 2012 R2," you can install Windows Server 2012 R2 as either Server with a GUI, which presents a full graphical user interface, or Server Core, which presents only a command prompt window.

Installing a Windows Server Core Computer

As explained in Chapter 1, Windows Server Core includes a minimal version of the server software without the GUI; you perform all configuration tasks from the command prompt. Follow this procedure to install Windows Server Core and perform initial configuration tasks:

1. Insert the Windows Server 2012 R2 DVD-ROM and turn on your computer. You should see a message informing you that Windows is copying temporary files; if not, you should access the BIOS setup program included with your computer and modify the boot sequence so that the computer boots from the DVD.

2. After a few minutes, you receive the Windows Server 2012 R2 screen shown in Figure 2-1. Click **Install now** to begin the installation.

Figure 2-1   Starting the installation of Windows Server 2012 R2.

3. Windows copies temporary files and then displays the Get important updates for Windows Setup screen shown in Figure 2-2. If you're connected to the Internet, select **Go online to install updates now (recommended)**.

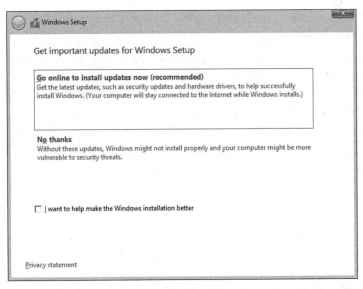

Figure 2-2 If you're connected to the Internet, you should select the option to get updates.

4. On the next **Install Windows** screen, click **Install now**.

5. You receive the options shown in Figure 2-3, which enable you to install the complete Standard or Datacenter version of Windows Server 2012 R2 with a GUI or Windows Server 2012 R2 Server Core. Select the **Windows Server 2012 R2 Datacenter (Server Core Installation)** option and then click **Next**.

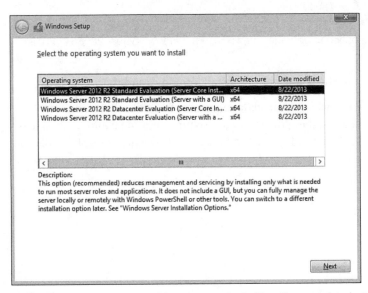

Figure 2-3 This screen enables you to select either the complete installation of Windows Server 2012 R2 or the Server Core option.

6. You are asked to accept the license terms. Select the check box labeled **I accept the license terms** and then click **Next**.

7. You receive the options shown in Figure 2-4 to upgrade or install a clean copy of Windows Server 2012 R2. Select Custom (advanced) to install a clean copy of Windows Server 2012 R2. The upgrade option is available only if you have started the installation from within Windows Server 2008, Windows Server 2008 R2, or the original version of Windows Server 2012.

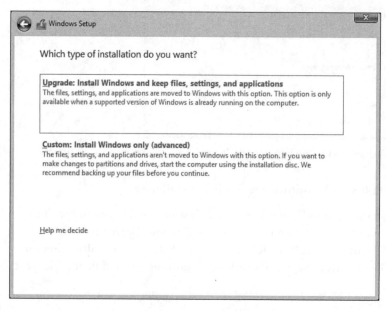

Figure 2-4   You have the option to upgrade when run from Windows Server 2008/R2/2012.

8. Select the disk on which you want to install Windows and then click **Next**.

9. Take a coffee break while the installation proceeds. This takes some time (particularly when installing on a virtual machine), and the computer restarts several times. As shown in Figure 2-5, Setup charts the progress of installation.

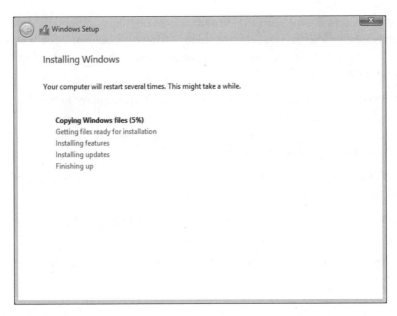

Figure 2-5   Windows Setup charts the progress of installing Windows Server 2012 R2.

10. After 15–30 minutes (depending on your hardware), Windows restarts a last time and informs you that your password must be changed before logging on for the first time. Click **OK**.

11. Type and confirm a strong password. When informed that the password is changed, click **OK**. After a minute or so, the desktop appears, containing a command window but no Start screen or desktop icons (see Figure 2-6). This is the standard Windows Server Core interface.

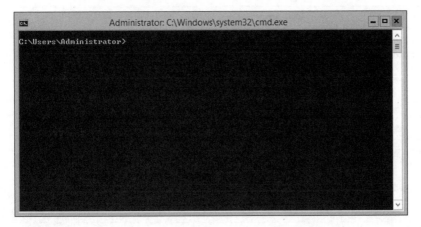

Figure 2-6   At startup, Windows Server Core 2012 R2 displays only a command window.

12. To set the correct time, type `control timedate.cpl`. By default, Server Core sets the time zone to Pacific Time. If you are in a different time zone, you will need to change this. Set the appropriate time zone, change the date and time if necessary, and then click **OK**.

13. Windows installs Server Core with a randomly generated computer name. To set a name of your choice, type `netdom renamecomputer %computername% /newname:ServerC1` (where, in this instance, `ServerC1` is the name you're assigning; substitute your desired server name).

14. Windows warns you that the rename process might have an adverse impact on some services. Type `Y` to proceed.

15. You are informed that the computer needs to be restarted in order to complete the rename. Type `shutdown /r /t 0` to reboot your server.

16. After the server reboots, press **Ctrl+Alt+Delete** and log on using the password you set in step 11.

Useful Server Core Commands

All configuration, management, and troubleshooting of Windows Server Core is done from the command line. Available utilities enable you to perform almost all regular configuration tasks in this fashion. In Windows Server 2012 and 2012 R2, many of the commands used with Server Core in Windows Server 2008 have been replaced by PowerShell cmdlets. Table 2-3 describes some of the more useful available commands.

Table 2-3   Useful Windows Server Core Commands and Cmdlets

Command	Meaning
`netdom join computername / domain:domainname`	Joins an Active Directory domain. You will be prompted for the username and password of a user with domain administrator privileges.
`Sconfig.cmd`	Configures and manages a series of common Server Core installation properties. See Figure 2-7.
`cscript scregedit.wsf`	Enables automatic updates.
`Get-WindowsFeature`	Displays roles and features currently installed on the server.
`Install-WindowsFeature`	Adds roles or features.
`Uninstall-WindowsFeature`	Removes roles or features.
`netsh interface IPv4`	Includes a series of subcommands that enable you to configure IPv4 networking.

Command	Meaning
netsh advfirewall	Includes subcommands that enable you to configure the Windows firewall.
Help	Provides a list of all available Windows Server Core commands.

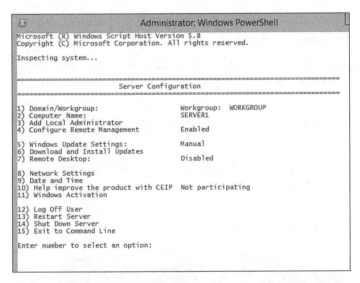

Figure 2-7   The sconfig.cmd utility enables you to perform many basic configuration actions on a Server Core computer.

Available commands also include most commands formerly used with MS-DOS and previous Windows versions. We discuss many Server Core commands and PowerShell cmdlets in various chapters of this book and other *Cert Guide* books in this series.

NOTE   For additional information on installing Windows Server Core, as well as any of these commands or other commands available in Windows Server Core, type the command name followed by /? or consult "Configure and Manage Server Core Installations" at http://technet.microsoft.com/en-us/library/jj574091.aspx. For additional information on the available Windows Server 2012 R2 installation options, refer to "Windows Server Installation Options" at http://technet.microsoft.com/library/hh831786.

Installing the Full GUI Server

Although Microsoft markets Server Core as being the default Windows Server 2012 R2 installation, the full GUI version still represents the most easily managed version of the server. The procedure for installing the full GUI server is the same whether you're installing directly from a DVD-ROM or a network share, except that you must have some type of network client installed on your computer to access a network share. The following procedure outlines installation from a DVD-ROM:

1. Follow the procedure outlined earlier for installing Windows Server Core until you receive the screen previously shown in Figure 2-3.

2. Select either **Windows Server 2012 R2 Standard (Server with a GUI)** or **Windows Server 2012 R2 Datacenter (Server with a GUI)**, and then click **Next**.

3. Complete steps 6–10 of the earlier procedure. Installation will take 15–45 minutes, depending on your hardware.

4. Type and confirm a secure password. Windows informs you that your password has been changed. Click **OK**.

5. Windows displays a Welcome message and prepares your desktop. Then the desktop with Server Manager shown in Figure 2-8 appears.

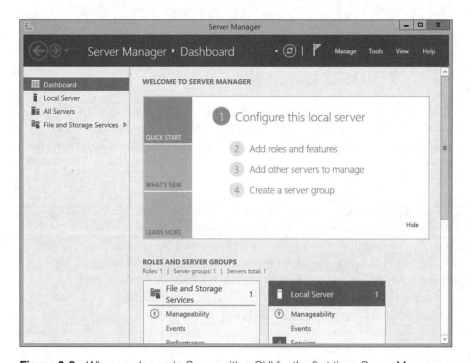

Figure 2-8 When you log on to Server with a GUI for the first time, Server Manager appears.

After you have performed the initial configuration steps, you will be prompted to press **Ctrl+Alt+Delete** and enter your password when you restart your server.

> **TIP**   When you shut down a Windows Server 2012 R2 computer, it displays the Shutdown Event Tracker dialog box, which asks you for a reason for shutting down the server. For learning purposes, it is helpful to disable this item. You can do so by typing `gpedit.msc` to open the Local Group Policy Object Editor. Navigate to Computer Configuration\Administrative Templates\System, right-click the **Display Shutdown Event Tracker** policy, and click **Properties**. On the dialog box that appears, click **Disabled** and then click **OK**.

Upgrading a Windows Server 2008 Computer

You can upgrade a computer running Windows Server 2008 R2 with Service Pack 1 (SP1) or later to Windows Server 2012 R2, provided that the computer meets the hardware requirements for Windows Server 2012 R2. You cannot upgrade a Windows Server 2003 or older computer or a computer running any client version of Windows to Windows Server 2012 R2.

To upgrade to Windows Server 2012 R2, proceed as follows:

1. While logged on to Windows Server 2008 R2 as an administrator, insert the Windows Server 2012 R2 DVD-ROM.

2. When the **Install Windows** screen appears, click **Install now**.

3. Select your operating system, either the standard or Windows Core version of Windows Server 2012 R2; then click **Next**.

4. Accept the licensing terms and then click **Next**.

5. On the **Which Type of Installation Do You Want?** page, select **Upgrade**.

6. Windows checks compatibility of your hardware and software and displays a compatibility report that informs you of any potential upgrade problems. Review this report and make any changes you feel are required. When you are ready to proceed, click **Next**.

7. Take a lunch break while the upgrade proceeds. This will take 60 minutes or longer, depending on your hardware configuration or use of virtual computing software. The server will reboot three or four times.

8. After the final reboot, log on using the password previously used in Windows Server 2008 R2. Windows prepares your desktop and displays the Server Manager tool as previously shown in Figure 2-8.

> **NOTE**   For additional information on upgrading to Windows Server 2012 R2 including a detailed list of supported upgrade paths, refer to "Upgrade Options for Windows Server 2012 R2" at http://technet.microsoft.com/en-us/library/dn303416.aspx.

Converting Between Core and GUI

You can convert the full GUI version of Windows Server 2012 R2 to Server Core or vice versa at any time; further, you can interconvert the GUI version between any of the three options described in Chapter 1.

Use the following procedure to convert the full GUI server to Server Core:

1. From the Search charm, type `powershell` and select **Windows PowerShell**.

2. Type the following cmdlet:

   ```
   Uninstall-WindowsFeature Server-Gui-Mgmt-Infra –Restart
   ```

3. A display on the PowerShell window tracks the removal process, which takes several minutes. A Configuring Windows features message then appears as the GUI is removed. After a few more minutes, the server restarts. When the logon screen appears, press **Ctrl+Alt+Delete** and log back on as an administrator.

Use the following procedure to convert a Server Core computer to run the full GUI:

1. From the administrative command prompt, type `powershell`.

2. Type the following command:

   ```
   Get-WindowsImage -ImagePath <path to wim>\install.wim
   ```

3. This command returns the index number for the server with a GUI image. Then type the following command:

   ```
   Install-WindowsFeature Server-Gui-Mgmt-Infra, Server-Gui-Shell –
   Restart -Source wim:<path to wim>\install.wim:<Index #>
   ```

4. Wait as Windows configures features and restarts; then press **Ctrl+Alt+Delete** and log back on as an administrator.

If you are converting a server that was originally installed in GUI mode back to GUI from Server Core, the procedure is slightly simpler. Use the following PowerShell command in place of those given in steps 2 and 3:

```
Install-WindowsFeature Server-Gui-Mgmt-Infra,Server-Gui-Shell
-Restart
```

To install the complete desktop experience on your server (including access to Windows Store apps as in Windows 8 or Windows 8.1), use the following PowerShell command and then restart your computer. This mode adds a link to Windows Store on the Start screen, as shown in Figure 2-9:

```
Install-WindowsFeature Desktop-Experience
```

Figure 2-9 The complete desktop experience in Windows Server 2012 R2 enables you to add Windows Store apps.

Installing the minimal server interface on your server requires you to remove the Start screen shell. Use the following PowerShell command and then restart your computer. You receive a command prompt window and the Server Manager console as previously shown in Figure 2-8.

```
Uninstall-WindowsFeature Server-Gui-Shell
```

Delegation of Server Administration

As an organization grows, administration of servers can become become quite overwhelming to manage. To help balance the workload and create a smooth support process, a delegation model should be implemented. Implementing a delegation model involves the following:

- Preparing for a delegation model
- Establishing delegate access
- Leveraging Active Directory
- Identifying administration tools

Preparing for a Delegation Model

Preparing for a delegation model requires some planning up front. Deciding how to manage your systems administration can be a frustrating task. The key to success is to define a model that best works for your situation, agree upon the long-term strategy, and discipline those involved to stick with the model. There are three basic strategies to select from when deciding how to manage your environment:

- **Decentralized:** This is typically designed for small mom-and-pop shops or even home offices. In this model, administrators are present at each site and all share the same responsibilities and access to the servers. This model typically introduces challenges with scalability and standardizations.

- **Centralized:** Typically found in medium to large organizations, the centralized model focuses on driving standards and consistent management from a central site or from a central group of administrators. Branch sites might employ desktop engineers who have been granted local admin rights to workstations but limited access to servers. In many cases, the centralized approach evolves to the decentralized model over time.

- **Shared/Delegated:** While a shared/delegated model can be used for an organization of any size, it is typically adopted by large/enterprise class organizations with a larger IT workforce. Containing characteristics of both decentralized and centralized models, the shared or delegated approach focuses on centralized policies and procedures governed by the enterprise admins. Enterprise admins "deputize" junior admins at each site to manage local servers and drive a consistent process among all sites. This approach is hierarchical in nature in that many layers of administration can be defined.

For example, the main office might contain the majority of the systems. These systems are managed by senior administrators or an enterprise admin group. Branch sites might contain locally significant servers such as file servers that are managed by site admins and/or the enterprise admin group. Desktop engineers might be delegated administrative access to all desktops but might escalate issues to site admins or even enterprise admins if necessary.

Establishing Delegate Access

Once a delegation model has been selected, the next step is to decide how to delegate access. Depending on the server, installed roles, and applications installed, there are different ways to delegate access. In some cases, applications or roles include an interface where elevated access is granted. In most other situations, local built-in groups can be used to grant different access to different delegates depending on their function.

For example, suppose you have delegated backup duties to a small team of junior administrators. To grant or delegate the necessary permissions, you might decide to nest, rather than add, the junior admins' domain accounts to the built-in local backup operators group on one or more servers. To help streamline this in larger organizations, you might consider additional layers of group nesting along with group policy to push down the elevated access to a group of servers. This method provides a more scalable solution as expanding delegate access is as simple as adding more junior admin accounts to a domain group. The domain group is then automatically added to the backup operators local group on the servers. Active Directory will be discussed in more detail later. Refer to Table 2-4 for a listing of built-in local groups and their functions.

Table 2-4 Built-in Local Groups

Group	Function
Access Control Assistance Operators	Remotely query permissions or authentication attributes for resources on the computer.
Administrators	Grants full access and control to the computer. Allows members to change and manage permissions and access to the computer.
Backup Operators	Ability to back up and restore files regardless of the permissions assigned to the folder or files. These users are unable to modify and manage permissions.
Certificate Services DCOM Access	Members are allowed to connect to Certificate Authorities.
Cryptographic Operators	Perform Cryptographic operations.
Distributed COM Users	Start, activate, and use DCOM objects.
Event Log Readers	Ability to read event logs on the computer.
Guests	Users are granted virtually no access to the system other than to use the Internet and basic applications. They are granted temporary profiles upon logon.
Hyper-V Administrators	Grants full control over Hyper-V.

Group	Function
IIS Users	Used by IIS Web Services.
Network Configuration Operators	Ability to make changes to TCP/IP Settings and release and renew IP addresses.
Performance Log Users	Manage and schedule performance counters logs and alerts on the computer.
Performance Monitor Users	Ability to monitor performance counters and read performance counter data.
Power Users	Typically used to provide elevated privileges for legacy applications.
Print Operators	Administer printers and print jobs on the server.
Remote Desktop Users	Members of this group are granted permission to log onto the computer remotely.
Replicator	Manages domain replication functions.
Users	Limited access to log on to the computer. Allows users to run applications, use local devices and peripherals but not make administrative changes.
WinRMRemoteWMIUsers	Ability to access WMI resources.

TIP   When delegating administrative tasks, it is a good practice to create separate delegate accounts for users. The idea is to operate on the principle of least privilege, meaning for normal operations you would use a standard user account with enough access to perform your job. When elevated privileges are required, invoke the run as function or log in with your delegate account. This reduces the risk of unintentional changes that could make for an unpleasant day for the admin.

Leveraging Active Directory

One of the major benefits of Active Directory is that you can split up administrative tasks among various individuals using the AD DS Delegation of Control Wizard. You can assign different sets of administrative responsibility to different users, and these can include segments of the directory structure such as OUs or sites. The following are several benefits of delegating administrative control:

- You can assign subsets of administrative tasks to users and groups.

- You can assign responsibility of a limited portion of the domain, such as OUs or sites, to users or groups.

- You can use a nested hierarchy of OUs for even more granular control over which users can perform certain administrative tasks.

- You can enhance network security by placing more restrictive limits on the membership of powerful groups such as Domain Admins, Enterprise Admins, and Schema Admins.

When designing your AD DS forest structure, you should keep in mind the administrative requirements of each domain. Each domain has the capability to contain a different OU hierarchy. The forest administrators, who are members of the Enterprise Admins group, are automatically granted the ability to create an OU hierarchy in any domain within the entire forest. Domain administrators, who are members of the Domain Admins group in each separate domain, by default are granted the right to create an OU hierarchy within their own domain.

When you initially create your OU design, you should do so to enable administration. After that, you should create any additional OUs required for the application of Group Policy and management of computers. Delegation of Control and management of AD DS are discussed in more detail later.

Identifying Administration Tools

The final step in delegating administrative duties is identifying the toolsets available to your delegates. Microsoft has provided us with the following tools to help with administrative tasks:

- **Server Manager:** Server Manager provides the ability to manage local or remote servers from a central location.

- **Windows PowerShell Web Access:** As we have seen previously, PowerShell is a powerful command-line tool that has been available since Windows Server 2008. As an improvement to Server 2012 R2, PowerShell now has the ability to be executed over the Web through the use of a Windows PowerShell Web Access Gateway. This is available as an installable feature through Server Manager.

NOTE   For additional information on installing and configuring PowerShell Web Access, refer to "Deploy Windows PowerShell Web Access" at http://technet. microsoft.com/en-us/library/hh831611.

- **Windows PowerShell Desired State Configuration (DSC):** PowerShell Desired State Configuration (DSC) is a PowerShell extension released with Windows Server 2012 R2 and Windows 8.1. We discuss DSC in more detail in the next section.

- **Microsoft Management Console (MMC):** As with previous versions of Windows, the MMC is still a powerful tool used by administrators to manage local and remote servers. You can create custom read-only MMC consoles with specific snap-ins containing only those tools required for the specific delegate function.

- **Remote Server Administration Tools:** Provides a set of tools to be used with client computers running Windows 8/8.1. It includes Server Manager, MMC snap-ins, PowerShell cmdlets, and additional command-line tools used to manage Windows Server 2012 R2 Core and Full installations. You can download Remote Server Administration tools from the Microsoft Download Center as a standalone installer.

NOTE   Before using administrative tools, you must first ensure that the necessary access rights have been granted and that you have addressed any prerequisites, such as .Net Framework 4.5, Windows Management Framework 4.0, or Firewall configurations.

Windows PowerShell Desired State Configuration

As mentioned previously, Windows PowerShell Desired State Configuration (DSC) was designed to enhance the levels of automation through the use of PowerShell 4.0. It helps administrators cut down on repetitive tasks by defining prebuilt configurations that accompany PowerShell 4.0 cmdlets. Configuration parameters are saved in a Managed Object File (MOF) and can be used as a baseline for comparison or as a template for new deployments. DSC is often used in the following situations:

- You need to verify or test applied system configurations against a configuration baseline defined in the DSC configuration.

- When using PowerShell to install or remove Server Roles/Features or installation packages based on specific configurations.

- You need to review or make changes to registry settings, environment variables, processes, or services.

- You need to manage local users/groups to ensure that they are configured according to DSC.

To function properly, DSC requires the following components:

- A strong knowledge of PowerShell

- Installation of the Windows PowerShell Desired State Configuration Service feature

- .NET Framework 4.5

- Windows Communication Foundation (WCF) Services

- Web Server (IIS) and related role services/features

- Clients running at least Windows 7 or Windows Server 2008 R2 with Windows Management Framework 4.0

Installing and Configuring DSC

DSC works via two basic methods: Pull and Push. The Pull method works through the use of a Pull Server. Using this method, you can configure a server as the Pull Server, which acts as central configuration repository storing the configuration data for computers. The Pull Server stores DSC resources required by the target computers, also known as *nodes*. In large environments, nodes can be configured to pull from the server as they come online. The second method is the Push method. In smaller implementations, a central server can be configured to Push DSC configurations. The down side is that this doesn't always guarantee that all nodes receive the updated configuration. As an administrator, you also have the ability to use a combination of both Pull and Push methods.

DSC works through the basis of defining configurations within scripts. Using Notepad, you can build a custom DSC configuration. Configurations contain several components, all of which are organized within a *configuration block*. The keyword **Configuration** tells PowerShell that a specific configuration is to follow. The use of braces **{ }** identify the start and end of the configuration. Together, both of these items create the foundation of a configuration block. The basic structure of a configuration block is

```
Configuration MyConfigName
{

}
```

Inside the configuration block, *node blocks* are identified. A node represents a computer in the environment. Nodes are used when you need to apply a configuration block to a specific computer or computers. Like configuration blocks, node blocks start and end with a brace **{ }**. Multiple node blocks can be created within a configuration block, although a configuration block does not have to contain any node blocks. Depending on the requirements, you might need to use node blocks.

```
Configuration MyConfigName
{
```

```
Node "MyComputer1"
    {

    }

}
```

Inside the node blocks, *resource blocks* can be identified. Resource blocks are used to configure specific resources. These can be configured manually, or you can use several prebuilt resources available within the PowerShell framework. Some of the built-in resources include

- **DSC Configuration Archive:** For working with compressed/archive files
- **DSC Configuration Environment:** For managing computer environmental configurations
- **DSC Configuration File:** For manging files and folders
- **DSC Configuration Group:** For managing local groups on target nodes
- **DSC Configuration Log:** For writing messages to the DSC event log
- **DSC Configuration Package:** For installing msi/exe packages
- **DSC Configuration Process:** For managing processes on target nodes
- **DSC Configuration Registry:** For managing registry keys on target nodes
- **DSC Configuration Role:** For adding or removing Windows features and roles on target nodes
- **DSC Configuration Script:** For running PowerShell script blocks on target nodes
- **DSC Configuration Service:** For managing services on target nodes
- **DSC Configuration User:** For managing local user accounts on target nodes

Resource blocks are identified by a resource name followed by an identifier. Again, use braces to establish the start/finish boundary. For example, to add configuration details to ensure that the Web-Server role is installed for **MyComputer1**, use the following syntax:

```
Configuration MyConfigName
{
    Node "MyComputer1"
        {
                WindowsFeature MyRoles
```

```
                              {
                              Ensure = "Present"
                              Name = "Web-Server"
                              }
                  }

}
```

After you have created the appropriate configurations, save it as a PowerShell script. To invoke the configuration, execute it via an administrative PowerShell session. Invoking the configuration creates the MOF file in the working directory containing the configuration block script. To execute the configuration, run the command:

```
Start-DscConfiguration -Wait -Verbose -Path .\MyConfigName
```

> **NOTE** The intent of this section was to provide a high-level overview of DSC and how to use it. There are a variety of configuration parameters and best practices that go beyond the scope of this *Cert Guide*. For more information on implementing DSC, refer to "Windows PowerShell Desired State Configuration Overview" at http://technet.microsoft.com/en-us/library/dn249912.aspx.

Configuring Offline Server Images

In any large-scale deployment, imaging technology will be one of your strongest allies. Microsoft has continued to evolve its imaging process through enhancements made to the Windows Deployment Services (WDS) role. WDS is covered in the *70-411 Cert Guide*, but in this section, we will assume you already have a prebuilt image and are looking to perform offline servicing of the image.

So what is meant by servicing an image, and why offline? Historically speaking, updates to images required the administrator to deploy a new computer from the image, run through any customizations or updates, repackage the image, and upload it back to the repository. This is often a lengthy process—especially when only minor updates are required. For these instances, Microsoft has provided the ability to inject updates to a Windows image file (.wim) or virtual hard disk (.vhd or .vhdx) via the command line. Scenarios in which images require updating include

- Enable or disable Windows roles and features
- Add or remove drivers or installable packages such as hotfixes
- Perform an inventory of installed packages, drivers, features, and so on

- Modify logging abilities to help post deployment troubleshooting

- Modify the offlineServicing section of an Unattend.xml answer file

- Configure international settings

- Upgrade the installation to a higher edition of Windows

Deployment Image Servicing and Management

Servicing an image offline requires an understanding of the Deployment Image Servicing and Management (DISM) tool. DISM is a command-line tool included in Windows Server 2012 R2. For previous installations of Windows it is also available within the Windows Automated Installation Kit (AIK), which can be downloaded from the Microsoft Download Center.

DISM takes the legwork out of the mix by enabling an administrator to mount the image file, similar to mounting a hard disk, and issue commands to update the image. When the updating is complete, changes are committed to the image and the file is unmounted, in which case the image is ready for the next deployment. Some key points and best practices to consider when using DISM:

- Must be run as administrator.

- Service an image offline whenever possible.

- If Windows image files are split or spanned across multiple types of media, you must copy them centrally to a single folder to service. Without this, mounting the image is not possible.

- Keep architecture consistent, meaning don't inject x64 drivers into x86 images.

- Remote image updates is not currently supported. To make any changes, you must first copy the Windows image to the local machine, perform the necessary updates, and then copy the image back to the repository.

- After deployment, use the system file checker **sfc.exe /verifyonly** option.

TIP   DISM is typically used for updating offline images, but it can also be used to update servers that are online especially in cases when you need a fast method to standardize or update to a higher edition of Windows.

There are several parameters you should understand when servicing images. Table 2-5 outlines some of the key parameters:

Table 2-5 Useful DISM Parameters

Command	Meaning
`/Get-ImageInfo`	Used to gather information from the image file such as index number, image name, description, and image size.
`/ImageFile`	Used to identify the location of the source image file.
`/Mount-Image`	Parameter used to mount the image. When mounting the image, you must also specify an in index number or the name associated with the image. This information can be extracted from the `/Get-ImageInfo` parameter.
`/MountDir`	Directory in which the image is mounted to. For optimal performance, this should be on the local computer that is updating the image.`Dism /Mount-Image /ImageFile:C:\TestImages\TestImage.wim /Name:"Image Name" /Mountdir:C:\MountedImage`
`/Cleanup-Mountpoints`	In some cases images might become locked/orphaned and are unable to be remounted. Use this switch when experiencing trouble with mounting images that might have been previously mounted.
`/Add-Package`	Adds one or more install packages or cabinet files (.cab) to a mounted image. When applying multiple packages, packages are listed in the order in which they should be installed. `/Add-Package /PackagePath:[package path\package.cab] /PackagePath:[second package path\package2.cab]`
`/Add-Driver`	Adds a driver to the offline image. For third-party drivers, you might choose the `/ForceUnsigned` switch.
`/Remove-Driver`	Removes a driver from the offline image.
`/Commit-Image`	Applies changes made to a mounted image and leaves the image mounted for additional changes.
`/Get-Packages`	Produces a list of Packages from the mounted image in the mount directory. This can also be piped > to a .txt file for easy reading.
`/Get-Features`	Produces a list of features by their case-sensitive name and their enabled/disabled status. This can also be piped > to a .txt file for easy reading. It's used in conjunction with **`/Get-FeatureInfo /FeatureName:[FeatureName]`** to output additional details for the feature.
`/Enable-Feature`	Enables a specific feature.
`/Disable-Feature`	Disables a specific feature.
`/Remove-Package`	Removes an installed package.

Command	Meaning
/Unmount-Image	Unmounts the image. Use the /commit or /discard switch to apply or cancel any changes made before the image is unmounted.
/Set-Edition	Used to change an offline windows image to a higher edition. This might also be done online with the /AcceptEula and /ProductKey switches.

NOTE   This list is introduces only a few of the DISM parameters. For a full list of options, refer to "Deployment Image Servicing and Management Command Line Options Reference" at http://technet.microsoft.com/en-us/library/hh825099.aspx.

Using DISM to Enable Remote Desktop Services

Now that you have an understanding of DISM and some of the key options, let's see it in action by enabling the Remote Desktop Services feature in an offline image. The first thing you need to do is obtain a copy of the source image. In this example, we will use one of the default Windows image files found on the Server installation media and extracted by a WDS server. Again, WDS is covered in more detail in the *70-411 Exam Cert Guide*. To enable a feature in an offline image, perform the following steps:

1. Gather identifying information from the image using the /Get-ImageInfo option as shown in Figure 2-10.

Figure 2-10 Dism /Get-ImageInfo

2. Using either the index number or name of the image, mount the image to a temporary mount directory. This will extract the contents of the image (Figure 2-11) to a directory structure in the temp mount directory specified. This process might take time depending on the speed of your computer.

```
PS C:\TestImages> dism /Mount-Image /ImageFile:c:\testimages\testimage.wim /Name:"Windows Server 2012 SERVERDATACENTER"
/MountDir:c:\mountedimage

Deployment Image Servicing and Management tool
Version: 6.2.9200.16384

Mounting image
[==========================100.0%==========================]
The operation completed successfully.
PS C:\TestImages>
```

Figure 2-11 Dism /Mount-Image.

3. Review the current state of the Remote-Desktop-Services feature. Shown in Figure 2-12, take notice that the feature is currently disabled.

```
PS C:\TestImages> dism /Image:c:\mountedimage /Get-FeatureInfo /FeatureName:Remote-Desktop-Services

Deployment Image Servicing and Management tool
Version: 6.2.9200.16384

Image Version: 6.2.9200.16384

Feature Information:

Feature Name : Remote-Desktop-Services
Display Name : Remote Desktop Services
Description : Add or remove Remote Desktop Services.
Restart Required : Possible
State : Disabled

Custom Properties:

ServerComponent\Description : <a href="TS_admin.chm::/html/2584b4b6-9185-4914-9f3f-9e60a72a3bda.htm">Remote Desktop Serv
ices</a> enables users to access virtual desktops, session-based desktops, and RemoteApp programs. Use the Remote Deskto
p Services installation to configure a Virtual machine-based or a Session-based desktop deployment.
ServerComponent\DisplayName : Remote Desktop Services
ServerComponent\EventQuery : RemoteDesktop.Events.xml
ServerComponent\Id : 18
ServerComponent\Type : Role
ServerComponent\UniqueName : Remote-Desktop-Services
ServerComponent\Version\Major : 6
ServerComponent\Version\Minor : 2
ServerComponent\BestPractices\Model\Id : Microsoft/Windows/TerminalServices

The operation completed successfully.
PS C:\TestImages> _
```

Figure 2-12 Dism /Get-FeatureInfo /FeatureName:Remote-Desktop-Services.

4. Enable the Remote-Desktop-Services feature in the offline image by executing the command shown in Figure 2-13.

```
PS C:\TestImages> dism /Image:c:\mountedimage /Enable-Feature /FeatureName:Remote-Desktop-Services

Deployment Image Servicing and Management tool
Version: 6.2.9200.16384

Image Version: 6.2.9200.16384

Enabling feature(s)
[==========================100.0%==========================]
The operation completed successfully.
PS C:\TestImages> _
```

Figure 2-13 Dism /Enable-Feature /FeatureName:Remote-Desktop-Services.

5. Verify that the feature has been enabled using the `Dism /Get-FeatureInfo` command as shown in Figure 2-14.

```
PS C:\TestImages> dism /Image:c:\mountedimage /Get-FeatureInfo /FeatureName:Remote-Desktop-Services

Deployment Image Servicing and Management tool
Version: 6.2.9200.16384

Image Version: 6.2.9200.16384

Feature Information:

Feature Name : Remote-Desktop-Services
Display Name : Remote Desktop Services
Description : Add or remove Remote Desktop Services.
Restart Required : Possible
State : Enabled

Custom Properties:

ServerComponent\Description : <a href="TS_admin.chm::/html/2584b4b6-9185-4914-9f3f-9e60a72a3bda.htm">Remote Desktop Serv
ices</a> enables users to access virtual desktops, session-based desktops, and RemoteApp programs. Use the Remote Deskto
p Services installation to configure a Virtual machine-based or a Session-based desktop deployment.
ServerComponent\DisplayName : Remote Desktop Services
ServerComponent\EventQuery : RemoteDesktop.Events.xml
ServerComponent\Id : 18
ServerComponent\Type : Role
ServerComponent\UniqueName : Remote-Desktop-Services
ServerComponent\Version\Major : 6
ServerComponent\Version\Minor : 2
ServerComponent\BestPractices\Model\Id : Microsoft/Windows/TerminalServices

The operation completed successfully.
PS C:\TestImages> _
```

Figure 2-14 Change Verification—`Dism /Get-FeatureInfo /FeatureName:Remote-Desktop-Services`.

6. Commit changes to the image and unmount the **.wim** file, as shown in Figure 2-15. This will repackage the image file with the changes made. It might take some time depending on the speed of your computer.

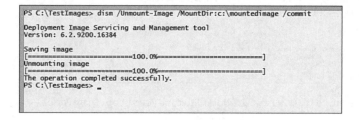

Figure 2-15 `Dism /Unmount-Image /commit`.

NOTE When unmounting images, it is important to close all windows and applications, especially File Explorer windows. This will help prevent locks during the unmounting process.

Configuring Remote Server Roles

As discussed previously, remote management of servers is extremely helpful for an administrator, especially in scenarios in which your organization is driving a centralized management approach or if you are managing a group of Server Core installations.

Before remote management can occur, the remote servers must be configured to enable remote management. This is on by default for new installations but can be changed by navigating to the Local Server properties of Server Manager as shown in Figure 2-16.

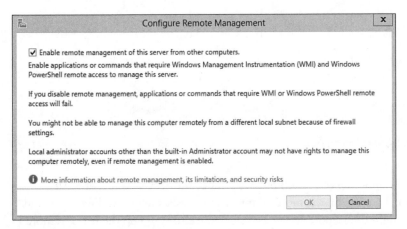

Figure 2-16 Server Manager Remote Management.

Similarly, remote management can be also be configured using the PowerShell command `Configure-SMRemoting.exe -Enable` or the `-Disable` switch if choosing to disable the service.

> **NOTE**   To enable remote management on legacy systems, you might be required to perform additional configuration steps, such as enabling WMI through the Windows Firewall service. For more information, refer to "Manage Multiple, Remote Servers with Server Manager" at http://technet.microsoft.com/en-us/library/hh831456.aspx.

Once enabled for remote management, use the **Add other servers to manage** feature from the Server Manager Dashboard. The Add Servers dialog enables you to search for remote servers using Active Directory by importing a list from a text file or by using DNS as shown in Figure 2-17.

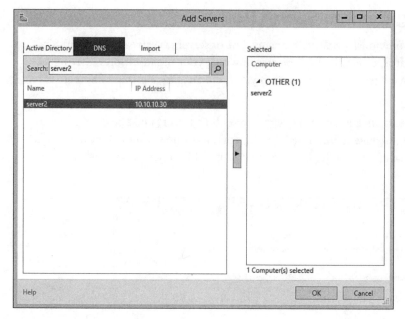

Figure 2-17 Add Servers Dialog Box.

After adding a remote server, it will be listed under the Server Manager > All Servers group. To perform a remote administrative task, such as Adding Roles and Features, highlight the remote server and right-click to bring up the list of remote management options as shown in Figure 2-18.

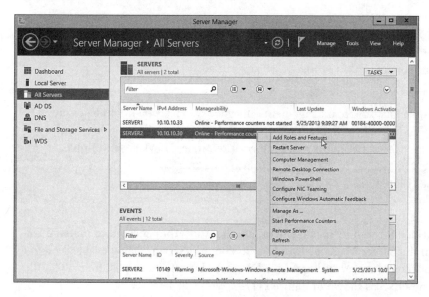

Figure 2-18 Adding Roles and Features Remotely.

NOTE   In situations where different security boundaries—such as managing between workgroups or domains—exist, you might consider using the **Manage As** function to first supply the necessary authoritative credentials.

From this point, step through the Add Roles and Features Wizard as you have done previously. The only difference this time is to select the remote server previously added. To ensure the proper remote server is selected, take note of the destination server listed in the upper-right corner of the dialog box, as shown in Figure 2-19.

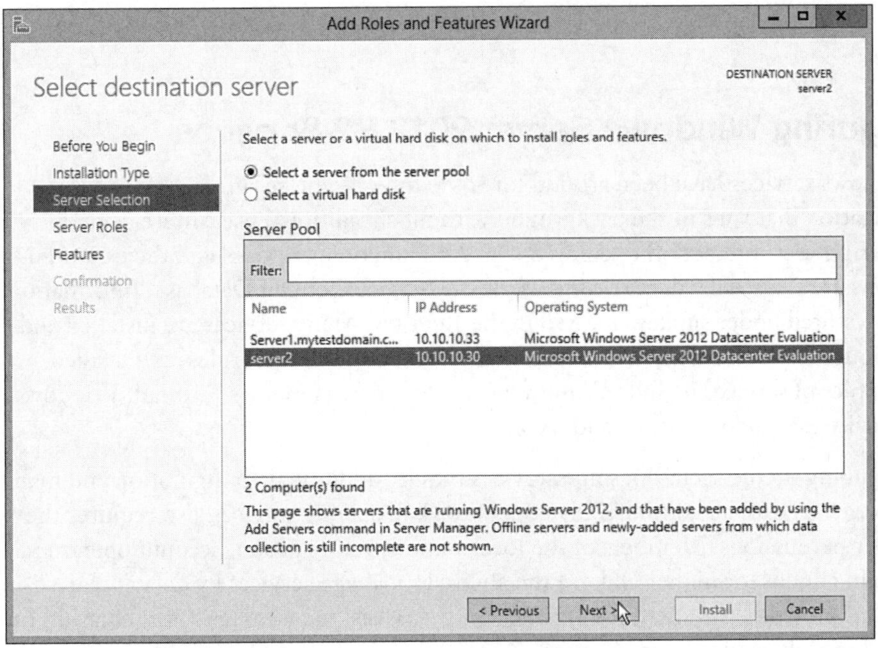

Figure 2-19   Adding Roles and Features to Destination Server.

After you have installed the role, you now have the ability to manage and configure services associated with the role centrally from Server Manager on your managing server. In addition to Server Manager, PowerShell can be another powerful tool to simplify the installation and management of server roles remotely.

Using PowerShell, an administrator can perform a series of commands. Some common commands are outlined in Table 2-6.

Table 2-6 PowerShell Remote Server Commands

Command	Meaning
`Get-WindowsFeature -ComputerName` `[remote computer name]`	Retrieves a list of roles and features installed on the remote server specified
`Install-WindowsFeature -Name` `[feature name] -ComputerName` `[remote computer name] -Restart`	Installs a specific feature to the destination computer listed. Issues a restart if required
`Uninstall-WindowsFeature -Name` `[feature name] -ComputerName` `[remote computer name] -Restart`	Removes a specific feature to the destination computer listed. Issues a restart if required.

Configuring Windows Server 2012 R2 Services

Windows services have been around for some time. If you recall, a service is an application that runs in the background without a traditional user interface or requiring user interaction to complete its core function. Services and their configurations are stored in a database known as the Service Control Database. Information is also stored under subkeys located in the Registry. Many services are installed and configured by default when the operating system or additional roles are installed. Examples of services include Windows Print Spooler, Windows Firewall, Windows Event Log, Windows Time, and so on.

Depending on the scenario, some services require additional configuration and management. As with all administrative operations, managing services also requires the proper permissions. Members of the local administrators group, account operators, domain admins, or higher all have the ability to manage services by default. Microsoft has provided two methods for managing services, the `services.msc` snap-in for the Microsoft Management Console (MMC) and the Service Controller configuration `sc config` command. An administrator will use these methods to perform the following:

- Local and remote administration of services

- Configuration of custom developed services

- Start, stop, pause, resume, or disable services

- Configure recovery actions if a service fails

- Run services as a specific user

- Enable or disable services for certain hardware profiles

- View service status and details

Services.msc

To manage services via a GUI, use the Services.msc snap-in. The services snap-in, as shown in Figure 2-20, can be launched by searching for services.msc from the Charms bar or by navigating to **Start > Administrative Tools > Services**.

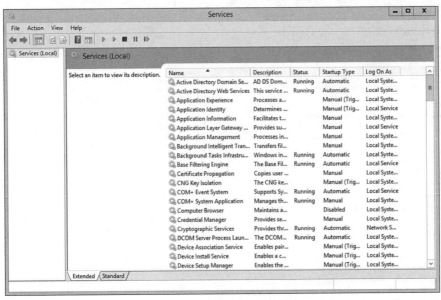

Figure 2-20   Services Snap-in for Microsoft Management Console.

In the instances where services need to be managed remotely from a central console, you can add the Services snap-in to a custom Microsoft Management Console. To do this, launch the MMC application from the Search charm, add the Services snap-in to the console, and specify the name of another computer or browse to it using the **Browse** button as shown in Figure 2-21.

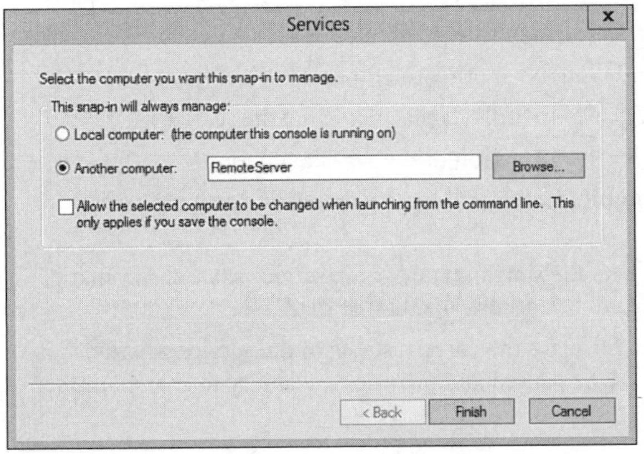

Figure 2-21   Remote Services Management.

Regardless of local or remote, a handful of items are configurable from the Services snap-in. Each service listed has a series of configurable properties. For example, Figure 2-22 illustrates the Properties dialog box for the Windows Firewall service (MpsSvc).

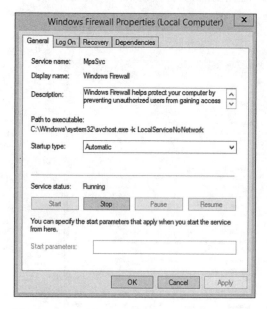

Figure 2-22   Windows Firewall (MpsSvc) Properties Dialog Box.

As you can see, several configurable items are grouped into different tabs as outlined in Table 2-7.

Table 2-7   Configurable Properties for Services

Property Tab	Description
General	Used to view information about the service such as: ■ **Service name:** Windows short name for the service ■ **Display name:** User-friendly display name for the service ■ **Description:** Brief explanation of the service function ■ **Path to executable:** Local path for the executable or binary of the service ■ **Startup type:** Sets the startup type for the service such as automatic, automatic with a delayed start, manual, or disabled ■ **Service status:** Displays the current status of the service whether it is running, stopped, or paused and provides the ability to change the service status

Property Tab	Description
Log On	Used to configure the account used to start the service upon boot up. In most cases, this is defaulted to the Local Service or System built in accounts. If a specific account has been delegated the ability to run the service, this tab provides the ability to supply the authoritative credentials.
Recovery	Provides recovery options and the automated responses if the service fails.
Dependencies	Lists the dependant and depending services or applications for the specific service.

SC Commands

For local or remote management through the command line, Microsoft has included the ability to interface with the Service Controller using the **C:\Windows\System32\SC.exe** application. Launch the application by opening an Admin Command Prompt by right-clicking the **Start** button and choosing **Command Prompt (Admin)**. SC.exe is particularly useful when working with Server Cores and for testing/troubleshooting issues. Commonly used SC commands are listed in Table 2-8.

Table 2-8   Common SC Commands

Command	Meaning
`SC Query`	Queries a server for Service Status. Outputs information such as Service Name, Display Name, Type, and State of the service. `SC [\\ServerName] Query`
`SC [Start, Stop, Pause, Continue]`	Executes command to start, pause/continue, or stop a service. `SC [\\ServerName] [Start/Stop/ Pause/Continue] [ServiceName]`
`SC Create`	Creates a new service in the Service Control Managers database. The startup type, location to the binary path, display name, and so on are among the configuration options for this command.
`SC Config`	Configures local or remote services. `SC [\\ServerName] config [ServiceName] [options]` **Common Options:** ■ *Start*=[boot, auto, demand, disabled]
`SC delete`	Deletes a service. `SC [\\ServerName] delete [ServiceName]`

Command	Meaning
SC description	Provides or updates the user friendly name, or description of a service. **SC** [\\ServerName] **description** [ServiceName] [Description]
SC failure	Sets the services automatic recovery options if a failure occurs. **SC** [\\ServerName] **failure** [ServiceName] [Options] **Common Options:** ■ *Reset=* [x, where x is the period of time measured in seconds in which the error count will be reset back to zero] ■ *Reboot=* [message to be broadcasted upon failure] ■ *Command=* [command to be executed upon failure] ■ *Actions=* [Specifies the actions and time in which they will occur such as run, restart, and reboot]

NOTE   These are only a few of the options available for the SC command. For a complete list, refer to "SC" at http://technet.microsoft.com/en-us/library/bb490995.aspx.

Configuring NIC Teaming

NIC Teaming, also known as Load Balancing/Fail Over (LBFO), is a strategy used to increase network availability and overall performance. Multiple network interface cards are joined together and operate as a single entity. Previously, NIC Teaming was left for the manufacturers to provide a tool. Today, NIC Teaming is included in Windows Server 2012 R2 to provide the following capabilities:

■ **High Availability:** A server can contain multiple network cards, each connected to a different network switch part of the same network segment. This scenario provides high network link availability in the event of a single NIC failure, single switch failure, or single link failure.

■ **Increased Throughput:** Multiple network interface cards can be teamed together to provide increased throughput or load-balancing capabilities. The aggregation of multiple links provides a "larger pipe" to connect to the network.

Configure NIC Teaming via GUI

You can launch the NIC Teaming configuration interface, as shown in Figure 2-23, from the Server Manager Local screen. To configure NIC Teaming via GUI, perform the following steps:

1. From the NIC Teaming interface, highlight the available adapters to be added to the team as shown in Figure 2-23.

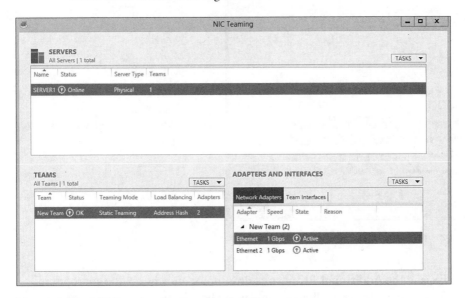

Figure 2-23   NIC Teaming Configuration Interface.

2. Once highlighted, select **Add to New Team** from the **Tasks** drop-down list. This will launch the New team dialog box.

3. Type a Team name in the NIC Teaming dialog box as shown in Figure 2-24. Confirm that all appropriate adapters are checked.

Figure 2-24   New Team Dialog Box.

4. Expand the **Additional Properties** drop-down and choose the appropriate Teaming mode. The following modes can be selected:

- **Static Teaming:** This mode requires custom configurations on the switch and host to identify the links as being part of the team. Static Teaming is considered a Switch Dependent mode because it depends on the switch for configuration. It is used for custom scenarios with supported switches where more granular or manual control is required.

- **Switch Independent:** Refers to the ability of the NIC Team to manage the connections to the switches and keeps track of the teams' connection state. This is the most common teaming method as it supports just about any Ethernet switch. This option enables the NIC Team to split adapters' connections between one or multiple switches.

  Because the Team manages the connection states, Switch Independent mode also provides an option for Active/Active or Active/Standby teaming. In Active/Active, all links are used for load balancing and throughput. For Active/Standby teaming, one link can be designated as the active link where others are remaining passive. The passive links stand by and take over during a failover event resulting from the active link failing.

- **LACP:** Link Aggregation Control Protocol (LACP) is a Switch-Dependent mode used to dynamically identify and aggregate links between a host and switch. An enterprise class managed switch is required.

5. Choose the appropriate load balancing mode from the following options:

   - **Address Hash:** Load balances outbound network traffic across all active NICs. Inbound traffic is received by only one NIC in the team. This mode is typically seen with web servers.

   - **Hyper-V Port:** Provides improved support for load balancing between virtual machines (VMs). Hyper-V works with the NIC Team to load balance and deliver VM traffic over specific NICs.

6. Select the appropriate Standy adapter by selecting a specific adapter or choosing **None** where all adapters remain active.

7. Confirm the Primary team interface. This enables you to choose the default or specific Virtual Local Area Network (VLAN).

8. Click **OK** when complete.

After you have successfully configured a NIC Team, a new logical adapter will be available for management under the Network and Sharing Center. From here, you can manage adapter settings much like you have done previously with a traditional adapter. In the event that you decide to remove the NIC Team, the NIC Team user interface will return the adapters to the previous state prior to teaming.

> **NOTE**   There are many scenarios and configurations for NIC Teaming. For a complete installation and configuration guide, refer to "Windows Server 2012 R2 NIC Teaming Deployment and Management" available from the Microsoft Download Center at http://www.microsoft.com/en-us/download/details.aspx?id=40319.

Configure Basic NIC Teaming via PowerShell

You can configure NIC Teams by issuing PowerShell commands. To create a new NIC Team, execute the following command:

```
New-NetLbfoTeam [Team Name], Ethernet, Ethernet 2
```

Once issued, the NIC Team will be established and enabled in the default Switch Independent mode. To remove the NIC Team, execute the command:

```
Remove-NetLbfoTeam [Team Name]
```

> **NOTE**   For a complete list of PowerShell cmdlets refer to "NIC Teaming Cmdlets in PowerShell" at, http://technet.microsoft.com/en-us/library/jj130849(v=wps.620).aspx.

Exam Preparation Tasks

Review All the Key Topics

Review the most important topics in the chapter, noted with the key topics icon in the outer margin of the page. Table 2-9 lists a reference of these key topics and the page numbers on which each is found.

Table 2-9   Key Topics for Chapter 2

Key Topic Element	Description	Page Number
Table 2-2	Describes the minimum hardware requirements for installing Windows Server 2012 R2.	40
Step list	Shows you how to install the Server Core version of Windows Server 2012 R2.	42
Figure 2-3	You can select either the Server Core version or the Server with a GUI.	43
Table 2-3	Summarizes several more common commands used in configuring Server Core.	46
Step list	Shows you how to install the Server with a GUI version of Windows Server 2012 R2.	48
Step list	Shows you how to convert your server from Server with a GUI to Server Core.	50
Step list	Shows you how to convert your server from Server Core to Server with a GUI.	50
Table 2-4	Listing of local groups built into Windows Server 2012 R2.	53

Key Topic Element	Description	Page Number
Step list	Shows you tasks to complete when servicing offline images.	62
Step list	Shows you how to create a new NIC team using the NIC Teaming interface.	73
Paragraph	Shows you how to configure NIC Teaming via PowerShell.	75

Complete the Tables and Lists from Memory

Print a copy of Appendix B, "Memory Tables" (found on the CD), or at least the section for this chapter, and complete the tables and lists from memory. Appendix C, "Memory Tables Answer Key," is also on the CD and includes completed tables and lists to check your work.

Definitions of Key Terms

Define the following key terms from this chapter, and check your answers in the glossary.

Desired State Configuration (DSC), Failover, Load Balance, Sconfig.cmd, Windows PowerShell

This chapter covers the following subjects:

- **Designing storage spaces:** Planning is one of the most important aspects for any deployment. This section introduces storage spaces and the many benefits they bring to the table, including the support for disk enclosures and tiered storage under Windows Server 2012 R2.

- **Configuring Basic and Dynamic Disks:** This section provides an overview of basic and dynamic disks and how to manage them within Windows.

- **Configuring MBR and GPT Disks:** This section discusses the importance of disk signatures and partition tables and when to use each type.

- **Managing Volumes:** Taking a deeper look into basic and dynamic disks, this section identifies the various types of basic volumes and advanced disk configurations with the use of dynamic disks.

- **Creating and Mounting Virtual Hard Disks (VHDs):** This section provides you with an understanding of virtual hard disks and how to manage them in your environment using tools such as Disk Management.

- **Configuring Storage Pools and Disk Pools:** This section provides step-by-step instructions on how to implement storage pools and virtual disks.

CHAPTER 3

Configuring Windows Server 2012 R2 Local Storage

The Microsoft 70-410 exam assesses your ability to configure and administer local storage on Windows Server 2012 R2. This chapter reviews basic disk fundamentals and advanced disk configurations and provides a framework for you to identify the appropriate storage strategy for your servers.

"Do I Know This Already?" Quiz

The "Do I Know This Already?" quiz enables you to assess whether you should read this entire chapter or simply jump to the "Exam Preparation Tasks" section for review. If you are in doubt, read the entire chapter. Table 3-1 outlines the major headings in this chapter and the corresponding "Do I Know This Already?" quiz questions. You can find the answers in Appendix A, "Answers to the 'Do I Know This Already?' Quizzes."

Table 3-1 "Do I Know This Already?" Foundation Topics Section-to-Question Mapping

Foundations Topics Section	Questions Covered in This Section
Designing Storage Spaces	1
Configuring Basic and Dynamic Disks	2
Configuring MBR and GPT Disks	3
Managing Volumes	4
Creating and Mounting Virtual Hard Disks (VHDs)	5–7
Configuring Storage Pools and Disk Pools	8–10

1. Which storage space configuration should you use if you need to provide fault tolerance for a three-drive configuration?

   a. Simple

   b. Parity

   c. Mirror

   d. RAID 1

2. Which are the following scenarios require dynamic disks? (Choose all that apply.)

   a. You need to create a mirrored volume.

   b. You need to create a simple volume.

   c. You need to create four partitions on a single drive.

   d. You need to configure software RAID on your server.

3. You have recently purchased a 4-TB drive that you want to add to your server. Which partition type must you use to address this new volume?

   a. MBR

   b. GPT

   c. Storage pool

   d. VHD

4. You have been asked to design a local storage solution that offers fast read access for your files and offers protection against a single drive failure. Which RAID level should you use?

   a. RAID 0

   b. RAID 1

   c. RAID 2

   d. RAID 5

5. You need to create a 3-TB virtual hard disk. Which format should you use?

   a. Thin provisioning

   b. .VHDX

   c. Fixed provisioning

   d. .VHD

6. You need to create a portable VHD to use between your Windows Server 2008 and Windows Server 2012 R2 computers. Which format should you use?

    a. vDisk

    b. .VHDX

    c. .VHD

    d. .vfile

7. Which command-line tool can be used to mount and dismount virtual disks?

    a. `fdisk`

    b. `DiskPart`

    c. `chkdsk`

    d. `fixmbr`

8. Which of the following tools can be used to create storage pools?

    a. Disk Management

    b. Storage Configuration Manager

    c. File and Storage Services

    d. WDS

9. What is the name of the default storage pool that contains a listing of physical disks installed on your server?

    a. Primordial

    b. Default storage pool

    c. Unallocated

    d. Disk0

10. You need to configure your server's storage to provide storage for two separate applications. Application A requires 500 GB of storage, and Application B requires 200 GB of storage. You have purchased four 200-GB drives. You need to make sure that you provision enough storage from day one and that the storage for each application does not interfere with any other. Each answer represents part of a solution. (Choose two.)

   a. Use the Disk Management snap-in to create two mirrored volumes.

   b. Create a storage pool using File and Storage Services and use all four 200-GB drives.

   c. Create a storage pool using the Storage Pool Manager.

   d. Create two virtual disks using fixed provisioning.

   e. Create two virtual disks using thin provisioning.

   f. Use the Disk Management snap-in to create a new storage pool.

Foundation Topics

Designing Storage Spaces

Although the cost of storage has come down over the years, we always seem to find ourselves looking for more space to land our files. As a new capability for Windows Server 2012 R2, Microsoft has included a concept known as *storage spaces*. Storage spaces allow for the creation of virtual disks from a pool of storage created by grouping standard physical disks. Storage spaces provide the following benefits:

- Optimal storage allocation

- Improved administrative control

- Scalability

- High availability

Optimal Storage Allocation

Historically speaking, servers used local or direct attached storage. As you needed more space, you would have to purchase additional drives and, in some cases, a new server. Similarly, to separate storage for different applications, you might be required to stand up a separate server. The overcommitment of storage and resources becomes quite costly over time. To help provide a more cost-effective and scalable solution, storage pools can be configured to help you maximize storage investments.

A *storage pool* is a group of physical disks combined to create a shared pool of storage. The concept of pooled storage provides you with more granular control over your storage investment by providing the ability to allocate just the right amount of storage to your server. This strategy helps to reduce overcommitting storage. Storage provisioning is covered in more detail later this chapter.

Once pooled, storage can be allocated as one large volume, or it can be carved up into smaller segments known as storage spaces. Storage spaces enable you to configure smaller virtual hard disks (VHDs), which are discussed later, and allocate virtual disks to different servers or as separate volumes within the same server.

One of the key points of storage pools is that they can be designed to expand as needed. For example, suppose you are installing Windows Server 2012 R2 with the Hyper-V role. You purchase five 2-TB drives. From here, you might decide you need to create one virtual file server and one virtual Exchange server. Both will run as guests on your Hyper-V server. You might decide to split the storage equally between the virtual machines (VMs), but this might not be an optimal use of your storage depending on your current and future needs. Alternatively, you could consider creating a 10-TB storage pool. From here, you might decide that you only need 2 TB for Exchange and 1 TB for the file server to start out. With your 10-TB storage pool, you can carve up a 2-TB virtual drive for Exchange and a 1-TB virtual drive for your file server. Each drive will be given its own storage space from the pool. In the event that you need to add more storage to either server, you can add storage by drawing down from the remaining storage pool.

Improved Administrative Control

Storage pools and storage spaces help reduce administrative overhead of managing separate physical storage arrays. Fewer moving parts correlate to lower administrative costs and in many situations fewer headaches. Secondly, storage pools provide more granular administrative control as they can take advantage of Access Control Lists (ACLs) for the purpose of delegated administration. This is particularly helpful if you need to present a portion of the pool to different servers or separate administrators.

Scalability

Storage pools and storage spaces provide a more scalable solution over legacy storage strategies. The use of virtual disks allows for easier data migrations, which in many cases can occur in a nondisruptive manner.

Furthermore, unlike traditional physical disks, storage pools allow for dynamic expansion. If you are running low on space or if your pool dries up, additional storage can be added to the pool with little effort. Physical storage can be added or mixed from a variety of disk types, whether 10,000/15,000 RPM SATA drives, solid state, and so on, depending on your performance and capacity needs. The following disk types and configurations are supported:

- Serial attached drives such as SCSI or SAS

- SATA drives

- JBOD enclosures

- RAID enclosures with disabled RAID functionality

- USB-attached drives

- Clustered storage appliances

- Physical disks must be at least 4 GB

- Disks must be blank and unformatted

High Availability

Storage spaces can be designed and configured for high availability (HA) scenarios. Depending on the situation, storage pools can be designed using one of the configurations listed in Table 3-2.

Table 3-2 Storage Space Configurations

Configuration	Details	Scenario
Simple	Stripes data across physical disks.	Used in situations where high availability is not required, but maximum storage and throughput are.
Mirror	Requires a minimum of two physical disks to protect from a single disk failure and at least five physical disks to protect from two disk failures. As data is written, a duplicate copy is striped across multiple drives. Storage capacity is reduced with the increased redundancy. Windows Server 2012 R2 now enables the use of parity space for failover clusters.	The default and most commonly used configuration.
Parity	Requires a minimum of three physical disks to protect from a single disk failure. Data and parity information is striped across physical disks. Takes advantage of data journaling to keep track of the writes should an unplanned shutdown occur.	Used in scenarios that use sequential write methods such as a backup to disk solution. Due to its journaling feature, this is often used in scenarios in which you need to reduce chances of data corruption.
Dual Parity	Introduced under Windows Server 2012 and continued in Windows Server 2012 R2, dual parity provides the ability to add disks to store additional parity information.	Used when you need to protect from two simultaneous disk failures.
Storage Tiers	Windows Server 2012 R2 provides the ability to mix different disk types within a single disk enclosure, such as a JBOD, to create a cost-effective, tiered storage solution.	Tiered storage enables frequently accessed data to be automatically and transparently moved to faster drives such as solid state drives while data that is infrequently accessed is moved to slower, less costly disks such as high-capacity SATA drives.

Configuration	Details	Scenario
Write-back cache	Server 2012 R2 includes a write-back cache option that leverages solid state drives present in the configured storage space.	Used to increase protection and data loss due to power failures or lags in disk write activity. In a large environment, small random writes hammer away at the disk. To speed up the write process, solid state drives can be used as a write buffer to keep up with the random access workload.

Configuration of storage pools and virtual disks is discussed later in this chapter.

Configuring Basic and Dynamic Disks

Now that you have an understanding of storage spaces and storage pools, let's take a few moments to review the basics. When you first install Windows Server 2012 R2, the hard disk on which you install Windows is set up as a *basic disk*. When you add a new hard disk to your computer, this disk is also recognized as a basic disk. This disk type is the one that has existed ever since the days of MS-DOS. Starting with Windows 2000, Microsoft offered a new type of disk called a *dynamic disk*. This disk type offers several advantages over the basic disk, including the following:

- You can create specialized disk volumes on a dynamic disk, including spanned, striped, mirrored, and RAID-5 volumes. Basic disks are limited to primary and extended partitions and logical drives.

- You can work with and upgrade disk volumes on-the-fly, without the need to reboot your computer.

- You can create an almost unlimited number of volumes on a dynamic disk. A basic disk can only hold a total of four primary partitions or three primary partitions plus one extended partition.

Dynamic disks have their disadvantages, however:

- The disk does not contain partitions or logical drives and therefore can't be read by another operating system.

- On a multiboot computer, the disk might not be readable by legacy operating systems.

- Laptop computers do not support dynamic disks.

As with previous versions of Windows Server, there will be times when an administrator needs to make changes to one or more of the disks. For Windows Server 2012 R2, Microsoft has retained the Disk Management snap-in for the Computer Management console. As shown in Figure 3-1, Disk Management is your primary tool for managing and configuring both physical and virtual disks. Configuring disks through Disk Management is covered in more detail in the proceeding sections.

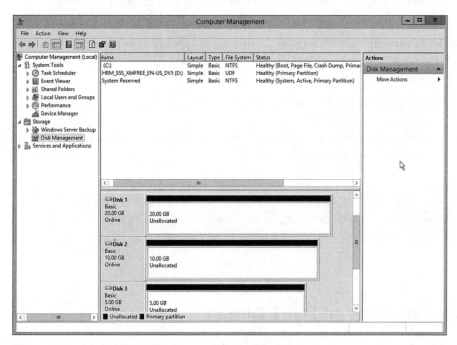

Figure 3-1   Computer Management > Disk Management.

The volume properties of a disk, as displayed in Figure 3-1, provide you with a status display that can help you in troubleshooting disk problems. The following volume statuses can appear:

- **Healthy:** This status is normal and means the volume is accessible and operating properly.

- **Active:** This status is also normal. An *active partition* is a partition or volume on a hard disk that has been identified as the primary partition from which the operating system is booted.

- **Failed:** This status means the operating system could not start the volume normally. Failed usually means the data is lost because the disk is damaged or the file system is corrupted. To repair a failed volume, physically inspect the computer to see whether the physical disk is operating. Ensure that the underlying disk(s) has an Online status in Disk Management.

- **Formatting:** This status is temporary, appearing only while the volume is being formatted.

- **Unknown:** This status means you've installed a new disk and have not created a disk signature or that the boot sector for the volume is corrupt, possibly because of a virus. You can attempt to repair this error by initializing the underlying disk by right-clicking the disk and selecting **Initialize** from the shortcut menu.

- **Data Incomplete:** This status appears when a disk has been moved into or out of a multidisk volume. Data is destroyed unless all the disks are moved and imported on the new computer.

- **Healthy (At Risk):** This status indicates I/O errors have been detected on an underlying disk of the volume but that data can still be accessed. The underlying disk probably shows a status of Online (Errors) and must be brought back online for the volume to be corrected.

> **NOTE**   Although it is better suited to manage virtual disks, Server Manager also provides the ability to perform basic disk and volume tasks. This is covered in more detail later in this chapter.

Configuring MBR and GPT Disks

After installing a new disk, you will need to ensure that a valid disk signature is present or that the disk is configured with the appropriate partition table. As with previous versions, Windows Server 2012 R2 includes two partition styles:

- **Master boot record (MBR):** Uses a partition table that describes the location of the partitions on the disk. The first sector of a master boot record (MBR) disk contains the MBR plus a hidden binary code file that is used for booting the system. This disk style supports volumes of up to 2 terabytes (TB) with up to four primary partitions or three primary partitions plus one extended partition that is subdivided into any number of logical drives.

- **GUID partition table (GPT):** Uses extensible firmware interface (EFI) to store partition information within each partition, and includes redundant primary and backup partition tables to ensure structural integrity. This style is recommended for disks larger than 2 TB in size and for disks used on Itanium-based computers. Not all previous Windows versions can recognize this disk style, however.

When you add a new disk of less than 2 TB size, it is added as an MBR disk. You can convert an MBR disk to a GPT using either Disk Management or the DiskPart tool, provided there are no partitions or volumes on the disk. To use Disk Management, right-click it and select **Convert to GPT Disk**. To use DiskPart, proceed as follows:

1. Open an administrative command prompt, type `DiskPart` and accept the User Account Control (UAC) prompt. The DiskPart command window appears.

2. Type `list disk` to get the disk number of the disks on your system.

3. Type `select disk` *n* where *n* is the number of the disk you want to convert.

4. Typing `convert gpt` DiskPart informs you that it has successfully converted the selected disk to GPT format.

If you want to convert a GPT disk back to MBR, the procedures are the same. You must back up all data and delete all volumes on the disk before performing the conversion. In Disk Management, right-click the disk and select **Convert to MBR Disk**. In DiskPart, use the same steps and type `convert mbr` in the last one.

Managing Volumes

After a new disk has been installed and a partition table has been written, it will appear in Disk Management as a basic disk. Windows Server 2012 R2 enables you to create a new partition (also called a simple volume) from the free space on a new or existing disk. This partition can be a primary, extended, or logical volume. Keep in mind that a single basic disk can contain up to four primary partitions or three primary partitions plus an extended partition; the extended partition can contain any number of logical drives. Use the following procedure to create a partition:

1. Launch Computer Management from Server Manager.

2. Select **Disk Management** in the left pane.

3. Locate the disk in the right pane that contains the unallocated space where the new volume will reside.

4. Right-click the unallocated space of the disk, and select **New Simple Volume** from the shortcut menu.

5. The New Simple Volume Wizard starts. Click **Next**.

6. On the Specify Volume Size page, type the size of the partition in megabytes and then click **Next**.

7. On the Assign Drive Letter or Path page shown in Figure 3-2, accept the drive letter provided or use the drop-down list to select a different letter. Then click **Next**.

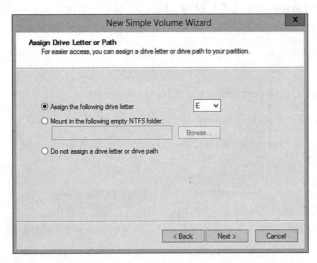

Figure 3-2   You can assign a drive letter to your partition or mount it in an empty NTFS folder.

8. On the Format Partition page shown in Figure 3-3, select the file system (FAT, FAT32, or NTFS) to format the partition. Provide a volume label name or accept the default of New Volume (this name will appear in the Computer window). If formatting with NTFS, you can modify the allocation unit size and/or enable file and folder compression. When done, click **Next**.

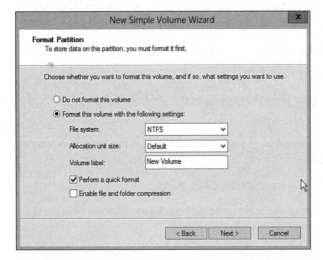

Figure 3-3   You are given several choices for formatting a new partition.

9. Review the information provided on the completion page and then click **Finish**. Windows Server 2012 R2 creates and formats the partition and displays its information in the Disk Management snap-in.

On a basic disk, Disk Management also enables you to perform several other management activities. You can extend, shrink, or delete volumes as necessary. Extending a volume adds any unallocated space to the volume. Right-click the volume and select **Extend Volume**. The Extend Volume Wizard informs you what space is available and enables you to add more space or select a smaller amount of space, as shown in Figure 3-4. Modify the amounts in MB as required, click **Next**, and then click **Finish** to extend the volume.

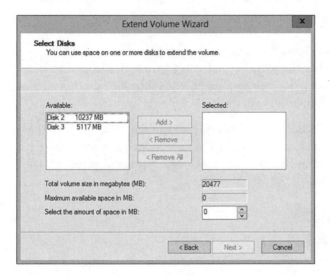

Figure 3-4   The Extend Volume Wizard helps you extend a volume on a basic or dynamic disk.

NOTE   If you add space on another disk from the Available column in the Extend Volume Wizard, you will be creating a spanned volume. The wizard will ask you to convert the disks to dynamic storage. More about this later in this chapter.

Shrinking a partition enables you to free up space to be used on a different partition. To do so, right-click the desired partition and select **Shrink Volume**. In the Shrink Volume dialog box shown in Figure 3-5, type the amount of space by which you want to shrink the volume (note the size after shrink to avoid over shrinking the volume). Then click **Shrink**.

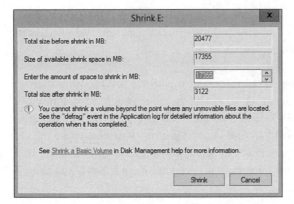

Figure 3-5   The Shrink Volume dialog box lets you shrink a partition or volume.

To view how a partition is configured, you can look at its properties in the Disk Management utility. Right-click the partition and select **Properties** from the short-cut menu. The Properties dialog box that appears has the following tabs (not all tabs will appear if the disk is not formatted with the NTFS file system):

- **General:** As shown in Figure 3-6, this tab provides an immediate view of the space allocation on the disk in a pie chart. The General tab also lets you to type a volume name, compress the drive to save disk space, and enable files on the drive to be indexed.

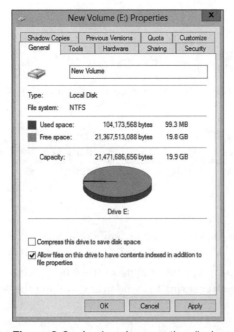

Figure 3-6   A volume's properties displays its space allocation.

- **Tools:** This tab has the following options:
  - **Error checking:** Windows Server will inform you as to whether you need to scan the drive for errors. You have the option to scan the drive and decide whether to fix any errors found.
  - **Optimize and defragment drive:** Executes a GUI to analyze and optimize the drives fragmentation level.
  - **Back up:** By clicking the **Back up now button**, Windows Server launches the Windows Server Backup console that enables you to perform a local backup or subscribe to the online Windows Azure Backup.
- **Hardware:** Displays the storage device hardware for the computer. You can obtain properties for any storage device, similar to that obtained from Device Manager, by selecting it and clicking **Properties**.
- **Sharing:** Enables you to share the disk so that others can access information on it.
- **Security:** Enables you to assign access permissions to files and folders on the disk.
- **Shadow Copies:** Enables you to allow Shadow Copies on the volume, alter the Shadow copy schedule, and configure storage limits for the Shadow Copies.
- **Previous Versions:** Enables you to locate older versions of files or folders that might have been created from Windows Backup or the Volume Shadow Copy Service.
- **Quota:** Enables you to assign disk quotas to users on the disk. This lets you limit the amount of space used on the disk by an individual user, who will receive a Disk Full message if he attempts to use more space than assigned to his quota.

You can delete a logical drive or partition easily from within the Disk Management utility. Simply right-click the logical drive and select **Delete Volume** from the shortcut menu. As shown in Figure 3-7, a prompt appears to warn you to verify that your data is backed up and that this action will destroy all data.

Figure 3-7   The Disk Management utility enables you to delete a partition or logical drive.

Converting Disks

When you created the simple volume, you might have noticed additional volume options (see Figure 3-8), such as:

- New Spanned Volume

- New Striped Volume

- New Mirrored Volume

- New RAID 5 Volume

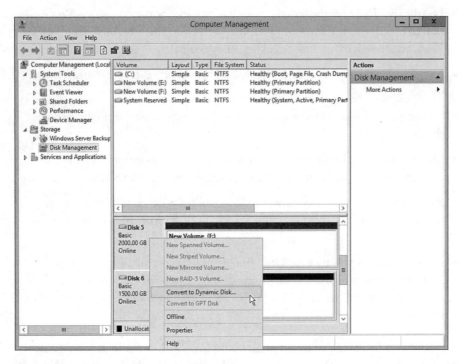

Figure 3-8   Dynamic disk conversion prompt.

By default, new disks are added as basic disks. Depending on the requirements, you might need to create one of the more advanced volumes shown in Figure 3-8. To use one of these configurations, you must first convert basic disks to dynamic. The process to convert a basic disk to a dynamic disk requires that you have a minimum of 1 MB of available space at the end of the disk. Best practices state that when you make changes to a disk configuration, you should back up the data before starting, just in case you need to restore it after you are finished. Even so, converting a basic disk to a dynamic disk should not have any effect on your data.

> **WARNING**   To convert a dynamic disk back to basic, you must first back up all data on the disk and delete all volumes. Then right-click the disk in Computer Management and select **Convert to Basic Disk**. The conversion proceeds and the display in Disk Management is updated within a few seconds.

You can convert a basic disk to dynamic at any time. Any partitions that are on the disk are converted to simple volumes in this process. To perform a conversion, you must be logged on as an administrator of the computer. Then follow these steps:

1. Using the Disk Management snap-in found within the Computer Management console, right-click the disk to be converted to dynamic, and select **Convert to Dynamic Disk**.

2. If more than one hard disk is present, the dialog box shown in Figure 3-9 appears. Select any additional disks you want to convert to dynamic and then click **OK**.

Figure 3-9   You can convert any of all of your disks to dynamic storage at the same time.

3. The Disks to Convert dialog box shows you the disks that will be converted. Click **Convert** to proceed.

4. Disk Management warns you that you will be unable to start installed operating systems except the current boot volume (see Figure 3-10). Click **Yes** to proceed.

Figure 3-10   You are warned that you will be unable to start other operating systems if you convert to dynamic storage.

5. The disk is converted to dynamic, and the display in Disk Management is updated accordingly.

When you convert a basic disk to a dynamic disk, the existing partitions are converted to simple volumes and fault-tolerant volumes are converted into dynamic volumes. Dynamic volumes can be changed on-the-fly, as the name "dynamic" implies. A dynamic volume is a unit of storage initially created from the free space on one or more disks. Table 3-3 lists the volume types available on a dynamic disk.

Table 3-3   Dynamic volume types.

Volume Type	Number of Disks	Configuration	Fault Tolerance
Simple	1	A single region or multiple concatenated regions of free space on a single disk.	None
Spanned	2–32	Two or more regions of free space on 2–32 disks linked into a single volume. Can be extended. Cannot be mirrored.	None
Striped	2–32	Multiple regions of free space from two or more disks. Data is evenly interleaved across the disks, in stripes. Known as RAID Level 0.	None
Mirrored	2	Data on one disk is replicated on the second disk. Cannot be extended. Known as RAID Level 1.	Yes, with maximum capacity of the smallest disk
RAID-5	3–32	Striping with parity. Data is interleaved equally across all disks, with a parity stripe of data also interleaved across the disks. Also known as RAID-5.	Yes, with maximum capacity of the number of disks minus one (if you have five 200-GB disks, your volume would be 800 GB)

RAID Volumes

The acronym *RAID* stands for Redundant Array of Independent (or Inexpensive) Disks—it is a series of separate disks configured to work together as a single drive with a single drive letter. You have already seen three of the most common types of RAID arrays in Table 3-3: RAID 0 (disk striping), RAID 1 (mirroring), and RAID-5 (disk striping with parity). Other versions of RAID also exist but are generally unused; you are unlikely to see these referenced on the 70-410 exam.

Creating a RAID 0 Volume

A RAID 0 (striped) volume contains space on 2–32 separate hard disks. Data is written in 64-KB blocks (*stripes*) to each disk in the volume, in turn. A striped volume offers considerable improvement in read/write efficiency because the read/write heads on each disk are working together during each I/O operation. A striped volume offers a maximum amount of space equal to the size of the smallest disk multiplied by the number of disks in the volume. However, the striped volume does not offer fault tolerance; if any one disk is lost, the entire volume is lost. Note that the system or boot volume cannot be housed on a striped volume.

You can create a striped volume by using 2–32 separate hard disks in Disk Management. Use the following procedure:

1. In Disk Management, right-click any one disk to be made part of the striped volume, and select **New Striped Volume**.

2. The New Striped Volume Wizard starts and displays the Select Disks page shown in Figure 3-11. The disk you initially selected appears under Selected. Select the disks you want to use from the **Available** column, and then click **Add**.

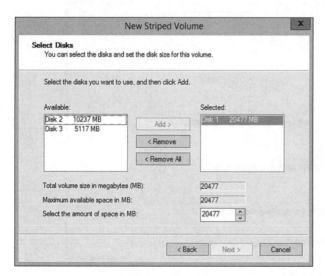

Figure 3-11   You need to select at least two disks to create a striped volume.

3. Disks you add appear in the Selected column. If you want to change the amount of space to be allocated, modify the value under **Select the amount of space in MB**. When done, click **Next**.

4. From the Assign Drive Letter or Path page, accept the default, choose another drive letter, or select the option to mount the volume in an empty NTFS folder if desired. Then click **Next**.

5. Choose the desired options in the Format Volume page, and then click **Next**.

6. Review the information on the completion page, and then click **Finish**.

7. If any of the disks to be used in the volume are configured as basic disks, you receive the same message warning you that you will be unable to boot other operating systems, as shown previously in Figure 3-10. To create your volume, you must click **Yes** and convert these disks to dynamic storage, as discussed earlier.

8. The volume is created and formatted, and appears in the Disk Management snap-in display, as shown in Figure 3-12.

Figure 3-12   New striped volume.

> **NOTE**   While you can use different-sized drives, your stripe is created using the smallest drive. The remaining space on the larger drive will appear as unallocated free space.

WARNING   Remember that RAID-0 is *not* fault tolerant. RAID-0 writes data in 64-KB blocks to each disk in the array sequentially, thereby improving read/write performance. However, if you lose any one of the disks in the array, all data is lost and you must restore the data from a backup after replacing the lost disk and re-creating the array.

Creating a Spanned Volume

You can extend storage space on an existing volume to a new disk by creating a spanned volume. This is essentially a volume that spans two or more disks and enables you to add space without the need to specify a new drive letter. Note that the spanned volume is even less fault tolerant than a simple volume—if any one disk fails, all data is lost from all disks and must be restored from backup.

To create a spanned volume, right-click the desired volume and select **Extend Volume**. From the Extend Volume Wizard, select the available disk(s) and complete the steps in this wizard, as previously described and shown in Figure 3-4.

Creating a Mirrored Volume

A mirrored volume contains two disks, each of which is an identical copy of the other, thereby providing fault tolerance at the expense of requiring twice the amount of disk space. You can use a mirrored volume to provide fault tolerance for the system and boot volumes, as well as any data volumes.

Creating a mirrored volume is similar to that of creating a striped volume. Use the following procedure:

1. In Disk Management, right-click any one disk to be made a part of the mirrored volume and select **New Mirrored Volume**.

2. Steps displayed by the New Mirrored Volume Wizard are similar to those of the New Striped Volume Wizard and outlined in the previous procedure. When you have completed the procedure, the mirrored volume appears in the Disk Management display.

Creating a RAID-5 Volume

A RAID-5 volume is similar to a striped volume in that data is written in 64-KB stripes across all disks in the volume. However, this volume adds a parity stripe to one of the disks in the array, thereby providing fault tolerance. The parity stripe rotates from one disk to the next as each set of stripes is written. The RAID-5 volume offers improved read performance because data is read from each disk at the same time; however, write performance is lower because processor time is required to calculate the parity stripes. You cannot house the system or boot volumes on a RAID-5 volume.

Creating a RAID-5 volume is also similar; remember that you must have at least three disks to create this type of volume. Select **New RAID-5 Volume** from the right-click options and follow the steps presented by the New RAID-5 Volume Wizard.

> **NOTE**   For more information on how RAID-5 volumes function, refer to "RAID-5 Volumes" at http://technet.microsoft.com/en-us/library/cc938485.aspx.

Managing and Troubleshooting RAID Volumes

Several things can go wrong with RAID volumes. Spanned and striped volumes are particularly vulnerable; as has already been mentioned, failure of any one disk in the volume renders the entire volume useless and data must be restored from a backup. If one disk in a mirrored volume fails, you can break the mirror and use the data on the other disk as a simple volume. If one disk in a RAID-5 volume fails, the system reconstructs the missing data from the parity information and the volume is still usable, but without fault tolerance and with reduced performance until the failed disk is replaced. If more than one disk in a RAID-5 volume fails, the volume has failed and must be restored from a backup after the disks have been replaced.

Besides the volume statuses already described for partitions on basic disks and simple volumes, Disk Management can display the following messages with RAID volumes:

- **Resyncing**: Indicates that a mirrored volume is being reinitialized. This status is temporary and should change to Healthy within a few seconds.

- **Data Not Redundant** or **Failed Redundancy:** For a mirrored or RAID-5 volume, this status usually means that half of a mirrored volume was imported, or that half is unavailable, or that only part of the underlying disks of a RAID-5 volume were imported. You should import the missing disk(s) to re-create the volume. You can also break the mirror and retain the half that is functioning as a simple volume. If you have all but one of the underlying disks of a RAID-5 volume, you can re-create the RAID-5 volume by adding unallocated space of a different disk.

- **Stale Data:** This status is shown when you import a disk that contains a mirrored volume half, or a portion of a RAID-5 volume, with a status other than Healthy before it was moved. You can return the disk to the original PC and rescan the disk to fix the error.

Creating and Mounting Virtual Hard Disks

Established back in 2003, the virtual hard disk (.VHD) format continues to grow in popularity. With the release of Windows Server 2008, Microsoft included native support for the use of .VHD files. Previously, you were only able to use .VHD files with Microsoft Virtual PC or third-party applications. VHDs are files stored on a server that make up contents of a virtual hard drive. Much like a physical hard drive, VHDs can contain operating system files, applications, and user data.

VHDs are stored on local physical drives. One or more VHD of different capacities can be added and can be assigned a unique drive letter. You can create as many VHDs as your physical storage allows, or until you run out of drive letters if presenting as a local volume. VHDs offer the following benefits:

- Ability to operate multiple servers and different operating systems using Hyper-V

- Complements storage pools, described in the next section

- Ability to divide local storage into multiple hard disk drives

- Granular control of allocating physical storage

- Easier backups and restores of data through the backup of the .VHD file(s)

- Support for native VHD boot, which enables a physical Windows 7, Server 2008 R2, or newer computers to mount and boot from an operating system contained within the .VHD file

- Provides an easier method to expand or shrink volumes

- Seamless data migration between servers via copying .VHD files

- Improved deployments of standard images or data sets to multiple computers

- Improved support for virus/malware removal though offline scanning of .VHD files (offline files can be mounted on a working computer for offline scans and file manipulation)

As you can see, there are many benefits of using virtual hard disks. One of the major drawbacks for .VHD files is that they support drives of up to only 2040 GB. To go beyond this limitation, Microsoft has created a newer version of the virtual hard disk format with the release of Windows Server 2012. Although Microsoft retained support for .VHD files, it has introduced a new .VHDX format. Both are supported under Windows Server 2012 R2. Although older versions of Windows do not support this format, .VHDX offers the following improvements:

- Supports up to 65-TB files.

- VHDX files are created with a 4 K block size to improve performance.

- Updated structure to help prevent data loss during unintentional power failures and to improve storage footprint on the physical disk using what is known as a *trim*.

- Ability to store custom metadata about the file.

Creating VHDs

Virtual hard disks can be created using the Disk Management snap-in, through Hyper-V, and through Server Manager File and Storage Services. In this section we focus on using Disk Management because Hyper-V and File and Storage Services are covered later. To create VHDs, perform the following steps:

1. Launch the Disk Management snap-in from the Computer Management console.

2. Right-click **Disk Management** and select **Create VHD**. Similarly, you can select this option from the **More Actions** drop-down list. This will launch the Create and Attach Virtual Hard Disk dialog box, as shown in Figure 3-13.

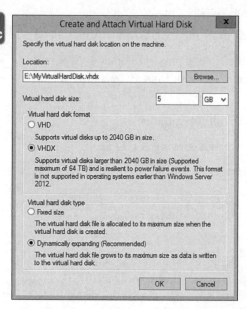

Figure 3-13   The Create and Attach Virtual Hard Disk dialog box.

3. Complete the dialog box by filling in or selecting the following:

- **Location:** Specify the location on the local server in which the virtual hard disk file will be stored.

- **Virtual hard disk size:** Specify the size of the hard disk in MB, GB, or TB.

- **Virtual hard disk format:** Select the appropriate virtual hard disk format based your situation. Refer to the section "Creating and Mounting Virtual Hard Disks," for guidance. In this example, we focus on the new .VHDX format.

- **Virtual hard disk type:** Select either Fixed size or Dynamically expanding. This is also referred to as *thin* or *fixed* provisioning, as you will see later in this chapter. Dynamically expanding disks will start out small and grow as data is written. If data is deleted, the virtual disk does not reduce in size without administrator intervention. Refer to Table 3-4 for commands used to shrink virtual hard disks.

4. Click **OK** when you are ready to create the virtual hard disk. Windows will create the virtual hard disk. If you browse to the storage location containing your virtual hard disk, you will see one large file present, as shown in Figure 3-14.

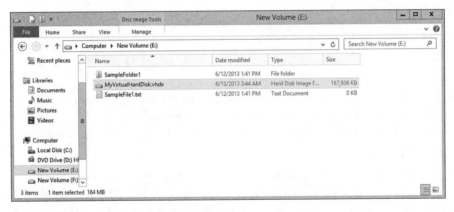

Figure 3-14   .VHDX file stored on local disk.

5. After your virtual hard disk has been established, it is presented under Disk Management as an unknown or uninitialized disk. From here, you will be able to establish a partition table, create, expand, or shrink volumes as if this were a physical disk.

Mounting VHDs

One of the benefits of using virtual hard disks is that they can be mounted and unmounted relatively quickly. This is helpful in situations where you need to transfer virtual disks between computers. To mount virtual hard disks, perform the following steps:

1. Copy the virtual hard disk file to your local computer, network-attached storage appliance, or storage area network depending on your configuration. It is important to note that you should copy the file where there is sufficient bandwidth and storage available to contain the virtual disk.

2. Using Disk Management, select **Attach VHD** under the **more actions** dropdown list.

3. Browse for the location of the virtual hard disk file and select **OK**. If desired, select the read only check box to prevent any accidental changes, as shown in Figure 3-15.

Figure 3-15 Attach VHD.

4. Once attached, the virtual hard disk and its contents will appear under Disk Management. If a partition or drive letter was established previously, Windows will assign a drive letter and make the virtual disk contents available through File Explorer.

5. To detach the virtual hard disk, right-click the drive in Disk Management and select **Detach VHD**. This will unmount the virtual hard disk and remove it from File Explorer. Once removed, the file is unlocked and can be copied or moved.

Managing VHDs with DiskPart

When mounting virtual hard disk, the DiskPart command-line tool is commonly used. Table 3-4 lists some commonly used DiskPart commands when dealing with virtual hard disks.

Table 3-4 DiskPart commands

Command	Description
`Attach vdisk`	Used to mount a virtual hard disk so that it is visible and accessible on the computer. If the VHD has a partition, Windows will assign it a drive letter and make its contents available via File Explorer.
`Compact vdisk`	Used to reduce the physical size of a dynamically expanding VHD. As data is written to dynamically configured virtual disks, the file size increases on the physical disk. When data is removed, the virtual disk does not automatically shrink in overall file size on the physical disk.
`Detach vdisk`	Unmounts or detaches the VHD and removes it from your local drive list. Once detached, the VHD and its contents can be moved to alternative locations.
`Expand vdisk`	Used to expand a virtual disk.

NOTE   Table 3-4 highlights the more commonly used DiskPart commands. For more information, refer to "DiskPart" at http://technet.microsoft.com/en-us/library/bb490893.aspx.

Configuring Storage Pools and Disk Pools

Previously we provided an overview of what storage pools are and how they enhance our server computing environments. Up until this point, you have probably spent most of your time planning for your storage requirements. Now it's time to put your plans in motion. Building a storage pool and creating a home for your data involves the following tasks:

- Configure a storage pool
- Create storage spaces
- Create volumes

You can complete each of these tasks using the File and Storage Services panel of Server Manager.

Configuring a Storage Pool

To configure a storage pool, perform the following steps:

1. Open **Server Manager** and click **File and Storage Services**.

2. Click **Storage Pools** from the navigation pane.

3. Windows includes a default pool that is named the primordial pool, as shown in Figure 3-16. The default pool shows you all available physical disks that can be configured with a pool on your server. This includes newly added disks. If no disks are available for configuration, then your disks do not meet the requirements for storage pools, as discussed previously. If you add a hot swap disk, select the **Rescan** option from the **Tasks** drop-down list to rescan for the new disks.

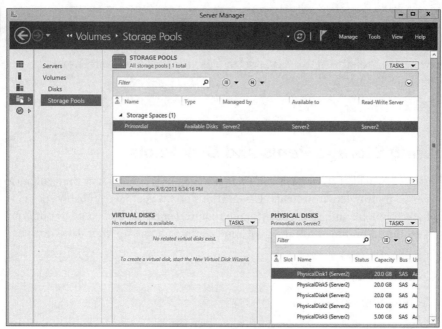

Figure 3-16   File and Storage Services Storage Pools.

4. Click the **Tasks** list under **Storage Pools** and click **New Storage Pool**. This will launch the New Storage Pool Wizard as shown in Figure 3-17. Click **Next** to continue.

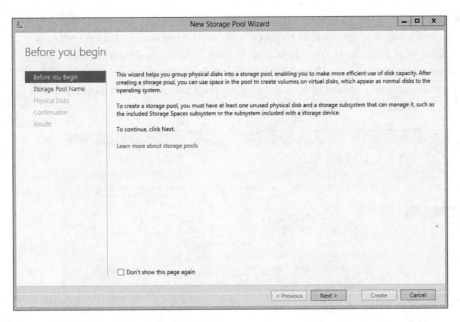

Figure 3-17 New Storage Pool Wizard.

5. Enter a storage pool name and description if desired, and select the primordial pool containing the available disks you want to use, as shown in Figure 3-18. Click **Next** when complete.

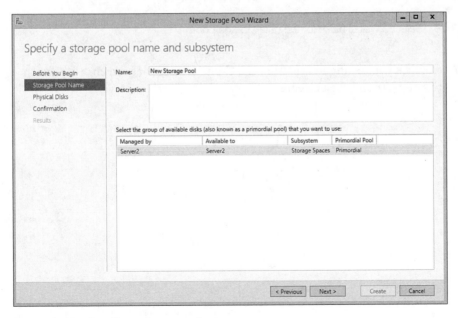

Figure 3-18 Specify a storage pool name.

6. Figure 3-19 shows the next screen where you can select the physical disks to use for the storage pool. If required, one or more disks can be selected and designated as a hot spare. This is used for hardware resilience, as described earlier in this chapter. You also can choose to add a hot spare later by adding an additional physical disk to the storage pool and marking it as a hot spare. Click **Next** when finished.

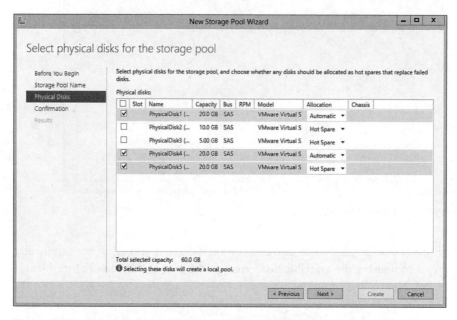

Figure 3-19   Select physical disks for the new storage pool.

7. Confirm your configuration from the Confirm selections screen, as shown in Figure 3-20, and click **Create**.

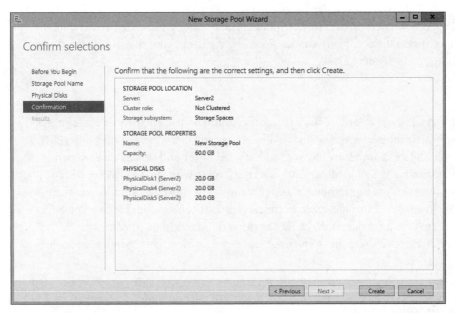

Figure 3-20 Confirm storage pool selections.

8. After the new storage pool has been created, you will be presented with a View results screen, as shown in Figure 3-21. Click **Close** when complete. Note, if you are ready to start carving up your storage pool, check the box to create a virtual disk when this wizard closes.

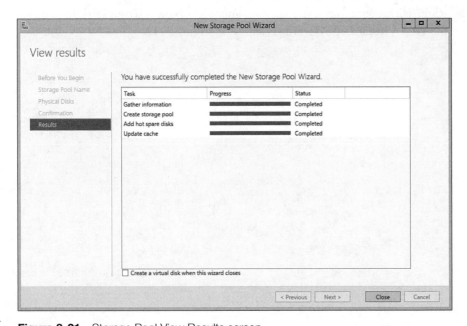

Figure 3-21 Storage Pool View Results screen.

> **NOTE** As discussed earlier, storage pool capacity can be expanded at any time by adding physical disks. This is accomplished by right-clicking the storage pool and choosing **Add Physical Disk**.

> **NOTE** As discussed earlier, storage pools can utilize disk enclosures containing disks of different performance levels. The disks can be configured into different tiers where data is automatically moved between faster and slower disks depending on the current I/O load demand. Tiering begins with the `New-StorageTier` cmdlet but requires some thought and planning. For more information on using disk enclosures and storage space tiering, refer to "Step-by-step for Storage Spaces Tiering in Windows Server 2012 R2" at http://blogs.technet.com/b/josebda/archive/2013/08/28/step-by-step-for-storage-spaces-tiering-in-windows-server-2012-r2.aspx.

Creating Storage Spaces

After creating a storage pool, you will need to allocate one or more storage spaces or virtual disks to your server. You can do this by performing the following steps:

1. Open **Server Manager** and click **File and Storage Services**.

2. Click on **Storage Pools** from the navigation pane.

3. Right-click a configured storage pool and select **New Virtual Disk** to launch the New Virtual Disk Wizard, as shown in Figure 3-22.

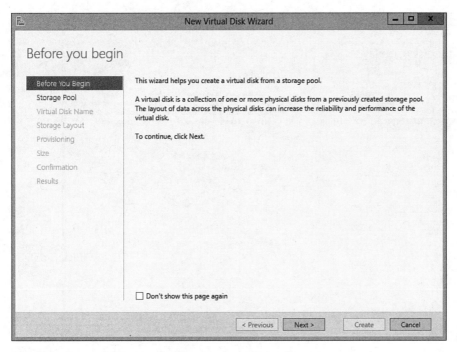

Figure 3-22 New Virtual Disk Wizard.

4. Click **Next** to continue to the Select the Storage Pool screen. Choose the appropriate storage pool, and click **Next**.

5. Specify the virtual disk name and provide an optional description; then click **Next**.

6. The next screen asks you to select the storage layout from three options, as shown in Figure 3-23. As discussed earlier in this chapter, each option provides a different level of resiliency and storage capacity.

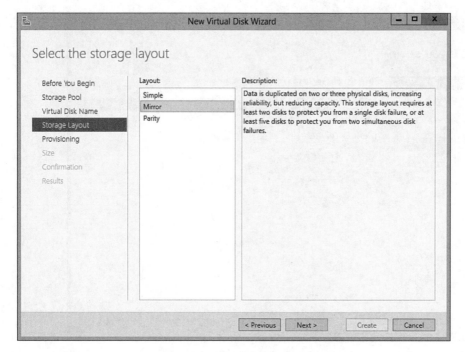

Figure 3-23   Select the storage layout for the new virtual disk.

7. After choosing the storage layout, you will be presented with two options for the provisioning type, as shown in Figure 3-24. Select the option that best meets your needs and click **Next**. For this example, we will use fixed provisioning as the default. You can choose from the following:

   ■ **Thin:** Storage is taken from the pool on an as-needed basis. The more data you write to your virtual disk, the smaller the storage pool becomes. Although this maximizes storage usage, you must be careful not to over-commit or overallocate storage.

   ■ **Fixed:** The size of the new virtual disk is allocated using the same amount of storage from the storage pool. For example, if you create a 20-GB virtual disk, 20 GB is consumed from the storage pool. Even though storage might be "wasted," you can always guarantee that you won't overcommit your storage and allocate more than your pool has available.

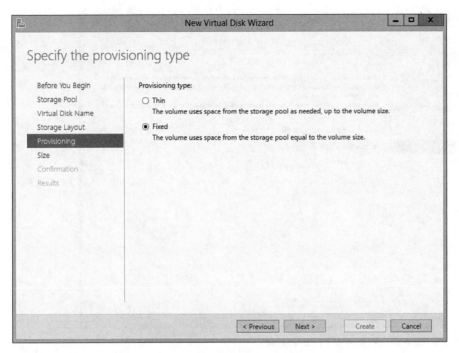

Figure 3-24   Specify the provisioning type for the new virtual disk.

8. After a provisioning type is chosen, the next step is to specify the size of the virtual disk. Figure 3-25 shows the total storage pool free space and provides you with the ability to enter the size of your virtual disk. For this example, we will create a 20-GB virtual disk. Click **Next** to continue.

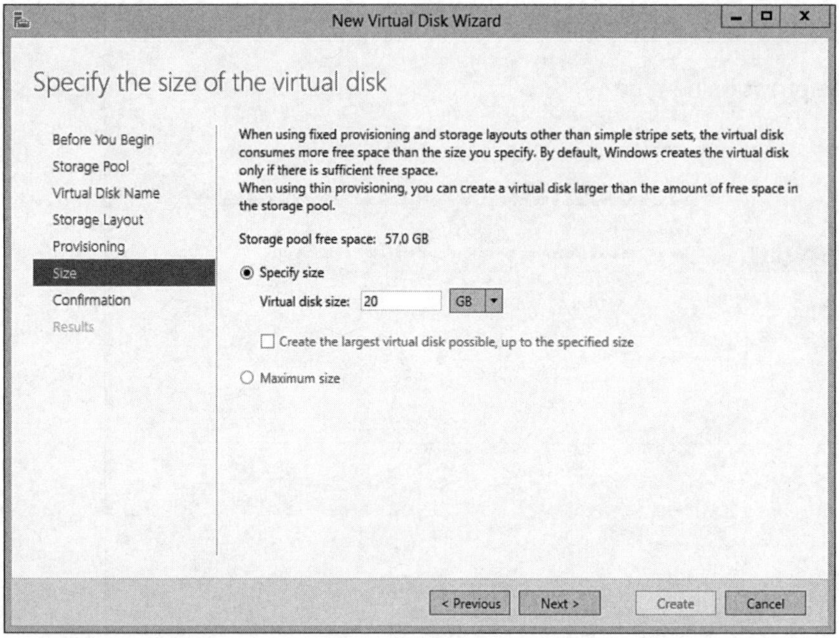

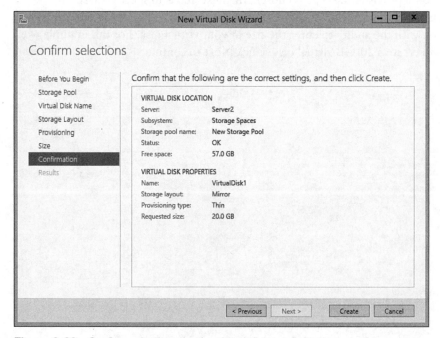

Figure 3-25   Specify the size of the virtual disk.

9. Confirm your virtual disk configuration, as shown in Figure 3-26, and click **Create**.

Figure 3-26   Confirm selections for the virtual disk configuration.

10. The New Virtual Disk wizard will create and initialize the virtual disk as shown in Figure 3-27. Upon completion, you will be asked to close the window, where by default, you will be stepped through creating a new volume on the virtual disk. Click **Close** when you are ready to proceed.

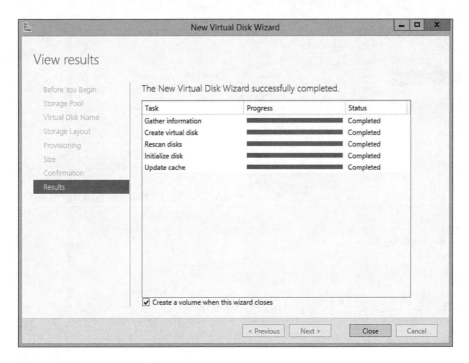

Figure 3-27   New virtual disk results.

> **NOTE**   At this point, your new virtual disk has been presented to the operating system and can be managed via File and Storage Services and the Disk Management snap-in, as covered previously. Use these tools for tasks such as extending, shrinking, or deleting the virtual disk.

Creating and Managing Volumes

After you have created a new storage space/virtual disk, the next step is to configure one or more volumes on the virtual disk. If you have just created a new virtual disk, Windows will present you with the New Volume Wizard; otherwise you can manage volumes via the Server Manager storage pools panel. To create a new volume, perform the following:

1. After the New Volume Wizard launches, click **Next** to continue. Select the server and disk on which to create the volume and click **Next** (see Figure 3-28).

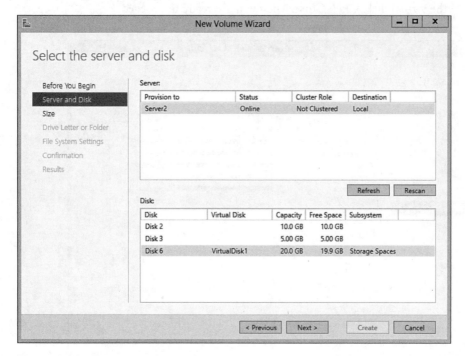

Figure 3-28   Select the server and disk from the New Volume Wizard.

2. Enter the volume size and click **Next**.

3. Specify a drive letter or specify a path in which to mount the volume as shown in Figure 3-29. Click **Next** to continue.

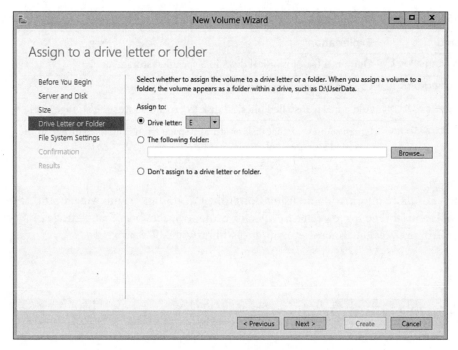

Figure 3-29   Assign a drive letter or folder for the volume.

4. Select a file system setting and allocation unit size, and supply an optional **Volume** label; then click **Next**.

5. From the Confirm Selections screen, verify that all configurations are correct and click **Create**.

6. Once completed, your new volume will be accessible and ready for use.

NOTE   Remember, you can also extend, shrink, or delete volumes as covered earlier.

Using PowerShell

As with most administrative functions, Microsoft has provided a handful of Power-Shell cmdlets for managing storage pools and storage spaces. Table 3-5 contains a few of these commands.

Table 3-5 PowerShell Cmdlets for Managing Storage Pools

Command	Explanation
`Get-StoragePool`	Outputs a list of physical disks in a specified storage pool
`New-StoragePool`	Creates a new storage pool
`Add-PhysicalDisk`	Add a newly installed physical disk to expand an existing storage pool
`New-VirtualDisk`	Creates a new virtual disk or storage space from available storage in the specified storage pool

NOTE For more information on using PowerShell to configure and manage storage pools and storage spaces, refer to "Deploy Storage Spaces on a Stand-Alone Server" at http://technet.microsoft.com/en-us/library/jj822938.aspx.

Exam Preparation Tasks

Review All the Key Topics

Review the most important topics in the chapter, noted with the key topics icon in the outer margin of the page. Table 3-6 lists a reference of these key topics and the page numbers on which each is found.

Table 3-6 Key Topics for Chapter 3

Key Topic Element	Description	Page Number
Table 3-2	Describes the various storage space configurations	85
List	Shows the advantages of dynamic disks	86
List	Shows the disadvantages of dynamic disks	86
List	Describes the MBR and GPT partition styles	88
Figure 3-9	Shows the process to convert from basic to dynamic disks	95
Table 3-3	Lists and explains the various dynamic volume types	96
List	Describes the benefits of virtual hard disks	101
Figure 3-13	Shows how to create and attach a virtual hard disk	102

Key Topic Element	Description	Page Number
Table 3-4	Describes the commonly used DiskPart commands	105
Figure 3-16	Shows the default primordial storage pool	106
Figure 3-17	Shows how to configure a new storage pool using the new Storage Pool Wizard	107
Figure 3-24	Shows the two options for provisioning virtual disks	113
Table 3-5	Describes the PowerShell commands to manage storage pools	118

Complete the Tables and Lists from Memory

Print a copy of Appendix B, "Memory Tables" (found on the CD), or at least the section for this chapter, and complete the tables and lists from memory. Appendix C, "Memory Tables Answer Key," is also on the CD and includes completed tables and lists to check your work.

Definitions of Key Terms

Define the following key terms from this chapter, and check your answers in the glossary.

Basic Disk, DiskPart, Dynamic Disk, Fixed Provisioning, GPT, MBR, Mount, RAID, Storage Pool, storage space, Thin Provisioning, VHD.

This chapter covers the following subjects:

- **Shared Folders in Windows Server 2012 R2:** This section introduces the concept of file sharing and discusses the available file sharing options and the permissions you can assign to shared folders on your server.

- **Offline Files:** This section shows you how to configure the Offline Files feature, which enables you to provide the capability for users to access shared files and folders when not connected to the server at which they are located.

- **Creating and Configuring Work Folders:** Work Folders is a new Windows Server 2012 R2 role service that offers a simplified means of synchronizing user data on a file server with client computers and other devices maintained by users on your network. This section shows you how to configure servers and client computers for Work Folders.

- **NTFS Permissions:** This section introduces the permissions you can assign to files and folders stored on partitions formatted with the NTFS file system. It then goes on to discuss how permissions assigned at different levels interact with one another, as well as the effective permissions a user receives when accessing a shared resource across the network.

- **Access-Based Enumeration of Files and Folders:** This section describes the function of access-based enumeration of files and folders and shows you how to enable or disable the feature.

- **Configuring Volume Shadow Copy Service (VSS):** This section reviews VSS, best practices for using VSS, and how to enable and configure it under Windows Server 2012 R2.

- **Configuring NTFS Quotas:** This section reviews NTFS Quotas and shows you how to manage and configure Quotas using File Explorer and File Server Resource Manager.

CHAPTER 4

Configuring Access to Files and Shares

All businesses use data of some kind. This might be inventory databases, product spreadsheets, images, Word documents, or other types of data. But these are all files that must be available to everyone who needs them to perform their job. Further, it is just as important that the individuals who really need these files to perform their jobs are the only ones who should be able to access them. And of those who can access them, only certain individuals should have the capability to modify them. Making sure that files on your network are properly available is one of the big jobs of the network specialist, and the File and Storage Services role in Windows Server 2012 R2 provides you with a complete set of tools that help you do the job to the best of your abilities. You learned about the new Storage Spaces feature in Chapter 3, "Configuring Windows Server 2012 R2 Local Storage," and now you look at how you can share data with computers across the network and control who is able to access and/or modify this data. This chapter and the ones to follow provide you with the resources and the know-how to administer and protect files and folders on your Windows Server 2012 R2 network.

"Do I Know This Already?" Quiz

The "Do I Know This Already?" quiz enables you to assess whether you should read this entire chapter or simply jump to the "Exam Preparation Tasks" section for review. If you are in doubt, read the entire chapter. Table 4-1 outlines the major headings in this chapter and the corresponding "Do I Know This Already?" quiz questions. You can find the answers in Appendix A, "Answers to the 'Do I Know This Already?' Quizzes."

Table 4-1   "Do I Know This Already?" Foundation Topics Section-to-Question Mapping

Foundations Topics Section	Questions Covered in This Section
Shared Folders in Windows Server 2012 R2	1–4
Offline Files	5
Creating and Configuring Work Folders	6
NTFS Permissions	7–11
Access-Based Enumeration of Files and Folders	12
Configuring Volume Shadow Copy Service (VSS)	13
Configuring NTFS Quotas	14–15

1. You need to create a shared folder on your Windows Server 2012 R2 computer that users on a UNIX server require access to. You want to configure access-denied assistance and quotas on this share. So you start the New Share Wizard from Server Manager. Which of the following options should you choose?

   a. **SMB Share–Quick**

   b. **SMB Share–Advanced**

   c. **SMB Share–Applications**

   d. **NFS Share–Quick**

   e. **NFS Share–Advanced**

2. Which of the following are valid permissions you can set for shared folders? (Choose three.)

   a. Full Control

   b. Modify

   c. Change

   d. Read and Execute

   e. Read

3. You are working at a computer running the Server Core version of Windows Server 2012 R2 and want to share a folder. Which command should you use?

   a. `Share`

   b. `Net share`

   c. `Net user`

   d. `Netsh`

4. You are configuring security permissions for a folder on your Windows Server 2012 R2 computer, and you want other users to be able to view files and run programs in the folder, but you do not want these users to be able to edit or delete files in the folder. Which permission should you assign?

   a. Full Control

   b. Modify

   c. Change

   d. Read

   e. Read and Execute

5. You have configured the Offline Files option on your Windows Server 2012 R2 computer and want to ensure that all available files on a network share are available for caching by users at remote computers running Windows Vista, Windows 7, Windows 8, or Windows 8.1. Which option should you enable?

   a. **Only the files and programs that users specify will be available offline**

   b. **Enable BranchCache**

   c. **All files and programs that users open from the shared folder are automatically available offline**

   d. **Optimize for performance**

6. You would like to enable users to access their work-related documents from external locations without the need to create a virtual private network (VPN) connection. Your network includes a Windows Server 2012 R2 file server. All users have client computers that run Windows 8.1. Which of the following actions do you need to perform to accomplish this task? (Choose all that apply.)

   a. Configure Offline Files on the file server.

   b. Enable BranchCache on the file server.

   c. Set up Work Folders on the file server.

   d. Obtain a server certificate from a trusted certification authority for the file server.

   e. Obtain a client certificate from a trusted certification authority for each client computer.

   f. Install Work Folders client software on each client computer.

   g. Configure each client computer with the email address or URL that enables access to the file server.

7. You have granted a user named Alice the Read NTFS permission on a folder named Documents. Alice is also a member of the Interns group, which has been explicitly denied the Full Control NTFS permission on the Documents folder. What is Alice's effective permission on this folder?

    a. Full Control.

    b. Modify.

    c. Read.

    d. Alice does not have access to the folder.

8. You have configured a folder with the basic NTFS permission of Read. Which of the following special access permissions are included in this permission? (Choose all that apply.)

    a. Traverse folder/execute file

    b. List folder/read data

    c. Read attributes

    d. Read extended attributes

    e. Delete

    f. Read permissions

    g. Take ownership

9. You have created a shared folder named Documents on your Windows Server 2012 R2 computer, which is a member server in your company's AD DS domain. You have assigned the Engineers global group the Full Control NTFS permission to this share. In addition, you have assigned the Interns group the Read permission to a subfolder of the Documents folder that is named Specifications. You do not want the members of the Interns group to be able to modify this folder. What should you do?

    a. Access the Advanced Security Settings dialog box for the Specifications folder and click the **Disable inheritance** command button. On the Block Inheritance dialog box that appears, select **Remove all inherited permissions from this object**.

    b. Access the Advanced Security Settings dialog box for the Specifications folder and click the **Disable inheritance** command button. On the Block Inheritance dialog box that appears, select **Convert inherited permissions into explicit permissions on this object**.

   c. Access the Security tab of the Permissions dialog box for the Specifications folder. In this dialog box, select the **Interns** group and then select the **Full Control** permission under the Deny column.

   d. You do not need to do anything because you have not granted any other permission to the Interns group.

10. You have granted a user named Peter the Full Control NTFS permission on a shared folder named Documents on your Windows Server 2012 R2 computer, which also has the Read shared folder permission granted to Everyone. Peter will be accessing this folder across the network on his computer. What is Peter's effective permission on this folder?

   a. Full Control.

   b. Modify.

   c. Read.

   d. Peter does not have access to the folder.

11. You have granted a user named Fred the Full Control NTFS permission on a shared folder named Documents on your Windows Server 2012 R2 computer, which also has the Read shared folder permission granted to Everyone. Fred will be accessing this folder on your computer. What is Fred 's effective permission on this folder?

   a. Full Control.

   b. Modify.

   c. Read.

   d. Fred does not have access to the folder.

12. What is the proper syntax for hiding a Windows share from network users?

   a. `Share!`

   b. `Share`

   c. `Share$`

   d. `$Share`

13. You have received reports that VSS has slowed down access to your file server. What should you do to improve performance when using VSS?

    a. Modify the default shadow copy schedule to occur every hour and increase the storage assigned to shadow copies.

    b. Modify the default shadow copy schedule to occur less frequently or after hours.

    c. Add more RAM to your server.

    d. Add a second network interface card.

14. You have been tasked with controlling storage on your file server. You need to control the amount of user personal data stored on the server. How can you accomplish this?

    a. Using Disk Configuration, enable NTFS Quotas per Server.

    b. Using File Resource Server Manager, enable NTFS Quotas.

    c. Using File Explorer, enable disk compression.

    d. Using File Server Resource Manager, enable NTFS Quotas.

15. What NTFS Quota configuration should you enable to actively notify users that they are nearing their Quota limit?

    a. Deny disk space to users exceeding quota limit.

    b. Limit disk space.

    c. Set warning level.

    d. Log event when user exceeds his warning level.

Foundation Topics

Shared Folders in Windows Server 2012 R2

Computers are networked together so that they can share data. In other words, you are sharing a folder from one computer so that users at other computers on the network can access its information. And users on any computer can access applications, data, and user home folders wherever they connect to the network. In addition, you can use network application folders for configuring and upgrading software, thereby maintaining applications at centralized locations rather than on client computers. Each user can have his own home folder on the server, which provides a place for storing his own personal information. You can also share other resources such as printers so that users can print to a printer not directly attached to his computer.

Understanding the File and Storage Services Role in Windows Server 2012 R2

Unlike the situation in Windows Server 2008, where you had to install the File Services role, the File and Storage Services role is installed by default in Windows Server 2012 and Windows Server 2012 R2, and cannot be removed. You will learn more about most of the capabilities of the File and Storage Services role in this chapter, the chapters to come, and the *Cert Guide* books for exams 70-411 and 70-412. Table 4-2 presents a brief summary of the more important capabilities of the File and Storage Services role and the enhancements provided by Windows Server 2012 and Windows Server 2012 R2:

Table 4-2   New/Updated Features for File and Storage Services in Windows Server 2012 and Windows Server 2012 R2

Feature/ Functionality	Description	Windows Server 2012	Windows Server 2012 R2
File Server Resource Manager (FSRM)	A set of tools that enable you to manage resources used by files and folders on your server by performing such tasks as limiting the amount of space used by users, restricting the types of files being saved, and monitoring the amount of storage used. Updates to FSRM in Windows Server 2012 R2 include improvements in file classification and management, customized `Access Denied` messages for Windows 8/8.1 clients, and Dynamic Access Control (which helps you to control and audit access to files and folders on your server). You will learn more about FSRM in the *Cert Guide* book for exam 70-411.	X	X

Feature/ Functionality	Description	Windows Server 2012	Windows Server 2012 R2
Distributed File System (DFS)	Simplifies the logical grouping of shared resources on multiple servers by making them available within a single tree structure. Also included is DFS replication, which optimizes the synchronization of shared resources among multiple locations on your network, thereby providing load balancing and fault tolerance for user access to these resources. Enhancements for Windows Server 2012 R2 include a new Windows PowerShell module, a new DFS Replication WMI provider, faster replication when high bandwidth is available, improvements in conflict resolution and preexisting data recovery, and capabilities for rebuilding corrupted databases without data loss.	X	X
Data Deduplication	A new role feature that reduces the amount of duplicate blocks of data in storage. This enables you to store more data in a volume of a given size, compared to older volumes that used Single Instance Storage or NTFS file system compression. Possible improvement in data storage utilization ranges from a 2:1 ratio on general-purpose file servers up to as high as 20:1 for virtualization data, such as VHD files.	X	X
Services for Network File System (NFS)	Enables file sharing among servers running Windows and UNIX. Added in Windows Server 2012 R2 is an NFS module for Windows PowerShell with several new cmdlets specific to NFS.	X	X
Support for Resilient File System (ReFS)	ReFS is a new file system in Windows Server 2012 R2 that provides a cost-effective platform for maximum data availability that scales efficiently to very large data volumes. Combined with the new Storage Spaces feature, ReFS provides a highly available, scalable, and resilient data access system for modern information storage needs.	X	X
Support for Server Message Block (SMB) 3.0	SMB is a network file sharing protocol that enables applications to read and write data and request information from programs on network servers. SMB applications are enabled to read and write files on the network server, and to communicate with programs configured to receive SMB client requests.	X	X

Feature/ Functionality	Description	Windows Server 2012	Windows Server 2012 R2
Storage Manager for SANs	A role feature that assists you in creating and managing physical and logical storage solutions pertaining to storage area networks (SANs) that include Fibre Channel and iSCSI disk drive subsystems.	X	X
Share and Storage Management	A role feature that facilitates administration of shared resources. Included is Access-Based Enumeration, which enables the display of only those files and folders that a user is entitled to access according to share and security permissions granted to her account.	X	X
Storage Pools and Storage Spaces	As discussed in Chapter 3, Windows Server 2012 R2 includes support for the creation of Pooled Storage that can be divided into one or more Storage Spaces using Virtual Disks.	X	X
Windows Search Service	A role feature that indexes files and folders to facilitate rapid searching by users when connecting to shared folders.	X	X
Transactional NTFS	Enables sequential operations on a file volume running NTFS to be performed as a single transaction. This means that all steps in the sequential operation must succeed for the transaction to be completed; if any step fails, the previous steps in the transaction are rolled back.	X	X
Work Folders	Enables users to store and access work data on personal computers, tablets, smartphones, and other devices, and access this data in a consistent manner.		X
iSCSI Target Server	Using the Internet SCSI (iSCSI) standard, provides block storage to other servers and applications on the network. Improved in Windows Server 2012 to include virtual disk enhancements, manageability enhancements in cloud services, and improved optimization for disk-level caching.	X	X

NOTE   For more information on new features of File and Storage Services in Windows Server 2012 and Windows Server 2012 R2, refer to "File and Storage Services Overview" at http://technet.microsoft.com/en-us/library/hh831487.aspx. Also see "What's New in File Server Resource Manager" at http://technet.microsoft.com/en-us/library/dn383587.aspx.

Creating a Shared Folder

The Shares subnode in the File and Storage Services utility simplifies the task of creating shared folders. Use the following procedure:

1. From the Server Manager Dashboard, select **File and Storage Services**. You see the Servers page shown in Figure 4-1.

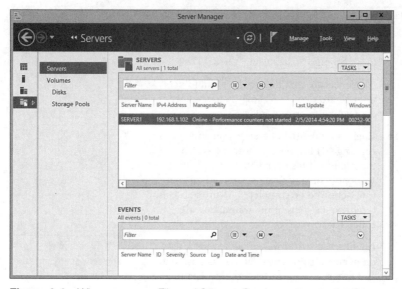

Figure 4-1   When you open File and Storage Services, you see the Servers page, which displays information about all servers on the network.

2. Select the Shares node from the left pane. When first opened, you are informed that there are no shares. Click the link labeled **To** create a file share, start the New Share Wizard. If the Shares node is not visible, select the **Volumes** node and then select **New Share** under the Tasks list. If this option is not available, select the link labeled **Start the Add Roles and Features Wizard**. Then follow the steps presented to install (refer to Figure 1-6 in Chapter 1, "Introducing Windows Server 2012 R2," for more information). After completing this procedure, the New Share task should be available under the Tasks list.

3. After completing either of the procedures in step 2, the New Share Wizard starts with the Select the profile for this share page, as shown in Figure 4-2. Select from one of the following options, and then click **Next**:

- **SMB Share–Quick:** Uses SMB to provide basic file sharing with shared folder and NTFS permissions. This is the default sharing option in Windows Server 2012 R2.

- **SMB Share–Advanced:** Adds access to services provided by File Server Resource Manager to the basic SMB sharing protocol, including configuration of folder owners for access-denied assistance, default classification of data, and the enabling of quotas.

- **SMB Share–Applications:** Enables sharing settings used by Hyper-V, certain databases, and many other applications.

- **NFS Share–Quick:** As already mentioned, NFS is a file sharing protocol used when sharing files with UNIX servers. This option includes basic sharing permissions.

- **NFS Share–Advanced:** Adds access to services provided by File Server Resource Manager to the basic NFS sharing protocol, similar to those mentioned for advanced SMB sharing.

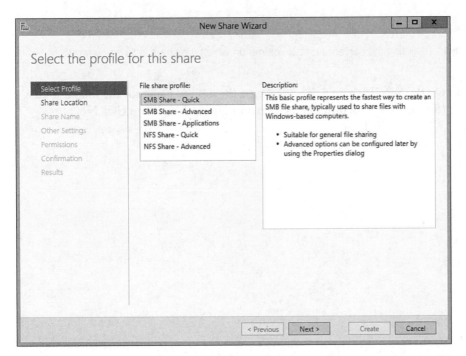

Figure 4-2   The New Share Wizard provides a choice of five file share profiles.

4. From the Select the server and path for this share page shown in Figure 4-3, select the server and volume where you want to create the share, and then click **Next**.

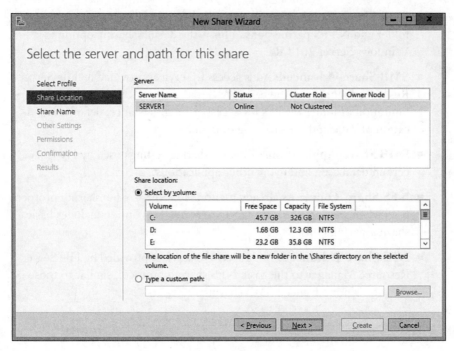

Figure 4-3   Selecting the server and disk volume on which the share is to be created.

5. On the Specify share name page, type the desired name for the shared folder (for example, **Documents**, as shown in Figure 4-4). Then click **Next**.

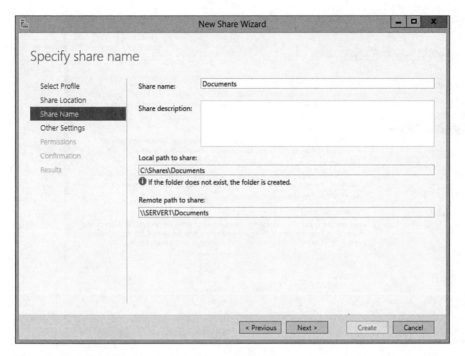

Figure 4-4   Specifying the name of the shared folder.

6. On the Configure share settings page shown in Figure 4-5, select options for access-based enumeration, offline file caching, and data encryption as desired; then click **Next**.

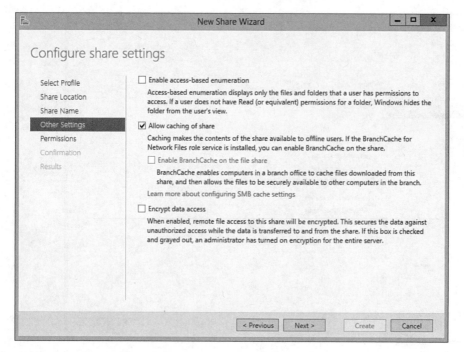

Figure 4-5   The Configure share settings page enables you to select additional file sharing options.

7. On the Specify permissions to control access page, click **Customize permissions** if you want to modify the default permissions. Shared folder permissions are discussed later in this section. When finished, click **Next**.

8. The Confirm selections page provides a summary of the options you've configured. Review these options and click **Previous** if you need to modify them. When finished, click **Create** to create the shared folder.

9. You are informed that the share has been created. Click **Close** to finish the wizard and return to Server Manager, which now displays the shared folder in the right pane.

Using the Network and Sharing Center to Configure File Sharing

First introduced in Windows Vista and Server 2008 and continued in Windows 7, 8, 8.1, and Windows Server 2012/R2, the Network and Sharing Center, shown in Figure 4-6, brings all networking tasks together in a single convenient location. You can configure connections to other computers and networks; share folders, printers, and media; view devices on your network; set up and manage network connections; and troubleshoot problems from this location.

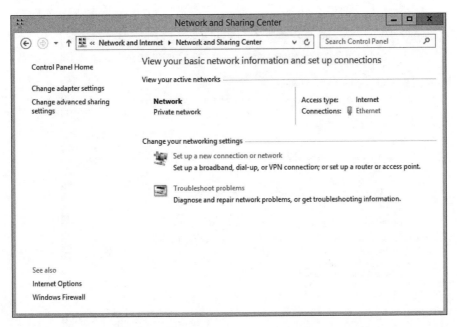

Figure 4-6   The Network and Sharing Center provides a centralized location for configuring network properties.

You can open the Network and Sharing Center by using any of the following methods:

- In the Search charm, type `network and sharing` in the Search text box. Then **select Network and Sharing Center** from the list that appears.

- In the Settings charm or the Start screen, select **Control Panel**. On the Control Panel home page, click **Network and Internet**, and then click **Network and Sharing Center** or **View network status and tasks**.

- Right-click **Start** and select **Control Panel**. Then proceed as previously stated.

From the Network and Sharing Center, you can perform actions related to the sharing of resources on your computer with others on the network. Click **Change advanced sharing settings** to obtain the Advanced sharing settings dialog box shown in Figure 4-7. Among other networking options, you can specify the following file-sharing options (note that the available options depend on the network profile in use):

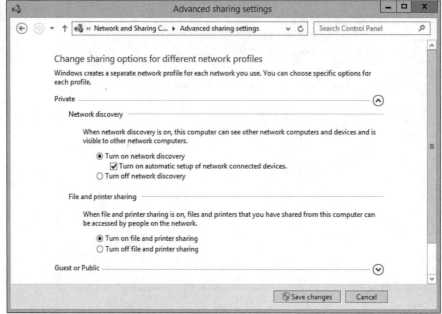

Figure 4-7 The Advanced sharing settings dialog box enables you to configure several global file and folder sharing settings.

- **Network discovery:** Enables the computer to locate other computers and devices on the network and enables these computers to locate your computer. It is expected that you would never turn this option off on a server.

- **File and printer sharing:** Enables the Standard Folder Sharing model, thereby allowing others on the network to access shared files on your computer and print from printers attached to your computer. This is the normal sharing model used by servers and will be discussed in detail later in this section.

- **Public folder sharing:** Enables the Public Folder sharing model, thereby allowing others on the network to access files in your Public folders of each Windows library (Documents, Pictures, Videos, and Music). This is a simplified folder sharing model that is not normally used on a server-based computer.

- **Password protected sharing:** Increases security by limiting access of shared files and printers to only those who have a user account and password on your computer. You would normally keep this option turned on at a server.

Sharing Files, Folders, and Printers

Shared folders are folders on the local hard drive that other users on a network can connect to. For the exam, it is critical that you understand how to manage and troubleshoot connections to shared resources, how to create new shared resources, and how to set permissions on shared resources. The process that Windows Server 2012 R2 uses to share folders is that an administrator selects a folder, regardless of its location in the local folder hierarchy, and shares it through the Sharing tab of the folder's Properties dialog box.

To share files with other users across the network, you must manually do so for each folder containing the files that you want to share. To share a folder with other network users, use the following procedure:

1. In File Explorer, navigate to the folder, right-click it, select **Share with**, and then click **Specific people**. The File Sharing dialog box opens, as shown in Figure 4-8.

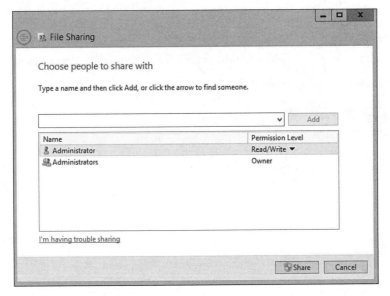

Figure 4-8   The File Sharing dialog box enables you to choose those you want to share a file with.

2. Type the name of a user with whom you want to share the folder, and then click **Add**. The name appears in the Name list with a default permission level of Read.

3. To share with another user, repeat step 2 as many times as required. When finished, click **Share**.

4. To modify the permission assigned to a user, click that user and select either **Read** or **Read/Write**, as desired. To remove a user from the list, click the user and select **Remove**. When done, click **Share** to apply your changes.

To remove a shared folder, right-click the folder and select **Share with > Stop sharing**.

Modifying Shared Folder Properties

When sharing files and folders with other users across a network, your computer becomes vulnerable to both unintentional and intentional attacks. Not only can the data simply be viewed for malicious purposes, such as corporate spying, but it also can be altered or destroyed on purpose or accidentally. For this reason alone, you should always grant the most restrictive permissions necessary for a network user to conduct work on those files. Granting just enough permission without being too lenient requires careful consideration. If you are too stringent, users can't get their jobs done. If you are too lenient, the data is at risk.

Use the following procedure to modify shared folder properties:

1. In a File Explorer window, right-click the shared folder and select **Properties**.

2. Click the **Sharing** tab (see Figure 4-9).

Figure 4-9   The Sharing tab of a folder's Properties dialog box enables you to modify shared folder properties.

3. Click **Advanced Sharing**. The Advanced Sharing dialog box shown in Figure 4-10 appears. This dialog box provides the options that are summarized in Table 4-3.

Table 4-3   Shared Folder Options in Windows Server 2012 R2

Option	Description
Share this folder	Click to start sharing the folder.
Share name	This is the folder name that remote users will employ to connect to the share. It will appear in a user's File Explorer window, or the user can access it by typing *computername**sharename* at the Run command or in the address bar of an Explorer window.
Comments	This information is optional and identifies the purpose or contents of the shared folder. The comment appears in the Map Network Drive dialog box when remote users are browsing shared folders on a server.
User limit	This sets the number of remote users who can connect to a shared resource simultaneously, reducing network traffic. For Windows Server 2012 R2, the limit is set to 77216 by default.
Permissions	Permissions can be assigned to individual users, groups, or both. When a directory (folder) is shared, you can grant each user and each group one of the three types of permissions for the share and all of its subdirectories and files or choose to specifically deny them those permissions.
Caching	Enables offline access to a shared folder. Available settings in the Offline Settings dialog box are discussed later in this chapter.

Figure 4-10   The Advanced Sharing dialog box enables you to configure several properties of shared folders.

4. To add another share name, click **Add** under the Share name section. (If this command button is dimmed, ensure that the Share this folder option is selected and click **Apply**.) An additional share name enables users to access the shared folder under this name. Type the required share name. You can also change the maximum number of simultaneously accessing users with this share name. To do so, type the required number or use the arrows to select a number. In Windows Server 2012 R2, the maximum number of users is set to 16777 by default. When finished, click **OK**.

5. To change shared folder permissions, click **Permissions**. This displays the Permissions for (folder name) dialog box shown in Figure 4-11. By default, the creator of the share receives Full Control permission and other users receive the Read permission. Click **Add** to add another user or group and then modify this user's permissions as desired. Click **OK** when finished. Table 4-4 describes the available shared folder permissions.

Table 4-4   Shared Folder Permissions

Permission	Description
Full Control	Users are allowed to perform any task on the folder or its constituent files, including modifying their individual attributes and permissions used by others accessing them.
Change	Users are allowed to view and modify files but not change the attributes of the shared folder itself. This is equivalent to Read/Write, as described earlier in this section.

TIP   If you select permissions from the Deny column, you are explicitly denying access to that user or group. Such an explicit denial overrides any other permissions allowed to this group. Remember this fact if users experience problems accessing any shared resources across the network.

Permission	Description
Read	Users are allowed to view but not modify files.

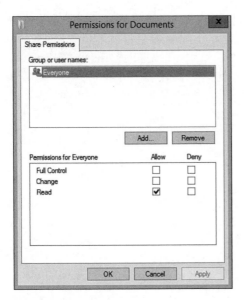

Figure 4-11   The Permissions for (folder name) dialog box enables you to configure permissions that apply to users accessing the folder across the network.

6. To set granular security permissions on the folder, click the **Security** tab of the folder's Properties dialog box and modify the settings in the dialog box shown in Figure 4-12 as required. These permissions apply to everyone accessing the folder either locally or across the network; more restrictive permissions configured here override those configured from the Sharing tab. These settings are discussed later in this chapter.

Figure 4-12   The Security tab of a folder's Properties dialog box enables you to configure granular permissions for users and groups accessing the folder.

7. When you are finished, click **Close** to close the Properties dialog box. You can also click **Apply** to apply your changes and continue making modifications.

Mapping a Drive

Mapping a network drive means associating a shared folder on another computer with a drive letter available on your computer. This facilitates access to the shared folder. Proceed as follows to map a drive:

1. In any File Explorer window, right-click **Network** from the list in the left side of the window and then select **Map network drive**.

2. In the Map Network Drive Wizard shown in Figure 4-13, select the drive letter to be assigned to the network connection for the shared resource from the Drive drop-down box. Drive letters being used by local devices are not displayed in the Drive list. You can assign up to 24 drive letters.

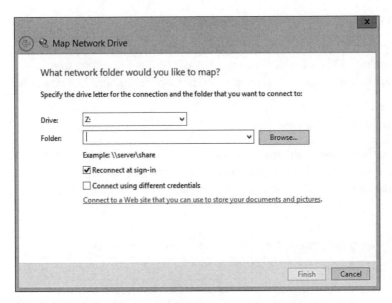

Figure 4-13   Mapping a network drive.

3. In the Folder box, enter a Universal Naming Convention (UNC) path to specify the network path to the computer and the shared folder. For example, to connect to the shared folder Documents on a computer named Server2, type `\\Server2\Documents`. You can also click **Browse** to find the shared folder and then select the desired path.

4. Select a connection option, as follows:

   ■ **Reconnect at sign-in:** This option is enabled by default and creates permanent connections. It reconnects the user to the shared folder each time the user logs on unless the user manually disconnects from the resource.

   ■ **Connect using different credentials:** This option enables you to connect to a shared folder using a different user account. This option is useful if you are at another user's computer and need to connect to a resource to which the currently logged-in user does not have the appropriate access.

5. Click **Finish**.

Using the net share Command to Manage Shared Folders

Windows Server 2012 R2 provides the `net share` command that you can use to manage shared folders. This is useful if you need to use scripts for automating administrative tasks, or for sharing folders at a Server Core computer. The syntax is as follows:

```
net share [sharename] [/parameters]
```

In this command, *sharename* is the name of the shared resource, and */parameters* refers to any of a series of parameters that you can use with this command. Table 4-5 describes several of the more common parameters used with this command.

Table 4-5   Several Common Parameters Used with the `net share` Command

Parameter	Description
`/users:number`	Specifies the maximum number of users who can access the shared resource at the same time. Specify unlimited to allow the licensed limit of users.
`/cache:option`	Enables offline caching as discussed in the next section, according to the value of *option*: **Documents:** Specifies automatic reintegration of documents **Programs:** Specifies automatic reintegration of programs **Manual:** Specifies manual reintegration **None:** Advises the client that caching is inappropriate
`/delete`	Stops sharing the specified resource.
`/remark:"text"`	Adds a descriptive comment. Enclose the comment (*text*) in quotation marks.

Note that you can also use this command without any parameters to display information about all the shared resources on the local computer.

Offline Files

The Offline Files feature in Windows Server 2012, Windows Server 2012 R2, Windows 8, and Windows 8.1 originated with Windows 2000 and XP. This feature enables a user to access and work with files and folders stored on a network share when the user is disconnected from that share. For example, such a situation could occur when the user is working from a laptop on the road or at home. This feature ensures that users are always working with the most recent version of their files.

When you enable Offline Files, this feature makes anything you have cached from the network available to you. It also preserves the normal view of network drives and so on, as well as shared folder and NTFS permissions. When you reconnect to the network, the feature automatically synchronizes any changes with the versions on the network. Also, changes made to your files while online are saved to both the network share and your local cache.

Offline files are stored on the local computer in a special area of the hard drive called a *cache*. More specifically, this is located at **%systemroot%\CSC**, where **CSC** stands for client-side caching. By default, this cache takes up 10 percent of the disk volume space.

You need to configure both the server and the client computer to use the Offline Files feature. Keep in mind that, in this sense, the "server" refers to any computer that holds a shared folder available to users of other computers. Besides a server running Windows Server 2008/R2, or Windows Server 2012/R2, this might be a computer running Windows Vista Business, Enterprise, or Ultimate; Windows 7 Professional, Enterprise, or Ultimate, or Windows 8 or 8.1 Pro or Enterprise.

NOTE   For more information on new features of Offline Files in Windows 8/8.1 and Windows Server 2012/R2, refer to "Folder Redirection, Offline Files, and Roaming User Profiles overview" at http://technet.microsoft.com/en-us/library/hh848267.aspx.

Configuring Servers for Offline Files

To enable the caching of files stored on a shared folder, you need to configure the shared folder on the server and specify the type of caching available. The following procedure shows you how to perform these tasks on a Windows Server 2012 R2 computer.

1. Right-click the shared folder and select **Properties**.

2. On the Sharing tab of the folder's Properties dialog box, click **Advanced Sharing**.

3. On the Advanced Sharing dialog box, click **Caching** to open the Offline Settings dialog box shown in Figure 4-14.

Figure 4-14   The Offline Settings dialog box provides several options for enabling offline caching in Windows Server 2012 R2.

   4. Select from the following options, and then click **OK**:

- **Only the files and programs that users specify are available offline:** Requires that a user connecting to the share specifically indicate the files to be made available for caching. This is the default setting.

- **Enable BranchCache:** Enables computers in a branch office to cache downloaded files and then securely serve these files to other branch office client computers.

- **No files or programs from the shared folder are available offline:** Effectively disables the Offline Files feature.

- **All files and programs that users open from the shared folder are automatically available offline:** Makes every file in the share available for caching by a remote user. When a user opens a file from the share, the file is downloaded to the client's cache and replaces any older versions of the file.

- **Optimize for performance:** Enables expanded caching of shared programs so that users can run them locally, thereby improving performance. Note that this option does not provide any enhancement for client computers running Windows Vista or newer.

   5. Click **OK** to close the Advanced Sharing dialog box, and then click **Close** to close the Properties dialog box for the shared folder.

NOTE   For more information on the available server options for Offline Files, refer to "Configure Offline Availability for a Shared Folder" at http://technet. microsoft.com/en-us/library/cc732663.aspx. Although written for Windows Server 2008 R2, the Offline Files settings have remained unchanged in Windows Server 2012 R2.

Configuring Client Computers

By default, the Offline Files feature is enabled on the client computer. A client computer running Windows Vista, Windows 7, Windows 8, or Windows 8.1 provides the Offline Files dialog box, which provides options for managing offline files at the client computer, including the use of the Sync Center for synchronizing offline file content.

To cache all available files from a network share to which you have connected a computer running Windows Vista, Windows 7, Windows 8, Windows 8.1, or Windows Server 2008/R2/ 2012/R2, right-click the shared folder icon and select **Always available offline**. This automatically caches all available files without your having to open them first. You can also synchronize your cached files manually when you are connected to the network share. To do so, right-click the shared folder icon and select **Sync > Sync Selected Offline Files**.

Configuring Offline File Policies

Group Policy makes available a series of policy settings. In Local Group Policy Editor or Group Policy Management Editor, navigate to **Computer Configuration\ Policies\Administrative Templates\Network\Offline Files** to display the policy settings shown in Figure 4-15. Note that some of the policy settings available here are applicable to computers running older Windows versions only and are provided for backward compatibility purposes. Table 4-6 describes the more important policy settings relevant to Windows Server 2012 R2 and Windows 8.1 computers that you should be aware of.

Table 4-6   Offline File Policies

Policy	Description
Specify administratively assigned Offline Files	Specifies network files and folders that are always available offline. Type the UNC path to the required files.
Configure Background Sync	Enables you to control synchronization of files across slow links. You can configure sync interval and variance parameters, as well as blackout periods when sync should not occur.

Policy	Description
Limit disk space used by Offline Files	When enabled, limits the amount of disk space in MB used to store offline files.
Allow or Disallow use of the Offline Files feature	Determines whether users can enable Offline Files. When enabled, Offline Files is enabled and users cannot disable it; when disabled, Offline Files is disabled and users cannot enable it.
Encrypt the Offline Files cache	When enabled, all files in the Offline Files cache are encrypted.
Remove "Make Available Offline" command	Prevents users from making network files and folders available offline. Even when enabled, Windows still caches local copies of files on network shares that are designated for automatic caching.
Remove "Make Available Offline" for these files and folders	Enables you to specify the UNC path to shared files and folders for which you want to block the Make Available Offline command.
Enable Transparent Caching	Controls caching of offline files across slow links. You can specify a network latency value above which network files are temporarily cached. More about this policy in the next section.
Configure slow-link mode	Controls background synchronization across slow links and determines how network file requests are handled across slow links.
Configure Slow link speed	Specifies the threshold link speed value below which Offline Files considers a network connection to be slow. Specify the value in bits per second divided by 100; for example, specify 1280 for a threshold of 128,000 bps.

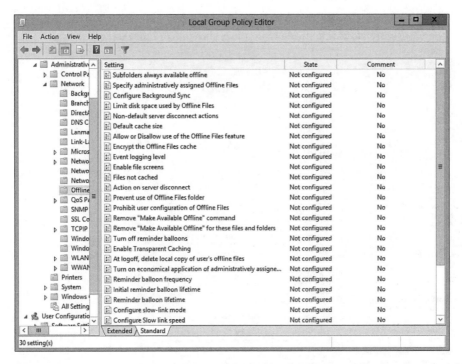

Figure 4-15   You can configure a large number of policy settings related to the use of Offline Files.

Using the Always Offline Mode

New to Windows Server 2012 and Windows 8, and continued in Windows Server 2012 R2 and Windows 8.1, is the Always Offline mode that enables faster access to cached files and redirected folders in an Active Directory Domain Services (AD DS) environment. Enabling this mode reduces bandwidth usage because users are always working offline even when connected to the network.

Use the following steps to enable the Always Offline mode:

1. Access the Group Policy Management Editor focused on a Group Policy object (GPO) focused on the desired domain, site, or organizational unit (OU).

2. Navigate to the **Computer Configuration\Policies\Administrative Templates\Network\Offline Files** node.

3. Right-click the **Configure slow-link mode policy** and select **Edit** to display the Configure slow-link mode dialog box shown in Figure 4-16.

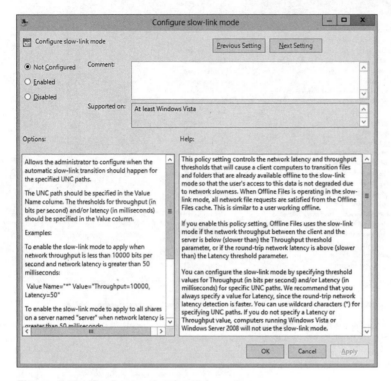

Figure 4-16   Configuring the slow-link mode.

4. Select **Enabled**.

5. Scroll through the Options section of this dialog box to click **Show** at the bottom of this section.

6. From the Show Contents dialog box, specify the file share for which the Always Offline mode should be enabled, as shown for **\\server2\documents** in Figure 4-17.

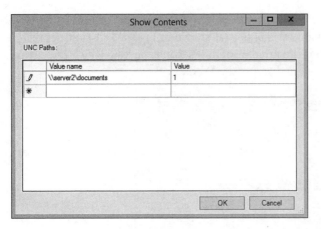

Figure 4-17   Specifying a shared folder that should always be available offline.

7. In the Value column, specify a latency value in milliseconds (as shown in Figure 4-17 for 1 millisecond), and then click **OK**.

8. Click **OK** to close the Configure slow-link mode dialog box.

> **NOTE**   For more information on the Always offline mode, refer to "Enable the Always Offline Mode to Provide Faster Access to Files" at http://technet.microsoft.com/en-us/library/hh968298.aspx.

Configuring Transparent Caching of Offline Files

Introduced with Windows Server 2008 R2 and Windows 7 and continued in Windows Server 2012, Windows Server 2012 R2, Windows 8, and Windows 8.1 is the concept of *transparent file caching*. It enables client computers to temporarily cache files obtained across a slow WAN link more aggressively, thereby reducing the number of times the client might have to retrieve the file across the slow link. Use of transparent caching also serves to reduce bandwidth consumption across the WAN link. Prior to Windows Server 2008 R2 and Windows 7, client computers always retrieved such a file across the slow link.

The first time a user accesses a file across the WAN, Windows retrieves it from the remote computer; this file is then cached to the local computer. Subsequently, the local computer checks with the remote server to ensure that the file has not changed and then accesses it from the local cache if its copy is up-to-date. Note that this type of file caching is temporary; clients cannot access these files when they go offline.

You can configure the Enable Transparent Caching policy so that clients can perform transparent caching. Enable this policy (as shown in Figure 4-18) and set the network latency value, which is the number of milliseconds beyond which the client will temporarily cache files obtained across the WAN.

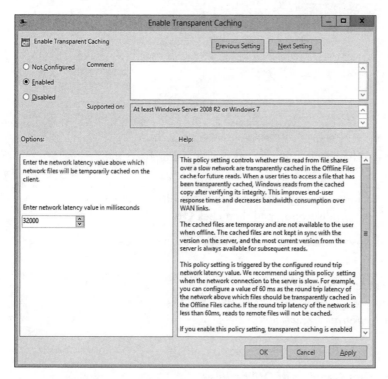

Figure 4-18 Enable the Enable Transparent Caching policy setting so that clients can temporarily cache files obtained across a slow WAN link.

Creating and Configuring Work Folders

Work Folders is a new role service within File and Storage Services in Windows Server 2012 R2 that enables users to automatically and seamlessly synchronize work-related documents with a file server. Users can synchronize work data to any computer running Windows 8.1 or a personal device, such as a tablet running Windows RT 8.1, while maintaining compliance with company security policies. All data is stored on a specially configured folder on the file server that includes subfolders for each user. For example, a user might save her data at her desktop computer and then access the data on her home computer or tablet while offline. At home, she makes changes to this data and saves them on her device. The next day on returning to the office, the data is automatically synchronized to the file server.

Similar to Folder Redirection or Offline Files, Work Folders enables synchronization of work documents with a file server; however, Work Folders extends synchronization capabilities to include user-owned computers and devices not normally connected to the corporate network without the need for remote access connection technologies such as DirectAccess or virtual private networks (VPNs). Further, cloud technologies such as Microsoft OneDrive are not required (users can sync personal data with the cloud using OneDrive or other technologies).

The following are several of the important capabilities of Work Folders:

- Provide a single point of access to data on a user's computers and devices running Windows 8.1 or Windows RT 8.1. It is planned to extend this functionality to Windows 7 computers and additional devices such as iPads in the future.

- You can deploy Work Folders alongside other file server technologies, including folder redirection, offline files, and home folders.

- Assists users in keeping work and personal information separate from each other.

- Maintains data encryption during synchronization activities and enables corporate data wipe by means of data management services such as Windows Intune. You can use security policies to ensure that Work Folders are encrypted and a lock screen password is in use.

- You can manage user data using available file server management technologies, including disk quotas and file classification.

The following are functionalities included with Work Folders:

- **Work Folders role service:** Enables you to set up shared folders that store work data on a Windows Server 2012 R2 computer. You can also monitor data being stored and manage sync shares and user access.

- **Work Folders PowerShell cmdlets:** Includes a comprehensive set of cmdlets for managing Work Folders on Windows Server 2012 R2 computers.

- **Integration with client computers:** Provides Work Folders functionality on computers and devices running Windows 8.1 or Windows RT 8.1. Included is a Control Panel applet that sets up and monitors Work Folders, integration with File Explorer, and a sync engine that facilitates file transfer with the file server.

- **Work Folders app for devices:** Apps are currently in development that will enable popular devices such as iPads and Android to access information stored in Work Folders.

Enabling and Configuring Work Folders

As already mentioned, Work Folders is available as a role service within File and Storage Services server in Windows Server 2012 R2. Use the following procedure to enable Work Folders:

1. From the Server Manager Dashboard, click **Manage** > **Add roles and features**.

2. If you receive the Before you begin page, click **Next** to bypass this page.

3. On the Select installation type page, leave the default of role-based or feature-based installation selected, and then click **Next**.

4. Select the server on which you want to install Work Folders (by default, this is the local server), and then click **Next**.

5. On the Select server roles page, expand the **File and Storage Services** node; then expand the **File and iSCSI Services** subnode.

6. As shown in Figure 4-19, select **Work Folders**, and then click **Next**.

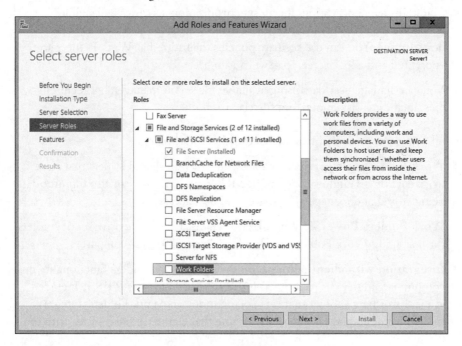

Figure 4-19   Selecting the Work Folders role service.

7. If you receive a message box informing that you need to add IIS Hostable Web Core, click **Add Features** to proceed.

8. Click **Next** to receive the Confirm installation selections page. Review the information provided, and then click **Install** to proceed.

9. The Installation progress page tracks the progress of installing Work Folders and IIS Hostable Web core. When informed that installation has succeeded, click **Close**.

You can also use the following PowerShell cmdlet to set up Work Folders:

```
Add-WindowsFeature FS-SyncShareService
```

Installing the Work Folders role service adds the Work Folders page to File and Storage Services in Server Manager. In addition, the Windows Sync Shares service and the SyncShare Windows PowerShell module are installed on the file server. After installing this service, you need to configure the shared folder from which users will synchronize their work data. Use the following procedure:

1. From the Server Manager Dashboard, click **File and Storage Services** > **Work Folders**.

2. You are informed that there are no sync shares. Click the link labeled **To create a sync share for Work Folders**; this starts the New Sync Share Wizard.

3. The wizard begins with a Before you begin page. Note the information provided about creating sync shares, and then click **Next**.

4. On the Select the server and path page shown in Figure 4-20, specify the local path where user subfolders will be stored. You can also click the **Select by file share** radio button to use a shared folder provided on this page, or click **Browse** to locate a suitable folder. When finished, click **Next**.

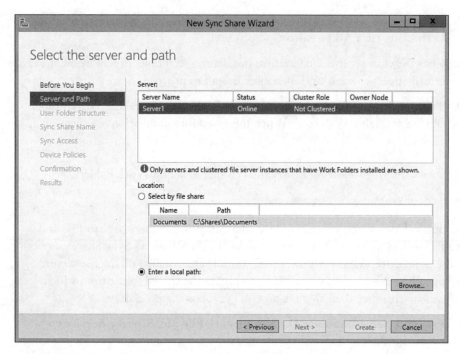

Figure 4-20   Specifying the path to the Work Folders share.

5. On the Specify the structure for user folders page shown in Figure 4-21, select one of the options provided for naming user-based subfolders; then click **Next**.

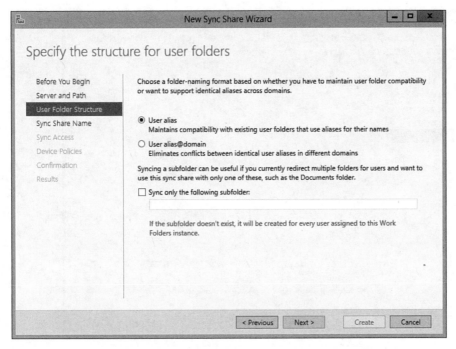

Figure 4-21   Specifying a naming format for user subfolders in the Work Folders share.

6. On the Enter the sync share name page, provide a name and optional description, and then click **Next**.

7. On the Grant sync access to groups page shown in Figure 4-22, click **Add** to display the Select User or Group dialog box shown in Figure 4-23. Type the name of the user or group you want to grant access to, and then click **OK**. Repeat as required to add users or groups. When finished, click **Next**.

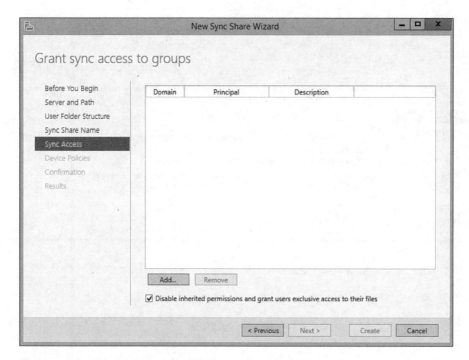

Figure 4-22   The Grant sync access to groups page enable you to specify users or groups that are permitted to sync data to the Work Folders share.

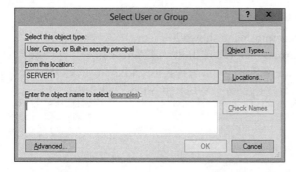

Figure 4-23   The Select User or Group dialog box enables you to specify groups that are permitted to sync to the Work Folders share.

8. You see the Specify device policies page, which enables you to select either or both of the following policies. Select the desired policies, and then click **Next**.

   ■ **Encrypt Work Folders:** Encrypts all documents with the Enterprise ID. This is the user's primary SMTP email address. The use of a different key to encrypt Work Folders ensures the security of documents on client devices and enables an administrator to wipe Work Folders as necessary, for example, if the users' device is lost or stolen.

- **Automatically lock screen and require a password:** Requires a password policy with a minimum password length of 6, an autolock screen policy set to 15 minutes or less, and a maximum password retry of 10 or less. If a device does not meet these polices, the user will be unable to set up Work Folders on her device.

9. On the Confirm selections page, review the settings you've specified. If necessary, click **Previous** to make changes. When finished, click **Create**.

10. The wizard charts the progress of setting up Work Folders. When informed that the process is finished, click **Close**.

The following items are also needed to enable users to sync to the Work Folders share across the Internet:

- **A server certificate for each file server hosting the Work Folders share:** You should use certificates granted by a public certification authority (CA) that is trusted by your users. For more information, refer to the *Cert Guide* for exam 70-412.

- **Firewall proxy or gateway access rules that enable access to the server across the Internet:** For more information, refer to Chapter 19, "Configuring Windows Firewall."

- **A publicly registered DNS domain name with the ability to create additional public records:** For more information, refer to Chapter 12, "Deploying and Configuring Domain Name System (DNS)."

Ideally, you should also have an AD DS forest that includes Windows Server 2012 R2 schema extensions that support automatic referral of computers and devices to the correct file server. If using Active Directory Federation Service (AD FS) authentication, you need to include the appropriate AD FS infrastructure.

Configuring Client Computers for Work Folders

Client computers use Secure Sockets Layer (SSL) to connect to the server. Consequently, you need to install an SSL certificate on the server. Use the following procedure on a client computer running Windows 8.1 to set up Work Folders:

1. In Control Panel, click **System and Security** > **Work Folders**.

2. The Work Folders applet opens. Click **Set up Work Folders**.

3. The Enter your work email address page shown in Figure 4-24 opens. Type your email address in the space provided. Alternatively, click the **Enter a Work Folders URL instead** link and type the URL you've been given. When finished, click **Next**.

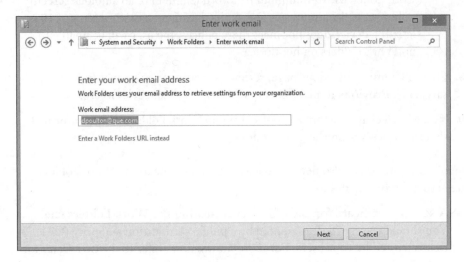

Figure 4-24   Use your work email address to access the Work Folders server.

4. A Windows Security dialog box displays. Enter your work-based username and password, and then click **OK**. This step is not required if your computer is joined to your company's AD DS domain.

5. The Introducing Work Folders page displays a default path to a local Work Folders location. Accept the default location or click **Change** to enter an alternative location. When finished, click **Next**.

6. The Security policies page displays security policies that were configured when setting up Work Folders on the server, as done in the previous procedure. To accept these policies, select the check box provided; then click **Set up Work Folders**.

Windows configures Work Folders and displays an icon in File Explorer. You can work with this folder as you would any other library or folder; any subfolders and files you place here are automatically synced to the file server.

> **NOTE**   For more information on configuring Work Folders, refer to "Work Folders Overview" at http://technet.microsoft.com/en-us/library/dn265974.aspx and "Introducing Work Folders on Windows Server 2012 R2" at http://blogs.technet.com/b/filecab/archive/2013/07/10/introducing-work-folders-on-windows-server-2012-r2.aspx. You can also configure Work Folders using PowerShell cmdlets; for more information, refer to "Sync Share Cmdlets in Windows PowerShell" at http://technet.microsoft.com/en-us/library/dn296644%28v=wps.630%29.aspx.

NTFS Permissions

Earlier in this chapter, you learned how to share folders and configure permissions that you can attach to shared folders. These permissions apply only when you access the folders across the network. Windows Server 2012 and Windows Server 2012 R2 provide another means to secure files and folders on the local computer. The New Technology File System (NTFS) that has existed since the early days of Windows NT enables you to secure and manage access to resources on both a network level and on a local level. These NTFS file and folder permissions are also known as *security permissions*; they can apply to both files and folders, and they apply on your computer to files and folders whether a folder is shared or not shared at all. Keep in mind, however, that although Windows Server 2012 and Windows Server 2012 R2 support FAT and FAT32 partitions, NTFS permissions apply only on partitions that are formatted using NTFS. Because you are already familiar with shared folder permissions, we will use that as a jumping-off point to describe NTFS permissions.

NTFS File and Folder Permissions

Like the shared folder permissions, which you can assign to users and groups, NTFS permissions for a folder control how users access a folder and the files contained within it. NTFS folder permissions are designed to control what the user can do with these files. If no explicit permissions are assigned to a folder, a user cannot access that folder at all.

Windows stores an access control list (ACL) with every file and folder on an NTFS partition. The ACL is a list of users and groups that have been granted access for a particular file or folder, as well as the types of access that the users and groups have been granted. Collectively, these kinds of entries in the ACL are called access control entries (ACEs). If you think of the ACL as a list, it isn't hard to conceive that a list contains entries of various kinds. Windows uses the ACL to determine the level of access a user should be granted when he attempts to access a file or folder.

Table 4-7 describes the standard NTFS file and folder permissions in detail.

Table 4-7   NTFS File and Folder Permissions

Permission	What a User Can Do on a Folder	What a User Can Do on a File
Full Control	Change permissions, take ownership, and delete subfolders and files. All other actions allowed by the permissions listed in this table are also possible.	Change permissions, take ownership, and perform all other actions allowed by the permissions listed in this table.
Modify	Delete the folder as well as grant that user the Read permission and the List Folder Contents permission.	Modify a file's contents and delete the file as well as perform all actions allowed by the Write permission and the Read and Execute permission.
Read & Execute	Run files and display file attributes, owner, and permissions.	Run application files and display file attributes, owner, and permissions.
List Folder Contents	List a folder's contents, that is, its files and subfolders.	n/a
Read	Display file names, subfolder names, owner, permissions, and file attributes (Read Only, Hidden, Archive, and System).	Display data, file attributes, owner, and permissions.
Write	Create new folders and files, change a folder's attributes, and display owner and permissions.	Write changes to the file, change its attributes, and display owner and permissions.

Applying NTFS Permissions

It is simple to apply NTFS permissions, as the following procedure shows:

1. Right-click a folder or file and select **Properties**.

2. Select the **Security** tab of the Properties dialog box. Also known as the ACL Editor, the Security tab enables you to edit the NTFS permissions for a folder or file (see Figure 4-25).

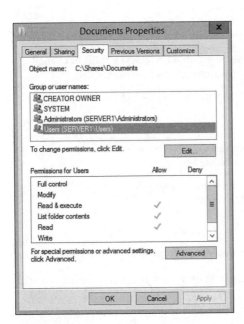

Figure 4-25   The Security tab of a file or folder's Properties dialog box displays its security permissions.

3. Click **Edit** to display the dialog box shown in Figure 4-26. You can configure the permissions described in Table 4-8.

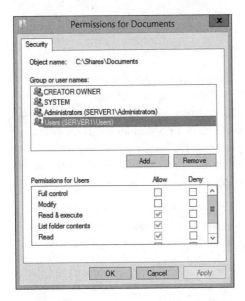

Figure 4-26   The Permissions for (file/folder name) dialog box enables you to configure security permissions.

Table 4-8   Security Tab Options

Option	Description
Group or Usernames	Start by selecting the user account or group for which you want to change permissions or that you want to remove from the permissions list.
Permissions for Authenticated Users	Select the **Allow** check box to allow a permission. Select the **Deny** check box to deny a permission.
Add	Click **Add** to open the Select Users or Groups dialog box to select user accounts and groups to add to the Name list.
Remove	Click **Remove** to remove the selected user account or group and the associated permissions for the file or folder.

4. When finished, click **OK** to return to the Security tab shown in Figure 4-25.

5. If you need to configure special permissions or access advanced settings, click **Advanced**. The next section discusses these permissions.

> **NOTE**   You can also configure NTFS permissions from the command line by using the **icacls.exe** utility. This utility is useful for scripting permissions configuration or for configuring permissions at a Server Core computer. For more information on this utility, refer to "Icacls" at http://technet.microsoft.com/en-us/library/cc753525.aspx.

Specifying Advanced Permissions

For the most part, the standard NTFS permissions are suitable for managing user access to resources. There are occasions where a more specialized application of security and permissions is appropriate. To configure a more specific level of access, you can use NTFS special access permissions. The NTFS standard permissions are actually combinations of the special access permissions. For example, the standard Read permission is comprised of the List folder/read data, Read attributes, Read extended attributes, and Read permissions special access permissions.

In general, you will only use the standard NTFS permissions already described. In exceptional cases, you might need to fine-tune the permissions further, and this is where the special access NTFS permissions come in. To configure special access permissions, use the following steps:

1. From the Security tab of the appropriate file or folder, click **Advanced** to access the Advanced Security Settings dialog box.

2. Click **Change Permissions** to display the Advanced Security Settings dialog box shown in Figure 4-27.

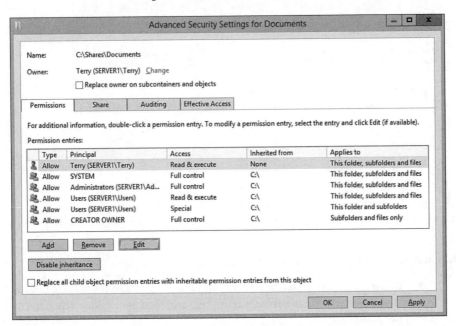

Figure 4-27   The Advanced Security Settings dialog box displays information about the permissions currently assigned to the file or folder and enables you to add or edit permissions.

3. Select the user or group account for which you want to apply special access permissions; then click **Edit** (if available) to display the Permission Entry dialog box shown in Figure 4-28.

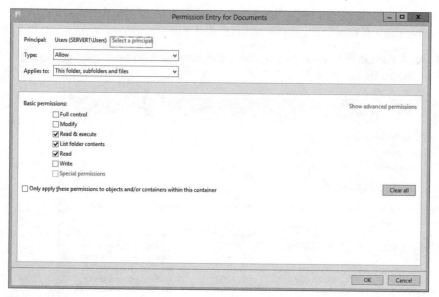

Figure 4-28   Configuring file and folder permissions from the Permission Entry dialog box.

4. Configure the following options as required:

   ■ **Principal:** The user account or group name appears in this dialog box, but you can select a different one in the scroll box by clicking the Select a principal link.

   ■ **Type:** Select **Allow** or **Deny** as required.

   ■ **Applies to:** You can adjust the level in the folder hierarchy at which the special permissions apply and are inherited. When permissions are not being inherited from a parent folder, you can choose between **This folder, subfolders and files,** or any one or two of these components.

   ■ **Basic Permissions:** Enables you to allow or deny (according to the Type option you've selected) the basic permissions as described previously in Table 4-7.

   ■ **Only apply these permissions to objects and/or containers within this container:** Here you can adjust a particular folder's properties so that files and subfolders inherit their permissions from the folder you are working on. Selecting this option propagates the special access permissions to files and folders within and below your current location in a folder hierarchy.

   ■ **Clear All:** You can clear all selected permissions.

5. When finished, click **OK**.

To configure advanced permissions, select the link labeled **Show advanced permissions**. As shown in Figure 4-29, the Permission Entry dialog box displays the special access file and folder permissions that you can configure from the Permission Entry dialog box. Table 4-9 describes these permissions:

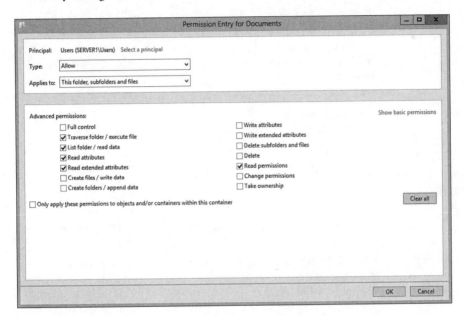

Figure 4-29   Configuring advanced permissions from the Permission Entry dialog box.

Table 4-9   NTFS Special Access Permissions

Folder Permission	What a User Is Allowed to Do	File Permission	What a User Is Allowed to Do
Full control	Includes all special access permissions.	Full control	Includes all special access permissions.
Traverse folder	Navigate through folders that a user normally can't access to reach files or folders that the user does have permission to access.	Execute file	Run executable files.
List folder	View files or subfolders.	Read data	View data in a particular file.

Folder Permission	What a User Is Allowed to Do	File Permission	What a User Is Allowed to Do
Read attributes	View folder attributes. These attributes are defined by NTFS.	Read attributes	View file attributes. These attributes are defined by NTFS.
Read extended attributes	View extended folder attributes. Extended attributes are defined by software and can vary.	Read extended attributes	View extended file attributes. Extended attributes are defined by software and can vary.
Create files	Create files within a folder.	Write data	Write changes to or overwrite a file.
Create folders	Create subfolders.	Append data	Make changes to the end of a file by appending data. Does not allow changing, deleting, or overwriting existing data.
Write attributes	Change the attributes of a folder, such as read-only or hidden. Attributes are defined by NTFS.	Write attributes	Change the attributes of a file, such as read-only or hidden. Attributes are defined by NTFS.
Write extended attributes	Change the extended attributes of a folder. Extended attributes are defined by programs and can vary.	Write extended attributes	Change the extended attributes of a file. Extended attributes are defined by programs and can vary.
Delete subfolders and files	Delete subfolders, even if the Delete permission has not been granted on the subfolder.	Delete subfolders and files	Delete files, even if the Delete permission has not been granted on the file.
Delete	Delete a folder or subfolder.	Delete	Delete a file.
Read permissions	Read permissions for a folder, such as Full Control, Read, and Write.	Read permissions	Read permissions for a file, such as Full Control, Read, and Write.

Folder Permission	What a User Is Allowed to Do	File Permission	What a User Is Allowed to Do
Change permissions	Change permissions for a folder, such as Full Control, Read, and Write.	Change permissions	Change permissions for a file, such as Full Control, Read, and Write.
Take ownership	Take ownership of a folder.	Take ownership	Take ownership of a file.

Taking ownership is a very special type of access permission. In Windows Server 2012 R2, as with previous Windows servers dating back to Windows NT, each NTFS folder and file has an owner. Whoever creates a file or folder automatically becomes the owner and, by default, has Full Control permissions on that file or folder. If that person is a member of the Administrators group, then the Administrators group becomes the owner. The owner possesses the ability to apply and change permissions on a folder or file that she owns, even if the ACL does not explicitly grant her that ability. This does make it possible for the owner of a particular file or folder to deny Administrators access to a resource. But an administrator can exercise the optional right to take ownership of any resource to gain access to it, if this becomes necessary.

In Table 4-7, which described the standard access permissions, you might have noticed that a standard permission such as Modify enables a user to do more than one thing to a file or folder. A special-access permission typically enables a user to do one thing only. All special permissions are encompassed within the standard permissions.

Configuring NTFS Permissions Inheritance

All NTFS permissions are inherited—that is, they pass down through the folder hierarchy from parent to child. Permissions assigned to a parent folder are inherited by all the files in that folder, and by the subfolders contained in the parent folder as well. Unless you specifically stop the process of files and folders inheriting permissions from their parent folders, any existing files and subfolders and any new files and subfolders created within this tree of folders will inherit their permissions from the original parent folder. To use the fancy term, permissions are *propagated* all the way down the tree.

Windows Server 2012 R2 lets you modify this permissions inheritance sequence if necessary. To check whether permissions are being inherited and to remove permissions inheritance, use the following procedure:

1. From the Advanced Security Settings dialog box previously shown in Figure 4-27, click the **Disable inheritance** command button.

2. The Block Inheritance dialog box shown in Figure 4-30 appears and prompts you to specify one of the following permissions inheritance options:

    ■ **Convert inherited permissions into explicit permissions on this object:** Select this link to add existing inherited permissions assigned for the parent folder to the subfolder or file. This action also prevents subsequent permissions inheritance from the parent folder.

    ■ **Remove all inherited permissions from this object:** Select this link to remove existing inherited permissions assigned to the parent folder to the subfolder or file. Only permissions that you explicitly assign to the file or folder will apply.

    ■ **Cancel:** Click **Cancel** to abort the operation and restore the Allow inheritable permissions from parent to propagate to this object check box.

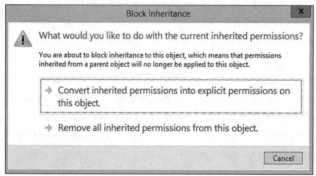

Figure 4-30   If you choose to remove permissions inheritance, you will need to decide how they are going to be applied.

3. You are returned to the Advanced Security Settings dialog box. Click **OK** or **Apply** to apply your changes.

Taking Ownership of Files and Folders

In certain cases, you might need to grant the special Take Ownership permission to a user account. This can be valuable if a user is taking over responsibilities and resources from another individual. A user with the Full Control NTFS permission or the Take Ownership special permission can take ownership of a file or folder from the folder's Properties dialog box, as follows:

1. From the Security tab of the folder's Properties dialog box previously shown in Figure 4-25, click **Advanced**. The Advanced Security Settings dialog box previously shown in Figure 4-27 displays the current owner on the Owner line near the top.

2. To change ownership, click **Change**.

3. You see the Select User or Group dialog box as previously shown in Figure 4-23. Type the username of the desired owner from the list displayed, and then click **OK**. If necessary, click **Locations** to locate a user or group from another server or AD DS domain.

4. You are informed that if you have just taken ownership, you will need to close and reopen the object's Properties dialog box to view or change permissions.

5. Click **OK** to accept this message, and then click **OK** again to close the Advanced Security Settings dialog box.

Effective Permissions

Users who belong to more than one group might receive different levels of permission. Both shared folder and NTFS permissions are cumulative. Your effective permissions are a combination of all permissions configured for your user account and for the groups of which you are a member. In other words, the effective permission is the least restrictive of all permissions that you have. For example, if you have Read permissions for a given file but are also a member of a group that has Modify permissions for the same file, your effective permissions for that file or folder would be Modify.

However, there is one important exception to this rule. If you happen to be a member of yet another group that has been explicitly denied permissions to a resource (the permission has been selected in the Deny column), then your effective permissions will not allow you to access that resource at all. Explicit denial of permission always overrides any allowed permissions.

Putting the two types of permissions together, the rules for determining effective permissions are simple:

- At either the shared folder or NTFS permissions level by itself, if a user receives permissions by virtue of membership in one or more groups, the *least restrictive* permission is the effective permission. For example, if a user has Read permission assigned to his user account and Full Control permission by virtue of membership in a group, he receives Full Control permission on this item.

- If the user is accessing a shared folder over the network and has both shared folder and NTFS permissions applied to it, the *most restrictive* permission is the effective permission. For example, if a user has Full Control NTFS permission on a folder but accesses it across the network where he has Read shared folder permission, her effective permission is Read.

- If the user is accessing a shared folder on the computer where it exists, shared folder permissions do not apply. In the previous example, this user would receive Full Control permission when accessing the shared folder locally.

- If the user has an explicit denial of permission at either the shared folder or NTFS level, he is denied access to the object, regardless of any other permissions he might have to this object.

> **TIP** It is important to remember that specifically denying permission to a file within a folder overrides all other file and folder permissions configured for a user or for a group that might contain that user's account. There is no real top-down or bottom-up factor to consider when it comes to denying permissions. If a user is a member of a group that has been denied a permission to a file or folder, or if a user's individual account has been denied a permission to a particular resource, that is what counts. If you are denied access to a folder, it does not matter what permissions are attached to a file inside the folder because you cannot get to it.

Viewing a User's Effective Permissions

Windows Server 2012 R2 enables you to view a user or group's effective permissions. This is most useful in untangling a complicated web of permissions received by a user who is a member of several groups. Use the following procedure:

1. From the Security tab of the folder's Properties dialog box previously shown in Figure 4-25, click **Advanced**, and then click the **Effective Access** tab on the Advanced Security Settings dialog box (previously shown in Figure 4-27).

2. Click **Select a user** to display the Select User or Group dialog box previously shown in Figure 4-23.

3. Enter the appropriate user or group, and then click **OK**.

4. This user or group name appears on the Effective Access tab. To display the user or group's effective permissions, click **View effective access**.

5. As shown in Figure 4-31, the Effective Access tab displays the effective permissions for the selected user or group. Click **OK** to close this dialog box.

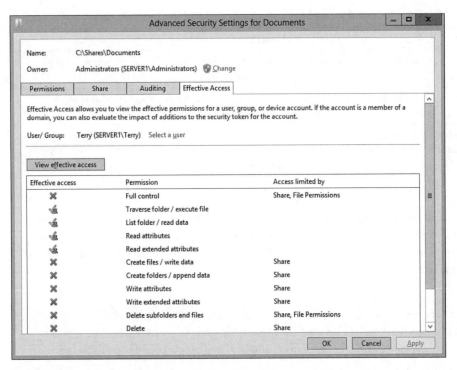

Figure 4-31   You can view a user or group's effective permissions to a resource from the Effective Access tab of the Advanced Security Settings dialog box.

Copying and Moving Files and Folders

When you copy or move a file or folder that is configured with NTFS permissions, those NTFS permissions can change. The action that occurs depends on whether you are copying the file or folder or whether you are moving the file or folder.

Copying Files and Folders with NTFS Permissions

When you copy a file or folder that is configured with NTFS permissions, those NTFS permissions can change. If you are copying files and folders to a place where the NTFS permissions match exactly, the permissions will stay the same. There are no exceptions to this rule. The potential for change is always there, however, when you copy files and folders with NTFS permissions. To ensure that NTFS permissions are applied effectively on your computer, you will need to keep in mind how copying can change NTFS permissions. There are essentially three possible outcomes, as outlined in Table 4-10.

Table 4-10   The Effect of Copying Files or Folders on Their NTFS Permissions

Action	Result
Copy a file or folder within the same partition	The copy inherits the NTFS permissions of the destination folder.
Copy a file or folder from one NTFS partition to another NTFS partition	The copy inherits the NTFS permissions of the destination folder.
Copy a file or folder from an NTFS partition to a FAT or FAT32 partition	The copy of a file or folder loses its NTFS permissions completely. NTFS permissions cannot apply anywhere else but on an NTFS partition.

To copy files from an NTFS partition, you need to have at least the Read permission for the originating folder. To complete the copy operation so that the copied versions are written to disk, you need to have at least the Write permission for the destination folder.

CAUTION   A close look at Table 4-10 should alert you to the fact that copying a file or folder from an NTFS partition to a FAT or FAT32 partition will strip the file or folder of its NTFS permissions and make it fully available to all users at the local computer.

Moving Files and Folders with NTFS Permissions

Moving files with NTFS permissions might change those permissions. Depending on the circumstances, especially the destination of the move, the permissions might change or stay the same. As outlined in Table 4-11, there are also three possible outcomes.

Table 4-11   The Effect of Moving Files or Folders on Their NTFS Permissions

Action	Result
Move a file or folder within the same partition	The file or folder retains its NTFS permissions, regardless of the permissions that exist for the destination folder.
Move a file or folder from one NTFS partition to another NTFS partition	The file or folder inherits the NTFS permissions of the destination folder.
Move a file or folder from an NTFS partition to a FAT or FAT32 partition	The file or folder loses its NTFS permissions completely. NTFS permissions cannot apply anywhere else but on an NTFS partition.

To move files within an NTFS partition or between two NTFS partitions, you need to have at least the Modify permission for the originating folder. To complete the move operation so that the moved versions are written to disk, you need to have at least the Write permission for the destination folder. The Modify permission is required at the source so that source files and folders can be deleted after the files or folders are safely relocated to their new home.

> **NOTE**   After you have had time to think about how copying and moving files and folders affects NTFS permissions, there is an easy way to remember how all these possible outcomes will work. One simple sentence can serve to summarize what is going on—"Moving within retains." The only sure way to retain existing NTFS permissions during a copy or move operation is to move files within a single NTFS partition. All the other options hold a very real potential for altering NTFS permissions.

Using the Mouse to Copy or Move Objects from One Location to Another

Keep in mind the following facts about dragging objects between locations:

- When you use the mouse to drag an object from one folder to another on the *same* partition, you are *moving* that object.

- If you drag the object to a folder on *another* partition, you are *copying* that object.

- If you hold down the Ctrl key while dragging, you are *copying* the object, whether it is to the same or another partition.

- You can also right-drag the object. In this case, when you release the mouse button, you have the choices of copying the object, moving it, or creating a shortcut to the object in its original location.

Practical Guidelines on Sharing and Securing Folders

When you share folders, it is important to control how they are used. To control the use of shared folders, you should be aware of how shares are applied in Windows Server 2012 R2. The following facts should be kept in mind.

- **Denying permissions overrides all other shared permissions that can be applied to a folder:** If a user is part of a group that is denied permission to access a particular resource, that user will not be able to access that resource, even if you grant her user account access to the share.

- **Multiple permissions accumulate:** You might be a member of multiple groups, each with a different level of permissions for a particular shared resource. Your effective permissions are a combination of all permissions configured for your user account and the groups of which you are a member. As a user, you might have Read permissions for a folder. You might be a member of a group with Change permissions for the same folder. Your effective permissions for that folder would be Change. If you happen to be made a member of yet another group that has been denied permissions to a folder, then your effective permissions will not allow you to access that folder at all. That is the one important exception to this rule.

- **Copying or moving a folder alters the shared permissions associated with that folder:** When you copy a shared folder, the original shared folder is still shared, but the copied folder is not. When you move a shared folder to a new location anywhere, that folder is no longer shared by anyone.

- **When you share a folder that is located on an NTFS volume, you will still need to consider the NTFS permissions that apply to that folder:** There might already be NTFS permissions in place on a folder that you are in the process of sharing. You will need to consider how your NTFS and shared folder permissions combine. (See the next item.) If there aren't any NTFS permissions on that folder, you might need to configure NTFS permissions for your shared folder or it is possible that no one will be able to access it.

- **When shared folder and NTFS file and folder permissions combine, the most restrictive permissions apply:** When both NTFS and shared folder permissions apply to the same folder, the more restrictive permission is the effective permission for that folder. Do not lose sight of the fact, however, that shared folder permissions have no effect on users that are logged into the computer locally.

- **When a folder resides on an NTFS volume:** You will need at least the NTFS Read permission to be able to share that folder at all.

Access-Based Enumeration of Files and Folders

As discussed previously, access-based enumeration (ABE) enables the display of only those files and folders that a user is entitled to access according to share and security permissions granted to her account. This feature applies to viewing files and folders in a shared folder over the network. It does not apply when viewing files or folders while browsing the server locally.

There are two methods to enable access-based enumeration:

- **Shared Folder Wizard:** Access-based enumeration can be enabled during initial configuration of a new share using the Shared Folder Wizard, as you have learned previously. Under the Configure Share Settings screen as shown in Figure 4-5, confirm that the Enable access-based enumeration check box has been checked.

- **Modifying an Existing Share:** Access-based enumeration might be modified after a share has been established through the File and Storage Services section of Server Manager.

If at any time you need decide to enable or disable access-based enumeration, you can do so by performing the following steps:

1. Open Sever Manager and navigate to the **File and Storage Services** section.

2. Click the **Shares** tab.

3. Right-click the shared folder or volume and then click **Properties**. Similarly, you can also use the **Tasks** drop-down menu.

4. Expand **Settings** to allow you to enable or disable access-based enumeration by checking or unchecking the setting box, as shown in Figure 4-32.

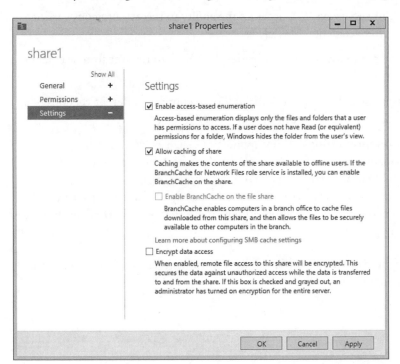

Figure 4-32   You can modify properties of a share using the Shares tab of File and Storage Services.

5. Click **Apply** and then **OK** when complete.

> **NOTE**   Individual shares can be created and hidden from network browsing by appending a $ at the end of the share name. For example, Share1 will be visible, but Share1$ will be created as a hidden share.

Configuring Volume Shadow Copy Service

If you recall from previous releases of Windows Server, Volume Shadow Copy Services (VSS) creates point-in-time copies, known as *snapshots*, of user files located on server shares. With just a few clicks, users can roll back to previous versions of the files. Shadow copies are created based on configurable intervals. The amount of copies stored on the server depends on available storage and the rate of file change. VSS provides the following benefits:

- **Lower administrative overhead:** VSS empowers users with the ability to recover previous versions of their files.

- **Deleted file recovery:** VSS provides the ability to recover previous versions of the file after accidental file deletes.

- **File overwrite recovery:** VSS provides the ability to recover from accidental file overwrites.

- **File comparison:** VSS provides the ability to compare different versions of a file and track changes between the versions.

- **Application integrations:** Many applications such as Windows Server Backup, Shadow Copies for Shared Folders, System Restore, and so on take advantage of the VSS core services to create point-in-time copies of data or configurations for easy recovery. This is especially useful in situations where snapshots allow in use data, applications, or even Hyper-V virtual machines to be backed up.

There are many moving parts built in to the VSS infrastructure. Table 4-12 outlines the core components:

Table 4-12 VSS Infrastructure Components

Component	Function
VSS Service	Primary component that manages VSS interaction between the operating systems and other VSS components.
VSS Requester	Component that requests the creation of shadow copies. This can include the Windows backup application or VSS for Shared Folders (discussed later).
VSS Writer	Component responsible for guaranteeing data consistency as snapshots are created.
VSS Provider	Component that creates and maintains the shadow copies. This is built in to many operating systems and in some cases hardware appliances.

NOTE For more information on how the Volume Shadow Copy Service works, refer to "Volume Shadow Copy Service" at http://technet.microsoft.com/en-us/library/ee923636.aspx.

Configuring Shadow Copies of Shared Folders

To enable and configure Shadow Copies of shared folders, perform the following steps:

1. Create a custom MMC console and add the **Shared Folders** snap-in or launch the **Computer Management** console from the Administrative Tools folder.

2. From the console tree, right-click **Shared Folders**. From the All Tasks menu, click **Configure Shadow Copies**. This will launch the Shadow Copies configuration dialog box shown in Figure 4-33. Shadow Copies can also be configured through File Explorer by accessing the properties of a local volume.

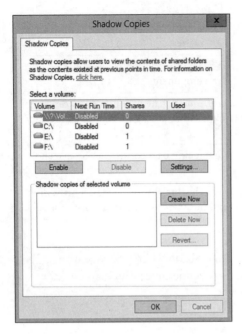

Figure 4-33   Shadow Copies Configuration dialog box.

3. Under **Select a volume**, highlight the volume for which you want to enable Shadow Copies and click **Enable**.

4. Windows will prompt you to confirm you want to enable shadow copies and use the default schedule and settings, as shown in Figure 4-34. Click **Yes** to proceed.

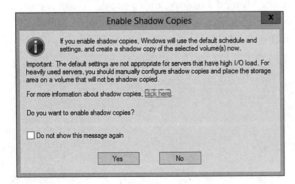

Figure 4-34   Shadow Copies Enable prompt.

5. The default schedule will scan the volume for changes and create shadow copies at 7:00 a.m. and noon every day. The default storage for shadow copies is on the same volume and is allocated 10% of the available space. Depending on your server load, you might choose a less or more frequent schedule and/or allocate additional storage to provide capacity for more copies. To modify these settings as shown in Figure 4-35, highlight the specific volume and click **Settings**.

Figure 4-35   Modify settings for Shadow Copies.

NOTE   Shadow Copies of Shared Folders is enabled on a per-volume basis so you are unable to target specific folders.

NOTE   Shadow Copies under Server Core installations can be configured and managed using the `vssadmin` command. For more information, refer to "VSSadmin" located at http://technet.microsoft.com/en-us/library/cc754968(v=ws.10).aspx.

Guidelines for Using VSS

While it might seem simple, there are several guidelines for enabling and using VSS:

- Always be sure to continue to back up your data on a regular basis. VSS is not designed to be a replacement for regular data backups, but it can be considered a complement to it.

- Consider server I/O load when determining an appropriate schedule. If you are currently experiencing higher I/O load, choose a less frequent shadow copy schedule.

- Consider how often users request file restores to determine frequency or how much storage you will need for shadow copies. A maximum of 64 shadow copies per volume can be stored. If you reach the 64-copy limit or storage runs out, older shadow copies will be deleted to make room for new versions.

- Know that when a file is restored to a previous version, permissions remain the same. If a file was accidentally deleted, file permissions will be reset to the default permissions for the folder.

- Avoid using shadow copies on volumes that use mount points because the mounted drive and its data will not be included in the shadow copies.

- When possible, use a separate volume or even storage space to contain shadow copies.

- If a volume must be deleted, ensure that all shadow copy tasks are removed and disable shadow copy services for that volume before deleting the volume.

- For optimal file fragmentation, format the source volume for the shadow copies using a 16-KB allocation unit size.

- If you need to restore a previously backed-up shadow copy volume, be sure to restore the data to the same volume to avoid the risk of duplicate snapshots.

Configuring NTFS Quotas

First introduced in Windows 2000, and improved with each successive server version, is the concept of disk quotas. This feature allows an administrator to set a limit on the amount of disk space used by an individual user. Added with Windows Server 2008 is the use of File Server Resource Manager (FSRM) to enable quotas on shared folders within disk volumes, together with additional mechanisms for notifying users who are approaching or exceeding their quota limits. Both quotas and FSRM have been carried over into Windows Server 2012 and Windows Server 2012 R2.

Using FSRM, you can send a warning to users when they reach a certain level of disk usage, and you can write an event to the event log if a user attempts to exceed his quota. When you have enabled disk quotas, Windows Server 2012 R2 also collects disk usage statistics for all users enabled on the volume, thus allowing the administrator to keep track of disk usage. Thereby, the administrator can manage disks more efficiently and prevent users from "hogging" disk space.

You can enable disk and volume quotas from File Explorer or from the FSRM console. Enabling quotas from File Explorer permits you to set different quotas for different users; the quotas apply to all folders within the specified volume. Enabling quotas from FSRM, on the other hand, permits you to set quotas that apply to given folders (such as shares) on the server; however, you cannot specify different quota levels for different users when using FSRM.

Using File Explorer to Enable Disk Quotas

File Explorer lets you to enable quotas on a per-volume, per-user basis. Use the following procedure to enable disk quotas from File Explorer:

1. In File Explorer, right-click the volume on which you want to enable disk quotas, and then select **Properties**.

2. In the Properties dialog box, click the **Quota** tab to display disk quota information.

3. On the Quota Properties dialog box, select the **Enable quota management** check box. Then specify values for the quota parameters described in Table 4-13 and shown in Figure 4-36.

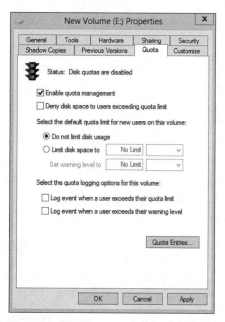

Figure 4-36   You can enable disk quotas on given disks.

4. Quota Management also provides the ability to configure quota entries for specific users. Click the **Quota Entries** button to view or modify quotas configured on the volume, including the user name, amount of space used, quota limit, warning level, and percent used.

5. After making any changes and closing the Quota Entries dialog box, click **OK** or **Apply**. A Disk Quota message box (see Figure 4-37) warns you that the disk will be rescanned and that this can take several minutes.

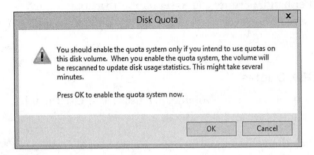

Figure 4-37 You are warned that the disk volume will be rescanned to update disk usage.

6. Click **OK** to close this message box and start the scan.

Table 4-13 describes the options available on the Quota tab of the disk's Properties dialog box.

Table 4-13 Disk Quota Configuration Options

Option	Description
Enable quota management	Enables quota management and enables the other options so you can configure them.
Deny disk space to users exceeding quota limit	When users exceed their quota, they receive an Out of disk space message and they cannot write further data.
Do not limit disk usage	Select this option when you do not want to limit the amount of disk space used.
Limit disk space to	Configures the disk space limit per user.
Set warning level to	Configures the amount of disk space that a user can write before receiving a warning.
Log event when a user exceeds their quota limit	Writes an event to the Windows system log on the computer running disk quotas whenever a user exceeds her quota limit.
Log event when a user exceeds their warning level	Writes an event to the Windows system log on the computer running disk quotas any time a user exceeds her quota warning level, not her actual quota.

When the disk quota system is active, a user checking the properties of the volume where it is enabled sees only the amount of space permitted on the quota; the available space is the permitted space minus the space already used. If a user tries to copy a file that is larger than the allowed space, he receives a message that the file cannot be copied. In addition, an event is written to the event log if you have selected the appropriate check box described in Table 4-13. You can view usage statistics by clicking the **Quota Entries** button.

> **NOTE**   You can enable quotas only on volumes formatted with the NTFS file system. Only administrators can enable quotas, but they can permit users to view quota settings.

> **TIP**   Set appropriate quotas on all volumes that a user can access. Provide warnings to the users, and log events when they exceed their quota limit and/or warning level.

Using FSRM to Enable Quotas

FSRM provides a more comprehensive set of options for enabling quotas. You can enable quotas on shared folders as well as volumes, and you can define templates that can be used for setting common quota definitions across multiple servers and shares. FSRM enables you to create the following types of quotas:

- **Hard quota:** Denies additional disk space to a user exceeding her quota limit and generates notifications when data saved reaches configured thresholds. Equivalent to selecting the **Deny disk space to users exceeding quota limit** option previously shown in Figure 4-36.

- **Soft quota:** Only generates the configured notifications when data saved reaches configured thresholds. Equivalent to clearing the previously mentioned option.

FSRM can generate notification actions that are similar to those already discussed for file classification, including email notifications, logged events, execution of commands or scripts, or generation of storage reports. Use the following procedure to create a quota:

1. Install the File Server Resource Manager Role using Server Manager.

2. Launch FSRM from within Administrative Tools.

3. Expand the **Quota Management** node in FSRM to reveal the Quotas and Quota Templates subnodes.

4. Right-click **Quotas** and select **Create Quota**. The Create Quota dialog box shown in Figure 4-38 appears.

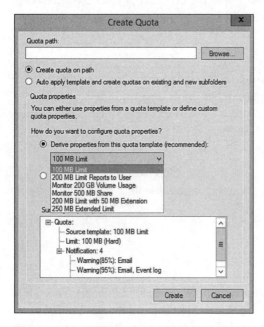

Figure 4-38   FSRM provides several default options for creating a shared folder-based quota.

5. Type or browse to the desired volume or folder.

6. If you have a quota template configured, select the **Auto apply** template and create quotas on existing and new subfolders option. Otherwise, leave the default of **Create quota on path** selected.

7. Select an option for configuring quota properties from the drop-down list shown in Figure 4-38, or select the **Define custom quota properties** radio button for specifying additional options.

8. When finished, click **Create** to create and enable the quota.

Using FSRM to Create Quota Templates

Previously released with Windows Server 2008 R2, Windows Server 2012 R2 also provides the capability of defining *quota templates*. If you recall, you can apply standard storage limits and notification thresholds to many volumes and folders on servers throughout your organization. In addition, you can automatically update all quotas based on your template simply by editing the template. This enables you to create a standard user quota template that limits each user's storage on the user's personal folder; you can easily modify all users' limits by editing this template.

FSRM provides several default quota templates that you can use or modify to suit your needs. You can also create a new quota template by performing the following procedure:

1. Select the **Quota Templates** subnode in the console tree of FSRM. The details pane displays the default quota templates.

2. Right-click **Quota Templates** and select **Create Quota Template**. The Create Quota Template dialog box shown in Figure 4-39 appears.

Figure 4-39   Using FSRM to create a custom quota template.

3. If you want to copy the properties of a default quota template, select it from the drop-down list provided and click **Copy**.

4. Type a name and optional description for the template in the text boxes provided.

5. Specify a space limit (in KB, MB, GB, or TB), and select whether to enable a hard or soft quota.

6. Click **Add** to configure notification thresholds. The Add Threshold dialog box enables you to send email messages to users and administrators, write events to the event log, execute commands or scripts, or generate reports. Options available are similar to those available with other FSRM actions. Click **OK** when finished.

7. When finished, click **OK** to close the Create Quota Template dialog box and add your custom template to the list in the details pane of FSRM.

> **NOTE**   For more information on using FSRM to configure quotas, refer to "Working with Quotas" at http://technet.microsoft.com/en-us/library/dd758768(WS.10).aspx.

> **TIP**   You should be aware that you can set quotas by user only by configuring them from File Explorer; conversely, you can set quotas by shared folder only by configuring them from FSRM. An exam question might test your knowledge of this fact.

Some Guidelines for Using Quotas

The following are a few guidelines for using quotas on Windows Server 2012 R2 file servers:

- If you need to specify different quotas for different users, use File Explorer to configure quotas. Conversely, if you need to specify quotas that apply to shared folders, use FSRM to configure quotas.

- When installing applications, use the Administrator account rather than your own user account. That way, the space used by the applications will not be charged against your quota if you have one.

- If you want to use disk quotas only to monitor disk space usage, specify a soft quota by clearing the **Deny disk space to users exceeding quota limit** check box in File Explorer or by selecting the **Soft quota** option in FSRM. That way, users are not prevented from saving important data.

- Be aware that the use of hard quotas might cause applications to fail. Using FSRM to configure hard quotas provides additional reports and warnings that alert you to situations where quota limits are being approached and enable you to take action as needed.

- Monitor the space used and increase the limits for those users who need larger amounts of space. When using FSRM, set up additional folders with less restrictive limits applied to users with access permissions for these folders.

- Set quotas on all shared volumes, including public folders and network servers, to ensure appropriate use of space by users.

- If a user no longer stores files on a certain volume, delete her disk quota entries. You can do this only after her files have been moved or deleted or after someone has taken ownership of them.

NOTE You should be aware that NTFS file compression actually has no particular effect on the amount of quota space available to such a user. Disk quotas are calculated based on the amount of space occupied by uncompressed folders and files, regardless of whether files are compressed or not compressed.

Exam Preparation Tasks

Review All the Key Topics

Review the most important topics in the chapter, noted with the key topics icon in the outer margin of the page. Table 4-14 lists a reference of these key topics and the page numbers on which each is found.

Table 4-14 Key Topics for Chapter 4

Key Topic Element	Description	Page Number
List	Describes new and improved capabilities of the File and Storage Server role in Windows Server 2012 R2.	127
Figure 4-2	Shows the five file share profile options in Windows Server 2012 R2.	131
Figure 4-7	The Advanced sharing settings dialog box enables you to configure several global file sharing options.	136
Figure 4-8	Shows you how to choose people to share with from File Explorer.	137

Key Topic Element	Description	Page Number
Table 4-3	Describes important file sharing options available in Windows Server 2012 R2.	139
Table 4-4	Describes shared folder permissions.	140
Table 4-6	Describes several offline file policies available in Windows Server 2012 R2.	147
List	Describes important capabilities of Work Folders.	153
Step list	Shows you how to install Work Folders.	154
Step list	Shows you how to configure client computers for Work Folders.	159
Table 4-7	Describes NTFS permissions available on files and folders.	162
Figure 4-25	Shows security permissions displayed on the Security tab.	163
Figure 4-29	Shows you how to configure advanced NTFS permissions.	167
Figure 4-30	Shows the available options for configuring permissions inheritance.	170
List	Describes how effective permissions are determined from a combination of share and NTFS permissions configured at different levels.	171
Figure 4-31	Displaying a user or group's effective permissions.	173
Figure 4-32	Displays the Enable/Disable option for access-based enumeration.	177
Table 4-12	Lists the components of VSS.	179
List	Shows you how to configure Shadow Copies of Shared Folders.	179
List	Describes best practices and guidelines for using VSS.	182
Step List	Shows how to use File Explorer to enable disk quotas.	183
Table 4-13	Lists Disk Quota configuration options.	184
List	Lists steps to create quotas using FSRM.	185
List	Describes guidelines for using quotas.	188

Complete the Tables and Lists from Memory

Print a copy of Appendix B, "Memory Tables" (found on the CD), or at least the section for this chapter, and complete the tables and lists from memory. Appendix C, "Memory Tables Answer Key," is also on the CD and includes completed tables and lists to check your work.

Definitions of Key Terms

Define the following key terms from this chapter, and check your answers in the glossary.

Access control list, Always offline mode, File and Storage Services role, Network File System (NFS), New Technology File System (NTFS), NTFS permissions, Offline Files, Quota, Server Message Block (SMB), Shared folders, Shared folder permissions, Snapshot, Synchronizing files, VSS, Work Folders

This chapter covers the following subjects:

- **Printing Terminology in Windows Server 2012 R2:** This section introduces key terminology and concepts you must be aware of to administer printers. It also reviews the actions that occur when a user submits a print job.

- **Installing, Sharing, and Publishing Printers:** This section shows you how to install the Print and Document Services server role and goes on to cover the installation, sharing, and publication of printers.

- **Configuring Drivers Including the Easy Print Driver:** This section covers the V4 Printer Driver model and how to configure and manage print drivers including the Easy Print Driver.

- **Managing and Troubleshooting Printers:** Print servers and printers come with a large array of properties you must be aware of to effectively manage a corporate printing environment. This section introduces you to the management of these properties as well as the topics of granting permissions to printers and print servers and troubleshooting common printer problems.

CHAPTER 5

Configuring and Monitoring Print and Document Services

Resources on a Windows Server 2012 R2 network go beyond the subject of files and folders that have been the focus of Chapter 4, "Configuring Access to Files and Shares." An important component of any business network is the capability to print documents in a timely and accurate manner, and Windows Server 2012 R2 provides the Print and Document Services server role to assist administrators in setting up print servers and keeping printing capabilities operating properly. Typically, a print server is a computer to which you connect a print device and share so that many people across your network, and even across the Internet, can print to the printer.

In any case, clients that print to the printer can be running a variety of platforms and not just Windows systems. Windows Server 2012 R2 supports hundreds of print devices from a large number of printer manufacturers. This chapter introduces you to management of printers, a very important topic both in real life and on the 70-410 exam.

"Do I Know This Already?" Quiz

The "Do I Know This Already?" quiz enables you to assess whether you should read this entire chapter or simply jump to the "Exam Preparation Tasks" section for review. If you are in doubt, read the entire chapter. Table 5-1 outlines the major headings in this chapter and the corresponding "Do I Know This Already?" quiz questions. You can find the answers in Appendix A, "Answers to the 'Do I Know This Already?' Quizzes."

Table 5-1 "Do I Know This Already?" Foundation Topics Section-to-Question Mapping

Foundations Topics Section	Questions Covered in This Section
Printing Terminology in Windows Server 2012 R2	1–2
Installing, Sharing, and Publishing Printers	2–5
Configuring Drivers Including the Easy Print Driver	6–7
Managing and Troubleshooting Printers	8–12

1. In Microsoft terminology, which of the following is the best definition of a printer?

    a. The program that converts graphic commands into instructions that the physical print device is able to understand.

    b. The physical (hardware) device that produces the printed output.

    c. The computer that handles the printing process on the network.

    d. The software (logical) interface between the operating system and the physical print device.

2. Your print server is configured so that print jobs are copied to a reserved area within the system root folder of the computer before being sent to the print device. What is this action called?

    a. Preprinting

    b. Spooling

    c. Creation of an enhanced metafile (EMF)

    d. Routing

3. You have purchased a new print device for your company's network. The print device is equipped with its own network adapter so that it can be directly connected to the network. You have attached the print device to the network and are at the print server and want to install it. Which program should you use? (Each correct answer represents a complete solution. Choose two answers.)

    a. The Print Management snap-in

    b. The Add Roles and Features Wizard in Server Manager

    c. File Explorer

    d. Device Manager

    e. Control Panel Devices and Printers

4. You have installed and shared a new printer on your Windows Server 2012 R2 computer, which is configured with the Print and Document Services server role. Users printing documents from Windows 7, 8, or 8.1 computers receive their documents properly, but users printing from Windows XP computers receive documents full of illegible characters. What should you do?

   a. From the Sharing tab of the Properties dialog box for the printer, select the **Render print jobs on client computers** option.

   b. From the Sharing tab of the Properties dialog box for the printer, click **Additional Drivers**. Then select drivers for Windows XP from the Additional Drivers dialog box, and click **OK**.

   c. From the Security tab of the Properties dialog box for the printer, add a group that contains the users of Windows XP computers and grant them the Manage Documents permission.

   d. Install a new printer from the Print Management snap-in. Configure this printer to point to the same print device and provide a unique share name that references users of Windows XP computers.

5. You are responsible for printers connected to Windows Server 2012 R2 print servers in your company's AD DS domain. These servers are configured as member servers in the domain. You have installed a printer that should be accessible to computers in the Graphics department but not to computers in other departments of the company. All resources in this department are located in the Graphics organizational unit (OU). What should you do?

   a. From the Sharing tab of the printer's Properties dialog box, select the **List in the directory** option.

   b. Right-click this printer in the details pane of the Print Management snap-in and select **List in Directory**.

   c. Right-click this printer in the details pane of the Print Management snap-in and select **Deploy with Group Policy**. Select a GPO that is linked to the Graphics OU and select the option labeled The users that this GPO applies to (per user).

   d. Right-click this printer in the details pane of the Print Management snap-in, and select **Deploy with Group Policy**. Select a GPO that is linked to the Graphics OU, and select the option labeled **The computers that this GPO applies to (per machine)**.

6. You are the administrator for your print server. You need to configure your server to enable clients to print if your print server is offline. What should you do?

    a. Enable Offline Printing.

    b. Enable Branch Office Direct Printing.

    c. Configure an alternative TCP/IP Address for the printer.

    d. Enable Branch Cache.

7. You are responsible for your Remote Desktop Server environment. You need to configure your servers to enable client printer redirection with the least amount of administrative effort. How should you configure your printer redirection policies?

    a. Enable the Do not allow client printer redirection policy setting.

    b. Disable the Do not allow client printer redirection policy setting.

    c. Configure the Use Terminal Services Easy Print printer driver first setting.

    d. Download and install the manufacturer driver on all Remote Desktop Servers. Enable the group policy setting to only use certified vendor drivers.

8. You are responsible for the print servers and printers on your company's network. You have configured a shared printer (HP40001) on Server1. Server2 also has an identical shared printer (HP40002). HP40001 on Server1 experiences a catastrophic paper jam. There are a number of jobs waiting to be printed in Server1's print queue. How can you ensure that these print jobs will be printed without the need to ask the users to resubmit their print jobs to Server2?

    a. From the Ports tab of the HP40001 Properties dialog box, select **Enable printer pooling**. Include HP40002 and HP40001 in the pool.

    b. Rename the shared printer HP40001 to HP40002.

    c. In the printers folder on the Server1, add a network printer called HP40003 pointing to HP40002 on Server2. Rename printer HP40001 to HP4000X. Then rename HP40003 to HP40001.

    d. Select the **Ports** tab of the HP40001 Properties dialog box, click **Add Port**, select **Local Port**, click **New Port**, and assign the UNC name \\Server2\HP40002 to the new port.

9. The boss is fed up with waiting for her documents to print and wants to be sure the account statement prints immediately when it is needed. What is the simplest thing to do so this will happen properly?

   a. Ask her secretary to come in at 7 a.m. and print the account statement.

   b. When she needs to print the account statement, have her go to the printer properties and click **Cancel All Documents** before printing the document.

   c. Configure a printer that points to the same print device and has the priority set at 99. Configure this printer's permissions so that only the boss has the Print permission and direct her to print the account statement on this printer.

   d. Configure her user account to have the Prioritize Documents permission.

10. You are responsible for maintaining the printers on your company's AD DS network, which includes 1 domain with 3 print servers and 12 printers. You have purchased a powerful new computer and installed Windows Server 2012 R2 and the Print and Document Management server role. You would like to consolidate all the existing printers on the new server. What should you do to accomplish this task with the least amount of administrative effort?

   a. At each existing print server, select the **Export printers to a file** option. Complete the steps in the Printer Migration Wizard that starts to save printer export information to a file. Then at the new server, select the **Import printers from a file** option. Then use the Printer Migration Wizard to import the previously exported printer information.

   b. Use Windows Server Backup at each existing print server to back up the contents of the print server. Then at the new server, use Windows Server Backup to restore the information that was backed up from each existing print server.

   c. Connect to the %systemroot%\system32\spool\printers folder on each existing print server and copy the contents of this folder to the same folder on the new print server. Repeat this task at each of the remaining print servers.

   d. At the new print server, run the Printer Installation Wizard to install each of the printers in turn, selecting the **Search the network for printers** option to ensure that you've selected and installed the printers.

11. You are a tech support specialist at your company. A Windows Server 2012 R2 computer is configured as a print server. This server supports several types of printers, including color ink-jet and laser models. After updating the driver for the color ink-jet printers, users report that their print jobs printed at either the color ink-jet or laser printers contain unintelligible characters. Checking the website for the color ink-jet printer manufacturer, you notice that they have withdrawn the latest driver and will be issuing one within a few days. What action should you take to enable users to print from the laser printer with the least amount of delay?

   a. Install new printers for the laser print device at another server running Windows Server 2012 R2.

   b. Open Device Manager on the print server and access the Driver tab of the laser printer's Properties dialog box. Then click the **Roll Back Driver** button.

   c. From the Print Management snap-in at the print server, right-click the driver and select **Set Driver Isolation > None**.

   d. From the Print Management snap-in at the print server, right-click the driver and select **Set Driver Isolation > Isolated**.

12. You are responsible for several printers installed on a Windows Server 2012 R2 print server on your network, which is configured as a workgroup. You would like to allow a secretary named Evelyn to have the ability to view and manage print queues, but you do not want her to have any other administrative capabilities on the network. What should you do?

   a. Access the Security tab of the Print Server Properties dialog box and add Evelyn to list of usernames or group names. Then select the **View Server**, **Print**, **Manage Documents**, and **Manage Printer** permissions under the Allow column.

   b. Access the Security tab of the Print Server Properties dialog box and add Evelyn to list of usernames or group names. Then select the **View Server** and **Manage Server** permissions under the Allow column.

   c. Open the Computer Management snap-in and select the **Groups** sub-node under the Local Users and Groups node. Then add Evelyn's user account to the Print Operators group.

   d. Open the Computer Management snap-in and select the **Groups** sub-node under the Local Users and Groups node. Then add Evelyn's user account to the Power Users group.

Foundation Topics

Printing Terminology in Windows Server 2012 R2

We are all used to thinking of a printer as the machine that spews out printed pages. But Microsoft has its own terminology (which it has used ever since the days of Windows NT and 9x), which you need to be aware of. Table 5-2 describes the official Microsoft definitions:

Table 5-2 Printing Terminology Used by Windows Computers

Term	Description
Printer	The software (logical) interface between the operating system and the print device. In other words, a printer is part of the software and a print device is hardware. What this means is that a printer is the way that Windows sees where it is sending print jobs. This is true for all Windows versions, client or server.
Print device	The physical (hardware) device that produces the printed output. This device can be connected directly to your computer using a parallel (LPT) port, a USB connection or a wireless connection such as infrared (IR) or Bluetooth, or it can be attached to the network by means of its own network interface card.
Print server	The computer that controls the entire printing process on a Windows network. The print server handles printing requests from all its clients. It can be running either a server operating system, such as Windows Server 2008, 2012, or 2012 R2, or a client, such as Windows XP, Vista, 7, 8, or 8.1; however, print servers on client operating systems are limited to 10 concurrent connections.
Print driver	The program that converts graphics commands into instructions a given type of print device can understand. New in Windows Server 2012 is the V4 print driver model, which includes changes to printer sharing called Enhanced Point and Print. With this driver model, the print server no longer needs to act as a driver distribution point. Also new is the Easy Print driver, which enables users on Remote Desktop sessions to print to local print drivers.
Printer ports	The software interface (such as LPT1) between the computer and the print device.
Print queue	A waiting area where print jobs are stored and sequenced as they await the print device. Jobs are sequenced according to the order in which they are received as well as priority settings that are discussed later in this chapter.

Key Topic

Term	Description
Print spooling	The act of writing the contents of a print job to disk before sending it on to the print device. This can improve performance by eliminating the print device as a bottleneck that ties up the operating system or an application until the entire print job is output by the print device. In Windows 8.1 and Windows Server 2012 R2, the default folder for spooling is located at **%systemroot%\system32\spool\printers**. You can change this location by altering the print server properties (Advanced tab) or the appropriate key in the Registry.

TIP   Remember that Microsoft considers a *printer* to be the software interface between the print server and the physical print device, and a *print device* to be the actual hardware device that produces the printed output. This convention is used on Microsoft exams.

The Printing Process

When a user selects **File > Print** from an application, a series of steps must be completed for the printed document to appear. These steps have remained much the same over all recent versions of Windows and are as follows:

1. When the user selects **File > Print**, a new print job is created, which includes all of the data, and eventually the printer commands that the system requires to output a document.

2. The client computer queries the print server for a version of the print driver for the default or a selected printer. If necessary, the most recent version of the driver is downloaded to the client computer.

3. The graphics device interface (GDI) and the printer driver may convert the print job into a rendered Windows enhanced metafile (EMF). (The GDI is the component that provides network applications with a system for presenting graphical information.) The GDI actually does double duty by producing WYSIWYG (what you see is what you get) screen output as well as printed output.

4. Windows can convert the application's output (the print job) into either a metafile or a RAW format. (The RAW format is ready to print and requires no further rendering.) The driver then returns the converted print job to the GDI, which delivers it to the spooler.

5. The client side of the spooler (Winspool.drv) makes a remote procedure call (RPC) to the server side of the spooler (Spoolsv.dll). If a network-connected server is managing the print device, the spooler hands off the print job to the spooler on the print server. Then that spooler copies the print job to a temporary storage area on that computer's hard disk. This step does not take place for locally managed print jobs. In that case, the job is spooled to disk locally.

6. The print server receives the job and passes it to the print router, Spoolss.dll. (You should not confuse a router in this context with the device that directs network packets from one subnetwork to another.)

7. The router checks the kind of data it has received and passes it on to the appropriate print processor component of the local print provider, or the remote print server if the job is destined for a network printer.

8. The local print provider can request that the print processor perform additional conversions as needed on the file, typically from EMF to RAW. (Print devices can only handle RAW information.) The print processor then returns the print job to the local print provider.

9. If a separator page is being used, the separator page processor on the local print provider adds a separator page to the print job and then passes the print job on to the appropriate print monitor. All recent versions of Windows support three types of print monitors—language, local port, and remote.

   - **Language monitor:** Provides the communications language used by the client and printer. In the case of bidirectional printers, this monitor enables you to monitor printer status and send notifications such as **paper tray empty**.

   - **Local port monitor (Localspl.dll):** Controls parallel, serial, and USB I/O ports where a printer may be attached and sends print jobs to local devices on any of these ports.

   - **Remote port monitor:** Enables printing to remote printers. An example is the LPR port monitor, which can be used as an alternative to the standard port monitor for UNIX print servers.

10. The print monitor communicates directly with the print device and sends the ready-to-print print job to the print device.

11. The print device receives the data in the form it requires and translates it to a bitmap, producing printed output.

Though it might seem complicated, this sequence is designed to make printing more efficient and faster in a networked environment. In particular, the burden of spooling is distributed between client and server computers.

New Features of Print and Document Services in Windows Server 2012 R2

Microsoft has introduced several new and updated features in Windows Server 2012 R2. Table 5-3 presents a brief summary of these features:

Table 5-3   New/Updated Features for Print and Document Services in Windows Server 2012 and Windows Server 2012 R2

Feature/ Functionality	Description	Windows Server 2012	Windows Server 2012 R2
Branch Office Direct Printing (BODP)	Enables the rendering of a print job on the computer where it was created and then sent directly to a local printer, rather than using a remote print server in a head office as an intermediary. Optimizes bandwidth utilization across slow WAN links.	X	X
Event logging for BODP	When you deploy BODP with event logging, print jobs are logged and events written to Event Viewer on the remote print server, despite the fact that Windows sends these jobs directly to the local printer without other intervention from the print server. This logging is enabled by default when you deploy BODP; however, you can disable or reenable logging with Windows PowerShell cmdlets.		X
Printer migration for Web Services for Devices (WSD) print devices	Updated in Windows Server 2012 R2, the Print Management console or the command line tool **PrintBRM.exe** enables you to back up, restore, and migrate WSD print devices. Printer migration enables you to back up and restore the local computer or a remote WSD print server.		X
Roaming settings that include printer connections	Windows Server 2012 R2 now includes printer connections in the roaming settings of users logging onto Windows 8.1 or Server 2012 R2 computers using Microsoft accounts. This simplifies the process of accessing shared printers to which they have previously connected.		X

Feature/ Functionality	Description	Windows Server 2012	Windows Server 2012 R2
Easier printing in Windows RT and Windows RT 8.1	New included print class drivers provided with Windows RT enable support for many printers. However, the print servers must be configured with version 4 (v4) print drivers. New to Windows 8.1 and Windows Server 2012 R2 is easier connection to shared printers, even if they are configured with v3 print drivers.	X	X
Near Field Communication (NFC) connections to printers	New to Windows 8.1 and Windows Server 2012 R2 is NFC technology that facilitates short-range wireless communications. Windows PowerShell cmdlets enable you to create NFC tags for existing hardware that advertise a printer, simplifying clients' discovery and installation of printers.		X
Common framework for PIN-protected printing support by independent hardware vendors (IHVs)	Windows 8.1 and Windows Server 2012 R2 enable a new common framework for PIN-protected printing that helps to prevent unauthorized use of printing resources. You can configure printing queue defaults in the Print Management console or by using Windows PowerShell. You can specify that users will be prompted to enter a PIN when printing from Windows Store applications.		X
Print and Fax services now include user access logging	Previously, you were only able to log printer access by means of client computer IP addresses. Windows Server 2012 R2 now enables you to log each user that utilizes print and fax services by both IP address and username. This enables you to obtain more accurate accounting of printer and fax usage, and validate print usage against licensing agreements. Also included are Windows PowerShell cmdlets for viewing logging information.		X

NOTE   For more information on new Windows Server 2012 R2 print and document service features, refer to "What's New in Print and Document Services in Windows Server 2012 R2" at http://technet.microsoft.com/en-us/library/dn434036.aspx.

Installing, Sharing, and Publishing Printers

By itself, Windows Server 2012 R2 is a very capable print server that provides a large range of capabilities for working with printers and documents, much like the capabilities that were included with previous Windows Server versions. Microsoft added the Print Services server role in Windows Server 2008, which provided enhanced capabilities for sharing printers on the network and centralizing printer and print management tasks into its own Microsoft Management Console (MMC) snap-in. Windows Server 2012 R2 replaces this role with the Print and Document Services role, which adds scanning management to the list of capabilities. In addition, this role enables the use of Type 4 printer drivers, direct printing to print devices located in branch offices, Web Services for Devices (WSD) secure printing, and support for the Open XML Paper Specification (OpenXPS) document format. You can use PowerShell to manage printers by means of the Print Management Windows PowerShell module.

NOTE For additional introductory information on the Print and Document Services server role, including information on new and updated features in Windows Server 2012 and 2012 R2, refer to "Print and Document Services Overview" at http://technet.microsoft.com/library/hh831468. You can also obtain detailed step-by-step procedures for setting up printing in Windows Server 2012 by downloading "Test Lab Guide—Demonstrate Windows Server "8" Beta Print and Document Services," available at http://www.microsoft.com/en-us/download/details.aspx?id=29021.

Installing the Print and Document Services Role

Use the following procedure to install the Print and Document Services server role on a Windows Server 2012 R2 computer:

1. From the Manage menu in Server Manager, select **Add Roles and Features**.

2. The Add Roles and Features Wizard starts with the Select installation type page. Ensure that Role-based or feature-based installation is selected, and then click **Next**.

3. On the Select destination server page, select the server or virtual hard disk (VHD) on which you want to install this role, and then click **Next**.

4. From the Select server roles page, select **Print and Document Services**.
   As shown in Figure 5-1, you are informed that several additional tools are
   required to manage Print and Document Services. Click **Add features**.

Figure 5-1   When you select the Print and Document Services role, you are informed of the
features that must be installed to support the role.

5. You are returned to the Add Roles and Features Wizard. Click **Next**.

6. If you want to add more features from the Select features page, select these
   features. Then click **Next**.

7. The Print and Document Services page shown in Figure 5-2 provides additional information that you should note about this server role. Read and make
   a note of the information provided on this page; then click **Next**.

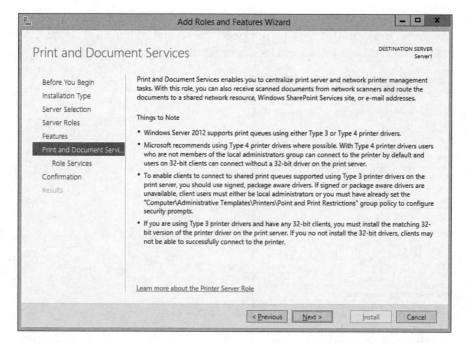

Figure 5-2   The Print and Document Services page provides noteworthy information on this server role.

8. The Select Role Services page shown in Figure 5-3 enables you to select additional role services. The Print Server role service is included by default. If desired, select one or more of the following role services, and then click **Next**:

- **Distributed Scan Server:** Enables the server to receive and manage documents that users have scanned from network-based scanners

- **Internet Printing:** Enables Internet-based users to create print jobs and send them to a website on the server that will print them on a network-based print device

- **LPD Service:** Enables UNIX clients to use the LPR utility to print documents to Windows-based printers on the network

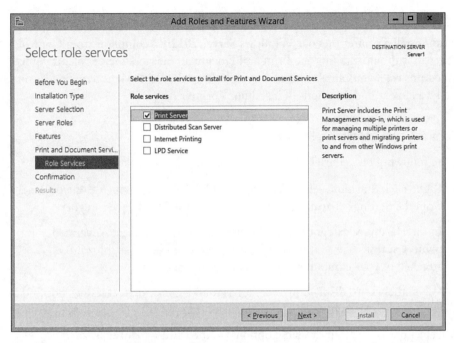

Figure 5-3   You can select optional role services from the Select Role Services page.

9. On the Confirm Installation Selections page, click **Install**.

10. The Installation Progress page tracks the progress of installing the Print and Document services server role. When informed that the installation is complete, click **Close**.

When finished, the Print Management snap-in is accessible from the Dashboard view of Server Manager or by typing `print management` into the Search charm. This snap-in enables you to perform a variety of printer management tasks on printers installed on computers running any recent version of Windows. This chapter covers a large range of tasks you can perform from this snap-in.

NOTE   For more information on installing the Print and Document Services server role, refer to "Install Print and Document Services" at http://technet.microsoft.com/en-us/library/jj134159.aspx.

Installing Printers

You can install a printer on your Windows Server 2012 R2 computer from Control Panel even without installing the Print and Document Services server role. If you've installed this role, you can also install a printer from the Print Management snap-in. We take a look at both methods of installing a printer here.

Using Control Panel to Install a Printer

Use the following procedure to install a printer from Control Panel:

1. Right-click **Start** and select **Control Panel**. You can also open Control Panel from the Settings charm. In either case, select the **Hardware** category.

2. In the Hardware category under Devices and Printers, select **Advanced printer setup**. The Add Printer Wizard starts and searches for printers attached to your computer or accessible on the network.

3. When the wizard displays printers it has found, click **Next**. If it does not find a printer, click **Search again** and then click **Next**.

4. Select one of the four available options on the **Find a printer by other options** page shown in Figure 5-4; then click **Next**.

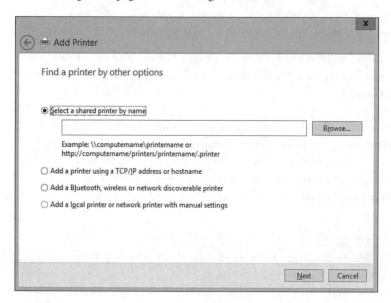

Figure 5-4   Windows Server 2012 R2 provides several additional options for locating and installing a printer.

5. If you select the **Add a Bluetooth, wireless, or network discoverable printer** option, Windows searches for network printers. Select the desired printer and then click **Next**. If you select the **Add a local printer or network printer with manual settings** option, the Add Printer page asks you to select a printer port. Select the port to which the printer is attached and then click **Next**.

6. The Install the printer driver page displays. Select the make and model of the print device for which you're installing the printer (as shown in Figure 5-5), and then click **Next**. To install a driver from an installation CD, click **Have Disk** and follow the instructions provided.

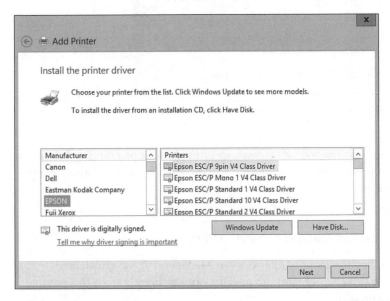

Figure 5-5   Selecting the make and model for which you're installing a printer.

7. The Type a printer name page provides a default name for the printer. Accept this or type a different name, and then click **Next**.

8. The Printer Sharing page shown in Figure 5-6 enables you to share the printer. Accept the share name or type a different name if necessary. Optionally, type location and comment information in the text boxes provided (this information helps users when selecting a network printer). When finished, click **Next**.

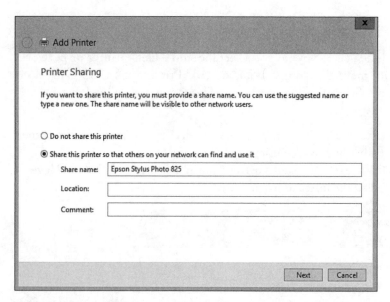

Figure 5-6   You are provided with options for sharing your printer.

9. You are informed that you've successfully installed your printer. Click **Print a test page** to print a test page if desired to confirm printer installation. When done, click **Finish**.

Using the Print Management Console to Install a Printer

When you've installed the Print and Document Management server role as described earlier in this chapter, you can install a printer directly from this console. Use the following procedure:

1. From the Tools menu in Server Manager, select **Print Management** to open the Print Management console.

2. Expand the **Print Server** node to locate your print server.

3. Right-click your print server and select **Add Printer**. The Network Printer Installation Wizard starts and displays options, as shown in Figure 5-7.

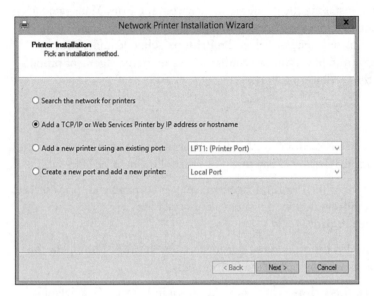

Figure 5-7   The Network Printer Installation Wizard facilitates installation of printers on the network.

4. Select the appropriate option and then click **Next**.

5. If you select the **Add a TCP/IP or Web Services Printer by IP address or hostname** option, specify the hostname or IP address as well as the port name on the Printer Address page; then click **Next**. If you select the **Search the network for printers** option, the Network Printer Search page appears and displays the printers it finds. Select the desired printer and then click **Next**.

6. On the Printer Driver page, select the make and model of the print device for which you're installing the printer and then click **Next**.

7. The Type a printer name page provides a default name for the printer. Accept this or type a different name, and then click **Next**.

8. The Printer Sharing page provides options similar to those previously shown in Figure 5-6 that are provided when installing from Control Panel. Specify the required options and then click **Next**.

9. If you see a page asking for printer-specific configuration options, select the required options and then click **Next**. Options provided depend on the make and model of the print device associated with the printer you're installing.

10. You are informed that you've successfully installed your printer. Click **Finish**.

When you're finished installing the printer (whether from the Print Management snap-in or from Control Panel), the printer is displayed in the details pane of the Print Management snap-in when you select the **Printers** subnode under the node for your print server. From here, you can configure a series of management properties as described in the sections to follow.

Sharing Printers

As indicated in the previous section, you can share a printer at the time you install it. You can configure printer sharing at any time. Use the following procedure:

1. In the console tree of the Print Management snap-in, expand your print server and select the **Printers** node. All printers configured for your server will appear in the details pane.

2. Right-click your desired printer and select **Manage Sharing**. This opens the printer's Properties dialog box to the Sharing tab.

3. Select the **Share this printer** check box. As shown in Figure 5-8, a default share name is provided automatically; accept this or type a different share name, as desired.

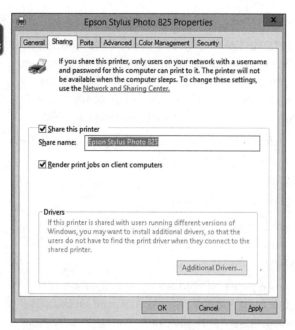

Figure 5-8 You can share your printer from the Sharing tab of the printer's Properties dialog box.

4. If users connecting to this printer are running different versions of Windows (including 32-bit as opposed to 64-bit Windows versions), click **Additional Drivers** to install drivers required by these users. From the Additional Drivers dialog box that appears, select the required drivers and click **OK**.

5. If client computers have the processing power for handling the print rendering process, select the check box labeled **Render print jobs on client computers**. To have the print server handle this processing load, clear this check box.

6. Click **OK**.

If you haven't installed the Print and Document Services server role, you can perform the same task from the Devices and Printers applet in Control Panel. Right-click your printer and select **Printer Properties**. This brings up the same Properties dialog box; select the **Sharing** tab as shown previously in Figure 5-8 and follow the same procedure as outlined here.

TIP   Unreadable output indicates incorrect printer drivers. If the printer produces a series of unintelligible characters rather than the expected output, the problem lies in the printer driver. Check with the manufacturer of the print device and ensure that you have installed the correct printer drivers.

Publishing Printers in Active Directory

If your print server is part of an Active Directory Domain Services (AD DS) domain, you can publish the printer to facilitate the task of users locating printers installed on the server. In the Print Management snap-in, right-click your printer and select **List in Directory**, as shown in Figure 5-9.

If your print server is in an AD DS domain, the Sharing tab previously shown in Figure 5-8 also includes a List in the directory checkbox. You can also select this check box to publish your printer in AD DS.

If you want to remove your printer from AD DS, right-click it and select **Remove from Directory**, or clear the **List in the directory** check box.

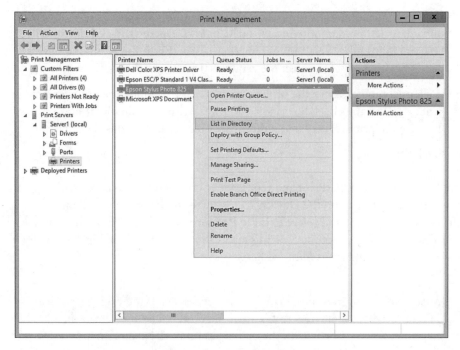

Figure 5-9   Publishing a printer in Active Directory.

You can also use the `pubprn.vbs` script to publish a printer in AD DS from the command line. The syntax is as follows:

```
Cscript Pubprn.vbs {<ServerName> | <UNCPrinterPath>}
"LDAP://CN=<Container>,DC=<Container>"
```

In this command, `<ServerName>` specifies the name of the server hosting the printer to be published. If omitted, the local server is assumed. `<UNCPrinterPath>` represents the UNC path to the shared printer being published. `"LDAP:// CN=<Container>,DC=<Container>"` specifies the path to the AD DS container where the printer is to be published.

For example, to publish a printer named `HPLaserJ` located at Server1 to the Printers container in the `que.com` domain, use the following command at Server1:

```
Cscript Pubprn.vbs \\Server1\HPLaserJ LDAP://
CN=Printers,DC=Que,DC=com"
```

> **TIP**   Published printers can be viewed using Active Directory Users and Computers. To ensure that you can see printers, you might need to configure your console view to show Users, Contacts, Groups, and Computers as containers.

Using Group Policy to Deploy Printer Connections

Group Policy enables you to deploy printers in an AD DS domain environment, automatically making printer connections available to users and computers in the domain or organizational unit (OU). Use the following procedure to add printer connections to a Group Policy object (GPO):

1. In the details pane of the Print Management snap-in, right-click the desired printer and select **Deploy with Group Policy**. (This option is visible in Figure 5-9 previously shown.)

2. The Deploy with Group Policy dialog box shown in Figure 5-10 opens. Click **Browse** and locate an appropriate GPO. If necessary, you can also create a new GPO for storing the printer connections.

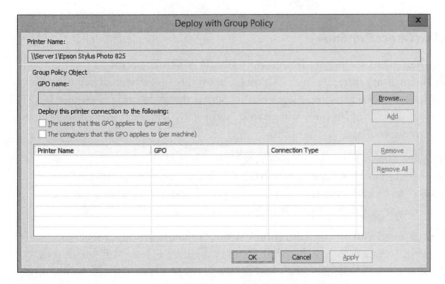

Figure 5-10   Using Group Policy to deploy printer connections.

3. Select either or both of the following options for deploying printer connections to users or computers, as required:

   - Select **The users that this GPO applies to (per user)** to deploy to groups of users, enabling these users to access the printer from any computer to which they log on.

   - Select **The computers that this GPO applies to (per machine)** to deploy to groups of computers, enabling all users of the computers to access your printer.

4. Click **Add**.

5. Repeat steps 2–4 to deploy the printer connection settings to another GPO, if required.

6. Click **OK**. You are informed that the operation has been performed successfully. Click **OK** again.

> **TIP**   You can perform nearly all of the tasks described in this section using PowerShell. This enables you to script frequently used procedures and to perform print configuration tasks at a Server Core computer. For more information, refer to "Print Management Cmdlets in Windows PowerShell" at http://technet.microsoft.com/en-us/library/hh918357.aspx.

Branch Office Direct Printing

In cases where print servers are hosted centrally, WAN links become a key component for the printing infrastructure. Although central management of print servers is a benefit, it comes with some cost. Printing across the WAN might require larger connections, which can become quite costly—especially when the idea of redundant circuits comes into play.

Branch Office Direct Printing is a new technology included in Windows Server 2012 and updated in Windows Server 2012 R2. It was designed to help reduce bandwidth costs by reducing the amount of printing traffic that would traverse WAN links. Branch Office Direct Printing provides the following benefits:

- **Lower bandwidth requirements:** Client computers are able to use the central print server to query the printer and authenticate, but print data is sent directly from the client to the print device. This is accomplished through print drivers that support Client Side Rendering (CSR). The fact that print data does not have to be spooled and processed by the print server and then sent back to the print device to print translates into lower bandwidth utilization.

- **Lower server load:** By printing directly to print devices, the client assumes the role of managing the print data thus reducing the workload of your central print server.

- **Branch site printing resilience:** If a WAN link fails, Branch Office Direct Printing allows clients to continue to print directly to the print device through the use of cached printer information.

NOTE   Branch Office Direct Printing is only supported by Windows 8/8.1 and Windows Server 2012/R2 clients. Any clients prior will still be able to use the print server but not take advantage of the Client Side Rendering functionality.

NOTE   Branch Office Direct Printing only works with network attached printers and is not supported by third-party printer applications or printer pooling.

Use the following procedure to configure Branch Office Direct Printing:

1. Open the **Print Management Console** and expand **Print Servers**.

2. Expand the appropriate print server and then expand **Printers**.

3. Right-click the shared printer and select **Enable Branch Office Direct Printing**, as shown in Figure 5-11.

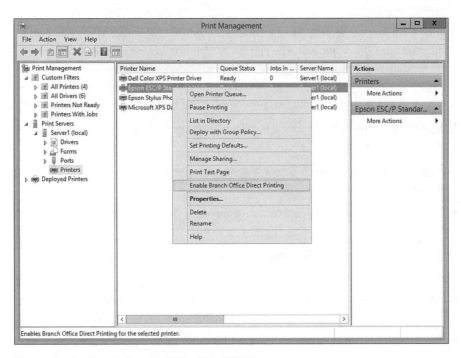

Figure 5-11   Enable Branch Office Direct Printing

Configuring Drivers Including the Easy Print Driver

With the release of Windows 2000, Microsoft established a standard for printing model for drivers that they've identified as the V3 Model of drivers. The V3 Model relied heavily on manufacturers to produce specific drivers for each make and model of printer. Each driver was responsible for the configuration and management of the printer's specific functions.

Printer Driver Challenges

As with most implementations, over time requirements change and printing infrastructures tend to become more complicated. As you add printers to your print server or introduce Remote Desktop Services into your environment, driver compatibility becomes virtually the number one headache for any administrator. You often find yourself spending most of your day battling conflicting drivers, driver names and third-party applications installed with the printer driver package. To make matters worse, you then have to integrate both 32- and 64-bit drivers in the same environment.

Beginning with the V3 Model, these challenges continued through Windows Server 2003 but became a bit easier with the release of Windows Server 2008 and the V4 printing model. The V4 printing model eliminated many of the previous struggles with printer drivers. Windows Server 2012 R2 continues to leverage the V4 Model, but includes some additional benefits, described here:

- **Driver isolation:** Driver files are isolated from each other to prevent any file-name conflicts.

- **Multiple device support:** A single driver has the ability to support multiple devices.

- **Smaller footprint:** V4 Driver files are typically smaller in size than V3 drivers.

- **Transparent client architecture:** Printer sharing does not require separate installations for 32- and 64-bit clients.

- **Ease of deployment:** V4 Drivers can be distributed by Windows Update or Windows Software Update Services (WSUS).

- **Modified point and print:** With previous operating systems and driver models, clients that connect to shared printers would attempt to locate the appropriate printer driver based on matching the device HardwareID with the appropriate PrinterDriverID. If a good match was found, the driver would be installed locally on the client. With the V4 Model, if a suitable match is not found, the client will connect to the printer using the enhanced Point and Print Driver. The enhanced Point and Print Driver is a universal, cross-platform driver that provides basic print functionality for most printers.

Installing Print Server Drivers

Use the following procedure to install drivers to your print server:

1. Open the **Print Management Console** and expand **Print Servers**.

2. Expand the appropriate print server, and then right-click **Drivers** and select **Add Driver**.

3. The Add Printer Driver Wizard opens with a Welcome page. Click **Next**.

4. On the Processor Selection page, select the processor (**x64** or **x86**) on computers that will use this driver, and then click **Next**.

5. On the Printer Driver Selection page shown in Figure 5-12, browse for the appropriate driver or supply the driver by clicking **Have Disk**. Then click **Next**.

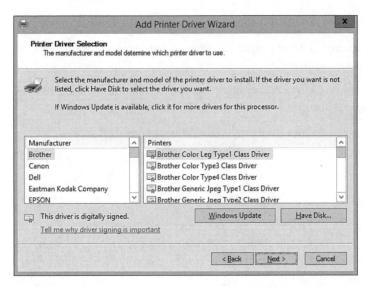

Figure 5-12   Selecting a printer driver for installation on the print server.

6. On the Completing the Add Printer Driver Wizard page, click **Finish**. The driver is added to the list in the details pane of the Print Management snap-in.

Easy Print Driver

Similar to the concept of the enhanced Point and Print driver, the Easy Print Driver is used with Remote Desktop Services, formerly known as Terminal Services. As client computers connect, their local printers can be redirected into the Remote Desktop session. This means that printers configured on the client computer are automatically carried into the remote desktop or Terminal Server session. Print jobs submitted while logged on to the remote desktop session are passed back to the client computer where they are printed to the specific print device.

There have been several improvements to Remote Desktop/Terminal Server printing over the years. Today, the Windows Server 2012 R2 Remote Desktop Server attempts to use the Easy Print Driver, which is a universal, cross-platform driver introduced in Windows Server 2008. If the client device or printer does not support this driver, the server attempts to locate and use a more suitable driver match from its local driver repository. Specific printer model drivers can be installed on the terminal server using the driver install method discussed previously. This can become an administrative burden depending on the number of terminal servers and drivers you'll need to manage. The Terminal Services Easy Print driver offers the following functionality:

- More reliable printing services for RemoteApp and Remote Desktop sessions

- Support for legacy and current printer drivers without requiring additional drivers on the Terminal Servers

- Better printer enumeration and mapping process through a per-session basis as opposed of a per-user basis

- Improved printer capabilities over previous editions of terminal services printing

Configuring Easy Print Driver

You can configure Easy Print Driver settings using local or Group Policy. When dealing with multiple servers, Group Policy is a more suitable approach. You can configure Easy Print Driver and Terminal Server printing settings under the following Group Policy location:

Computer Configuration\Policies\Administrative Templates\Windows Components\Terminal Services\Terminal Server\Printer Redirection

Group Policy is covered in more detail later, but Table 5-4 outlines the group policy settings related to printer redirection.

Table 5-4   Terminal Server Group Policy Settings for Printing

Policy	Details	Requirements
Do not allow client printer redirection	This policy enables you to configure whether or not to allow local client printers from being redirected into the Remote Desktop session. When this option is configured, other policy settings for printer redirection are ignored.	At Least XP Pro or Server 2003
Do not set default client printer to be default printer in a session	This policy enables you to configure whether or not the client default printer is mapped and configured as the default printer in the Remote Desktop session.	At least XP Pro or Server 2003
Redirect only the default client printer	When configured, this policy will only redirect and map the default client printer into the Remote Desktop session.	Windows 2008 or Greater
Specify terminal server fallback printer driver behavior	This policy enables you to configure how the terminal server manages the redirected printer driver. By default, this option is disabled and the terminal server does not use any alternative or fallback printer driver. If a driver is not found, no printers are mapped into the session. If this policy is enabled, you can configure the terminal server to use a standard PCL or PS driver if a more suitable native print driver is not found.	Windows Server 2003 with SP1
Use Terminal Services Easy Print printer driver first	When configured, this policy enables the Terminal Services Easy Print driver to be used when mapping all client printers. If the client printer is not compatible with the Easy Print driver, the terminal server looks in its own printer driver pool to try to find a more suitable driver for the client printer.	Windows Server 2008 or Greater

Managing and Troubleshooting Printers

There are several factors that must be considered in administering printers. Like any other shared resources, you can assign permissions to them and audit their usage. As well, you can set up special printing configurations such as printer pools.

You can configure multiple printers for one print device to handle different types of jobs. Furthermore, lots of things can go wrong with print jobs. Complaints from users that they cannot print or are denied access can make up a significant portion of a network administrator or support specialist's job.

Using the Printer Properties Dialog box

Each printer has associated with it a Properties dialog box that enables you to perform a large quantity of management tasks. You have already seen how to share a printer or publish it in AD DS. This section discusses several additional tasks you can perform from this dialog box. Right-click the printer in the details pane of the Print Management snap-in and select **Properties**, or right-click the printer in the Control Panel Devices and Printers applet and select **Printer properties** to bring up this dialog box. In addition to the tabs discussed here, some printers show additional tabs; for example, color printers possess a Color Management tab that enables you to adjust color profile settings. Some printers have a Version Information tab, which merely displays version information and contains no configurable settings.

General Tab

Use the General tab to rename the printer or modify the Location and Comment fields you supplied when installing the printer. You can also print a test page or modify printer preferences from this tab; click **Preferences** to open a dialog box that enables you to adjust settings such as print quality; paper source, type, and size; maintenance factors such as print head cleaning; and so on. Appearance of, and options included in, this dialog box vary according to print device make and model.

Ports Tab and Printer Pooling

Shown in Figure 5-13, the Ports tab enables you to select various available ports to which a document will be printed. Documents will print to the first available selected port. Click **Add Port** to bring up a dialog box that displays available port types and enables you to add new ports. From here you can add a new TCP/IP port for accessing a network printer; a wizard is provided to guide you through the required steps. Options for configuring port options and deleting unneeded ports are also available.

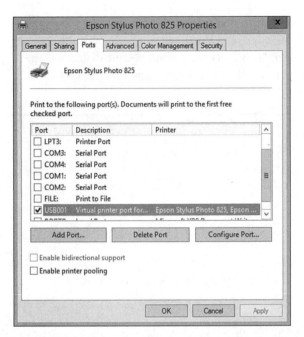

Figure 5-13   The Ports tab of the printer's Properties dialog box enables you to configure printer ports and printer pooling.

The Ports tab also enables you to configure *printer pooling*. A printer pool is a group of print devices that are connected to a single printer through multiple ports on the print server. These print devices should be the same make and model so that they use the same printer driver. This method is useful because it allows pooling of similar print devices. In high-volume print situations, if one print device is busy, print jobs directed to a printer can be spooled to another available print device that is part of the printer pool and printing jobs are completed more quickly. To configure printer pooling, specify a different port for each print device in the printer pool. Then select the check box labeled **Enable printer pooling** and click **OK**.

To client computers, the printer pool appears as though it were a single printer. When users submit print jobs to the printer pool, the jobs are printed on any available print device. You should position the physical print devices in close proximity to each other so that the user does not have to search for print jobs. Enabling separator pages is a best practice that you should follow so that the users can locate their print jobs rapidly and conveniently.

This tab also enables you to redirect a printer should a problem occur with its print device and you need to take it offline for maintenance. Redirecting a printer on the print server redirects all documents sent to that printer. However, you cannot redirect individual documents. To do so, click **Add Port**, and on the Printer Ports dialog box, select **Local Port**; then click **New Port**. In the Port Name dialog box that appears, enter the UNC or URL path to the other printer, and then click **OK**.

> **TIP** Configuration changes to the available ports on any print server affect all printers set up on that server. Also note that it is a good idea to locate all the print devices that make up a printer pool in the same general area of your operation. People won't need to roam the halls of your organization in search of printed jobs.

Advanced Tab

The Advanced tab enables you to control the availability of the printer and configure drivers and spool settings. Available settings on this tab are shown in Figure 5-14 and described in Table 5-5.

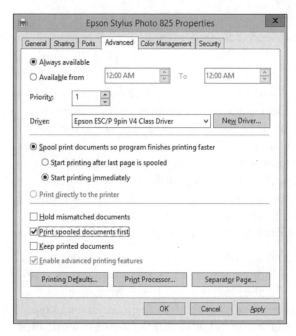

Figure 5-14 The Advanced tab of the printer's Properties dialog box enables you to control availability, priority, and spooler settings.

Table 5-5   Configurable Advanced Printer Properties

Setting	Description
Always available and available from	Enables you to specify the hours of the day when the printer is available. For example, you can configure a printer that accepts large jobs to print only between 6:00 p.m. and 8:00 a.m. so that shorter jobs can be printed rapidly. Jobs submitted outside the available hours are kept in the print queue until the available time.
Priority	Enables you to assign a numerical priority to the printer. This priority ranges from 1 to 99, with higher numbers receiving higher priority. The default priority is 1. For example, you can assign a printer for managers with a priority of 99 so that their print jobs are completed before those of other employees.
Spool print documents so program finishes printing faster	Enables spooling of print documents. Select from the following: Start printing after last page is spooled—Prevents documents from printing until completely spooled. Prevents delays when the print device prints pages faster than the rate at which they are provided. Start printing immediately—The default option, causes documents to be printed as rapidly as possible.
Print directly to the printer	Sends documents to the print device without first writing them to the print server's hard disk drive. Recommended only for nonshared printers.
Hold mismatched documents	The spooler holds documents that do not match the available form until this form is loaded. Other documents that match the form can print.
Print spooled documents first	Documents are printed in the order that they finish spooling, rather than in the order that they start spooling. Use this option if you have selected the Start printing immediately option.
Keep printed documents	Retains printed jobs in the print spooler. Enables a user to resubmit a document from the print queue rather than from an application.
Enable advanced printing features	Turns on metafile spooling and presents additional options like page order and pages per sheet. This is selected by default and should be turned off only if printer compatibility problems arise.
Printing Defaults command button	Selects the default orientation and order of pages being printed. Users can modify this from most applications if desired. Additional print device–specific settings may be present.
Print Processor command button	Specifies the available print processor, which processes a document into the appropriate print job. Available print processors are described in "Print Processor" at http://technet.microsoft.com/en-us/library/cc976744.aspx.
Separator Page command button	Enables you to specify a separator page file, which is printed at the start of a print job to identify the print job and the user who submitted it. This is useful for identifying printed output when many users access a single print device.

TIP   You can configure different printers associated with the same print device so that a managers' print jobs are printed before those of other users or so that long print jobs wait until after hours to prevent tying up a print device for an extended period of time. To do this, simply assign a priority of 99 to the managers' printer and 1 to the printer used by all other users. Also assign permissions so that only the managers can print to their printer.

Security Tab and Printer Permissions

Just as you can assign permissions to files and folders as you learned in Chapter 4, you can assign permissions to printers. Printers have access control lists (ACLs) that you can modify in the same manner. Use the following steps to configure a printer's permissions from the Security tab of its Properties dialog box:

1. Select the **Security** tab of the printer's Properties dialog box, as shown in Figure 5-15.

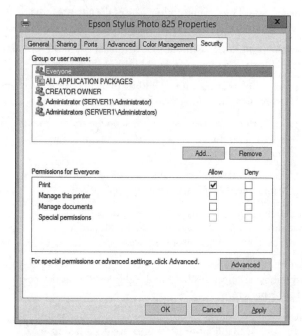

Figure 5-15   The Security tab of the printer's Properties dialog box enables you to configure printer permissions.

2. If you need to add users or groups to the ACL, click **Add** to open the Select Users, Computers, or Groups dialog box.

3. In this dialog box, click **Advanced**, and then click **Find now** to locate the required users or groups. You also can use the fields in the Common Queries area of the dialog box to narrow the search for the appropriate object.

4. Select one or more users or groups in the list and then click **OK**. This returns you to the Security tab of the printer's Properties dialog box.

5. Select the permissions you want to allow or deny from the available list. Table 5-6 describes the available permissions.

6. If you need to assign special permissions or check the effective permissions granted to a specific user, click **Advanced**. The options available are similar to those discussed in Chapter 4 for files and folders.

7. When you are finished, click **OK** or **Apply** to apply your settings.

Table 5-6   Windows Server 2012 R2 Printer Permissions

Permission	Description
Print	Enables users to connect to the printer to print documents and control settings for their own documents only. Users can pause, delete, and restart their own jobs only.
Manage this printer	Enables users to assign forms to paper trays and set a separator page. Users can also pause, resume, and purge the printer; change printer properties and permissions; and even delete the printer itself. Also enables users to perform the tasks associated with the Manage Documents permission.
Manage documents	Enables users to pause, resume, restart, and delete all documents. Users can also set the notification level for completed print jobs and set priority and scheduling properties for documents to be printed.
Special permissions	Similar to NTFS security permissions discussed in Chapter 4, the three default printer permissions are made up of granular permissions. Click **Advanced** to bring up the Advanced Security Settings dialog box, from which you can configure these permissions if required.

NOTE   The act of managing print jobs includes the two actions of resuming and restarting print jobs. Resuming a print job means to restart the job from the point at which it was paused—for example, to add more paper to the printer. Restarting a print job means to restart it from the beginning—for example, when the print job is being printed on the wrong type of paper. You can perform either of these tasks by right-clicking the print job in the print queue and selecting the appropriate option.

TIP   Print permissions behave in much the same fashion as file and folder permissions. As with file and folder permissions, printer permissions are cumulative, with the user receiving the sum of all permissions granted to any groups to which he belongs. If you explicitly deny a permission to a user or group by selecting a check box in the **Deny** column, this denial overrides any other allowed permissions the user might have, in exactly the same manner as discussed in Chapter 4 for file and folder permissions.

Migrating Print Queues and Printer Settings

The Print Management snap-in enables you to export print queues, printer settings, printer ports, and language monitors and then import these settings to another print server. Doing so enables you to consolidate multiple print servers or replace an older server.

Use the following procedure to perform a print migration:

1. In the console tree of the Print Management snap-in, expand the **Print servers** node, right-click the print server whose queues you want to export, and select **Export printers to a file**. The Printer Migration Wizard starts.

2. On the Review the list of items to be exported page shown in Figure 5-16, verify the objects listed that will be exported and then click **Next**.

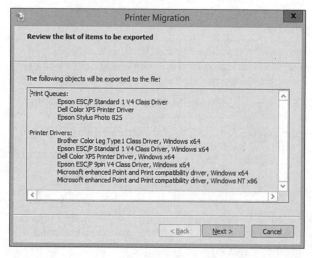

Figure 5-16   The Printer Migration page informs you of the items that will be exported.

3. On the Select the file location page, type the path to the required file or click **Browse** to locate an appropriate file. The file you specified will be saved with a `.printerExport` extension.

4. The Exporting page tracks the progress of the export and then displays an Export complete message. This page also informs you of any errors that might have occurred. You can obtain information on any errors from Event Viewer by clicking the **Open Event Viewer** command button provided on this page. This button opens Event Viewer to a Printer Migration Events subnode that displays events related to the migration process. When done, click **Finish**.

NOTE   For more information on Event Viewer, refer to the *Cert Guide* book for exam 70-411. You can also refer to the links contained in "Event Viewer How To..." at http://technet.microsoft.com/en-us/library/cc749408.aspx.

Use the following steps to import the print queue to the new server:

1. In the console tree of the Print Management snap-in, expand the **Print servers** node, right-click the print server whose queues you want to import, and select **Import printers from a file**. The Printer Migration Wizard starts.

2. On the Select the file location page, type or browse to the location of the `.printerExport` file to be imported.

3. On the Review the list of items to be imported page, review the list of objects that will be imported, and then click **Next**.

4. On the Select import options page, select the following import options:

   - **Import mode:** Select **Keep existing printers** to maintain the settings on any existing printers that are installed on this print server, or select **Overwrite existing printers** to restore printer information from the backup file and overwrite the settings for existing printers on this print server.

   - **List in the directory**—Select **List printers that were previously existed** to maintain the current listing of printers in AD DS; select **List all printers** to add newly imported printers to the listing in AD DS; or select **Don't list any printers** to clear the listing of printers in AD DS.

   - Select the **Convert LPR Ports to Standard Port Monitors** check box to convert Line Printer Remote (LPR) printer ports to the faster Standard Port Monitor when performing the import operation.

5. Click **Next**.

6. The Importing page tracks the progress of the import operation and displays an Import Complete operation when finished. This page also informs you of any errors that might have occurred. You can obtain information on any errors from Event Viewer by clicking **Open Event Viewer** as previously described for the export action. When done, click **Finish**.

> **NOTE**   You can also migrate printer queues and settings from the command line by using the `Printbrm.exe` command. For more information on exporting and importing print queues and settings, refer to "Migrate Print Servers" at http://technet.microsoft.com/en-us/library/cc722360.aspx.

Isolating Printer Drivers

First introduced in Windows Server 2008 R2 and continued in Windows Server 2012 R2 is the capability to configure printer driver components to run in a process that is isolated from other processes, including the spooler process. Doing so improves the reliability of the Windows print service by preventing a faulty printer driver from stopping all print operations on the print server. In previous Windows Server versions, printer drivers ran in the same process as the spooler; if a driver component were to fail, all print operations from the server would be halted.

Driver isolation is specified by an INF file that installs the printer driver. If this file indicates that the driver being installed supports driver isolation, the installer automatically configures the driver to run in an isolated process. This is specified by a `DriverIsolation` keyword in the INF file. If this variable is set to 2, the driver supports driver isolation; if it is omitted or set to 0, the driver does not support driver isolation.

To configure driver isolation, select the **Drivers** subnode under the print server in the Print Management snap-in. Right-click the driver and select **Set Driver Isolation > Isolated**, as shown in Figure 5-17. To disable driver isolation, select **None** or **Shared**.

> **NOTE**   For more information on printer driver isolation, refer to "Printer Driver Isolation" at http://msdn.microsoft.com/en-us/library/ff560836(VS.85).aspx.

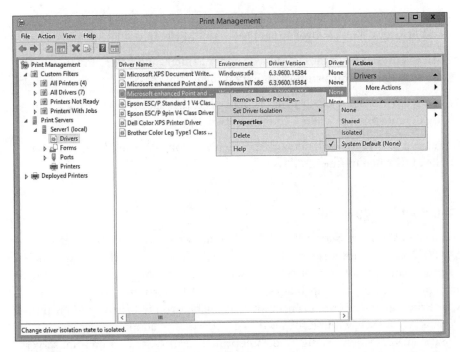

Figure 5-17   Configuring printer driver isolation.

TIP   Sometimes you might have a server on which you've installed different types of printers such as laser, color laser, or color ink-jet. Enabling printer driver isolation enables you to ensure that if a driver problem is encountered with one printer type, users can continue to use other printers of a different type on the same server.

Configuring Location-Aware Printer Settings

Introduced in Windows Server 2008 R2 and continued in Windows Server 2012 and Windows Server 2012 R2 is the concept of location-aware default printer settings. Users with mobile computers running Windows 7 Professional, Enterprise, or Ultimate or Windows 8 or 8.1 Pro or Enterprise can configure a different default printer according to the network to which they are connected. For example, a user can specify a default printer when in the office and a different default printer set for home. The laptop automatically selects the correct default printer according to the current location of the user.

Use the following procedure on a Windows 8.1 computer to configure location-aware printing:

1. In the Hardware and Sound category of Control Panel, select **View devices and printers**. The Control Panel Devices and Printers applet opens.

2. Select a printer from those displayed under Printers and Faxes, and then click the **Manage default printers** option on the menu bar.

3. From the Manage Default Printers dialog box that appears, select the **Change my default printer when I change networks** radio button.

4. Select a printer for each network to which you connect, click **Add**, and then click **OK** when finished.

Delegating Print Management

Introduced in Windows Server 2008 R2 and Windows 7 and continued in Windows Server 2012 and Windows Server 2012 R2 and Windows 8/8.1 is the ability to delegate print management tasks directly to users who are not members of a group with built-in print management capabilities, such as the Administrators, Server Operators, or Print Operators group. This capability enables you to balance administrative workloads across users without the need to grant excessive administrative capabilities; it also enables you to configure default printer security settings on print servers so that new printers inherit these settings automatically as you install them.

The Security tab of the print server's Properties dialog box includes the following permissions, which enable you to delegate print management tasks:

- **View Server:** Enables users to view the print server, including the printers that are managed by the server. By default, the Everyone group is granted this permission.

- **Manage Server:** Enables users to create and delete print queues with already installed drivers, add or delete ports, and add or delete forms. By default, administrators and the Interactive group are granted this permission. A user who has been granted this permission is referred to as a *delegated print administrator*.

You need to be a member of the Administrators group or running with administrative privileges to create a delegated print administrator. Use the following procedure:

1. In the console tree of the Print Management snap-in, right-click the print server and select **Properties**.

2. Select the **Security** tab to display the default permissions.

3. Click **Add** to add the user or group to which you want to delegate users, type the required user or group name, and then click **OK**. The user or group is added to the list in the Security tab.

4. Select this user or group and then select the check box under the Allow column for **Manage Server** (this also selects the **View Server** permission).

5. Also select the **Print**, **Manage Documents**, and **Manage Printers** permissions in the Allow column, as shown in Figure 5-18.

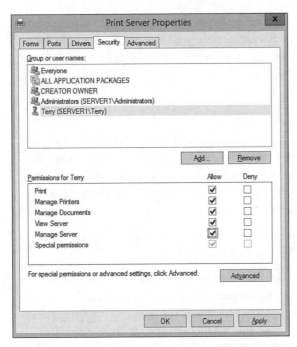

Figure 5-18   The Security tab of the print server's Properties dialog box enables you to delegate administrative control of printers attached to the server.

6. To delegate just the ability to add printers, follow step 3 to add the user or group, and then select only the **Manage Server** and **Print** permissions (this also selects the **View Server** permission).

7. To delegate just the ability to manage existing print queues, follow step 3 and then select the **View Server**, **Print**, **Manage Documents**, and **Manage Printer** permissions.

8. When finished, click **OK** to apply the permissions and close the Security tab of the Print Server Properties dialog box.

> **NOTE**   For more information on delegating administrative control of printers, refer to "Assigning Delegated Print Administrator and Printer Permission Settings in Windows Server 2012" at http://technet.microsoft.com/en-us/library/jj190062.aspx. Included in this reference are tables describing the tasks that users granted the various permissions in the print server's Security tab are entitled to perform.

Troubleshooting Printer Problems

Lots of things can go wrong in a print job's journey from an application to a print device, with stops in between at the operating system and its print drivers. By having reviewed the printing process described at the beginning of this chapter, you can often locate the source of printing problems.

Some Common Problems

When a user complains that he cannot print, the first thing to do is check the physical aspects of the print device, such as the cable, power, and paper. If you need to check more advanced print device–related problems, refer to *CompTIA A+ 220-801 and 220-802 Authorized Cert Guide* (by Mark Edward Soper, Scott Mueller, and David L. Prowse) for more suggestions.

`Access Denied` errors usually indicate that printer permissions are not configured correctly or that they are not configured to the user's liking.

If the printed document comes out garbled, someone has installed an incorrect print driver. You should ensure that the correct driver for the problematic client is installed (Click **Additional Drivers** on the Sharing tab of the printer's Properties dialog box to add a driver.) Occasionally this problem can result from a resource conflict with the parallel port or a damaged printer cable. Check the printer cable for damage; also check for conflicts using Device Manager.

Sometimes print jobs get stuck in the spooler. You might notice that no print jobs are coming out and the hard drive on the print server appears to be thrashing. If this happens, you need to stop and restart the spooler service. Use the following procedure:

1. In the console tree of Server Manager, expand the **Configuration** node and select **Services**. This displays the list of services in the details pane.

2. Right-click **Print Spooler** and select **Stop**.

3. Right-click it again and select **Start**. This clears the jammed print job from the queue and allows other print jobs to print.

You can modify spool settings on a per-printer basis, making the printing process more efficient. The Advanced tab of the printer's Properties dialog box contains several settings previously shown in Figure 5-14 and described in Table 5-5 that you can modify to optimize the spool process if necessary.

Printer Port Problems

Improperly configured printer ports can cause printing failures. Errors can occur if a user configures a computer to print directly to the printer or to use bidirectional printing when the print device does not support these functions.

TCP/IP printing, like the protocol itself, is subject to connectivity problems that require a good grounding in the TCP/IP protocol as provided in Chapter 10, "Configuring IPv4 and IPv6 Addressing." If TCP/IP port problems occur, try configuring the standard TCP/IP port monitor for your printer. You might need to reconfigure the standard port monitor port from the printer's Properties dialog box. On the Ports tab of this dialog box (previously shown in Figure 5-13), click **Configure Port**. You might need to check with the manufacturer of the print device to see whether it supports Simple Network Management Protocol (SNMP). Printers use SNMP to return print status. On print devices that support SNMP, printer status is returned to the user, including errors that occur during printing. If a print device does not support SNMP, you will receive either a generic printing error message or no error message when a printing error occurs.

You might need to add an additional TCP/IP port using the procedure described earlier in this chapter. You also might need to verify the port name and the printer name or IP address in the Ports tab of the printer's Properties dialog box. To do so, click **Configure Port** and make the required modifications in the Configure Standard TCP/IP Port Monitor dialog box that appears. Then click **OK** and click **Close** to close the printer's Properties dialog box.

Enabling Notifications

The Print Management snap-in enables you to set up filters that can respond to printers encountering problem conditions such as paper jams or running out of paper. Such a filter can perform an action such as sending an email to an administrator, running a script, or so on.

Use the following procedure to set up a filter for notification purposes:

1. In the console tree of the Print Management snap-in, right-click **Custom Filters** and select **Add New Printer Filter**. This starts the New Printer Filter Wizard.

2. On the Printer Filter Name and Description page, type a name and optional description, and then click **Next**.

3. On the Define a filter page shown in Figure 5-19, specify values for the filter criteria, as follows:

   ■ **Field:** Specify a characteristic for the print server, queue, or status. By specifying Queue Status, you can evaluate a printer's current status.

   ■ **Condition:** Specify a Boolean characteristic, such as "is exactly," "begins with," "contains," or several others. Available conditions depend on the Field value.

   ■ **Value:** The value to be matched for the criteria to be met.

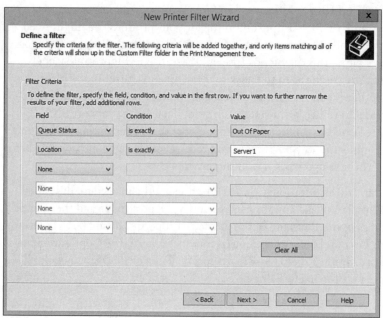

Figure 5-19   Defining a filter that alerts you to an out-of-paper condition on any printer attached to a server named Server1.

4. When finished specifying the appropriate criteria, click **Next** to display the Set Notifications (Optional) page.

5. On this page, select **Send e-mail notification** and type one or more email addresses of individuals to be notified in the format account@domain. Also type the email address of the sender, the name or IP address of the SMTP server that will relay the message, and the message text to be included in the

email. If you want to run a script, select **Run script** and type the path to the required script, or click **Browse** to locate the script. Use the **Additional arguments** field to include any required script parameters.

6. When done, click **Finish**.

Exam Preparation Tasks

Review All the Key Topics

Review the most important topics in the chapter, noted with the key topics icon in the outer margin of the page. Table 5-7 lists a reference of these key topics and the page numbers on which each is found.

Table 5-7   Key Topics for Chapter 5

Key Topic Element	Description	Page Number
Table 5-2	Describes important terms that you might otherwise confuse with regard to printing	199
List	Shows you how to install the Print and Document Services server role	204
List	Shows you how to install a printer from Control Panel	208
Figure 5-7	Shows you how to use the Network Printer Installation Wizard to install a network-based printer	211
Figure 5-8	Shows you how to share a printer	212
Figure 5-10	Shows you how to deploy a printer connection using Group Policy	215
Figure 5-11	Shows you how to enable Branch Office Direct Printing	217
Table 5-5	Describes configurable advanced printer properties	225
Table 5-6	Describes printer permissions	227
Paragraph	Describes printer driver isolation	230
List	Shows you how to delegate print management tasks	232
Figure 5-19	Shows you how to set up a printer notification filter	236

Complete the Tables and Lists from Memory

Print a copy of Appendix B, "Memory Tables" (found on the CD), or at least the section for this chapter, and complete the tables and lists from memory. Appendix C, "Memory Tables Answer Key," is also on the CD and includes completed tables and lists to check your work.

Definitions of Key Terms

Define the following key terms from this chapter, and check your answers in the glossary.

Branch Office Direct Printing, Easy Print Driver, Local printer, Location-aware printing, Network printer, Print device, Print driver, Print driver isolation, Print pooling, Print queue, Print server, Print spooler, Printer, Printer pool, Printer priority

This chapter covers the following subjects:

- **Configuring WinRM:** This section introduces WinRM and its function with respect to remote management of servers. Also covered is the configuration and use of WinRM.

- **Configuring Down-Level Server Management:** This section outlines the steps required to configure previous versions of Windows so they can be used with current versions of PowerShell and Server Manager.

- **Configuring Multiple Server Management:** This section discusses the use and configuration of Windows Server 2012 R2 Server Manager to support and manage multiple servers from a central location, including nondomain joined servers.

- **Remote Management of Server Core Machines:** This section provides an overview of the tools available for remotely managing Server Core installations. It offers best practices and step-by-step instructions on configuring servers for remote management, including how to install and configure Remote Server Administration Tools, the Microsoft Management Console, and PowerShell for remote administration.

- **Configuring Daily Management Tasks:** This section provides you with an overview of Task Scheduler and Active Directory Administrative Console and how they help provide efficiency gains for managing daily or repeat tasks.

CHAPTER 6

Configuring Remote Management of Servers

The Microsoft 70-410 exam assesses your ability to configure and prepare Windows Server 2012 R2 installations for remote management. This chapter focuses on the various remote access methods, how to use the tools, and how to prepare your server installations to allow remote access.

"Do I Know This Already?" Quiz

The "Do I Know This Already?" quiz enables you to assess whether you should read this entire chapter or simply jump to the "Exam Preparation Tasks" section for review. If you are in doubt, read the entire chapter. Table 6-1 outlines the major headings in this chapter and the corresponding "Do I Know This Already?" quiz questions. You can find the answers in Appendix A, "Answers to the 'Do I Know This Already?' Quizzes."

Table 6-1 "Do I Know This Already?" Foundation Topics Section-to-Question Mapping

Foundations Topics Section	Questions Covered in This Section
Configuring WinRM	1–2
Configuring Down-Level Server Management	3–4
Configuring Multiple Server Management	5–6
Remote Management of Server Core Machines	7–9
Configuring Daily Management Tasks	10

1. You need to enable the WS-Management listener service with the least amount of administrative effort. Which command should you execute?

   a. `Enable WSManagement`

   b. `WinManagement enable quickconfig`

   c. `Winrm quickconfig`

   d. `Winrs autostart`

2. Using the WS-Management listener service, which command can you execute to retrieve the IP Address configuration for ServerB?

   a. `Winrs -r:ServerB ipconfig`

   b. `Psremote -exec ServerB ipconfig`

   c. `Get ipconfig -ServerB`

   d. `Netsh ServerB`

3. What is the PowerShell cmdlet to enable remote management on down-level servers?

   a. `Enable-RemoteLegacy -Force`

   b. `Set PSremoting enable`

   c. `Psexec remote enable`

   d. `Enable-PSremoting -Force`

4. Which of the following is not supported by Server Manager?

   a. Ability to manage Windows Server 2008 Servers

   b. Ability to restart servers

   c. Ability to launch PowerShell

   d. Ability to manage Windows Server 2003 Servers

5. You have spent hours customizing Server Manager. With the least amount of administrative effort, what can you do to save a copy of your configuration in the event of a failure?

   a. Create a full backup of your server.

   b. Export Server Manager settings.

   c. Enable Clustering Services.

   d. Enable Server Manager settings logging during startup.

6. You have recently installed Windows Server 2012 R2. You try to use RDP via a client machine, but are unable to connect. What should you check?

   a. Install the Remote Desktop Services role.

   b. Reinstall the server and select the **Server Core** option.

   c. To connect to a server using RDP, you must select the **Allow remote connections to this computer** check box under System Properties.

   d. That your client is Windows 7 or higher.

7. You need to manage your Server Core installation remotely from your Windows 8.1 client. Which tool(s) can you use?

   a. Remote Administration Tools for Windows

   b. Remote Server Administration Tools

   c. Server Manager for Clients

   d. Admin Pack for Servers

8. You attempt to use MMC to manage the Event Viewer on a remote server and receive a message stating that the RPC Server is unavailable or that the server cannot be accessed. You confirm that you are able to ping the remote server. What should you check?

   a. Ensure that the Windows Firewall has the appropriate rule group enabled.

   b. Verify that the service is set to manual.

   c. Verify that the Event Viewer has the security log enabled.

   d. Verify that you are using MMC 3.0.

9. Which PowerShell cmdlet is used to retrieve information about a specific function?

   a. `Get`

   b. `Invoke`

   c. `Disable`

   d. `Enable`

10. Which tools can you use to streamline and simplify daily management tasks for your Windows Servers? (Choose all that apply.)

   a. Event Viewer

   b. Task Scheduler

   c. Disk Management

   d. PowerShell

   e. Active Directory Administrative Center

   f. DHCP

   g. Process Explorer

Configuring WinRM

Windows Remote Management (WinRM) is Microsoft's version of the WS-Management protocol. The WS-Management protocol is an open standard for querying and exchanging management data between devices that use this protocol. It relies on specifications established under the Simple Object Access Protocol (SOAP). SOAP defines the structure to exchange information using XML-formatted data that is exchanged typically using Web Services (HTTP/HTTPS) or in some cases Simple Mail Transfer Protocol (SMTP).

When Microsoft created WinRM, their goal was to leverage existing technologies to create a command-line application that by default communicated over TCP port 80. This later changed to TCP 5985 under Server 2008 R2. Still useful with Windows Server 2012 R2, WinRM provides the following benefits:

- **Remote PowerShell Administration:** WinRM is the foundation for executing PowerShell cmdlets received from remote management computers.

- **Execute custom scripts:** Scripts can be used to query data and perform management tasks using the Windows Management Interface (WMI).

- **Manage Remote Hardware:** Through the use of management controller interfaces, servers can be managed even in cases where the operating system might be malfunctioning.

Installation and Configuration of WinRM

To start using WinRM, a couple of prerequisites must be addressed. First, the WinRM service must be installed and configured with the appropriate listener ports. Secondly, the Windows Firewall must be configured to allow incoming request for WS Management listener service. These items can be addressed through the use of the `winrm` command-line tool. Several configuration options are available via the `winrm` command. To configure WinRM with the default settings, perform the following steps:

1. On the target server, open a command prompt as an Administrator.

2. Execute `Winrm quickconfig`. You will be prompted as to whether you want to configure WinRM using the default settings. Press **Y** followed by **Enter** to continue. WinRM will be configured as shown in Figure 6-1.

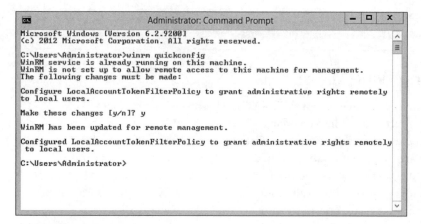

Figure 6-1   Enabling WinRM.

By default, the WinRM command-line tool performs the following actions:

- Starts the WinRM service and configures it for autostart
- Creates a WS-Management listener service using TCP 5985
- Creates a Windows Firewall exception for the listener service (see Figure 6-2)

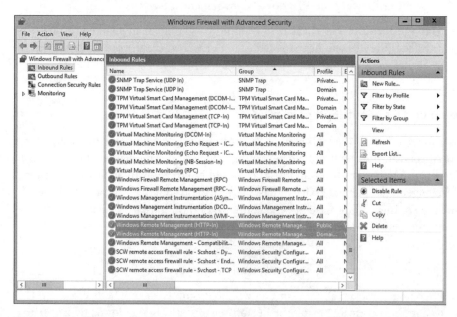

Figure 6-2   Windows Firewall with Advanced Security Inbound Windows Remote Management firewall rules.

Although WinRM has many uses, Table 6-2 outlines the most commonly used options.

Table 6-2 WinRM Options

Command	Explanation
Winrm get	Retrieves management information
Winrm set	Modifies management information
Winrm create	Creates a new instance of a management resource
Winrm delete	Removes an instance of a management resource
Winrm enumerate	Lists all instances of a management resource
Winrm help	Retrieves additional information related to configuration, execution, and management of winrm commands on local or remote machines.
Winrm invoke	Executes a method on a management resource
Winrm identify	Determines whether a WS-Management implementation is running on a remote machine
Winrm quickconfig	Applies the default configuration of WinRM and allows it to accept WS- Management requests from other remote machines.

NOTE For more information, refer to "Configure Remote Management in Server Manager" at http://technet.microsoft.com/en-us/library/hh921475.aspx.

Windows Remote Shell

The Windows Remote Shell (WinRS) is the client component used in conjunction with WinRM. WinRS enables you to administer a server installation, including Server Core, remotely via the command line. It relies on the WinRM service to execute commands remotely. To use WinRS, you must ensure the following requirements are met:

- Your local computer must be Windows Vista or higher.

- You must enable the WinRM listener on your servers.

- Windows Firewall exceptions must have been made.

- You must have the appropriate access to execute remote commands.

> **NOTE** To use WinRS, you must be logged on to the client computer with an account that is authorized to execute the remote command. If not, you might be required to use the `winrs` `-u` and `-p` switches to supply the username and password combination for an authorized account.

The basic syntax for the WinRS command is **`winrs` `-r`:** `[remote computer]` `command`. For example, if you need to retrieve the IP Address of ServerB, execute the following command from ServerA:

```
winrs -r:ServerB ipconfig
```

> **NOTE** To confirm WinRM functionality, use the `Test-WSMan [remote computer]` command.

Configuring Down-level Server Management

As with previous versions of Windows, when you begin to deploy Windows Server 2012 R2, there will be a period of time in which previous versions must coexist. One of the great things about Windows Server 2012 R2 is that we can continue to manage our previous or "down-level" installations of Windows Server 2008 and Windows Server 2008 R2. Down-level installations can be managed using Server Manager or Remote Server Administration Tools, both of which are discussed in more detail later.

To begin managing a down-level installation, the following prerequisites must be met:

- On each down-level server you want to manage, install the Windows Management Framework 4.0—available from the Microsoft Download Center.

- Ensure that the latest service pack has been installed for the Windows Server 2008 installations.

- Install .NET Framework 4.5 on each down-level server. To ensure that performance data is readable from down-level installs, install the performance update hotfix on each down-level server. For more information, refer to Knowledge Base article KB2682011 located at http://support.microsoft.com/kb/2682011.

- Install and configure the WinRM service on each down-level server as covered previously in this chapter.

- Enable Windows PowerShell remote management on each down-level server by executing the cmdlet `Enable-PSremoting -Force` in a Windows PowerShell window.

After all prerequisites have been addressed, you will be able to add remote servers from Server Manager or Remote Server Administration tools.

Preparing Down-level Server Core Installations

If you are managing down-level Server Core installations, the same prerequisites apply; however, each down-level Server Core installation requires additional features to be installed using the `dism /online /enable-feature–[feature name]` command. Using the `dism` command, install the following features:

- `MicrosoftWindowsPowerShell`

- `MicrosoftWindowsPowerShell-WOW64`

- `NetFx2-ServerCore`

- `NetFx2-ServerCore-WOW64`

Configuring Multiple Server Management

Remote management of servers is extremely helpful for an administrator—especially in scenarios in which your organization is driving a centralized management approach or if you are managing a group of Server installations. Although many tools are available for server management, Server Manager provides a quick and easy-to-use interface for this function.

Using Server Manager for Remote Management

While Server Manager has been used since the release of Windows Server 2008, Microsoft has enhanced the ability to manage multiple servers from within a single console. Server Manager runs in the Minimal Server Graphical Interface, so if you have removed this feature, you will need to reinstall it before continuing. Server Manager can be used to perform a variety of Administrative tasks as outlined here:

- Add/Remove remote servers to manage

- Create and manage server groups

- Install/Uninstall roles, role services, and features

- Start management tools such as PowerShell or MMC Snap-ins

- Manage remote servers with different credentials using the Manage As function

- Start/Stop Windows Services

- Configure Network Settings, Users, Groups, Remote Desktop Services, and so on

- Identify server status, events, and troubleshoot issues

- Restart servers

NOTE Server Manager can show the online/offline status for only legacy Windows Server 2003 servers.

Configuring Server Manager

As we covered previously, before any remote management can occur, the remote servers must be configured to enable remote management. Down-level installations require some additional preparations, although it is much simpler to manage Windows Server 2012/2012 R2 installations. By default, remote management using Server Manager is enabled. This can be changed by navigating to the Local Server properties of Server Manager as shown in Figure 6-3.

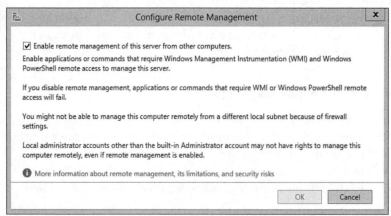

Figure 6-3 Server Manager Remote Management.

Similarly, remote management can be also be configured using the PowerShell command `Configure-SMRemoting.exe –Enable`.

This command is exclusive to Windows Server 2012 installations. As mentioned in the previous section, Enable-PSremoting -Force can be used for down-level installations.

> **NOTE**   To enable remote management on legacy systems, you might be required to perform additional configuration steps such as enabling WMI through the Windows Firewall service. For more information, refer to "Manage Multiple, Remote Servers with Server Manager" at http://technet.microsoft.com/en-us/library/hh831456.aspx.

Once enabled for remote management, use the **add other servers to manage** feature from the Server Manager Dashboard. The Add Servers dialog box enables you to search for remote servers using Active Directory by importing a list from a text file or by using DNS as shown in Figure 6-4.

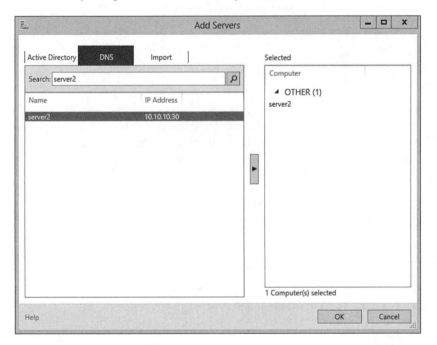

Figure 6-4   Add Servers Dialog.

After adding a remote server, it will be listed under the Server Manager > All Servers group. To list available administrative tasks, highlight the remote server and right-click to display remote administration options as shown in Figure 6-5.

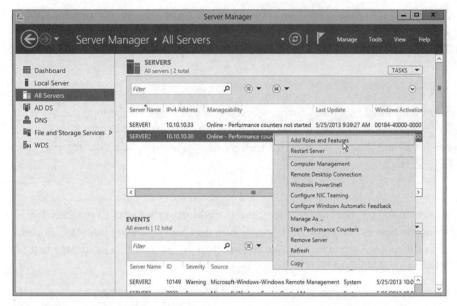

Figure 6-5 Remote Administration Menu.

Manage Nondomain Joined Servers

In situations where there are different security boundaries, such as managing nondomain joined servers, you will need to use the Manage As function within Server Manager to first supply the necessary authoritative credentials. Shown in Figure 6-6, failing to properly authenticate can result in one or more of the following conditions:

- Server Manager Notification messages indicating authentication failures due to authentication scheme differences

- Missing server informational details or the inability to refresh details for specifics servers listed under the All Servers dashboard

- `Access is denied` message when trying to perform remote management tasks such as remote computer management

Figure 6-6 Access is denied when trying to manage a non-domain joined server.

To manage nondomain joined servers or any server with a different authentication scheme, perform the following steps:

1. Right-click the server and select **Manage As** from the drop-down list as shown in Figure 6-7.

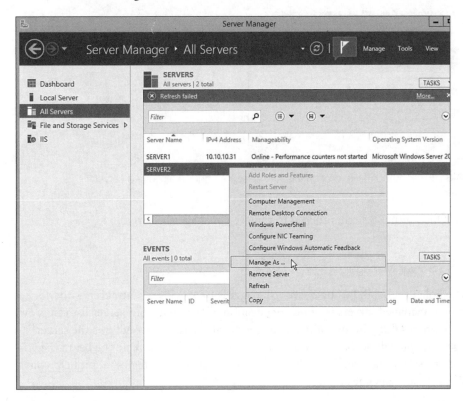

Figure 6-7   Invoking Manage As within Server Manager.

2. In the Windows Security dialog box shown in Figure 6-8, enter the user account and password with rights on the selected server. Optionally, you also can choose to remember the credentials.

Figure 6-8   Enter authoritative credentials to manage a nondomain joined server.

    3. Once authenticated, proceed to remotely manage the server.

Organizing Server Manager

The whole idea behind using Server Manager is to provide a central repository or listing of managed servers in your organization. Over time, your server list can grow quite large resulting in difficulty locating a specific server. Secondly, as the server list grows, you will probably agree that you can't afford to recreate the list in the event of a system failure. The following Server Manager strategies might help you address these challenges:

- **Create Custom Groups:** Custom groups can be created to organize and contain servers of the same type. For example, you might choose to create a File Server Group that contains all of your file servers. Similarly, you might choose to organize by operating system type, location, or any other criteria that best suits your needs. Using the Manage menu button, select the **Create Server Group** option to open the Create Server Group dialog box as shown in Figure 6-9. Enter a Server Group name and select or query the server to be added to the group.

  Newly created server groups will appear on the left side of the Dashboard, as shown in Figure 6-10. Servers can be added or removed from groups at any time.

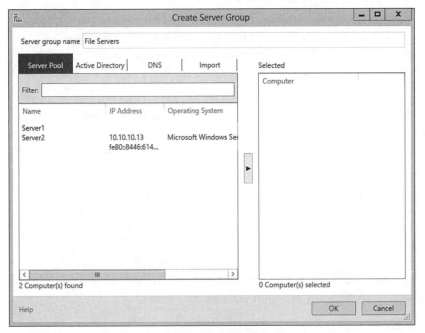

Figure 6-9   Server Manager Create Server Group.

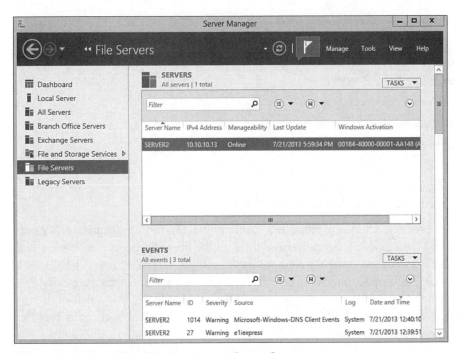

Figure 6-10   Server Manager Dashboard: Server Groups.

- **Export Server Manager Settings:** Server Manager settings can be backed up and restored to alternative management stations. This is particularly helpful in an unplanned recovery situation or if you simply want to copy settings to another server or client workstation containing Server Manager. Server Manager settings are stored in a `ServerList.xml` file along with a `User.config` file located under the following paths:

  - `%appdata%\Microsoft\Windows\ServerManager\ServerList.xml`

  - `%appdata%\Local\Microsoft_Corporation\`
    `ServiceManager.exe_StrongName_GUID\6.2.0.0\user.config`

- **Server Manager Properties:** Using the Server Manager Properties dialog box (available from the Manage button), you might choose to specify a data refresh period. Depending on how many servers you are managing, you might choose to create a more or less frequent refresh period. The more servers you have, the longer it will take to refresh, so a more frequent refresh interval can result in performance issues. If you do not want to have Server Manager start automatically upon logon, enable the check box for **Do not start Server Manager automatically at logon** as shown in Figure 6-11.

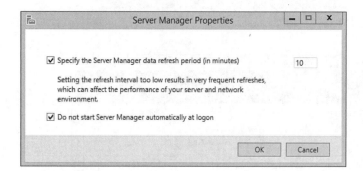

Figure 6-11   Server Manager Properties.

Enabling Remote Desktop Using Server Manager

As with previous editions of Windows, Remote Desktop for Administration is a useful tool. When enabled and authorized through the firewall, clients can connect to a Full GUI installation using the Remote Desktop Protocol (RDP) over TCP 3389. A Remote Desktop Connection client (mstsc.exe) is included in current operating systems today. Microsoft also provides a Remote Desktop MMC snap-in that enables you to create a list of servers where you can simply double-click the specific server to connect via RDP.

To enable remote connections on your Windows Server 2012 R2 installation, perform the following steps:

1. Open **Server Manager**.

2. In the left pane, click **Local Server**.

3. When the local server properties appear, click the **Remote Desktop status** link to switch from the default disabled state.

4. The System Properties dialog box opens, as shown in Figure 6-12. Click **Allow remote connections to this computer**; then click **OK**.

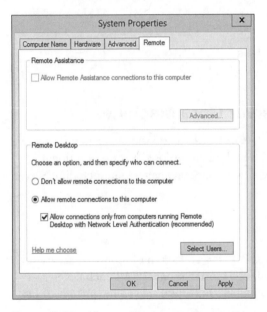

Figure 6-12   Allow remote connections to this computer.

5. You will be prompted that a Remote Desktop Firewall exception will be enabled. Click **OK** to continue.

6. Click the **Select Users** button to add/remove users that are authorized to use Remote Desktop to log in to the server. By default, members of the Remote Desktop Users and Administrators groups have access. Click the **Add** or **Remove** button to add or remove users as appropriate, and click **OK** as shown in Figure 6-13.

Figure 6-13   Add/Remove Remote Desktop Users.

Remote Management of Server Core Machines

Earlier in this chapter we discussed the use of WinRM and the use of WinRS to manage remote servers. In this section, we take a closer look at some additional tools and practices for configuring servers for remote management, including Server Core installations.

Remote Server Administration Tools

Remote Server Administration Tools (RSAT) is a collection of tools that are useful for managing Server Core as well as Full GUI installations. RSAT includes Server Manager, MMC snap-ins, PowerShell cmdlets, and additional command-line tools used to manage remote computers.

As a best practice, RSAT should be installed on a dedicated management server or client computer to limit the amount of access or load on production servers.

NOTE   RSAT tools are included as an installable feature under the Windows Server Full GUI installation, or they can also be downloaded from Microsoft and installed under Windows 8/8.1. They cannot be run from a Windows Server Core computer.

Installing RSAT on Client Workstations

You can install Remote Server Administration Tools by completing the following steps on a Windows 8.1 client management workstation:

1. Download and install the Remote Server Administration Tools for Windows 8.1, which is available from the Microsoft Download Center.

2. When prompted to install the update for Windows, click **Yes** to install the package.

3. Read the license agreement and accept the terms by clicking **I Accept**.

4. After the installation wizard completes, click **Close**.

5. Once installed, RSAT can be enabled or disabled as a Windows Feature. To do this, navigate to **Control Panel**, and click **Programs**.

6. Click **Turn Windows features on or off**.

7. Under the Windows Features dialog box, expand **Remote Server Administration Tools**.

8. Expand **Role Administration Tools** or **Feature Administration Tools** depending on what you want to disable or enable. By default, all administration tools are installed as shown in Figure 6-14.

Figure 6-14   Windows Features: Remote Server Administration Tools for Windows 8.1.

9. Select or deselect the appropriate tools, and click **OK**.

After the Remote Server Administration Tools have been installed and enabled, you will be able to access Server Manager, Active Directory, PowerShell, and other snap-ins for MMC, as shown in Figure 6-15.

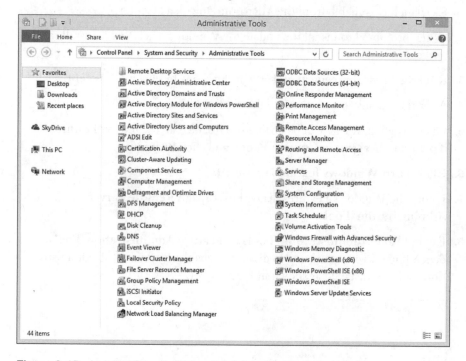

Figure 6-15   Installed Remote Server Administration Tools for Windows 8.1.

NOTE   To manage a Server Core Installation using RSAT, you must first configure the Windows Firewall.

Microsoft Management Console

As with previous versions of Windows, the Microsoft Management Console (MMC) is still a powerful tool used by administrators to manage local and remote servers, including Server Core installations. Custom read-only MMC consoles can be created with specific snap-ins containing only those tools required for the specific delegate function. With the release of Windows Server 2008, Microsoft introduced us to version 3.0 of the MMC. In the latest version, MMC 3.0 includes the following new features:

- **Action pane:** The action pane is located on the right side of the console. It lists all actions available to users.

- **Improved dialog boxes:** The Add/Remove snap-in dialog has been updated to allow for better snap-in organization

- **Improved error handling:** This version of MMC provides additional error handling notices and provides the ability to take specific actions when the errors occur.

The Microsoft Management Console is available and can be accessed by launching the MMC.exe application. If you are using a client workstation such as Windows 8.1, a wide array of MMC snap-ins are installed as part of the Remote Server Administration Tools package.

MMC Options for Delegation

An administrator not only can use MMC for local and remote management, but can also use it for delegation of administrative control, as we discussed in Chapter 2, "Installing and Configuring Windows Server 2012 R2." As with previous versions, MMC 3.0 provides the ability to create custom or limited views for the specific MMC snap-ins. Once snap-ins have been configured and added to the console, the console can be saved as a .MSC file and distributed to delegates.

For example, you might decide to delegate the ability for local site admins to manage a specific portion of Active Directory. After you configure the appropriate permissions in Active Directory, you might decide to author a custom MMC snap-in for Active Directory Users and Computers. Perhaps you want to allow the site administrator to view only a specific OU. This can be accomplished by creating a custom filter and limiting the access for the console. Delegation of Control for Active Directory is discussed later. MMC offers the following console configuration modes and options:

- **Author mode:** Grants users full access to all MMC functionality, which includes the ability to add or remove snap-ins, create new windows, create taskpad views and tasks, and view all areas of the console tree. This is the mode that is enabled by default for all new consoles. Typically consoles are set up by an administrator and then locked down by changing the mode to one of the user access modes.

- **User mode—Full access:** Prevents users from adding or removing snap-ins or changing snap-in properties. Users have full access to the tree.

- **User mode—limited access, multiple window:** Prevents users from accessing areas of the tree that are not visible in the snap-in console windows.

- **User mode—limited access, single window:** Opens the snap-in console in single-window mode and prevents users from accessing areas of the tree that are not visible in the single snap-in console window.

- **Do not save changes to this console (check box):** Regardless of what is changed, the console is not saved. Changes will be lost upon the next time it opens.

- **Allow the user to customize views (check box):** When checked, this option allows the user to customize console views, including enabling filters.

You can configure Console Options via the Options menu item of the MMC File menu as shown in Figure 6-16.

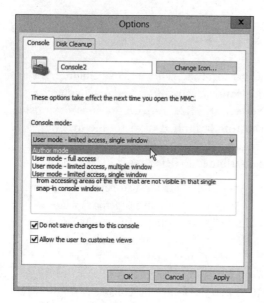

Figure 6-16   MMC Console Options.

After you create a custom MMC console, lock it down using the appropriate console option and/or filters using the View menu, simply save the console as an .MSC file, and distribute it accordingly. Delegates will be able to manage local or remote servers assuming the following criteria has been met:

- Delegates have been granted proper access to the server or resources.

- Windows Firewall has been configured to accept MMC connections.

Configuring Windows Firewall

To use MMC to manage Server Core, you must first create Advanced Firewall rules to permit access. The following `Netsh` command is the basic syntax required:

```
Netsh advfirewall firewall set rule group="[Rule Group Name]" new
enable=yes
```

You must specify a specific Rule Group Name to tell the Windows Firewall what traffic you want to allow. If security is not a major concern, you might also choose a blanket approach, enabling the Remote Administration Rule Group, which allows remote access for all supported MMC snap-ins. To enable Remote Administration on Server Core installations, issue the command `netsh advfirewall firewall set rule group="Remote Administration" new enable=yes`.

Even though many MMC snap-ins are available, not all are available by default for managing Server Core. Many of the administrative tasks for Server Core are completed via command-line applications or PowerShell cmdlets, as discussed previously. Table 6-3 lists the more commonly used MMC snap-ins supported by Server Core. The table also lists the appropriate Firewall Rule Group Name required to complete the `Netsh` configuration. Additional snap-ins might be available depending on the roles/features enabled for your server. Nevertheless, the same concept applies. If you need to manage a remote server, ensure that you have granted the proper access and have configured the firewall appropriately.

Table 6-3   MMC Snap-Ins and Firewall Rule Group Names

MMC Snap-In	Rule Group Name(s)	Description
Event Viewer	Remote Event Log Management	Provides the ability to review and manage Event Viewer logs remotely.
Reliability and Performance	Performance Logs and Alerts File and Printer Sharing	Provides the ability to manage server performance counters remotely.
Services	Remote Service Management	Allows you to start, stop, and manage services on the remote server.
Shared Folders	File and Printer Sharing	Provides the ability to manage shared folders and resources on a remote File and Print server.
Task Scheduler	Remote Scheduled Tasks Management	Enables the ability to manage scheduled tasks on a remote server.
Windows Firewall with Advanced Security	Windows Firewall Remote Management	Enables remote ability to manage the Windows Firewall. This is helpful if you need to modify the remote server to allow connections for other MMC snap-ins and services.

> **NOTE** Some snap-ins such as Disk Management require additional configuration to enable MMC management of a Server Core installation. For more information, refer to "Using MMC Snap-ins and RSAT" at http://technet.microsoft.com/en-us/library/dd163507.aspx.

Using MMC for Remote Management

To use MMC for remote server management, perform the following steps:

1. Using the **Windows Search** charm or **Run** bar from the Start right-click menu, launch `MMC.exe`. This will open an empty MMC console, as shown in Figure 6-17.

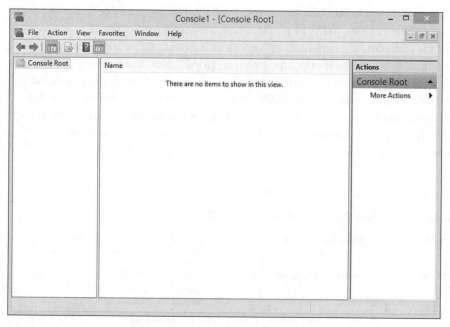

Figure 6-17 Microsoft Management Console.

2. From the File menu, click **Add/Remove Snap-in** to bring up a list of all available snap-ins as shown in Figure 6-18.

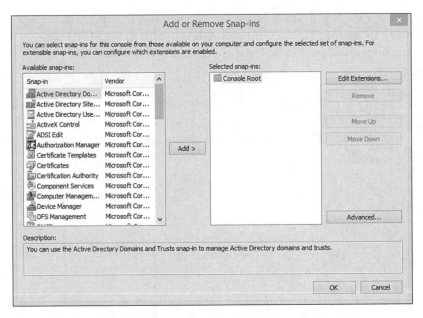

Figure 6-18   MMC Add/Remove Snap-in dialog box.

3. Select one or more snap-ins and then click the **Add** button. In this example, we will select **Services** to remotely manage services on a remote server.

4. If the snap-in allows for remote management, you might be presented with a dialog box to specify the local or remote computer you want to manage. In this example, we will manage Server2 from a Windows 8.1 Client with RSAT installed as shown in Figure 6-19. Click **Finish** when you have finished adding the server name.

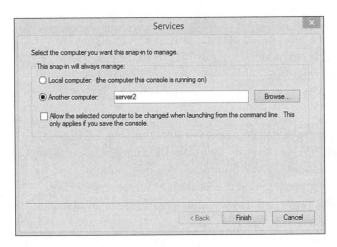

Figure 6-19   Select Computer to Manage.

5. If desired, add more snap-ins as you've done previously in Step 3. After you have added all appropriate snap-ins, click **OK** to return to the MMC console. Any snap-ins added will be listed in the MMC Console as shown in Figure 6-20.

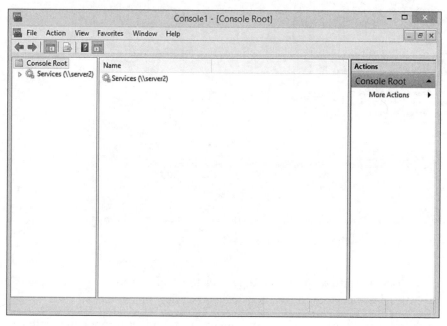

Figure 6-20 Custom MMC Console.

6. Expand the console tree to view the snap-in details for the remote server as shown in Figure 6-21.

NOTE For more information on how to use MMC for remote administration, creating custom consoles, and best practices, refer to "Microsoft Management Console 3.0" at http://technet.microsoft.com/en-us/library/cc709659.aspx.

NOTE MMC is designed to be used in a domain environment; however, in a workgroup environment with different security boundaries, you might be required to use the Run As function for a custom MMC console. You might also need to adjust Windows Firewall settings, ensure that the Secondary Logon services are started, and ensure that an account with the appropriate permissions is available on the workgroup computers.

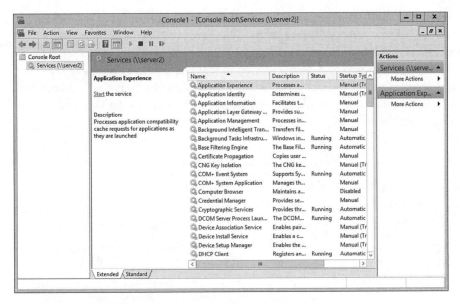

Figure 6-21   Remote Management of the Services Snap-in.

Windows PowerShell

As we have seen previously, PowerShell is a powerful command-line tool that has been available since Windows Server 2008. Microsoft has included Version 3.0 with the release of Windows Server 2012 and Version 4.0 with 2012 R2. A wide range of commands are used to manage servers via PowerShell and are discussed throughout this book. Microsoft has provided the ability to send and execute PowerShell cmdlets to remote computers using WinRM as we discussed earlier in this chapter. To use PowerShell to manage remote computers, the following must be considered:

- Ensure that WinRM is installed and running.

- Remote Management must be enabled on the Server Core Installation by executing the command `Enable-psremoting`. Not all cmdlets require this. For example, `Get` cmdlets do not require this level of access.

- Ensure that .NET Framework is installed.

- Although it's not required, the same version of PowerShell should be installed on both the local and remote server. Older versions can limit what can be configured remotely.

- The appropriate level of administrative access must be enabled for the service or resource.

- The appropriate firewall rules must be enabled.

After you have confirmed access and enabled Remote Administration on Server Core installation, a series of PowerShell cmdlets are available to facilitate Remote Administration. One of the most powerful cmdlets is the PSSession cmdlet. This cmdlet functions similar to a Telnet session in that you connect directly to the remote server. Once connected, you virtually have full access to run all commands as if you were sitting in front of the Server Core console. Some of the more common cmdlets are outlined in Table 6-4.

Table 6-4   PowerShell Basic Cmdlets for Remote Administration

Cmdlet	Description	Examples
Get	Used to retrieve or get information about a specific function	**Get-Process:** To retrieve or get a list of processes running on a computer
		Get-Service: To retrieve or get a list of services running on a computer
		Get-EventLog: Enables you to manage event logs and retrieve events contained within those event logs
		Get-WmiObject: Retrieves information from the Windows Management Instrumentation (WMI) such as specific hardware or software information
Invoke	Enables you to run a single command on one or more computers. As commands are executed, a remote session is established and disconnected upon completion. This cmdlet is particularly helpful for automating some manual tasks.	**For Commands:** *Invoke-Command -ComputerName [Computer1, Computer 2] - ScriptBlock {command}* **For Scripts:** *Invoke-expression c:\testscript\ testscript.ps1*
PSSession	Similar to a Telnet session, PSSession creates a persistent connection to a remote computer. From here you can execute virtually any command that you could if you were logged on locally. Commands can be executed until you exit the session using the Exit-PSSession command.	**New-PSSession:** *New-PSSession -ComputerName [remote computer]* **Get-PSSession:** List active sessions **Enter-PSSession:** Switch between sessions **Exit-PSSession:** Exists a session

NOTE   For a full listing of PowerShell cmdlets and how to use them, refer to "Windows PowerShell User's Guide" available at: http://technet.microsoft.com/en-us/library/cc196356.aspx.

NOTE   For more information on the new release of PowerShell, refer to "What's New in Windows PowerShell" at http://technet.microsoft.com/en-us/library/hh857339.aspx.

Windows PowerShell Web Access

PowerShell Web Access is a new function available under Windows Server 2012. Using Web Access, you can create a secure central portal to use PowerShell Sessions, cmdlets, and scripts to manage a remote computer. One of the major benefits of using the Web is that it can be accessed by a wide range of browsers and client devices, including smartphones, tablets, shared kiosk computers, and so on. Although this is convenient, opening up anything over the Internet should be approached with caution due to the potential security concerns.

PowerShell Web Access works via a Windows PowerShell Web Access Gateway. The gateway is essentially a web server with the Web Access Gateway Role/Feature components installed. The server typically sits in a DMZ between the Client/Internet and the internal servers. To act as a Web Access Gateway, the web server must meet the following prerequisites:

- Server running Windows Server 2012 or Windows Server 2012 R2

- Internet Information Services (IIS) role installed

- .NET Framework 4.0

To install PowerShell Web Access, perform the following steps:

1. From an administrative PowerShell session, execute the command
   ```
   Install-WindowsFeature -Name WindowsPowerShellWebAccess
   -ComputerName [computer name] -InclueManagementTools -Restart.
   ```

2. After the install, you will be prompted to review a readme file containing setup instructions for configuring the gateway. For your convenience, the file is saved under C:\Windows\Web\PowerShellWebAccess\wwwroot\Readme.txt.

> **NOTE**   PowerShell Web Access goes beyond the scope of this book and the
> 70-410 Exam. For a complete configuration guide, refer to "Install and Use Win-
> dows PowerShell Web Access" at http://technet.microsoft.com/en-us/library/
> hh831611.aspx.

Configuring Daily Management Tasks

Repetitive tasks are often tedious and are probably one of the most dreadful things
an administrator has to deal with. To help automate some of the daily tasks, Microsoft has created a couple of tools for us.

Task Scheduler

Task Scheduler is a MMC snap-in that enables you to schedule and automate tasks
to perform a specific action at a specific time. It can also be used to trigger an event
as a follow-up to another event occurring. For example, suppose you need to restart
your server every day at 2 a.m. One option is to set your alarm clock every morning
at 2 a.m. just to restart the server. On the other hand, using a scheduled task to run
automatically seems a bit easier.

Tasks can be configured to run under a specific local or domain service account.
Here are a few components associated with Task Scheduler:

- **Triggers:** A *trigger* is a set of criteria that when met executes a specific task.
  Triggers can be based on a schedule, logon event, or startup event; during
  a period of inactivity; upon session connect/disconnect or workstation lock/
  unlock, and so on.

- **Actions:** An *action* refers to an event that occurs after a trigger is set. Actions
  include starting a program such as a script, sending an email, displaying an
  alert, and so on.

- **Conditions:** Enable you to specify how the actions should be taken. Conditions include items such as idle times, current power state, and whether the
  task should stop if the computer is on battery power.

- **Settings:** Specifies additional settings such as what to do if the task fails or if
  the schedules are missed due to the computer being offline.

The layout of Task Scheduler is similar to that of other MMC snap-ins as shown in
Figure 6-22.

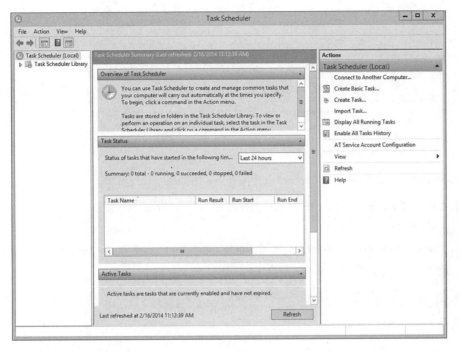

Figure 6-22   Task Scheduler.

You will notice the Task Scheduler Library on the left pane. This is where all of your scheduled tasks are stored. You have the ability to create custom folders for storing and organizing your tasks. In the center pane, you will notice the list of active tasks. Highlight the task to configure triggers, actions, conditions, and so on. On the far right pane is a list of Actions. Table 6-5 outlines the available actions.

Table 6-5   Task Scheduler Actions

Action	Description
Create Basic Task	Basic wizard used to create a task with specifying only basic settings, which include only the trigger and action.
Create Task	Full wizard that enables you to create a task specifying security settings, triggers, task recovery options, scheduling, conditions, and so on.
Import Task	Allows the importing of a task from a saved .XML file.
Display All Running Tasks	Shows all running tasks, when they started, how long they ran for, the current state, and the location of the task.
Disable All Task History	When clicked, task history is disabled. Click again to reenable.

Action	Description
New Folder	Creates a folder to store or group configured tasks.
View	Customizes the appearance of the Task Scheduler console.
Refresh	Refreshes the console to display changes in events or tasks.
Help	Calls the console help tool that displays links to Task Scheduler information available on TechNet.

To schedule a task with Task Scheduler, perform the following steps:

1. Open **Task Scheduler** from the Server Manager Tools menu or via Administrative Tools.

2. On the right pane, click **Create Basic Task**. The Create Basic Task Wizard will appear as shown in Figure 6-23.

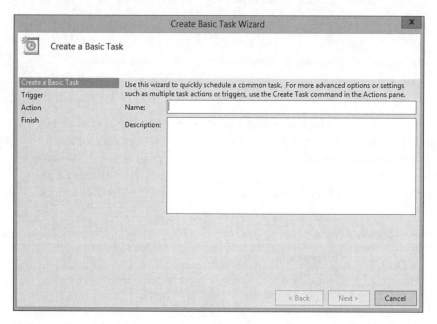

Figure 6-23   Create Basic Task Wizard.

3. Type a name for the task and a description, and click **Next**.

4. For this example, we will create a task called Open Notepad that will open Notepad upon logon. Select the **When I log on** radio button for the trigger as shown in Figure 6-24. Click **Next** to continue.

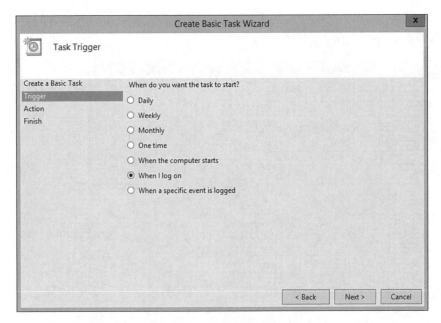

Figure 6-24 Create Basic Task Wizard: Configure Trigger.

5. For the Action, select **Start a program** as shown in Figure 6-25; click **Next**.

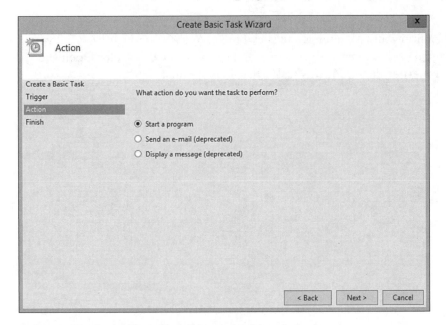

Figure 6-25 Create Basic Task Wizard: Configure Action.

6. Browse to the path of the program or script—in this case `Notepad.exe`. Click **Next** as shown in Figure 6-26.

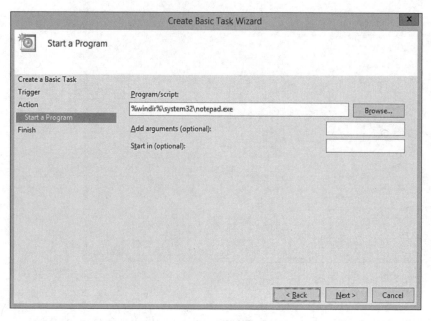

Figure 6-26   Create Basic Task Wizard: Start a Program.

7. Confirm your task settings and click **Finish**. As shown in Figure 6-27, if you would like to review the properties of the task, check the box for **Open the Properties dialog for this task when I click Finish.**

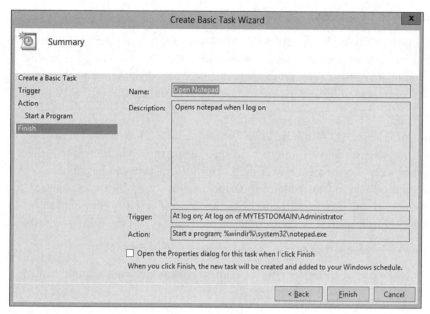

Figure 6-27 Create Basic Task Wizard: Finish.

8. Refresh the Task Scheduler console to see your newly created task as shown in Figure 6-28.

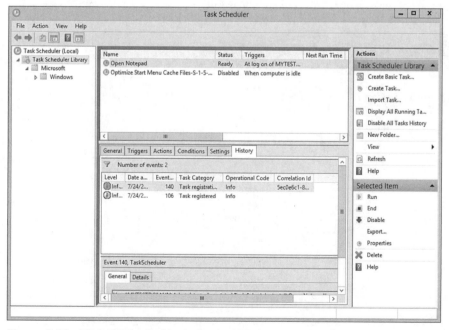

Figure 6-28 Task Scheduler Newly Created Task.

Active Directory Administrative Center

Released under Windows Server 2008 R2, Microsoft created the Active Directory Administrative Center. This tool provided a method for administrators to simplify and even automate routine tasks that are normally managed via Active Directory Users and Computers. The underlying technology controlling this tool is Windows PowerShell.

In the current release, AD Administrative Center includes a PowerShell History function. This function logs all actions performed using the GUI, but records the events as they were executed via PowerShell. This information can be copied to Notepad and modified to be used later to script specific events. The code output from this function can also be used later with the Active Directory Module for PowerShell. AD Administrative Center can be used to perform the following tasks:

- Create and manage user accounts, groups, computers, and OUs

- Connect to one or more domains or domain controllers from a single console

- Filter and query Active Directory data

Active Directory Administrative Center is installed by default when the Active Directory Domain Services (AD DS) role is installed via Server Manager or when Remote Server Administration Tools are installed. AD Administrative Center, shown in Figure 6-29, is accessed via Administrative Tools or from the Tools menu under the Server Manager\AD DS dashboard item.

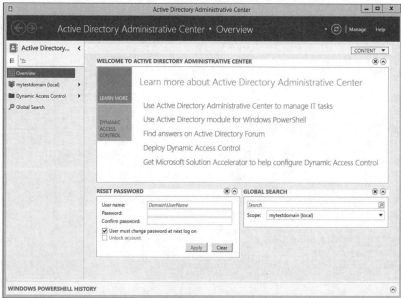

Figure 6-29 Active Directory Administrative Center.

From the Overview screen, AD Administrative Center provides some quick links to learn more about the tool and how to use it as well as links to configure Dynamic Access Control. Although tested on the 70-412 exam, Dynamic Access Control enables you to define criteria in which specific events can be triggers. For example, if a user account is created with the Department attribute matching "Information Technology," Active Directory Administrative Center can be configured to automatically grant access to IT resources upon account creation. With Dynamic Access Control, you can perform the following tasks using Active Directory:

- **Create a claim type:** A claim type sets the definition for matching specific criteria. We can define our claim type so that the Department attribute in Active Directory contains "Information Technology." From here, we can trigger an event if the claim type is true.

- **Create a resource property:** A resource property describes or classifies a specific characteristic of a resource such as a file or folder. It is used to define target resources and permissions when creating central access rules.

- **Create a central access rule:** A central access rule defines how permissions are assigned to resources defined within the resource property.

- **Create a central access policy:** A central access policy contains one or more central access rules that determines who should have access to the resource.

> **NOTE**   This section provided an overview of Dynamic Access Control. For more information, refer to "Dynamic Access Control—Scenario Overview" at http://technet.microsoft.com/en-us/library/hh831717.aspx.

Exam Preparation Tasks

Review All the Key Topics

Review the most important topics in the chapter, noted with the key topics icon in the outer margin of the page. Table 6-6 lists a reference of these key topics and the page numbers on which each is found.

Table 6-6 Key Topics for Chapter 6

Key Topic Element	Description	Page Number
Table 6-2	Describes the different commands associated with WinRM	247
Figure 6-3	Shows you how to enable Remote Management using Server Manager	250
List	Shows you the steps to manage nondomain joined servers	253
Figure 6-9	Shows you how to create a Server Group	255
Table 6-3	Listing of common MMC Snap-ins and corresponding Firewall Rule Groups	263
List	Shows you how to use MMC for Remote Management	264
List	Lists prerequisites and considerations for using PowerShell for Remote Management	267
Table 6-4	Lists commonly used cmdlets for remote administration using PowerShell	268
Table 6-5	Describes the actions available from Task Scheduler	271
List	Lists the tasks required to schedule a basic task	272
Figure 6-29	Shows you the Active Directory Administrative Center	276

Complete the Tables and Lists from Memory

Print a copy of Appendix B, "Memory Tables" (found on the CD), or at least the section for this chapter, and complete the tables and lists from memory. Appendix C, "Memory Tables Answer Key," is also on the CD and includes completed tables and lists to check your work.

Definitions of Key Terms

Define the following key terms from this chapter, and check your answers in the glossary.

Active Directory Administrative Center, MMC, RSAT, Task Scheduler, WinRM, WinRS

This chapter covers the following subjects:

- **Introduction to Hyper-V:** This section provides an introduction to Hyper-V and the new functions available with the release of Windows Server 2012 R2. The section also covers the process to install and configure the Hyper-V role under Windows Server 2012 R2.

- **Creating and Configuring Virtual Machine Settings:** This section walks you through creating and configuring generation 1 and 2 virtual machines. It also provides you with the framework for managing virtual machines and virtual hardware using Hyper-V Manager.

- **Configuring Dynamic Memory:** This section provides an overview of dynamic memory and how it is used to optimize pooled memory.

- **Configuring Smart Paging:** Memory is something that is typically depleted early on in a virtual environment. Running out of memory creates some challenges for any administrator. This section demonstrates the use of smart paging and how it is used in a virtual implementation.

- **Configuring Resource Metering:** As more companies leverage cloud technologies, managing resources and determining how to allocate costs becomes a tedious task. This section shows you how Hyper-V resource metering can help simplify these tasks.

- **Configuring Guest Integration Services:** This section provides an overview of Guest Integration Services and how they improve your virtual experience. It also outlines steps required to install and configure integration services.

CHAPTER 7

Configuring Hyper-V

If we look back several years, managing a server room or data center was often a time-consuming task for an IT technician. As the demand for new servers increased, so did the amount of racking, stacking, cabling, and configuring of physical servers. It was often hard to react at a moment's notice. Today, many of these headaches go away with the use of virtual servers. With the release of Windows Server 2012 R2, Microsoft has made working with virtual computers even easier. This chapter reviews Hyper-V and demonstrates how seamless it is to configure virtual machines today.

"Do I Know This Already?" Quiz

The "Do I Know This Already?" quiz enables you to assess whether you should read this entire chapter or simply jump to the "Exam Preparation Tasks" section for review. If you are in doubt, read the entire chapter. Table 7-1 outlines the major headings in this chapter and the corresponding "Do I Know This Already?" quiz questions. You can find the answers in Appendix A, "Answers to the 'Do I Know This Already?' Quizzes."

Table 7-1 Do I Know This Already?" Foundation Topics Section-to-Question Mapping

Foundations Topics Section	Questions Covered in This Section
Introduction to Hyper-V	1–2
Creating and Configuring Virtual Machine Settings	3–7
Configuring Dynamic Memory	8
Configuring Resource Metering	9
Configuring Guest Integration Services	10

1. The underlying mechanism responsible for managing virtual machines is known as a:

    a. Virtual machine supervisor

    b. Hypervisor

    c. vProcessor

    d. Hyper-V machine processor

    e. Hyperserver

2. You are looking to introduce virtualization into your organization. Which are valid methods for installing Hyper-V? (Choose all that apply.)

    a. Install the Hyper-V role using Server Manager.

    b. Install Microsoft Virtual PC 2012.

    c. Download and install the standalone version of Hyper-V Server 2012.

    d. Boot to the Windows Server 2012 installation media and select Hyper-V.

3. What must you do to properly move the checkpoint folder for a virtual machine? Each answer represents part of the solution. (Choose all that apply.)

    a. Suspend the virtual machine.

    b. Move the virtual machine to a new storage location.

    c. Delete any existing checkpoints.

    d. Copy any existing checkpoints.

    e. Specify a new Checkpoint File Location under the virtual machine settings.

4. You need to install the RemoteFX 3D Video adapter driver for your virtual machine. Which role is required to use this driver?

    a. Remote Desktop Virtualization

    b. 3D Streaming Video

    c. Video Bus Virtualization

    d. HDFX Virtualization

5. You are looking to delegate control to junior systems administrators. With the least amount of administrative privilege, how can you delegate junior admins the ability to manage and administer your Hyper-V server?

   a. Add the users to the Domain Administrators group.

   b. Add the users to the Power Users group.

   c. Add the users to the Server Operators Group.

   d. Add the users to the Hyper-V Administrators group.

6. You install a legacy virtual network adapter on a newly created generation 1 virtual machine. You notice that network performance for your virtual machine is operating much slower than expected. What should you do?

   a. Remove Guest Integration Services.

   b. Add a second legacy virtual network adapter.

   c. Remove the Legacy Network Adapter and install a Network Adapter instead.

   d. Increase the memory for the virtual machine.

7. You are managing a Hyper-V host with three virtual machines. You need to ensure that VM1 is always given priority to the hosts processor. What should you do?

   a. Modify the resource control options for VM1.

   b. Add additional virtual processors to VM1.

   c. Reduce the processors on all virtual machines except for VM1.

   d. Add virtual memory to VM1.

8. Which virtual machine setting allows virtual machines to consume additional memory from those virtual machines that are underutilized or idle?

   a. Guest Integration Services

   b. Resource Metering

   c. Smart Paging

   d. Dynamic Memory

9. You need to configure your virtual machine to track memory, CPU and network usage. What should you configure?

    a. Smart paging

    b. Resource metering

    c. Guest usage tracking

    d. Dynamic memory

10. You notice poor response time for keyboard and mouse input on your virtual machine. What is most likely the problem?

    a. Integration Services is not installed.

    b. The input device is not supported by Windows.

    c. Dynamic Memory is disabled.

    d. There is not enough start-up memory configured for the virtual machine.

Introduction to Hyper-V

What exactly is Hyper-V? Hyper-V is Microsoft's version of a *hypervisor*. A hypervisor, also referred to as a *virtual machine manager*, is the entity responsible for managing virtual machines (VMs). Hyper-V enables you to host virtual machines within your server computing environment.

Hyper-V is available in two configurations:

- **Role Based:** Hyper-V can be installed as a role running on a Windows Server Core or Full GUI installation.

- **Standalone:** Hyper-V can also be installed as a standalone server product that does not require an installation of Windows Server. Hyper-V Server 2012 R2 is available as a downloadable package from the Microsoft Download Center.

As a role-based installation, the hypervisor is installed on top of the Windows Server operating system. In the standalone server product, the hypervisor is integrated into a customized stripped-down Windows Server Core like platform. This allows for a smaller footprint without the overhead of other applications or Windows Server operating system components.

In either case, Hyper-V uses the latest 64-bit hardware-assisted processors enabling you to host one or more virtual servers within a physical server. Each virtual server, known as a *guest*, will operate independently as if it was its own physical server. Guests will consume resources from your physical Hyper-V Server, known as a *host*. Hosts can be standalone or clustered and contain local storage or even use shared storage platforms. Microsoft's Hyper-V provides the following benefits to an organization:

- **Shared resources:** Hyper-V enables you to pool physical resources and dynamically adjust based on workload and demand for additional services. In a sense, Hyper-V provides you with a cloud environment in your organization.

- **Consolidated hardware:** Underutilized or legacy servers can be consolidated into fewer physical hosts. This reduces energy costs, administrative costs, and overall total cost of ownership.

- **Disaster recovery/business continuity:** Hyper-V provides the ability for easier restores and rollbacks should an unplanned event occur.

- **High availability:** With a clustering type solution, Hyper-V can be configured for high availability (HA).

- **Improved desktop experiences:** Hyper-V enables you to deploy a Virtual Desktop Infrastructure (VDI). This allows applications and workstation images to be managed centrally and rapidly deployed.

- **Testing and development:** Hyper-V enables you to create separate environments that can be used for testing and development activities.

What's New in Hyper-V Server

Microsoft has made several improvements to Hyper-V with the release of Windows Server 2012 and Windows Server 2012 R2. Table 7-2 outlines some of these improvements.

Table 7-2   What's New or Improved in Hyper-V

Function	Windows Server 2012/ Hyper-V Server 2012	Windows Server 2012 R2/ Hyper-V Server 2012 R2
Client Hyper-V	New function enables you to create and manage VMs under Windows 8. Windows 8 clients include the ability to turn the Hyper-V feature on or off via Programs and Features located under Control Panel.	New function enables you to create and manage VMs under Windows 8.1. Windows 8.1 clients include the ability to turn the Hyper-V feature on or off via Programs and Features located under Control Panel.
Hyper-V module for PowerShell	New feature that enables you to create and manage Hyper-V using Windows PowerShell	No further improvements.
Hyper-V Replica	New ability that enables you to replicate VMs between different storage areas and even data centers for Disaster Recovery purposes.	Update that enables an extended replica or third server that can be configured to receive a copy of the VMs.
Live Migration	Updated function that enables you to perform one or more live migrations of VMs.	Updated to enable administrators to select performance options when moving VMs to a different server.
Improved Scalability	The current version of Hyper-V supports additional resources for creating guest servers with larger capacities.	No further improvements.
Storage Migration	A new feature that enables you to move virtual hard disks containing the VM to a different storage area without incurring any downtime.	No further improvements.

Function	Windows Server 2012/ Hyper-V Server 2012	Windows Server 2012 R2/ Hyper-V Server 2012 R2
Virtual Fibre Channel	New function that enables you to connect your Hyper-V server to a Fibre channel storage array from within the guest operating system.	No further improvements.
Virtual Hard Disk Format	Increased support for larger virtual hard disks up to 64 TB.	No further improvements.
Virtual Switch	Added support for monitoring, forwarding, and filtering packets.	No further improvements.
Shared virtual hard disk	No further improvements.	New feature that enables clustering of virtual machines by using shared virtual hard disk VHDX files.
Resize virtual hard disk	No further improvements.	Updated to enable the resizing of virtual hard disks while the VM is running.
Storage Quality of Service	No further improvements.	New function that provides Quality of Service (QoS) for storage. This ensures that I/O load on one VM does not impact others.
Virtual machine generation	No further improvements.	New function that detects the level of virtual hardware present and enables additional features such as PXE boot for later Gen2 virtual hardware.
Automatic Virtual Machine Activation	No further improvements.	New function that enables VMs to be activated automatically without having to manage product keys.
Integration Services	No further improvements.	New service has been added to enable an administrator to copy internal VM files to a running VM without shutting down.
Export	No further improvements.	Updated function that enables you to export a virtual machine checkpoint while the VM is running. This is helpful when copying a production server to a test lab.

Function	Windows Server 2012/ Hyper-V Server 2012	Windows Server 2012 R2/ Hyper-V Server 2012 R2
Failover Clustering	No further improvements.	Updated function that allows Hyper-V to provide better abilities to detect hardware failures and relocate VM's to alternate hardware before the VM is interrupted unexpectedly.
Enhanced Session Mode	No further improvements.	New function that allows for redirection of local resources such as printers, USB devices, and other plug and play equipment in a VM.
Linux Support	No further improvements.	Updated support for Linux VM backups.
Management	No further improvements.	Alternate solution to allow older versions of Hyper-V to manage newer versions.

> **NOTE** For a full listing of New and Updated features, refer to "What's New in Hyper-V for Windows Server R2" at http://technet.microsoft.com/en-us/library/dn282278.aspx and "Hyper-V Overview" at http://technet.microsoft.com/library/hh831531.

Installing the Hyper-V Server Role

Hyper-V is available as an installable server or as a role within a Windows Server 2012 R2 Core or Full GUI installation. For the 70-410 exam, we will focus on the Hyper-V Role. Before installing, you must ensure that your hardware meets the minimum requirements as shown in Table 7-3.

Table 7-3 Minimum Hardware Requirements for Hyper-V

Hardware	Requirements
Processor	Minimum 1.4-GHz, 64-bit processor with hardware-assisted virtualization. Most processors today include a virtualization option that can be enabled/disabled through the System Setup or BIOS.
Memory	512 MB minimum to support the installation, but you will need additional RAM if you intend to set up guest operating systems.

Hardware	Requirements
Network Adapters	At least one adapter is required, but two or more is preferred.
Storage	While the storage required to accommodate the Role is minimal, you will require local or shared storage to support guest operating systems. If you are using the standalone product, you will require storage on the dedicated server.

After you confirm the minimum hardware requirements, you can proceed to install Hyper-V. To install Hyper-V, perform the following steps:

1. From Server Manager, pull down the **Manage** menu and click **Add Roles and Features** to launch the Add Roles and Features Wizard.

2. At the Before you begin screen, click **Next**.

3. On the Select installation type screen, choose **Role-based** or **feature-based** installation and click **Next**.

4. On the Select destination server screen, select the destination server and click **Next**.

5. Select **Hyper-V** from the Select server roles screen. Confirm the installation of the additional features, and click **Add Features** as shown in Figure 7-1. Click **Next** to continue.

Figure 7-1   Add Roles and Features Wizard.

6. Click **Next** on the Select features screen. At this point, you do not need to select any additional features to be installed on the selected server.

7. Click **Next** on the Hyper-V screen, as shown in Figure 7-2.

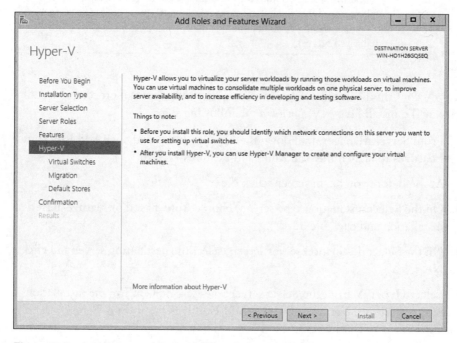

Figure 7-2   Add Roles and Features Wizard—Hyper-V screen.

8. On the Virtual Switches screen shown in Figure 7-3, select one or more network adapters to bind to the virtual switch. Click **Next** to continue..

NOTE   To provide improved throughput or isolate VM traffic, it is recommended that you install and use multiple network interface cards.

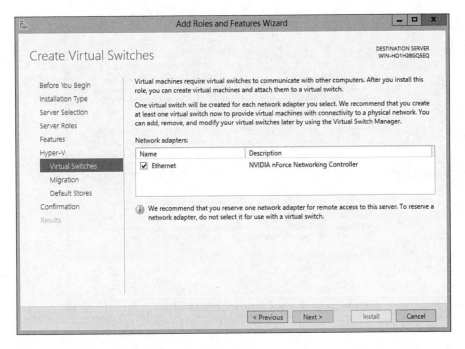

Figure 7-3   Select virtual network adapters.

9. The next step presented in the wizard is the Virtual Machine Migration screen (see Figure 7-4). This screen enables you to configure Hyper-V to send and receive live migrations of virtual machines on this server. This function is primarily used with a Hyper-V cluster where VMs, while running, move between cluster hosts. As noted in Figure 7-4, you can configure this later when you are ready to configure a cluster. Click **Next** to continue.

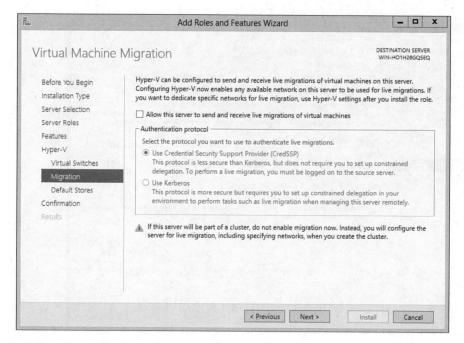

Figure 7-4 Migration settings.

10. On the Default Stores screen, select the default location to store virtual hard disk files for your virtual machines, as shown in Figure 7-5. Earlier in this book we discussed storage pools and storage spaces. For scalability, consider storing virtual servers and disks in a storage pool as opposed to a local disk. Click **Next** to continue.

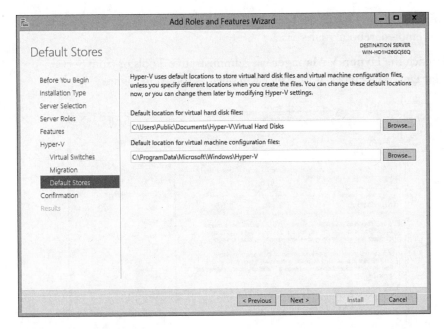

Figure 7-5   Default stores.

11. Click **Install** at the Confirm installation selections screen shown in
Figure 7-6.

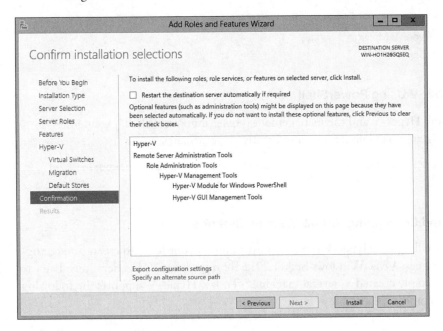

Figure 7-6   Hyper-V Role Confirmation screen.

12. After the Hyper-V role has been installed, click **Close** on the Results screen. If prompted, reboot your server.

13. Launch the **Hyper-V Manager** via Administrative Tools or from Server Manager. The Hyper-V Manager will open as shown in Figure 7-7.

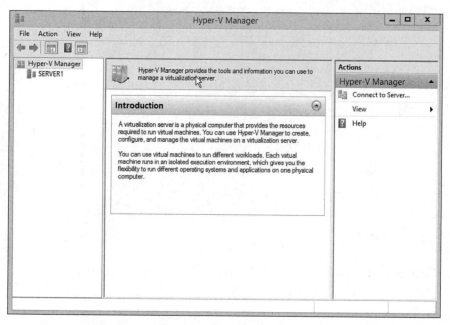

Figure 7-7   Hyper-V Manager.

Install Hyper-V Using PowerShell

To install Hyper-V and the management tools using PowerShell, execute the following command under an administrative PowerShell session:

```
Install-WindowsFeature -Name Hyper-V -ComputerName [computername]
-IncludeManagementTools -Restart
```

Creating and Configuring Virtual Machine Settings

After installing the Hyper-V role, the next thing on your list is to create and config-ure your guest VMs. Windows Server 2012 R2 introduces VM generations. Prior to this, we simply created a "virtual machine." Today, Hyper-V supports the following VM generations:

- **Generation 1:** Generation 1 VMs use the same virtual hardware used with previous versions of Windows Server and Hyper-V. These VMs utilize a Hyper-V Basic Input Output System (BIOS) similar to that of legacy x86 physical computers. VMs support booting from legacy IDE controllers, legacy network adapters, basic peripherals, and limited support for other bootable devices.

- **Generation 2:** Generation 2 VMs provide new functionality for VMs. They utilize a Unified Extensible Firmware Interface (UEFI) as opposed to a BIOS. This enables VMs to support a wide range of CPU architectures and drivers, booting from larger disks with different partition tables, and PXE boot capabilities.

  Generation 2 VMs are configured to use Secure Boot by default. This function is intended to reduce the likelihood of executing unauthorized code during the boot process. Generation 2 VMs also support additional boot capabilities such as booting from a SCSI virtual hard disk, SCSI virtual DVD, or PXE environment by using a standard network adapter.

  Generation 2 VMs are supported by Windows Server 2012, Windows Server 2012 R2, and 64-bit versions of Windows 8/8.1.

Before selecting a generation, there are several things that you must consider:

- Virtual IDE controllers and virtual floppy disks .vfd have been removed from generation 2 VMs.

- COM ports are not available in generation 2 VMs by default. You can, however, configure them via PowerShell using the Set-VMComPort cmdlet.

- Secure Boot is enabled by default for generation 2 VMs. You can modify this while the VM is powered off.

- RemoteFX is not supported by generation 2 VMs.

- You cannot attach a physical CD/DVD drive to a generation 2 VM. Only ISO image files are supported.

- Generation 2 VMs only support VHDX virtual hard drives. If you have a legacy VHD, you must convert the virtual hard drive using Hyper-V or the Convert-VHD PowerShell cmdlet.

- Generation 2 VMs can support and resize VHDX files up to a 64 TB.

- Generation 2 VMs support up to eight network adapters.

TIP   Once a virtual machine is created, you cannot change its generation. Make sure to determine requirements prior to creating a new virtual machine. Generation 2 virtual machines are not supported by operating systems prior to Windows Server 2012.

NOTE   For more information, refer to "Generation 2 Virtual Machine Overview" at http://technet.microsoft.com/en-us/library/dn282285.aspx and "Virtual Machine Specifications for Hyper-V in Windows Server 2012 R2" at http://technet.microsoft.com/en-us/library/dn592184.aspx.

Configuring a Virtual Machine

To create a VM, perform the following steps:

1. Log in with the appropriate credentials. By default, administrators and members of the Hyper-V Administrators group have the ability to manage Hyper-V.

2. Open Hyper-V Manager. Locate your Hyper-V server in the left pane. Right-click the server and select **New Virtual Machine**. This will open the New Virtual Machine Wizard shown in Figure 7-8.

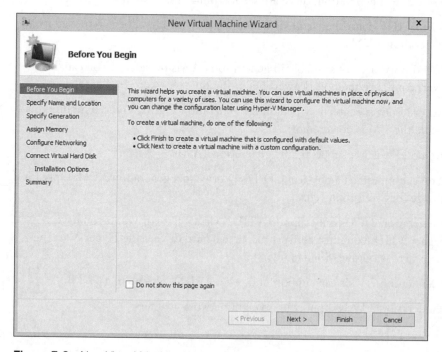

Figure 7-8   New Virtual Machine Wizard.

3. Click **Next** at the Before You Begin screen.

4. The next screen will ask you to specify the VM name and location. The name given is not the computer name, but the name displayed in Hyper-V Manager. As a best practice, you might consider naming the VM using the same display name as the computer name.

   By default, the location selected will be the default location you chose during the installation of the Hyper-V role. You might also choose to store the VM in a different location if you have a specific location for this particular VM. For this example, leave the default location, enter a **Name** and click **Next** as shown in Figure 7-9.

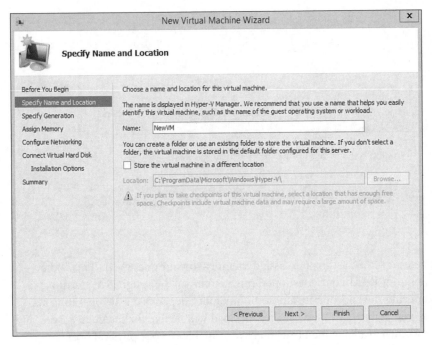

Figure 7-9   Specify name and location for a new VM.

5. On the Specify Generation screen, select the generation of the new VM you are creating. You can choose between Generation 1(default) and Generation 2. For this example, select **Generation 2** as shown in Figure 7-10. Click **Next** to proceed.

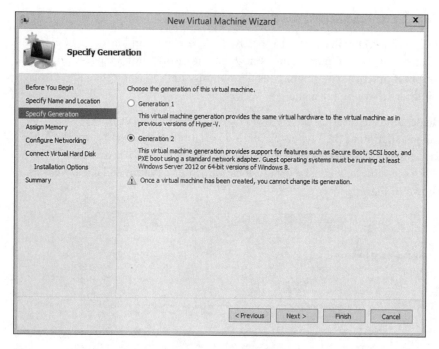

Figure 7-10   Choosing a generation of the new VM.

TIP   After the VM has been created, you cannot change its generation.

6. The next screen asks you to assign memory to your guest VM. This is the amount of RAM your guest operating system will be assigned at startup. Choosing the appropriate amount of memory depends on the operating system you plan to install, what the workload will be like for the guest server, and how much available memory you have available in your physical host.

Remember, virtual guests consume resources from the physical host. If you plan to install and run multiple virtual guests on the same physical host, you will need to supply the physical host with additional RAM so that it can be shared. In this screen you also have an option to use Dynamic Memory. This will be covered in the next section. Enter a value for **Startup memory** in megabytes (MB) as shown in Figure 7-11 and click **Next** to continue.

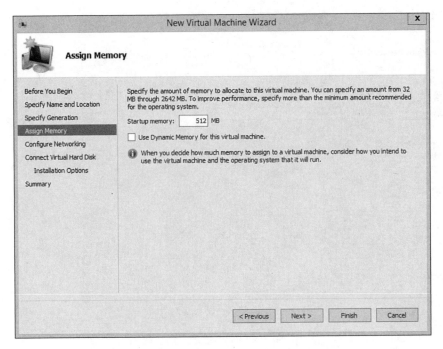

Figure 7-11   Assigning startup memory to a VM.

7. The next screen will ask you to configure Networking. Each new VM will be configured with a virtual network adapter. In this screen you might have several options to choose from depending on the network adapters installed and any existing virtual network configurations. You can even accept the default, which is Not Connected, as shown in Figure 7-12.

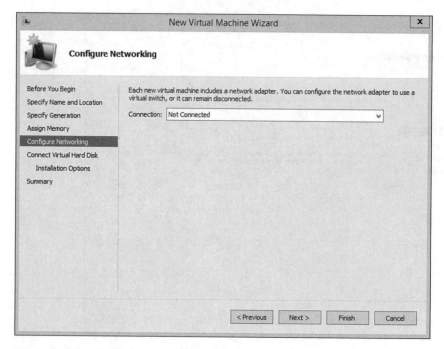

Figure 7-12   Connecting virtual network adapters.

Depending on your Hyper-V host configuration, you might have different options, but in most installations there are three basic types of connection settings:

- **Not connected:** Meaning your VM will not have its network adapter connected. Think of it as leaving your network cable unplugged.

- **Private Network:** Your network adapter is connected to a virtual switch that is accessible only by the VMs connected to the private network. This option is often helpful for lab/testing environments.

- **Specific Network Interface Card:** Your physical host might have multiple network adapters that can be connected to different networks on your physical LAN. Use this setting if you want your VM to share the same physical network. It will receive an IP address from your LAN allowing access to both local and Internet resources.

8. The next screen will enable you to connect a virtual hard disk (VHD) as shown in Figure 7-13.

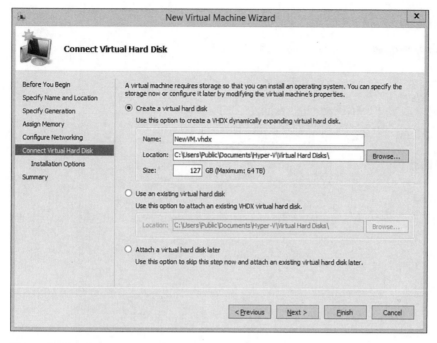

Figure 7-13   Connect a virtual hard disk to a VM.

Select one of the following options from the Connect Virtual Hard Disk screen:

- **Create a virtual hard disk:** Select this option to create a new virtual hard disk using the new dynamically expanding VHDX format. When selected, you will be able to specify a name for the VHD, select a location to store the VHD and specify the size of the VHD in gigabytes (GB).

- **Use an existing virtual hard disk:** Select this option if you have an existing VHD or VHDX formatted virtual hard disk. You will be able to browse for the location of the VHD file.

- **Attach a virtual hard disk later:** Select this option to skip this step now and attach a VHD at a later time.

9. In this example, select to **Create a virtual hard disk**, accept the default name, enter 127 GB as the size, and click **Next**. You will be presented with Installation Options as shown in Figure 7-14. At this screen, you will have the option to install an operating system later, from a bootable image file (.iso), or from a network installation server (only if you chose to connect a network adapter in step 7). Select the appropriate option and click **Next**.

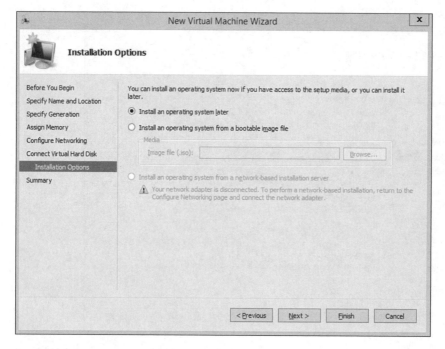

Figure 7-14   Installation options for a new VM.

CAUTION   As discussed previously, generation 2 VMs do not allow you to select physical CD/DVD drives or virtual floppy disk .vfd files as the Media type. If you require these sources, step back through the New Virtual Machine Wizard and specify to create a generation 1 VM. Only then will this screen include options for installing from physical CD/DVD or virtual floppy disk files. Remember, you will not be able to take advantage of the generation 2 benefits, and after the VM has been created, you cannot switch between generations.

10. Review the new VM settings from the summary screen and click **Finish** as shown in Figure 7-15. Hyper-V will create your new VM and prepare it for the installation media based on the settings specified in step 7.

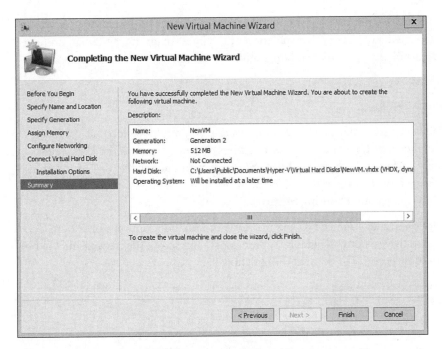

Figure 7-15   Virtual Machine Summary screen.

11. Using the Hyper-V Manager, right-click the name of the VM and then click **Connect**. This will open the Virtual Machine Connection window shown in Figure 7-16.

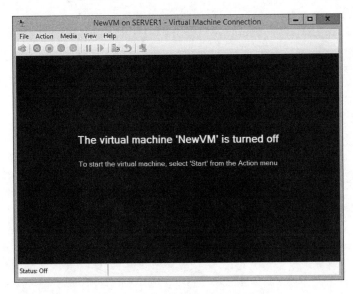

Figure 7-16   Virtual Machine Connection window.

12. Click **Start** on the Action menu. The VM will power up and locate the appropriate media to begin the installation of the guest operating system. Complete the installation as you would on a physical server.

Virtual Machine Settings

After you have installed a guest operating system, you might decide that you need to modify the virtual hardware or other settings as they pertain to the VM. You can modify VM settings from the **File** > **Settings** menu under the VM connection window shown previously in Figure 7-16, or by right-clicking on the VM name in Hyper-V Manager and choosing **Settings**.

Whether you decide you need to add memory; modify boot options; or add or remove hard drives, network adapters, processors, and so on, the Settings dialog box shown in Figure 7-17 will be your tool of choice.

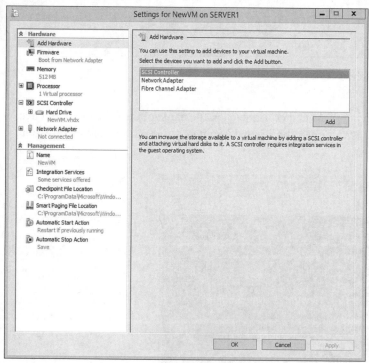

Figure 7-17   Virtual machine settings.

Table 7-4 outlines the various settings available to modify for a VM. Take notice of the differences between Generation 1 and Generation 2 VMs. After making a change, click the **Apply** button to apply the changes, and then click **OK** to close Settings.

NOTE In some cases you might need to schedule a shutdown for the VM before the settings can be modified.

Table 7-4 Virtual Machine Configurable Settings

Setting	Generation 1	Generation 2
Add Hardware	Use this setting to add devices to your VM. Devices can include SCSI controllers, network adapters, legacy adapters, Fibre Channel adapters, and video adapters. The RemoteFX 3D Video adapter hardware option is available only when the Remote Desktop Virtualization role is enabled and you have a suitable video adapter installed in the host server.	Similar to Generation 1, but you can only add SCSI controllers, network adapters, or Fibre Channel adapters. RemoteFX and legacy adapters are no longer available.
BIOS	Modify the virtual BIOS boot device startup order using floppy, CD-ROM, or IDE. The BIOS for Generation 1 VMs is based off of the American Megatrends (AMI) BIOS on an emulated Intel 440BX chipset.	N/A
Firmware	N/A	Enable/Disable Secure Boot allows you to modify the boot order between the different virtual hard disk .vhdx files or network adapter if using PXE boot.
Memory	Configure startup RAM, dynamic memory, and memory weight. Supports up to 1 TB of RAM per VM.	Same as Generation 1.

Setting	Generation 1	Generation 2
Processor	Modify the number of virtual processors based on the number of physical processors available on the computer. You might also choose to set limits on processor priority given to the VM. This is helpful when multiple VMs are competing for resources. **Note:** Under the Resource Control section of the Processor settings, you can reserve a percentage of the physical processor for the VM, allocate a percentage of total system resources, limit the processor, establish a weight/priority, or even limit the processor functionality for use with legacy operating systems such as Windows NT.	Same as Generation 1.
IDE Controller	You can add/remove hard drives and or CD/DVD drives to your IDE controller. If a hard drive is chosen, you might choose to link to a specific physical disk or add a virtual disk. Depending on your configuration, you might also choose to add controllers containing multiple hard drives. For CD/DVD, you have the option to mount to a different physical optical drive or specify an image file (.iso).	N/A
SCSI Controller	You can add/remove SCSI controllers and drives. Boot from SCSI is not supported.	You can add/remove SCSI controllers and drives. SCSI is now the standard for Generation 2 VMs (including bootable).

Setting	Generation 1	Generation 2
Legacy Network Adapter	Specify the configuration of a legacy network adapter attached to the physical host. In most cases, legacy adapters are used to perform network-based installations of the guest operating system, or if you are unable to install integration services on the guest operating system. **Tip:** It is important to note that legacy network adapters operate at slower speeds and do not support bandwidth throttling.	N/A
Network Adapter	Specify the configuration for the VM network adapter. Provides the option to configure your network adapter for different virtual switches and enable advanced features such as bandwidth management.	Same as Generation 1.
COM	Allows you to configure the virtual COM port to communicate with the physical computer. Emulates up to two serial ports that can be mapped to local named pipes and files.	No longer available by default, but can be configured via PowerShell using the `Set-VMComPort` cmdlet.
Diskette Drive	Specify a virtual floppy disk file to use (`.vfd`) if you need to boot to or access legacy floppy disks.	N/A
Management	Edit the name and notes for the VM.	Same as Generation 1.
Integration Services	Add or remove services that you want Hyper-V to offer the VM.	Same as Generation 1.
Checkpoint File Location	Specify the folder to store checkpoint files for the virtual machine. **Tip:** To change the location of the checkpoint folder, you must remove all existing checkpoints contained in the folder.	Same as Generation 1.
Smart Paging File Location	Specify the folder to store the smart paging files for the virtual machine	Same as Generation 1.

Setting	Generation 1	Generation 2
Automatic Start Action	Configure start action settings for the virtual machine that occur after the physical computer starts. Depending on the services the virtual machine provides, you may need to configure your host to automatically start one or more virtual machines. For example, if your virtual machine provides services such as file and print sharing, Windows Deployment Services, DHCP, and so on, you may want to configure the automatic startup option. Options include automatic start based on previous state, always automatically start, and delayed start.	Same as Generation 1.
Automatic Stop Action	Configure the action for the virtual machine to take when the physical computer shuts down. Options include saving the virtual machine state, turning off the virtual machine, or shut down the guest operating system.	Same as Generation 1.

NOTE   Generation 2 virtual machines no longer support Legacy Network Adapters. A standard network adapter must be used with generation 2 virtual machines. Standard network adapters are also referred to simply as "network adapters."

Additional Virtual Machine Components

To complement the various hardware components, Hyper-V includes a series of software components designed to optimize VM performance. Although there are several software components, the following list shows those relevant to the 70-410 exam:

- **Microsoft Hyper-V Virtual Machine Bus:** This component provides a channel to communicate between the VM and the host.

- **Microsoft Hyper-V Network Adapter:** Responsible for working with the physical NIC to control inbound/outbound network traffic.

- **Microsoft Hyper-V Video:** Supports and manages video data.

- **Microsoft Hyper-V Virtual Keyboard:** Supports and manages keyboard input.

- **Microsoft Hyper-V Input:** Supports and manages devices in compliance with human interface device (HID), such as a mouse.

- **Automatic Virtual Machine Activation:** Enables a Windows Server 2012 R2 guest operating system to automatically activate the product license if the host is Windows Server 2012 R2 Datacenter.

- **Enhanced Session Mode:** Covered in more detail in the next section, this feature allows Hyper-V to redirect local resources such as keyboard, video, mouse, and other local resources to the VM.

> **NOTE**   For more information, refer to "Virtual Machine Specifications for Hyper-V in Windows Server 2012 R2" at http://technet.microsoft.com/en-us/library/dn592184.aspx.

Enhanced Session Mode

Hyper-V now supports redirecting local resources such as keyboard, video, mouse, audio, printers, clipboard, USB devices, drives, plug-and-play devices, and so on to a VM session. These devices are redirected from the computer interacting with the Virtual Machine Connection window. Enhanced Session Mode uses a Remote Desktop Connection session for user inputs, but the traffic (and any traffic generated from connected peripherals) is tunneled through the virtual machine bus (VMBus). Because of this, an active network connection on the VM is not required.

This feature is enabled by default in Client Hyper-V under Windows 8.1 and disabled by default on Hyper-V in Windows Server 2012 R2.

Enhanced Session Mode is particularly useful in the following scenarios:

- Where you are required to use a smart card to sign in to the VM

- When you need to connect local peripherals such as a printer, USB drives, and so on to the VM

- When troubleshooting a VM where you are unable to use standard remote access methods

To configure Enhanced Session mode, perform the following steps:

1. Open Hyper-V Manager, select the host server, and select **Hyper-V Settings** from the Actions pane or Actions menu. Select the option for **Allow enhanced session mode** under Enhanced Session Mode Policy as shown in Figure 7-18.

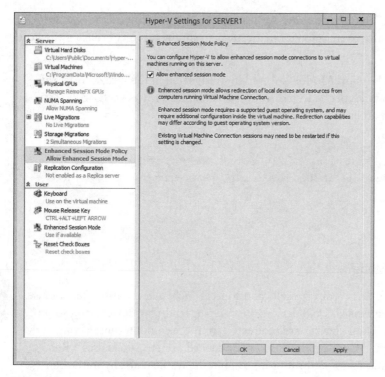

Figure 7-18   Allow Enhanced Session Mode.

2. On the guest operating system, ensure that **Remote Desktop Services** is enabled and that the account logged in with is a member of the local Remote Desktop Services group or local Administrators group.

3. Ensure that **Guest Integration Services** is enabled and running on the guest operating system.

4. When these conditions are met, use the Virtual Machine Connection window to connect to a VM. Hyper-V will use Enhanced Session Mode to interact with the guest operating system. The Virtual Machine Connection window will prompt you to configure the Display and Local Resources, as shown in Figures 7-19, 7-20, and 7-21.

   As an option, you might choose to save settings for future connections to this VM. Settings are stored in a separate file for each VM under `%appdata%\roaming\Microsoft\Windows\Hyper-V\Client\1.0`.

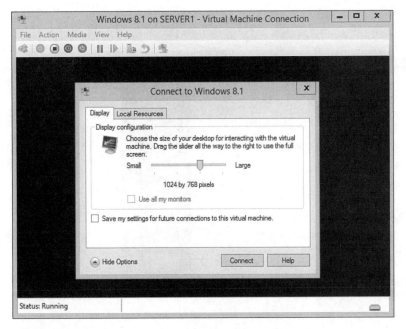

Figure 7-19   Enhanced Session Mode display settings.

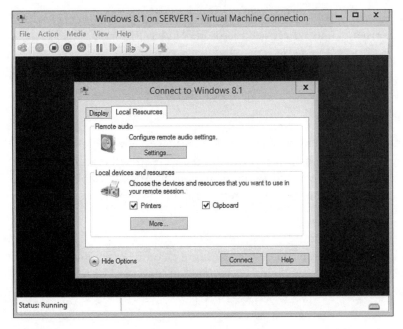

Figure 7-20   Enhanced Session Mode local resources.

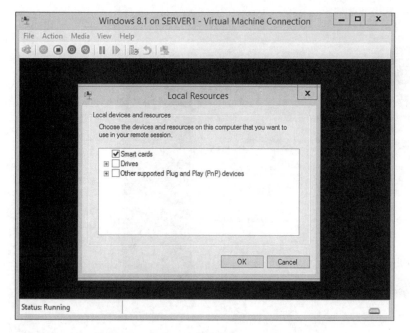

Figure 7-21   Enhanced Session Mode more local resources.

> **NOTE**   For more information, refer to "Virtual Machine Connection – Enhanced Session Mode Overview" at http://technet.microsoft.com/en-us/library/dn282274.aspx.

Managing Virtual Machines

There are several things an administrator can do to manage a VM. From the connection window shown previously in Figure 7-16, there are several tasks to choose from under the menu bar. We will focus on the Action, Media, and Clipboard items, but also know that you can configure View settings and invoke the Help menu when in need.

> **NOTE**   Depending on the current state of the VM, not all of the menu items will be available. The Clipboard menu item is not present until the VM has been started.

Virtual Machine Actions

We have already looked at the Settings under the File menu. The Action menu (see Figure 7-22) contains the following items:

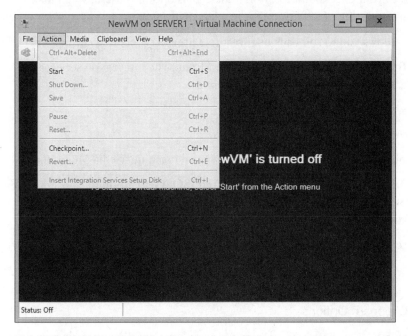

Figure 7-22 Virtual Machine Connection Action menu.

- **Ctrl+Alt+Delete:** Sends the Ctrl+Alt+Delete sequence to the VM. Use the Ctrl+Alt+End combination on the Host to send the Ctrl+Alt+Delete sequence to the VM.

- **Start:** Powers up or starts the VM.

- **Shut Down:** Initiates a guest operating system shutdown or graceful shutdown. All running processes are completed before the system powers down.

- **Turn Off:** Available after a VM is powered on, the turn off option cuts the power to the VM similar to a hard shutdown.

- **Save:** Saves the current state of the VM. Processor and memory resources are freed up and made available for other VMs.

- **Pause:** Suspends the state of a VM. Memory is not freed up, but processing resources are made available for other VMs.

- **Reset:** Resets the VM and restarts it. Similar to pressing a reset button on a physical computer. A hard restart is performed.

- **Checkpoint:** Previously known as a snapshot, a checkpoint creates a point in time backup of the VM state and configuration. The backup is written to disk. Multiple checkpoints can exist depending on available storage space assigned to your checkpoint location folder. This option is useful when making changes, testing new software, or in a lab environment.

- **Revert:** Allows you to roll back or revert to a previously created checkpoint.

- **Insert Integration Services Setup Disk:** Mounts the integration services setup disk to enable you to add/remove services.

Virtual Machine Media Options

You can complete the following tasks using the virtual machine Media Menu item:

- **DVD Drive:** Enables you to eject a mounted ISO (Generation 2), a insert a new ISO (Generation 2), or switch to a specific physical optical drive (Generation 1).

- **Diskette Drive:** Allows you to eject or mount a different virtual floppy disk (Generation 1).

Virtual Machine Clipboard Options

Available when a VM has been started, you can complete the following tasks using the VM Clipboard Menu item:

- **Type clipboard text:** Enables you to insert or paste the contents of the clipboard generated from a copy command on a different VM or the Hyper-V host.

- **Capture screen:** Enables you to capture the screen into the clipboard similarly to the print screen function. This is useful when documenting or building a testing environment.

Configuring Dynamic Memory

Introduced with Windows Server 2008 R2 SP1, Hyper-V Dynamic Memory is an option to enhance memory utilization for VMs. It helps free up memory in the pool by reallocating a portion of RAM assigned to idle or underutilized VMs. This ultimately helps reduce cost by allowing you to squeeze more VMs onto a single host. It also provides you with more flexibility to support a dynamically changing environment. You can configure dynamic memory via the following methods:

- Upon creation of a new VM

- By modifying the memory settings of an existing VM that is in a powered off state

You can enable Dynamic Memory options in the VM Settings dialog box by selecting the **Enable Dynamic Memory** check box as shown in Figure 7-23.

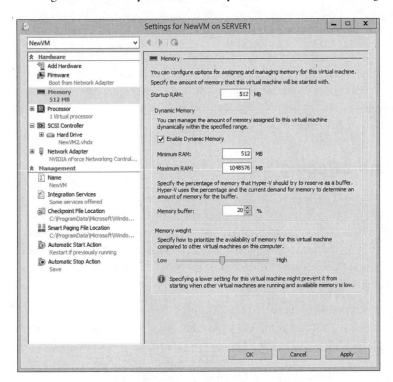

Figure 7-23   Virtual machine dynamic memory.

When a new VM is configured, you will specify initial startup memory. The startup memory is the amount of RAM required to start up and run a VM in a steady state of normal operation. Additional memory is required upon startup due to loading all drivers, services, and core operating system components. As the startup routine normalizes, you might find that the memory consumption drops and eventually levels off.

As workload increases, additional RAM is assigned to the VM based on the workload needs. The Dynamic Memory option enables you to specify a minimum and maximum amount of RAM to be allocated to the VM. The minimum memory setting is used to reserve memory for the VM. It is the minimum required for the VM.

During periods of high load, additional memory is allocated from the physical pool maximum. Under periods of low utilization, memory is released from the VM and is given back to the pool.

When multiple VMs operate under higher load, Hyper-V enables you to configure *memory buffers* and *memory weights*. A memory buffer allows you to reserve a percentage of memory for the VMs. Memory weight allows you to specify how to prioritize the use of available memory for one VM over other VMs. VMs configured with a higher memory weight will have priority over those with lower weights.

Choosing the appropriate configuration is not always a science. You might need to tweak memory settings until you find the correct combination for your environment. If you find yourself overallocating memory or that there is just too much contention for resources, you might need to consider expanding your Hyper-V cluster by adding more physical resources.

Configuring Smart Paging

In the previous section, we discussed the use of the minimum memory option. Although conserving memory is important, it does come with some challenges. In situations where you establish a minimum memory requirement that is less than the VM startup memory, you can experience difficulty restarting the VM. In some cases you can receive a failure. To resolve this, Windows Server 2012 introduced a new feature known as Smart Paging.

With Smart Paging, Hyper-V ensures that the difference between minimum and startup memory is available using a temporary page file stored on the disk. Similar to paging on a physical computer, Smart Paging comes with the risk of degraded performance. Smart Paging is a temporary process in that the page files are created only when needed and are deleted when additional memory is available.

Smart Paging is an automatic function; however, the location of the Smart Paging files can be configured under the VM Settings dialog box. Located under the Management group, the Smart Paging File Location can be altered as shown in Figure 7-24.

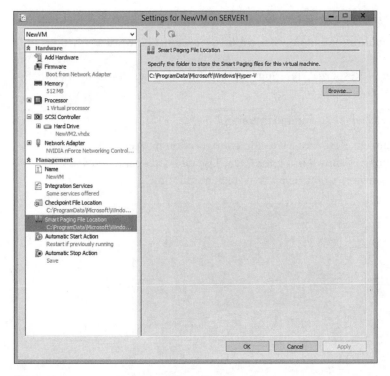

Figure 7-24 Virtual Machine Smart Paging.

Configuring Resource Metering

As you continue to grow your Hyper-V clusters, you might find it cumbersome to manage current resource usage and track historical usage. This becomes increasingly difficult as you support different segments of your business or perhaps different customers under your Hyper-V cluster. Tracking usage for each server, department, or customer historically required several tools and manual calculations. Hyper-V Resource Metering provides a simpler, streamlined solution for gathering this type of data.

Windows Server 2012 R2 enables Hyper-V administrators to retrieve historical data on the usage of VM resources. Using PowerShell Hyper-V cmdlets and API's available in the Virtualization WMI Provider, the following metrics can be gathered:

- Average CPU and memory usage
- Minimum and maximum memory usage

- Maximum disk space allocated to a VM

- Total inbound/outbound network traffic for a virtual network adapter

To enable Hyper-V Resource Metering, execute the following PowerShell cmdlets on each Hyper-V host:

1. Open PowerShell as an administrator.

2. View the current Resource Metering configuration by executing the `Get-VM` cmdlet as shown in Figure 7-25. Use `Get-VM -ComputerName [Hyper-V Server]` to retrieve a remote configuration.

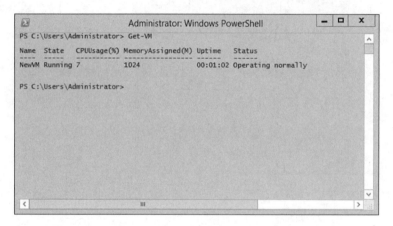

Figure 7-25 `Get-VM Configuration.`

3. Enable Resource Metering for the specific VM by typing `Enable-VMResourceMetering [VMName]`. This will begin gathering data for the specific VM. To enable Resource Metering for all VMs, pipe the `Get-VM` command to `Enable-VMResource Metering` using the command `Get-VM | Enable-VMResourceMetering`.

4. To produce a report of VM Data, execute the command `Measure-VM [VMName]` as shown in Figure 7-26.

To generate a report for all virtual machines, pipe the results from `Get-VM` to `Measure-VM`. To do this, execute the command `Get-VM | Measure-VM`.

NOTE Use the `Reset-VMResoruceMetering` cmdlets to reset statistics and the `Disable-VMResourceMetering` cmdlets to disable resource utilization statistics for one or more VMs.

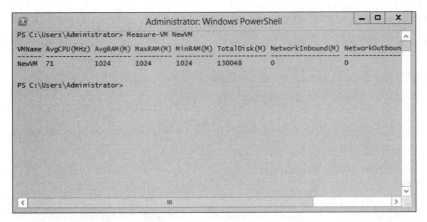

Figure 7-26   VM Resource Metering Report.

Configuring Guest Integration Services

Guest Integration Services is a suite of tools that you can install after the guest operating system has been configured. Guest Integration Services, more commonly known as *Integration Services*, is designed to optimize the performance of a VM. Upon installation, generic operating system drivers for keyboard, video, mouse, network, disk controllers, and so on are replaced with versions optimized for Hyper-V.

From a high level, Hyper-V was designed into two partitions that take on a parent/child relationship in hierarchy. To bridge the gap between the parent (host) and child (guest), Microsoft created the Hyper-V Integration Services suite. Integration Services provide the following benefits:

- **Improved peripheral responses:** Mouse response and user experience are improved when working with Virtual Machine Connection windows.

- **Improved virtual drivers:** Guests are able to interface directly with host hardware.

- **Time synchronization:** Time is synchronized between clients and the host operating systems.

- **Improved host-level logging of failed guests:** Using a heartbeat service, the host is able to detect when guest VMs lock up or fail. Heartbeats are sent to the guest, and if a response is not received, an alert is sent and logged for an administrator to take action.

- **Host-based shutdown:** Hyper-V includes a host initiated shutdown service whereby the administrator issues a shutdown command from the Hyper-V host, which then initiates a guest level shutdown. With this service, you are not required to log in to a guest VM to initiate a shutdown.

■ **Host-based snapshot backups:** Using a Shadow Copy service, Hyper-V integration services allows snapshots of guest VMs to be taken from the host. This service streamlines VM backups.

■ **Host/Guest data exchange:** Using a data exchange service, hosts and guests are able to exchange configuration information from the registry.

Table 7-5 lists the various services that make up the suite of Integration Services.

Table 7-5 Hyper-V Guest Integration Services.

Setting	Description
Operating System Shutdown Service	Responsible for managing host-initiated shutdowns of guest VMs.
Time Synchronization Service	Service used to synchronize guest time clocks with the host.
Data Exchange Service	Enables the exchange of registry information between guests and hosts.
Heartbeat Service	Maintains a heartbeat between the host and each guest VM to ensure that the guest is operational.
Backup (Volume Snapshot) Service	Manages Shadow Copy services that allow for snapshot processing for point-in-time backups. This service also works hand in hand with backup applications.

You can install Integration Services by performing the following steps:

1. Using Hyper-V Manager, power on and log on to the VM.

2. Select **Install Integration Services Setup Disk** from the Action menu. Hyper-V will mount the preconfigured ISO image on the guest CD/DVD Drive. Windows will present an AutoPlay dialog box similar to the Windows 8.1 AutoPlay dialog box shown in Figure 7-27.

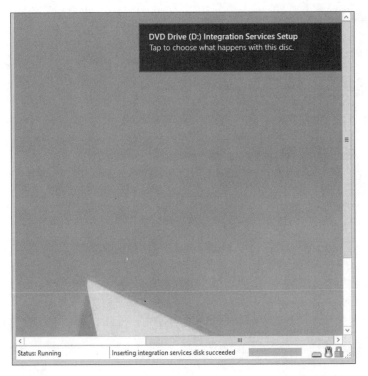

Figure 7-27   Guest Integration Services Setup Disk AutoPlay.

3. Click the option to **Install Hyper-V Integration Services**.

4. Windows will install the application and prompt you to restart the system to complete the installation. Click **Yes** to restart.

NOTE   Some operating systems, such as Windows 8.1, include a copy of Guest Integration Services so you might receive a warning that they are already installed.

5. Once restarted, your guest VM will take advantage of all integration services by default. To enable/disable specific services, use the **Settings** dialog box for the VM as shown in Figure 7-28.

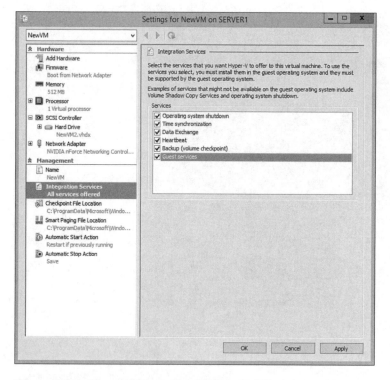

Figure 7-28   Changing Integration Services for VMs.

NOTE   Hyper-V Integration Services will appear under the Windows Services snap-in and can be managed like any other installed service.

Exam Preparation Tasks

Review All the Key Topics

Review the most important topics in the chapter, noted with the key topics icon in the outer margin of the page. Table 7-6 lists a reference of these key topics and the page numbers on which each is found.

Table 7-6 Key Topics for Chapter 7

Key Topic Element	Description	Page Number
Table 7-2	Lists the new or improved features for Hyper-V	286
List	Lists the steps to install Hyper-V	289
Paragraph	Describes the process to install Hyper-V using PowerShell	294
List	Lists the differences between generation 1 and generation 2 VMs	295
List	Lists the steps to configure a VM	296
Figure 7-17	Shows the VM settings screen	304
Table 7-4	Describes the settings that can be configured for a VM	305
Paragraph	Provides an overview of Enhanced Session Mode	309
List	Describes the various actions available for managing VMs	313
Figure 7-23	Shows the different VM memory options including enabling the dynamic memory option	315
Paragraph	Describes the benefits and configuration of Smart Paging	316
List	Provides instructions on how to enable Hyper-V Resource Metering	318
Table 7-5	Lists the Integration Services available for VMs	320
List	Lists the process to install Hyper-V Integration Services	320

Complete the Tables and Lists from Memory

Print a copy of Appendix B, "Memory Tables" (found on the CD), or at least the section for this chapter, and complete the tables and lists from memory. Appendix C, "Memory Tables Answer Key," is also on the CD and includes completed tables and lists to check your work.

Definitions of Key Terms

Define the following key terms from this chapter, and check your answers in the glossary.

Dynamic Memory, Enhanced Session Mode, Guest, Guest Integration Services, Host, Hyper-V, Hypervisor, Smart Paging, Resource Metering.

This chapter covers the following subjects:

- **Creating and Configuring Virtual Hard Disks and Differencing Drives:** This section begins with a review of virtual hard disk formats, specifically the current VHDX format. It continues to discuss the various disk types, when to use each type, and how to configure virtual hard disks using Hyper-V Manager. The section concludes with a more in-depth look at the various management tasks associated with virtual hard disks, including the importing/exporting and migration of virtual hard disk data.

- **Configuring Pass-through Disks:** This section introduces you to pass-through disks and provides instructions on how to configure them with guest virtual machines.

- **Managing Checkpoints:** Checkpoints, previously known as "Snapshots," are one of the most useful features used with virtual machines. This section shows you how to create point-in-time checkpoints and revert the virtual machine to a previous state. It also provides an overview of how Hyper-V simplifies the management of multiple checkpoints.

- **Implementing Virtual Fibre Channel Adapters:** This section describes the use of virtual fibre channel adapters and their integration with Hyper-V's Virtual SAN function. It continues to show you how to configure guest virtual machines so that they can properly communicate with one or more storage area networks.

CHAPTER 8

Creating and Configuring Virtual Machine Storage

In Chapter 3, "Configuring Windows Server 2012 R2 Local Storage," you learned how storage spaces and storage pools provide additional capabilities for local storage. Chapter 3 also provided an overview of virtual hard disks (VHDs) and how they are managed under disk management. This chapter will focus on the specifics on how to create, configure, and manage virtual machine (VM) storage for different scenarios for your Hyper-V infrastructure.

"Do I Know This Already?" Quiz

The "Do I Know This Already?" quiz enables you to assess whether you should read this entire chapter or simply jump to the "Exam Preparation Tasks" section for review. If you are in doubt, read the entire chapter. Table 8-1 outlines the major headings in this chapter and the corresponding "Do I Know This Already?" quiz questions. You can find the answers in Appendix A, "Answers to the 'Do I Know This Already?' Quizzes."

Table 8-1 "Do I Know This Already?" Foundation Topics Section-to-Question Mapping

Foundations Topics Section	Questions Covered in This Section
Creating and Configuring Virtual Hard Disks and Differencing Drives	1–4
Configuring Pass-through Disks	5
Managing Checkpoints	6–7
Implementing Virtual Fibre Channel Adapters	8

1. You need to install a new virtual disk for one of your guest operating systems. You need to ensure that you do not overcommit storage. Which virtual disk type is best for this requirement?

   a. Dynamically expanding

   b. .VHD

   c. NTFS

   d. Fixed size

2. When deleting data on a dynamically expanding disk, what is the impact to the physical host and what should you do to fix it? (Each answer represents part of the solution. Choose two.)

   a. Convert the virtual hard disk to a fixed size.

   b. Use diskpart to convert the disk to a dynamic disk.

   c. Host storage fragmentation.

   d. Delete any existing checkpoints.

   e. Compact the virtual hard disk file.

   f. Expand the virtual hard disk file.

   g. Host data corruption.

3. You need to share the contents of a virtual hard disk between multiple guest virtual machines. What can you do?

   a. Establish a parent/child relationship and configure the virtual hard disk containing the files as the parent disk.

   b. Convert the virtual hard disk to a fixed-sized disk.

   c. Establish a dynamically expanding disk relationship between the virtual machines.

   d. Add a second virtual hard disk and configure a virtual mirror.

4. Which of the following are valid virtual hard disk management tasks? (Choose all that apply.)

   a. Compact

   b. Erase

   c. Inspect

   d. Shrink

   e. Undo

   f. Update

   g. Reconnect

5. You have just installed a 2-TB disk in your Hyper-V host. You initialize the disk and ensure that it is online. You need to use this new drive as a pass-through disk on your guest virtual machine. When you configure the virtual machine storage, you are unable to add it as a pass-through disk. What should you do?

   a. Convert the disk to a fixed-size virtual disk.

   b. Upgrade the host disk to a dynamic disk.

   c. Take the disk offline on the host.

   d. Upgrade Guest Integration Services.

6. You are responsible for managing a production SQL server. Each month, you deploy necessary Windows Updates to the server. Before deploying the updates, you create a checkpoint of the virtual machine. Over time, users report that the SQL server has slowed down significantly. What should you do?

   a. Increase the processor priority for the virtual machine.

   b. Delete all old checkpoints for the virtual machine.

   c. Implement a Hyper-V host cluster.

   d. Add additional storage to accommodate additional checkpoints.

7. Your Hyper-V host is connected to two storage area networks: one for production and the other for development. The host has four HBAs installed, two connected to the production SAN and two connected to the development SAN. You need to connect your guest virtual machine to the development SAN. What do you need to do to begin this process?

   a. Disconnect the links connecting to the production SAN.

   b. Configure NIC Teaming.

   c. Create a Virtual Fibre Channel SAN configured for the development HBAs.

   d. Remove Guest Integration Services.

8. You have recently installed an application that has crashed your server. What can you do to restore the previous configuration with little downtime?

   a. Restore from tape backup.

   b. Restart with the Windows Server 2012 installation media and repair the install.

   c. Redeploy the server from a WDS image and reconfigure all applications.

   d. Revert to a previous checkpoint for the virtual machine.

Foundation Topics

Creating and Configuring Virtual Hard Disks and Differencing Drives

As you have seen previously, virtual hard disks provide several benefits and can be formatted in either the legacy .VHD format or the new .VHDX format. In this section, we will focus on the .VHDX format and how drives can be created using Hyper-V Manager. If you recall, .VHDX drives provide the following enhancements:

- Support up to 64-TB disks.

- VHDX files are created with a 4 K block size to improve performance.

- Updated structure to help prevent data loss during unintentional power failures and to improve storage footprint on the physical disk using what is known as a *trim*.

- Ability to store custom metadata about the file.

Hyper-V Manager enables you to create and manage VHDs and make them available to virtual machines. There are three types of VHDs that can be created: fixed-size, dynamically expanding, and differencing.

Fixed-Size Disks

If you recall from Chapter 3, a fixed-size disk allocates all storage for the VHD during the time in which the hard disk is created. The size of the fixed disk is specified upon creation and doesn't change unless an administrator intervenes. The following points should be considered when using fixed-sized disks:

- Fixed-sized disks offer better random write performance due to the static and predictable nature of storage allocation.

- Fixed-size disks are recommended for servers running applications with high levels of disk activities.

- Fixed-sized disks are recommended for production usage, especially when storage is pooled and available for multiple VMs.

To create a fixed-size VHD using Hyper-V Manager, perform the following steps:

1. Open Hyper-V Manager.

2. From the Actions Pane, expand **New** and select **Hard Disk**. Hyper-V Manager will open the New Virtual Hard Disk Wizard, as shown in Figure 8-1. Similarly, VHDs can be added to a preexisting VM by modifying the IDE/SCSI controller settings for the specific VM.

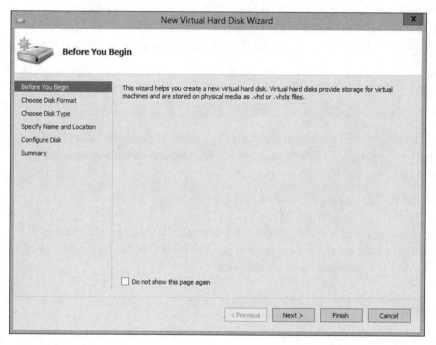

Figure 8-1   New Virtual Hard Disk Wizard.

3. Click **Next** on the Before You Begin Screen.

4. Select **VHDX** for the disk format and click **Next**.

5. Select the **Fixed-size disk type** as shown in Figure 8-2, and click **Next**.

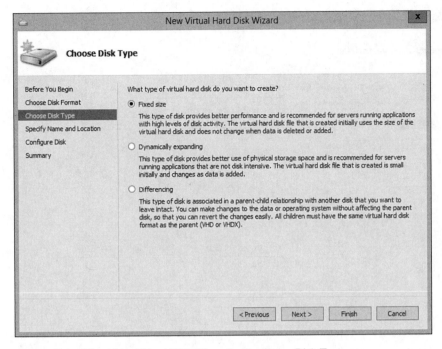

Figure 8-2   New Virtual Hard Disk Wizard—Fixed-size Disk Type.

6. Specify the name and location for the VHD file as shown in Figure 8-3. This is the location in which the VHD file and its contents will be stored. If you recall previously, this can be a local disk, storage pool, or even a network-attached storage location.

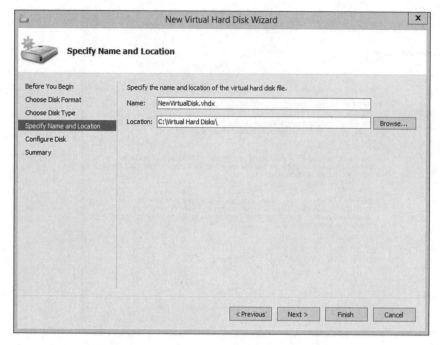

Figure 8-3   New Virtual Hard Disk Wizard—Specify Name and Location.

7. Specify how to configure the virtual disk as shown in Figure 8-4. Hyper-V enables you to create a blank virtual disk up to the maximum size available on the host, or you might choose to copy the contents of an existing physical disk or another VHD. In this example, choose to create a new blank VHD, accept the default size of 127 GB, and click **Next**.

> **NOTE**   Copying the contents of a physical disk to a new VHD provides you with a quick and easy way to make the contents of your physical disk portable. Once copied to the virtual disk, simply copy the VHD file to an external medium or transmit across the network to another server.

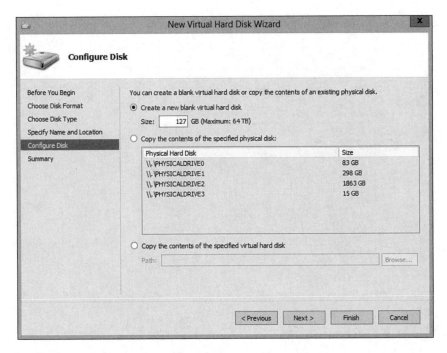

Figure 8-4   New Virtual Hard Disk Wizard—Configure Disk.

8. Click **Finish** on the Summary screen to complete the process of creating a new VHD.

9. After the VHD has been created, it can be attached to a local physical machine using the Disk Management snap-in as discussed in Chapter 3, or it can be added to a VM using the Virtual Machine Settings dialog box shown in Figure 8-5.

Figure 8-5   Add VHD to VM.

TIP   The VM NewVM shown in Figure 8-5 is a generation 1 VM. You can identify this by the presence of a BIOS, COM ports, DVD drive, and diskette drive.

Dynamically Expanding Disks

The second type of VHD available for selection is the dynamically expanding disk.
If you recall, dynamically expanding disks start out with a small footprint, typically
only a few kilobytes, and dynamically grow up to the size specified during creation.
Upon creation, the VHD header/footer allocation table information is written. The
VHD file increases as data is written and the drive expands to accommodate storing the data. The following points should be considered when using dynamically
expanding disks:

- These disks are often recommended for use with data that does not require a
  high volume of disk activities.

- Dynamically expanding disks are recommended for testing or development
  environments.

- Dynamically expanding disks introduce a risk of storage overcommit because any VM can grow to consume all available physical storage.

- When deleting data, an administrator must use a compact function to shrink the virtual disk. Failing to do this will result in physical host storage fragmentation.

To create a dynamically expanding VHD using Hyper-V Manager, follow the same steps as you would to create a fixed-size VHD except select **Dynamically expanding** for the disk type as shown in Figure 8-6.

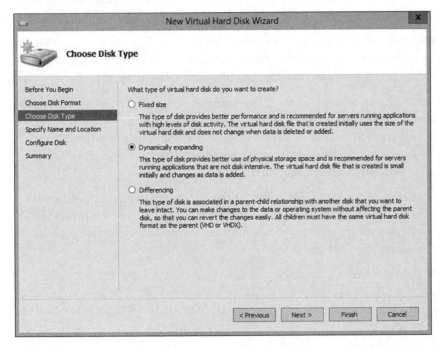

Figure 8-6   New Virtual Hard Disk Wizard—Dynamically Expanding Disk Type.

Differencing Disks

A differencing disk, also known as a *differencing drive* or *child disk*, is a VHD that is used to store changes made to a parent disk. In other words, differencing disks are the child in a parent/child relationship. When you first create a VM, you configure a VHD and install your operating system along with any applications. At some point you might decide to take advantage of differencing disks.

A differencing disk is nothing more than a separate disk that is linked to the original or parent disk. Without a parent, the differencing disk is simply a nonbootable disk with some random data on it. It is not possible to use a differencing disk without a parent. Its purpose is to track changes to the parent disk and redirect all writes to the differencing disk. Differencing disks provide the following benefits:

- Differencing disks reduce storage overhead as operating system, applications, and common data is stored only once.

- Differencing disks can be used for development purposes in that they enable you to test changes under different VMs that link up to the same parent disk configuration.

- Differencing disks provide additional control by allowing you to store write operations on different physical storage platforms. This can be used to improve performance by enabling you to spread disk I/O load.

- Because all writes occur on the differencing disk, this solution allows for quick rollback to the original system state by deleting the existing and relinking a new differencing disk to the parent disk. Similarly, alternative differencing disks can be relinked to the parent with just a few clicks. This enables you to flip between different configuration states.

- Differencing disks are helpful when deploying virtual desktop infrastructures where the operating system and core applications are stored on a parent disk and all user-specific storage, profile information, and configuration settings are stored on separate child disks.

- Differencing disks are helpful if you need to share the same data set, rather than contents, of a specific VHD file with multiple VMs. The shared data can be stored on the parent disk that is then available to all VMs configured with a differencing disk.

Differencing disks can be assigned in a couple of ways. The key point to remember is that you need a parent VHD that is configured with the appropriate settings, applications, and so on.

If you have a parent hard drive from a preconfigured VM, you might choose to copy the VHD file to a specific folder on your Hyper-V server or network share. All differencing disks created will be able to link to the parent VHD file.

If you have just created the parent VM containing the parent VHD, you might also choose to modify the parent VM and replace the parent hard disk with a new differencing disk. In this example, we will assume that we have just created a new Windows 8 parent VM containing the parent VHD. To create and configure a differencing disk for this parent disk, perform the following steps:

1. Open Hyper-V Manager.

2. Locate the parent VM to which you want to add the differencing disk and select **Settings**.

3. Click the appropriate parent hard drive under the IDE Controller, and click **New** as shown in Figure 8-7.

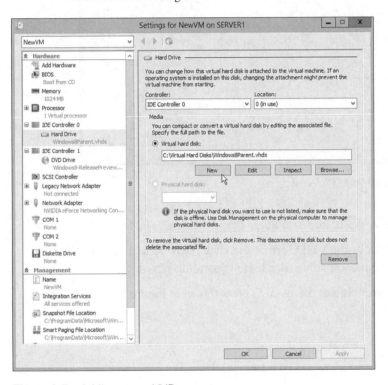

Figure 8-7   Adding a new VHD.

4. This will open the New Virtual Hard Disk Wizard shown in Figure 8-8. The New Virtual Hard Disk Wizard can also be accessed via the Actions Pane from Hyper-V Manager as shown earlier.

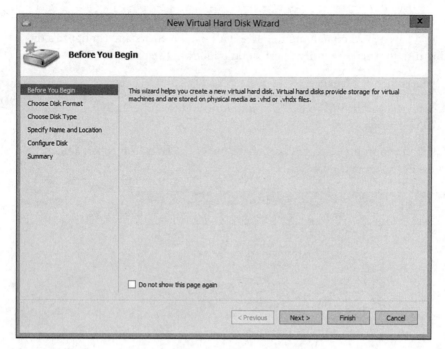

Figure 8-8   New Virtual Hard Disk Wizard.

5. Click **Next** at the Before You Begin Screen.

6. Select **VHDX** as the VHD format and click **Next**. Remember, VHDX formats are not compatible with legacy operating systems.

7. Select **Differencing** as the Disk Type as shown in Figure 8-9. Click **Next** to continue.

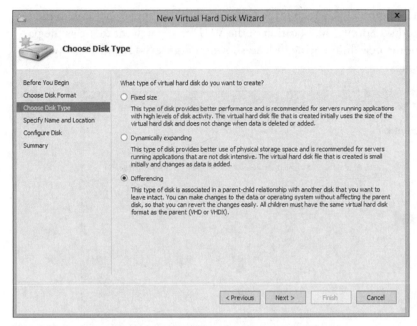

Figure 8-9   New Virtual Hard Disk Wizard—differencing disk type.

8. Specify the **Name** and **Location** for the differencing disk as shown in Figure 8-10. Click **Next** to continue.

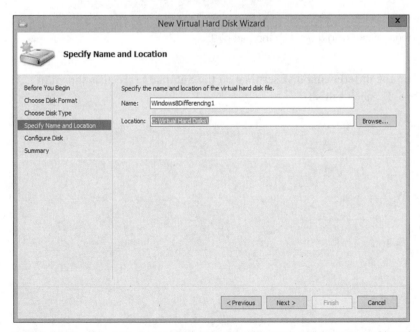

Figure 8-10   New Virtual Hard Disk Wizard—differencing disk name and location.

9. The Configure Disk screen is the key to establishing the proper link to the parent disk. Specify the Location of the VHD that you want to use as the parent for the new differencing disk, as shown in Figure 8-11, and click **Next** to continue.

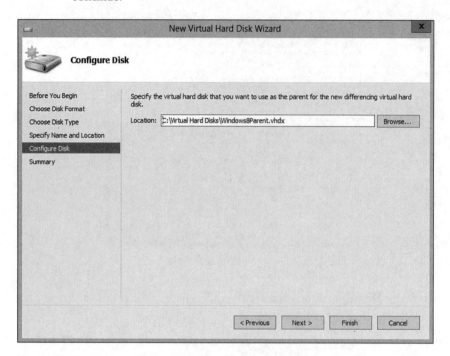

Figure 8-11   Linking differencing disks with the parent disk.

10. Confirm the differencing disk settings on the Summary screen as shown in Figure 8-12; click **Finish**.

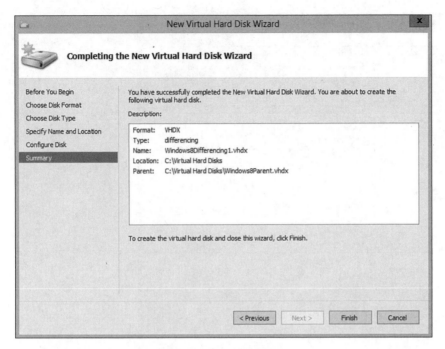

Figure 8-12   Differencing Disk Summary screen.

11. Review the updated settings for the VM and take notice that the VHD is now configured to use the newly created differencing disk as shown in Figure 8-13. Click **OK**.

Figure 8-13   VM using differencing disk.

12. Also take note that the differencing disk appears as any other VHD under File Explorer. The parent hard disk containing the operating system and applications is significantly larger at this point as shown in Figure 8-14. At this point, the differencing disk simply contains header/footer information and the link information to the parent VHD.

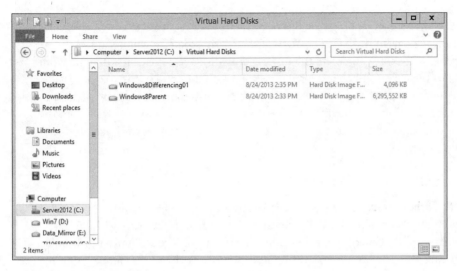

Figure 8-14   Differencing disk versus parent disk.

13. Power up the VM and begin writing data. Review File Explorer and take note that the parent VHD has not changed, but the file size for the child differencing disk has grown as shown in Figure 8-15.

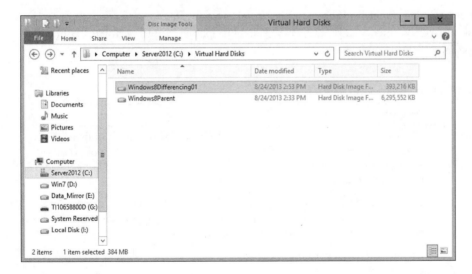

Figure 8-15   Differencing disk growth.

> **NOTE** After a differencing disk has been established, write events will no longer occur on the parent disk. Any changes such as writes/deletes will be stored on the differencing disk. If you delete the differencing disk and replace it with a new one linked to the parent, all changes will revert back to the state of the parent disk. Subsequent writes/changes will occur on the new differencing disk. If you delete files or applications on the differencing disk, these files are not removed from the parent disk and will be available again if a new differencing disk is linked to the parent.

> **NOTE** If the parent disk is destroyed or moved, the link for the differencing disk will no longer work. In addition, you can link multiple differencing disks to the same parent disk. Either create additional VMs with differencing disks or modify an existing VM and browse to a different differencing disk. This can be helpful from a development/test standpoint or if you are using a virtual desktop infrastructure where you want to deploy a standard base image but store user customizations on a separate disk.

Virtual Hard Disk Management

Over time you might find that you need to alter your VHDs, perform maintenance tasks, or verify functionality. Hyper-V Manager enables you to perform a handful of tasks as shown in Table 8-2.

Table 8-2 Hyper-V Virtual Hard Disk Management

Task	Description
Compact	Compacts the file size of a VHD. Typically helpful with the use of dynamically expanding disks. After data is deleted from the VHD, use the compact task to eliminate white space and reduce the VHD file size. This option does not alter the storage capacity defined for the VHD.
Convert	Converts a VHD between fixed-sized and dynamically expanding by copying the contents to a new VHD. The new VHD can be configured to use a different type and format than the original hard disk.
Expand	Expands the capacity of the VHD.
Merge	Merges the changes stored in a differencing disk into the parent disk or a new disk. Helpful when accepting changes after development activities.
Shrink	Reduces the storage capacity of the VHD.
Inspect	Inspects the VHD for any errors. Also used to determine the disk type and format.

Task	Description
Reconnect	After a parent-child relationship has been established, any changes to the parent disk, such as altering the path, will invalidate the relationship. If this happens, the child disk will need to reconnect to the parent. After inspecting the child disk and recognizing a failure, the reconnect option will be available.

NOTE Depending on the current configuration, formatting, or disk type selected, not all options are available.

Compacting a Virtual Hard Disk

Compacting a VHD allows you to reclaim space on the physical disk that was previously consumed by a dynamically expanding VHD. To compact a VHD, perform the following steps:

1. Open Hyper-V Manager.

2. Highlight a VM and select **Settings** under the Actions pane.

3. Select the virtual hard drive and click the **Edit** button located under the VHD path, as shown in Figure 8-16.

Figure 8-16 Edit a VHD.

> **NOTE**   If the New, Edit, or Browse button is grayed out under Windows Server 2012, ensure that the VM is powered off. Changes to the VHD cannot be made with the VHD file mounted unless you have Windows Server 2012 R2.

4. After you select to edit a VHD, the Edit Virtual Hard Disk Wizard appears as shown in Figure 8-17.

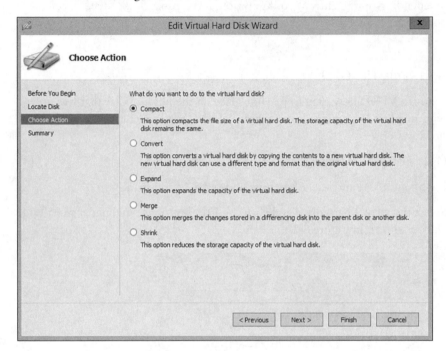

Figure 8-17   Edit Virtual Hard Disk Wizard.

5. Select **Compact** and click **Next**.

6. On the Summary screen, click **Finish** to begin the compact.

Converting a Virtual Hard Disk

Because .VHDX files are not supported by operating systems prior to Windows Server 2012, you might need to convert a VHD to .VHD format so it can be supported under an older operating system. Furthermore, this task is also helpful when converting from a fixed-sized to a dynamically expanding disk. To convert a VHD, perform the following steps:

1. Open Hyper-V Manager and pull up the **Settings** dialog box for the VM as you have done previously.

2. Click the **Edit** button under the VHD to launch the Edit Virtual Hard Disk Wizard as shown previously.

3. Select **Convert** and click **Next**.

4. If you want to change the disk format, select a new format under the **Choose Disk Format** screen shown in Figure 8-18; click **Next**.

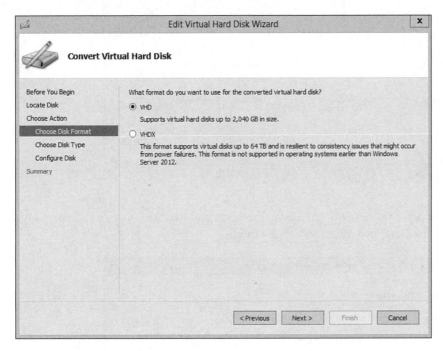

Figure 8-18   Choose Disk Format.

5. If you want to change the disk type, select a new type in the **Choose Disk Type** dialog box shown in Figure 8-19; then click **Next**.

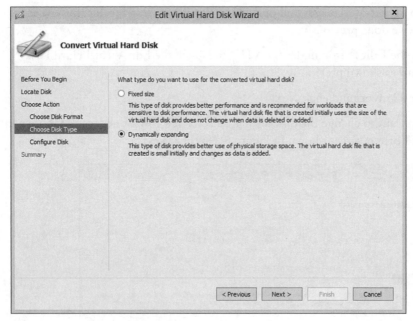

Figure 8-19   Choose Disk Type.

6. As shown in Figure 8-20, specify the name and location to store the new copy of the converted VHD and click **Finish**.

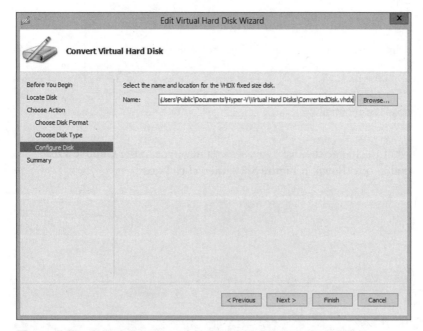

Figure 8-20   Selecting a name and location for the converted VHD.

7. Hyper-V will convert the hard disk and make it available for use. Simply modify the VM, browse for the newly converted file, and apply the changes to the Settings dialog box.

Expanding a VHD

Hyper-V Manager provides the capability to expand the capacity of VHDs. To expand a VHD, perform the following steps:

1. Open Hyper-V Manager and pull up the **Settings** dialog box for the VM as you have done previously.

2. Click the **Edit** button under the VHD to launch the Edit VHD Wizard as shown previously.

3. Select **Expand** and click **Next**.

4. Enter a new size to expand the virtual disk to on the Configure Disk screen as shown in Figure 8-21. Click **Next** to continue.

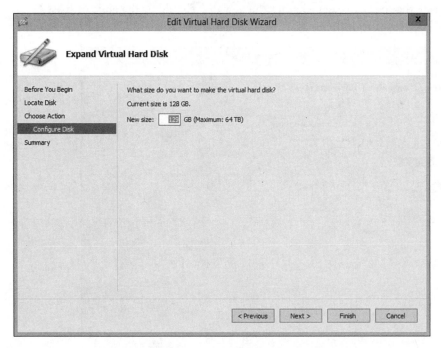

Figure 8-21   Expanding a VHD.

5. On the Summary screen, click **Finish** to complete the operation.

Merging Differencing Disks with Parent Disk

If you are using differencing disks for testing or perhaps as part of a virtual desktop infrastructure, you might need to commit the changes back to the parent disk. This will essentially update the parent disk and establish an updated master image. Or, perhaps you want to create a new version of the parent disk and keep the old one. In either case, Hyper-V Manager enables you to merge changes with the parent or a new disk by performing the following steps:

1. Open Hyper-V Manager and pull up the **Settings** dialog box for the VM as you have done previously.

2. Click the **Edit** button under the VHD to launch the Edit VHD Wizard as shown previously.

3. Select **Merge** and click **Next**.

4. On the Merge Changes from Differencing Disk screen, select either the option to merge **To the parent VHD** or to merge **To a new VHD** as shown in Figure 8-22. If you choose the new VHD option, specify the location to store the file and select whether the new disk should by dynamic or fixed. Click **Next** to continue.

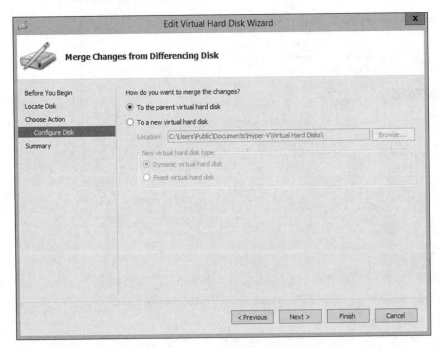

Figure 8-22   Merging a differencing hard disk.

5. On the Summary screen, click **Finish** to complete the operation.

> **NOTE**   Depending on how large the parent disk is and how much data has been written to the differencing disk, it can take some time to merge the changes.

Shrinking VHDs

To shrink the overall capacity of a VHD, perform the following steps:

1. Open Hyper-V Manager and pull up the **Settings** dialog box for the VM as you have done previously.

2. Click the **Edit** button under the VHD to launch the Edit VHD Wizard as shown previously.

3. Select **Shrink** and click **Next**.

4. On the Summary screen, click **Finish** to complete the operation.

Inspecting VHDs

From time to time, you might want to check the VHD for any errors. You might also need to identify the disk type or formatting type. Hyper-V provides an Inspect function where you can view the properties of the VHD from within Hyper-V. To inspect a VHD, perform the following steps:

1. Open Hyper-V Manager and pull up the **Settings** dialog box for the VM as you have done previously.

2. Instead of using the Edit button, click the **Inspect** button under the VHD to inspect the VHD for errors or to retrieve information. Hyper-V will inspect the VHD and present a dialog box showing the VHD Properties, as shown in Figure 8-23. Any errors will be displayed in the dialog box.

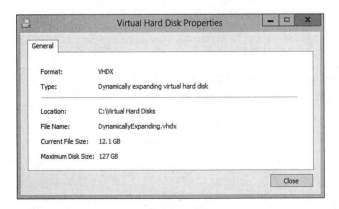

Figure 8-23   VHD properties after inspecting it.

> **NOTE**   In the event that the parent hard disk in a parent/child relationship becomes inaccessible or moved, the inspect function will warn you that the VHD chain is broken. You will need to perform a reconnect on the differencing disk to relink the differencing disks to the parent.

Reconnecting a Differencing Disk to the Parent Disk

To reconnect a differencing disk to a parent disk, perform the following steps:

1. Open Hyper-V Manager and pull up the **Settings** dialog box for the VM as you have done previously.

2. Click the **Inspect** button under the VHD section. A failed link to the parent VHD will result in an error message, including the option to reconnect, as shown in Figure 8-24.

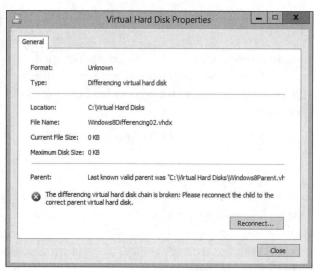

Figure 8-24   Differencing disk with a broken chain to the parent disk.

3. Click the **Reconnect** button to launch the Edit VHD Wizard as shown in Figure 8-25. The wizard will step you through reconnecting the VHD.

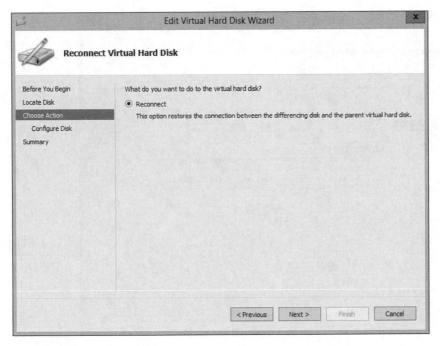

Figure 8-25   Reconnect the VHD.

4. Click **Next** on the Reconnect VHD screen.

5. Browse to the location of the appropriate parent VHD as shown in
   Figure 8-26. Hyper-V will present you with the previously known location of
   the parent virtual disk, including the filename. Browse to the correct location
   and click **Next**. If the parent disk ID is not the original parent for the differencing disk, the IDs might not match. To force a reconnect, click the **Ignore
   ID mismatch** check box and accept the risk of corrupt data or data loss. Use
   this only when no other options exist.

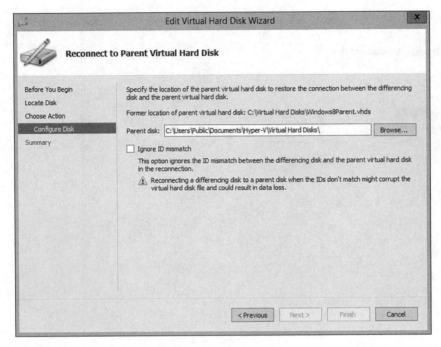

Figure 8-26   Reconnect VHD—Specify Location.

6. Click **Finish** on the Summary screen to complete the operation.

7. To confirm functionality, click the **Inspect Parent** button as illustrated in Figure 8-27.

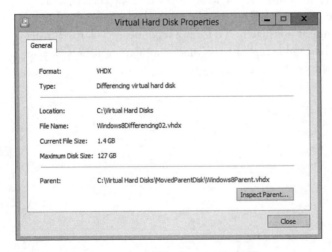

Figure 8-27   Reconnect VHD—Inspect Parent.

Hard Disk Sharing

Hard disk sharing is a new feature released with Windows Server 2012 R2. In the new version, Hyper-V enables you to share a VHD between multiple VMs. Sharing a VHD provides the ability to enable shared storage for guest VM failover. This is particularly helpful for providing high availability (HA) to virtual production servers such as SQL or file servers.

Previously, clustering occurred at a higher level and VMs had to rely on the physical storage and server infrastructure. To take advantage of shared hard disks, the following requirements must be met:

- VHDs must use the .VHDX format for the shared data drive.

- The operating system must be Windows Server 2012 or 2012 R2.

- Windows Server 2012 R2 Integration Services must be installed on the guest.

- Although technically not required, you should establish a Hyper-V failover host cluster to ensure HA.

NOTE   Guest clusters and shared VHDs fall outside of the current scope of the 70-410 exam. For a complete deployment guide, refer to "Deploy a Guest Cluster Using a Shared Virtual Hard Disk" at http://technet.microsoft.com/en-us/library/dn265980.aspx.

Storage Quality of Service

A new feature in Windows Server 2012 R2 is Storage Quality of Service (Storage QoS). Hyper-V now includes the ability to control and monitor disk performance, which is particularly useful in cloud implementations.

Storage QoS enables you to specify maximum input/output operations per second (IOPS) for a VHD. This ensures that no single VM overloads the disk infrastructure with read/write operations. Similarly, a low end threshold can be established to alert an administrator that the VM is not operating as fast as it could from a disk perspective.

To configure Storage QoS, perform the following steps:

1. Open Hyper-V Manager and pull up the **Settings** dialog box for the VM as you have done previously.

2. Expand the **SCSI Controller** and select **Advanced Features** under the Hard Drive.

3. In the Advanced Features pane, click **Enable Quality of Service management** as shown in Figure 8-28.

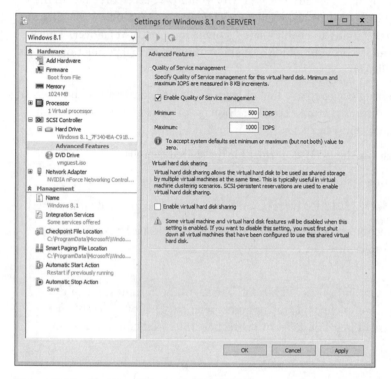

Figure 8-28   Enabling Storage Quality of Service.

4. Specify a **Minimum IOPS value** and a **Maximum IOPS value** other than 0, which is the default. You might need to refer to the disk storage vendor specifications to determine maximum IOPS supported by each drive in the array.

5. Click **Apply** and then click **OK**.

NOTE   For more information on Storage QoS, refer to "Storage Quality of Service for Hyper-V" at http://technet.microsoft.com/en-us/library/dn282281.aspx.

Importing, Exporting, Migrating, and Replicating Virtual Machines

In addition to managing VHDs, Hyper-V provides more advanced data and VM-level tasks, including these:

- **Moving VMs between Hyper-V hosts:** If you need to perform maintenance on a particular host, Hyper-V allows you to move VMs to different hosts.

- **Moving VM storage:** This enables you move the VM data, checkpoints, VHDs, and so on to one or more locations locally or on a completely separate shared storage medium.

- **Hyper-V replica:** This feature allows you to replicate your VMs to standby hosts for disaster recovery or migration situations.

- **Import/Export VMs:** This enables you to import/export preconfigured VMs between hosts.

Moving Virtual Machines and Virtual Machine Storage

To move a VM, the Hyper-V Live Migration service must be enabled and configured. Live Migration requires a Hyper-V host cluster for optimal configuration; however, it can be configured without a failover cluster. The purpose of Live Migration is to enable you to move a running VM between servers running Hyper-V. The kicker to this is that the move occurs without any noticeable downtime or impact to the users.

To configure Live Migrations, modify the Hyper-V Settings on Hyper-V hosts using the **Hyper-V Settings** link under the Actions menu. You can configure global settings for the Hyper-V host as shown in Figure 8-29. Also available on this menu are configurable options for Storage Migrations and Replication.

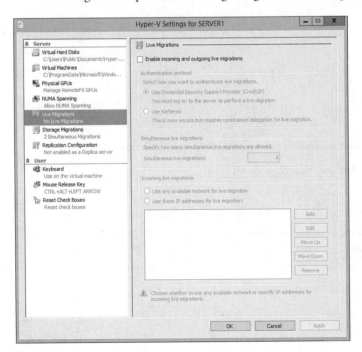

Figure 8-29   Hyper-V Host Settings—Live Migrations.

Hyper-V Live Migrations and movement of storage are covered on the 70-412 exam, "Configuring Advanced Windows Server 2012 Services." To launch the Move Wizard, perform the following steps:

1. Open Hyper-V Manager and select the VM you want to move.

2. Click the **Move** link on the Actions pane. This will open the Move Wizard.

3. Click **Next** to continue.

4. Select the appropriate move action you want to perform as indicated in Figure 8-30.

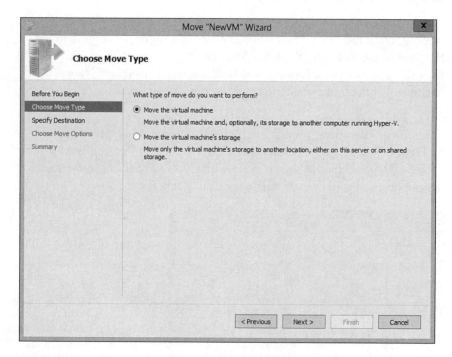

Figure 8-30   Move Virtual Machine Wizard.

NOTE   For more information on Live Migrations, refer to "Virtual Machine Live Migration Overview" at http://technet.microsoft.com/en-us/library/hh831435.aspx.

Hyper-V Replica Feature

Although it's covered on the 70-412 exam, it is good to know that the Hyper-V Replica feature enables administrators to replicate VMs from one host to another. This is particularly useful in disaster recovery or business continuity situations. You can configure Hyper-V Replica to replicate the VM from your primary datacenter host to a standby datacenter host across a WAN link.

Once configured, Hyper-V Replica keeps track of all write operations on the primary VM. As data is written, the service replicates changes to the Replica server via HTTP.

NOTE   For more information on the Hyper-V Replica Feature, refer to "Step 1: Prepare to Deploy Hyper-V Replica"" at http://technet.microsoft.com/en-us/library/jj134153.aspx.

Import/Export Virtual Machines

If you decide to move a VM to a different host or perhaps need to distribute a copy of a configured VM, Hyper-V Manager provides you with a more manual process for doing so. To export a VM, perform the following steps:

1. Shut down the guest and power off the VM if it is currently running.

2. Open **Hyper-V Manager** and select the VM you want to export.

3. Using the Actions pane, select **Export** to open the Export Virtual Machine dialog box.

4. Specify the path to the location on the disk to which you want to export the VM, as shown in Figure 8-31.

Figure 8-31   Exporting the VM.

5. Click the **Export** button to begin the export process. Hyper-V will create a subfolder with the name of the VM and begin to copy the VM and its data to the directory. Review the progress by viewing the **Status** bar under the center pane of Hyper-V Manager.

6. When the export reaches 100%, you will notice multiple folders placed in the export folder as shown in Figure 8-32. One folder will contain all existing checkpoints for the VM; another folder will contain the VHDs; and the last folder will contain the XML file containing the VM configuration settings.

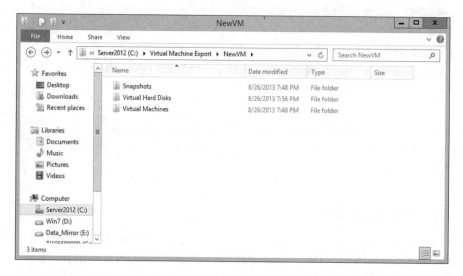

Figure 8-32   Folders containing exported VM data.

> **TIP**   Windows Server 2012 R2 now enables you to export a VM while it is still powered and running. This is useful in situations where you might need to back up the VM or clone it for testing and development purposes.

To import a VM, perform the following steps:

1. Launch **Hyper-V Manager**.

2. From the far-left pane, click the Hyper-V server into which you want to import the VM.

3. Using the Actions pane, click **Import Virtual Machine** to launch the Import Virtual Machine Wizard shown in Figure 8-33.

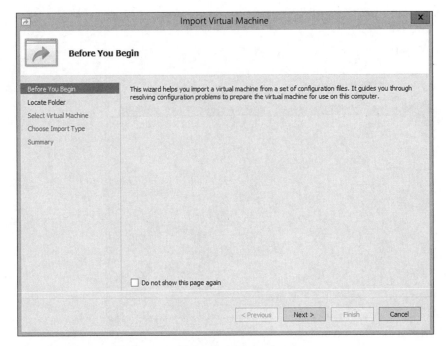

Figure 8-33   The Import Virtual Machine Wizard.

4. At the Before You Begin screen, click **Next**.

5. On the Locate Folder screen, specify or browse to the folder containing the VM to import and click **Next**.

6. On the Select Virtual Machine Screen, select the VM to import as illustrated in Figure 8-34. If you have multiple VMs that were previously exported into a central folder, you will see all available VMs. Click **Next** to continue.

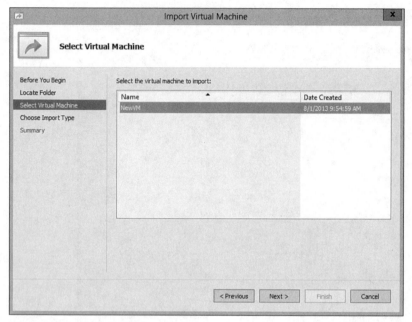

Figure 8-34 Select the VM to import.

7. From the Choose Import Type screen, select the appropriate method for importing the VM as shown in Figure 8-35.

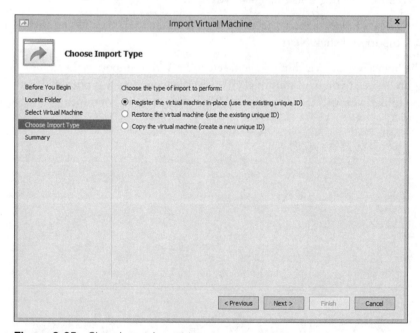

Figure 8-35 Choosing an import type.

All VMs must have a unique ID, much like a SID with Active Directory. Select **Register the virtual machine in-place (use the existing unique ID)** if you simply need to reconnect a VM and its configuration to Hyper-V Manager. This is helpful if Hyper-V Manager loses its connection/registration with the VM. Select **Restore the virtual machine (use the existing unique ID)** if you want Hyper-V to re-register the VM and restore the data. Select **Copy the virtual machine (create a new unique ID)** if you want to create a copy of the VM. This is helpful in situations where you treat the source files as a template. Click **Next** to continue.

8. If you choose to restore a copy, accept the default storage location or specify a destination for the configuration, checkpoint, and Smart Paging data as shown in Figure 8-36. To alter the default locations, select the checkbox to **Store the VM in a different location** and then modify the paths appropriately. Click **Next** to continue.

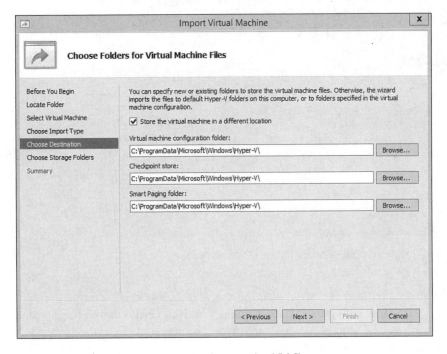

Figure 8-36   Choosing a destination for restoring VM files.

> **NOTE**   The default location for storing VMs, checkpoints, configurations, and Smart Paging settings can be specified for each Hyper-V host by modifying the Hyper-V Settings under the Actions pane of Hyper-V Manager.

9. When restoring a copy, you will be asked to choose a location to store the VHDs as shown in Figure 8-37. Accept the default server location or specify a new location on the Choose Folders to Store VHDs screen. Click **Next** to continue.

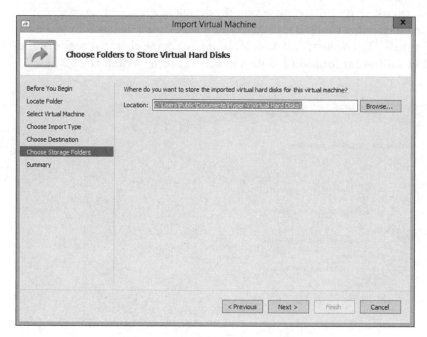

Figure 8-37   Choosing a destination for restoring VM hard disks.

10. From the Summary screen, confirm source files to import and destination folders to store configuration settings and VM data. Click **Finish** to begin the import process. Once imported, the VM will be accessible from the Hyper-V Server Manager console.

Configuring Pass-Through Disks

Pass-through disks are physical disks mapped through Hyper-V and granted exclusively for use with guest VMs. The guest VM is granted full access to the storage while the Hyper-V server sees the storage as an *offline* raw storage entity that is not assigned any drive letter. The offline state enables the guest to own the storage.

Pass-through disks are created using a couple of methods. They can be configured using locally attached storage connected to the Hyper-V host, or they can be configured using a Hyper-V host provisioned with a storage area network (SAN) logical unit (LUN). In either case, the Hyper-V server treats the storage the same and exclusive access is given to the specific guest VM.

When using pass-through disks, the following points should be considered:

- Pass-through disks tend to provide increased performance due to guests accessing raw disks without the added overhead of the virtualization layer. This is especially helpful for servers that demand high levels of I/O activities such as an SQL server.

- Pass-through disks are often more useful when you have large volumes of data. There are more options with respect to backups available for pass-through disks.

- Pass-through disks cannot be used with removable drives.

- Checkpoints and other host-based Shadow Copy providers, including those included with third-party backup providers, do not support pass-through disks. Traditional file-level backups are required to protect data stored on pass-through disks.

- Live Migrations without user impact are not possible with pass-through disks.

- Pass-through disks might put an increased workload on the VM.

To configure a pass-through disk, perform the following steps:

1. Install and configure additional storage on the Hyper-V host. Depending on your requirements, this can be additional disks added to the host, an external directly attached storage array, or even network-attached storage or SAN.

2. Using Disk Management, initialize the disk if it reports as being Not Initialized. This can be done by right-clicking the disk and selecting **Initialize Disk**.

3. Establish a partition table using MBR or GPT as we have seen previously.

4. Once initialized, ensure that the disk is in an Offline state and is not assigned any drive letters as shown in Figure 8-38.

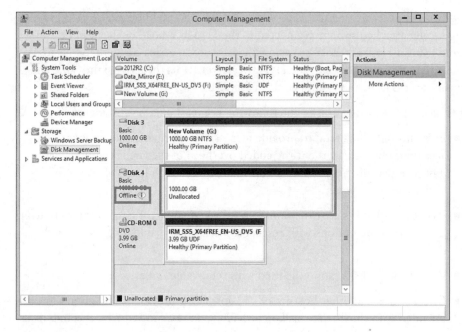

Figure 8-38   Pass-through disk offline.

5. Launch Hyper-V Manager and open the **Settings** for the VM to which you want to add the pass-through disk.

6. Add a new hard drive instead of creating a new VHD or browsing for one. Select the radio button for **Physical hard disk** as shown in Figure 8-39. Select the physical disk that corresponds to the pass-through disk that was added to the Hyper-V Server and click **Apply**.

7. Hyper-V will add the pass-through disk to the VM. The pass-through disk will appear like any other drive under the guest VM. Import the drive and assign a drive letter like you would any other disk.

NOTE   In this example, a VHD was used to simulate a pass-through disk. To properly use a pass-through disk, you will need to use local storage or network-attached storage. The drive must be in an offline state for the guest to receive exclusive access to it.

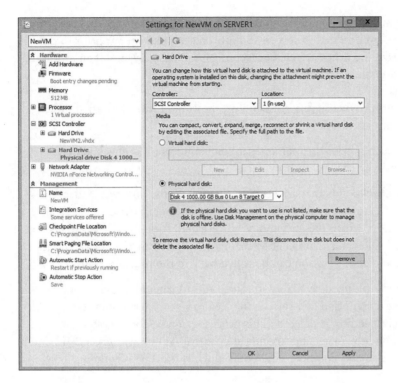

Figure 8-39   Adding a physical hard disk to a VM.

Managing Checkpoints

Virtual machine checkpoints (previously known as *snapshots*) are used to capture the state, data, and configuration of a VM. They are used to quickly revert to a previous state of the VM with just a few clicks. With the release of Windows Server 2012, Hyper-V enables you to merge checkpoints and apply them while the VM is running with little impact to the users. This is possible via the new Live Migration feature. Live Migration must be enabled and configured appropriately to take advantage of minimal to no downtime. In previous versions of Windows Server, the VM would pause when reverting to a previous checkpoint. These capabilities have been carried forward in Windows Server 2012 R2.

Depending on available storage, you can create multiple checkpoints at different points in time. The ability to restore the state of a VM helps in the following scenarios:

- For development/testing environments that require an "undo" function.

- As a safety net when deploying Windows Updates, applications, or configuration changes to production servers. Simply create a checkpoint prior to the change; make the necessary changes; confirm functionally; and if an unwanted result occurs, simply revert to the previous state.

While checkpoints provide significant benefits, they might introduce the following challenges to your organization:

- Raw disks such as pass-through disks are not supported by checkpoints or similar third-party snapshot providers.

- The more checkpoints that are created, the greater the disk I/O is for the VM. This is because Hyper-V needs to keep track of all data changes from the point in time at which the checkpoint was created. It essentially has to keep a journal with all events that occur so that each change can be undone and the VM, data, and configuration can be rolled back to the previous state.

- If checkpoints fill up all available storage, the VM can enter a saved state to prevent data corruption. To restore the VM to a normal running state, checkpoints might need to be deleted. This process can take considerable time depending on how many checkpoints are present. Windows Server 2012 and 2012 R2 enable checkpoints to be removed while the VM is running.

TIP   To change the default checkpoint folder for a VM, modify the VM settings and specify a new path under the Checkpoint File Location management setting.

Creating and Reverting to a Previous Checkpoint

Checkpoints can be created with just a few clicks. Similarly, reverting a VM to the last or previous state is also an easy task. To create and revert to a previous checkpoint, perform the following steps:

1. To create a checkpoint, select the VM in Hyper-V Manager.

2. Using the Actions pane, select the **Checkpoint** link. Hyper-V will create a checkpoint and store the data in the default checkpoint folder specified for the VM.

NOTE   To change the default checkpoint folder for a VM, modify the VM settings and specify a new path under the Checkpoint File Location management setting.

3. To revert the VM to the previous checkpoint, select the **Revert** link under the Actions pane for the VM.

4. Hyper-V will ask you to confirm the revert process. Click **Revert** to continue.

Managing Multiple Checkpoints

Depending on available storage, multiple—up to 50—checkpoints can be stored for each VM. You even have the ability to create snapshot trees. For example, you can create top-level checkpoints for major changes and sub-snapshots under each branch. To organize checkpoints and provide a process for managing them, Hyper-V Manager displays a listing of checkpoints in a hierarchical tree format in the center pane as shown in Figure 8-40.

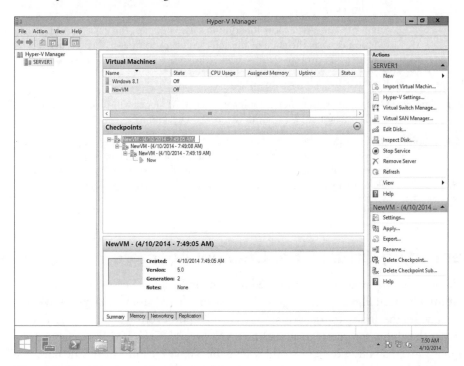

Figure 8-40   Virtual machine checkpoints.

From here, you can select a checkpoint and select one of several options under the Actions pane for the selected checkpoint. Table 8-3 provides an overview of the actions available.

Table 8-3   Hyper-V Checkpoint Pane Tasks

Task	Description
Settings	Displays information contained within the checkpoint file. This includes all hardware, management, and configuration settings for the VM.
Apply	Applies the selected checkpoint to the VM. Hyper-V Manager will ask you to select one of the following settings when applying the snapshot: ■ **Take Checkpoint and Apply:** Creates a new checkpoint before applying or reverting to the selected one ■ **Apply:** Does not create a new checkpoint, but simply applies and reverts to the selected one ■ **Cancel:** Cancels the operation and does not apply the selected checkpoint
Export	Similar to the VM export function discussed earlier, the export checkpoint function exports the state of the selected checkpoint as a VM. Hyper-V Manager will prompt you to specify the location for the exported VM.
Rename	Renames the selected checkpoint.
Delete Checkpoint	Deletes the selected checkpoint. Hyper-V Manager will prompt you to confirm whether you want to delete the checkpoint.
Delete Checkpoint Subtree	Deletes the selected checkpoint and the entire subtree. Hyper-V Manager will prompt you to confirm the selection. This action can be useful in situations where checkpoints fill up the available storage. With just a few clicks, many or all checkpoints can be deleted to free up space.

Implementing Virtual Fibre Channel Adapters

As discussed earlier, one of the supported features and, in some cases, a requirement for advanced Hyper-V strategies is the use for shared storage. Hyper-V Manager provides the ability to use virtual fibre channel ports within a guest VM. This provides the ability for guests to access the SAN directly. Each VM fibre channel adapter is given an unique ID or world wide name (WWN) and world wide port name (WWPN), which is used to identify the adapter and grant access to the presented storage on the storage network.

The integration with fibre channel adapters also enables advanced features such as guest level clustering, live migration (discussed previously), virtual SANs, and multipath I/O (MPIO).

NOTE   The Virtual Fibre Channel function supports the use of the N_Port ID Virtualization (NPIV) T11 standard for sharing physical ports between multiple VMs.

Virtual SAN Support

Virtual SAN Support for Hyper-V is used to bridge the gap between guest VMs and the physical SAN. The purpose is to identify physical links associated with a SAN; group them under a single named entity, known as a virtual SAN; and configure virtual fibre channel adapters to use the named entity.

Because hosts might be connected to one or more SANs, Hyper-V enables you to associate a virtual fibre channel adapter with one or more physical connections using the virtual SAN. For example, you could have one Hyper-V host with four host bus adapters (HBAs). An *HBA* is essentially a network interface card for storage networks. In this scenario, the Hyper-V host could have two physical links connected to a production SAN and two physical links connected to a development SAN. If you want Guest1 to only access the production SAN, then you would need to create a virtual SAN named Production, for example. The "Production" virtual SAN would then be linked and associated with the two physical HBAs physically connected to the production SAN.

Each storage vendor has a specific process that you must follow to configure the storage for the host. Although the specifics are out of scope for the 70-410 exam, use the following steps as a guideline to enable communications between the guest and SAN:

1. As a prerequisite, ensure that the physical HBA is installed in the host per the manufacturer's installation procedure. Ensure that all physical connections are made and that the host is authorized to communicate with the SAN as per the SAN configuration procedures.

2. Launch **Hyper-V Manager**.

3. Highlight the Hyper-V host containing the VMs.

4. From the Actions pane, select **Virtual SAN Manager**. This will launch the Virtual SAN Manager dialog box for the host as shown in Figure 8-41.

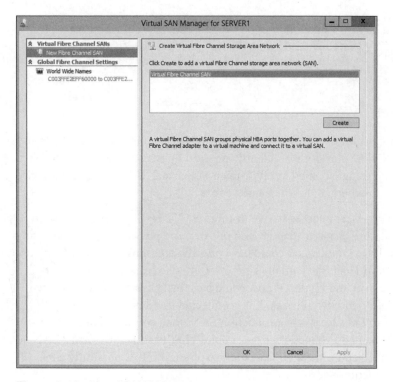

Figure 8-41   Virtual SAN Manager.

5. Enter the name for the virtual SAN and select the HBAs associated with the virtual SAN. If you do not see any HBAs listed, refer to Step 1 and ensure that all physical connections have been made and that the drivers are installed properly.

6. Use the WWNs and WWPNs to identify the HBAs and physical ports that the host uses to connect to the storage network.

7. When the virtual SAN is configured, add a fibre channel adapter to the VM. To do this, open the **Settings** dialog box for the VM and choose to add a new fibre channel adapter under **Hardware**.

8. Once installed, configure the virtual fibre channel adapter to connect to the appropriate virtual SAN as shown in Figure 8-42.

9. Power up the VM and complete the process to initialize and format the newly recognized disk. Windows Server 2012 R2 will see the new disk as if it were a local disk.

Figure 8-42   Installing a virtual fibre channel adapter.

Advanced Fibre Channel Adapter Features

Hyper-V and Windows Server 2012 R2 accommodate enterprise-class fibre channel features, which include the following:

- **Multipath I/O:** Windows Server 2012 R2 provides the ability to use multipath I/O. MPIO is used to provide a level of redundancy between the VMs and the storage network. Multiple fibre channel ports on the host connect to the storage network. Guest VMs can be configured to use multiple virtual fibre channel adapters to increase throughput and take advantage of the multiple paths from the host to the storage network.

- **Offload Data Transfer:** Enterprise-class storage systems include the ability to offload specific data transfer tasks to separate paths to the guest. For example, the offload function can be used in situations where checkpoints initiated by the host actually transfer data within the SAN using the storage processors on the SAN as opposed to the resources on the guest/host or even the production network. Hyper-V 2012 R2 is aware and fully supports the offload data transfer technology.

Exam Preparation Tasks

Review All the Key Topics

Review the most important topics in the chapter, noted with the key topics icon in the outer margin of the page. Table 8-4 lists a reference of these key topics and the page numbers on which each is found.

Table 8-4   Key Topics for Chapter 8

Key Topic Element	Description	Page Number
List	Describes the considerations for using fixed-size disks	329
List	Shows you how to create a fixed-size disk	330
List	Describes the considerations for using dynamically expanding disks	334
List	Shows you how to create a dynamically expanding disk	336
List	Describes the benefits of differencing disks	337
List	Shows you how to create and assign differencing disks	337
Table 8-2	Lists the management tasks for VHDs	344
Figure 8-24	Shows you the result of a broken link for differencing disks	352
List	Lists the steps to configure Storage Quality of Service	355
List	Shows you how to configure a pass-through disk	365
Table 8-3	Lists the various tasks available for managing checkpoints	370
Paragraph	Describes a scenario to explain the use of a virtual SAN	371
Figure 8-42	Installing a virtual fibre channel adapter	373

Complete the Tables and Lists from Memory

Print a copy of Appendix B, "Memory Tables" (found on the CD), or at least the section for this chapter, and complete the tables and lists from memory. Appendix C, "Memory Tables Answer Key," is also on the CD and includes completed tables and lists to check your work.

Definitions of Key Terms

Define the following key terms from this chapter, and check your answers in the glossary.

Checkpoint, Dynamically Expanding Disk, Differencing Disk, Fixed-size Disk, Host Bus Adapter, Multipath I/O, Pass-through disk, Storage QoS, Virtual Fibre Channel Adapter, Virtual SAN.

This chapter covers the following subjects:

- **Network Virtualization Using Hyper-V:** This section begins with an overview of Hyper-V Network Virtualization (HNV). It introduces the concept of cloud computing and discusses the various components of HNV. The section concludes with step-by-step instructions on creating and configuring the different virtual switch types.

- **Optimizing Virtual Network Performance:** Meeting performance expectations is critical to any server implementation. This section lists some strategies and configuration options that can be leveraged to maximize virtual machine network performance.

- **Configuring MAC Addresses:** This section begins with a recap of MAC addresses and how to properly identify them. It continues to discuss the use of dynamic MAC address pools and how to configure them in Hyper-V. The section concludes with the benefits of using static MAC addresses and MAC address spoofing.

- **Configuring Network Isolation:** This section discusses the purpose of network isolation and how to properly configure a virtual switch to isolate one or more virtual machines.

- **Configuring Virtual Network Adapters:** This section describes the various types of virtual network adapters, including virtual NIC teams and how they are used with Hyper-V Network Virtualization. The section concludes by providing you with an overview of the advanced network adapter features, including virtual switch extensions and useful PowerShell cmdlets used to configure HNV.

CHAPTER 9

Creating and Configuring Virtual Networks

Previously, we've been focusing on server virtualization in which multiple virtual servers run on a physical server. Each virtual server operates as if it were its own physical server. In this chapter, we discuss Hyper-V network virtualization (HNV) in which multiple virtual networks operate with a physical network. Each virtual network operates independently as if it were its own physical network.

Much like the physical network, virtual networks also require planning and specific configurations to meet the needs of your organization. This chapter will provide you with a foundation for Hyper-V network virtualization. It will provide you with an understanding of key concepts and provide you with the skills required to prepare you for the 70-410 exam.

"Do I Know This Already?" Quiz

The "Do I Know This Already?" quiz enables you to assess whether you should read this entire chapter or simply jump to the "Exam Preparation Tasks" section for review. If you are in doubt, read the entire chapter. Table 9-1 outlines the major headings in this chapter and the corresponding "Do I Know This Already?" quiz questions. You can find the answers in Appendix A, "Answers to the 'Do I Know This Already?' Quizzes."

Table 9-1 "Do I Know This Already?" Foundation Topics Section-to-Question Mapping

Foundations Topics Section	Questions Covered in This Section
Network Virtualization Using Hyper-V	1–5
Optimizing Virtual Network Performance	6
Configuring MAC Addresses	7–8
Configuring Network Isolation	9
Configuring Virtual Network Adapters	10–11

1. Which of the following are benefits of Hyper-V network virtualization? (Choose all that apply.)

   a. Ability to create public clouds

   b. Ability to create private clouds

   c. Reduced scalability

   d. Increased cost through consolidation of resources

   e. Ability to create hybrid clouds

   f. Ability to deploy resources on demand

2. Hyper-V vetwork virtualization allows you to create NIC teams. Which PowerShell cmdlet provides this ability?

   a. `New-NetSwitchTeam`

   b. `Set-NetSwitch Team`

   c. `NetSwitchTeam -Enable`

   d. `New-NICTeam -Enable`

3. Which Hyper-V Virtual Switch feature enables you to send a copy of inbound/outbound traffic to a destination virtual machine?

   a. MAC address spoofing

   b. Port mirroring

   c. Network load balancing

   d. Port virtual local area network

4. You need to allow your virtual machine to communicate with all new servers on your physical network. Which Hyper-V virtual switch type should you use?

   a. Internal

   b. Private

   c. Local

   d. External

5. You are planning on reconfiguring a Hyper-V host to meet changes in business requirements. Your Hyper-V host contains four NICs configured in a NIC Team. You need to configure two virtual machines to use an external switch, one virtual machine to use an internal switch, and three virtual machines to use a private switch for a lab. What is the first thing you need to do to accomplish this?

   a. Assign the NIC Team to the internal, external, and private virtual switches.

   b. From a PowerShell session, remove the NIC Team configuration by executing the `Remove-NetLbfoTeam` cmdlets.

   c. Upgrade Guest Integration Services

   d. Remove one network adapter from the team as NIC and reserve it for host management traffic.

6. Users complain of slow network performance using virtual servers. What can you do to maximize virtual machine network performance? (Choose all that apply.)

   a. Disable TCP Offloading for virtual network adapters.

   b. Configure and use the legacy network adapter driver.

   c. Configure and use the Hyper-V synthetic network adapter.

   d. Enable Single Root I/O Virtualization.

   e. Reduce the CPU cores assigned to the virtual machine.

   f. Reduce the overcommitted memory assigned to the virtual machine.

7. You have an application that requires a license key that is tied to the MAC address of a virtual network adapter. What can you do to ensure that the application remains properly licensed during virtual machine migrations?

   a. Configure a dynamic MAC address pool for the virtual machine.

   b. Configure MAC address spoofing.

   c. Configure a static MAC address for the virtual machine.

   d. Configure a legacy network adapter for the virtual machine.

8. You are deploying a new web server configured in a load balancing cluster. You need to ensure that connectivity is not lost when the incoming web requests are alternated between servers. Which Hyper-V network virtualization feature should you configure?

   a. Dynamic MAC address pool

   b. MAC address spoofing

   c. Static MAC address

   d. Legacy network adapter

9. Which of the following are valid PVLAN modes for configuring network isolation? (Choose three.)

   a. Isolated

   b. Private

   c. External

   d. Promiscuous

   e. Community

   f. Team

10. You need to block rogue DHCP servers from handing out addresses to your virtual machines. Which advanced adapter feature should you configure?

   a. Access control list

   b. DHCP guard

   c. Port mirroring

   d. Router guard

11. Which PowerShell cmdlet retrieves the VLAN configuration for a virtual machine?

   a. `Get-VMSwitchExtension`

   b. `Get-VMNetworkAdapterAcl`

   c. `Get-VMNetworkAdapterVlan`

   d. `Show VLAN`

Foundation Topics

Network Virtualization Using Hyper-V

With the release of Windows Server 2012 R2, Microsoft has continued to drive the use of virtual machines (VMs) and cloud-based computing. As organizations grow, the demand for servers and shared computing environments continues to increase. To keep up with the dynamic nature of today's businesses, Microsoft has empowered organizations with the ability to create cloud computing environments using Hyper-V network virtualization (HNV).

HNV allows multiple customers, known as *tenants*, to use a portion of the shared computing environment. Network virtualization offers the following benefits:

- Ability to create public, private, or hybrid clouds
- Lower cost through consolidation of resources, including datacenters
- Improved scalability
- Centralized and simplified management
- Ability to keep up with dynamic changes
- Empowers customers to deploy resources on demand
- Ability to provide hosting services and bill according to resource usage

NOTE   The specifics of cloud services fall outside the scope of the 70-410 exam. Refer to the Windows Azure home page at https://www.windowsazure.com/en-us/solutions/ or "Server and Cloud Platform" at http://www.microsoft.com/en-us/server-cloud/windows-server/.

Many components make up the HNV infrastructure. Some of these we will discuss in more detail throughout this chapter. At its core, the HNV is divided into the following spaces:

- **Customer address space:** HNV allows multiple customers or tenants to own and manage a group of virtual machines (VMs) configured in a virtual datacenter. The VMs are grouped together under a dedicated virtual network. The tenants have full control of the virtual network and servers connected to it. This concept creates a dedicated area of ownership known as the customer address space.

- **Provider address space:** The provider address spaces contains all hardware and physical connections required to provide processing power and connectivity to the customer address space. The provider refers to either the information technology group within a company-owned private cloud, or it can refer to a hosting organization that manages a public cloud containing one or more customers or tenants.

Before we take a deeper dive as to what makes HNV work, let's review some of the new and updated features for HNV. Table 9-2 outlines the new features for HNV under Windows Server 2012 and those that are new or updated under Windows Server 2012 R2.

Table 9-2   New/Updated Features for Hyper-V Network Virtualization

Feature/ Functionality	Description	Windows Server 2012	Windows Server 2012 R2
Hyper-V Network Virtualization Gateway	A gateway service that allows multiple tenants to connect to their servers using VPN and forwarding functions.		X
Hyper-V Virtual Switch Extensions/ Architecture	Microsoft has integrated new features into the HNV architecture that provide the ability to forward packets to the appropriate destination based on details in the packets.	X	X
Network Diagnostics	Ability to perform diagnostics on the virtual network.	X	X
Dynamic IP Address Learning	Allows Hyper-V to learn about the IP addresses of a VM so that it can isolate different instances of DHCP, DNS, and Active Directory.		X
Windows NIC Teaming	Enables you to team multiple network adapters to combine bandwidth or provide redundancy within the virtual environment. Configured using the NIC Teaming GUI or via the PowerShell `New-NetSwitchTeam` cmdlet.	X	X
NVGRE Encapsulated Task Offload	Allows for the use of network virtualization using generic routing encapsulation (NVGRE). This increases performance by taking advantage of physical network adapters that offload processing decisions from the CPU to the NIC.	X	X

Planning for Network Virtualization

Planning is the most important aspect for implementing network virtualization. Remember, you will be creating a shared environment, so taking some things into account prior to implementation will ensure that all your requirements as well as the customer requirements are met. Whether you are planning for server workload, clustering requirements, or even how to bill the customer, designing the appropriate solution takes some work. Some of the planning aspects, such as virtual hardware and storage allocation, have been discussed previously, but there are some additional items you must think about. Before you implement network virtualization using Hyper-V, you should take the following into consideration:

- Requirements for host clustering, shared storage, redundancy within the physical datacenter, and data protection

- Requirements for virtual network interface cards

- Requirements for virtual switches

- How to configure virtual network interface cards for proper connectivity

- How to configure subnets and virtual local area networks (VLANs)

- Specific requirements for media access control (MAC) addresses

- The need to isolate IP address and subnet configurations or integrate with the physical network

- How you will manage virtual networks and integration with System Center 2012 R2 for a cloud computing infrastructure

NOTE   System Center is introduced in the 70-411 *Cert Guide*. If you would like to know more, refer to "What's New in System Center 2012 R2" at http://technet.microsoft.com/en-us/library/dn249519.aspx.

Network Virtualization Components

Several components make up the HNV infrastructure. We have discussed some of the components previously. HNV begins with configured VMs powered by one or more Hyper-V physical hosts. In most cloud scenarios, a Hyper-V cluster is configured with a highly available and redundant server and storage infrastructure. The VMs contain guest operating systems where application data is stored. The guest VMs use virtual network adapters enabling them to communicate on the physical network. What we have not discussed is how VMs communicate within a virtual network.

NOTE   The purpose of the information discussed under the next several headings is to provide you with an overview of HNV. For more details, refer to "Hyper-V Network Virtualization technical details" at http://technet.microsoft.com/en-us/library/jj134174.aspx and "Windows Server 2012 Hyper-V Network Virtualization Survival Guide" at http://social.technet.microsoft.com/wiki/contents/articles/11524.windows-server-2012-hyper-v-network-virtualization-survival-guide.aspx.

Virtual Network

A virtual network is a boundary containing one or more virtual subnets that provides connectivity for VMs. In a shared environment, multiple datacenters exist so a mechanism is needed to separate them. This is exactly what a virtual network does.

If you look back to when servers were only physical, moving any server between datacenters or subnets often required the tedious task of re-IP addressing all servers. The reason being was that there was always some application, firewall settings, or network policy that prevented you from simply moving servers. HNV reduces or in some cases removes this headache.

One of the major benefits of network virtualization is the ability for the VMs and virtual network to own IP address ranges that are independent from the physical network. This allows for seamless consolidation into a cloud solution. The ability to consolidate datacenters without requiring servers to be assigned new IP addresses allows for faster consolidation and lower risk of downtime. To the business, faster consolidation means lower total cost of ownership for the datacenters.

Hyper-V Virtual Switch

A core element of the virtual network is the Hyper-V virtual switch. The virtual switch is a software function of Hyper-V that is responsible for layer 2 switching activities. Windows Server 2012 R2 introduces the following new features for the Hyper-V virtual switch:

- **PowerShell support:** Ability to configure and manage the Hyper-V virtual switch via PowerShell cmdlets.

- **Multiple virtual NICs:** Ability to use multiple NICs for increased throughput.

- **New security features:** New features such as port access control lists (ACLs), MAC address spoofing, router guard, DHCP guard, and IPSec task offload are supported.

- **Port virtual LAN (PVLAN) and Trunk Mode:** Ability to isolate VMs, networks, and their associated network traffic.

- **Port mirroring:** Ability to send a copy of inbound/outbound traffic to a monitoring server.

- **Receive side scaling (RSS) and dynamic virtual machine queue (D-VMQ):** Ability to spread network traffic across multiple CPU cores as well as use queues to improve performance when sending large amounts of data to specific VMs.

- **Dynamic load balancing of network traffic:** Ability to balance network traffic load between NICs or a NIC team.

- **Integration with third-party extensions:** Ability to incorporate third-party extensions to enhance the functionality of the virtual switch.

- **Improved network tracing:** As data is sent through the virtual switch, additional informational packets are sent containing switch and port configuration information for ease of support.

NOTE   The list of new features was provided as an overview. Some of the topics will be covered in more detail later in this chapter. For more information on the new features for the Hyper-V Virtual Switch, refer to "What's New in Hyper-V Virtual Switch in Windows Server 2012 R2" at http://technet.microsoft.com/en-us/library/dn343757.aspx or "What's New in Hyper-V Virtual Switch in Windows Server 2012" at http://technet.microsoft.com/en-us/library/jj679878.aspx.

With respect to configuring the virtual switch, there are three virtual network switch types to select from:

- **External:** Creates a virtual switch that binds to the physical network adapter so that the VMs can access a physical network.

- **Internal:** Creates a virtual switch that can be used only by the VMs that run on the physical computer and between the VMs and the physical computer. An internal switch does not allow for connectivity to a physical network connection.

- **Private:** Creates a virtual switch that can be used only by the VMs that run on the physical computer.

Selecting the appropriate switch type depends on the practical application for the virtual network. Table 9-3 outlines the different virtual switch types and the suggested uses for them.

Table 9-3 Selecting a Virtual Switch Type

Virtual Switch Type	Practical Uses and Considerations for Communication Activities
External	■ Provides connectivity between a VM and VMs on the same physical server. ■ Provides connectivity between a VM and other VMs on the same virtual network/subnet. ■ Provides connectivity between a VM and servers on the host LAN or external to the host LAN. ■ Useful if your production environment is comprised of both physical and virtual servers. ■ Requires a physical network adapter on the host machine to facilitate communication with the physical or external network.
Internal	■ Provides connectivity between a VM and VMs on the same physical server. ■ Provides connectivity between a VM and other VMs on the same virtual network/subnet. ■ Useful for lab/development scenarios. ■ Does not require a physical network adapter on the host machine. As a result, external communication is not possible.
Private	■ Provides connectivity between a VM and VMs on the same physical server. ■ Does not allow communication between the a VM and the host operating system. ■ Useful in cloud scenarios where you need to isolate VMs from the host and/or external resources. ■ May also be useful if you need to create an isolated network such as to test domain migrations or application upgrades.

> **NOTE** For more information, refer to "Hyper-V—What are the uses for different types of virtual networks" at http://blogs.technet.com/b/jhoward/archive/2008/06/17/hyper-v-what-are-the-uses-for-different-types-of-virtual-networks.aspx.

Virtual Subnets

Like physical subnets, each subnet within a virtual network contains a specific subnet addressing scheme. To identify a virtual subnet, HNV assigns a virtual subnet ID (VSID). The VSID enables address ranges to be reused with different virtual networks even if the virtual resources run on the same host. The host identifies the subnet by the VSID and associates it with a specific virtual network.

The subnets *within* a virtual network must contain unique address ranges that do not overlap. As with physical networks, each subnet is isolated to a single broadcast domain. Each subnet is associated with a routing domain ID (RDID). This configuration results in functionality similar to a VLAN—as we've become accustomed to—with managing physical networks. To communicate between subnets, a routing function is required.

Routing

To enable communications between subnets within a virtual network, HNV uses a routing function that is available on the host. In many cases, a virtual datacenter is assigned specific hosts to make up a cluster for the tenant. As a result, the host is able to act as the router to route between virtual subnets within the virtual network assigned to the tenant. This allows for all traffic to remain within the host as the routing boundary. The default gateway in a virtual network is typically the lowest address for the subnet. In most cases, this is the .1 address for a default Class C /24 subnet. In the cases where the tenant's network requires outside access, such as for Internet use or even VPN access into their address space, HNV includes a Virtualization Gateway function.

Hyper-V Network Virtualization Gateways

HNV gateways provide the following benefits for an HNV implementation:

- Enable remote access, such as VPN, into the isolated virtual networks

- Enable inbound/outbound access for Internet-related services such as for browsing or hosted HTTP/FTP services

- Enable site-to-site VPN communication for hybrid cloud scenarios in which some company resources exist in the shared provider space while other resources exist within the tenant's local server room/datacenter

- Provide load-balancing capabilities

- Enable access between tenants for collaboration or partnerships

NOTE   For more information on how to design and configure HNV gateways, refer to "Hyper-V Network Virtualization Gateway Architectural Guide" at http://technet.microsoft.com/en-us/library/jj618319.aspx.

Hyper-V Network Virtualization Policy Management

Windows Server 2012 R2 includes the ability for applications such as Microsoft System Center 2012 R2 to integrate with Hyper-V for management purposes. Management tools leverage Windows RM and WMI to gather performance and usage data and can interface directly with the virtual infrastructure to make changes via web-driven portals.

Configuring Virtual Network Switches

To configure a virtual network switch, Hyper-V Manager provides a Virtual Switch Manager tool. Using this tool, you can add/remove virtual switches, manage available switch extensions, and modify global network settings, including MAC address assignments. The next several headings provide you with step-by-step instructions on how to create and configure virtual switches.

Creating an External Virtual Network Switch

To create an external virtual network switch, perform the following steps:

1. Open Hyper-V Manager and select a Hyper-V host.

2. From the Actions pane, click the **Virtual Switch Manager** link to launch the Virtual Switch Manager, as shown in Figure 9-1. You will notice a default switch exists. This is created when the Hyper-V role is installed and configured.

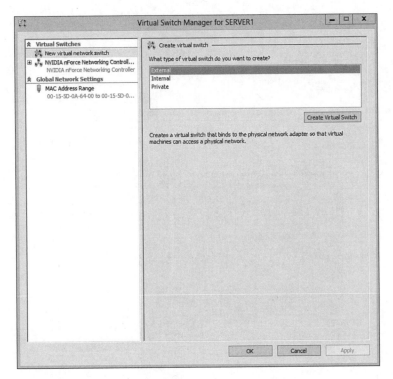

Figure 9-1   Virtual Switch Manager.

3. Select **External** as the virtual switch type, and click the **Create Virtual Switch** button. Hyper-V will create a new virtual switch with the ability to connect to resources externally.

4. Enter a **Name** and optional **Notes** for the virtual switch, as shown in Figure 9-2.

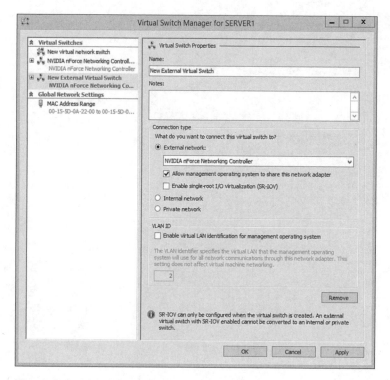

Figure 9-2   Virtual Switch Manager—New Virtual Switch.

5. Select the **Connection type** for the external network. In other words, choose the appropriate physical adapter connected to the physical network that you need to access. If your physical host takes advantage of NIC Teaming, you will be able to select the team.

> **NOTE**   If you are using a NIC Team, the Hyper-V host will treat the NIC Team as one logical switch. As a result, you can connect the team to only one virtual switch. If you need to connect the host to multiple virtual switches, you will need to install additional physical interfaces or split the NIC Team up. You can do this via the GUI or by executing the `Remove-NetLbfoTeam` cmdlet.

6. Depending on your requirements, you also can configure some of the following options:

   ■ **Allow management operating system to share this network adapter:** This setting controls whether you want to use the physical network adapter to access the operating system running the Hyper-V role. This option is helpful in isolating the host operating system from being able to communicate with VMs or the physical network.

- **Enable single-root I/O virtualization (SR-IOV):** The single-root I/O virtualization option enables the virtual network to access physical resources and functions of the physical network interface cards. The benefit of this is that the virtual network traffic is able to bypass the software layer of the virtual switch and access the physical interface for improved performance. You can create SR-IOV only when the virtual switch is created. As a result, you cannot convert a switch with SR-IOV enabled to internal or private.

- **Enable virtual LAN identification for management operating system:** This option enables you to specify an identification number that is used to isolate network traffic from the host operating system. As a prerequisite, you must configure a VLAN on the physical network to be used and associated with the virtual switch.

7. Click **Apply** to save the virtual switch configuration.

8. Hyper-V will warn you that pending changes may disrupt network connectivity, as shown in Figure 9-3. Click **Yes** to continue.

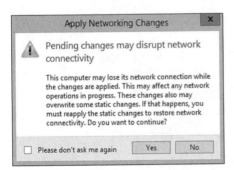

Figure 9-3   Applying a virtual network switch configuration.

NOTE   If a physical adapter is already associated with an existing virtual network switch, you will not be able to associate it with another virtual network switch. You might need to add more NICs to the host to accommodate multiple configurations.

Creating an Internal Virtual Network Switch

To create an internal virtual network switch, perform the following steps:

1. Follow the previous instructions to launch the Virtual Switch Manager.

2. Select **Internal** as the virtual switch type and click the **Create Virtual Switch** button.

3. Enter a **Name** and optional **Notes** similar to the previous instructions.

4. You will notice that with Internal network as the selected connection type, you are unable to associate it with a physical NIC or apply additional connection type options, as shown in Figure 9-4.

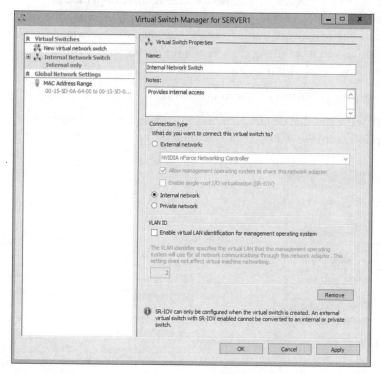

Figure 9-4 Internal virtual network switch configuration.

5. Select and specify an optional VLAN ID if your environment is capable of supporting this.

6. Click **Apply** to save the virtual switch configuration.

7. Hyper-V will warn you that pending changes may disrupt network connectivity. Click **Yes** to continue.

Creating a Private Virtual Network Switch

To create an isolated private virtual network switch, perform the following steps:

1. Follow the previous instructions to launch the Virtual Switch Manager.

2. Select **Private** as the virtual switch type and click the **Create Virtual Switch** button.

3. Enter a **Name** and optional **Notes** similar to the previous instructions.

4. You will notice that with Private network as the selected connection type, you are unable to associate it with a physical NIC, apply additional connection type options, or specify VLAN IDs, as shown in Figure 9-5.

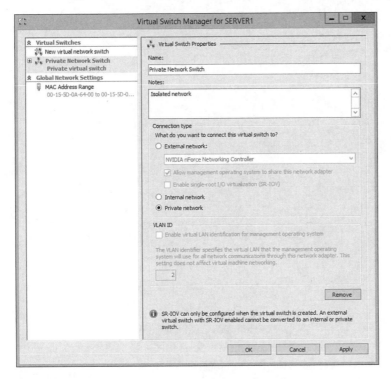

Figure 9-5   Private virtual network switch configuration.

5. Click **Apply** to save the virtual switch configuration.

6. Hyper-V will warn you that pending changes may disrupt network connectivity. Click **Yes** to continue.

Removing a Virtual Network Switch

To remove a virtual network switch, perform the following steps:

1. Follow the previous instructions to launch the Virtual Switch Manager.

2. Select the virtual network switch name listed under **Virtual Switches**.

3. Click the **Remove** button on the right pane.

4. Virtual Switch Manager will indicate the pending removal of the virtual network switch by graying out the screen and striking through the text containing the VM name, as shown in Figure 9-6.

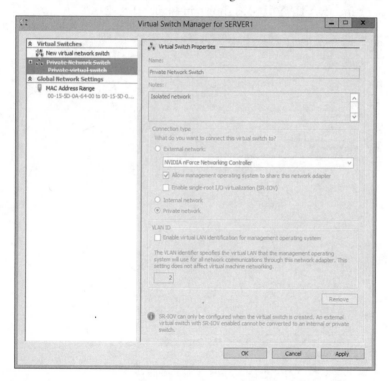

Figure 9-6   Removing a virtual network switch configuration.

5. Click **Apply** to remove the virtual switch configuration.

6. Hyper-V will warn you that pending changes may disrupt network connectivity. Click **Yes** to continue.

7. After removing a virtual network switch, you might need to update all VMs that previously used the switch. This action is similar to removing a physical switch from a network closet, leaving all patch cables hanging. The virtual network adapter under each affected VM will display a configuration error, as shown in Figure 9-7. To correct the issue, connect the virtual network adapter to a virtual network switch or create a new virtual network switch as you have done previously.

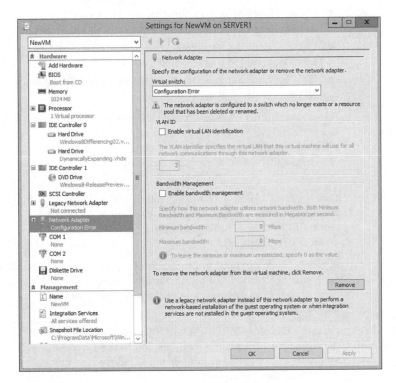

Figure 9-7   Virtual network adapter configuration error.

Optimizing Virtual Network Performance

As with any implementation, you want to get the most bang for your buck. There are a handful of things that you can do to achieve the most of your virtual network. Table 9-4 lists some best practices for optimizing a virtual network. It is important to understand that not all options are a good fit for every situation. Depending on your environment, you might use some or all of these options to improve performance.

Key Topic

Table 9-4 Optimizing Virtual Networks

Task	Details
Configure NIC Teaming on the Hyper-V host	Use multiple NICs teamed together to deliver a multilink solution to improve throughput and failover capabilities.
Enable single root I/O virtualization	Windows Server 2012 R2 and Windows 8.1 allow VMs to share physical PCIe devices. It enables the VM to directly access the physical NIC and access network resources. ■ On the Hyper-V host, use the PowerShell cmdlet `GetNetAdapterSriov` to review the capabilities. ■ Use the command `New-VMSwitch -Enableiov` to create an IOV supported virtual switch. ■ Use the command `Enable-NetAdapterSriov` to enable IOV on the physical network adapter.
Implement bandwidth management and quality of service	If you have limited resources, consider limiting bandwidth for low priority VMs. This ensures that a larger slice of the pie is available for more critical VMs. Also consider implementing QoS to classify, tag, and prioritize traffic based on different policies.
Implement storage quality of service	Discussed in Chapter 8, "Creating and Configuring Virtual Machine Storage," storage QoS is a new feature in Windows Server 2012 R2 that enables administrators to control and monitor virtual disk performance.
Configure virtual machines on the same host to use a private virtual network	If your VMs do not need to communicate with your host, configure all VMs to use a private virtual network. This will keep all traffic isolated and prevent the host from processing the packets.
Disable TCP offloading for virtual machine network cards	Disable TCP offloading, including IPSec task offloading under the virtual network adapter hardware acceleration settings. Similarly, this can also be done via the Windows Registry under the following keys: ■ HKEY_LOCAL_MACHINE\System\ CurrentControlSet\Services\TCPIP\Parameters\ DisableTaskOffload Set this value to 1 to disable task offloads from the TCP/IP transport. ■ HKEY_LOCAL_MACHINE\System\ CurrentControlSet\Services\Ipsec\EnabledOffload Set this value to 0 to disable Internet Protocol security (IPsec) offloads.
Configure a guest virtual machine to use the Hyper-V synthetic network adapter	Hyper-V synthetic network adapters are designed to reduce CPU overhead when network traffic is passed. Synthetic adapters may not be supported by legacy operating systems prior to Windows Server 2008.

Task	Details
Enable offloading capabilities for the physical network adapter driver	Depending on the adapter, physical NICs can include a TCP offloading capability that helps reduce CPU overhead and improve network processing. ■ Hyper-V under 2012 R2 supports LargeSend offload (LSOv1, LSOv2) and TCP checksum offload (TCPv4, TCPv6).
Leverage multiple network adapters when using multiple virtual network switches	For situations in which high network load is expected, consider using multiple network adapters and multiple virtual network switches to provide additional resources to the inventory of VMs.
When using multiple physical network cards on a Hyper-V host, dedicate one or more processors to specific network cards	In some cases, you might consider establishing processor affinity in which you dedicate specific logical processors or cores to different network adapters. Hyper-V supports what is known as a Dynamic Virtual Machine Queue. This feature automatically scales the number of processors in use based on the level of network activity. This can help balance the workload.
Enable VLAN tagging for the Hyper-V synthetic network adapter	Hyper-V synthetic adapter using VLAN tagging offers significantly better performance.
Enable Virtual Machine Queues	Enable VMQ for virtual machines that receive higher loads of incoming data. While it should be used sparingly, this feature may help the host manage incoming data streams destined for one or more virtual machines.
Install high end network adapters on the Hyper-V host	Install enterprise class high speed NICs on the Hyper-V host. Lock in the speed to the maximum setting and avoid auto negotiate if possible. It is important to use a duplex, speed and flow control settings that are compatible with the Layer 2 switch that the host is connected to.

NOTE   Table 9-4 lists only a handful of optimizations available for VMs. For a full guide, download the performance guide "Performance Tuning Guidelines for previous versions of Windows Server" at http://msdn.microsoft.com/en-us/library/windows/hardware/dn529134 and "Performance Tuning Guidelines for Windows Server 2012 R2" at http://msdn.microsoft.com/library/windows/hardware/dn529133.aspx.

Configuring MAC Addresses

As a recall, a media access control (MAC) address is an unique ID assigned to each network interface card (NIC) by the manufacturer. It is also referred to as the physical address of a NIC. The MAC address is a Layer 2 network address used by switches to learn where devices are and to which ports they are connected.

A MAC address is a 48-bit hexadecimal value that is composed of six groups of two hex digits separated by either a hyphen or colon depending on the application. One of the easiest ways to identify the MAC address is to issue the `ipconfig /all` command, as shown in Figure 9-8.

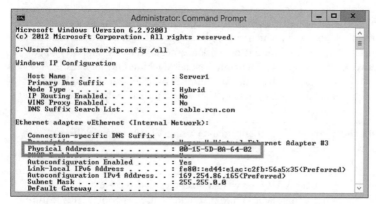

Figure 9-8   Display MAC address using `ipconfig /all`.

So we've just stated that MAC addresses are tied to a physical adapter. What does that mean for our virtual NICs? Despite the virtual hardware layer, Hyper-V treats the virtual network adapters as if they were physical. Meaning, all virtual network adapters are assigned a MAC address. Using Hyper-V, you can configure a VM to use either a dynamic or static MAC address for each adapter.

Dynamic MAC Addresses

The default option is to use a dynamic MAC address, meaning that Hyper-V will generate an initial MAC address for the network adapter. Each time a new virtual network adapter is created, the Hyper-V host will assign it a MAC address from a preconfigured pool.

If any issues occur or changes are made to the virtual NIC, Hyper-V may need to regenerate a new MAC address to ensure proper Layer 2 connectivity. The following situations will cause Hyper-V to regenerate a MAC address:

- The VM currently uses a MAC address that falls outside of the dynamic range configured for the Hyper-V host. This can occur when moving VMs between hosts or during a VM import process.

■ If a VM is resumed from a suspended or saved state, Hyper-V might need to regenerate a MAC address especially if it has been down for some time and the MAC address was assigned to another VM.

NOTE If Hyper-V needs to regenerate a MAC address, the virtual network adapter will remain offline until the VM is rebooted. This ensures that Hyper-V is able to modify the configuration for the virtual network interface.

As an administrator, you have the ability to define the range of MAC addresses that can be assigned dynamically to virtual network adapters. To configure or modify the dynamic address range, perform the following steps:

1. Open **Hyper-V Manager** and open **Virtual Switch Manager**.

2. Select **MAC Address Range** under Global Network Settings.

3. Specify a **Minimum MAC Address Range** and **Maximum MAC Address Range** in the right pane, as shown in Figure 9-9.

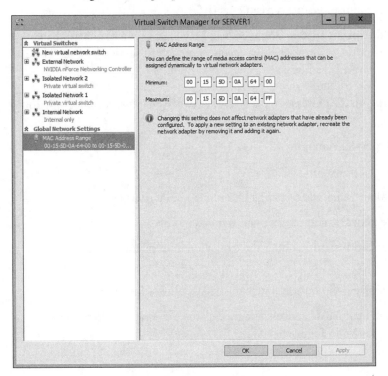

Figure 9-9   Configure dynamic MAC address range.

4. When completed, click **Apply** to commit the changes.

Static MAC Addresses

For specific instances, Hyper-V enables you to configure a static MAC address. Once configured, the static MAC address will not change unless you manually configure it. Unlike the dynamic configuration, Hyper-V will not be able to change the address after it is configured. An administrator might consider assigning a static MAC address to a VM for the following situations:

- **DHCP reservations:** Typically DHCP is not recommended for servers, but suppose you have a virtual workstation that needs to be managed via a DHCP reservation. Consider establishing a static MAC address on the network adapter for the VM. This ensures that the DHCP reservation continues to function if the VM is moved between hosts.

- **Custom licensing:** Some manufacturers license their products using the workstation or server's MAC address as part of the license activation process. Assigning a static MAC address will keep the product activated even if the VM moves between hosts. Before implementing static MAC addresses, always verify that the manufacturer supports virtualization and that you are in compliance with end user license agreements (EULAs).

- **Traffic and content filters:** Some devices may enable you to control bandwidth, filter traffic, or provide some levels of quality of service by controlling traffic based on MAC address.

To configure static MAC addresses for a virtual network adapter, complete the following steps:

1. Launch **Hyper-V Manager**.

2. Shut down and power off the guest VM.

3. Select a VM and click the **Settings** link under the Actions pane.

4. Expand the network adapter that you want to modify.

5. Click **Advanced Features** under the expanded options for the Network Adapter.

6. Select the **Static** radio button under the MAC address heading.

7. Accept the default MAC address assigned as the new static address or specify a new one, as shown in Figure 9-10.

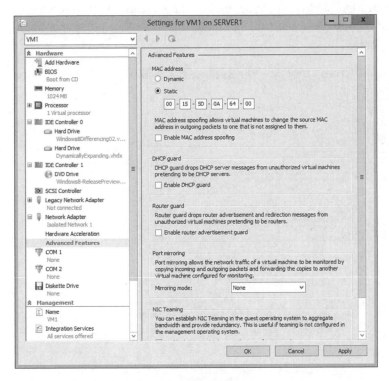

Figure 9-10 Configure a static MAC address.

8. Click **Apply** to save the changes.

9. **Click OK** to close the window and proceed to power up the VM.

10. Confirm the static MAC address by issuing `ipconfig /all` from a command prompt.

MAC Address Spoofing

MAC address spoofing enables VMs to change the source MAC address in outgoing packets to one that is not assigned to them. This is particularly useful for scenarios in which you need to configure a virtual NIC Team (discussed later in this chapter) or use network load balancing (NLB). NLB enables multiple servers to function in a load balancing cluster, such as with web or FTP servers.

Depending on the configuration, each host in the cluster might use its own MAC address or might use the cluster MAC address. Depending on the configuration and which your network switch supports, you may need to enable MAC address spoofing. To enable MAC address spoofing, modify the Advanced Features setting of a virtual network adapter and select the option to Enable MAC address spoofing, as shown in Figure 9-11.

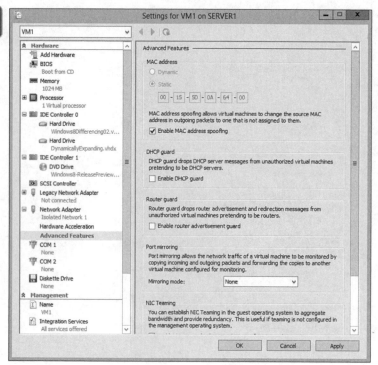

Figure 9-11 Enable MAC address spoofing.

Once enabled, it is important to ensure that your network switch is properly configured to accommodate the NLB and MAC address spoofing configurations. Refer to your switch manufacturer configuration guides for proper configuration steps.

> **NOTE** For more information on configuring NLB, refer to "Network Load Balancing Overview" at http://technet.microsoft.com/en-us/library/hh831698.aspx.

Configuring Network Isolation

Earlier in this chapter, you learned about creating private virtual switches to isolate VMs from the host or external resources. To take it one step further, Windows Server 2012 R2 enables you to leverage VLANs to provide connectivity to different subnets associated with your physical network. VLANs, combined with firewall/router ACLs, will provide you with an option to isolate VMs.

Virtual Switch Trunking

By default, a virtual switch port is untagged, meaning no VLAN is associated with the port. Depending on your needs, you might decide to implement VLANs and assign a switch port to a specific VLAN. Before you implement VLANs, it is important to understand the port modes available. You may configure a port using one of the following port modes:

- **Access:** Access mode tells the virtual switch on which VLAN to configure the VM's switch port. Use this mode when you need to communicate with only devices on the assigned VLAN.

- **Trunk:** When a port is configured as a trunk, the virtual switch/VM is able to see traffic from other VLANs similarly to a physical switch trunk port.

- **Untagged:** By default, ports are not tagged with any VLAN information.

Hyper-V enables you to configure a virtual switch for the use of VLAN trucking. If you recall, when a device is in a VLAN, it is allowed to communicate with only other devices in the same VLAN. To enable communication between VLANs, a router is required. If you plan on placing a VM in a specific VLAN, you will need to configure a virtual switch trunk. When configured as a trunk, the switch port receives traffic from all VLANs in the allowed VLAN list. To configure and enable VLAN trunking, perform the following steps:

1. Configure a trunk port on the physical switch. Refer to your switch manufacturer's installation and configuration guide for specifics.

2. Connect the Hyper-V host to the switch.

3. Configure a virtual switch network as you have done previously. As a recommended configuration step under the Virtual Switch Properties, select **Enable virtual LAN identification for management operating system** as seen previously in Figure 9-2.

4. Configure the VM with a network adapter connected to the virtual switch.

5. On the Hyper-V host, open PowerShell as an administrator.

6. Issue the command `Set-VMNetworkAdapterVlan -VMName [VM Name] -Trunk -AllowedVlanIdList [1-10] -NativeVlanId 2`. Hyper-V will allow the VM to use the trunk to carry information from VLANs 1–10, and it will use Native VLAN 2 for communicating with the operating system and other devices on the native VLAN.

7. To review the configuration, execute the cmdlet `Get-VMNetworkAdapterVlan`. This will produce a list of all configured VMs, their configured network adapters, their port modes, and the allowed VLANs configured.

8. In the properties of the virtual network adapter, select the **Enable virtual LAN identification** option shown previously in Figure 9-7, and specify the VLAN identifier to be used for all network communications through the adapter.

Using PVLANs for Isolation

In the case of a shared cloud-based solution, HNV allows you to further isolate VMs at the port level on the virtual switch. This enables you to isolate specific customer traffic, isolate specific customer VMs, and enable customers to use the same IP address ranges without overlapping or impacting other customers or VMs. The mechanism responsible for this is known as port virtual local area network (PVLAN).

PVLANs were designed to overcome the limitation of traditional VLANs. Traditional VLANs enable you to create up to 4,095 unique VLAN IDs. In a multitenant cloud scenario, you wouldn't want to limit the amount of customers you could support. By using a PVLAN, you could essentially configure each tenant subnet or, in extreme cases, each individual port connecting a single VM as their own PVLAN completely. The concept of PVLAN is similar to that of a private VLAN in the physical world.

A PVLAN is nothing more than a switch property that an administrator can configure. Each PVLAN is assigned a primary and a secondary PVLAN ID. The primary VLAN is essentially the original VLAN of the virtual switch/port. You can configure the secondary PVLAN ID in one of the following modes:

- **Isolated:** Isolates the configured port so that no other device can communicate with it. Typically, isolated ports communicate with only specific ports associated with a gateway, firewall, or router.

- **Promiscuous:** Allows communication with all ports in the PVLAN (including all devices/servers). This is typically used when you need to communicate between external servers, devices, routers, backup servers, management/monitoring workstations, and so on.

- **Community:** Communicates with ports in the same community (primary VLAN) and any promiscuous ports in the PVLAN.

Configure PVLAN Ports

To configure PVLAN ports for network isolation, perform the following steps on the Hyper-V host:

1. Before beginning, review the current trunk/VLAN configuration on the Hyper-V host by executing the PowerShell cmdlet `Get-VMNetworkAdapterVlan`.

2. If the VM you are configuring is on a VLAN that is unintended, clear any existing VLAN configurations by executing the PowerShell cmdlet `Set-VMNetworkAdapterVlan -VMName [VM Name] -Access -VlanId 2`. This will clear any trunk configurations on the virtual port for the VM. The `Set-VMNetworkAdapter Vlan -VMName` command will configure the VM on VLAN 2 using an access port configuration.

3. Execute the cmdlets `Get-VMNetworkAdapter -VMName [VM Name]` to retrieve information about the network adapters connected to the VM specified. The command will return information including the virtual network adapter names, virtual switch names, MAC addresses, IP addresses, and the status of the interfaces.

4. Next, configure the PVLAN mode and configure both primary and secondary VLAN IDs. Depending on the isolation requirements, issue one of the following commands:

   - **Isolated:** To configure an isolated PVLAN, issue the command
     `Set-VMNetworkAdapterVlan -VMName [VM Name]`
     `-VMNetworkAdapterName [Adapter Name] -Isolated`
     `-PrimaryVlanId 2 -SecondaryVlanID 10`.

     This command configures an isolated PVLAN for the VM and network adapter specified. The Primary VLAN used for management will be configured for VLAN 2, while the secondary VLAN will be assigned VLAN 10.

   - **Promiscuous:** To configure a PVLAN that is able to communicate with other PVLANs, set the VM port to trunk mode and enable the appropriate VLANs in the allowed list. Then issue the command
     `Set-VMNetworkAdapterVlan -VMName [VM Name] -Promiscuous`
     `-PrimaryVlanId 2 -SecondaryVlanIdList 3-10`.

     This command enables Promiscuous mode for PVLAN communications for the VM specified. The Primary VLAN used for management will be configured for VLAN 2, while the secondary VLANs that the VM is able to communicate with are 3–10.

- **Community:** To configure a PVLAN using the community mode, issue the command `Set-VMNetworkAdapterVlan -VMName [VM Name] -VMNetworkAdapterName [Adapter Name] -Community -PrimaryVlanId 2 -SecondaryVlanID 10`.

    This command configures the PVLAN using community mode for the VM and adapter specified. The Primary VLAN, VLAN 2 identifies the community (including management). The Secondary VLAN is used to communicate with any promiscuous ports in VLAN 10.

5. Review the updated configuration by executing the cmdlet `Get-VMNetworkAdapterVlan -VMName [VM Name]`.

Configuring Virtual Network Adapters

Hyper-V supports two types of virtual network adapters. When configuring VMs, you might notice that there is a legacy network adapter and a network adapter. These adapters are also referred to as an *emulated* network adapter and a *synthetic* network adapter, respectively. Although they both offer the same core function—which is to provide network connectivity to the guest operating system—there are some significant differences:

- **Emulated network adapter:** The emulated network adapter, also referred to as a *legacy network adapter*, uses a legacy driver to support legacy operating systems. It offers the most compatibility but is limited in functionality. Emulated adapters perform slowly and are unable to take advantage of bandwidth throttling or hardware acceleration capabilities. Emulated network adapters are also used to perform network-based installations of the guest operating system or when integration services are not installed on the operating system.

- **Synthetic network adapter:** The synthetic network adapter, also displayed as *network adapter*, uses a custom driver specifically designed to work with Hyper-V. Synthetic drivers require Guest Integration Services to be installed, and when installed, the adapter is able to take advantage of hardware acceleration and bandwidth throttling capabilities.

- **Virtual Machine NIC Team:** In addition to a physical NIC team, discussed in Chapter 2, "Installing and Configuring Windows Server 2012 R2," Windows Server 2012 and 2012 R2 enable you to create a virtual NIC team using up to two virtual network adapters up to two virtual network switches. This provides additional redundancies at the virtual hardware layer designed to reduce unplanned downtime.

Even if one virtual network adapter becomes disconnected, connectivity is not disrupted because another virtual network adapter configured in the virtual NIC team is connected to a different virtual network switch.

Regardless of which network adapter you install, to add a new network adapter to a VM, modify the settings of the specific VM and use the Add Hardware link to add either a network adapter or legacy network adapter, as shown in Figure 9-12.

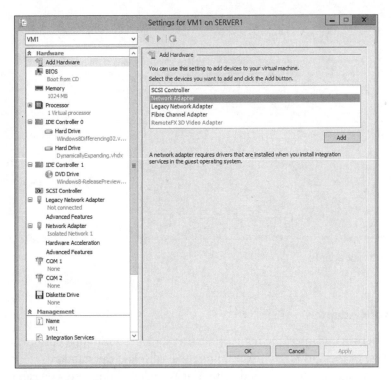

Figure 9-12   Add hardware—network adapters.

Configuring an Emulated (Legacy) Network Adapter

Once installed, you can configure a couple of options for a legacy network adapter, as shown in Figure 9-13. The most important of which is the virtual switch to which you want to connect the legacy adapter. If desired, you also can enable VLAN IDs for the adapter.

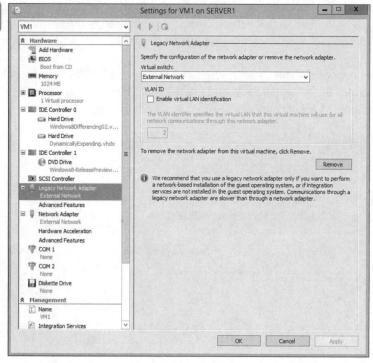

Figure 9-13   Legacy network adapter.

Configuring a Network Adapter

Unlike the legacy network adapter, the network adapter includes additional options, taking full advantage of the optimized driver. Figure 9-14 displays the standard options and the additional options for Bandwidth Management. From here, you can specify the minimum and maximum bandwidth to restrict utilization for the VM.

Figure 9-14   Network adapter bandwidth management.

NOTE   Use the `Set-VMNetworkAdapter` PowerShell cmdlets to configure bandwidth options.

You may also notice that the network adapter includes a section for configuring Hardware Acceleration. The Hardware Acceleration options, as shown in Figure 9-15, enable you to configure networking tasks that can be offloaded to a physical network adapter, thus reducing CPU overhead.

Figure 9-15   Network adapter hardware acceleration.

You can enable the following settings to leverage hardware acceleration options:

- **Enable virtual machine queue:** Virtual machine queue (VMQ) is a physical storage queue available on supported physical adapters. The VMQ function helps the host server manage incoming data destined for one or more VMs. The physical adapter places incoming packets in the queue until the data stream captures enough data for the virtual adapter to process more quickly. The guest operating system must be Windows Server 2008 R2/Windows 7 or higher to take advantage of this feature. This feature should be used sparingly and for those VMs with heavy inbound requests.

- **Enable IPsec task offloading:** IPsec is used to secure incoming and outgoing network traffic. While it protects your valuable data, network bandwidth may take a hit due to the additional overhead required to ensure secure communications. In addition to this, IPsec runs extensive algorithms to encrypt the data. The stronger the encryption, the greater the calculations. As a result, CPUs tend to work harder, which also reduces the amount of processing power for other applications or functions. To improve performance, some physical adapters include an offload function. When enabled, the calculations that once occurred on the CPU can now be handled by a dedicated processor on the NIC. Hyper-V's synthetic driver works with the physical adapter to leverage these technologies at the virtual network adapter level.

- **Enable SR-IOV:** Single-root I/O virtualization is a new function included in Windows Server 2012 and Windows 8. Also available under Windows Server 2012 R2 and Windows 8.1, this function allows for the sharing of PCIe network adapters between VMs. When enabled, it allows VMs to directly access network resources as if it were using the physical adapter directly. To use this function, you must have a physical network adapter that supports this feature.

Configure a Virtual NIC Team

Virtual NIC teams are created using the same process as described in Chapter 2. The only difference is that you must configure one or more physical NIC or NIC Teams and one or more virtual network switches to be used by the virtual network adapters. You must also enable NIC Teaming under the VM's Network Adapter Advanced Features, as shown in Figure 9-16.

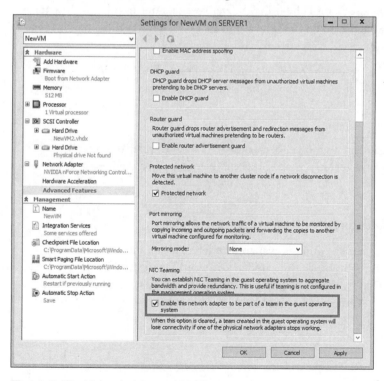

Figure 9-16 Network Adapter NIC Teaming

Before configuring a virtual NIC Team, consider the following:

- **Enable MAC spoofing:** Because virtual network adapters are tied to a specific physical NIC, different MAC addresses are used. MAC address spoofing ensures that traffic flows properly in the event of a failover event. You should enable MAC spoofing prior to configuring the virtual NIC Team.

- **SR-IOV:** Data is delivered directly to the network interface card without passing it through the networking stack. As a result, the NIC team cannot see the data or redirect it to an alternative path in the team. As a result, SR-IOV is not supported.

- **Remote Direct Memory Access (RDMA):** RDMA is a new underlying technology introduced with Windows Server 2012. It was added to increase network performance, typically with virtual machine Live Migrations by enabling the network adapter to transfer data directly to or from an application memory to the network without the need to use the buffers built in to the operating system. This function is not compatible with virtual NIC Teams.

- **TCP offloading:** Discussed earlier, TCP offloading reduces data processing load from the host's CPU by using the network adapter to process the data. TCP offloading is sometimes referred to as TCP chimney offload. This function is not supported with virtual NIC Teams.

- **Physical NIC requirements:** A minimum of one physical NIC is required to function, but at least two must be used to support fault tolerance and high availability.

> **NOTE** For more information on configuring NIC Teams, refer to "NIC Teaming Overview" at http://technet.microsoft.com/en-us/library/hh831648.aspx.

Advanced Adapter Features

In addition to the standard options available under each adapter type, Hyper-V includes several configurable options under Advanced Features (shown previously in Figure 9-16). Depending on your requirements, you may need to enable one or more Advanced Features for a VM. Table 9-5 provides an overview of these features.

Table 9-5 Adapter Advanced Features

Feature Heading	Configurable Option	Description
MAC address	Enable MAC address spoofing	Allows VMs to change the source MAC address in outgoing packets to one that is not assigned to them. Often necessary with the use of network load-balancing clusters. Also available under the MAC address heading are options for switching between Dynamic/Static MAC addresses.
DHCP guard	Enable DHCP guard	Used to block rogue DHCP servers. This setting drops DHCP server messages from unauthorized VMs.
Router guard	Enable router advertisement guard	This setting is used to block rogue routers. When enabled, it drops router advertisements and redirection messages from unauthorized VMs with routing services installed.
Port mirroring	Port mirroring	This feature allows network traffic from VMs to be monitored by copying incoming and outgoing packets. Copied packets are forwarded to a VM that contains traffic monitoring applications such as Wireshark. You can configure this feature using the following mirroring modes: ■ **None:** Default option that essentially means this feature is disabled and packets are not copied. ■ **Destination:** This tells Hyper-V that this VM is the destination VM where all copied packets are forwarded. The destination is the VM containing the packet analyzing or monitoring software. ■ **Source:** Virtual machines configured as a source will copy all incoming/outgoing packets and forward it to the destination. **Note**: As a general practice, specify one VM as a dedicated destination VM. You can configure multiple sources to forward packets to the destination.
NIC Teaming	Enable this network adapter to be a part of a team in the guest operating system	Enables you to establish a NIC team within the guest operating system. This is particularly helpful in situations where the host may not have a NIC team or perhaps you may not have the authority to make changes on the host.

In addition to the network switch types, Hyper-V Virtual Switch Manager provides the ability to enable/disable virtual switch extensions. Virtual switch extensions are essentially add-on features that allow direct integration between the guest and host for providing additional capabilities for the virtual switch.

As a new feature under Windows Server 2012, also included in Windows Server 2012 R2, extensions support the implementation of port ACLs. ACLs enable you to implement firewall-level protection and enforce specific security policies for cloud implementations. Port ACLs enable you to permit or deny traffic in or out of a VM. Traffic is filtered based on IPv4 or IPv6 addresses, MAC address, and IP address ranges. With Windows Server 2012 R2, specific TCP/UDP ports can be filtered. Port ACLs are applied using the `Add-VMNetworkAdapterAcl` PowerShell command.

> **NOTE**   For more information on creating security policies with extended port ACLs, refer to "Create Security Policies with Extended Port Access Control Lists for Windows Server 2012 R2" at http://technet.microsoft.com/en-us/library/dn375962.aspx.

Extensions come in the form of third-party plug-ins or can be homegrown, depending on the needs of your organization. They can be installed (bound), removed (unbound), and configured via Windows PowerShell cmdlets. The `Get-VmSwitchExtension` PowerShell cmdlet enumerates the Hyper-V virtual switch extensions currently bound to an instance of the virtual switch. This cmdlet also reports whether the extension is enabled—as the extension may be bound but not actively enabled.

Use the cmdlets `Enable-VMSwitchExtension` and `Disable-VMSwitchExtension` to enable/disable the extension.

For the GUI folks, you can also enable/disable extensions via the Virtual Switch Manager, as shown in Figure 9-17.

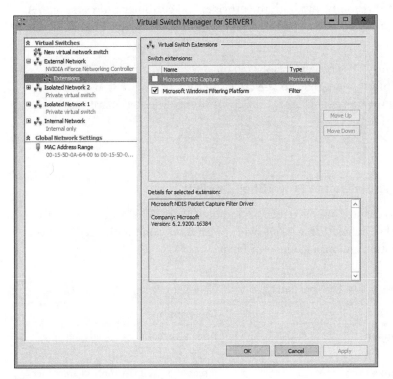

Figure 9-17   Virtual switch extensions.

Some hardware vendors might provide specific extensions for better VM integration with their equipment. For most scenarios, the default extensions suffice. Windows Server 2012 and 2012 R2 include the following switch extensions by default:

- **Microsoft NDIS capture:** Microsoft's version of the Network Driver Interface Specification (NDIS). NDIS is an application programming interface (API) that allows software vendors to create applications that interface with Layer 2 of the OSI model. Applications leveraging NDIS are typically designed around the capturing and monitoring of traffic.

- **Microsoft Windows Filtering Platform:** Used as a framework for integrating filtering functions. The Windows Filtering Platform (WFP) is a set of APIs that enable software vendors to create applications to filter and modify TCP/IP packets, monitor, or even authorize connections.

As an improvement under Windows Server 2012 R2, Microsoft has made it easier for third-party extensions to integrate with the Hyper-V virtual switch. With a change in the underlying architecture of the data flows, HNV under 2012 R2 provides increased visibility into both the provider and customer address spaces. As a result, this opens up additional possibilities for third-party integrations.

> **NOTE** The specifics of switch extensions fall outside of scope for the 70-410 exam. For more information, refer to "Overview of the Hyper-V Extensible Switch" at http://msdn.microsoft.com/en-us/library/windows/hardware/ hh582268(v=vs.85).aspx.

Hyper-V Network Virtualization PowerShell Cmdlets

Throughout this chapter, we have seen a handful of PowerShell cmdlets used to configure virtual switches. Table 9-6 provides a listing of commonly used cmdlets for the configuration and management of HNV.

Table 9-6   Useful PowerShell Cmdlets for Hyper-V Network Virtualization

Cmdlet	Description
Add-VMNetworkAdapter	Adds a virtual network adapter to a VM.
Add-VMNetworkAdapterAcl	Creates an ACL to apply against the traffic through a VM network adapter.
Add-VMSwitch	Adds a virtual switch.
Add-VMSwitchExtensionPortFeature	Adds a new feature to a virtual network adapter. It is also used to configure built-in virtual switch features.
Add-VMSwitchExtensionSwitchFeature	Adds a feature supported by a virtual switch extension.
Connect-VMNetworkAdapter	Connects a virtual network adapter to a specific virtual switch.
Disable-VMSwitchExtension	Disables a virtual switch extension.
Enable-VMSwitchExtension	Enables a virtual switch extension.
Get-VMNetworkAdapter	Queries and lists details about a virtual network adapter and the management operating system.
Get-VMNetworkAdapterAcl	Retrieves the ACL configuration for a virtual network adapter.
Get-VMNetworkAdapterFailoverConfiguration	Retrieves the IP address of a virtual network adapter that is used when the VM fails over.

Cmdlet	Description
Get-VMNetworkAdapterVlan	Retrieves VLAN configuration applied to a virtual network adapter.
Get-VMSwitch	Produces a list of configured virtual switches on a Hyper-V host.
Get-VMSwitchExtension	Lists the extensions for a virtual switch.
Get-VMSwitchExtensionPortData	Retrieves the status of a virtual switch extension feature applied to a network adapter.
Get-VMSwitchExtensionPortFeature	Lists the features configured on a virtual network adapter.
Get-VMSwitchExtensionSwitchData	Retrieves the status of a virtual switch extension feature applied on a virtual switch.
Get-VMSwitchExtensionSwitchFeature	Lists the features configured on a virtual switch.
Get-VMSystemSwitchExtension	Lists the switch extensions installed on a Hyper-V host.
Get-VMSystemSwitchExtensionPortFeature	Gets the port-level features supported by a virtual switch extension.
Get-VMSystemSwitchExtensionSwitchFeature	Retrieves the switch level features on a Hyper-V host.
New-VMSwitch	Creates a new virtual switch on a Hyper-V host.
Remove-VMNetworkAdapter	Removes a specific virtual network adapter.
Remove-VMNetworkAdapterAcl	Removes an ACL applied to the traffic for a virtual network adapter.
Remove-VMSwitch	Removes a virtual switch.
Remove-VMSwitchExtensionPortFeature	Removes a virtual switch feature from a network adapter.
Remove-VMSwitchExtensionSwitchFeature	Removes a feature from a virtual switch.
Rename-VMNetworkAdapter	Renames a specific virtual network adapter.
Rename-VMSwitch	Renames a specific virtual switch.
Set-VMNetworkAdapter	Used to configure features of the virtual network adapter.

Cmdlet	Description
`Set-VMNetworkAdapterFailoverConfiguration`	Configures an IP address of a virtual network adapter that will be used for failover capabilities.
`Set-VMNetworkAdapterVlan`	Configures VLAN settings for a virtual network adapter.
`Set-VMSwitch`	Configures a virtual switch.
`Set-VMSwitchExtensionPortFeature`	Configures a feature on a virtual network adapter.
`Set-VMSwitchExtensionSwitchFeature`	Configures a feature on a virtual switch.

NOTE   Table 9-6 lists provides an overview of the more commonly used Power-Shell cmdlets. For a full listing of cmdlets and information on cmdlets syntax, refer to "Hyper-V Cmdlets in Windows PowerShell" at http://technet.microsoft.com/en-us/library/hh848559.aspx.

Exam Preparation Tasks

Review All the Key Topics

Review the most important topics in the chapter, noted with the key topics icon in the outer margin of the page. Table 9-7 lists a reference of these key topics and the page numbers on which each is found.

Table 9-7   Key Topics for Chapter 9

Key Topic Element	Description	Page Number
Table 9-2	Lists the new and updated features for HNV	382
List	Outlines the new features and capabilities for the Hyper-V virtual switch	384
Table 9-3	Lists the virtual switch types and outlines the practical uses for each type	386
List	Shows you how to configure virtual network switches	388
Table 9-4	Provides a listing of the tasks and options to configure to optimize virtual networks	396

Key Topic Element	Description	Page Number
Figure 9-9	Shows you how to configure a dynamic MAC address range	399
Figure 9-10	Shows you how to configure a static MAC address for a VM	401
Figure 9-11	Shows you how to enable MAC address spoofing	402
List	Lists the various port modes for a virtual switch	403
List	Provides instructions on how to configure virtual trunks, get VLAN information, and enable VLAN identifications for the virtual network adapter	403
List	Lists the different network isolation modes available	404
List	Provides instructions on how to configure PVLAN ports using PowerShell cmdlets	405
List	Describes the virtual network adapter types available	406
Figure 9-13	Displays the legacy network adapter options available for configuration	408
Figure 9-14	Displays the additional configurable options for the virtual network adapter	409
List	Lists the virtual network adapter hardware acceleration options	410
Table 9-5	Outlines the virtual network adapter advanced features	413
Figure 9-17	Shows the default virtual switch extensions available in Hyper-V under Windows Server 2012 R2	415
Table 9-6	Lists commonly used PowerShell cmdlets for HNV	416

Complete the Tables and Lists from Memory

Print a copy of Appendix B, "Memory Tables" (found on the CD), or at least the section for this chapter, and complete the tables and lists from memory. Appendix C, "Memory Tables Answer Key," is also on the CD and includes completed tables and lists to check your work.

Definitions of Key Terms

Define the following key terms from this chapter, and check your answers in the glossary.

Customer Address Space, Hyper-V Network Virtualization, MAC Address, NIC Team (*virtual*), Provider Address Space, PVLAN, Tenant.

This chapter covers the following subjects:

- **Concepts of TCP/IP:** TCP/IP is a complex stack of related networking protocols. This section introduces the various protocols involved and explains their relationship with one another.

- **IPv4 Addressing:** Version 4 of the IP protocol has been used for many years and is still common today. This section describes the 32-bit IPv4 address classes and shows you how to configure your computer for IPv4 addressing.

- **IPv6 Addressing:** With the increasingly large number of computers and other devices that connect to the Internet, IPv4 is running out of addresses. The 128-bit IP version 6 was developed to alleviate this problem. In this section you are introduced to the various types of IPv6 addresses that are available. You then learn how to configure your computer with IPv6 and connect to other computers using either IPv4 or IPv6.

- **Interoperability Between IPv4 and IPv6 Addresses:** It is not expected that IPv4 will go away at any time in the near future, so you must be able to handle connections between computers running on either version of the IP protocol. Transition technologies such as ISATAP, 6to4, and Teredo have been developed to handle connections between IPv4 and IPv6 networks. Microsoft expects you to be familiar with these technologies for the 70-410 exam.

- **Resolving IPv4 and IPv6 Network Connectivity Issues:** Many factors can result in an inability to access other computers on the network or in intermittent connectivity. This section introduces common troubleshooting techniques you should be aware of when your computer cannot connect to others.

CHAPTER 10

Configuring IPv4 and IPv6 Addressing

At its heart and soul, computer networking is all about getting computers to talk to one another and exchange information. And for computers to talk to one another, they must know how to contact each other. When I want to talk to another person across the city, the country, or the world, I pick up the phone and dial their number. In the same fashion, a computer wanting to talk to another one must dial its number. That number is the computer's IP address. In his first career as an environmental scientist, one day in the 1980s a fellow scientist in another agency told the senior author that he could send some data from his computer to the author's if he entered a series of numbers that he dictated to him. That series of numbers was an IP address, and that was his first exposure to TCP/IP. Upon transitioning to a computer networking career with Windows NT, he quickly discovered that he needed to use and be proficient with TCP/IP to operate large networks and the Internet. Although considered by Microsoft as an elective, the exam offered by Microsoft in TCP/IP networking in Windows NT was really mandatory for anyone who wanted to become proficient in server and network management.

Beginning with Windows 2000 and becoming much more so with successive versions of Windows Server, TCP/IP came into its forefront as the primary networking protocol, relegating other networking protocols such as NetBEUI to the museum. In fact, Microsoft made TCP/IP the required networking protocol for Active Directory. This is largely because of Active Directory's dependence on the domain name system (DNS) to provide the computer name and address resolution for all resources in Active Directory. In reading this book to prepare for the 70-410 exam, you will learn about all the latest Windows Server 2012 R2 networking technologies used by businesses to keep users connected with each other and their data, regardless of where they are accessing the network from and the tasks they are expected to perform.

For many years, version 4 of the IP protocol with its 32-bit addressing scheme provided an abundant supply of IP addresses for all the computers wanting to access the Internet. However, the Internet Engineering Task Force (IETF) foresaw the day that IPv4 would run out of address space and began the introduction of version 6 of this protocol, featuring a 128-bit address space in the late 1990s. Simply known as IPv6, this protocol provides for 128-bit addressing, which allows for a practically infinite number of possible addresses. Because IPv4 is still in common use, Microsoft expects you to know how to configure both IPv4 and IPv6 for the 70-410 exam, and this chapter presents a comprehensive introduction to both versions of the TCP/IP networking protocol.

"Do I Know This Already?" Quiz

The "Do I Know This Already?" quiz enables you to assess whether you should read this entire chapter or simply jump to the "Exam Preparation Tasks" section for review. If you are in doubt, read the entire chapter. Table 10-1 outlines the major headings in this chapter and the corresponding "Do I Know This Already?" quiz questions. You can find the answers in Appendix A, "Answers to the 'Do I Know This Already?' Quizzes."

Table 10-1   "Do I Know This Already?" Foundation Topics Section-to-Question Mapping

Foundations Topics Section	Questions Covered in This Section
Concepts of TCP/IP	1
IPv4 Addressing	2–5
IPv6 Addressing	6–7
Interoperability Between IPv4 and IPv6 Addresses	8–10
Resolving IPv4 and IPv6 Network Connectivity Issues	11–13

1. At which layer of the TCP/IP reference model does the TCP protocol operate?

    a. Network

    b. Presentation

    c. Internet

    d. Transport

    e. Network Interface

2. You need to ensure that your IPv4-enabled computer can access other subnets on your company's network, as well as the Internet. Which addressing component should you ensure is specified properly?

   a. IP address

   b. Subnet mask

   c. Default gateway

   d. DNS server address

   e. WINS address

3. Your computer is configured with the IP address 131.107.24.5. To which class does this IP address belong?

   a. A

   b. B

   c. C

   d. D

   e. E

4. Your network is configured to use DHCP for assignment of IP addresses and other TCP/IP configuration information such as DNS server addresses. Which of the following options should you ensure are selected in the Internet Protocol Version 4 (TCP/IPv4) Properties dialog box? (Choose two.)

   a. **Obtain an IP address automatically**

   b. **Use the following IP address**

   c. **Obtain DNS Server address automatically**

   d. **Use the following DNS server addresses**

5. Your computer is configured to use the IPv4 address 169.254.183.32. Which system is being used by your computer?

   a. Automatic Private Internet Protocol Addressing (APIPA)

   b. Dynamic Host Configuration Protocol (DHCP)

   c. Alternate IP configuration

   d. Private IPv4 network addressing

6. Your company has transitioned to using the IPv6 protocol, and you are responsible for configuring Internet servers that need direct access to the Internet. Which of the following types of IPv6 addresses should you use for this purpose?

    a. Global unicast

    b. Link-local unicast

    c. Site-local unicast

    d. Multicast

    e. Anycast

7. Your computer is using an IPv6 address on the fe80::/64 network. Which type of IPv6 address is this?

    a. Global unicast

    b. Site-local unicast

    c. Link-local unicast

    d. Teredo

8. You are responsible for adding IPv6 to your company's network. Two computers that are separated by an IPv4-only network infrastructure are configured with the IPv6 addresses of fe80::5efe:172.16.21.3 and fe80::5efe:192.168.12.51, respectively. Which of the following address types is being used to ensure IPv6-IPv4 connectivity in this example?

    a. ISATAP

    b. Teredo

    c. 6to4

    d. IPv4-mapping

9. You have configured a Windows Server 2012 R2 computer with the Internet Connection Sharing (ICS) feature to enable IPv6 forwarding on both the 6to4 tunneling and private interfaces. Which of the following networking components is configured on this machine?

    a. 6to4 host

    b. 6to4 router

    c. 6to4 host/router

    d. 6to4 relay

10. Which of the following is a valid Teredo address?

   a. 2003:414:ab86:731f::230:1:45ab

   b. 3ffe:831f::ab86:731f:230:1:45ab

   c. 2001::ce49:7601:2cad:dfff:7c94:fffe

   d. 2002::ce49:7601:2cad:dfff:7c94:fffe

11. Your computer is configured to use DHCP on the IPv4 network 192.168.4.0 but is unable to connect to other computers. You run `ipconfig /all` and notice that the computer is using the address 169.254.231.98. You must try again immediately to connect to other network computers. Which parameter of the `ipconfig` command should you use?

   a. `/release`

   b. `/renew`

   c. `/flushdns`

   d. `/displaydns`

12. Computers on your network are configured to use static IP addresses. Your computer has been able to connect to the network most mornings when you start up, but one morning when you do not arrive until 9:30 a.m., your computer is unable to connect. Which of the following is the most likely reason for this problem?

   a. Your computer is configured with an IP address that is a duplicate of another one that has started up first.

   b. Your computer is using APIPA.

   c. Your computer is configured with an incorrect subnet mask.

   d. Your computer is configured with an alternative IP address and is using the alternative.

13. You are using the `ping` command to verify connectivity on your IPv6 network. You want to verify connectivity with a machine whose IPv6 address is fe80::9f:00ff:3a87:e364. Which of the following should you do? (Each answer represents part of the solution. Choose three.)

   a. Run the `ipconfig /displaydns` command.

   b. Run the `netsh interface ipv6 show interface` command.

   c. Run the `netsh interface ipv6 show neighbors` command.

   d. Run the `netsh interface ipv6 delete neighbors` command.

   e. Type `ping fe80::9f:00ff:3a87:e364 %<ID>`, where `<ID>` is the zone ID for the sending interface.

Foundation Topics

Concepts of TCP/IP

You might think of TCP/IP as a single networking protocol. However, this is not true—TCP/IP is actually a suite, or stack, of networking protocols that has been developed over the past several decades to provide a robust, scalable mechanism for networking computers both on a local and long-distance scale. Before introducing the components of the TCP/IP protocol stack, let's take a quick look at how this protocol stack came to be.

TCP/IP History in Brief

In the late 1960s, the Advanced Research Projects Agency (ARPA) of the U.S. Department of Defense began sponsoring research into connecting geographically remote computers (ARPA was later renamed The Defense Advanced Research Projects Agency [DARPA]). TCP/IP began its development as part of ARPANET, a U.S. Department of Defense (DOD) packet-switched, wide area network (WAN). ARPANET's initial reason for existence was to connect 4 mainframe computers located at the University of California at Los Angeles, Stanford Research Institute, University of California at Santa Barbara, and University of Utah. The network was gradually extended, and by 1981, was comprised of 200 mostly academic and research-oriented sites.

In the 1980s minicomputers and microcomputers were also evolving and growing in power and complexity. Many of these machines ran on Berkeley Software Distribution (BSD) UNIX. It was actually at the U.S. government's urging that the TCP/IP protocol was incorporated into the BSD version of UNIX. The sharing of knowledge could be made easier if everyone involved (and their computers) used a common set of communication protocols. Whatever the government's motives might have been, the Internet is in part a result of this coming together and this standardization.

Several of the more important milestones of the early development of TCP/IP include the following:

- **1970:** ARPANET began to use the Network Control Protocol (NCP).

- **1973:** Request for Comment (RFC) 454 described the File Transfer Protocol (FTP).

- **1974:** Detailed specifications for TCP were defined.

- **1981:** RFC 1791 described the IP protocol standard.

- **1982:** The Defense Communications Agency (DCA) and ARPA established TCP and IP as the TCP/IP protocol suite.

- **1983:** ARPANET began to use TCP/IP instead of NCP.

- **1984:** The Domain Name System (DNS) was introduced to provide a common name resolution standard for computers on the Internet.

NOTE   RFCs are officially registered documents that describe the internal workings of the Internet, including all standards and enhancements pertaining to TCP/IP versions 4 and 6. They propose revisions and enhancements to its present standards and methods. IETF working groups oversee the development, revision, and acceptance of each RFC. The beginnings of IPv4 were described in RFC 791; many additional RFCs have been published that describe other components of and improvements to IPv4 throughout the years. IPv6 was first described in RFC 1884, and was updated in RFCs 2373 and 3513.

The TCP/IP Protocol Stack

You can generally describe network protocols as being implemented in layers. The bottom layer typically deals with the physical aspects of networking. As one ascends through the layers, functions and descriptions become increasingly less physical and more abstract. A model that is commonly used to describe networking functionality is the Open Systems Interconnection (OSI) reference model, which segregates networking functions into a series of seven layers, each of which specifies protocols and interfaces that work together to provide all network communications, both within the local area network (LAN) and globally across the Internet.

NOTE   For more information on the OSI model and the functions of each of its layers, refer to "The OSI Model's Seven Layers Defined and Functions Explained" at http://support.microsoft.com/kb/103884. You can also refer to any textbook on computer networking or the CompTIA Network+ exam.

The Four-Layer TCP/IP Model

TCP/IP protocols correspond to a four-layer reference model, as shown in Figure 10-1. Here also, the four layers represent related standards. These standards serve to define the architecture of a TCP/IP network. They also define how TCP/IP communicates. The four layers that comprise the TCP/IP protocol suite are

Application, Transport, Internet, and Network Interface. Each layer corresponds to one or more layers of the seven-layer OSI model as shown in the diagram. If you remember your networking essentials, you are aware that logical communication takes place between the corresponding layers of a reference model as found on two machines on a network. That is, the Application layer on one machine has important things to say to the Application layer on another machine.

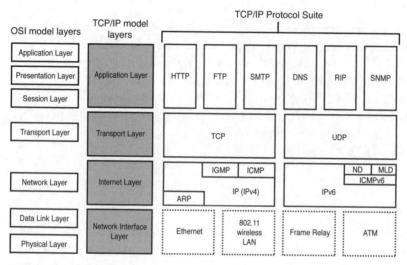

Figure 10-1   TCP/IP architecture is built in four layers.

Physical communication takes place between adjacent layers within the reference model on one machine. For example, the Transport layer passes information to and receives information from the Internet layer as found on one machine. A basic familiarity with the layers helps to understand how TCP/IP operates.

The Application Layer

Like the OSI model's Application layer, this layer is the access point that applications use to begin communicating with the network. Most applications conform to a client/server architecture. This layer defines numerous protocols (HTTP, FTP, SMTP, DNS, RIP, and SNMP) used by applications to communicate across the network; more applications that use this layer are always in development.

The Transport Layer

Transmission Control Protocol (TCP) and User Datagram Protocol (UDP) are the two protocols that operate at the Transport layer. They are principally responsible for enabling delivery of packets transmitted by the Network layer.

TCP is the protocol used for connection-oriented, reliable communication between two hosts—typically involving large amounts of data. Note that a *host* includes any device on the network (such as a computer, switch, or router) that is configured for TCP/IP. User Datagram Protocol (UDP) is used for non-connection-oriented communications with no guarantee of delivery—typically small, short bursts of data. Applications that are using UDP data are responsible for checking their data's integrity.

The Internet Layer

The Internet layer is primarily concerned with the routing and delivery of packets. This layer corresponds closely to the OSI Network layer. Both versions 4 and 6 of the Internet Protocol (IP) operate at this layer.

Routing is accomplished mainly by means of IP. Other protocols that function at the Internet Layer are the Internet Control Messaging Protocol (ICMP), Internet Group Management Protocol (IGMP), Address Resolution Protocol (ARP), Neighbor Discovery (ND) protocol, and Multicast Listener Discovery (MLD) protocol.

The Network Interface Layer

The network interface layer provides an interface for the layer above it to the network media. This layer controls the way frames are ultimately built and sent out on to the network media (Ethernet cables, network adapter cards, wireless cards, and so on) or received from the network media and sent to the upper layers. It is also responsible for controlling how frames are received from the network media and transmitted to the upper layers. The Network Interface layer needs to furnish an interface enabling the Internet layer to communicate with it from above. The Internet layer, in turn, is responsible for communicating directly with the Network Interface layer below.

The TCP/IP Component Protocols

As already described and shown in Figure 10-1, the TCP/IP protocol suite consists of a large number of component protocols. The following sections introduce these protocols.

Transmission Control Protocol

The *Transmission Control Protocol (TCP)* provides connection-oriented, reliable communication between two hosts, typically involving large amounts of data. This kind of communication also involves acknowledgements that data has been correctly received. TCP works by establishing a connection, or session, between two hosts before transmitting data. Once established, this connection is maintained for the duration of a session. The connection is closed at the end of session.

TCP is described as a reliable protocol because it makes every effort to deliver data to its destination. TCP accepts messages from upper-layer protocols and provides an acknowledged connection-oriented delivery service to the Transport layer at a remote host. Operating at the Transport layer, TCP provides a reliable and guaranteed delivery mechanism to a destination host. TCP can guarantee delivery of packets by tracking the transmission and error-free receipt of individual packets during communication. TCP reliability is the result of TCP assigning a sequence number to each data segment transmitted. TCP also informs upper network layers of errors if it cannot transmit data successfully. In addition, TCP is responsible for ensuring that data is sent in the proper sequence. TCP uses a checksum feature to validate both the packet header and its data for correctness. If a packet is lost or corrupted during transmission, TCP is responsible for initiating a retransmission of that packet. All the characteristics of TCP mentioned in this paragraph add overhead in terms of transmission speed and processing.

User Datagram Protocol

The *User Datagram Protocol (UDP)* is used for fast, non-connection-oriented communications with no guarantee of delivery, typically small, short bursts of data. It guarantees neither delivery nor correct sequencing of packets. Applications using UDP data transmission are responsible for checking their data's integrity. UDP operates with less overhead than TCP. It is also used sending data from a single source to multiple destinations.

In general, UDP is best for handling transmission of large amount of data where a dropped packet or two is not a major catastrophe. This can also include streaming and multimedia applications that require fast delivery of large amounts of data. Users of these applications won't notice that a few bits are out of place in a sound or picture. Digital media are still far more accurate in terms of reproduction than their analog alternatives.

Internet Protocol

The *Internet Protocol (IP)* handles, addresses, and routes packets between hosts on a network. It performs this service for all other protocols in the TCP/IP protocol suite.

IP is a connectionless protocol. Connectionless protocol transmissions occur without a pre-established path between the source and destination. This means that packets can take different routes between the source and destination. Packets might arrive at their destinations by different paths and in random order. They can also be duplicated or delayed. Although there is no way to guarantee delivery, IP will always make a "best effort" to deliver packets using the limited means at its disposal.

This best effort does not include acknowledgement for data that is received. Nor is the sender or receiver informed by IP when a packet goes missing or is sent out of sequence. Instead, the higher layer protocols, particularly TCP, take on the job of ensuring packets reach their destination without error and making acknowledgements in general.

By default, IP always first checks to see whether the destination IP address involved is for a local or remote host. If the destination address is identified as a local one, IP sends the packet directly to the host. If the destination address is a remote one, IP looks first to the local routing table for a route to the destination host or network. If IP cannot find a path in the routing table, it sends the packet to the source host's default gateway (assuming one is configured).

Address Resolution Protocol

Within the TCP/IP protocol suite, other protocols are used by IP for special tasks. For two systems to communicate across a TCP/IP network, the system sending the packet must map the address of the destination computer to the physical or media access control (MAC) address, which is a unique 12-digit hexadecimal number that is burned into ROM on every network adapter card. The *Address Resolution Protocol (ARP)* detects and updates a table that matches physical addresses with IP addresses. This table is cached or stored in RAM for a limited time.

Internet Control Message Protocol

The *Internet Control Message Protocol (ICMP)* is used to deliver messages to hosts on a TCP/IP network. ICMP is specifically responsible for reporting errors and messages regarding the delivery of IP datagrams. It is not responsible for error correction. Higher-layer protocols use information provided by ICMP to recover from transmission problems. Network administrators might also be able to use ICMP to detect network problems. ICMP is required in every IPv4 network implementation; IPv6 networks use a newer implementation of this protocol, ICMPv6.

Internet Group Management Protocol

The *Internet Group Management Protocol (IGMP)* is used at the host level to report host group memberships to local multicast routers. IGMP provides membership in a multicast group to individual TCP/IP hosts. Multicasting is a limited form of broadcasting because broadcasts are directed to only members of the multicast group.

These machines are also assigned special network addresses by TCP/IP. When using IGMP, a computer or other device sends a single copy of a message to a multicast service provider as a single operation. The service provider delivers that message to members of a group specified in the transmission. Note that IGMP is used in IPv4 only; on IPv6 networks, IGMP has been replaced by MLD, which serves to manage multicast groups on IPv6 networks.

Application Layer Protocols

The following protocols, located within the Application Layer of the four-layer TCP/IP model, provide ancillary application-related services to their host computers:

- **Hypertext Transfer Protocol (HTTP):** Provides a file transfer capability for web-based pages as requested by a browser.

- **File Transfer Protocol (FTP):** Provides bidirectional file transfers between a Windows-based computer and any TCP/IP host running FTP server software.

- **Simple Mail Transfer Protocol (SMTP):** Provides a simple service for transferring email messages and their attachments.

- **Domain Name System (DNS):** Resolves hostnames on the Internet and local networks to IP addresses. DNS is such an important technology on Windows networks that we spend four chapters on this topic.

- **Routing Internet Protocol (RIP):** Used by routers to exchange routing information across IP subnetworks. Windows Server 2012 R2 supports the updated version of this protocol, RIPv2.

- **Simple Network Management Protocol (SNMP):** Gathers network management information from network devices, such as routers, bridges, and servers, and provides this information to network management consoles.

You will study most of these protocols in detail in later chapters of this *Cert Guide* or in the *Cert Guide* for exam 70-411.

NOTE   For additional information on the component protocols in the TCP/IP protocol suite and their functions, refer to "Chapter 2–Architectural Overview of the TCP/IP Protocol Suite" at http://technet.microsoft.com/en-us/library/bb726993.aspx. Also refer to "IPv4 Protocols" for information on packet headers at http://technet.microsoft.com/en-us/library/dd392264(WS.10).aspx. You should note that the components and functionality of TCP/IP in Windows Server 2012

R2 are unchanged from TCP/IP in Windows Server 2008 R2.For more information on networking in general for Windows Server 2012 R2, refer to "Networking Overview" at http://technet.microsoft.com/en-us/library/hh831357.aspx and references cited therein.

New and Improved Networking Technologies in Windows Server 2012 R2

Microsoft has improved on many networking technologies in Windows Server 2012 R2. The following is a brief summary of these improvements:

- **802.1X authenticated wired and wireless network access:** Several new features and capabilities have been added, including the extension of the use of passwords for wired Ethernet access, the support for improved wireless bandwidth using the 802.11ac protocol, and the capability for wirelessly projecting your laptop or tablet screen to large monitors and TVs. Use of employee-owned wireless devices is possible with the need to enter passwords only once.

- **Improvements to DNS:** DNS servers in Windows Server 2012 R2 provide enhanced zone-level statistics, enhanced support for DNSSEC, and enhanced Windows PowerShell cmdlets and parameters.

- **Improvements to DHCP:** Microsoft has added new features and capabilities to DHCP in Windows Server 2012 R2. Included are DNS registration enhancements, which enable you to use DHCP policies to configure conditions based on clients' FQDN. Workgroup computers can be registered to DHCP using a guest DNS suffix. As well, new Windows PowerShell cmdlets are available.

- **Enhancements to Hyper-V networking:** Microsoft has introduced many updates to Hyper-V network virtualization, including hybrid cloud and private cloud solution enhancements and new features and capabilities to the Hyper-V virtual switch.

- **Improvements to Remote Access:** Microsoft has added new features and capabilities to the Routing and Remote Access (RRAS) server role and the DirectAccess role service in Windows Server 2012 R2 and Windows 8.1. Included are multitenant, site-to-site VPN Gateway, Multitenant Remote Access VPN Gateway, Border Gateway Protocol (BGP), and Web Application Policy, as well as supporting client features for Windows 8.1 computers.

- **Virtual Receive-side scaling:** This is a new feature introduced in Windows Server 2012 R2 that enables the load from a virtual network adapter to be distributed across multiple virtual processors in a virtual server.

- **Windows Server Gateway:** New to Windows Server 2012 R2, this feature is a virtual machine–based software that enables Cloud Service Providers and Enterprises to enable datacenter and cloud network traffic routing between physical and virtual networks, including the Internet.

> **NOTE** For additional information on new networking technologies in Windows Server 2012 R2, refer to "What's New in Networking in Windows Server 2012 R2" at http://technet.microsoft.com/en-us/library/dn313100.aspx, together with references cited therein.

IPv4 Addressing

IPv4 is installed as the default TCP/IP networking protocol in Windows Server 2012 R2. Much of IPv4 is transparent to users when you've configured it properly. The administrator might need to configure the address information applied to the network interface. Table 10-2 describes this address information:

Table 10-2 IPv4 Addressing Components

Addressing Component	Description
IP address	The unique, logical 32-bit address, which identifies the computer (called a *host* or *node*) and the subnet on which it is located. The IP address is displayed in dotted decimal notation (each decimal represents an octet of binary ones and zeroes). For example, the binary notation of an address can be 10000000.00000001.0000 0001.00000011, which in dotted decimal notation is written as 128.1.1.3.
Subnet mask	The subnet mask is applied to an IP address to determine the subnetwork address and the host address on that subnet. All hosts on the same subnet must have the same subnet mask for them to be correctly identified. If a mask is incorrect, both the subnet and the host address will be wrong. (For example, if you have an IP address of 128.1.1.3 and an incorrect mask of 255.255.128.0, the subnet address would be 128.1.0 and the host address would be 1.3. If the correct subnet mask is 255.255.255.0, then the subnet address would be 128.1.1 and the host address would be 3.)
Default gateway	The address listed as the default gateway is the location on the local subnet to which the local computer will send all data meant for other subnets. In other words, this is the IP address for the local network side of the router that is capable of transmitting the data to other networks.

Addressing Component	Description
DNS server address	The IP address to which names of IP hosts are sent so that the DNS server will respond with an IP address. This process is called *name resolution*. DNS is a distributed database of records that maps names to IP addresses, and vice versa.
Windows Internet Name Service (WINS) address	The WINS server address is the location where network computers send requests to resolve NetBIOS names to IP addresses. WINS is used on Microsoft Windows networks where older Windows computers or applications require NetBIOS name resolution. When a user types in a NetBIOS name, such as JACKSPC, the computer sends the name to the WINS server. Because WINS is a flat-file database, it returns an IP address or a `Name not found` message. WINS server addresses, like DNS server addresses, are optional.

Static IPv4 Addressing

IP addresses indicate the same type of location information as a street address within a city. A building on a street has a number, and when you add it to the street name, you can find it fairly easily because the number and the street will be unique within that city. This type of address scheme—an individual address plus a location address—enables every computer on a corporate network or the Internet to be uniquely identified.

A static IP address is one that is manually assigned to a computer on the network. Certain computers require static IP addresses because of their functions, such as routers or servers. Client computers are more often assigned dynamic addresses because they are more likely to be moved around the network or retired and replaced. DSL and cable modem users are usually given a static IP address, whereas dial-up users are provided with dynamic addresses.

IP addresses consist of two parts—one that specifies the network and one part that specifies the computer. These addresses are further categorized with classes, as described in Table 10-3.

Table 10-3   IPv4 Address Classes

Class	Dotted Decimal Hosts per Range	Default Subnet Mask	First Octet Binary	Usage	Number of Networks	Number of Hosts per Network
A	1.0.0.0– 126.255.255.255	255.0.0.0	0xxxxxxx	Large networks and ISPs	128	16.777.214
B	128.0.0.0– 191.255.255.255	255.255.0.0	10xxxxxx	Large or mid-size ISPs	16,384	65,534
C	192.0.0.0– 223.255.255.255	255.255.255.0	110xxxxx	Small networks	2,097,152	254
D	224.0.0.0– 239.255.255.255	N/A	1110xxxx	Multicasting	N/A	N/A
E	240.0.0.0– 254.255.255.255	N/A	1111xxxx	Reserved for future use	N/A	N/A

NOTE   The concept of loopback testing is the usage of a predefined IP address that a computer can dial itself up to see whether the TCP/IP stack is properly set up. If TCP/IP is configured, you should be able to run the `ping 127.0.0.1` command when troubleshooting a connectivity problem. More about this command is provided later in this chapter.

The portion of the address that decides on which network the host resides varies based on the class, and, as you will see further on, the subnet mask. In the following list, the uppercase *N*s represent the part of the IP address that specifies the network, and the lowercase *C*s represent the part of the address that specifies the computer. This explains why there are differing numbers of networks per class and different numbers of hosts per network, as listed in Table 10-3.

- **Class A:** NNNNNNNN.cccccccc.cccccccc.cccccccc

- **Class B:** NNNNNNNN.NNNNNNNN.cccccccc.cccccccc

- **Class C:** NNNNNNNN.NNNNNNNN.NNNNNNNN.cccccccc

These address portions coincide with the default subnet masks for each address class. A Class A subnet mask is 255.0.0.0, a Class B subnet mask is 255.255.0.0, and a Class C subnet mask is 255.255.255.0.

Take, for example, the IP address 192.168.5.137 on a default Class C network. In binary notation, this address is as follows:

11000000 10101000 00000101 10001001

The network portion of the address is the first three octets—11000000 10101000 00000101—and the host portion is represented by the final octet—10001001. This division follows directly from the information provided in Table 10-3.

In recent years, it has become popular to use *Classless Interdomain Routing (CIDR)*, also known as the *slash notation* or *CIDR notation*, to refer to the number of bits represented by the network portion of the IP address. This provides a simple means of defining a network address and subnet mask together; simply suffix the network address with a slash (/) followed immediately by the number of bits in the network portion of the address. Table 10-4 compares the different notations of the default subnet masks for Class A, B, and C networks.

Table 10-4   Default Subnet Masks in Different Notations

Class	Binary Subnet Mask Notation	Decimal Subnet Mask Notation	CIDR Notation
A	11111111 00000000 00000000 00000000	255.0.0.0	/8
B	11111111 11111111 00000000 00000000	255.255.0.0	/16
C	11111111 11111111 11111111 00000000	255.255.255.0	/24

Subnetting and Supernetting in IPv4

IPv4 does not restrict you to the default subnet masks already introduced for Classes A, B, and C networks. If it did, the use of IP address space would be extremely inefficient and IPv4 addresses would have been exhausted decades ago. By employing subnetting, you can divide the address space of your network into subnets of an efficient size that relates to the number of hosts that each subnet must support.

Using Subnetting to Divide a Network

The process of *subnetting* enables you to reconfigure which portion of the subnet mask constitutes the network portion and which portion constitutes the host portion. When you apply the subnet mask to the IP address by using a bitwise logical AND operation as discussed in the previous section, the result is a network number. A bitwise logical AND operation adds the bit, whether 1 or 0, to the corresponding bit in the subnet mask. If the subnet mask bit is a 1, the corresponding IP address bit is passed through as a result. If the subnet mask bit is a 0, a zero bit is passed through. For example, if the IP address is 141.25.240.201 with the default Class B subnet mask of 255.255.0.0 or /16, you will have the following:

- IP address: = 10001101.00011001.11110000.11001001

- Subnet mask = : 11111111.11111111.00000000.00000000

- Result from bitwise logical AND

- Network: = 10001101.00011001.00000000.00000000

This shows the network address as 141.25.0.0 and the host address to 0.0.240.201. If you add bits to the mask, you will be able to have additional subnetworks when you perform a bitwise logical AND, and each subnetwork will have fewer hosts because fewer bits are available for the host portion of the address. If you use the same address and add five bits to the subnet mask, you would receive the following:

- IP address: = 10001101.00011001.11110000.11001001

- Subnet mask: = 11111111.11111111.11111000.00000000

- Result from bitwise logical AND

- Network: = 10001101.00011001.11110000.00000000

In this case, the subnet mask changes the network address to 141.25.240.0 or /21. The host address changes to 0.0.0.201. Other IP addresses that are under the default Class B subnet mask that would otherwise be part of the same network, such as 140.25.192.15 and 140.25.63.12, are now on different subnets.

For an organization with a large number of physical networks where each requires a different subnet address, you can use the subnet mask to segment a single address to fit the network. You can easily calculate how many subnets and hosts you will receive when you subnet a network. To calculate the number of subnets, use the formula 2^s, where s is the number of bits in the subnet portion of the address. 2^s is the number 2 raised to the power of the number of subnet bits. To calculate the number of hosts available on each subnet, use the formula 2^h-2, where h is the number of bits in the host portion of the address. 2^h is the number 2 raised to the power of the number of host bits, and that result minus 2 (the addresses represented by all 1s and all 0s) equals the available hosts. Therefore, if you have a subnet of 5 bits as previously shown, you are able to achieve $2^5 = 32$ subnets. Because there are 11 bits left for host addresses, each subnet will have $2^{11}-2 = 2048-2 = 2,046$ hosts.

Table 10-5 compares the number of networks and hosts provided by subnetting a Class B network. You should be easily able to compute similar numbers for other network classes.

Table 10-5 Subnetting a Class B Network

Dotted Decimal Subnet Mask	CIDR Notation	Number of Subnets	Number of Hosts per Subnet
255.255.128.0	/17	2	32766
255.255.192.0	/18	4	16382
255.255.224.0	/19	8	8190
255.255.240.0	/20	16	4094
255.255.248.0	/21	32	2046
255.255.252.0	/22	64	1022
255.255.254.0	/23	128	510
255.255.255.0	/24	256	254

NOTE For more information on subnetting Class A, B, and C IPv4 networks, refer to "Host and Subnet Quantities" at http://www.cisco.com/en/US/tech/tk365/technologies_tech_note09186a0080093f33.shtml.

TIP Be sure you understand the various notations of IPv4 subnet masks thoroughly, both for the 70-410 exam and for the real world. You are most likely to encounter questions on the exam that ask you to determine the subnet mask that will accommodate a given number of hosts.

NOTE For more information on subnetting, refer to "Subnetting" at http://technet.microsoft.com/en-us/library/cc958834.aspx. For more information on all aspects of IP addressing, refer to "Chapter 3—IP Addressing" at http://technet.microsoft.com/en-us/library/bb726995.aspx.

Using Supernetting to Provide for Additional Hosts on a Network

The process of subnetting as outlined in the preceding section enables you to subdivide a network according to the number of hosts on each segment. But you might encounter the opposite problem—you might require a larger number of hosts than what a given network can accommodate. Suppose you are responsible for an organization that requires IPv4 addressing for as many as 2,000 hosts. Recall from Table 10-3 that a Class C network can accommodate up to 254 hosts, so your company would require 8 separate Class C networks or a single Class B network. However, the latter, which can accommodate 65,534 hosts, would be wasteful of IPv4 addresses. So the Internet Assigned Numbers Authority (IANA) assigns your company a contiguous block of 8 Class C network addresses that you combine to form a single network. This practice is known as *supernetting*. In doing so, a company can "supernet" 2 (or more) Class C addresses to put more than 254 hosts on a single physical network. Supernetting is the process of subtracting bits from the default subnet mask. This adds bits to the host portion, increasing the number of hosts available. CIDR is used in conjunction with supernetting so that only a single routing table entry is required for the 8 Class C networks assigned in this example. A possible CIDR notation for the network in this example could be 192.168.1.0/21. Table 10-6 shows how you can supernet several Class C networks together:

Table 10-6   Supernetting a Class C Network

Dotted Decimal Subnet Mask	CIDR Notation	Number of Network Addresses Combined	Number of Hosts Accommodated
255.255.192.0	/18	64	16382
255.255.224.0	/19	32	8190
255.255.240.0	/20	16	4094
255.255.248.0	/21	8	2046
255.255.252.0	/22	4	1022
255.255.254.0	/23	2	510

NOTE   For more information on supernetting, refer to "Planning Supernetting and Classless Interdomain Routing (CIDR)" at http://technet.microsoft.com/en-us/library/cc783978(WS.10).aspx.

Understanding Private IPv4 Networks

IPv4 specifications define sets of networks that are specified as *private IPv4 networks*. The private IP address classes are used on private networks that do not need to be accessed directly from the public Internet. Internet routers are preconfigured to not forward data that contains these IP addresses. Table 10-7 describes these networks.

Table 10-7 *Private IPv4 Network Addresses Defined in* IETF RFC 1918

Class	Dotted Decimal Address Range	First Octet Binary	Network Prefix	Number of Networks	Number of Hosts per Network
A	10.0.0.0–10.255.255.255	1010	/8	1	16,777,214
B	172.16.0.0–172.31.255.255	10101100	/12	16	65,534
C	192.168.0.0–192.168.255.255	11000000	/16	256	254

Dynamic IP Addressing

Dynamic IP addresses are provided to a computer when it needs to be connected to the network. The provider is the Dynamic Host Configuration Protocol (DHCP) server. Such an IP address is leased for a specified period of time (the administrator specifies this time period when configuring the DHCP server), and when the lease is up, the IP address is placed back in an IP address pool and can be delivered to another computer. You will learn more about DHCP and dynamic IP addressing in Chapter 11, "Configuring Dynamic Host Configuration Protocol (DHCP)."

Configuring IPv4 Address Options

You can configure TCP/IP version 4 on a Windows Server 2012 R2 computer either manually or dynamically. The default method is to dynamically configure TCP/IP. If the infrastructure includes DHCP services that deliver IP addresses to network computers, then a Windows Server 2012 R2 computer can connect upon logon with the default configuration of the network adapter. However, if you need to apply a static IPv4 address and other parameters (which is required for servers that provide infrastructure services, such as DHCP or DNS servers or domain controllers), your only option is to manually configure the network adapter. Use the following procedure to configure your server with a static IPv4 address:

1. In the Search charm, type `Network`. Select **Network and Sharing Center** from the list that appears. You can also access the **Control Panel** by selecting it from the Start screen or by right-clicking **Start** and choosing **Control Panel**. In either case, then select **View network status and tasks** under Network and Internet. Any of these actions opens the Network and Sharing Center.

2. From the left side of the Network and Sharing Center, click **Change adapter settings**. This opens the Network Connections page, as shown in Figure 10-2.

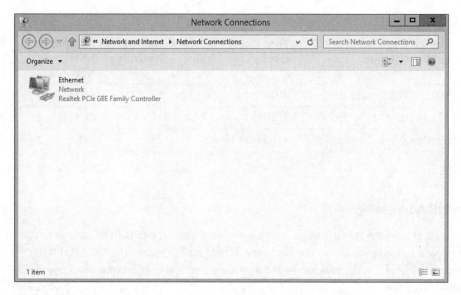

Figure 10-2   The Network Connections page displays the network connections configured for your computer.

3. Right-click the connection that represents the adapter you are going to configure, and select **Properties**. The Ethernet Properties dialog box opens, as shown in Figure 10-3.

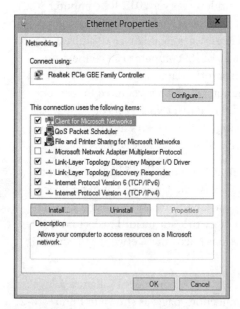

Figure 10-3   The Ethernet Properties dialog box enables you to configure TCP/IP addressing options.

4. Click to select **Internet Protocol Version 4 (TCP/IPv4)**. (You might need to scroll through other services to reach this item.) Click **Properties**. The Internet Protocol Version 4 (TCP/IPv4) Properties dialog box opens, as shown in Figure 10-4.

Figure 10-4 The Internet Protocol Version 4(TCP/IPv4) Properties dialog box lets you define manual or dynamic IPv4 address information.

5. To use DHCP services, you should make certain that **Obtain an IP address automatically** is selected, and if the DHCP server provides extended information—including the DNS server information—you also should select **Obtain DNS server address automatically**. To manually configure the IP address, click **Use the following IP address**.

6. In the IP address box, type the address that will function on the current network segment. For example, if the network segment uses a Class C address 192.168.1.0 with a subnet mask of 255.255.255.0 and you've already used 192.168.1.1 and 192.168.1.2, you could select any node address from 3 through 254 (255 is used for broadcasts), in which case you would type `192.168.1.3`.

7. In the Subnet mask box, type the subnet mask. In this case, it would be `255.255.255.0`.

8. In the Default gateway box, type the IP address that is assigned to the router interface on your current segment that leads to the main network or the public network. For example, suppose that the IP address of the router on your

segment is 192.168.1.1 and the IP address of the router's other interface is 12.88.54.179. In the Default gateway box, you would type `192.168.1.1`.

9. To configure an alternative IP address on a computer configured to use DHCP, click the **Alternate Configuration** tab. Then enter the required IP address, subnet mask, default gateway, and DNS and WINS server information.

10. Click the **Advanced** button. The Advanced TCP/IP Settings dialog box opens, as shown in Figure 10-5.

Figure 10-5 The Advanced TCP/IP Settings dialog box enables you to control granular IP addressing options.

11. If you require more than one IP address for a computer, such as for hosting two different websites, you can configure the additional IP addresses in this dialog box by clicking the **Add** button. You cannot configure any additional IP addresses if you are using DHCP.

12. If your network segment is connected to more than one router leading to the main or outside networks, you can configure these gateway addresses in the Default Gateways section by clicking the **Add** button.

13. When finished, click **OK** twice and then click **Close** to return to the Network Connections dialog box.

NOTE If you have configured your server to receive an IP address from DHCP and the observed IPv4 address is in the range of 169.254.0.1–169.254.255.254, your server has been unable to access the DHCP server and has used Automatic Private Internet Protocol Addressing (APIPA) to assign itself an IP address. Although possibly useful on a small LAN, this is usually a symptom of network connectivity problems. Refer to the section "Resolving IPv4 and IPv6 Connectivity Issues" later in this chapter for troubleshooting information.

TIP An alternate configuration as described in Step 9 of the preceding procedure is useful with a portable computer that might move to a network without a DHCP server. If such a computer is unable to locate a DHCP server, it defaults to the alternate IP configuration rather than assigning itself an APIPA address.

Using the Command Line to Configure IPv4 Addressing Options

Windows Server 2012 R2 introduces many new PowerShell cmdlets that enable you to configure TCP/IP-based networking. These commands are useful for scripting network configuration for a series of computers and are the only means of configuring TCP/IP options at a machine running the Server Core option of Windows Server 2012 R2.

Windows Server 2012 R2 still supports the `netsh` command that enables you to configure TCP/IP networking and addressing options from the command line. However, Microsoft recommends that you use the newer PowerShell cmdlets to configure networking in Windows Server 2012 R2, and these recommendations are sure to be reflected in questions asked on the 70-410 exam and other Windows Server 2012 R2 exams. Note, however, that you can execute `netsh` commands from within the PowerShell interface.

Table 10-8 describes many useful cmdlets for Windows Server 2012 R2 TCP/IPv4 networking:

Table 10-8 Windows Server 2012 R2 IPv4 Cmdlets

Cmdlet	Description
`Get-NetIPAddress`	Displays information about IP address configuration
`Get-NetIPInterface`	Displays information about IP interface properties
`Get-NetIPv4Protocol`	Displays information about the IPv4 protocol configuration
`Get-NetNeighbor`	Displays information about the neighbor cache for IPv4 and IPv6

Cmdlet	Description
Get-NetRoute	Displays the IP routing table
Get=NetTCPConnection	Displays information about current TCP connection statistics
Get-NetTCPSetting	Displays information about TCP settings and configuration
New-NetIPAddress	Creates an IP address and its corresponding configuration properties
New-NetNeighbor	Creates a neighbor cache entry for IPv4 and IPv6
New-NetRoute	Creates an entry in the IP routing table
Remove-NetIPAddress	Deletes an IP address and its corresponding configuration properties
Remove-NetNeighbor	Deletes a neighbor cache entry for IPv4 and IPv6
Remove-NetRoute	Deletes an entry or entries (IP routes) from the IP routing table
Set-NetIPAddress	Edits IP address configuration properties for an existing IP address
Set-NetIPInterface	Edits IP interface properties
Set-NetIPv4Protocol	Edits information about the IPv4 protocol configuration
Set-NetNeighbor	Edits information about a neighbor cache entry
Set-NetRoute	Edits an entry or entries in the IP routing table
Set-NetTCPSetting	Edits TCP settings and configuration

To obtain the proper syntax of any of these cmdlets, as well as additional information about the usage of each cmdlet, use the **Get-Help** *<cmdlet_name>* cmdlet, where *<cmdlet_name>* is the name of the desired cmdlet.

> **NOTE**   For more information on all TCP/IP cmdlets available for Windows Server 2012 R2, refer to "Net TCP/IP Cmdlets in Windows PowerShell" at http://technet.microsoft.com/library/hh826123.aspx. Use the links associated with each cmdlet to obtain syntax information for the selected cmdlet.

> **NOTE**   For additional information on netsh commands, refer to "Netsh Technical Reference" at http://technet.microsoft.com/en-us/library/cc725935(WS.10). aspx and "Netsh Overview" at http://technet.microsoft.com/en-us/library/ cc732279(WS.10).aspx. Though written for Windows Server 2008, these commands are still applicable on servers running Windows Server 2012 and Windows Server 2012 R2.

IPv6 Addressing

The 128-bit addressing scheme used by IPv6 enables an unimaginably high number of 3.4×10^{38} addresses, which equates to a total of 6.5×10^{23} addresses for every square meter of the Earth's surface. Consequently, this is a complicated addressing scheme, as described in the following sections.

By default, versions of Windows prior to Windows Server 2008 have used version 4 of the IP protocol, simply known as IPv4. With its 32-bit address space, this version has performed admirably well in the 25+ years since its initial introduction. However, with the rapid growth of the Internet in recent years, its address space has approached exhaustion and security concerns have increased. In fact, a news story in February 2011 reported that the last five blocks of IPv4 addresses had been allocated to the five Regional Internet Registries (RIRs), which will distribute these addresses to ISPs. Consequently, the IETF introduced version 6 of the IP protocol with RFC 1883 in 1995 and added RFCs 2460, 3513, and 4193 in more recent years.

The introduction by the IETF of 128-bit IPv6 addressing provides for a practically infinite number of possible addresses, as well as the following benefits:

- **An efficient hierarchical addressing scheme:** IPv6 addresses are designed to enable an efficient, hierarchical, and summarizable routing scheme, making way for multiple levels of ISPs.

- **Simpler routing tables:** Backbone routers on the Internet are more easily configured for routing packets to their destinations. Routing is discussed in the *Cert Guide* book for exam 70-411.

- **Stateful and stateless address configuration:** IPv6 simplifies host configuration with the use of stateful address configuration (configuring IP addresses in the presence of a DHCP server) or the use of stateless address configuration (configuring IP addresses in the absence of a DHCP server). Stateless address configuration enables the automatic configuration of hosts on a subnetwork according to the addresses displayed by available routers.

- **Improved security:** IPv6 includes standards-based support for IP Security (IPsec). In fact, IPv6 requires IPsec support. You can configure IPsec connection security rules for IPv6 in the same fashion as with IPv4. IPsec is discussed further in Chapter 19, "Configuring Windows Firewall."

- **Support for Link-Local Multicast Name Resolution (LLMNR):** This enables IPv6 clients on a single subnet to resolve each other's names without the need for a DNS server or using NetBIOS over TCP/IP.

- **Improved support for Quality of Service (QoS):** IPv6 header fields improve the identification and handling of network traffic from its source to destination, even when IPSec encryption is in use.

- **Extensibility:** You can add extension headers after the IPv6 packet header, which enable the inclusion of new features as they are developed in years to come.

By using a TCP/IP implementation known as the Next Generation TCP/IP stack (first included with Windows Vista), both Windows Server 2012 R2 and Windows 8.1 enable a dual IP layer architecture that allows the operation of both IPv4 and IPv6 at the same time. Unlike with Windows XP and older Windows versions, Windows Server 2012 R2 does not require you to install a separate IPv6 component; IPv6 is installed and enabled by default.

NOTE   For more introductory information on IPv6, refer to "Internet Protocol Version 6 (IPv6) Overview" at http://technet.microsoft.com/en-us/library/hh831730(v=ws.11).

IPv6 Address Syntax

Whereas IPv4 addresses use dotted-decimal format as explained earlier in this chapter, IPv6 addresses are subdivided into eight 16-bit blocks. Each 16-bit block is portrayed as a 4-digit hexadecimal number and is separated from other blocks by colons. This addressing scheme is referred to as *colon-hexadecimal*.

For example, a 128-bit IPv6 address written in binary could appear as follows:

0011111111111110 1111111111111111 0010000111000101
0000000000000000 0000001010101010 0000000011111111
1111111000100001 0011101000111110

The same address written in colon-hexadecimal becomes 3ffe:ffff:21a5:0000:00ff:fe21:5a3e. You can remove any single set of contiguous leading zeros, converting this address to 3ffe:ffff:21a5::ff:fe21:5a3e. This process is known as *zero compression*. In this notation, the block that contained all zeros appears as : :, which is called *double-colon*. You can always figure out how many blocks of zeros are contained within a double-colon because all IPv6 addresses consist of eight 16-bit blocks.

CAUTION   You can have only one double-colon notation within any IPv6 address. This is to prevent ambiguity in the number of blocks that contain all zeros at any given part of the address.

IPv6 Prefixes

Corresponding to the network portion of an IPv4 address is the prefix, which is the part of the address containing the bits of the subnet prefix. IPv6 addresses do not employ subnet masks, but rather use the same CIDR notation used with IPv4. For example, an IPv6 address prefix could be 3ffe:ffff:21a5::/64, where 64 is the number of bits employed by the address prefix.

Types of IPv6 Addresses

IPv6 uses the following three types of addresses:

- **Unicast:** Represents a single interface within the typical scope of unicast addresses. In other words, packets addressed to this type of address are to be delivered to a single network interface. Unicast IPv6 addresses include global unicast, link-local, and unique local addresses. Two special addresses are also included—unspecified addresses (all zeros or ::, equivalent to the IPv4 address of 0.0.0.0) and the loopback address, which is 0:0:0:0:0:0:0:1 or ::1 (which is equivalent to the IPv4 address of 127.0.0.1). By default, all unicast addresses are divided into a 64-bit network component and a 64-bit host component.

- **Multicast:** Represents multiple interfaces to which packets are delivered to all network interfaces identified by the address. Multicast addresses have the first eight bits set to 1s, so they begin with `ff`.

- **Anycast:** Also represents multiple interfaces. Anycast packets are delivered to a single network interface that represents the nearest (in terms of routing hops) interface identified by the address.

Table 10-9 provides additional details on the IPv6 classes and subclasses:

Table 10-9 IPv6 Address Classes and Subclasses

Class	Address Prefix	Additional Features	First Binary Bits	Usage
Global unicast	2000::/3	Use a global routing prefix of 45 bits (beyond the initial 001 bits) that identifies a specific organization's network, a 16-bit subnet ID (which identifies up to 65,536 subnets within an organization's network), and a 64-bit interface ID (which indicates a specific network interface within the subnet)	001	Globally routable Internet addresses that are equivalent to the public IPv4 addresses

Class	Address Prefix	Additional Features	First Binary Bits	Usage
Link-Local unicast	fe80::/64	Equivalent to APIPA-configured IPv4 addresses in the 169.254.0.0/16 network prefix	111111101000	Nonroutable addresses used for communication between neighboring nodes on the same subnet. These addresses are assigned automatically when you configure automatic addressing in the absence of a DHCP server
Unique local IPv6 unicast	fc00::/7	Prefix followed by a local (L) flag, a 40-bit global ID, a 16-bit subnet ID, and a 64-bit interface ID	11111100	Provide addresses that are private to an organization but unique across all the organization's sites
Multicast	Ff	Use the next 4 bits for flags (Transient[T], Prefix [P], and Rendezvous Point Address[R]), the following 4 bits for scope (determines where multicast traffic is forwarded), and the remaining 112 bits for a group ID	11111111	Multiple interfaces to which packets are delivered to all network interfaces identified by the address
Anycast	(from unicast addresses)	Assigned from the unicast address space with the same scope as the type of unicast address within which the anycast address is assigned	(varies)	Only utilized as destination addresses assigned to routers

Consider the following sample IPv6 addresses:

- **2003:414:ab86:731f::230:1:45ab:** This is a global unicast address in which 2003:414:ab86 represents the global routing prefix specifying the organizations site, 731f is a subnet identifier, and 0:230:1:45ab represents the host ID. Note that the presence of multiple 0s is implied by the presence of the double-colon.

- **fe80::cc33:456a:3719:1234%8:** This is a link local address in which the host ID is cc33:456a:3719:1234; included at the end of each link local address (but not part of the actual address itself) is a zone ID specified in the form %ID

(%8 in this example). This ID appears when you run the `ipconfig` command; it specifies the network interface and is typically equal to the interface index of the interface connected to the link on which the destination is located. It distinguishes the networks to which a computer with multiple network adapters is connected. Windows Server 2012 R2 assigns a zone ID according to a parameter called the interface index for each network interfaces. To view a list of interface indexes on a computer, open a command prompt and type `netsh interface ipv6 show interface`.

- **fd12:cde6:1208:9::f92b:** This is a unique local address in which the first 7 bits are all 1s; the eighth bit is also 1, which is the local (L) flag. The next 40 bits are 02:cde6:1208 and represent a global network ID, which is a randomly generated, site-specific value. The 16-bit subnet ID has a value of 0009; its use is for further subnetting the internal network in an analogous manner to the IPv4 subnetting discussed previously. Finally the last 64 bits are 0:0:0:f92b, which specifies the unique host interface ID. Again, the 0s are represented by the double-colon.

NOTE You might also find mention of the site-local IPv6 address class. This address class was equivalent to the private IPv4 addresses mentioned in Table 10-7; however, site-local addresses have been deprecated as of 2004. Refer to "Deprecating Site Local Addresses" at http://tools.ietf.org/html/rfc3879 for more information.

Connecting to a TCP/IP Version 6 Network

You can let IPv6 configure itself automatically with a link-local address described previously in Table 10-9. You can also configure IPv6 to use an existing DHCP server or manually configure an IPv6 address as required. Configuration of IPv6 addresses is similar to the procedure used with configuration of IPv4 addresses, as the following procedure shows:

1. In the Search charm, type `network`. Select **Network and Sharing Center** from the list that appears.

2. From the left side of the Network and Sharing Center, click **Change adapter settings**. This opens the Network Connections page, as previously shown in Figure 10-2.

3. Right-click the connection that represents the adapter you are going to configure, and select **Properties**.

4. Click to select Internet Protocol Version 6 (TCP/IPv6). (You might need to scroll through other services to reach this item.) Click **Properties**. The Internet Protocol Version 6 (TCP/IPv6) Properties dialog box opens, as shown in Figure 10-6.

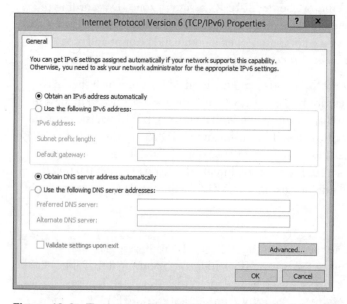

Figure 10-6 The Internet Protocol Version 6 (TCP/IPv6) Properties dialog box lets you define manual or dynamic IPv6 address information.

5. To use DHCP, ensure that the **Obtain an IPv6 address automatically** radio button is selected. If the DHCP server provides DNS server information, ensure that the **Obtain DNS server address automatically** radio button is also selected. You can also select these options to configure IPv6 automatically with a link-local address using the address prefix fe80::/64 previously described in Table 10-9.

6. To manually configure an IPv6 address, select **Use the following IPv6 address**. Then type the IPv6 address, subnet prefix length, and default gateway in the text boxes provided. For unicast IPv6 addresses, you should set the prefix length to its default value of 64.

7. To manually configure DNS server addresses, select **Use the following DNS server addresses**. Then type the IPv6 addresses of the preferred and alternate DNS server in the text boxes provided.

8. Click **Advanced** to display the Advanced TCP/IP Settings dialog box shown in Figure 10-7.

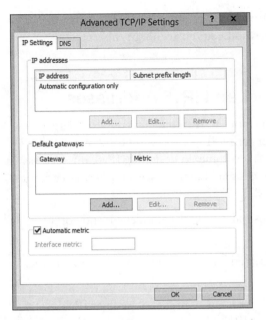

Figure 10-7   The Advanced TCP/IP Settings dialog box enables you to control granular IPv6 addressing options.

9. As with IPv4, you can configure additional IP addresses if you are not using DHCP. Click **Add** and type the required IP address in the dialog box that appears.

10. As with IPv4, if your network segment is connected to more than one router, configure additional gateway addresses in the Default gateways section by clicking the **Add** button.

11. When finished, click **OK** until you've returned to the Network Connections dialog box.

TCP/IPv6 PowerShell Cmdlets

You can use PowerShell to configure most of the properties of IPv6 connections in much the same way as already discussed for IPv4. Most of the cmdlets described in Table 10-8 function for IPv6 just as they do for IPv4. Use the `Get-NetIPv6Protocol` cmdlet to obtain information about the IPv6 protocol configuration and the `Set-NetIPv6Protocol` cmdlet to modify information about the IPv6 protocol configuration.

Although now less recommended than previously, you can still use the `netsh` tool with the `interface IPv6` subcommand to configure IPv6 from the command

line. For more information, refer to "IPv6 Configuration Information with the
`Netsh.exe` Tool" at http://technet.microsoft.com/en-us/library/bb726952.
aspx#EBAA.

Interoperability Between IPv4 and IPv6 Addresses

Many organizations are considering the move to IPv6 but currently have large
numbers of servers and client computers using IPv4 addressing technology. Indeed,
nodes using IPv4 will be with us for years to come. In designing IPv6, this fact was
recognized early in the process and the designers adopted several transition criteria
into the recommendations outlined in RFC 1752:

- You can upgrade existing IPv4 hosts at any time and independently of other
  devices on the network.

- You can add new IPv6-only hosts at any time without dependencies on other
  hosts or devices.

- After IPv6 is set up, existing IPv4 hosts can continue to use their IPv4
  addresses without the need for new IPv6 addresses.

- It should be easy to upgrade existing IPv4 hosts to IPv6 or deploy new IPv6
  hosts without much additional preparation.

To assist in upgrading networks to IPv6, the following node types were defined in
RFC 2893:

- **IPv4 node:** Uses IPv4 but can also be an IPv6/IPv4 node

- **IPv6 node:** Uses IPv6 but can also be an IPv6/IPv4 node

- **IPv4-only node:** Uses IPv4 and cannot support IPv6

- **IPv6-only node:** Uses IPv6 and cannot support IPv4

- **IPv6/IPv4 node:** Uses both IPv4 and IPv6

To assist in the migration from IPv4 to IPv6 and their coexistence, the following
address types were defined:

- Compatibility addresses

- Intra-Site Automatic Tunnel Addressing Protocol (ISATAP) addresses

- 6to4 addresses

- Teredo addresses

The following sections introduce these address types.

Compatibility Addresses

The following two types of compatibility addresses are defined for nodes that communicate on IPv4 and IPv6 networks:

- **IPv4-compatible addresses:** Nodes communicating between IPv4 and IPv6 networks can use an address represented by 0:0:0:0:0:0:*w.x.y.z*, where *w.x.y.z* is the IPv4 address in dotted-decimal. This IPv4 address simply becomes the last 32 bits of the 128-bit IPv6 address.

- **IPv4-mapped address:** An IPv4-only node is represented as ::ffff:w.x.y.z to an IPv6 node. This address type is used only for internal representation and is never specified as a source or destination address of an IPv6 packet.

ISATAP Addresses

As defined in RFC 4214, ISATAP is a tunneling technology that enables unicast IPv6 connectivity between IPv6/IPv4 hosts across an IPv4 intranet. You do not need to perform any manual configuration actions on an ISATAP host; ISATAP addresses are created using standard autoconfiguration mechanisms.

An ISATAP address utilizes the locally administrative interface identifier ::0:5efe:*w.x.y.z*, where *w.x.y.z* is any private unicast IPv4 address, or ::200:5efe:*w.x.y.z*, where *w.x.y.z* is a public IPv4 unicast address. You can combine either of these ISATAP identifiers with any 64-bit unicast IPv6 prefixes including link-local, unique local, and global prefixes already described in Table 10-9.

For example, suppose you have two ISATAP hosts, Computer1 and Computer2, that are separated by an IPv4-only network infrastructure, as shown in Figure 10-8. These machines have been configured with the IPv4 addresses 172.16.21.3 and 192.168.12.51, as shown. When the IPv6 protocol is added to the network, these computers are automatically configured with the ISATAP addresses of fe80::5efe:172.16.21.3 and fe80::5efe:192.168.12.51, respectively. When Computer1 sends an IPv6 message to Computer2 using Computer2's link-local ISATAP address, the source and destination addresses for the IPv4 and IPv6 packet headers are as shown in Figure 10-8.

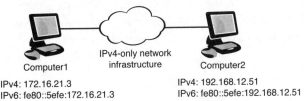

IPv4: 172.16.21.3
IPv6: fe80::5efe:172.16.21.3

IPv4: 192.168.12.51
IPv6: fe80::5efe:192.168.12.51

Figure 10-8   A sample ISATAP configuration.

You can use the `ping` command to test connectivity between these two hosts. For example, you can use the following command at Computer1 to test its connectivity to Computer2:

```
ping fe80::5efe:192.168.12.51%ZoneID
```

Where `ZoneID` is used in the destination address to specify the interface index of the interface from which the `ping` command is sent. The purpose of the `ZoneID` variable is to eliminate ambiguity when a server has more than one interface connected to a network. The ISATAP tunneling interface uses the link-local ISATAP address combined with the destination IPv4 address (which is the last 32 bits of the destination IPv6 address). More information about the `ping` command is provided later in this chapter.

> **TIP**   When you see the `5efe` block within an IPv6 address, this identifies the address as being an ISATAP address.

Configuring an ISATAP Host

The ISATAP client's interface is automatically configured when the client can resolve the ISATAP name from DNS. Either you can configure an ISATAP client with the address of the ISATAP router or it can resolve this address using DNS, as follows:

- You can configure the client with the address of the ISATAP router. If the client can use DNS to resolve ISATAP, it automatically configures its ISATAP tunnel interface. The ISATAP router publishes the network address of its interface.

- You can also publish the address of the ISATAP router in DNS using the keyword ISATAP in the router's host (A) record—for example, `isatap.que.com`. This enables the client to automatically locate the ISATAP router. You will learn more about DNS in Chapter 12, "Deploying and Configuring Domain Name System (DNS)."

Configuring the ISATAP router involves using a series of `netsh interface` commands to enable IPv4 routing. The topic of configuring routing and routing tables is a component of exam 70-411 and is discussed in the *Cert Guide* book for this exam.

6to4 Addresses

Two nodes running both IPv4 and IPv6 across an IPv4 routing infrastructure use this address type when communicating with each other. You can form the 6-to-4 address by combining the prefix 2002::/16 with the 32-bit public IPv4 address to form a 48-bit prefix of the form 2002:*wwxx:yyzz*::/48 in the case of a public IPv4 address *w.x.y.z*. The 6to4 address is completed with a 16-bit subnet ID and a 64-bit interface ID. This tunneling technique is described in RFC 3056; it is similar to ISATAP in the fact that it tunnels IPv6 traffic within an IPv4 packet.

By using 6to4, you can assign global IPv6 addresses to your corporate computers, which can reach IPv6 locations on the Internet without the need to obtain a connection to the IPv6 Internet or use an IPv6 global address prefix supplied by an Internet service provider (ISP).

Within the 6to4 addressing framework, you can have the following components, all of which can connect with each other by means of 6to4 tunnels:

- **6to4 host:** Includes any host configured with at least one 6to4 address with the 2002::/16 address prefix. These hosts do not require any manual configuration; the 6to4 address is created automatically using autoconfiguration.

- **6to4 router:** Includes any IPv6/IPv4 router that uses a 6to4 tunneling interface to forward 6to4 addressed traffic between 6to4 hosts and routers, host/routers, or relays on the IPv4 Internet. These routers might need additional manual configuration.

- **6to4 host/router:** Includes IPv6/IPv4 hosts that use 6to4 tunneling to exchange 6to4-addressed traffic with other 6to4 routers, host/routers, or relays on the IPv4 Internet. Unlike 6to4 routers, these host/routers do not forward traffic for other 6to4 hosts. An example could be a Windows Server 2012 R2 computer that is directly connected to the Internet and assigned a public IPv4 address. When a public IPv4 interface is assigned to the host's external interface, IPv6 automatically configures a 6to4 address with a 2002::/16 route that forwards all 6to4 traffic to IPv6 destinations encapsulated with an IPv4 header. A DNS query is also performed to obtain the IPv4 address of a 6to4 relay on the IPv4 Internet.

- **6to4 relay:** Includes IPv6/IPv4 routers that forward 6to4 addressed traffic between 6to4 routers and 6to4 host/routers on the IPv4 Internet and hosts on the IPv6 Internet. Such computers utilize the Internet Connection Sharing (ICS) feature to enable IPv6 forwarding on both the 6to4 tunneling and private interfaces. A 64-bit IPv6 subnet prefix of the form 2002:*wwxx:yyzz: InterfaceIndex*::/64 is also determined, where *InterfaceIndex* is the interface index of the private interface.

When using 6to4 on a host configured with a public IPv4 address, a 6to4 interface is automatically enabled and assigned a unique global public IPv6 address of the form 2002:*wwxx:yyzz::wwxx:yyzz*, where *wwxx:yyzz* is the hexadecimal representation of the host's IPv4 address. For example, an IPv4 address of 200.19.144.6 translates to the hexadecimal equivalent of c813:9006, and the corresponding 6to4 address is 2002:c813:9006::c813:9006. You can use the `ping` command in a fashion similar to that already described for ISATAP to send a packet across the 6to4 tunnel and validate connectivity.

> **NOTE**   For information on `netsh` commands used for manual configuration of 6to4 routers and ISATAP routers, refer to "Manual Configuration for IPv6" at http://technet.microsoft.com/en-ca/library/bb878102.aspx.

Teredo Addresses

Teredo is a tunneling communication protocol that enables IPv6 connectivity between IPv6/IPv4 nodes across network address translation (NAT) interfaces, thereby improving connectivity for newer IPv6-enabled applications on IPv4 networks. Teredo sends IPv6 packets using IPv4-based UDP methodology. Teredo is described in RFC 4380. Because NAT devices are generally unable to handle protocol 41 traffic, IPv4-encapsulated IPv6 traffic is unable to cross the typical NAT interface, thereby preventing the use of 6to4 as an IPv6 transition technology. To enable this flow of IPv6 traffic, Teredo encapsulates the IPv6 packet as an IPv4 UDP message that includes both IPv4 and UDP headers, enabling the tunneling of information between hosts separated by one or more NAT devices.

Teredo makes use of a special IPv6 address that includes the following components in the sequence given:

- A 32-bit Teredo prefix, which is 2001::/32 in Windows Vista/7/8/8.1 and Windows Server 2008/R2/2012/R2

- The 32-bit IPv4 address of the Teredo server involved in creating this address

- A 16-bit Teredo flag field and an obscured 16-bit UDP port interface definition of the external NAT port of the host

- A 32-bit obscured external IPv4 address corresponding to all Teredo traffic across the Teredo client interface

A computer running Windows 8/8.1 or Windows Server 2012/R2 includes a Teredo client that is enabled but inactive by default. To activate Teredo, you must install an application that recognizes Teredo on the computer or configure Windows Firewall to enable Teredo on a per-application basis. After activation, the Teredo client obtains information such as the type of NAT device in use, thereby setting up and maintaining a communication tunnel for the Teredo client through its NAT device.

Initial negotiation of communication between the Teredo client and server involves the following:

- The Teredo client connects to the Teredo server.

- The server determines the type of NAT the host is behind. To do this, you must configure the server with two consecutive IPv4 addresses, so that it can determine the type of NAT in use.

- Then the server can provide the address of the client's Teredo tunnel.

You can use the following sample command to enable the client for Teredo:

```
netsh interface ipv6 set Teredo enterpriseclient servername
```

Note that in this command, the `enterpriseclient` keyword describes a type variable that directs Teredo to skip managed network detection. Specify the name of the server (for example, `teredo.que.com` for the que.com domain) at `servername`. At the Teredo server, ensure that a DNS entry is included. Then add a second IPv4 address to the Teredo server, which is used for NAT detection, and enable the Teredo server and its tunneling interface.

> **NOTE**   For more information on Teredo, refer to "Teredo Overview" at http://technet.microsoft.com/en-us/library/bb457011.aspx. More information on compatibility addresses and technologies used for transition to IPv6 is available in "Internet Protocol Version 6, Teredo, and Related Technologies in Windows 7 and Windows Server 2008 R2" at http://technet.microsoft.com/en-us/library/ee126159(WS.10).aspx. A comprehensive description of the technologies discussed in this section is found in "IPv6 Transition Technologies" at http://technet.microsoft.com/en-us/library/bb726951.aspx. Settings described in these articles apply equally well to Windows 8 and Windows Server 2012 R2.

Using Group Policy to Configure IPv6 Transition Technologies

On a Windows 8.1 or Windows Server 2012 R2 computer, you can use Group Policy to configure settings for ISATAP, 6to4, and Teredo settings. In an Active Directory Domain Services (AD DS) environment, this enables you to configure settings applicable to all computers in the domain, site, or organizational unit (OU).

To do this, access the Group Policy Management Editor focused on the appropriate Group Policy object (or the Local Group Policy Editor in a nondomain environment) and navigate to the **Computer Configuration\Policies\Administrative Templates\Network\TCP/IP Settings\IPv6 Transition Technologies** node.

You receive the settings shown in Figure 10-9. To enable any policy, right-click the desired policy and choose **Edit**, as shown for the 6to4 Relay Name policy in Figure 10-10. Select **Enabled** and specify any options pertaining to the policy being configured. You can also enable IP-HTTPS, which is a tunneling technology that uses IP-Hypertext Transfer Protocol Secure (HTTPS) to enable IP connectivity to a remote network and is useful if a client behind a NAT device is unable to create a Teredo tunnel. For more information on all the IPv6 transition technology policies, consult the help information provided with each policy's dialog box, as shown for the 6to4 Relay Name policy in Figure 10-10.

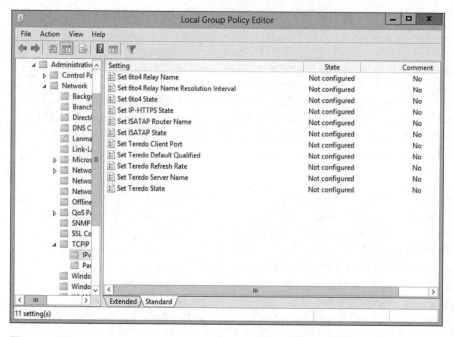

Figure 10-9   You can configure IP transition technology policies using Group Policy in Windows Server 2012 R2.

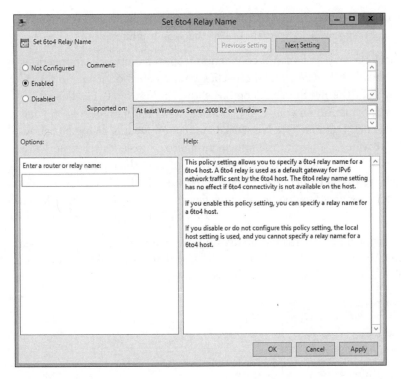

Figure 10-10   Configuring the 6to4 Relay Name policy in Windows Server 2012 R2.

Resolving IPv4 and IPv6 Network Connectivity Issues

With any type of computer network, connectivity problems can and do occur whether you have configured your network to use IPv4, IPv6, or both. You should be aware of the types of problems that you might encounter, and the steps to use for determining the source of the problem and the means to correct it.

Windows Server 2012 R2 Network Diagnostics Tools

Windows Server 2012 R2 provides several tools that are often useful in trouble-shooting network and Internet connectivity failures. These tools provide wizards that ask questions as to what problems might exist and suggest solutions or open additional troubleshooters.

The Network and Sharing Center provides a comprehensive networking problem troubleshooter. Select a problematic network connection and click **Diagnose this connection** from the Network Connections dialog box to start a wizard that attempts to locate and troubleshoot networking problems. If the wizard is unable to identify a problem, it suggests additional options that you might explore.

You can also check the status of a LAN connection from the Network Connections page previously shown in Figure 10-2. Right-click your connection icon and select **Status** to display the Ethernet Status dialog box shown in Figure 10-11. This dialog box provides information on your LAN connectivity. To obtain details on your LAN connection, click **Details**. The Network Connection Details dialog box shown in Figure 10-12 provides a subset of the information also provided by the `ipconfig` command discussed in the next section. To view or configure the properties of the connection, click the **Properties** button shown in Figure 10-11. This takes you to the same Ethernet Properties dialog box discussed earlier in this chapter and shown in Figure 10-3.

If you suspect a problem, click the **Diagnose** button shown in Figure 10-11 to open a troubleshooter. You will be informed of any problem that exists, such as a disconnected network cable or malfunctioning network adapter card.

Figure 10-11   The Ethernet Status dialog box provides information on the connectivity of your LAN connection.

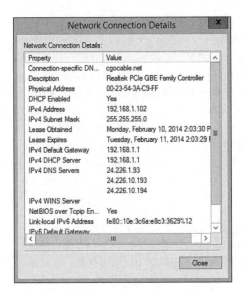

Figure 10-12   The Network Connection Details dialog box provides IPv4 and IPv6 configuration information.

Using TCP/IP Utilities to Troubleshoot TCP/IP

The TCP/IP protocol suite includes a number of tools that can help you isolate the source of connectivity problems. Windows Server 2012 R2 incorporates these tools as command-line executables. Each tool is different in what information it provides and when you might want to use it.

When you are troubleshooting a connectivity problem, remember that sometimes the problem is the hardware—a failed network adapter, a failed port on the hub, a failed switch, and so on. If the communication is between two physical segments, it could be a problem with the router between them. And if you were able to communicate in the past, and now cannot, the most likely suspect is a configuration change on one of the computers and the second most likely is that a piece of equipment has failed. To check whether there is an adapter failure, you can look at Device Manager.

ARP

After data reaches the segment on which the IP address resides, it needs to discover the MAC address of the machine. As introduced earlier in this chapter, ARP is the protocol in the TCP/IP suite that resolves IP addresses to MAC addresses by creating an Address Resolution table in each host that transmits data on the network segment.

The ARP command is useful for viewing the ARP cache. If two hosts on the same subnet cannot even ping each other successfully, try running the **arp -a** command on each computer to see if they have the correct MAC addresses listed for each other. You can determine a host's MAC address by using **ipconfig /all**. If another host with a duplicate IP address exists on the network, the ARP cache might have had the MAC address for the other computer placed in it. In addition, if you cannot contact a host or connect to an unexpected host, the results of this command will help in determining the source of the connectivity problems. Arp -d can be used to delete an entry that might be incorrect. Entries can be added using arp -s.

FTP

File Transfer Protocol (FTP) is not normally considered to be a troubleshooting tool. Sometimes you need to make certain that a protocol is able to move data from one network segment to another and this utility can help out in a pinch because it verifies TCP specifically, as well as all the protocols down to the Physical layer of the stack.

If you want to verify whether TCP is functioning across a router, you can use FTP to download a file from an FTP server on another subnet.

Ipconfig

Windows Server 2012 R2 uses the ipconfig utility without any additional param-eters to display summary information about the IP address configuration of its net-work adapters. When you are experiencing a problem with connectivity, this is the first thing you should check (besides the link lights on the network adapter). If you are using DHCP, you can see whether the adapter was able to obtain an IP address lease. If you are using a static IP address, you can verify and validate whether it has been configured correctly. You can use ipconfig with the following switches:

- ipconfig /all: Displays a comprehensive set of IPv4 and IPv6 address data for all network adapters including IPv6 Teredo interfaces, as shown in Figure 10-13. Use this command to see whether an adapter has been misconfigured or the adapter did not receive a DHCP lease. You can also determine whether the IP address the computer is using has been provided by APIPA; check the Autoconfiguration Enabled line of this output. If this line states Yes and the IP address is 169.254.0.1–169.254.255.254, you are using an APIPA address. This is also true if you observe an IPv6 address on the fe80::/64 network. Out-put can be redirected to a file and pasted into other documents by using stan-dard Windows commands, for example, ipconfig /all > ipstatus.txt.

Figure 10-13 The `ipconfig /all` command provides a comprehensive set of TCP/IP configuration information.

- `ipconfig /release`: Releases the current DHCP lease. Use this command to remove an IP address that is misconfigured or when you have moved from one network to another and the wrong IP address is still leased to the adapter.

- `ipconfig /release6`: Same as the `/release` switch for IPv6.

- `ipconfig /renew`: Renews (or tries to renew) the current DHCP lease. Use this command to see whether the computer can contact the DHCP server.

- `ipconfig /renew6`: Same as the `/renew` switch for IPv6.

- `ipconfig /displaydns`: Displays the contents of the DNS cache. Use this command when the computer connects to the wrong network.

- `ipconfig /flushdns`: Flushes the contents of the DNS cache. Use this command when the computer connects to the wrong network and you see incorrect entries after using the `ipconfig /displaydns` command.

- **ipconfig /registerdns:** Refreshes all adapters' DHCP leases and re-registers the DNS configuration. Use this command when the computer has temporarily disconnected from the network and you have not rebooted it.

- **ipconfig /showclassid** *adapter:* Shows the DHCP class ID. If you use the asterisk (*) in place of *adapter*, you see the DHCP class ID for all adapters.

- **ipconfig /setclassid** *adapter:* Changes the DHCP class ID for an adapter. If you use the asterisk (*) in the place of *adapter*, you set the DHCP class ID of all adapters.

Nbtstat

The Nbtstat utility is used on networks that run NetBIOS over TCP/IP. This utility checks to see the status of NetBIOS name resolution to IP addresses. You can check current NetBIOS sessions, add entries to the NetBIOS name cache, and check the NetBIOS name and scope assigned to the computer.

Netstat

The Netstat command-line tool enables you to check the current status of the computer's IP connections. If you do not use switches, the results are port and protocol statistics and current TCP/IP connections. Netstat -a displays all connections and listening ports, even those not presently involved in a connection. This enables you to check whether a connection to a remote host that does not appear to be responding is hung. Netstat -r displays the route table, plus active connections. The -n switch tells netstat not to convert addresses and port numbers to names. The -e switch displays Ethernet statistics and can be combined with the -s switch, which shows protocol statistics.

You should use Netstat to look for the services that are listening for incoming connections if you have already checked the IP configuration and, though it is correct, the computer still displays a connectivity problem.

Nslookup

Name Server Lookup, or Nslookup, is a command-line utility that communicates with a DNS server. There are two modes to Nslookup—interactive and noninteractive. The interactive mode opens a session with a DNS server and views various records. The noninteractive mode asks for one piece of information and receives it. If more information is needed, a new query must be made.

Ping

Ping is a valuable tool for determining whether there is a problem with connectivity. The ping command uses an ICMP echo packet at the Network layer—the default is to send a series of four echoes in a row—transmitting the packets to the IP address specified. The Echo returns an acknowledgment if the IP address is found. The results are displayed in the command window. If an IP address is not found, you see only the response Request timed out. You see similar results to those shown in Figure 10-14, where the first address that was pinged was found and the second address was not found. The ping command indicates how long each packet took for the response. You can use the ping command to determine whether a host is reachable, and to determine whether you are losing packets when sending/receiving data to a particular host.

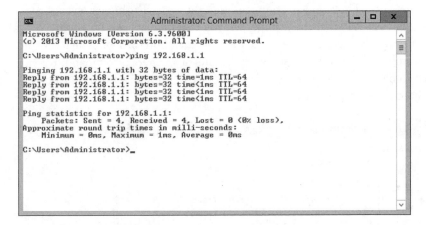

Figure 10-14   The ping command displays its results in a command window.

ping also has several command-line options. Type **ping -?** to see the available options. For example, ping enables you to specify the size of packets to use, how many to send, whether to record the route used, what TTL value to use, and whether to set the "don't fragment" flag.

You can use the ping command to determine whether the internal TCP/IP protocol stack is functioning properly by pinging the loopback testing address. The command for IPv4 is

ping 127.0.0.1.

For IPv6, the command is ping ::1.

> **NOTE**   Firewall settings can prevent you from receiving responses from pinged hosts. In Windows Server 2012 R2, by default you cannot ping other computers on your network. We take a look at configuring firewall settings and policies in Chapter 19.

Tracert

When you have a problem communicating with a particular host, yet you have determined that your computer is functioning well, you can use `tracert` (Trace Route) to tell you how the data is moving across the network between your computer and the one that you are having difficulty reaching. `tracert` uses the IP TTL field and ICMP error messages to determine the route from one host to another through the network. The `tracert` command offers a somewhat higher level of information than `ping`. Rather than simply tell you that the data was transmitted and returned effectively, as `ping` does, `tracert` logs each hop through which the data was transmitted. Figure 10-15 shows the results of a `tracert` command. Keep in mind that some network routers strip out or refuse to reply to `tracert` requests. When this happens, you see `Request timed out` messages.

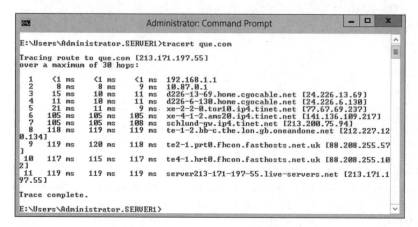

Figure 10-15   The `tracert` command provides detailed information about the path that data travels between two IP hosts.

pathping

The `pathping` command combines the actions of the `ping` and `tracert` utilities into a single command that tests connectivity to a remote host and maps the route taken by packets transmitted from your computer to the remote host. It also provides data on packet loss across multiple hops, thereby providing an estimate of the reliability of the communication links being used.

Troubleshooting IPv4 and IPv6 Problems

Many problems can result in your inability to reach other hosts on your local subnet, other subnets on your local network, or the Internet. The 70-410 exam will present you with scenarios in which you must figure out the cause of and solution to problems with IPv4 and IPv6 connectivity failures. We cover the use of the TCP/IP troubleshooting tools already presented to test connectivity and follow this up with additional suggestions you can use for troubleshooting connectivity problems, both on the 70-410 exam and in the real world.

A Suggested Response to a Connectivity Problem

Microsoft recommends a troubleshooting procedure for TCP/IP connectivity problems similar to the following:

1. Verify the hardware is functioning.

2. Run `ipconfig /all` to validate the IP address, subnet mask, default gateway, and DNS server and whether you are receiving a DHCP leased address.

3. Ping 127.0.0.1 or ::1, the loopback address, to validate that TCP/IP is functioning.

4. Ping the computer's own IP address to eliminate a duplicate IP address as the problem.

5. Ping the default gateway address, which tells you whether data can travel on the current network segment.

6. Ping a host that is not on your network segment, which shows whether the router will be able to route your data. By pinging the hostname, you can verify that DNS is resolving the name, and by pinging the IP address, you can verify network connectivity.

Additional possible troubleshooting steps you can use include the following:

- FTP a file from an FTP server not on your network, which tells you whether higher-level protocols are functioning. TFTP a file from a TFTP server on a different network to determine whether UDP packets are able to cross the router.

- Check the configuration of routers on a network with multiple subnets. You can use the `tracert` and `pathping` commands to verify connectivity across routers to remote subnets. Also use the `route print` command to check the configuration of routing tables in use.

- Clear the ARP cache by opening a command prompt and typing `netsh interface ip delete arpcache`.

- Check the computer's DNS configuration. You can also clear the DNS client resolver cache by using the `ipconfig /flushdns` command.

Many LAN connection problems can be traced to improper TCP/IP configuration. Before looking at the use of TCP/IP utilities for troubleshooting these problems, this section reviews briefly some of the problems you might encounter.

Network Discovery

Network Discovery is a tool enabled by default on Windows 8/8.1 and Windows Server 2012 R2 computers. For computers to be able to connect to one another, ensure that Network Discovery has not been turned off at either the source or destination computer. To check this setting, access the Network and Sharing Center and click **Change advanced sharing settings**, found in the list on the left side. As shown in Figure 10-16, you can configure a series of sharing options for different network profiles. Ensure that the **Turn on network discovery** option is selected, and then click **Save changes**.

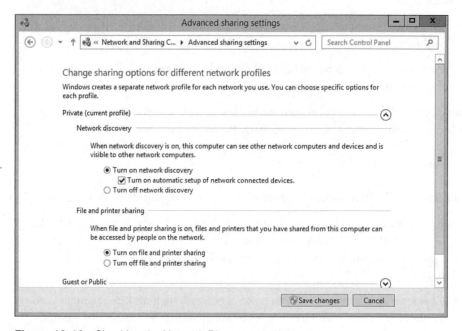

Figure 10-16 Checking the Network Discovery setting.

Incorrect IPv4 Address or Subnet Mask

Recall from earlier in this chapter that the subnet mask determines the number of bits assigned to the network portion of the IP address and the number of bits assigned to the host portion. Be aware of the fact that the network portion of the IP address must match properly on all computers within a network segment and that the subnet mask must be configured appropriately to ensure that the computer is able to determine whether the computer to which it is attempting to connect is on the same or a different subnet. An incorrect subnet mask can result in intermittent connections. Sometimes the connection works; sometimes it doesn't. Problems occur when the IP address of the destination host results in the packet being routed when it shouldn't be or when it is not routed when it should be.

For example, suppose you are at a computer configured with an IP address of 192.168.1.2 and a subnet mask of 255.255.255.0. If you want to reach a computer with the IP address of 192.168.2.1, the subnet mask indicates that this computer is located on a different subnet. Connection will take place across a router. If the computer you are at is configured with the same IP address but a subnet mask of 255.255.248.0, this would indicate that the destination computer with the IP address of 192.168.2.1 is on the same subnet. If, in fact, this computer is located across a router on another subnet, you will fail to connect to it. Router problems could also cause a failure to access a computer on another subnet.

Incorrect Default Gateway

The default gateway is the IP address of the near side of the router used to communicate with external networks. It is used only for outgoing communication. If specified incorrectly, the host can communicate with other hosts on the local network but is unable to communicate with external hosts. External hosts can send messages to the incorrectly configured host, but any return message will not reach the external host. In addition, when using DHCP, if the default gateway of the DHCP server is incorrectly specified, clients will be unable to contact the DHCP server to obtain IP address leases. This results in the clients being unable to contact anyone, as they will be configured with an inappropriate IPv4 address using APIPA or a link-local IPv6 address.

Unable to Connect to a DHCP Server

If you configure your computer to automatically receive an IPv4 address and the DHCP server is down, the computer will assign itself an APIPA address as already described. If you notice this when using `ipconfig /all`, check the connectivity to the DHCP server or contact an administrator responsible for this server.

Duplicate IP Address

If your computer is using an IP address that duplicates another computer on the network, you will be unable to connect to any computer on the network. When this happens, the first computer on the network performs properly but receives a message when the second computer joins the network. Ping your computer's IP address to check for this problem. This problem cannot occur if you are using DHCP to obtain an IP address automatically, or if your computer is configured for an IP address using APIPA.

Unable to Configure an Alternate TCP/IPv4 Configuration

The Alternate Configuration tab of the TCP/IPv4 Properties dialog box (refer to Figure 10-4) enables you to configure an alternative IPv4 address, which is useful in situations where you need to connect to a second network; for example, when you are using a portable computer and traveling to a branch office of your company. However, to use the alternative configuration, your primary connection must be set to obtain an IP address automatically. If this is not the case, this tab does not appear.

Using Event Viewer to Check Network Problems

One of Windows Server 2012 R2's standard troubleshooting tools is Event Viewer, which is incorporated into the Server Manager console. You can rely on this utility to be able to see errors and system messages. The ones that would be of most concern for a network problem are in the System Event log. You will learn about Event Viewer in the *Cert Guide* book for exam 70-411.

Additional Troubleshooting Hints When Using IPv6

When verifying IPv6 network connectivity, you might need to specify a zone ID for the sending interface with the `ping` command. The zone ID is a locally defined parameter that you can obtain from the `ipconfig /all` command or the `netsh interface ipv6 show interface` command. Using this zone ID, to verify connectivity with a machine whose IPv6 address is fe80::b3:00ff:4765:6db7, you would type `ping fe80::b3:00ff:4765:6db7%12` at a command prompt, if the zone ID is 12.

Before using `ping` to check IPv6 network connectivity, clear the neighbor cache on your computer. This cache contains recently resolved link-layer IPv6 addresses. To view this cache, open a PowerShell command window and type `Get-NetNeighbor`; to remove entries from it, type `Remove-NetNeighbor`.

NOTE   For further suggestions with regard to troubleshooting IPv6 network connectivity, refer to "The Cable Guy–March 2005" at http://technet.microsoft.com/en-us/library/bb878005.aspx.

Exam Preparation Tasks

Review All the Key Topics

Review the most important topics in the chapter, noted with the key topics icon in the outer margin of the page. Table 10-10 lists a reference of these key topics and the page numbers on which each is found.

Table 10-10   Key Topics for Chapter 10

Key Topic Element	Description	Page Number
Paragraphs	Introduce the various TCP/IP component protocols	429
Table 10-2	Describes important addressing components of TCP/IP version 4	434
Table 10-3	Describes the various IPv4 address classes	436
Table 10-4	Default subnet masks in different notations	437
Paragraph	Explains how to use subnet masks to separate the network and machine portions of an IPv4 address	437
Table 10-5	Describes subnetting	439
Table 10-6	Describes supernetting	440
Table 10-7	Describes private IPv4 networks	441
Step list	Explains how to configure a network adapter with a static IPv4 address	441
Figure 10-5	Shows the advanced TCP/IP settings you can configure	444
Paragraph	Introduces PowerShell cmdlets used to configure TCP/IP networking	445
List	Describes the major benefits achieved by using IPv6	447
Table 10-9	Explains IPv6 address classes and subclasses	449
Step list	Explains how to configure your computer to connect to an IPv6 network	451

Key Topic Element	Description	Page Number
Paragraph	Describes ISATAP addressing	455
Paragraph	Describes 6to4 addressing	456
Paragraph	Describes Teredo addressing	458
Figure 10-11	Using the Ethernet Status dialog box to check LAN connection status	462
Figure 10-13	Use of the `ipconfig /all` command	465
Step list	Describes a procedure that tests your computer's IP connectivity	469

Complete the Tables and Lists from Memory

Print a copy of Appendix B, "Memory Tables" (found on the CD), or at least the section for this chapter, and complete the tables and lists from memory. Appendix C, "Memory Tables Answer Key" is also on the CD and includes completed tables and lists to check your work.

Definitions of Key Terms

Define the following key terms from this chapter, and check your answers in the glossary.

6to4, Address Resolution Protocol (ARP), Anycast IPv6 address, Automatic Private IP Addressing (APIPA), Classless inter-domain routing (CIDR), Default gateway, Dynamic IP address, Global unicast IPv6 address, Host, Internet Protocol (IP), Intra-Site Automatic Tunnel Addressing Protocol (ISATAP), IP version 4 (IPv4), IP version 6 (IPv6), IP address, IPv4-compatible address, IPv4-mapped address, ipconfig, Link local IPv6 address, Multicast IPv6 address, Network Interface layer, Private IPv4 network, Static IP address, Subnet mask, Subnetting, Teredo, Transmission Control Protocol (TCP), User Datagram Protocol (UDP)

This chapter covers the following subjects:

- **How DHCP Works:** This section introduces the concept of DHCP and describes how the four-stage DHCP process works with IPv4. It follows this up by describing important new features of DHCPv6.

- **Installing and Configuring a DHCP Server:** DHCP in Windows Server 2012 R2 is installed as a server role. This section takes you through the process of installing a DHCP server, both from the Server Manager tool and from the command line.

- **DHCP Scopes and Options:** All DHCP servers have one or more scopes, which define the range of IP addresses available to clients. In this section you learn how to create scopes and configure the various options available at various levels.

- **Configuring PXE Boot:** This section shows you how to configure DHCP to accommodate PXE Boot scenarios such as with Windows Deployment Services. It also provides you with an understanding of the various troubleshooting tools available to properly diagnose and resolve DHCP issues.

- **Managing and Authorizing DHCP Servers:** This section discusses several additional tasks you should be familiar with, including authorizing DHCP servers in your environment as well as configuring and using DHCP Relay Agents.

CHAPTER 11

Configuring Dynamic Host Configuration Protocol (DHCP)

Chapter 10, "Configuring IPv4 and IPv6 Addressing," introduced you to the various types of Internet Protocol (IP) addresses use in modern computer networks. You learned that every computer on the network must have its own unique IP address, together with additional configuration options such as the subnet mask or IPv6 subnet prefix length, the default gateway, and other parameters. On a small network you could manually specify these options for each computer on the network, but what happens if you're responsible for networking hundreds or even thousands of computers? Attempting to maintain manual TCP/IP configuration for more than a handful of computers becomes an extreme headache. And this is where Dynamic Host Configuration Protocol (DHCP) comes to the rescue. DHCP automatically assigns these networking parameters and more to every computer on your network. It maintains a database of all configured options and prevents problems such as duplicate IP addresses and more from occurring. DHCP eliminates most of the problems associated with manual configuration because it can furnish all essential TCP/IP information to all DHCP-enabled clients on a TCP/IP network. When problems do arise, they are generally easier to trace on a DHCP-controlled network than on a manually configured one.

"Do I Know This Already?" Quiz

The "Do I Know This Already?" quiz enables you to assess whether you should read this entire chapter or simply jump to the "Exam Preparation Tasks" section for review. If you are in doubt, read the entire chapter. Table 11-1 outlines the major headings in this chapter and the corresponding "Do I Know This Already?" quiz questions. You can find the answers in Appendix A, "Answers to the 'Do I Know This Already?' Quizzes."

Table 11-1   "Do I Know This Already?" Foundation Topics Section-to-Question Mapping

Foundations Topics Section	Questions Covered in This Section
How DHCP Works	1–4
Installing and Configuring a DHCP Server	5–6
DHCP Scopes and Options	7–9
Configuring PXE Boot	10
Managing and Authorizing DHCP Servers	11–13

1. Your client computer running Windows 8.1 Enterprise is requesting an IPv4 address from the local network's DHCP server. Which of the following messages are exchanged between the two computers? (Choose all that apply; arrange your answers in the proper sequence in which the messages are exchanged.)

   a. DHCPREQUEST

   b. DHCPOFFER

   c. DHCPINFORM

   d. DHCPACK

   e. DHCPADVERTISE

   f. DHCPDISCOVER

2. By default, at what percentage of the lease time will a DHCP client first attempt to renew its lease?

   a. 50

   b. 80

   c. 87.5

   d. 95

3. An IPv6 client computer can automatically configure itself with a unique address by using router discovery without the use of a DHCPv6 server. What is this process called?

   a. Stateful address configuration

   b. Stateless address configuration

   c. Managed address configuration

   d. Automatic private IP addressing

4. Which of the following messages are exchanged between an IPv6 client computer and DHCPv6 server when requesting configuration information? (Choose all that apply; arrange your answers in the proper sequence in which the messages are exchanged.)

   a. Discover

   b. Offer

   c. Advertise

   d. Request

   e. Solicit

   f. Confirm

   g. Reply

5. Which of the following situations might result in a failure of DHCP to install properly on a Windows Server 2012 R2 computer? (Choose two.)

   a. The computer is configured with IPv6 only.

   b. The computer is configured to obtain an IP address automatically.

   c. The computer is not configured as a domain controller.

   d. You are logged on to the computer as a nonadministrative user.

6. You are installing DHCP on a server that runs the Server Core version of Windows Server 2012 R2. Which of the following commands should you run to install DHCP on this server? (Each correct answer represents a complete solution. Choose two answers.)

   a. `Start /w ocsetup DHCPServerCore`

   b. `Dism /online /enable-feature /featurename:DHCPServerCore`

   c. `servermanagercmd –install DHCPServerCore`

   d. `Install-WindowsFeature DHCPServerCore`

7. You are configuring options on your DHCP server that need to be applied to various subsets of the computers on your network. You realize that there are four levels at which these options can be applied. Which of the following represents the sequence in which these options are applied?

   a. Server, client, class, scope

   b. Server, scope, class, client

   c. Scope, class, client, server

   d. Client, server, scope, class

8. You would like all desktop computers to retain their IP leases for 14 days to reduce the network overhead on the DHCP server. At the same time, you would like laptop computers connecting from external locations to give up their leases within 12 hours. What should you do?

   a. Specify a user class option that sets the lease interval to 12 hours for all laptop computers.

   b. Specify a vendor class option that sets the lease interval to 12 hours for all laptop computers.

   c. For each laptop computer, specify a client option that sets the lease interval to 12 hours.

   d. Create a separate scope for all laptop computers and specify a scope option that sets the lease interval to 12 hours.

9. You have installed DHCP on a Windows Server 2012 R2 computer and are now creating a scope that will deploy IP addresses to computers on the 192.168.3.0/24 network. The network contains three file servers that must always have the IP addresses 192.168.3.100, 192.168.3.102, and 192.168.3.103. These servers should receive other IP configuration information from the DHCP server. What should you do? (Each answer represents part of the solution. Choose two.)

   a. Create an exclusion range on the scope that prevents these addresses from being assigned to client computers.

   b. Create two scopes, one that assigns the IP addresses 192.168.3.1 to 192.168.3.100 and the other that assigns the IP addresses 192.168.3.104 to 192.168.3.254.

   c. Create three reservations in DHCP, one for each of the three file servers.

   d. Configure each of the three file servers with static IP addresses.

10. As the network administrator for your company, you have been given the task of configuring your DHCP server to handle PXE requests to be used with deploying images to client computers. Which DHCP options will you need to configure? (Choose all that apply.)

   a. Option 50

   b. Option 66

   c. Option 70

   d. Option 67

   e. Option 76

11. You have installed DHCP on a Windows Server 2012 R2 computer that is a member server on your company's AD DS network and created a scope that is to assign IP addresses on the 192.168.4.0 network. The next day you notice that the DHCP server has not started and client computers on your network are autoconfiguring themselves with IP addresses on the 169.254.0.0 network. What do you need to do?

    a. Deactivate and reactivate the scope.

    b. Create a scope option that disables the use of APIPA.

    c. Promote the DHCP server to domain controller.

    d. Authorize the DHCP server in Active Directory.

12. You are responsible for managing a DHCP server on your company's network, which consists of two subnets separated by a legacy router. You have created two scopes, one for each subnet. The DHCP server is located on subnet A. Client computers on this subnet are receiving proper IP addressing information, but those on subnet B are autoconfiguring themselves with IP addresses on the 169.254.0.0 network. They cannot communicate with computers on the first subnet. What should you do?

    a. Install a DHCP relay agent on a server located on subnet A.

    b. Install a DHCP relay agent on a server located on subnet B.

    c. Specify a scope option for client computers on subnet B that specifies the IP address of the DHCP server.

    d. Specify the IP address of the DHCP server manually in the TCP/IP properties of each computer on subnet B.

13. You are responsible for ensuring that file and web servers on your company's network always are configured with the same IP address, so you are creating IP address reservations on your DHCP server. When you attempt to reserve an IP address for a server named WEB1, you receive a message stating `The specified DHCP client is not a reserved client`. What should you do to provide the proper IP address while ensuring that this server receives all other required options?

    a. Modify the DHCP scope to include the IP address to be reserved for WEB1.

    b. Configure a scope option that specifies the IP address to be reserved for WEB1.

    c. Locate the machine that is already using this IP address and type `ipconfig /release` at this machine so that the required IP address becomes available.

    d. Configure a static IP address for WEB1 instead.

Foundation Topics

How DHCP Works

DHCP works by providing IP addressing information from a pool of addresses called a *scope*, which is defined in the DHCP server's database. If a client accepts the address, it can use the address for a predefined period called a *lease*. If a client cannot obtain a lease of an IP address from a DHCP server, it cannot initialize TCP/IP normally.

DHCP used in Windows Server 2012 R2 is based on standards defined by the Internet Engineering Task Force (IETF), which set out specifications in Request for Comment (RFC) 2131, *Dynamic Host Configuration Protocol and RFC 2132: DHCP Options and BOOTP Vendor Extensions*. With the advent of IPv6, IETF provided the specifications for using DHCP on IPv6-based networks in RFC 3315, *Dynamic Host Configuration Protocol for IPv6 (DHCPv6)*. This section introduces you to the processes used by DHCP in configuring IPv4 and IPv6 clients; while conceptually similar, some important differences are present in the way IPv6 clients are configured.

> **NOTE**   For more information on DHCPv6, its specific advantages, and its message details, refer to "The Cable Guy—The DHCPv6 Protocol" at http://technet.microsoft.com/en-us/magazine/2007.03.cableguy.aspx.

What's New with DHCP in Windows Server 2012 and Windows Server 2012 R2

Table 11-2 introduces the new and updated technologies included with DHCP in Windows Server 2012 and Windows Server 2012 R2.

Table 11-2   New/Updated Features for DHCP

Feature/ Functionality	Description	Windows Server 2012	Windows Server 2012 R2
DHCP failover	Windows Server 2012 and Windows Server 2012 R2 enable you to set up two DHCP servers that lease IP addresses and other options in the same subnet or scope at the same time. This provides for fault tolerance and load balancing. The two servers exchange information so that they do not lease conflicting IP addresses. You will learn more about DHCP failover in the *Cert Guide* books for exams 70-412 and 70-413.	X	X

Feature/ Functionality	Description	Windows Server 2012	Windows Server 2012 R2
Policy-based lease assignment	Windows Server 2012 and Windows Server 2012 R2 enable you to define policies the DHCP servers will use to evaluate DHCP requests. These policies apply to a specific scope with a defined processing order, and you can define policies at the scope level or configure them to be inherited from policies defined at the server level. Policies are available for scenarios that include multiple device types, multiple computer roles, and virtualization. You can also have multiple policies affecting a single request or policies that are associated with multiple address scopes.	X	X
Windows PowerShell cmdlets	Windows Server 2012 provides 103 task-oriented cmdlets that enable you to configure and manage most properties of DHCP servers. Additional cmdlets have been added in Windows Server 2012 R2.	X	X
DNS registration enhancements	New in Windows Server 2012 R2, you can use the fully qualified domain name (FQDN) of DHCP clients as a basis for configuring DHCP policies. You can also register workgroup computers by means of a guest DNS suffix.		X
DNS PTR registration options	New to Windows Server 2012 R2, DHCP enables you to specify DNS registration of address (A) and pointer (PTR) resource records.		X

NOTE   For more information on new capabilities of DHCP in Windows Server 2012/R2, refer to "What's New in DHCP in Windows Server" at http://technet.microsoft.com/en-us/library/dn305900.aspx.

The Four-Phase DHCP IPv4 Leasing Process

The DHCP server and the DHCP client both need to go through a four-phase process before DHCP configures the client with a working set of TCP/IP parameters. Note that many of the communications are in the form of broadcasts. The broadcast nature of these communications can present a major problem if routers on an internetwork are not capable of forwarding these DHCP messages.

Figure 11-1 is a schematic view of the DHCP leasing process:

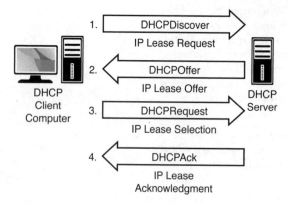

Figure 11-1   The four-step DHCP process.

The following sections describe the four DHCP communication phases. Note that the actual process, described at the packet level, uses slightly different terminology and can take a few more twists and turns than those briefly described here.

The client must use the IP lease process when it is in any of the following states:

- A client configured to use DHCP is initializing TCP/IP for the very first time.

- A client requests a specific IP address but the server has denied that IP address, as could occur if a DHCP server dropped a lease.

- The client had previously leased an IP address but has since released that IP address and now requires a new lease. This can occur when the user has typed the `ipconfig /release` and `ipconfig /renew` commands.

IP Lease Request (DHCPDISCOVER)

When an IPv4 client computer starts up and discovers that it requires an IP address, it initializes a limited version of TCP/IP and then broadcasts a request for the location of a DHCP server. This broadcast indicates to the listening server that the client needs IP addressing information. The broadcast packet sent by the

DHCP client at this stage contains the lease request, as well as the source address for the client, 0.0.0.0, and the destination address, which is the broadcast address 255.255.255.255. The packet also includes the client's hardware (MAC) address and computer name; recall that network communication often boils down to a hardware address of one kind or another. The inclusion of the hardware address reveals the origin of the request to DHCP servers.

The actual packet that the client issues to request an IP address from a DHCP server is called a DHCPDISCOVER packet. The DHCPDISCOVER packet and all that it contains represent the client's IP lease request.

IP Lease Offer (DHCPOFFER)

Any DHCP server with valid IP addressing information will respond to a needy DHCP client with an offer of IP addressing information. It responds with one of the unassigned IP addresses from a scope of addresses that are valid for that specific host. To be able to respond to a DHCPDISCOVER packet, a DHCP server must have valid IP configuration information for the client. Any DHCP server with valid IP information can respond to the client with a DHCPOFFER packet containing the following information:

- The client's hardware address (allows the unique identification of the DHCP client)

- An offered IP address

- An appropriate subnet mask

- A duration for the lease

- A server ID, which would be the IP address of the DHCP server

The server sends a DHCPOFFER packet to the client's hardware (MAC) address because the client does not yet have an IP address. Similar to other DHCP messages, this packet is sent as a broadcast message, which is converted to the MAC address on the network. The DHCP server is also smart enough to reserve the IP address it has just offered. This ensures that it will not offer it to another DHCP client, thus avoiding duplicate IP addresses. It is worth remembering that the world does not stand still during this process—a DHCP server might be handling DHCP traffic from multiple clients at any given time. Therefore, it needs to keep track of the IP addresses it is offering and dishing out.

IP Lease Selection (DHCPREQUEST)

The DHCP client selects the IP addressing information it requires from the first DHCPOFFER packet it receives—that is, the offer from the server quickest off the mark to supply the information. At this time, it broadcasts this information out onto the network. In this broadcast, the client requests the IP address the server has proposed for it. The explanation for including the IP address request in the broadcast is that the client could have received more than one offer if there are other DHCP servers on the network. By broadcasting its request, the client announces to any other DHCP servers that this client will not be accepting their offers. To further ensure that there is no confusion over which server's offer the client is accepting, the client includes the following additional information in the request packet:

- The IP address of the server, whose offer it accepted
- The client's hardware address
- The IP address the client is accepting

The name of the actual packet sent is a DHCPREQUEST packet. In addition to requesting a specific IP address from a DHCP server, this packet asks other DHCP servers on the network to withdraw their offers of an IP address if they have made any.

IP Lease Acknowledgment (DHCPACK)

The DHCP server responds to the client that made the selection by assigning IP addressing information to the client. After it has done so, it also acknowledges that it has assigned IP addressing information to that client through a special acknowledgement packet called a DHCPACK, which it sends to the client. This message contains a valid lease for an IP address and other configuration information, which a network administrator might have specified in a DHCP scope.

Occasionally, a DHCP lease request can be unsuccessful after the client has accepted a lease offered by the server. This can happen in situations such as the following:

- The IP address is not valid because the client has been moved to another subnet.
- The client is attempting to lease its previous IP address and the IP address is no longer available.

In either of these situations, the server would broadcast an unsuccessful (negative) acknowledgment packet or DHCPNACK. A client that receives a DHCPNACK must start the whole DHCP initialization process over from scratch. That is, it must broadcast another DHCPDISCOVER packet looking for a fresh IP address from any available DHCP server.

Renewing an IPv4 Lease

A DHCP server leases an IP address to the DHCP client for only a specified term. The default term is eight days. To continue using its leased IP address, a DHCP client will attempt to renew its lease before it expires. This will occur at default intervals during the life of the lease. It sends the renewal request automatically if TCP/IP is still initialized on the client. The client receives a response if it is still on the same network or subnet and is able to communicate with the DHCP server.

When 50 percent of the lease time has expired, a client will attempt to renew its lease with the DHCP server that provided its lease and configuration information. It makes the renewal attempt by sending a DHCPREQUEST packet directly to that DHCP server. If the DHCP server and the IP address are both available, the server will renew the client's IP addressing information by sending a DHCPACK to the client with the renewed lease duration and any updated configuration information. Upon receipt of the DHCPACK, the client updates its configuration.

If the client is unable to renew its lease with the original DHCP server at this time, it continues to use its currently leased IP address and any other configuration data it received from its DHCP server with the original lease. The client can still use the address because only 50 percent of the lease duration has expired.

If a client still does not have a renewed lease after 87.5 percent of the active lease period has gone by, it will attempt to communicate with any DHCP server on the network to secure IP addressing and configuration information by broadcasting a DHCPREQUEST packet. The listening DHCP servers can make two possible responses:

- Any DHCP server can respond with a DHCPACK message to renew the lease. However, the renewal is most likely to come from the DHCP server that originally leased the IP address, although the location of an IP address or an IP address scope is not tied to one DHCP server forever. For the record, it is possible for a DHCP client to renew the same IP address lease from a different DHCP server.

- Any DHCP server can respond with a DHCPNACK message. DHCPNACK messages force a client to reinitialize and to obtain a lease for a different IP address.

If the client cannot make contact with a DHCP server and consequently fails to maintain its lease, the client must discontinue use of the IP address and begin the entire process again by issuing a DHCPDISCOVER packet. If this is also not possible, it resorts to APIPA to give itself an IP address when the lease expires.

How DHCPv6 Works

IPv6 clients can use address autoconfiguration to automatically configure themselves without DHCPv6 using a link-local address and router discovery. This enables the host to determine the addresses of routers, servers, and other configuration parameters. The following types of address configuration can be used:

- **Stateless address autoconfiguration:** Uses Router Advertisement messages to configure link-local addresses and additional addresses by exchanging Router Solicitation and Router Advertisement messages with neighboring routers.

- **Stateful address autoconfiguration:** Uses a stateful address configuration protocol such as DHCPv6 to obtain non-link-local addresses and other IPv6 configuration parameters.

- **Both types of addresses:** Uses Router Advertisement messages that include address prefixes and stateful address configuration protocols.

Two address autoconfiguration flags are used to determine the use of stateful and stateless address autoconfiguration on an IPv6 network:

- **Managed Address Configuration (M) flag:** Determines when DHCPv6 is used to obtain IPv6 stateful addresses. When set to 0, DHCPv6 is not used and stateless addresses are obtained. When set to 1, DHCPv6 is used to assign stateful addresses to IPv6 clients.

- **Other Stateful Configuration (O) flag:** Determines how additional IPv6 configuration parameters are obtained. This includes such settings as the IPv6 addresses of Domain Name System (DNS) servers. When set to 1, DHCPv6 is used to obtain these types of information. If the M flag is set to 0 and the O flag is set to 1, a combination known as DHCPv6 stateless is being used, where DHCPv6 is assigning additional stateless configuration settings but not stateful addresses to IPv6 clients.

An IPv6 client attempts DHCPv6 configuration according to the values of the M and O flags in router advertisement messages. If the M flag is set to 1, the client requesting addressing information participates in a four-step process similar to that used with IPv4, as follows:

1. The client sends a Solicit message from its link-local address to the All_DHCP_Relay_Agents_and_Servers address of FF02::1:2. This message corresponds to the DHCPDISCOVER message used with IPv4.

2. A DHCP server receiving this message sends an Advertise message (which corresponds to the DHCPOFFER message) to the client. This message informs the client that the server can provide address and configuration settings.

3. The client sends a Request message to the server to request address and configuration settings (corresponding to the DHCPREQUEST message). If the client does not receive an Advertise message, it uses a stateless address configuration protocol to obtain IPv6 configuration information.

4. The DHCP server sends a Reply message (which corresponds to the DHCPACK message) to the client to confirm acceptance of the Request message and assignment of the IPv6 address and configuration settings.

NOTE   To extend an expiring IPv6 address lease, the DHCPv6 server will send a Renew message. Several other types of DHCPv6 messages are possible; for information on other DHCPv6 messages, refer to "DHCP Protocols" at http://technet.microsoft.com/en-us/library/dd145321(WS.10).aspx. This reference also provides information on the structure of various DHCPv6 messages. Though written for Windows Server 2008, information in this reference applies equally well to Windows Server 2012 and Windows Server 2012 R2.

TIP   To view the settings of the M and O flags, first obtain the index of the desired interface by using the `netsh interface ipv6 show interface` command. Then view the settings of the interface by using the `Netsh interface ipv6 show interface <number>` command, where `<number>` is the interface index (Idx) number. The results of the latter command include a large number of connection parameters for the specified interface. To configure a Windows Server 2012 R2 router to set the M flag to 1 in router advertisements, use the `netsh interface ipv6 set interface InterfaceName managedaddress=enabled` command. To set the O flag to 1, use the `netsh interface ipv6 set interface InterfaceName otherstateful=enabled` command.

Installing and Configuring a DHCP Server

In Windows Server 2012 R2, DHCP is installed and configured as a server role. Before installing DHCP, ensure that the server is configured with a static IP address that is compatible with the scope that you will be configuring for lease purposes. You can do this from the Properties dialog box for your network adapter, accessible from the Network and Sharing Center:

1. Ensure that you are logged on as an administrative user.

2. From the left panel, select **Change adapter settings**. This displays the Network Connections dialog box.

3. Right-click your network connection and select **Properties**.

4. From the Ethernet Properties dialog box that appears, select either **Internet Protocol Version 4 (TCP/IPv4)** or **Internet Protocol Version 6 (TCP/IPv6)** as required; then click **Properties**.

5. In the dialog box that appears, select the **Use the following IP address** option and then type the IP address, subnet mask or subnet prefix length, and default gateway. Click **OK** and then click **Close**.

Using Server Manager to Install DHCP

Use the following procedure to install DHCP on a Windows Server 2012 R2 computer:

1. From the Dashboard of Server Manager, click **Manage** > **Add Roles and Features**.

2. The Add Roles and Features Wizard starts with a Select installation type page. Select **Role-based** or **feature-based** installation, and then click **Next**.

3. On the Select destination server page, ensure that **Select a server from the server pool** option (the default) is selected, select your local server from the list displayed, and then click **Next**.

4. The Select Server Roles page enables you to select the roles you want to install on your server. Select **DHCP Server** (as shown in Figure 11-2). If you receive a dialog box asking to install features that are required for DHCP server, click **Add Features** to accept the installation of these features and return to the Select Server Roles page. Then click **Next**.

5. The Select Features page enables you to add more features if desired. Select any desired features (these are not required when performing this procedure for study purposes); then click **Next**.

6. The DHCP Server page shown in Figure 11-3 displays. Read the information provided. When you're ready to proceed, click **Next**.

7. The Confirm Installation Selections page that summarizes the options you've specified displays. Verify that these selections are complete, and then click **Install**.

8. The Installation Progress page tracks the progress of installing DHCP. When informed that the installation is complete, click **Close**.

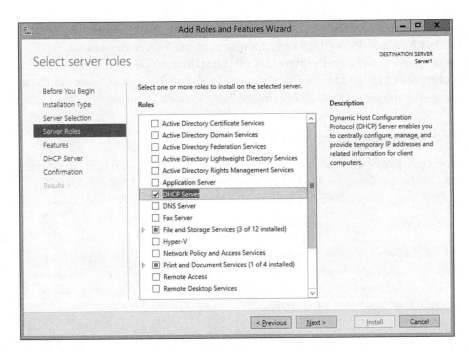

Figure 11-2   Selecting the DHCP server role.

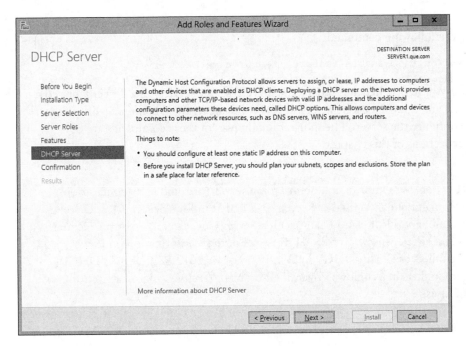

Figure 11-3   The DHCP Server page provides more information on DHCP.

After you've finished installing DHCP, the DHCP Microsoft Management Console (MMC) snap-in is added to the set of administrative tools accessed from the Start screen of a server configured with the full GUI installation option. A DHCP module is also present in the Dashboard of Server Manager. The remainder of this chapter discusses configuration of the options available from this console.

Using Windows PowerShell to Install DHCP

You can use PowerShell to install a server role or feature such as DHCP on a server running the Server Core version of Windows Server 2012 R2. To install DHCP, use the following PowerShell cmdlet:

```
Install-WindowsFeature DHCPServerCore
```

As was the case with Windows Server 2008 R2, you can also use the Deployment Image Servicing and Management (DISM.exe) tool in Windows Server 2012 R2 to install and configure server roles such as DHCP. Use the following command to install DHCP on a Server Core machine:

```
Dism /online /enable-feature /featurename:DHCPServerCore
```

Note that this command is case-sensitive and **DHCPServerCore** must be typed exactly as indicated.

On a computer running any of the GUI-based editions of Windows Server 2012 R2, use the following command:

```
Dism /online /enable-feature /featurename:DHCPServer
```

After you've installed and started the DHCP server service on a Server Core computer, you can use PowerShell cmdlets or the `netsh dhcp` command-line context to configure the server. The more common uses of these commands are covered in later sections of this chapter.

> **NOTE**   For more information on installing server roles and role services from the command line in Windows Server 2012 and Windows Server 2012 R2, refer to "Install Server Roles and Features on a Server Core Server" at http://technet.microsoft.com/en-us/library/jj574158.aspx. For more information on PowerShell cmdlets used with DHCP in Windows Server 2012 R2, refer to "DHCP Server Cmdlets in Windows PowerShell" at http://technet.microsoft.com/library/jj590751.aspx.

CAUTION   If you use Windows PowerShell to install DHCP on a server configured with a GUI option, the installation routine does not add the DHCP Management snap-in. You will have to use Windows PowerShell or remote server management tools to perform subsequent configuration of this DHCP server.

DHCP Scopes and Options

After you have installed and started the DHCP Server service, you need to configure a scope of configuration information. Every DHCP server requires at least one scope with a pool of IP addresses available for leasing to clients. You can create a scope for each physical subnet on your network and use this scope to define networking parameters such as the range of IP addresses and their subnet masks, lease duration values, scope options, and client reservation options. You can create multiple scopes to act as a backup method for other DHCP servers and for assigning IP addresses specific to a subnet, such as default gateway addresses.

Creating DHCP Scopes

Windows Server 2012 R2 provides the Create Scope Wizard to facilitate the creation of new scopes. Use the following procedure to create a new DHCP scope:

1. Open the DHCP console from the Start screen, the Server Manager Dashboard, or the Search charm.

2. If you receive a DHCP Post-Install configuration wizard page asking you to create security groups for delegation of DHCP server administration, click **Commit** and then click **Close** to complete this task.

3. In the console tree, expand the node for your server to reveal subnodes for IPv4 and IPv6. Select either **IPv4** or **IPv6** as required according to the scope you plan to create.

4. Right-click either **IPv4** or **IPv6** and select **New Scope**.

5. The New Scope Wizard starts with a Welcome page. Click **Next**.

6. On the Scope Name page, type a name (required) and optional description for the scope; then click **Next**.

7. On the IP Address Range page, specify the start and end points of the address range (as shown in Figure 11-4) to be provided by the scope. Change the subnet mask length and value if required, and then click **Next**.

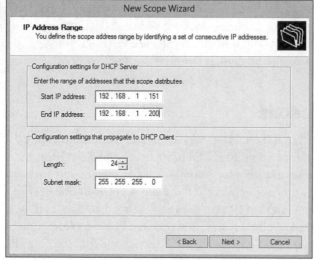

Figure 11-4 Specifying the range of IP addresses to be provided by the scope.

8. The Add Exclusions and Delay page shown in Figure 11-5 enables you to specify a range of addresses to be excluded from distribution to clients. This is useful to exclude IP addresses configured for servers or other devices with static IP addresses from being distributed. Specify the start and end IP addresses (as shown in Figure 11-5), click **Add**, and then click **Next**.

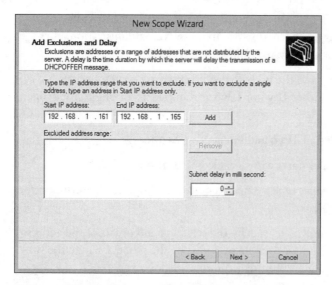

Figure 11-5 Specifying a range of IP addresses to be excluded from your scope.

9. The Lease Duration page enables you to choose how long a client is entitled to use an IP address from the scope. By default, this period is eight days. If you want, choose a different number of days, hours, and minutes for the lease duration period. Then click **Next**.

10. The Configure DHCP Options page shown in Figure 11-6 displays. Leave the default of Yes, I want to configure these options now selected to specify options for domain name, lease duration, and router location. Click **No, I will configure these options later to complete the wizard** and specify these options later. These options are discussed later in this section.

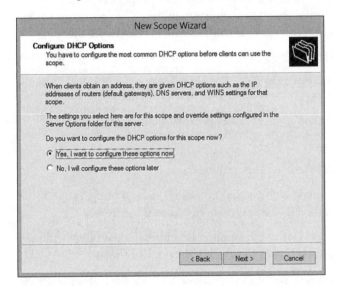

Key Topic

Figure 11-6   The wizard enables you to choose whether to specify several common options now or later.

11. When you've finished configuring these options, you are asked whether you want to activate the scope now. To provide IP addressing information to clients, you must activate the scope. Click **Yes, I want to activate this scope now**, and then click **Next**. Note that you do not receive this page if you've chosen the No, I will configure these options later option in Step 9; you will have to activate the scope after completing the wizard.

12. Click **Finish** to create your scope.

Creating an IPv6 scope is similar. After you've specified the name of the scope, the wizard asks for a scope prefix (refer to Table 10-9 in Chapter 10). It then asks whether you want to add exclusions (similar to Figure 11-5 for IPv4) and the lease duration.

> **NOTE** For more information on configuring DHCP including test lab procedures and scope creation, refer to "Step-by-Step: Configure DHCP Using Policy-based Assignment" at http://technet.microsoft.com/en-us/library/ hh831538.aspx.

Using Windows PowerShell to Create Scopes

PowerShell in Windows Server 2012 R2 provides the `Add-DhcpServerv4Scope` and `Add-DhcpServerv6Scope` cmdlets that enable you to create scopes on your DHCP server. This is useful for scripting tasks to be run from multiple servers or for working at a Server Core machine. Use the following cmdlet to create an IPv4 scope:

```
Add-DhcpServerv4Scope [-StartRange] <IPAddress> [-EndRange] <IPAddress>
[-SubnetMask] <IPAddress> [-Name] <String> [-ActivatePolicies <Boolean> ]
[-AsJob] [-CimSession <CimSession[]> ] [-ComputerName <String> ]
[-Delay <UInt16> ] [-Description <String> ] [-LeaseDuration <TimeSpan> ]
[-MaxBootpClients <UInt32> ] [-NapEnable] [-NapProfile <String> ]
[-PassThru] [-State <String> ] [-SuperscopeName <String> ]
[-ThrottleLimit <Int32> ] [- Type <String> ] [-Confirm] [-WhatIf]
[ <CommonParameters>]
```

In this cmdlet, the following parameters are required:

- `-StartRange <IPAddress>`: Defines the starting IP address of the range within the subnet from which the DHCP server should lease IP addresses

- `-EndRange <IPAddress>`: Defines the ending IP address of the range within the subnet from which the DHCP server should lease IP addresses

- `-SubnetMask <IPAddress>`: Specifies the subnet mask for the scope specified in IP address format

- `-Name<String>`: Specifies the name of the IPv4 scope being added

For definitions of the remaining (optional) parameters, refer to "Add-DhcpServerv4Scope" at http://technet.microsoft.com/en-us/library /jj590728.aspx.

For example, the following command adds a scope with a starting range of 10.2.2.1, an ending range of 10.2.2.254, a subnet mask of 255.255.255.0, and a scope name of MyScope:

```
Add-DhcpServerv4Scope -Name "MyScope" -StartRange 10.2.2.1 -EndRange
10.2.2.254 -SubnetMask 255.255.255.0
```

NOTE   You can also use `netsh` commands to perform DHCP management tasks from the command line, including creation of scopes, though Microsoft now favors the use of PowerShell cmdlets. For more information on using the `netsh` command-line tool for configuring and scripting DHCP, refer to "`Netsh` commands for DHCP" at http://technet.microsoft.com/en-us/library/cc787375(WS.10).aspx.

Specifying Exclusions

An *exclusion* is a range of IP addresses within a scope that you do not want to have used by DHCP in leasing addresses to clients. Typically, these are IP addresses of computers such as servers configured with static IP addresses.

You can create an exclusion when first creating a scope with the New Scope Wizard, as already described. Use the following procedure:

1. In the console tree of the DHCP console, double-click the required scope under the IPv4 node to expand it.

2. Select **Address Pool**, then right-click it, and select **New Exclusion Range**.

3. In the Add Exclusion dialog box, type the starting and ending IP addresses of the desired exclusion range in the **Start IP Address** and **End IP Address** fields; then click **Add**.

4. Repeat as needed to define additional exclusion ranges. When finished, click **Close**.

You can also use the `Add-DhcpServer4ExclusionRange` and `Add-DhcpServer6ExclusionRange` PowerShell cmdlets to create an exclusion from the command line. To create an exclusion range for an IPv4 scope, type the following:

```
Add-DhcpServerv4ExclusionRange [-ScopeId] <IPAddress> [-StartRange]
<IPAddress> [-EndRange] <IPAddress> [-AsJob] [-CimSession
<CimSession[]> ] [-ComputerName <String> ] [-PassThru] [-ThrottleLimit
<Int32> ] [-Confirm] [-WhatIf] [ <CommonParameters>]
```

In this command, `-ScopeId` *<IPAddress>* specifies the identifier of the IPv4 scope from which the IP addresses are being excluded, and `-StartRange` *<IPAddress>* and `-EndRange` *<IPAddress>* specify the IP addresses of the start and end points of the exclusion range. For definitions of the other (optional) parameters, refer to "Add-DhcpServerv4ExclusionRange" at http://technet.microsoft.com/en-us/library/jj590721(v=wps.620).aspx.

For example, to exclude the range 192.168.1.101 to 192.168.1.199, use the following command:

```
Add-Dhcpserverv4ExclusionRange -ScopeId 192.168.1.0 -StartRange
192.168.1.101 -EndRange 192.168.1.199
```

> **NOTE**   For more information on managing scopes in general, refer to "Managing DHCP Server Scopes" at http://technet.microsoft.com/en-us/library/dd183624(WS.10).aspx. Though written for Windows Server 2008, information in this reference also applies to Windows Server 2012 and Windows Server 2012 R2.

Configuring DHCP Scope Properties

Each scope you create on your DHCP server has a set of properties associated with it. Right-click the scope and select **Properties** to display the dialog box shown in Figure 11-7. The four tabs enable you to configure the following properties:

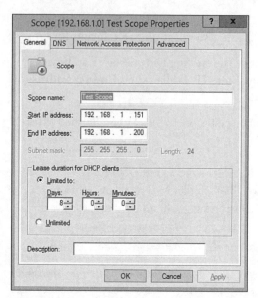

Figure 11-7   Configuring DHCP scope properties.

- **General tab:** Enables you to adjust the IP address range and lease duration, as shown in Figure 11-7.

- **DNS tab:** Enables you to automatically update the host (A) and pointer (PTR) records on the authoritative DNS servers. More information on this process is provided in Chapter 12, "Deploying and Configuring Domain Name System (DNS)."

- **Network Access Protection tab:** Enables you to set up Network Access Protection (NAP) settings for the scope. NAP is discussed in the *Cert Guide* for exam 70-411.

- **Advanced tab:** Enables you to select whether the scope provides IP addressing information to DHCP clients, BOOTP clients, or both. You can adjust the lease duration for BOOTP clients, which is 30 days by default.

Configuring DHCP Options

As already noted, the Create Scope Wizard enables you to specify several options related to the scope. DHCP in Windows Server 2012 R2 provides a considerable range of options you can use to specify additional TCP/IP-related parameters to client computers on your network. You can specify these options at any of the following four levels:

- **Server:** Specific for either IPv4 or IPv6, it serves as defaults for all scopes configured on the server.

- **Scope:** Applies only to the scope for which it is specified.

- **Option class:** Applies to all computers belonging to the defined option class. Option classes are discussed later in this chapter.

- **Client:** Applies only to the specified client computer.

Any option applied at a later stage in this sequence always overwrites a conflicting option that was applied earlier in this sequence. For example, server options are overwritten by any conflicting option applied at any of the other levels, and client options always overwrite other options applied at any level.

Table 11-3 summarizes the more important DHCP server options:

Table 11-3   Common DHCP Options

DHCP Option	Description
003 Router	Specifies the IP address of the default gateway.
006 DNS Servers	Specifies the IP addresses of the network's DNS name servers.
015 DNS Domain Name	Specifies the DNS domain name used for client reservations.
044 WINS/NBNS Servers	Specifies the IP addresses of the network's NetBIOS name servers.

DHCP Option	Description
046 WINS/NBT Node Type	Specifies the type of NetBIOS over TCP/IP name resolution to be used by the client: 1 = B-node (broadcast) 2 = P-node (peer) 4 = M-node (mixed) 8 = H-node (hybrid)
047 NetBIOS Scope ID	Specifies the local NetBIOS scope ID. Hosts can communicate only with other hosts configured with the same scope ID.
060 Vendor class Identifier	Specifies the vendor type and configuration of the DHCP client.
066 Boot Server Host Name	Specifies the hostname of the Trivial File Transfer Protocol (TFTP) server used in servicing PXE boot clients.
067 Boot File Name	Specifies the name of a boot image file on the TFTP server used in servicing PXE boot clients.

NOTE For a complete list of available DHCP options and their associated parameters, refer to "DHCP Tools and Options" at http://technet.microsoft.com/en-us/library/dd145324(WS.10).aspx and "RFC 2132–DHCP Options and BOOTP Vendor Extensions" at http://www.faqs.org/rfcs/rfc2132.html. Though written for Windows Server 2008, the options discussed are unchanged for Windows Server 2012 and Windows Server 2012 R2.

Server Options

As already noted, you can configure DHCP options at any of four levels. Use the following procedure to configure DHCP options at the server level:

1. In the console tree of the DHCP console, right-click **Server Options** under either IPv4 or IPv6 as required and select **Configure Options**.

2. From the General tab of the Server Options dialog box, select the option to be configured. The lower part of this dialog box expands to reveal parameters specific to the option selected, as shown in Figure 11-8 for the 003 Router option.

3. Click **Apply** to apply your changes, and then select another option as required. When finished configuring options, click **OK**.

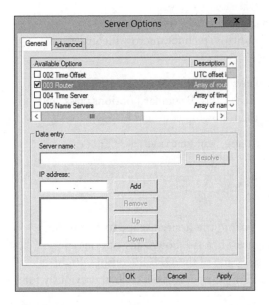

Figure 11-8   Configuring the 003 Router DHCP server option.

Note that if you specified any of these options while installing the DHCP server role, they will appear in the Server Options dialog box. You can modify any of these options simply by selecting the required option and making any needed changes.

You can also use the `-Add-DhcpServerv4OptionDefinition` and `-Add-DhcpServerv6OptionDefinition` cmdlets to add server options in versions 4 and 6 of DHCP, respectively. To add a server option in version 4 of DHCP, use the following cmdlet:

```
Add-DhcpServerv4OptionDefinition [-Name] <String> [-OptionId]
<UInt32> [-Type] <String> [-AsJob] [-CimSession <CimSession[]> ]
[-ComputerName <String> ] [-DefaultValue <String[]> ] [-Description
<String> ] [-MultiValued] [-PassThru] [-ThrottleLimit <Int32> ]
[-VendorClass <String> ] [-Confirm] [-WhatIf] [ <CommonParameters>]
```

In this cmdlet, the following parameters are required:

- `-Name <String>`: Specifies the name of the DHCPv4 option.

- `-OptionId <UInt32>`: Specifies the numerical identifier of the option, as previously mentioned in Table 11-3.

- `-Type <String>`: Specifies the data type of the values for this option. The acceptable values are `Byte`, `Word`, `Dword`, `DwordDword`, `IPAddress`, `String`, `BinaryData`, `EncapsulatedData`, and `IPv6Address`.

For the definitions of the other (optional) parameters, refer to "Add-DhcpServerv4OptionDefinition" at http://technet.microsoft.com/en-us/library/jj590734.aspx.

For example, to add a new option type named `Vendor Class Identifier` with code 60 and a `STRING` data type, join it to the DHCP standard options class, and assign it a default value of `c:\Temp`, use the following command:

```
Add-DhcpServerv4OptionDefinition -Name VendorClassIdentifier
-OptionId 60 -Type String -DefaultValue c:\Temp
```

Scope Options

To configure options at the scope level, expand the desired scope to reveal the Scope Options subnode, as shown in Figure 11-9. As shown, any options specified at the server level appear in the details pane of the DHCP console. Right-click this node, select **Configure Options**, and then proceed as described previously for server options.

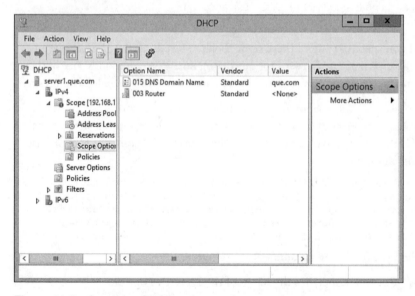

Figure 11-9   Specifying DHCP options at the scope level.

To set an IPv4 option value for the current scope from the command line, use the following Windows PowerShell 4.0 cmdlet:

```
Set-DhcpServerv4OptionValue [-OptionId] <UInt32> [-Value] <String[]>
[[-ScopeId] <IPAddress> ] [-AsJob] [-CimSession <CimSession[]> ]
[-ComputerName <String> ] [-Force] [-PassThru] [-PolicyName <String> ]
```

```
[-ReservedIP <IPAddress> ] [-ThrottleLimit <Int32> ] [- UserClass
<String> ] [-VendorClass <String> ] [-Confirm] [-WhatIf]
[ <CommonParameters>]
```

This cmdlet sets an IPv4 option value at the server, scope, or reservation level. In this command, `OptionID <UInt32>` specifies the numeric identifier of the option being configured (as specified in Table 11-3). `Value <String[]>` specifies one or more values of format `Byte`, `Word`, `DWord`, `DWordDword`, `IPAddress`, or `IPv6Address`. Other parameters are as defined previously for adding server options. For example, to set the default gateway for the scope at 192.168.0.0 to 192.168.0.1, use the following command:

```
Set-DhcpServerv4OptionValue -ScopeID 192.168.0.0 -OptionId 3 -Value 3
IPADDRESS 192.168.0.1
```

> **NOTE**   For more information on the Set-DhcpServerv4OptionValue cmdlet, refer to "Set-DhcpServerv4OptionValue" at http://technet.microsoft.com/en-us/library/jj590669.aspx.

Option Classes

DHCP in Windows Server 2012 R2 provides *option classes*, which facilitate the introduction of custom applications on enterprise networks. By specifying option classes, you can differentiate groups of DHCP clients and specify customized options that apply only to the specified group of clients. The following two types of option classes are available in Windows Server 2012 R2:

- **Vendor classes:** Used to identify a client's vendor type and configuration when obtaining a DHCP lease. You can use the vendor class ID option (code 60) to specify vendor classes. This option includes an identifier with a string of character data readable by the DHCP servers. Often used with vendor classes are standard reserved hardware and operating system codes defined in RFC 1700.

- **User classes:** Used to differentiate clients according to their type, such as desktop, laptop, or server computer. For example, you can group mobile computers into a specific class and apply options such as shorter lease times to only these computers by supplying them with the relevant class ID. You can also define class identifiers that specify information such as a client's software configuration, physical location within a building, operating system in use, and so on.

> **TIP** DHCP in Windows Server 2012 R2 provides for a default user class, to which all DHCP clients belong by default. Any options you define for this class automatically apply to all DHCP clients. Options assigned to this class can be overridden by options assigned to other user classes.

Use the following procedure to define a custom user class:

1. In the console tree of the DHCP console, right-click the **IPv4** or **IPv6** node as required under the DHCP server and select **Define User Classes**.

2. When defining a user class, the DHCP User Classes dialog box appears. As shown in Figure 11-10, three default user classes are provided. To define a new user class, click **Add**.

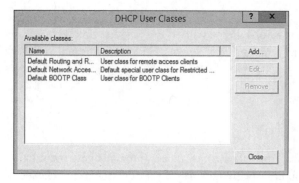

Figure 11-10 DHCP provides three user classes by default.

3. In the New Class dialog box that appears (see Figure 11-11), type the required information and then click **Add**.

You can define a custom vendor class using a similar procedure. Right-click **IPv4** or **IPv6** and select **Define Vendor Classes**.

To specify DHCP options for user or vendor classes, select the **Advanced** tab of either the Server Options or Scope Options dialog box (refer to Figure 11-8 for the Server Options dialog box). Specify the class ID to be assigned, and then configure the required options as described previously.

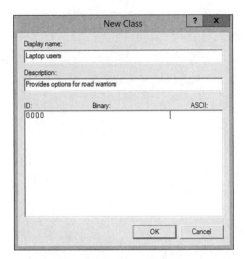

Figure 11-11   Specifying user class information.

NOTE   For more information on option classes, refer to "Understanding user and vendor classes" at http://technet.microsoft.com/en-us/library/cc737299%28v=WS.10%29.aspx. Although originally written for Windows Server 2003, the information provided is still applicable for all recent versions of Windows Server.

Client Reservations and Options

You can configure DHCP so that a DHCP server always assigns the same IP address to a client computer. This feature is known as a *client reservation*. It maps the IP address to a specific MAC address and is useful for configuring servers that must always be reached at the same IP address with a specified set of options. You can include client-specific options that override conflicting server- and scope-based options. Proceed as follows:

1. In the console tree of the DHCP console, expand the required scope to reveal the Reservations node.

2. Right-click this node and select **New Reservation**.

3. In the dialog box that appears (see Figure 11-12), type the correct IP address (for example, `192.168.1.163`) and MAC address (`ab-17-3f-42-69-7c`) for the reservation; then click **Add**.

Figure 11-12   Specifying a client reservation.

4. Repeat to add client reservations as needed. When finished, click **Close**.

5. To specify client-based options similar to those already mentioned for server and scope options, right-click the client reservation and select **Configure Options**.

You can also use the -Add-DhcpServerv4Reservation and -Add-DhcpServerv6Reservation PowerShell cmdlets to add client reservations in versions 4 and 6 of DHCP, respectively. To add a client reservation in version 4, use the following PowerShell cmdlet:

```
Add-DhcpServerv4Reservation [-ScopeId] <IPAddress> [-IPAddress] <IPAddress>
[-ClientId] <String> [-AsJob] [-CimSession <CimSession[]> ] [-ComputerName
<String> ] [-Description <String> ] [-Name <String> ] [-PassThru]
[-ThrottleLimit <Int32> ] [-Type <String> ] [-Confirm] [-WhatIf]
[ <CommonParameters>]
```

In this cmdlet, the following parameters are required:

- -ClientId <String>: Specifies the unique identifier (ID) for the client. Use the MAC address for Windows-based clients.

- -IPAddress < IPAddress>: Specifies the IPv4 address to be reserved for the client.

- -ScopeID < IPAddress>: Specifies the ID of the scope in which the reservation is being created.

For the definitions of the other (optional) parameters, refer to "Add-DhcpServerv4Reservation" at http://technet.microsoft.com/en-us/library/jj590686.aspx.

For example, to reserve the IP address 192.168.1.163 in the 192.168.1.0 scope for a server named MailServer1 and using the MAC address ab-17-3f-42-69-7c, use the following command:

```
Add-DhcpServerv4Reservation -ScopeId 192.168.1.0 -IPAddress
192.168.1.163 -ClientId ab-17-3f-42-69-7c -Description "MailServer1"
```

TIP   Remember that DHCP options are applied in the sequence server, scope, user class, and client reservation. Options applied at a later stage of this sequence always override those applied earlier.

DHCP Filters

With the release of Windows Server 2008 R2, Microsoft included a DHCP Filter function. Windows Server 2012 and Windows Server 2012 R2 continue this filter function. Using the filter, you can specify a MAC address or range and allow or deny IP address assignment on the network. This can be useful if you have a collection of servers, perhaps a development pool of virtual machines you don't want to receive IP addresses from DHCP Server A, for example. Using the filter function on your DHCP server, you can add the MAC addresses for each virtual server and create a deny rule. On the other hand, perhaps you have created a development DHCP server and want it to hand out addresses to only specific hosts. You can choose to create an allow rule for the specific MAC addresses. Although this process might work, it's not a guarantee because MAC addresses can be spoofed. To create a DHCP filter, perform the following steps:

1. In the DHCP console, right-click the **IPv4** node; then click **Properties**.

2. On the filters tab, select either **Enable Allow List** or **Enable Deny List**. Click **OK** to save the changes.

3. Right-click the **Allow/Deny** filter and select **New Filter**.

4. Enter the MAC address to the filter, specify a comment, and click **Add**.

5. Close the console when you have completed adding all MAC addresses to the filter.

Configuring PXE Boot

When using Windows Deployment Services (WDS) to install operating systems such as Windows 7, Windows 8, Windows Server 2008, or Windows Server 2012 R2 on new computers, the network interface card (NIC) of the new computer must be compliant with the Preboot Execution Environment (PXE). PXE enables a computer to access an image across the network to simplify and streamline installations. The computer connects to a WDS server, which then installs the operating system via the network without the need for a CD, DVD, or other media..

When the computer initializes a PXE boot, the PXE ROM requests an IP address from the DHCP server using the normal four-step process described earlier in this chapter. The DHCPDISCOVER message indicates to the server that the client computer is PXE-enabled, and after the client receives a valid IP address, it attempts to locate and connect to the WDS server to download a network boot program.

NOTE WDS is covered in more detail on the 70-411 exam. For more information on WDS and its use in deploying operating systems, refer to "Windows Deployment Services Getting Started Guide for Windows Server 2012" at http://technet.microsoft.com/en-us/library/jj648426.aspx.

Configuring DHCP Options for PXE

After you have configured WDS with appropriate images, you will need to ensure that your DHCP server is configured with options 066 and 067. These options enable clients to connect to the WDS server using PXE. To configure the options, perform the following steps:

1. In the console tree of the DHCP console, right-click **Server Options** under either IPv4 or IPv6 as required and select **Configure Options** as you did previously.

2. From the General tab of the Server Options dialog box, select option **066 Boot Server Host Name** as shown in Figure 11-13.

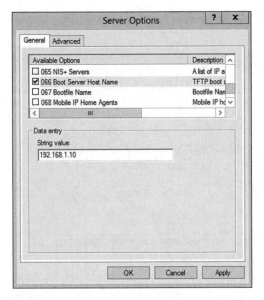

Figure 11-13   Configuring the 066 Boot Server Host Name DHCP server option.

3. Enter the IP address of the WDS Server in the **String value** text box.

4. Click **Apply** to apply your changes.

5. Select option **067 Bootfile Name** as shown in Figure 11-14.

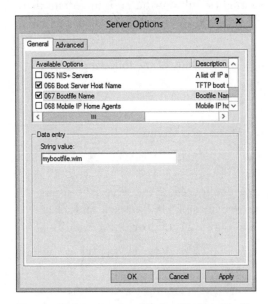

Figure 11-14   Configuring the 067 Bootfile Name DHCP server option.

6. Enter the appropriate path to your WDS image file in the **String value** text field.

7. Click **Apply** to apply your changes.

8. Click **OK** to complete the changes and close the dialog box.

> **TIP**   If your server contains both PXE and DHCP functions, you will need to configure DHCP Option 60 with a string containing PXEClient so PXE clients can communicate properly with WDS using an alternative port that does not conflict with those used by DHCP/BOOTP.

As mentioned previously, if you specified any of these options while installing the DHCP server role, they will appear in the Server Options dialog box. You can modify any of these options simply by selecting the required option and making any needed changes. Similarly, you can use PowerShell cmdlets to modify these options, as discussed earlier.

Monitoring and Troubleshooting a DHCP Server

As with any other server role, things can and do go wrong with a DHCP server. If problems occur with a DHCP server, client computers might not receive proper IP leases and network communication errors might result. Further, it is important that you know whether your DHCP server is encountering performance bottlenecks or other issues.

You can obtain DHCP server monitoring data from any of the following three locations:

- DHCP statistics
- Statistical information provided by Performance Monitor
- Events recorded by Event Viewer

DHCP statistics are provided for each scope configured on the server. To access DHCP statistics, right-click the required scope in the DHCP console and select **Display Statistics**. The dialog box shown in Figure 11-15 provides statistical information.

Server server2.mytestdomain.com Statistics

Description	Details
Start Time	9/16/2013 7:12:26 PM
Up Time	0 Hours, 20 Minutes, 6 Seconds
Discovers	9
Offers	9
Delayed Offers	0
Requests	1
Acks	1
Nacks	0
Declines	0
Releases	0
Total Scopes	1
Scopes with delay configured	0
Total Addresses	11
In Use	2 (18%)
Available	9 (81%)

Refresh   Close

Figure 11-15 Displaying DHCP statistical data.

When you install DHCP, a series of statistical counters is added to Performance Monitor. These counters enable you to track server performance and monitor server activity such as the number and types of messages sent and received by the server, the processing time required by the DHCP server to deal with requests sent to it, and whether message packets are being dropped because of internal server delays.

> **NOTE** For a more information, refer to "DHCP Failover Events and Performance" at http://technet.microsoft.com/en-us/library/dn338988.aspx.

Each time the DHCP server receives a lease request, offers a lease, or acknowledges or denies it, a record is written to the DHCP event log, which you can view in Event Viewer. Errors or warning messages encountered during this activity are also recorded, which enables you to locate and track problems related to the DHCP server. If disk space is causing a problem, you can move the database file to another location. By default, the database is stored at `%systemroot%\system32\dhcp`, as shown in Figure 11-16. Use the following procedure to move the database to another location:

Figure 11-16 The Properties dialog box for a DHCP server enables you to change the location of the database and backup files.

1. In the console tree of the DHCP snap-in, right-click the server and select **Properties**.

2. Click **Browse opposite the Database path field** to move the database file to another location.

3. You are warned that for the changes to take effect, the service must be stopped and restarted. Click **Yes** to continue.

4. Click **OK** to close the dialog box.

The following are a few problems you might encounter with a DHCP server, together with suggestions for resolution:

- **IP address conflicts:** This can occur if a user has manually configured a computer with a static IP address that is within the range of a DHCP scope. Ensure that the user selects the **Obtain an IP address automatically** option. If there is a reason that the chosen IP address must be retained, configure an exclusion so that the DHCP server does not lease this address. This error might also occur if more than one DHCP server is configured with overlapping scopes.

- **Failure to obtain an IP address reservation:** If you attempt to add a reservation for an IP address outside the range of a configured scope, you will receive a message stating `The specified DHCP client is not a reserved client.`

You must use an IP address that is contained within an existing scope when configuring an IP address reservation. Use an exclusion range to ensure that another client does not receive the same IP address.

- **Clients are unable to receive an IP address:** This might mean that all available IP addresses within the range of existing scopes have been allocated. You should extend the scope or create a new scope, according to the overall network configuration.

- **After restoring the DHCP server from backup, clients receive IP addresses that are already in use:** After restoring the DHCP server from backup, it might be unaware of which IP addresses it has leased from a given scope. The Conflict detection parameter is provided for this purpose. By default, this parameter is set to 0, which disables conflict detection. When this parameter is set to a nonzero value, the DHCP server uses the ping utility to test an IP address before leasing it to a client; the value represents the number of times the server performs this test. The value can range from 0 to 6. Higher values perform a more thorough test at the expense of server resources. To specify a value for this parameter, right-click the DHCP server in the console tree of the DHCP snap-in. From the Advanced tab of the Properties dialog box, type a value between 1 and 6 in the **Conflict detection attempts** text box, and then click **OK**.

- **Client obtains an inappropriate IP address:** Such an error can cause an inability to communicate on the network. This might occur if the client is connected to the wrong network or if the scope has been incorrectly configured. Check the scope configuration as well as the location of the client computer.

Managing and Authorizing DHCP Servers

Exam 70-410 tests your ability to perform several additional managerial tasks on your DHCP server, including the following:

- Authorizing the server in Active Directory
- Configuring DHCP relay agents

Authorizing a DHCP Server in Active Directory

In an Active Directory Domain Services (AD DS) domain, you must authorize the DHCP server in Active Directory before it can lease IP addresses. This is to prevent rogue DHCP servers from leasing improper IP addresses that would result in communication problems. When a domain controller or member server running DHCP starts up, it queries AD DS for the list of authorized servers as identified by their IP addresses. If its IP address is not present on this list, the DHCP Server service does not complete its startup sequence.

To authorize your DHCP server, you must be a member of the Enterprise Admins group. Use the following procedure:

1. At the top of the console tree of the DHCP console, right-click **DHCP** and select **Manage authorized servers**.

2. On the Manage Authorized Servers dialog box that appears, click **Authorize**.

3. On the Authorize DHCP Server dialog box, type the name or IP address of the server to be authorized, as shown in Figure 11-17; then click **OK**.

Figure 11-17   Authorizing a DHCP server in Active Directory.

4. Click **OK** to confirm the authorization. Assuming that the domain controller can be contacted and the appropriate privileges are used, DHCP Manager will place the server in the list of Authorized DHCP servers, as shown in Figure 11-18. Click **Close** when finished.

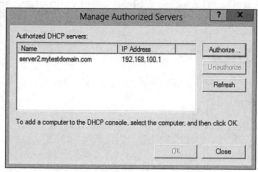

Figure 11-18   Authorized DHCP server.

To authorize your DHCP server from the command line, use one of the following methods:

- **Netsh:** In the Netsh dhcp add server *ServerDNS* ServerIP command, *ServerDNS* is the DNS domain name of the DHCP server to be authorized and *ServerIP* is the IP address of this server. Both parameters are required.

- **Add-DhcpServerInDC:** This PowerShell 4 cmdlet adds the computer running the DHCP service to the list of authorized DHCP servers in the domain. The basic syntax for the cmdlet is `Add-DhcpServerIn DC -DNSName [server name.mydomain.com]`.

> **NOTE** For a more information, refer to "How to Use Netsh.exe to Authorize, Unauthorize and List DHCP Servers in Active Directory" at http://support.microsoft.com/kb/303351 and "Add-DhcpServerInDC" at http://technet.microsoft.com/en-us/library/jj590712.aspx.

Configuring DHCP Relay Agents

Recall from earlier in this chapter that when a client computer starts up, it broadcasts a DHCPDISCOVER message to locate a DHCP server and obtain TCP/IP configuration information. What happens if there is no DHCP server on the subnet to which the client belongs? Broadcast messages do not cross routers to access servers on another subnet unless the router is compliant with the RFC 1542 standard "Clarifications and Extensions for the Bootstrap Protocol." Such a router can recognize and pass BOOTP broadcasts to other subnets, a feature known as BOOTP-forwarding. Note that nearly all current routers are RFC 1542 compliant, but you might still encounter legacy routers that are not compliant.

A *DHCP relay agent* is another means to forward BOOTP broadcasts to other subnets in search of a DHCP server. A DHCP relay agent is a Windows Server 2012 R2 computer configured with the Remote Access role (also known as Routing and Remote Access) to pass BOOTP broadcasts and is thereby compliant with RFC 1542. This server acts as a DHCP proxy by listening for DHCPDISCOVER broadcasts and translating them into DHCPINFORM messages that are directed to the IP addresses of all DHCP servers on adjacent subnets the DHCP relay agent knows about.

Before configuring a Windows Server 2012 R2 computer as a DHCP relay agent, you must set up the Remote Access Role and associated features. The installation of roles is covered in Chapter 2, "Installing and Configuring Windows Server 2012 R2." After installing the Remote Access Role, use the following procedure to configure a Windows Server 2012 R2 computer as an IPv4 DHCP relay agent:

1. Open the Routing and Remote Access (RRAS) snap-in by clicking **Start > Administrative Tools > Routing and Remote Access**.

2. From the console tree of the RRAS snap-in, expand **IPv4**, right-click the **General** subnode, and select **New Routing Protocol**.

3. From the New Routing Protocol dialog box, select **DHCP Relay Agent** (as shown in Figure 11-19); then click **OK**.

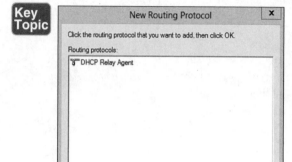

Figure 11-19   You must select DHCP Relay Agent from the New Routing Protocol dialog box.

4. DHCP Relay Agent is added to the console tree of the RRAS snap-in. Right-click it and select **New Interface**.

5. In the New Interface for DHCP Relay Agent dialog box shown in Figure 11-20, select the required network interface; then click **OK**.

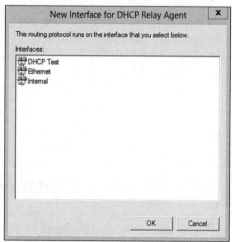

Figure 11-20   Configuring the DHCP Relay Agent.

6. Ensure that Relay DHCP packets is selected as shown in Figure 11-21, and then click **OK**.

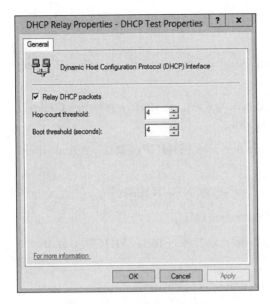

Figure 11-21 Relay DHCP packets.

7. Right-click **DHCP Relay Agent** and select **Properties**.

8. Shown in Figure 11-22, on the General tab of the DHCP Relay Agent Properties dialog box, type the IP addresses of the DHCP servers that will service the RRAS server's clients. Then click **Add** and click **OK**.

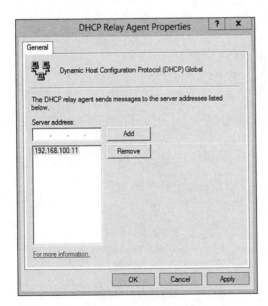

Figure 11-22 DHCP Relay Agent IPv4 Properties.

Configuring a DHCPv6 relay agent is slightly different, as the following procedure shows:

1. Open the RRAS snap-in by clicking **Start** > **Administrative Tools** > **Routing and Remote Access**.

2. From the console tree of the RRAS snap-in, expand **IPv6**, right-click **General**, and then click **New Routing Protocol**.

3. In the New Routing Protocol dialog box, select **DHCPv6 Relay Agent**; then click **OK**.

4. Right-click **DHCPv6 Relay** agent, and select **New Interface**.

5. Select the required interface, and then click **OK**.

6. In the DHCPv6 Relay Properties dialog box, select **Relay DHCP packets**; then click **OK**.

7. Right-click **DHCPv6 Relay Agent**, and select **Properties**.

8. You will notice two tabs, General and Servers. On the Servers tab shown in Figure 11-23, type the IPv6 addresses of the DHCP servers that will service the RRAS server's clients, click **Add**, and then click **OK**.

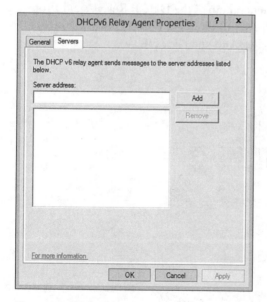

Figure 11-23   DHCP Relay Agent IPv6 properties.

Exam Preparation Tasks

Review All the Key Topics

Review the most important topics in the chapter, noted with the key topics icon in the outer margin of the page. Table 11-4 lists a reference of these key topics and the page numbers on which each is found.

Table 11-4   Key Topics for Chapter 11

Key Topic Element	Description	Page Number
Paragraphs	Describes the four-step DHCP lease process.	484
List	Describes DHCPv6 autoconfiguration options.	488
List	Describes how to install the DHCP server role.	490
List	Describes how to create a scope on the DHCP server.	493
Figure 11-4	You use the New Scope Wizard to define the range of IP addresses to be offered to clients.	494
Figure 11-6	You can configure DHCP options for your scope while creating it.	495
List	Describes the four levels at which you can create DHCP options.	499
Table 11-3	Describes the more common DHCP options.	499
List	Shows how to create server options.	500
List	Describes available option classes.	503
Figure 11-12	Shows how to configure a client reservation.	506
Figure 11-18	Shows how to authorize a DHCP server in Active Directory.	514
List	Lists the procedure to configure an IPv4 DHCP relay agent.	515
Figure 11-20	Shows how to create a DHCP Relay Agent.	516

Complete the Tables and Lists from Memory

Print a copy of Appendix B, "Memory Tables" (found on the CD), or at least the section for this chapter, and complete the tables and lists from memory. Appendix C, "Memory Tables Answer Key," is also on the CD and includes completed tables and lists to check your work.

Definitions of Key Terms

Define the following key terms from this chapter, and check your answers in the glossary.

Bootstrap Protocol (BOOTP), Broadcast, Client reservation, Dynamic Host Configuration Protocol (DHCP), DHCP options, DHCP relay agent, DHCP scope, Exclusion, Lease, Managed Address Configuration (M) flag, Multicast, Other Stateful Configuration (O) flag, Preboot Execution Environment (PXE), Reservation, Stateful address configuration, Stateless address configuration, User class, Vendor class

This chapter covers the following subjects:

- **Introduction to DNS:** This section provides you with background knowledge by introducing you to the fundamentals under which DNS is built. It then shows you how DNS works to resolve computer names to IP addresses in various situations that might be encountered.

- **Installing DNS in Windows Server 2012 R2:** This section shows you how to deploy and configure the DNS server role on a Windows Server 2012 R2 computer, both by using the Add Roles and Features Wizard and from the command line.

- **Zone Types and Their Uses:** This section introduces you to primary, secondary, and stub zones. It also shows you when you should use each zone type and discusses integration of these zones with Active Directory.

- **Configuring DNS Server Properties:** Each DNS server has a Properties dialog box associated with it from which you can configure a large number of server-specific properties. This section shows you how to configure DNS server forwarders; Root Hints; manage DNS cache; and debugging, logging, and monitoring functions.

- **Configuring Common Resource Records:** This section provides an overview of the commonly used resource record types, including A and PTR resource records. It also demonstrates how to configure additional resource records within DNS.

CHAPTER 12

Deploying and Configuring Domain Name System (DNS)

When you type an address like www.Microsoft.com into your web browser, the browser has to locate this name by finding the correct IP address associated with it. This requires a system of name resolution. Back in the early days of the Internet, when there were only a few hundred computers (or hosts) connected together in what was then a defense-oriented network that was also used by a few university researchers, a text-based file called HOSTS was developed that mapped hostnames directly to IP addresses. Whenever a new computer—either a server or a local workstation—was added to the Internet, a mapping was manually added to the HOSTS file. Historically, this worked well, especially for small networks. As networks grew, though, adding entries to a HOSTS file became a burden for administrators. As a result, DNS was created.

DNS has its beginnings in the Berkeley Internet Name Domain (BIND), developed at the University of California in Berkeley and originally defined in Request for Comments (RFCs) 1034 and 1035. As you will see, DNS was conceived as a hierarchical naming system, thereby allowing for an almost infinite possibility of expansion as more computers are added, limited only by the limitations of the IP addressing system itself. With the increasing use of IPv6, DNS has truly become an infinite system. In fact, ever since the inception of Active Directory in Windows 2000, a Microsoft domain running Active Directory Domain Services (AD DS) cannot function without DNS; if the DNS service becomes unavailable, users cannot log on or access any resources, such as servers or printers, until DNS is restored. Consequently, DNS is an extremely important component of any Microsoft domain and is therefore a well-tested topic on several Microsoft certification exams including 70-410.

"Do I Know This Already?" Quiz

The "Do I Know This Already?" quiz enables you to assess whether you should read this entire chapter or simply jump to the "Exam Preparation Tasks" section for review. If you are in doubt, read the entire chapter. Table 12-1 outlines the major headings in this chapter and the corresponding "Do I Know This Already?" quiz questions. You can find the answers in Appendix A, "Answers to the 'Do I Know This Already?' Quizzes."

Table 12-1   "Do I Know This Already?" Foundation Topics Section-to-Question Mapping

Foundations Topics Section	Questions Covered in This Section
Introduction to DNS	1–3
Installing DNS in Windows Server 2012 R2	4–5
Zone Types and Their Uses	6
Configuring DNS Server Properties	7–9
Configuring Common Resource Records	10

1. Which of the following are components of the DNS namespace? (Choose all that apply.)

   a. Root domains

   b. Top-level domains

   c. Second-level domains

   d. Hostnames

   e. NetBIOS names

2. Which of the following are valid fully qualified domain names (FQDNs)? (Choose all that apply.)

   a. SERVER1

   b. http://www

   c. www.certguide.com

   d. mailserver.acme.co.uk

   e. webserver.anydomain.

   f. fileserver1.mycompany.biz

3. Which of the following best describes the procedure followed during an iterative query for resolving a FQDN?

   a. A client sends a query to its local DNS server, which forwards the query to a DNS server hosted by the company's ISP. The latter server returns the appropriate IP address directly to the client.

   b. A client sends a query to its local DNS name server, which forwards the query to a DNS server that is authoritative for the hostname specified in the query. This DNS server forwards this information to a DNS server that is authoritative for the second-level domain, which in turn forwards the information to a DNS server that is authoritative for the top-level domain. Finally, this last DNS server returns the result to the local DNS name server, which returns the result to the client.

   c. A client sends a query to its local DNS name server, which forwards the query to a root name server. The root name server returns the IP address of a DNS server that is authoritative for the specified top-level domain. This server replies with the IP address of a DNS server that is authoritative for the specified second-level domain, which resolves the query and returns the result to the local DNS name server, which returns the result to the client.

   d. A client sends a query to a root name server, which forwards the query to a DNS server that is authoritative for the specified top-level domain. This server then forwards the query to a DNS server that is authoritative for the specified second-level domain. This next server forwards the query to a DNS server that is authoritative for the hostname, which resolves the query and returns the result to the client.

4. Which of the following tools can you use to install DNS on a Windows Server 2012 R2 computer? (Each correct answer represents a complete solution. Choose two.)

   a. Add Roles and Features Wizard

   b. Add Features Wizard

   c. Control Panel Add or Remove Programs

   d. The PowerShell `Add-WindowsFeature` cmdlet

   e. The `dnscmd` command

   f. DNS Manager

5. Which of the following is most likely to cause a problem when installing a DNS server?

    a. The server is not configured as a domain controller.

    b. The server is not configured with a static IP address.

    c. The server has only a single network adapter.

    d. The server is not configured with the Application Server role.

6. Which DNS zone type should you use if you require secure dynamic updates?

    a. Primary

    b. Active Directory Integrated

    c. Secondary

    d. Forward Lookup

7. Your company has entered into a partnership arrangement with another company, and you want to configure your company's DNS server to send queries for resources in the partner company to their DNS server. You need to ensure that requests for Internet resources do not go to the partner company DNS server. What should you do?

    a. Right-click the **Conditional Forwarders** node of the DNS snap-in and select **New Conditional Forwarder**. Then specify the DNS domain of the partner company and the IP address of their DNS server.

    b. On the Forwarders tab of your DNS server's Properties dialog box, specify the IP address and FQDN of the partner company's DNS server.

    c. Ask the administrator of the partner company's DNS server to specify the IP address and FQDN of your DNS server on the Forwarders tab of their DNS server's Properties dialog box.

    d. On the Root Hints tab of your DNS server's Properties dialog box, specify the IP address and FQDN of the partner company's DNS server.

8. You are responsible for configuring the DNS server on your network. Users at your company report that they are unable to access external websites. You check network connectivity and find that you can access external websites by IP address but not by name. Which of the following should you check at the DNS server?

   a. Conditional forwarders

   b. Root hints

   c. SRV records

   d. Round robin

9. You want to create a record of packets sent to and from your DNS server and store this information in a text file for later analysis. Which feature should you enable?

   a. DNS monitoring

   b. Event logging

   c. DNS Notify

   d. Debug logging

10. You need to create a friendly name for a helpdesk application that is hosted on Server1.mytestdomain.com. Which type of resource record can you use to create a friendly name for resolving to the application hosted on server1?

   a. A record

   b. CNAME record

   c. AAAA record

   d. PTR record

Foundation Topics

Introduction to DNS

Back in the early 1980s, computers on the Internet still used HOSTS files—as described in the introduction—to locate each other. However, around this time growth on the Internet really took off and it quickly became evident that this system could not be continued. So the Internet community came up with a solution of distributing the process of name resolution among a series of servers. And so the DNS system was born in 1984. At the same time a central clearinghouse for Internet names was established, called the Internet Network Information Center (InterNIC). In 1988, the Internet Assigned Numbers Authority (IANA) was created to keep track of Internet Protocol (IP) assignments. As applications or servers were created, vendors would register unique port numbers for their services.

Then in 1998, the Internet Corporation for Assigned Names and Numbers (ICANN; www.icann.org) was formed to coordinate and ensure that global Internet systems were assigned unique IP address spaces. Because of their interrelated activities, both IANA and InterNIC projects were reorganized the same year under the control of ICANN.

Today, a large series of name registrars have been accredited with ICANN for registering Internet names. IANA remains as a department of ICANN and oversees global IP address allocation and management of the DNS root zone as well as the .int and .arpa top-level domains.

So when you want to go to a website—for example, www.microsoft.com—you enter this name into your browser and a DNS query is sent to your local server. This query works its way up the hierarchy of DNS servers, as you will see shortly. It returns an IP address of 65.55.21.250 and makes the connection. Actually, to complete this connection, it must then use the Address Resolution Protocol (ARP) to locate the hardware, or MAC address, of the server that will respond to the query. But this is another matter. Likewise, when you need to access some resource such as a folder or printer located on another computer in your network, you use a program such as the Network and Sharing Center or type a UNC path such as \\server1\documents; a DNS query is used to resolve the computer name to its IP address. Furthermore, when you first log on to your computer on an AD DS network, the Netlogon service must access a domain controller to verify your credentials. The DNS naming scheme is used to create the structure of the AD DS namespace, permitting interoperability with Internet technologies; therefore, the concept of namespaces is central to Active Directory. By integrating this concept with the system's directory services, Active Directory facilitates the management of multiple namespaces that are often found in the heterogeneous software and hardware environments of corporate networks. Your client computer uses DNS to determine the location of resources, such as shared folders, printers, and so on, on the network. Again, DNS is used for this purpose.

The Hierarchical Nature of DNS

Nowadays, approximately one billion machines are hosting websites on the Internet! Imagine that number of machines referenced in a flat database—a HOSTS file containing references to all these machines would be at least tens of *gigabytes* in length! Imagine trying to search this file, let alone update it when a new machine was added to the Internet or replicate it to other servers.

So DNS was developed as a hierarchical name resolution system that is distributed among servers located around the world. It includes the following properties:

- **Companies registered with ICANN/IANA operate their own DNS servers, which describe their own machines to others on the Internet**: So when you point your browser to a location such as www.Microsoft.com, a machine owned by Microsoft and not one owned by ICANN responds to your request with the correct IP address. Only Microsoft has responsibility for these machines, and the only thing that ICANN knows about them is the correct IP addresses of all DNS servers operated by Microsoft.

- **ICANN/IANA functions as a central group to keep track of top-level Internet domain names and their DNS servers:** They keep a large database that contains the names of registered domains and the DNS servers that serve these domains. In turn, they delegate responsibility for managing down-level Internet domain names to various organizations responsible for these domains. Each of these organizations has the final say on registering Internet domain names; consequently, they will not register a name without knowing the IP addresses of at least two DNS servers that will be responsible for a new domain. So, for example, the operators of the .com top-level domain can tell you the IP addresses of several DNS servers operated by Microsoft that can provide the IP address of www.microsoft.com, or any other domain name such as search.Microsoft.com that Microsoft operates.

- **DNS server software is capable of referring queries to other DNS servers as required:** As you will see shortly, local DNS servers can refer queries to external locations to other DNS servers that can respond with an IP address. They actually do two jobs: resolving local or external queries for machines on your network and referring queries to external networks to the appropriate location.

■ **DNS servers can remember recently resolved names:** Because individuals tend to go to the same Internet sites frequently as opposed to going everywhere on the Internet at random, it is important that DNS servers can cache the results of recent name resolutions. Otherwise, think of the name resolution traffic that could result.

Let's look more closely at the hierarchical nature of DNS.

The hierarchical database of DNS, as represented schematically (and extremely simplified!) in Figure 12-1, is called the *domain namespace*. Within this namespace, every computer is identified by its fully qualified domain name (FQDN). Name servers themselves are grouped into different levels of domains and subdomains. Domains define the different levels of authority in the hierarchical structure of DNS.

Key Topic

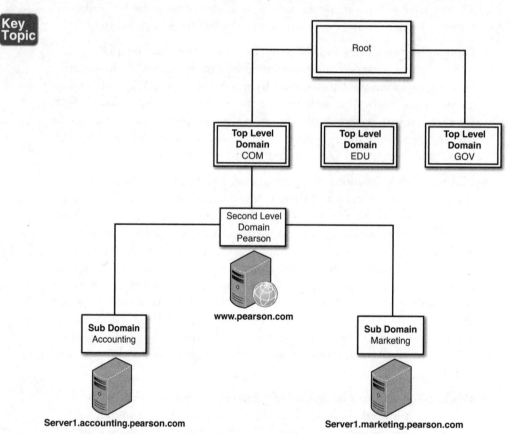

Figure 12-1   The hierarchical structure of DNS.

Root-level Domains

The top of the hierarchy is called the *root* domain. The root node uses a null label and is specified by "." (a period or dot). Connecting the top-level domains, it is not included in domain names.

Top-level Domains

Starting in the 1980s, ICANN set up a system of top-level domain names, including those described in Table 12-2. In more recent years, ICANN has expanded the series of top-level domain names, with currently about two dozen top-level domain names assigned. In addition, two-letter ISO standard country name abbreviations are used as top-level domains—for example, .ca for Canada and .au for Australia. A few countries sell space in their top-level domains. For example, .tv for Tuvalu sometimes is often linked to television broadcasts or programs.

Table 12-2   Original Top-level Domain Names

DNS Name	Type of Organization
.arpa	Used by Advanced Research Project Agency for reverse mapping of IP addresses to DNS domain names (for example, in-addr.arpa)
.com	Commercial (for example, microsoft.com for Microsoft Corporation)
.edu	Educational (for example, mit.edu for Massachusetts Institute of Technology)
.gov	Government (for example, whitehouse.gov for the White House)
.int	International organizations (for example, nato.int for NATO)
.mil	U.S. military operations (for example, army.mil for the Army)
.net	Networking organizations (for example, nsf.net for NSFNET)
.org	Noncommercial organizations, such as churches and charities (for example, unitedway.org)

Beginning in 2000 and continued into 2014, ICANN has introduced new top-level domains, so now more than 175 top-level domain names are in use across the Internet. Table 12-3 describes the more notable additional top-level domain names. Some of these are sponsored, meaning an organization is delegated some defining policy-formulation authority regarding the use of such a domain that ensures its appropriate usage (for example, ensuring that .edu domain names are limited to educational organizations). Others are unsponsored and operate under policies established by the global Internet community by means of processes sponsored by ICANN.

Table 12-3   Additional Top-level Domain Names

DNS Name	Type of Organization
.aero	Aviation-related organizations (for example, www.desktop.aero for Desktop Aeronautics, an aerospace consulting firm)
.biz	Businesses (introduced to take some load off the .com top-level domain; for example, cindyking.biz for Cindy King Social Media & Cross-Cultural Communication for International Businesses)
.coop	Cooperatives, wholly owned subsidiaries, and other organizations that support cooperatives (for example. Ica.coop for the International Co-operative Alliance)
.info	Informative Internet resource-related organizations (for example, mta.info for the New York Metropolitan Transit Authority)
.museum	Museums, museum associations, and individual members of the museum profession (for example, www.penn.museum for the University of Pennsylvania Museum of Archaeology and Anthropology)
.name	Individuals for representation of personal names, nicknames, pseudonyms, and so on; operated by VeriSign as of 2009 (for example, www.iranians.name for Persian Iranian Farsi Names for Boys and Girls)
.pro	Government-certified professionals such as lawyers, accountants, physicians, and engineers (for example, www.registry.pro for registration of businesses, professionals, and other entities around the world)

NOTE   For more information on the use and history of top-level domains, refer to "Top-Level Domains (gTLDs)" at http://www.icann.org/en/tlds/ and "Top-level domains" at http://technet.microsoft.com/en-us/library/cc784663(WS.10).aspx.

Second-level Domain Names

Under the top-level domains are additional groupings referred to as second-level domains. For example, pearson.com would be a second-level domain and is actually a subdomain of the .com top-level domain. Second-level domains can be divided into their own subdomains, for example accounting.pearson.com. In turn, these subdomains can be further subdivided and so on, up to a limit of 127 levels. Responsibility of designing, naming, and maintaining these lower-level domains or *subdomains*, rests with the administrator of the DNS server at the second-level domain. Authority for these subdomains can be delegated to organizations so that they can manage their own namespace. This is true at all levels of the DNS hierarchy.

Hostnames

Individual computers exist within a domain. Each computer in the domain must have its own name, referred to as the *hostname*. The combination of a hostname, an organization's domain name, and the Internet top-level domain name creates what is called a *fully qualified domain name (FQDN)* that is unique across the Internet. Hostnames used inside domains are added at the beginning of the domain name and are also referred to by their FQDNs. For example, a computer-called search in the Microsoft domain has a FQDN of search.Microsoft.com. The "www" is actually the name (or one of the names) used by a particular computer. Note that the maximum length of an FQDN is 255 characters.

In NetBIOS networking as used by older versions of Microsoft operating systems, no two computers can share the same NetBIOS name. The same is true regarding hostnames, but only insofar as every domain or subdomain is concerned. This is possible due to the hierarchical nature of DNS names. Because the FQDN contains both the hostname and domain name, two hosts from different domains can share the same hostname—for example, search.Microsoft.com and search.zdnet.com. Also note that NetBIOS names are derived from the first 15 characters of the hostname, so many organizations limit the hostname to 15 characters to prevent duplication of NetBIOS names.

The DNS Name Resolution Process

The three common types of queries a client can make to a DNS server are as follows:

- Recursive queries

- Iterative queries

- Reverse lookup queries

While discussing name resolution, keep in mind that a DNS server can be a client to another DNS server. They often are.

Both recursive and iterative queries try to do the same task in different ways. These are both types of forward lookup queries and are used to resolve a FQDN located somewhere on the Internet to its IP address. They are analogous to locating a phone number for a person whose name you know. A reverse lookup query is the opposite—given an IP address, it attempts to locate the FQDN of the host using this address. An analogy would be the locating of an individual or company that is using a known telephone number.

Recursive Queries

When you type an FQDN into the address field of your browser and press **Enter**, you are sending a query to the server configured as a preferred DNS server for the IP address of this FQDN. The name server receiving this query must respond with either the IP address for a name or an error stating that data of the requested type doesn't exist or that the domain name specified doesn't exist. The name server cannot simply refer the DNS client to another name server. This type of query is known as a *recursive query*.

A DNS client (often called a *resolver*) typically makes this type of query to a DNS server. Also, if a DNS server is configured to use a *forwarder* (this is another DNS server set up to handle requests forwarded to it), the request from this DNS server to its forwarder will be a recursive query. In other words, name servers that receive recursive requests need to do some digging on behalf of their clients. In networking terms, if all forward queries were recursive, there would be a lot more traffic on the network—a lot more activity. However, another option exists. The query can be referred onward to another DNS server. This option is known as an *iterative query* and is detailed in the next section.

Iterative Queries

In an *iterative query*, the queried name server provides the best answer it currently has to the resolver. A DNS server typically performs this type of query to other DNS servers after it has received a recursive query from a resolver. As a rule, clients don't make iterative queries. Upon receipt of an iterative query that it does not have a best answer for, a DNS server can respond by saying in effect "I can't help you, why don't you try someone else like…". This "someone else" is, of course, another DNS server. Figure 12-2 shows an example of recursive and iterative queries.

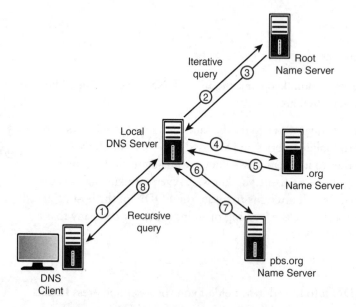

Figure 12-2   Recursive and iterative query.

The following steps occur during an iterative query:

1. The resolver sends a recursive DNS query to its local DNS server asking the DNS server to resolve the name www.pbs.org to an IP address. The client expects an answer from the local name server. It cannot be referred to another name server.

2. The local name server can't find the requested information in its zone files or its cache. It sends an iterative query for www.pbs.org to a root name server located up the DNS tree. Iterative queries are always directed elsewhere.

3. The root name server has authority for the root domain and sends back the IP address of a name server for the .org top-level domain.

4. The local name server sends an iterative query for www.pbs.org to the server that handles the .org top-level domain. (It is able to do this because it has been given the IP address of the .org server by the root name server.)

5. The .org name server responds to the local name server with the IP address of the name server that looks after the pbs.org domain.

6. The local name server sends an iterative query for the IP address of www.pbs.org to the pbs.org name server.

7. The pbs.org name server can resolve www an IP address within its domain. It replies to local name server with the IP address for www.pbs.org.

8. The local name server now has the exact information it needs to respond to the resolver. It sends the IP address of www.pbs.org to the resolver that needed the name resolved in the first place.

Note that a *zone* as mentioned in Step 2 of this procedure is a discrete portion of the Internet namespace for which a particular DNS server is primarily responsible.

Reverse Lookup Queries

You have seen how a forward lookup query works. In summary, the client sends the name to the DNS server and the DNS server replies with the IP address. But what if a resolver has the IP address and needed to know the hostname for a particular machine? In this instance, a resolver furnishes an IP address to the name server and requests that it be resolved to a hostname. This is the purpose of a *reverse lookup query*. In reverse lookup, the client sends the IP address to the DNS server and the DNS server replies with the name. Normally, a name server would need to perform an exhaustive search of all DNS domains to make sure it found the name that corresponded to an IP address. In our analogy, that would be like having a phone number and having to scan the phone book from A to Z looking for that phone number to find out the name of the individual associated with it. To do this, there needs to be a root server that maps IP addresses to names. In fact, there is such a server.

To address this problem, a special domain "in-addr.arpa" in the DNS namespace was created. Domain names, as we have learned, become more specific when moving from right to left. On the other hand, IP addresses become more specific when read from left to right. The most specific part of the IP address 172.48.4.23 is the 23. So if our name server and all the other name servers in DNS need to answer a question about a particular IP address, they should start in their own neighborhood at the most specific. They would need to trouble another name server only if their investigations didn't yield a result. This means that the record for the IP address 172.48.4.23 should read "backwards" as 23.4.48.172. That is, in fact, the kind of record in-addr.arpa contains. Such would also be true in resolving a phone number. The most specific part of the number 123-456-7890 is the 7890; you could resolve this by looking for the city or town in area code 123 whose numbers begin with the 456 prefix. Resolving the IP address works exactly the same way. The in-addr.arpa domain suffix is discussed in detail in RFC 2317.

What's New in Windows Server 2012 R2?

The concept of DNS and the name resolution process remains the same under Windows Server 2012 R2. There are a handful of improved and new features under Windows Server 2012 R2 and Windows 8.1 editions. Table 12-4 outlines some of the changes.

Table 12-4   Improved DNS Features

Feature/Functionality	Details
Improved DNSSEC Functionality	DNS Security Extensions (DNSSEC) provides additional capabilities for DNS security, such as secure dynamic updates of DNS records.
Improved PowerShell Support	PowerShell is closely integrated with dnscmd.exe for performing management tasks. The DNS Server Role can also be added or removed using PowerShell.
Improved DNS Zone Statistics	Additional statistics for resource records, zone transfers, and dynamic updates are available at the DNS Zone level.
Improved Client Response Time	The DNS query process has been improved to offer faster response times. DNS Cache structure has been optimized to allow for faster response times.

NOTE   For additional information on new DNS features, refer to "What's New in DNS Server in Windows Server 2012 R2" at http://technet.microsoft.com/en-us/library/dn305898.aspx.

Installing DNS in Windows Server 2012 R2

In Windows Server 2012 R2, DNS is present as a server role. You can install DNS on any server by using the Add Roles and Features Wizard. DNS now provides complete support for IP version 6 (IPv6). After you have installed DNS, the DNS Manager MMC snap-in is available in the Administrative Tools folder, from which you can perform all configuration activities associated with DNS. DNS Manager is also accessible via Server Manager.

Before installing DNS on your server, ensure that your server is configured to use a static IP address. You can do this from the Properties dialog box for your network adapter, accessible from the Network and Sharing Center:

1. From the left panel, select **Change adapter settings**.

2. Right-click your network connection and select **Properties**.

3. From the Local Area Connection Properties dialog box that appears, select either **Internet Protocol Version 4 (TCP/IPv4)** or **Internet Protocol Version 6 (TCP/IPv6)** as required; then click **Properties**.

4. In the dialog box that appears, select the **Use the following IP address** option and then type the IP address, subnet mask or subnet prefix length, and default gateway.

Use the following procedure to install DNS on a Windows Server 2012 R2 computer:

1. Open Server Manager and click **Add Roles and Features** from the Manage menu. This will launch the Add Roles and Features Wizard.

2. If you receive the Before You Begin page, click **Next**. Note that you can disable the appearance of this page by selecting the check box labeled **Skip this page by default**.

3. Select **Role-based** or **feature-based** installation at the Installation Type screen. Click **Next** to continue.

4. On the Select destination server screen, select a server from the server pool and click **Next**.

5. Select **DNS Server** under the Roles selection list, as shown in Figure 12-3. Click **Next** to continue. If prompted to install additional tools and features, click the **Add Features** button to continue.

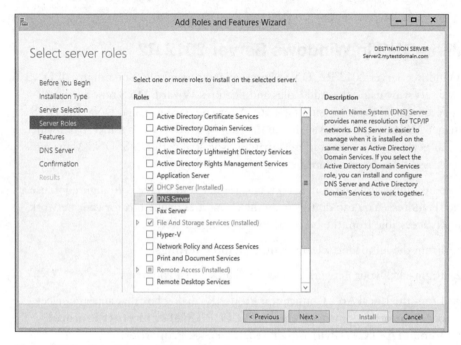

Figure 12-3   Selecting the DNS server role.

6. Click **Next** at the Features Screen. The wizard will display a DNS server informational screen with information about the DNS Server role. Click **Next** to continue.

7. The Confirm Installation Selections page informs you that the DNS server and associated features will be installed. You also have the option to check the box to Restart the destination server automatically if required. To proceed, click **Install**.

8. The Installation Progress page tracks the progress of installing DNS. When informed that the installation is complete, click **Close**.

> **NOTE**   The DNS Server role is typically selected during the installation of Active Directory Domain Services (AD DS) or via PowerShell by specifying the `InstallDns` parameter when using the `Install-ADDSDomainController` cmdlet. If the DNS Server is hosting Active Directory Integrated DNS Zones, you must install the AD DS role service on the server.

Using PowerShell to Install DNS

You can also install DNS on a Windows Server 2012 R2 computer via Windows PowerShell. Use the following command to install the DNS Server Role on a Windows Server 2012 R2 Full GUI or Server Core installation:

```
Add-WindowsFeature DNS
```

To remove DNS from a Windows Server 2012 R2 computer, use the following command:

```
Remove-WindowsFeature DNS
```

After installing DNS on a Server Core machine, you can manage DNS by using Server Manager's remote server management abilities or via PowerShell cmdlets.

Using PowerShell for DNS Server Administration

Previously under Windows Server 2008, DNS administrative tasks were performed from the command line using Dnscmd.exe. Under Windows Server 2012, including 2012 R2, Microsoft has included a ton of PowerShell cmdlets to manage virtually every aspect of the DNS server.

Table 12-5 summarizes the more frequently used PowerShell cmdlets for managing DNS.

Table 12-5 UsefulPowerShell DNS Cmdlets

Cmdlet	Description
Add-DnsServerConditionalForwarderZone	Adds a conditional forwarder to a DNS server
Add-DnsServerForwarder	Adds server-level forwarders to a DNS server
Add-DnsServerPrimaryZone	Adds a primary zone to a DNS server
Add-DnsServerResourceRecordA	Adds a type A resource record to a DNS zone
Add-DnsServerResourceRecordAAAA	Adds a type AAAA resource record to a DNS server
Add-DnsServerResourceRecordCname	Adds a canonical name (CNAME) record to a DNS server
Add-DnsServerResourceRecordPtr	Adds a type PTR resource record to a DNS zone
Add-DnsServerSecondaryZone	Adds a DNS server secondary zone

Cmdlet	Description
Add-DnsServerStubZone	Adds a DNS stub zone
Clear-DnsServerCache	Clears resource records from a cache on the DNS server
Clear-DnsServerStatistics	Clears all DNS server statistics
Get-DnsServer	Retrieves a DNS server configuration
Get-DnsServerCache	Gets DNS server cache settings
Get-DnsServerDiagnostics	Retrieves DNS event logging details
Get-DnsServerForwarder	Gets forwarder configuration settings on a DNS server
Get-DnsServerRecursion	Retrieves DNS server recursion settings
Get-DnsServerResourceRecord	Gets resource records from a specified DNS zone
Get-DnsServerRootHint	Gets root hints on a DNS server
Get-DnsServerScavenging	Gets DNS aging and scavenging settings
Get-DnsServerStatistics	Retrieves DNS server statistics
Get-DnsServerZone	Gets details of DNS zones on a DNS server
Get-DnsServerZoneAging	Gets DNS aging settings for a zone
Get-DnsServerZoneDelegation	Gets the zone delegations of a DNS server zone
Import-DnsServerResourceRecordDS	Imports DS resource record information from a file
Import-DnsServerRootHint	Copies root hints from a DNS server
Remove-DnsServerForwarder	Removes server-level forwarders from a DNS server
Remove-DnsServerResourceRecord	Removes specified DNS server resource records from a zone
Remove-DnsServerRootHint	Removes root hints from a DNS server
Remove-DnsServerForwarder	Removes server-level forwarders from a DNS server
Remove-DnsServerResourceRecord	Removes specified DNS server resource records from a zone
Remove-DnsServerRootHint	Removes root hints from a DNS server
Remove-DnsServerZone	Removes a zone from a DNS server

Cmdlet	Description
Restore-DnsServerPrimaryZone	Restores primary DNS zone contents from Active Directory or from a file
Restore-DnsServerSecondaryZone	Restores secondary zone information from its source
Set-DnsServer	Overwrites a DNS server configuration
Set-DnsServerCache	Modifies cache settings for a DNS server
Test-DnsServer	Tests that a specified computer is a functioning DNS server

NOTE   Table 12-5 provides only a handful of the frequently used PowerShell cmdlets available for managing DNS servers. For a complete listing of PowerShell cmdlets and how to use them, refer to "Domain Name System (DNS) Server Cmdlets in Windows PowerShell" at http://technet.microsoft.com/en-us/library/jj649850.aspx.

Zone Types and Their Uses

Each DNS name server stores information about a discrete portion of the Internet namespace. Such a portion is known as a *zone*, and the DNS server that is primarily responsible for each zone is considered to be *authoritative* for that zone. In other words, the DNS server is the main source of information regarding the Internet addresses contained within the zone. A zone can be considered a part of the big database that is DNS and can contain information on one or more AD DS domains. Zones are defined by who looks after maintaining the records that they contain. In Windows Server 2012 R2, DNS stores its zone data in one or more application directory partitions, each of which is an AD DS partition that contains application-specific data (in this case, DNS) that needs to be replicated throughout specified portions of the forest. This replication takes place by a process called *zone transfers*, which take place among all DNS servers in the forest.

When you first install AD DS and a DNS server, a default set of zones and subzones is installed (see Figure 12-4). You can use the New Zone Wizard to create additional zones, as required. Creating and managing zones is covered in more detail on the 70-411 exam.

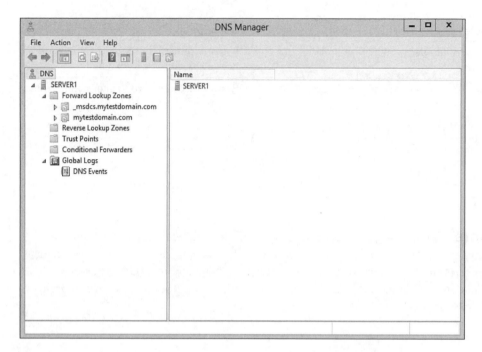

Figure 12-4   A default set of zones is included in DNS Manager when you create your domain.

TIP   You will notice additional folder groupings under the DNS console: Trust Points and Conditional Forwarders. These are covered on the 70-411 and 70-412 exams.

DNS Zone Types

Each DNS server provides for several types of zones, including primary, secondary, stub, and Active Directory-integrated. You can have forward and reverse lookup zones in each of these zone types. A *forward lookup zone* resolves a computer's FQDN to its IP address, whereas a *reverse lookup zone* resolves an IP address to the corresponding FQDN.

NOTE   For more information on how zones function, refer to "Understanding Zones" at http://technet.microsoft.com/en-us/library/cc725590.aspx.

Primary Zones

A *primary zone* is a master copy of zone data hosted on a DNS server that is the primary source of information for records found in this zone. This server is considered to be authoritative for this zone, and you can update zone data directly on this server. It is also known as a *master server*. If the zone data is not integrated with AD DS, the server holds this data in a local file named `<zone_name.dns>` that is located in the `%systemroot%\system32\DNS` folder. The server that hosts this zone is frequently called the *master server*.

Secondary Zones

A *secondary zone* is an additional copy of DNS zone data hosted on a DNS server that is a secondary source for this zone information. This server obtains the zone information from the server hosting the corresponding primary zone. Using secondary zones improves name resolution services on the network by providing redundancy and load balancing. The server that hosts a secondary zone is frequently called the *secondary server*.

Stub Zones

A *stub zone* contains source information about authoritative name servers for its zone only. The DNS server hosting the stub zone obtains its information from another server that hosts a primary or secondary copy of the same zone data. The following are several purposes of stub zones:

- Maintain a current list of delegated zone information within a hierarchy of DNS zones. A DNS server can host a parent zone at the primary or secondary level together with stub zones for its child zones and thereby have a list of authoritative DNS servers for the child zones.

- Provide improved name resolution by enabling a DNS server to rapidly locate the stub zone's list of name servers without the need for querying other servers to locate the appropriate DNS server.

- Simplify the administration of DNS by enabling the distribution of the list of authoritative DNS servers throughout a large enterprise network without the need for hosting a large number of secondary zones.

Active Directory-Integrated Zones

An *Active Directory-integrated zone* stores its data in one or more application directory partitions that are replicated along with other AD DS directory partitions. This helps to ensure that zone data remains up-to-date on all domain controllers hosting

DNS in the domain. Using Active Directory-integrated zones also provides the following benefits:

- It promotes fault tolerance because data is always available and can always be updated even if one of the servers fails. If a DNS server hosting a primary zone outside of AD DS fails, it is not possible to update its data because no mechanism exists for promoting a secondary DNS zone to primary.

- Each writable domain controller on which DNS is installed acts as a master server and enables updates to the zones in which they are authoritative; no separate DNS zone transfer topology is needed.

- Security is enhanced because you can configure dynamic updates to be secured; by contrast, zone data not integrated with AD DS is stored in plain-text files that unauthorized users could access, modify, or delete.

Either primary or stub zones can be integrated with AD DS. It is not possible to create an Active Directory-integrated secondary zone.

TIP   Keep in mind the properties of the various zone types. In particular, remember that you must have an Active Directory-integrated zone if you want to enable secure dynamic updates. Also remember that you can configure a secondary server with a copy of an Active Directory-integrated zone, but that this secondary zone copy is stored locally on that server and is not integrated with Active Directory. An exam question might ask which type of DNS zone is appropriate in a given scenario. The 70-410 exam tests your understanding of each zone type and DNS server properties, whereas the 70-411 exam tests your ability to create and configure each of the zone types.

GlobalNames Zone for Single-Label Resolution

Although it is not an actual zone type, a GlobalNames zone is the name of a primary zone used to enable *single-label* name resolution. In the NT4 days, we used Windows Internet Name Service (WINS) to resolve hostnames to IP addresses. This carried through Windows Server 2000 and in some cases Windows Server 2003. With the release of Windows Server 2008, Microsoft provided the ability to virtually eliminate WINS by using DNS and a GlobalNames zone. Still used today under Windows Server 2012 and 2012 R2, the GlobalNames zone can be populated with static records to provide backward compatibility for legacy name resolution. To use a GlobalNames zone, all DNS servers for the zone must be running at least Windows Server 2008.

Configuring DNS Server Properties

Every DNS server has a Properties dialog box that enables you to configure server properties that are applied to all zones hosted by the server. In the DNS Manager console, select the DNS server, right-click it, and select **Properties** to display this dialog box. The following sections describe the functions of the eight available tabs. Some of these are covered in more detail to satisfy the 70-410 exam objectives, while others are covered further on the 70-411 exam.

Interfaces Tab

On a multihomed DNS server, you can specify the IPv4 and IPv6 addresses of the network interfaces used by DNS to listen for queries from client computers. Doing so ensures that only servers and clients configured to use the specified IP addresses can query the DNS server. This is useful in the case of DNS servers that are also connected to the Internet; in such cases, you can ensure that only clients on the internal network can query your server for DNS name resolution. By default, the DNS server service listens on all IP interfaces on the server, including the following:

- Any additional IP addresses specified for a single network interface

- Individual IP addresses specified for separate interfaces when more than one interface is present on the server

To limit the interfaces to which the DNS server listens for queries, select the **Only the following IP addresses** option on the Interfaces tab, as shown in Figure 12-5. Select or deselect the specific IP address to be enabled on the server, and then click **Apply**.

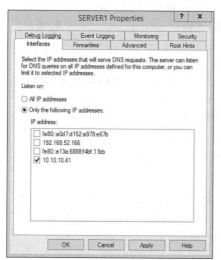

Figure 12-5   The Interfaces tab of the DNS server's Properties dialog box enables you to limit the interfaces on which the DNS server listens for queries.

Forwarders Tab

As already introduced, the act of forwarding refers to the relaying of a DNS request from one server to another one when the first server is unable to process the request. This is especially useful in resolving Internet names to their associated IP addresses. By using an external forwarder, the internal DNS server passes off the act of locating an external resource, thereby reducing its processing load and network bandwidth. The use of forwarding is also helpful for protecting internal DNS servers from access by unauthorized Internet users. It works in the following manner:

1. A client issues a request for an FQDN on a zone for which its preferred DNS server is not authoritative (for example, an Internet domain such as www.google.com).

2. The local DNS server receives this request but has zone information only for the internal local domain and checks its list of forwarders.

3. Finding the IP address of an external DNS server (such as one hosted by the company's ISP), it forwards the request to the external server (forwarder).

4. The forwarder attempts to resolve the required FQDN. If it is not able to resolve this FQDN, it forwards the request to another forwarder or uses an iterative query process to resolve the FQDN.

5. When the forwarder is able to resolve the FQDN, it returns the result to the internal DNS server by way of any intermediate forwarders, which then return the result to the requesting client.

You can specify external forwarders from the Forwarders tab of the DNS server's Properties dialog box, as shown in Figure 12-6. Click **Edit** to open the Edit Forwarders dialog box shown in Figure 12-7. In the **Click here to add an IP Address or DNS Name** space, specify the IP address of a forwarder and click **OK** or press **Enter**. The server will resolve this IP address to its FQDN and display these in the Forwarders tab. You can also modify the sequence in which the forwarding servers are contacted by using the **Up** and **Down** command buttons, or you can remove a forwarding server by selecting it and clicking **Delete**.

You can also specify forwarders from the command line by using the `Get/Add-DNSServerForwarder` PowerShell cmdlets as discussed earlier.

> **NOTE**   In addition to forwarding, DNS servers allow for *conditional* forwarding, which forwards DNS lookup requests to specific DNS servers based on specific domain names. Conditional forwarding is covered in more detail on the 70-411 exam.

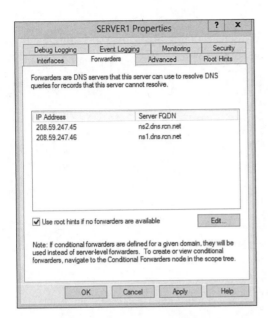

Figure 12-6 The Forwarders tab of the DNS server's Properties dialog box enables you to specify forwarders used by the current DNS server.

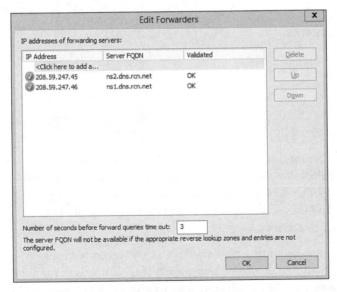

Figure 12-7 The Edit Forwarders dialog box enables you to add or remove forwarding servers or modify the sequence in which they are contacted.

Advanced Tab

The Advanced tab of the DNS server's Properties dialog box shown in Figure 12-8 contains a series of options you should be familiar with.

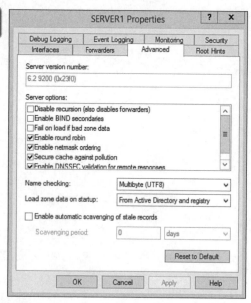

Figure 12-8   The Advanced tab of the DNS server's Properties dialog box enables you to configure several additional server options.

Server Options

The Server options section of this dialog box contains the following seven options, the last four of which are selected by default:

- **Disable recursion:** Prevents the DNS server from forwarding queries to other DNS servers. Select this check box on a DNS server that provides resolution services only to other DNS servers because unauthorized users can use recursion to overload a DNS server's resources and thereby deny the DNS server service to legitimate users.

- **Enable BIND secondaries:** During zone transfer, DNS servers normally utilize a fast transfer method that involves compression. If UNIX servers running a version of BIND prior to 4.9.4 are present, zone transfers will not work. These servers use a slower, uncompressed data transfer method. To enable zone transfer to these servers, select this check box. This option is relevant only if the network contains UNIX servers running BIND. For a pure Microsoft DNS setup, this option can remain cleared.

- **Fail on load if bad zone data:** When selected, DNS servers will not load zone data that contains certain types of errors. The DNS service checks name data using the method selected in the Name Checking drop-down list on this tab.

- **Enable round robin:** Enables round robin for use with multiple records for the same host.

- **Enable netmask ordering:** Prioritizes local subnets so that when a client queries for a hostname mapped to multiple IP addresses, the DNS server preferentially returns an IP address located on the same subnet as the requesting client.

- **Secure cache against pollution:** Cache pollution takes place when DNS query responses contain malicious items received from nonauthoritative servers. This option prevents attackers from adding such resource records to the DNS cache. The DNS servers ignore resource records for domain names outside the domain to which the query was originally directed. For example, if you sent a query for `que.com` and a referral provided a name such as `quepublishing.com`, the latter name would not be cached when this option is enabled.

- **Enable DNSSEC validation for remote responses:** Used to reduce the risk of DNS exploits by using digital signatures to validate DNS responses.

Name Checking

The Name checking setting (refer to Figure 12-8) enables you to configure the DNS server to permit names that contain characters that are not allowed by normal DNS standards outlined in RFC 1123. You can select the following options:

- **Strict RFC (ANSI):** Uses strict name checking according to RFC 1123 host naming specifications. Noncompliant DNS names generate error messages.

- **Non RFC (ANSI):** Permits nonstandard names that do not conform to RFC 1123 host naming specifications. ASCII characters that are not compliant to RFC 1123 specifications are accepted.

- **Multibyte (UTFB):** Enables the transformation and recoding of multibyte, non-ASCII characters according to Unicode Transformation Format (UTF-8) specifications. This is the default setting.

- **All names:** Permits names containing any types of characters.

If you receive an error with ID 4006 indicating that the DNS server was unable to load the records in the specified name found in the Active Directory-integrated zone, this means that the DNS name contains unsupported characters. You can resolve this problem by selecting the **All names** option and restarting the DNS service. This enables the DNS names to be loaded. If the names are improper, you can delete them and then reset the Name checking setting.

Loading Zone Data

When a DNS server containing an Active Directory-integrated zone starts up, it normally uses information stored in this zone and in the Registry to initialize the service and load its zone data. The Load zone data on startup option (refer to Figure 12-8) enables you to specify that the DNS server starts from the Registry only or from a file named `Boot` and located in the `%systemroot%\System32\Dns` folder. This optional file is similar in format to that used by BIND servers.

TIP   If you have improperly configured options on this tab and want to return to the default options, click the **Reset to Default** command button at the bottom of this tab and then click **Apply** to apply this change without closing the dialog box (or click **OK** to apply the changes and close the dialog box).

Root Hints Tab

As already discussed, a DNS server that is unable to resolve a name directly from its own database or with the aid of a forwarder sends the query to a server that is authoritative for the DNS root zone. The server must have the names and addresses of these servers stored in its database to perform such a query. These names and addresses are known as *root hints*, and they are stored in the `cache.dns` file, which is found at `%systemroot%\system32\dns`. This is a text file that contains resource records for every available root server.

When you first install DNS on a server connected to the Internet, it should download the latest set of root hints automatically. You can verify that this has occurred by checking the Root Hints tab of the server's Properties dialog box. You should see a series of FQDNs with their corresponding IP addresses, as shown in Figure 12-9.

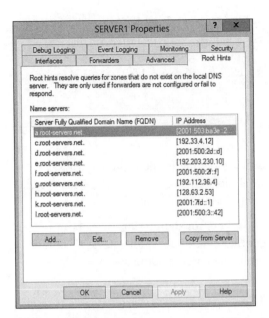

Figure 12-9   The Root Hints tab of the DNS server's Properties dialog box displays the names and IP addresses of the Internet root zones.

If your internal DNS server does not provide access to Internet name resolution, you can improve network security by configuring the root hints of the internal DNS servers to point to the DNS servers that host your root domain and not to Internet root domain DNS servers. To modify the configuration on this tab, perform one or more of the following actions:

- Click **Add** to display the New Name Server Record dialog box, from which you can manually type the FQDN and IP addresses of one or more authoritative name servers.

- Select an entry and click **Edit** to display the Edit Name Server Record dialog box, which enables you to modify it or add another IP address to an existing record.

- Select an entry and click **Remove** to remove a record.

- Click **Copy from Server** to copy a list of root hints from another DNS server. Type the DNS name or IP address in the dialog box that appears. This action is useful if your server was not connected to the Internet at the time DNS was installed.

> **TIP** If you need to ensure that clients cannot access the Internet, you can remove all root hints or even create a new DNS zone named ".". By creating a blank root zone, the DNS server assumes it is the root and is authoritative for all top-level domains. If no records exist in the root, the clients will be unable to resolve any address spaces outside of your network.

Debug Logging Tab

This tab enables you to configure packet-level logging for debugging purposes. Packets sent to and from the DNS server are logged to a text file named `dns.log`. This file is stored in the `%systemroot%\system32\dns` folder.

To enable debug logging, select the **Log packets for debugging** check box on the Debug Logging tab, which makes all other check boxes available, as shown in Figure 12-10. Table 12-6 describes the available logging options:

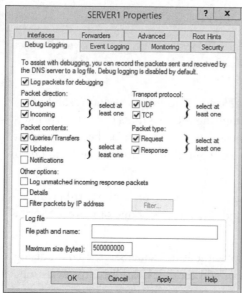

Figure 12-10 Configuring debug logging.

Table 12-6 DNS Debug Logging Options

Option	Description
Packet direction	Determines the direction of packets logged, incoming or outgoing or both.
Transport protocol	Select **UDP** to log the number of DNS requests received over a UDP port, and select **TCP** to log the number of DNS requests received over a TCP port.

Option	Description
Packet contents	Select at least one of the available options to determine the types of packets logged by the server: ■ **Queries/Transfers:** Logs packets containing standard queries, according to RFC 1034 ■ **Updates:** Logs packets containing dynamic updates, according to RFC 2136 ■ **Notifications:** Logs packets containing notifications, according to RFC 1996
Packet type	Determines whether the request or response (or both) packets are logged.
Other options	Select **Details** to enable logging of detailed information. Select **Filter** to limit the packets that are logged according to IP address. This logs packets sent from specific IP addresses to the DNS server or from the DNS server to these specific IP addresses (according to the incoming or outgoing choice).
Log file	Enables you to change the default file path, name, and maximum size. If the maximum size is exceeded, the DNS server overwrites the oldest logged data.

CAUTION   Configure debug logging only when absolutely necessary, only on required DNS servers, and only on a temporary basis. Its use is highly resource intensive. It is for this reason that debug logging is disabled by default.

To view the DNS log, first stop the DNS service by right-clicking the DNS server in DNS Manager and selecting **All Tasks > Stop**. Then open the log in either Notepad or WordPad. When you are finished, restart the DNS service by right-clicking the DNS server and selecting **All Tasks > Start**.

Event Logging Tab

The Event Logging tab of the DNS server's Properties dialog box, shown in Figure 12-11, enables you to control how much information is logged to the DNS log, which appears in Event Viewer. You can choose from one of the following options:

■ **No events:** Suppresses all event logging (not recommended).

■ **Errors only:** Logs error events only.

- **Errors and warnings:** Logs errors and warnings only.

- **All events:** Logs informational events, errors, and warnings. This is the default.

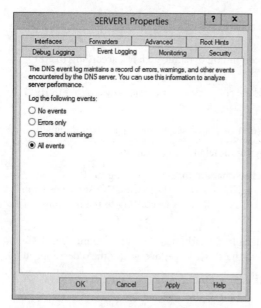

Figure 12-11   The Event Logging tab enables you to control the quantity of information that is logged to the DNS log in Event Viewer.

Selecting either the Errors only or Errors and warnings option might be useful to reduce the amount of information recorded to the DNS event log.

Monitoring Tab

The Monitoring tab enables you to perform test queries that verify the proper installation and operation of the DNS server. Shown in Figure 12-12, this tab enables you to perform two types of test queries:

- **Simple query:** The DNS client software performs a local query to a zone stored in the DNS server (including Active Directory-integrated zones).

- **Recursive query:** A recursive query is forwarded to another DNS server for resolution.

To perform these queries, select the check boxes as illustrated in Figure 12-12; then click the **Test Now** command button. The result is displayed in the Test results field directly below. Optionally, you can also schedule the test to occur automatically at preconfigured intervals by selecting the check box labeled **Perform automatic testing at the following interval** and then selecting a test interval in minutes or hours from the drop-down list.

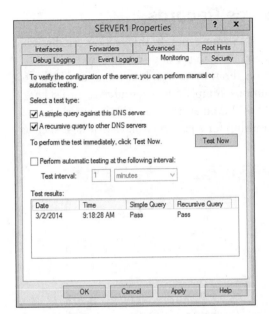

Figure 12-12   The Monitoring tab enables you to perform simple and recursive test queries against the DNS server.

Security Tab

The Security tab (see Figure 12-13) enables you to modify user/group abilities to manage specific DNS objects. From here, you can delegate control to different administrators.

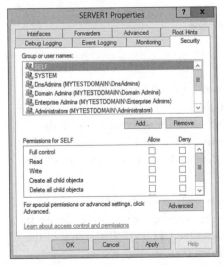

Figure 12-13   The Security tab enables you to modify user/group access to a DNS server.

Configuring Common Resource Records

Earlier you learned about the different DNS zone types. In this section, we discuss resource records and how to manage them. As with previous versions of DNS, each DNS name server stores information about devices and resources in which it is responsible for providing name resolutions. Simply put, a resource record such as that for SERVER2 shown in Figure 12-14 is an entry in the DNS zone that describes the name-to-IP address relationship for a particular device or host such as a workstation, server, or network device.

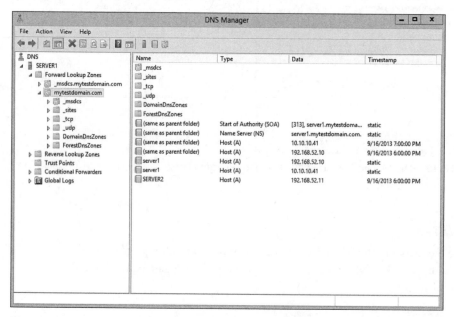

Figure 12-14   DNS resource records shown in a DNS zone.

DNS zones are populated with resource records via the following methods:

- **Dynamic Updates:** As a DHCP server hands out IP addresses, it registers the client hostname or FQDN and IP address with the DNS server. If the hostname or IP address changes, the DNS record is updated accordingly. The record for SERVER2 shown previously in Figure 12-14 is an example of a record registered dynamically. Take notice of the Timestamp in which the record was automatically created.

- **NIC Registration (static):** For computers with static IP addresses, the Microsoft Operating System attempts to register the connection's address in DNS if the option is enabled under the Advanced TCP/IP Properties of the network adapter. As the connection's address is registered, a static record is added to DNS such as that for server1 as shown in Figure 12-14. By issuing the `ipconfig /registerdns` command, the client will attempt to register or

reregister the connection in DNS. This is helpful if you change the hostname
or IP address and want to force an update of the record in DNS.

- **Manually:** DNS records can be created manually in the zone by an administrator. These records are static by nature and can be changed only by an administrator. If the hostname or IP address changes on a server, you must update the DNS record to ensure proper name resolution. Static records appear in DNS with a static timestamp as shown previously in Figure 12-14.

Also visible in Figure 12-14 are the two resource records automatically created whenever you use the New Zone Wizard to create a new zone: the SOA and NS resource records. The Start of Authority (SOA) record specifies the authoritative information about a DNS zone, such as the serial number, primary server, and responsible person, as well as other details about how the information in the zone is refreshed. The Name Server (NS) record identifies the FQDN of the authoritative DNS name server responsible for the DNS zone. Managing zones and specifics of SOA/NS records are covered in more detail on the 70-411 exam.

With most implementations involving a DNS server, resource records are populated using a combination of NIC registrations and the dynamic update process. Over time, you might come across the need to manually add a resource record in a DNS zone. DNS provides the ability to create different resource records for different needs. The different record types will be described over the next several sections.

To create a new manual DNS resource record, right-click your DNS zone and select the appropriate option from those shown in Figure 12-15.

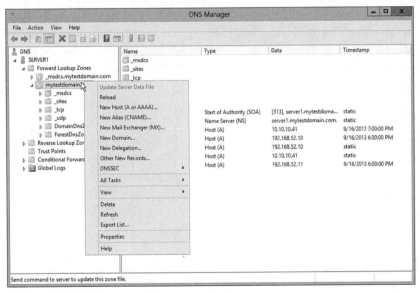

Figure 12-15   You can create new resource records in DNS by right-clicking your zone name and choosing the appropriate option.

New Host (A or AAAA) Records

A host resource record maps the FQDN of any computer (host) in the domain to its IP address. Normally, the appropriate host record is dynamically added or updated when the host obtains its IP configuration from DHCP. An A resource record is used on an IPv4 network, and an AAAA resource record is used on an IPv6 network; if your network is configured to use both IPv4 and IPv6, each host will have both A and AAAA resource records. However, if your network doesn't include a DHCP server, you will need to create your own host records. Further, a non-Windows computer, such as a UNIX server, cannot perform dynamic updates. So, you will need to create a host record for such a computer so clients can locate it by name.

Right-click the zone and select **New Host (A or AAAA)** to open the New Host dialog box shown in Figure 12-16. You need only enter the hostname (for example, `server3`) and IP address for the new host (for example, `192.168.52.12`). The FQDN is generated from the hostname you specified plus the zone you right-clicked. Additionally, select either or both of the following options as required and then click **Add Host** when complete:

- **Create associated pointer (PTR) record:** Automatically creates a PTR resource record, which enables reverse lookup queries to function. Recall that a reverse lookup query enables an IP address to be resolved to its associated FQDN.

- **Allow any authenticated user to update DNS records with the same owner name:** Enables an administrator to create a secure resource record for a new host that is not yet online and enables this resource record to be updated dynamically when the host comes online and uses DHCP to obtain its TCP/IP configuration. Normally, the host that requests an update receives permission to modify the resource record, but other administrative permissions are not enabled in the resource record's access control list (ACL).

Figure 12-16   The New Host dialog box enables you to create either A or AAAA resource records.

New Alias (CNAME)

A new alias or canonical name (CNAME) record is an alias for an existing host A or AAAA record in a DNS zone. CNAME records are useful if you need to create custom FQDNs or user-friendly names for a specific resource. For example, suppose you have a server named Server1 that hosts a helpdesk web application. Instead of instructing users to navigate to Server1.mytestdomain.com, you might create an alias for HelpDesk.mytestdomain.com. When clients resolve Helpdesk.mytestdomain.com, they are actually being routed to Server1.mytestdomain.com. CNAMEs are also helpful when migrating data from a legacy server to a new one. Suppose you have an application that is hard-coded to use a legacy server name. After the data is moved to a new server, you can create an alias with the old server name that points to the new server.

To create a CNAME record, right-click the DNS zone and select **New Alias (CNAME)**. This launches the New Resource Record dialog box shown in Figure 12-17. Type an alias name in the **Alias name** text box, and then browse to the Host record or specify the FQDN of the Host record. Optionally, you can choose to allow any authenticated user to update all DNS records with the same name.

Figure 12-17   The New Resource Record dialog box enables you to create a CNAME record.

New Mail Exchanger (MX)

The New Mail Exchanger (MX) Record identifies the mail exchange server responsible for managing mail flow in your organization. MX records are especially important when dealing with DNS servers responsible for the public IP address ranges
on the Internet. This allows for mail routing over the Internet, such as sending
email from a gmail.com account to a corporate mail server. As with other resource
records, right-click the DNS zone and select New Mail Exchanger (MX) to open
the New Resource Record dialog box shown in Figure 12-18. Enter the hostname
and specify the FQDN of the mail server.

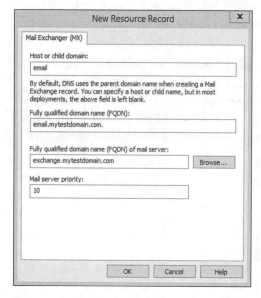

Figure 12-18 The New Resource Record dialog box enables you to create a CNAME record.

Additional New Resource Records

DNS in Windows Server 2012 R2 provides a large number of additional resource
records. Some of these records are discussed in more detail on the 70-411 exam. To
create one of the additional resource records, right-click an existing zone and select
Other New Records. This displays the Resource Record Type dialog box shown in
Figure 12-19.

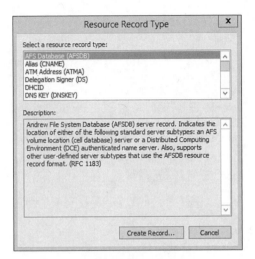

Figure 12-19 The Resource Record Type dialog box enables you to create any of the possible types of resource records in Windows Server 2012 R2 DNS.

Select the desired type of resource record, and click **Create Record** to open a dialog box that enables you to properly define the selected record type. Some of the available record types are as follows:

- **Service Locator Record (SRV):** Services such as Active Directory Domain Services or applications such as Microsoft Lync (formerly Office Communicator) use specific protocols that enable communication. To use these applications, they must use DNS to identify the location of the server that provides the service for clients. SRV records enable clients to use DNS to locate such services.

- **Pointer (PTR):** Pointer records are created automatically if you have specified this option in the New Host dialog box or if the appropriate option has been configured at the DHCP server for dynamic DNS. If not, select this option and specify the required octet(s) of the host's IP address; then specify or browse to the hostname that corresponds to this IP address (see Figure 12-20). PTR records can also be created under Reverse lookup zones.

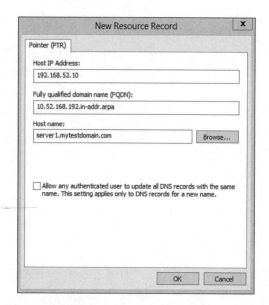

Figure 12-20   Creating a new PTR resource record.

> **NOTE**   For more information on the use of resource records, refer to
> "Resource records reference" at http://technet.microsoft.com/en-us/library/
> cc758321(v=ws.10).aspx.

Deleting Resource Records

Just as you can create resource records with a few clicks, you can delete them by
right-clicking the specific record in the zone and selecting **Delete**, as shown in
Figure 12-21. DNS Manager will prompt you to confirm whether you want to
delete the record. Please note that after the record is deleted, the clients will no
longer be able to resolve the resource using the deleted record.

> **NOTE**   To change a resource record previously created, right-click the record and
> select **Properties**.

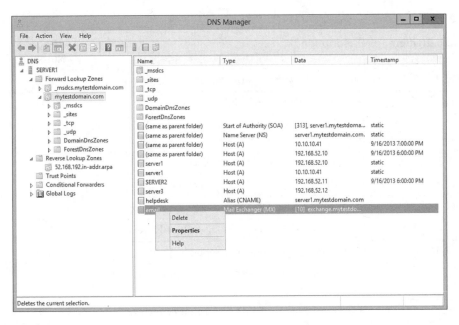

Figure 12-21   Deleting a resource record.

Using the Command Line to Create Resource Records

You can use Windows PowerShell cmdlets to create resource records from a Power-Shell session. Refer back to Table 12-5 for a listing of cmdlets used to manage resource records. The following command outlines the basic syntax to add a DNS resource record:

```
Add-DnsServerResourceRecord[type]  -Name  [record name]  -IPv4Address
[IP Address]  -ZoneName  [DNS Zone name]
```

Exam Preparation Tasks

Review All the Key Topics

Review the most important topics in the chapter, noted with the key topics icon in the outer margin of the page. Table 12-7 lists a reference of these key topics and the page numbers on which each is found.

Table 12-7   Key Topics for Chapter 12

Key Topic Element	Description	Page Number
Figure 12-1	Shows you how the Internet namespace is set up	530
Paragraph	Introduces the types of DNS queries	533
List	Describes the procedure for installing the DNS server role	537
Table 12-5	Lists commonly used DNS cmdlets	539
Figure 12-6	Shows how to specify DNS forwarders	547
Figure 12-8	Displays advanced DNS server configuration options	548
Figure 12-9	Shows you how to configure DNS Root Hints	551
Figure 12-10	Shows you how to configure debug logging	552
Figure 12-12	Shows you how to perform test queries against a DNS server	555
Paragraph	Introduces you to A and AAAA resource records	558
Figure 12-16	Shows you how to create an A or AAAA resource record	558
Paragraph	Describes alias (CNAME) resource records	559
Paragraph	Describes additional resource records commonly used	560

Complete the Tables and Lists from Memory

Print a copy of Appendix B, "Memory Tables" (found on the CD), or at least the section for this chapter, and complete the tables and lists from memory. Appendix C, "Memory Tables Answer Key," is also on the CD and includes completed tables and lists to check your work.

Definitions of Key Terms

Define the following key terms from this chapter, and check your answers in the glossary.

Conditional forwarding, DNS Manager, DNSSEC (Domain Name System Security Extensions), Domain Name System (DNS), Forward lookup query, Forwarding, Fully qualified domain name (FQDN), Hostname, Iterative query, Recursion, Reverse lookup query, Root hints

This chapter covers the following subjects:

- **The Building Blocks of Active Directory:** This section describes the components that Microsoft took from X.500 and LDAP to build the hierarchical structure that is Active Directory. It goes on to describe the logical building blocks Microsoft assembled in creating the structure of Active Directory.

- **Planning the Active Directory Namespace:** This section provides a basic introduction to best practices you should follow in planning and designing an Active Directory namespace that will serve your company properly both now and in the years to come.

- **Creating Forests and Domains:** In this section, you learn how to create your first domain controller in a new Active Directory forest. You then learn how to add domain controllers to your forest and create child domains.

- **Adding, Removing, and Upgrading Domain Controllers:** Many organizations are using Active Directory domains based on Windows 2003 and Windows Server 2008. This section takes you through the preparatory tasks you must perform before you can add a Windows Server 2012 R2 domain controller as well as the actual upgrading of older domain controllers. In addition, it introduces you to the concept of forest and domain functional levels, as well as the benefits of the newest Windows Server 2012 and Windows Server 2012 R2 functional levels.

- **Installing a Server Core Domain Controller:** You can use either Windows PowerShell or the `dcpromo.exe` command with an appropriate answer file to install AD DS on a Windows Server 2012 R2 Server Core computer.

- **Using the Install from Media Option:** This section provides an overview of IFM, how to configure an IFM package, and how to install a new domain controller using the IFM option.

- **Configuring Global Catalog Servers:** This section describes the uses for global catalog Servers and how to configure them.

- **Deploying Active Directory Infrastructure as a Service in Windows Azure:** The Microsoft Windows Azure cloud computing service enables you to deploy an entire AD DS forest or a portion thereof. This section introduces Windows Azure and shows you how to deploy domain controllers in Azure.

- **Troubleshooting Active Directory Installations:** After installing Active Directory, there are a handful of things you might want to configure. Before you head down that path, you might want to take some time to confirm basic functionality. This section discusses verifying your Active Directory installation and how to identify issues with Service Locator (SRV) records.

CHAPTER 13

Installing Domain Controllers

Active Directory has been with us for over a decade now and is firmly entrenched as Microsoft's forest and domain directory service. Microsoft built the Active Directory domain structure on the concepts of X.500 and Lightweight Directory Access Protocol (LDAP). Since its beginnings with Windows 2000, Active Directory has matured and gained new features, improved security and functionality, and ease of configuration and management. For those of you who have never worked with Active Directory, we begin this chapter with an introduction to the concepts involved in this directory service and then proceed with the installation of your first domain controller.

The act of installing Active Directory on a server is conceptually very simple. You need only run the Active Directory Domain Services (AD DS) Installation Wizard from the Add Roles and Features Wizard of Server Manager and provide answers to the questions the wizard asks. The actual act of installing AD DS, however, can be thought of as the tip of the iceberg. Before you install AD DS, you need to plan how Active Directory will fit into your company's corporate and geographical structure as well as your expectations for future growth and the potential for acquiring other companies. This chapter serves only as a basic introduction to the topic of planning.

"Do I Know This Already?" Quiz

The "Do I Know This Already?" quiz enables you to assess whether you should read this entire chapter or simply jump to the "Exam Preparation Tasks" section for review. If you are in doubt, read the entire chapter. Table 13-1 outlines the major headings in this chapter and the corresponding "Do I Know This Already?" quiz questions. You can find the answers in Appendix A, "Answers to the 'Do I Know This Already?' Quizzes."

Table 13-1   "Do I Know This Already?" Foundation Topics Section-to-Question Mapping

Foundations Topics Section	Questions Covered in This Section
The Building Blocks of Active Directory	1–2
Planning the Active Directory Namespace	3
Creating Forests and Domains	4–5
Adding, Removing, and Upgrading Domain Controllers	6–7
Installing a Server Core Domain Controller	8
Using the Install from Media Option	9
Configuring Global Catalog Servers	10
Deploying Active Directory Infrastructure as a Service in Windows Azure	11
Troubleshooting Active Directory Installations	12

1. Which of the following are logical components of an Active Directory structure? (Choose all that apply.)

   a. Forests

   b. Trees

   c. Sites

   d. Domains

   e. Organizational units (OUs)

   f. Global catalogs

2. On which of the following editions of Windows Server 2012 R2 can you install the AD DS role? (Choose all that apply.)

    a. Foundation

    b. Essentials

    c. Standard

    d. Datacenter

3. Which of the following are best practices that you should follow when planning an AD DS domain structure? (Choose all that apply.)

    a. Employ a test lab.

    b. Prepare thorough documentation.

    c. Keep everyone, including top managers, informed.

    d. Understand thoroughly the network's TCP/IP infrastructure.

    e. Develop and adhere to an adequate security policy.

    f. Know the capabilities of your WAN links.

4. Which of the following tools can you use to install AD DS on a server running Windows Server 2012 R2? (Choose all that apply.)

    a. The `dcpromo.exe` command using an answer file

    b. The `dcpromo.exe` command without any additional files

    c. The Configure Your Server tool

    d. Server Manager

    e. Windows PowerShell

5. Which of the following server roles is installed automatically by the Active Directory Domain Services Configuration Wizard if the wizard cannot find it on another server elsewhere on the network?

    a. Active Directory Certificate Services

    b. DHCP Server

    c. DNS Server

    d. Remote Access

6. Which of the following are not valid domain or forest functional levels for a domain controller running Windows Server 2012 R2? (Choose all that apply.)

   a. Windows 2000 mixed

   b. Windows 2000 native

   c. Windows Server 2003

   d. Windows Server 2008

   e. Windows Server 2008 R2

   f. Windows Server 2012 R2

7. You are the administrator of DC1, which is a Windows Server 2012 R2 domain controller in your company's domain. You are experiencing problems with DC1 and decide to run the Active Directory Domain Services Configuration Wizard again on this machine. What happens?

   a. A new copy of the AD DS software is installed.

   b. Two copies of the AD DS software will exist side-by-side.

   c. The domain controller is demoted to a member server.

   d. You receive an error message informing you that the wizard cannot be run again.

8. Your computer is running the Server Core edition of Windows Server 2012 R2. You want to promote this server to domain controller. What should you do? (Each correct answer presents a complete solution. Choose two answers.)

   a. Use Server Manager to run the Add Roles Wizard.

   b. Use the Initial Configuration Tasks window to run the Add Roles Wizard.

   c. Use the `Install-ADDSDomainController` cmdlet in Windows PowerShell.

   d. Use `dcpromo.exe` and specify the required parameters when prompted.

   e. Use `dcpromo.exe` together with an answer file that provides the required parameters.

   f. You cannot promote this server to domain controller without reinstalling Windows Server 2012 R2 as a full edition server.

9. You need to deploy a new Windows Server 2012 R2 domain controller DC2. DC1 is a Windows Server 2008 domain controller. What must you do first to use the install from media option for DC2?

   a. On DC1, create a new IFM package using the ntdsutil Create Full parameter.

   b. On DC2, create a new IFM package using the ntdsutil Create Full parameter.

   c. Upgrade DC1 to Windows Server 2012 R2.

   d. Upgrade DC1 to Windows Server 2008 R2.

10. Which of the following are features of a global catalog server? (Choose all that apply.)

   a. Validation of universal group memberships at logon

   b. Validation of site links

   c. Validation of UPNs across the forest.

   d. Validation of offline files

11. Which of the following can you do when deploying AD DS across a Windows Azure deployment? (Choose all that apply.)

   a. Deploy the forest root domain controller for a new forest.

   b. Deploy a replica domain controller for a forest hosted on your local network.

   c. Deploy a DNS server that provides service to an AD DS domain hosted in Windows Azure.

   d. Deploy a DHCP server that provides service to an AD DS domain hosted in Windows Azure.

   e. Deploy an entire domain controller including the database and SYSVOL folders on a single virtual disk.

12. Which file can you view to identify SRV records associated with a domain controller?

   a. `Primary.dns`

   b. `Secondary.dns`

   c. `netlogon.srv`

   d. `netlogon.dns`

Foundation Topics

The Building Blocks of Active Directory

Active Directory can support an almost unlimited scope of functions and capabilities in an enterprise network, from small-scale operations to a global-scale multidomain enterprises. Microsoft took the concepts of X.500 and LDAP and molded them with a series of new components to come up with Active Directory's structure. To this end, Active Directory embraces the following concepts:

- Namespace

- Object

- Container

- Schema

- Global catalog

- Partition

Each of these concepts is briefly discussed in the following sections.

Namespaces

The concept of a *namespace* originated with early incarnations of the Internet. This term refers to a bounded area within which a name is resolved or translated into information that is encompassed by the name. For an analogy, you can think of a telephone directory as a type of namespace in which names are resolved to phone numbers; its area is bounded within the city, county, or other geographic area served by the directory. An example in the computer world is that of a hostname that represents an IP address. Microsoft took this concept and expanded on it until it encompassed any type of information that anyone might have a need to locate. Further, Microsoft made this concept dynamic, so that when items were added, moved, or removed, the directory would reflect these actions. The result was Active Directory.

Namespaces can be either *flat* or *hierarchical*. Flat namespaces have only one level at which they store information, such as the NetBIOS naming concepts used in Windows NT 4. Hierarchical namespaces, as the name suggests, use several levels of name definition, such as those found in an Internet name, such as `www.sales.company.com`. Here, `.com` represents the top level, `company` represents a second-level domain, `sales` is a subdomain, and `www` is a web server name. As you are undoubtedly aware, DNS uses this type of namespace. The DNS naming scheme is used to create the structure of the Active Directory namespace, permitting interoperability with Internet technologies; therefore, the concept of namespaces is central to Active Directory. By integrating this concept with the system's directory services, Active Directory facilitates the management of multiple namespaces that are often found in the heterogeneous software and hardware environments of corporate networks.

The two types of namespaces are contiguous and disjointed. They are defined as follows:

- **Contiguous:** The name of child objects in the hierarchy contains the name of the parent object; for example, the relationship between domains within the same tree.

- **Disjointed:** The name of a child object in the hierarchy does not contain the name of the parent object; for example, the relationship between different trees in the same forest.

Objects

An *object* is any specific item that can be cataloged in Active Directory. Examples of objects include users, computers, printers, folders, and files. These items are classified by a distinct set of characteristics, known as *attributes*. For example, a user can be characterized by the username, full name, telephone number, email address, and so on. Note that in general, objects in the same container have the same types of attributes but are characterized by different values of these attributes. The Active Directory schema defines the extent of attributes that can be specified for any object.

The Active Directory service, in turn, classifies objects into *classes*. These classes are logical groupings of similar objects, such as users. Each class is a series of attributes that define the characteristics of the object.

Containers

A *container* is an object that is designed to hold other objects within the directory. A folder could be considered a container because it holds files and subfolders that are located beneath it. Like other objects, containers have their own attributes. Forests, trees, domains, and OUs are all different types of containers because they are all designed to contain other objects.

Schemas

The *schema* is a set of rules that define the classes of objects and their attributes that can be created in Active Directory. It defines which attributes can be held by objects of various types, which of the various classes can exist, and which object class can be a parent of the current object class. For example, the User class can contain user account objects and possess attributes such as password, group membership, home folder, and so on.

You can mark attributes as indexed, which means instances of the attribute are added to a searchable index and are more easily located by a user searching by the container in which the attributes are located. This feature improves search time but increases the size (and replication time) of the Active Directory database.

When you first install Active Directory on a server, a default schema is created, containing definitions of commonly used objects and properties such as users, computers, and groups. This default schema also contains definitions of objects and properties needed for the functioning of Active Directory.

The Active Directory schema is extensible—that is, you can define new types and attributes of directory objects, as well as new attributes for existing objects. In doing so, you can adapt the schema to a given type of business; for example, a wholesaler might want to add a warehouse object to the directory, including information specific to that business. Additions to the schema are implemented automatically and stored within the Active Directory database. Applications can be built to extend the schema and can use such extensions immediately.

WARNING   Modifying the schema is a serious business. Improper modifications to the schema can harm or disable the domain controllers or even the entire network. For this reason, Microsoft has included a group called Schema Admins. Only members of this group have the right to modify the schema.

Global Catalogs

The *global catalog* is a central information database that can hold data describing objects throughout the Active Directory forest namespace. Active Directory builds up the global catalog by replicating information between all domain controllers in the forest. In this way, a comprehensive and complete database of all available objects is automatically built up. To extend the telephone directory analogy mentioned earlier in this chapter, you can think of the global catalog as a Yellow Pages directory that facilitates your locating a specific type of resource, such as a color printer on the 17th floor of your building.

As well as providing a physical location that contains a subset of all information in each domain's Active Directory database, the global catalog is a service that permits the resolution of many common queries that originate from anywhere in the forest. It holds and organizes the common attributes used in search operations, such as user and group names, filenames, and so on. All information pertaining to universal groups, including their membership, is found here. Usernames are stored in the UPN format; in doing so, a user can log on to any computer in the forest by employing the UPN.

By default, Active Directory stores the global catalog on the first domain controller in a new forest. It is possible to either move or copy the global catalog to another domain controller.

Partitions

Active Directory is divided into several *partitions*—not to be confused with disk partitions—that enable the enterprise-level network to be scaled to enormous proportions while remaining manageable. A schema partition and a configuration partition are stored on all domain controllers within an Active Directory forest, and application and domain partitions are common to domain controllers within a domain. The roles of these partitions are as follows:

- **Domain partition:** This partition contains information about all objects such as users, groups, computers, and organizational units in a domain. It is replicated to all domain controllers within the domain, and a subset of this information is replicated to global catalog servers in the forest.

- **Schema partition:** This partition contains definitions of all objects and their attributes. Rules for creating and working with them are also located here. This partition is replicated to all domain controllers in the forest.

- **Configuration partition:** This partition contains information about the structure of Active Directory in the forest, including domains, sites, and services. It is also replicated to all domain controllers in the forest.

- **Application partition:** First introduced in Windows Server 2003, this partition contains application-specific data that needs to be replicated throughout specified portions of the forest. It can be replicated to a specific domain controller or to any set of domain controllers anywhere in the forest. In this way, it differs from the domain partition in which Active Directory replicates data to all domain controllers in that domain. It also contains DNS information for Active Directory-integrated DNS zones.

Naming Standards of X.500 and LDAP

Originating with X.500 and expanded upon by LDAP is a series of naming standards that define the path to any object that has been defined in the directory. As Active Directory uses LDAP as the protocol of choice for accessing objects in the directory, these naming paths and their components are important items that you should know to fully understand the capabilities of Active Directory. The naming paths include the distinguished names (DNs) and relative distinguished names. Additional identifiers that you should be familiar with include the User Principal Names (UPN) and Globally Unique Identifiers (GUID).

Distinguished Names

Each object in the LDAP inverted tree is uniquely identified by a DN that defines the complete path from the top of the tree to the object. The concept of distinguished names, which originated in the X.500 specifications, is a global one that was laid out with specific goals in mind:

- To provide an unambiguous representation of the name of any resource

- To provide a readily understood format for the majority of names

- To achieve an attractive representation of information within several layouts

- To clearly represent the contents of the object being defined

To achieve these goals, a series of X.500-based delimiters was developed with standard abbreviation names. The complete specification of distinguished names, including its complete syntax and full list of delimiters, is given in RFC 1779. The most common delimiters are as follows:

- CN = Common Name

- OU = Organizational Unit

- DC = Domain Component

- O = Organization Name

- C = Country Name

For any given object, the DN is a unique and unambiguous identification of the object and its location within the directory structure. In other words, two different objects can never have exactly the same DN. To specify a DN, include the name of the object itself, followed by the containers and parent containers holding the name in order. Note that a distinguished name can contain more than one of a given delimiter. The following is an example of a distinguished name:

```
CN=Tim Brown,OU=Inventory,DC=Que,DC=com.
```

> **NOTE**   Active Directory snap-in tools generally do not display the DN as shown in the previous paragraph. This is shown here to illustrate how LDAP recognizes the components of the DN. However, it is helpful to know the concept of the distinguished name and how objects fit together into the Active Directory hierarchy. You will see more of how this fits together as you progress through this training guide—for example, when you need to restore Active Directory objects.

Relative Distinguished Names

The relative distinguished name (RDN) is the most granular part of the distinguished name that identifies a specific attribute of the object itself. For example, in the DN given previously, the RDN is the first part—CN = Tim Brown. Within any given parent container, no two objects can have the same RDN. There can, however, be two objects within different containers that have the same RDN.

An analogy could be the fact that more than one city with the same name can exist, as long as the cities are located in different states, such as Springfield, Illinois, and Springfield, Massachusetts. The DNs for these cities could be as follows:

`CN=Springfield,OU=IL,C=US`

and

`CN=Springfield,OU=MA,C=US`

The CN in these examples defines the exact city as opposed to a different city such as Chicago or Boston; therefore, the CN is also the RDN here.

User Principal Names

In addition to the DN and RDN described previously, Active Directory uses the concept of UPN, which is introduced here as it is intimately related to these other names. The UPN is a shortcut name for the user that can be the same as a logon name or email address. For example, referring to the DN described previously, the UPN could be `TimB@inventory.que.com`.

Globally Unique Identifiers

Every object stored in Active Directory also has a unique identifier called the GUID, which is a 128-bit hexadecimal number assigned when the object is created in Active Directory. The GUID is stored in an attribute called objectGUID, which exists for every object in Active Directory. Unlike the DN or RDN, this identifier never changes even if you move or rename the object. For example, an employee leaves the company and is replaced; you want the new employee to have the same rights and privileges as the old one so you rename the user account; this account retains the GUID of the old account. However, if you were to delete an object and then later re-create another object with the same DN, the GUID would not be the same. This is the reason that if you deleted an object such as a user or group account and then must re-create it, you must re-create all properties and attributes associated with the object.

Security Identifiers

The security identifier (SID) is a value that uniquely identifies a security principal such as a user, group, service, or computer account within the Active Directory forest. When created, every account is issued a SID. These are used to identify security principals in Windows Server 2012 R2 for access control purposes. No two objects in the forest can have the same SID. A SID can change under certain circumstances, such as if a user is moved from one domain to another. Like the GUID, if you delete an object and later re-create an object with the same name, the SID would not be the same.

Active Directory Canonical Names

This is a version of the DN that Active Directory displays. The canonical name lists the RDNs from the root downward (that is, in reverse sequence to the DN); it also does not use the RFC 1779 naming attribute descriptors. However, it does use the DNS domain name. For the DN given previously, the Active Directory canonical name would be as follows:

```
Que.com/incentory/TimB
```

Logical Components of Active Directory

In creating the hierarchical database structure of Active Directory, Microsoft facilitated locating resources such as folders and printers by name rather than by physical location. These logical building blocks include domains, trees, forests, and OUs. The physical location of objects within Active Directory is represented by including all objects in a given location in its own site.

Because a domain is the basic unit upon which Active Directory is built, the domain is introduced first, followed by trees and forests (in which domains are located) and then OUs, which are containers located within a domain.

Domains

Similar to the case in Windows NT, the domain represents the core unit of the network structure. As in Windows NT, the domain is a logical grouping of computers that share a common directory database and security. However, whereas in Windows NT, each domain was a unit unto itself with no default trust relationship with other domains, in Active Directory, you can have a series of domains organized into larger units called *trees* and *forests*, with inherent trust relationships already built in to them. Individuals can be designated with administrative powers over a single domain or across an entire forest, and you can even configure trust relationships to external forests. Furthermore, Active Directory domains can hold millions of objects, as opposed to the Windows NT domain structure, which was limited to approximately 40,000 objects.

As in previous versions of Active Directory, the Active Directory database file (ntds.dit) defines the domain. Each domain has its own ntds.dit file, which is stored on (and replicated among) all domain controllers by a process called *multimaster replication*. The domain controllers manage the configuration of domain security and store the directory services database. This arrangement permits central administration of domain account privileges, security, and network resources. Networked devices and users belonging to a domain validate with a domain controller at startup. All computers that refer to a specific set of domain controllers make up the domain. In addition, group accounts such as global groups and domain local groups are defined on a domain-wide basis. Some benefits of using multiple domains are as follows:

- Domains can be considered as security boundaries. In other words, domain administrators can define access control lists (ACLs) that determine users' access rights and permissions to objects within the domain at the domain level. Also, each administrator has the authority to set security policy only within his domain.

- You can specify how resources in each domain can be accessed using Group Policy, which can be configured on a domain-wide basis. Group Policies have full control over all objects in the domain but do not have any authority over objects in other domains.

- You can configure domains along geographical lines; for example, a multinational company might organize its network with a domain for every country. In this manner, the company can deal with legal and other country-specific issues.

- You can configure domains along business lines, such as a parent company with a series of subsidiaries. This configuration simplifies reorganization should a subsidiary be sold or a new one acquired.

Trees

A *tree* is a group of domains that share a contiguous namespace. In other words, a tree consists of a parent domain plus one or more sets of child domains whose name reflects that of the parent. For example, a parent domain named `certguide.com` can include child domains with names such as `products.certguide.com`, `sales.certguide.com`, and `manufacturing.certguide.com`. Furthermore, the tree structure can contain grandchild domains such as `america.sales.certguide.com` or `europe.sales.certguide.com`, and so on, as shown in Figure 13-1. A domain called `que.com` would not belong to the same tree. Following the inverted tree concept originated by X.500, the tree is structured with the parent domain at the top and child domains beneath it.

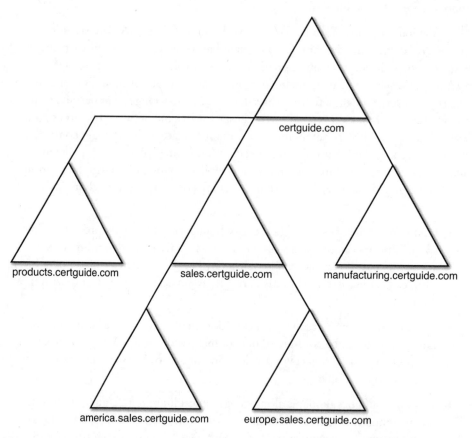

Figure 13-1   A tree consists of a group of domains that share a contiguous namespace, with the parent domain at the top.

All domains in a tree are linked with two-way, transitive trust relationships; in other words, accounts in any one domain can access resources in another domain, and vice versa. Refer to the *Cert Guide* book for exam 70-412 for more information on the types of trust relationships available and procedures for configuring them.

Forests

A *forest* consists of a group of domain trees that do not share a contiguous namespace. For example, you can have two trees with parent domains named `certguide.com` and `que.com`, as shown in Figure 13-2. Each tree can contain its own child domains within its namespace. Again, two-way transitive trust relationships exist between domains in the trees of a single forest. When you first create a new Active Directory structure, the first domain created is the forest root domain. Recalling the definition of namespace as a bounded area in which the directory can resolve names, the forest itself is also a namespace; in this case, it is a disjointed namespace. In other words, the two portions of the namespace do not share a name in common. By default, two-way transitive trust relationships exist between the parent domains in each tree throughout the forest. Again, these trust relationships do not need to be explicitly configured. In addition, all domains in the forest share a common schema, configuration, and global catalog.

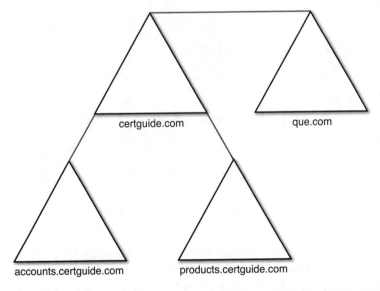

Figure 13-2   A forest is a group of trees that form a disjointed namespace.

In a forest, one domain has to be the forest root domain. The forest root domain is always the first domain created when a new forest is created.

Organizational Units

An *organizational unit (OU)* is a logical subgroup within a domain. It is convenient for locating resources used by a single work group, section, or department in a company and applying policies that apply to only these resources (see Figure 13-3). You can create a hierarchy of OUs and child OUs organized in much the same way as that of a hierarchy of folders, subfolders, and sub-subfolders on a disk. You can also delegate control of administrative activities to users within a single OU, such as creating and working with user accounts, groups, printers, and so on. Further, you can control users and computers within an OU by means of Group Policy; this is the smallest unit to which you can deploy Group Policy.

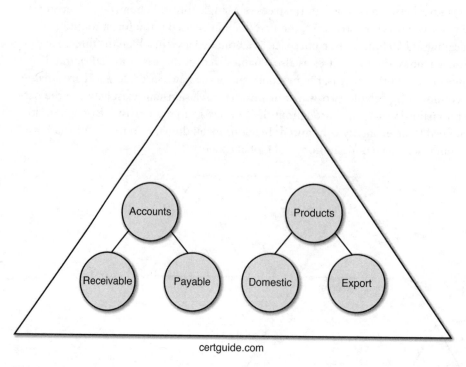

certguide.com

Figure 13-3 You can create hierarchies of OUs within your domain structure.

Each OU can contain any type of noncontainer object, such as users, groups, and computers. In addition, it can contain additional OUs within it. Therefore, you can build an OU hierarchy to any depth within the domain. You can also modify or remove a series of OUs. Within each OU, you can perform actions such as creating, moving, deleting, or modifying objects within the OU as easily as the OUs themselves.

Some uses of OUs are as follows:

- Apply different sets of policies to users with different requirements. For example, you might want to have a different desktop applied to accountants as compared to engineers. You can do this by specifying Group Policy objects (GPOs) that apply to the respective OUs.

- Delegate control of certain user and/or computer accounts to a subset of assistant administrators so that they can be responsible for accounts located within only a portion of the company and can perform activities such as resetting passwords and so on.

- Separate various types of objects. For example, you can use one OU to hold just client computers, another for member servers, another for domain controllers, and yet another for user and group accounts. In fact, Microsoft creates a default Domain Controller OU when you install Active Directory.

Physical Components of Active Directory

By contrast to the logical grouping of Active Directory into forests, trees, domains, and OUs, Microsoft includes physical components such as sites, domain controllers, global catalog servers, and operations masters. These items group components of a forest according to their physical locations as well as their particular functionalities in the forest.

Sites

Microsoft includes the concept of *sites* to group together resources within a forest according to their physical locations and/or subnets. A site is a set of one or more IP subnets that are connected by a high-speed, always available local area network (LAN) link. Figure 13-4 shows an example with two sites, one located in Chicago and the other in New York. A site can contain objects from more than one tree or domain within a single forest, and individual trees and domains can encompass more than one site. The use of sites enables you to control the replication of data within the Active Directory database as well as to apply policies to all users and computers or delegate administrative control to these objects within a single physical location. In addition, sites enable users to be authenticated by domain controllers in the same physical location rather than a distant location as often as possible. You should configure a single site for all work locations connected within a high-speed, always available LAN link, and designate additional sites for locations separated from each other by a slower wide area network (WAN) link.

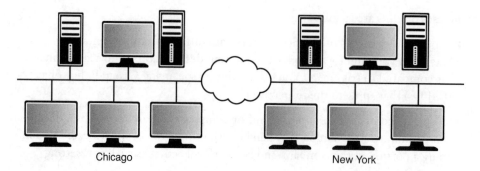

Figure 13-4 A site is a grouping of resources in one physical location and is distinct from any domain grouping.

Using sites permits you to configure Active Directory replication to take advantage of the high-speed connection. It also enables users to connect to a domain controller using a reliable, high-speed connection.

> **NOTE** The site topology of a network is different from the domain topology. Consequently, you can have one domain across more than one site, and you can have one site that contains multiple domains. You can even have multiple domains, each with portions thereof, on the same multiple sites.

Domain Controllers

Any server on which you have installed Active Directory is a *domain controller (DC)*. These servers authenticate all users logging on to the domain in which they are located, and they also serve as centers from which you can administer Active Directory in Windows Server 2012 R2. A domain controller stores a complete copy of all objects contained within the domain, plus the schema and configuration information relevant to the forest in which the domain is located. Unlike Windows NT, there are no primary or backup domain controllers. Similar to older Windows versions dating back to Windows 2000, all domain controllers hold a master, editable copy of the Active Directory database.

Every domain must have at least one DC. A domain can have more than one DC; having more than one DC provides the following benefits:

- **Fault tolerance:** If one domain controller goes down, another one is available to authenticate logon requests and locate resources through the directory.

- **Load balancing:** All domain controllers within a site participate equally in domain activities, thus spreading the load out over several servers. This configuration optimizes the speed at which requests are serviced.

Global Catalog Servers

The *global catalog* is a subset of domain information created for the purpose of enabling domain controllers in other domains in the same forest to locate resources in any domain. By default, the first domain controller installed in a new domain becomes a global catalog server. You can also designate additional domain controllers in the domain as global catalog servers. Doing so spreads out the task of locating resources between servers, thus facilitating response to user queries.

The global catalog server performs the following directory roles:

- **Locates objects within the forest:** When a user searches for objects such as people, folders, or printers, the global catalog enables her to locate objects in other domains within the forest. Active Directory automatically directs any search for the entire directory to the global catalog server.

- **Authenticates users by their UPNs:** When a user logs on to a domain other than his home domain using the UPN (for example, `user1@accounts.certguide.com` logging on to the `products.certguide.com` domain), the domain controller in the `products.certguide.com` domain contacts the global catalog server to obtain authentication information for this user.

- **Provides universal group membership information:** A universal group can include members from any domain in the forest, and its membership information, including permissions for resources assigned to it, is stored at the global catalog server. It supplies this information to a DC when a user who belongs to a universal group logs on. First introduced in Windows Server 2003, a DC can then cache this information to facilitate future logons by the same user.

Operations Masters

Microsoft designed Active Directory in such a fashion that you can perform most configuration activities from any domain controller. However, certain functions within the directory are restricted to specific domain controllers, which are known as *flexible single-master operations (FSMO) servers*, or simply as *operations masters*. These functions include the following:

- **Schema master:** Holds the only writable copy of the Active Directory schema. This is a configuration database that describes all available object and function types in the Active Directory forest. From an availability standpoint, the schema master is probably the least important role. Meaning, that the DC holding this role is required to be accessible only when schema updates are performed. For example, the schema must be updated during the deployment of Microsoft Exchange. To view the schema using the MMC, you must enable the .dll by executing the command `regsvr32 schmmgmt.dll` from a command prompt. Only one domain controller in the forest holds this role.

- **Domain naming master:** Ensures that any newly created domains are uniquely identified by names that adhere to the proper naming conventions for new trees or child domains in existing trees. This server must be online when adding or removing a domain in a forest. Only one domain controller in the forest holds this role.

- **PDC emulator:** It serves as a primary domain controller (PDC) for legacy servers, such as Windows NT 4.0 client computers, authenticating to the domain. Today, the PDC emulator functions to handle operations for legacy client logons and directory maintenance, including object changes or even password changes. A more current and critical function for this role is to act as a time synchronization master to synchronize the time on the remaining domain controllers in the domain. One domain controller in each domain holds this role. If you are planning any maintenance to this server, you might consider transferring the PDC emulator role to another domain controller in the domain using ntdsutil.exe.

- **Infrastructure master:** Updates references in its domain from objects such as domain group memberships to objects in other domains. If you add users from other domains into a group in your domain, you might notice that initially, the SID of the user account is displayed within the group. A few seconds later, the infrastructure master translates the SID into a friendly display name after it has looked up the necessary information. This server processes any changes in objects in the forest received from global catalog servers and replicates these changes to other domain controllers in its domain. One domain controller in each domain holds this role.

- **RID master:** Assigns security identifiers (SIDs) to objects created in its domain. A SID consists of a domain identifier common to all objects in its domain and a relative identifier (RID) that is unique to each object. This server ensures that no two objects have the same RID and hands out pools of RIDs to every domain controller in its domain. When moving objects between domains, you must start the move using the RID master of the domain containing the object. One domain controller in each domain holds this role.**NOTE**   Without functioning operations masters, an administrator will not be able to promote additional servers as domain controllers.

Ntdsutil

Ntdsutil.exe is a command-line tool used to manage Active Directory Domain Services and Active Directory Lightweight Directory Services. Administrators should take caution when using Ntdsutil. Ntdsutil.exe is most commonly used in the following situations:

- Perform database maintenance.

- Perform authoritative restores of deleted objects.

- Modify virtually any attribute of any object in the database.

- Manage and modify the FSMO roles. This can include transferring FSMO roles between online servers or seizing roles if a DC containing one or more roles fails unexpectedly. Seizing roles will enable you to force a specific DC to own a specific FSMO role.

- Manage directory partitions.

- Perform metadata cleanup of member servers, or even DCs that were removed without a clean demotion process.

- Manage directory snapshots.

NOTE   For more information on the use of Ntdsutil.exe, refer to "Ntdsutil" at http://technet.microsoft.com/en-us/library/cc753343.aspx.

NOTE   Without functioning operation masters, an administrator will not be able to promote additional servers as domain controllers. Furthermore, simple tasks such as logins can be impacted, especially if the server holding the PDC Emulator role is offline or inaccessible. You might be required to seize one or more FSMO roles to restore operation. When possible, it is always better to transfer roles.

New Features of Active Directory in Windows Server 2012 and Windows Server 2012 R2

As with previous versions of Active Directory, Microsoft has added new features and improved on others in Windows Server 2012 and Windows Server 2012 R2. Table 13-2 summarizes the more important improvements in Active Directory:

Table 13-2   New/Updated Features for Active Directory

Feature/ Functionality	Description	Windows Server 2012	Windows Server 2012 R2
Improved virtualization	Support for the capabilities of cloud-based computing has been added. In addition, Microsoft has improved the use of cloning for rapid deployment of virtual domain controllers.	X	X
Simplified deployment and upgrading	Microsoft has improved and streamlined the domain controller promotion wizard. This wizard is now integrated with Server Manager and supports the capabilities built in to Windows PowerShell. The wizard validates prerequisites, automates forest and domain preparation, and can install AD DS on a remote server.	X	X
Simplified management	Microsoft has added many new and improved management capabilities. These include a feature known as Dynamic Access Control (DAC), which enables you to centralize the management of access policies, directory attributes, file classification, and user and machine identities, all in one centralized location. Also, the Active Directory Administrative Center (ADAC) enables you to perform graphical tasks that automatically create the equivalent Windows PowerShell commands that you can use to create scripts that simplify the performance of repetitive administrative tasks.	X	X
AD DS platform improvements	Microsoft has improved the allocation and scaling of RIDs, deferred index creation, enhanced the Kerberos authentication protocol, and improved to Dynamic Access Control. The core functionality of the AD DS platform has also been improved.	X	X

Feature/ Functionality	Description	Windows Server 2012	Windows Server 2012 R2
Support for user-owned devices	Users are bringing more and more consumer devices such as smart phones and tablets to the workplace. Workplace Join in Windows Server 2012 R2 enables personal devices running Windows 8.1 and iOS to be authenticated to AD DS and become known to the corporate network. It also enables single-sign-on to workplace resources and applications.		X
Web Application Proxy	This is a new Remote Access role service in Windows Server 2012 R2 that enables access to websites and web-based applications by means of Active Directory Federation Services (AD FS) preauthentication. Users can connect to these applications and services from anywhere using Web Application Proxy.		X
Support for additional multifactor authentication and access control for sensitive applications	AD FS in Windows Server 2012 R2 enables improved multifactor authentication policies that facilitate user access to corporate resources while managing risks associated with these access types. Refer to the *Cert Guide* for exam 70-412 for more information on AD FS.		X

NOTE   For more information on the improvements to AD DS in Windows Server 2012 and Windows Server 2012 R2, refer to "What's New in Active Directory Domain Services (AD DS)" at http://technet.microsoft.com/en-us/library/hh831477.aspx and "What's New in Active Directory in Windows Server 2012 R2" at http://technet.microsoft.com/en-us/library/dn268294.aspx.

Planning the Active Directory Namespace

As already discussed, the domain is the primary administrative unit within an Active Directory namespace. Windows Server 2012 R2 uses the concept of domains to separate available resources among registered users. It is also the basic security unit, as you will see throughout this book, because many of the security requirements in

Active Directory are focused at the domain level. Therefore, it is important to begin the process of planning any company's Active Directory Domain Services (AD DS) namespace from the viewpoint of the domain structure.

All planning starts from the name of your company's root domain. Recall that each tree has a root domain located at the top of the inverted tree structure. All subdomains contain this root domain name in their own domain name. In addition, the first domain in the entire forest is not only a root domain, but is also the forest root. Also, the top-level domain names used on the Internet and defined in the DNS hierarchy are included. The latter is not an absolute requirement if you are planning a domain that has no Internet representation whatsoever, but what company these days does not have a presence on the Internet?

Therefore, it makes sense that your root domain can take the same name as your Internet domain name as registered with the Internet Corporation for Assigned Names and Numbers (ICANN) and Internet Assigned Numbers Authority (IANA), which took over in 1998 from InterNIC (Internet Network Information Center) as a master Internet domain registry. Consider a fictional company with an Internet domain name of `mycompany.biz`. Although you can use this name as your AD DS root domain name, it creates a risk of revealing your company's AD DS structure to the public Internet. Consequently, you might want to keep the internal name separate and use something like `mycompany.local` for the AD DS root domain name of the same fictional company.

Subdividing the Active Directory Namespace

You can subdivide your namespace within Active Directory in two ways:

- Separate domains
- Organizational units

In many instances, the use of separate domains or OUs would serve just as well as the other. In larger companies, the use of separate domains often arose from the limitations of the Security Accounts Manager (SAM) database in Windows NT. Because the AD DS database can hold millions of objects, this limitation is seldom of importance in AD DS design. For this reason, and because a single domain structure is the easiest type of structure to administer, this method is the best means of organizing your company's namespace if possible. There is no specific need to create separate domains for administrative functions, geographical sites, or departments in the company. Logically, you can handle this function by setting up a system of OUs. An internal system of OUs provides the following additional advantages:

- It can be administered either centrally or locally. The concept of delegation of control in AD DS facilitates the assignment of individuals as local administrators.

- User authentication is simpler and faster within a single domain environment, regardless of where a user is located.

- It is far simpler to modify when needed—for example, if your company is reorganized.

- It is flexible and can include an internal hierarchy of departments, sections, work units, and so on.

There are, however, reasons for using separate domains for discrete divisions of your company:

- This approach can facilitate decentralized administration of network resources.

- In the case of multiple Internet domain names, the domain can be built to mirror the Internet functionality.

- Multiple domains representing different geographical locations might reduce the amount of replication traffic across slow WAN links.

- User account requirements that vary among departments or locations, such as password complexity, are more easily handled with separate domains.

- International legal and language needs might be handled more easily by using separate domains.

- Very massive organizations can be broken down into a domain structure.

Administrative or Geographical Organization of Domains

You can organize a series of domains along either administrative or geographical means. For example, Figure 13-5 shows mycompany.biz organized along three administrative divisions—Accounting, Products, and Advertising—all reporting to a Management group. Contrast this with the company's main offices located in San Francisco, Dallas, Toronto, and Atlanta.

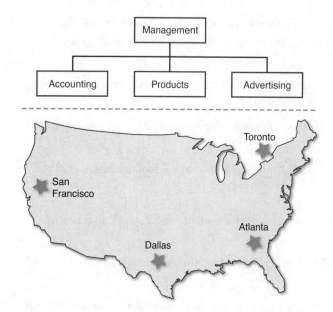

Figure 13-5   Administrative and geographical divisions of `mycompany.biz`.

You need to take into account conditions that favor either the administrative or geographical model. This can include the following factors:

- Plans for future offices in additional cities

- Projected growth of each of the company's divisions

- Potential for reorganization of the company along new departmental lines

- Requirements for centralized or decentralized administration of the company

- Needs for different security levels in either certain departments or certain offices

- Current or future use of one or more Internet DNS namespaces

Such factors suggest the best domain organization for your company's AD DS namespace.

Use of Multiple Trees

Within the AD DS forest, you can have one or more trees. As discussed earlier in this chapter, the main difference between trees and forests is that domains within a tree share a contiguous namespace, whereas domains located in different trees in the same forest have a disjointed namespace. Thus, `que.com` and `certguide.com` are root domains in two separate trees of the same forest.

In almost all multiple domain enterprises, it makes sense to employ a single tree. The major exception occurs when two companies merge and want to maintain their separate identities. Their identities, and indeed their Internet namespaces, are best served by having more than one tree in the forest.

NOTE   Another way of designing a multidomain forest is to employ an empty forest root domain, with a series of child domains representing administrative or geographical divisions of the company. The root domain contains only a small number of objects, and you can readily control membership in the Enterprise Admins and Schema Admins groups. The impact of business decisions, such as the spin-off or renaming of subsidiary companies, can be handled more readily. On the other hand, you must ensure that the forest root domain controllers are carefully secured and protected against disaster because their loss effectively destroys the entire forest structure.

Best Practices

Planning the AD DS domain structure is an act that has far-reaching implications. This process is something that cannot simply be decided by a few network administrators sitting down with a few diagrams of the network and company business structures. Rather, it must involve the company's senior and middle management as well as business strategy specialists and representatives from remote offices. If you use internally developed applications, representatives of the development team should be involved. The following guidelines will help you make your AD DS implementation proceed smoothly:

- **Know everything there is to know about the network:** Although this guideline might sound intuitive for senior administrators who have built the network from the ground up, those who have come on the scene more recently need to gather information about everything that must be accounted for in an AD DS plan.

- **Employ a test lab:** The lab should contain representative domain controllers, member servers, and client computers. Set up a mini version of your complete network, and engage the assistance of a representative set of users to test all facets of the implementation thoroughly.

- **Prepare thorough documentation:** This point can never be understated. Use tools such as Microsoft Visio to prepare diagrams of different levels of company detail, from the major administrative units down to the smallest workgroups. Visio is specifically designed for preparing administrative diagrams such as those required in this scenario. This exercise also helps in optimizing communication between technical individuals and top management.

- **Use an email distribution list to keep everyone informed:** When all concerned individuals have full access to the latest developments, unpleasant surprises are minimized.

- **Keep all employees informed:** Although the regular workers might not understand the details of what is happening, they should be informed of the summary points of any planned changes. They will then be much more able to cope with the changes. In addition, they could provide valuable feedback.

- **Ensure that all top managers know what's happening:** This point also can never be understated. This helps prevent unpleasant surprises and the need to redo portions of the planning process.

- **Understand thoroughly the network's TCP/IP infrastructure:** Your understanding helps in designing the network and DNS configuration that is the foundation of the AD DS infrastructure. It is especially true in developing the proper site structure, as you will study in the *Cert Guide* book for exam 70-412.

- **Develop and adhere to an adequate security policy:** Thoroughly review any security policy your company already has in place. Apply the policy's constraints to the proper design of your company's domain structure. Make any appropriate changes as you develop the AD DS infrastructure.

- **Know the capabilities of your WAN links:** If your network includes slow WAN links, test and monitor the use of these links before and during the AD DS implementation to ensure that you have the optimum configuration.

Creating Forests and Domains

After you have created a comprehensive plan for your organization's AD DS structure, you are almost ready to begin the installation. The first task you must perform is to install the first domain controller for the forest root domain.

Requirements for Installing Active Directory Domain Services

Before you can install AD DS, you must have at least one server that meets the following requirements:

- **Operating system:** The server must be running any edition (Foundation, Essentials, Standard, or Datacenter) of Windows Server 2012 R2.

- **Adequate hard disk space:** Beyond the space used for installing Windows Server 2012 R2, the server must have a minimum of 500 MB of disk space for the Active Directory database and SYSVOL folder, plus at least 100 MB for the transaction log files. The larger the proposed network, the more disk space is necessary, and in practical terms you should have several gigabytes of available space at a minimum. In particular, ensure that space is available for the Active Directory Recycle Bin, which holds deleted objects and their attributes until cleared.

- **A disk volume formatted with the NTFS file system:** This ensures security of the database; furthermore, it is required for the SYSVOL folder. Windows Server 2012 R2 creates an NTFS partition by default when installed.

TIP   It is strongly recommend that you use a fault-tolerant disk volume such as RAID-1 (disk mirroring) or RAID-5 (disk striping with parity) for the Active Directory files. This enables the domain controller to function in the event of a disk failure until the failed disk can be replaced. However, fault-tolerant disks are no substitute for regular backups of Active Directory. Backups are discussed in the *Cert Guide* for exam 70-411.

- **A DNS server:** Active Directory requires that a DNS server that supports service (SRV) resource records be present. This can be any server running Windows 2000 or later or a UNIX server running Berkeley Internet Name Domain (BIND) 4.9.7 or later. If you want to integrate the DNS database with Active Directory, you should install DNS on the same server on which you install AD DS. If the Active Directory installation wizard cannot find a suitable DNS server, you will be prompted to install one. DNS is discussed in Chapter 12, "Deploying and Configuring Domain Name System (DNS)."

- **Administrative privileges:** You must be logged on with an account that has the appropriate administrative privileges. For the first domain controller, this is a local administrator. To add a domain to an existing forest, you must be a member of the Enterprise Admins group in this forest, and to add a domain controller to an existing domain, you must be a member of the Domain Admins or Enterprise Admins group in this domain. Group memberships are discussed in Chapter 15, "Active Directory Groups and Organizational Units."

Installing Active Directory Domain Services

As in previous versions of Windows Server, Active Directory provides the Active Directory Installation Wizard that handles all aspects of installing or removing

Active Directory. As in Windows Server 2008, you install AD DS first in Windows Server 2012 or Windows Server 2012 R2 and then install a domain controller. You can install AD DS without installing a domain controller if you are configuring your server for a directory-related application such as Exchange Server. This section takes a look at the use of this wizard for installing different types of domain controllers.

You can start the Active Directory Installation Wizard from the Add Roles and Features Wizard in Server Manager or by using PowerShell cmdlets. The following sections describe the use of the Add Roles and Features Wizard for installing AD DS.

NOTE   Microsoft has depreciated `dcpromo.exe` beginning with Windows Server 2012 R2. You can still use this utility with an answer file for installing a domain controller in Windows Server 2012 R2. For more information, refer to "How to use unattended mode to install and remove Active Directory Domain Services on Windows Server 2008-based domain controllers" at http://support.microsoft.com/kb/947034.

New Forests

As already noted, the first domain installed is the root domain in its forest. You must be a local administrator on the server on which you install Active Directory to proceed. The following procedure describes the installation of the first domain:

1. From the Dashboard of Server Manager, click **Manage** > **Add Roles and Features**.

2. The Add Roles and Features Wizard starts with a Select installation type page. Ensure that the default of **Role-based** or **feature-based** installation is selected; then click **Next**.

3. On the Select destination server page, ensure that the **Select a server from the server pool** option (the default) is selected and select your local server from the list displayed. Then click **Next**.

4. The Select Server Roles page enables you to select the roles you want to install on your server. Select **Active Directory Domain Services** (as shown in Figure 13-6). If you receive a dialog box asking to install features that are required for AD DS, click **Add Features** to accept the installation of these features and return to the Select Server Roles page. Then click **Next**.

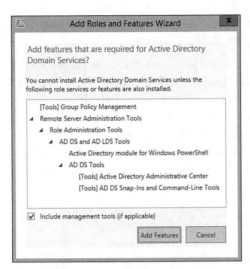

Figure 13-6 You can use the Add Roles and Features Wizard to begin the installation of AD DS.

5. On the Select Features page, select any additional sever features you want to install on the server, and then click **Next**.

6. The Active Directory Domain Services page shown in Figure 13-7 provides you with information and items to note about AD DS. Read the information provided. When finished, click **Next**.

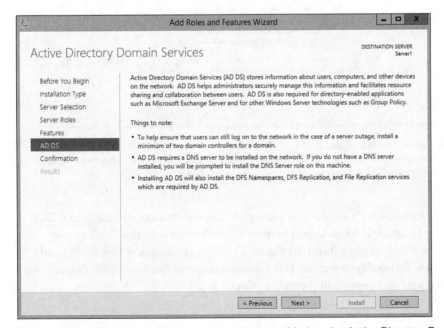

Figure 13-7 Note the information and cautions provided on the Active Directory Domain Services page of the Add Roles and Features Wizard.

7. Note the information provided on the Confirm installation selections page, and then click **Install** to begin installing Active Directory.

8. The wizard displays an Installation Progress page that charts the progress of installation. After a few minutes, it displays the page shown in Figure 13-8 that informs you that the AD DS role has been installed successfully. If you want to use the settings configured here on another server, click the link labeled **Export configuration settings**. To proceed with installing a domain controller, click the link labeled **Promote this server to domain controller**. If you want to promote the server later, click **Close** to exit the wizard and return to Server Manager.

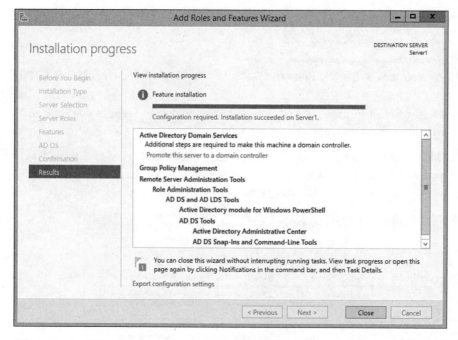

Figure 13-8   When the Add Roles and Features Wizard completes the installation of AD DS, you are provided with this page that informs you of the tools that have been installed and provides a link to begin promoting the server to domain controller.

9. After you click **Promote this server to domain controller**, the Active Directory Domain Services Configuration Wizard starts with the Deployment Configuration page shown in Figure 13-9. To create a new forest, click **Add a new forest**. Type the full DNS domain name of the forest root domain (for example, que.com), and then click **Next**.

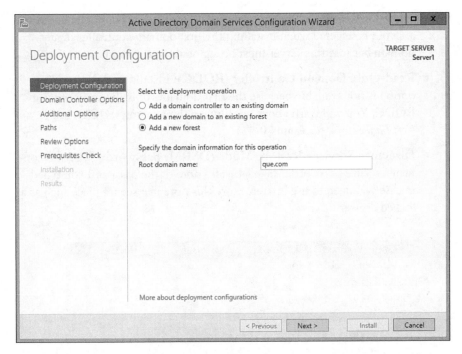

Figure 13-9   The Active Directory Domain Services Configuration Wizard provides you with choices of adding a domain controller to an existing domain, adding a new domain to an existing forest, or creating a new forest.

NOTE   You should not use a single-level domain name when creating your forest root. Best practices for naming your AD DS root domain stipulate that domain names should consist of two or more labels separated by the dot "." character. For more information, refer to "Deployment and operation of Active Directory domains that are configured by using single-label DNS names"" at http://support.microsoft.com/kb/300684.

10. The wizard displays the Domain Controller Options page shown in Figure 13-10. Configure the following options, and then click **Next**:

- **Forest and Domain functional levels:** You have four available functional levels for both the forest and domain. These determine the features AD DS will support, as well as the operating system permitted on domain controllers. The available domain and forest functional levels are discussed later in this chapter.

- **DNS Server:** Installs DNS on this server. This option is selected by default when first installing AD DS because DNS is required for Active Directory.

- **Global Catalog:** Installs a global catalog server. This option is not available but is selected when installing the first domain controller in any domain because this server must be a global catalog server.

- **Read-Only Domain Controller (RODC):** Installs an RODC. This option is not available because the first domain controller cannot be an RODC. You will learn about installing and managing RODCs in the *Cert Guide* book for exam 70-411.

- **Directory Services Restore Mode (DSRM) password:** Type and confirm a secure password. Make a careful note of the password you typed in case you need to use it later. Store this note in a secure place such as a locked drawer.

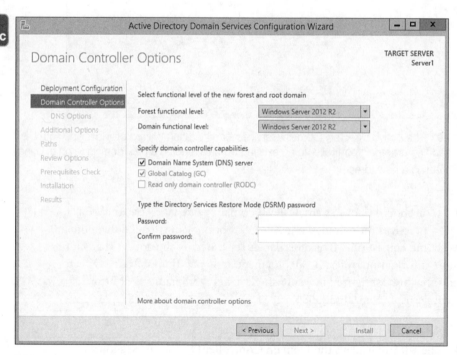

Figure 13-10 The Domain Controller Options page enables you to specify several important options.

11. If you are installing DNS on the server, you will see the DNS Options page, which enables you to specify DNS delegation options. You might receive a message informing you that a delegation for the DNS server will not be created if you are installing DNS on this server. If so, you should manually create this delegation later. If available and desired, select the **Create DNS delegation** check box, and then click **Next**.

12. The Additional Options page enables you to modify the NetBIOS domain name used by pre-Windows 2000 client computers to authenticate to the domain. Change this name if necessary, and then click **Next**.

13. Confirm the locations provided for the database, log files, and SYSVOL folders as displayed on the Paths page. If you want to change any of these locations, type the desired path or click **Browse**. When finished, click **Next**.

> **TIP** When setting up a domain controller on a production network, you should place the database and log folders on a separate drive from the SYSVOL folder. The reason for doing so is to improve only I/O performance; this does not improve security or fault tolerance, as an exam question might lead you to believe.

14. The wizard provides a Review Options page, shown in Figure 13-11. Review the information provided on this page. If you want to change any settings, click **Previous** and make the appropriate changes. If you want to export information to a PowerShell script, click **View script** and save this script with an appropriate pathname and filename. When done, click **Next** to continue.

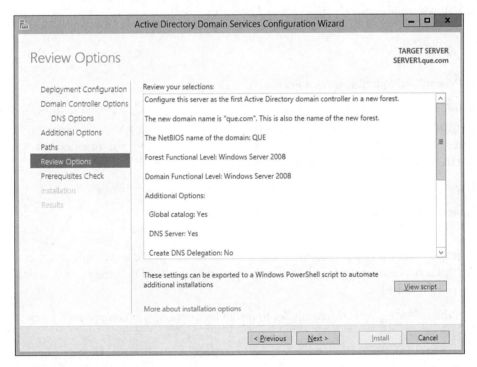

Figure 13-11   The wizard provides a Review Options page that enables you to review the settings you've specified.

15. After a minute or two, the wizard displays a Prerequisites Check page, which informs you of any prerequisites you might need to validate before the domain controller installation proceeds. Review the information presented on this page, and correct any problems that might be displayed. Also make note of any cautionary messages that appear. When ready to proceed, click **Install**.

16. The wizard proceeds to promote the server to domain controller. Note any messages that might appear on the Progress section of the Installation page. When the Results page appears, verify that the server was successfully promoted to domain controller. The server will restart automatically to complete the installation process.

> **NOTE**   For more information on installing AD DS and promoting your server to domain controller, refer to "Install Active Directory Domain Services (Level 100)" at http://technet.microsoft.com/en-us/library/hh472162.aspx, "Install a New Windows Server 2012 Active Directory Forest (Level 200)" at http://technet.microsoft.com/en-us/library/jj574166.aspx, and "Step-by-Step Guide for Setting Up Windows Server 2012 Domain Controller" at http://social.technet.microsoft.com/wiki/contents/articles/12370.step-by-step-guide-for-setting-up-windows-server-2012-domain-controller.aspx.

Using PowerShell to Install a New Forest Root Domain

Windows PowerShell enables you to install AD DS and promote servers to domain controllers. You need to use this method if you are promoting a Server Core computer to domain controller. As with the GUI-based installation, you first need to install the AD DS server role and then perform the promotion.

Use the following PowerShell cmdlet to install the AD DS server role:

```
Install-windowsfeature -name AD-Domain-Services
-IncludeManagementTools
```

In this cmdlet, the -name parameter specifies installation of the server role and the -IncludeManagementTools parameter specifies that the AD DS management tools are to be installed.

Use the following PowerShell cmdlet to install the first domain controller in a new forest:

```
Install-ADDSForest [-SkipPreChecks] -DomainName <string>
-SafeModeAdministratorPassword <SecureString> [-CreateDNSDelegation]
[-DatabasePath <string>] [-DNSDelegationCredential <PS Credential>]
[-NoDNSOnNetwork] [-DomainMode <DomainMode> { Win2008 | Win2008R2 |
 Win2012 | Win2012R2}] [-DomainNetBIOSName <string>] [-ForestMode
<ForestMode> { Win2008 | Win2008R2 | Win2012 | Win2012R2}] [-InstallDNS]
[-LogPath <string>] [-NoRebootOnCompletion] [-SkipAutoConfigureDNS]
[-SYSVOLPath] [-Force] [-WhatIf] [-Confirm] [<CommonParameters>]
```

Only the domain name is absolutely required. All other parameters (mentioned in
square brackets) are optional. Table 13-3 describes the more important parameters of
the Install-ADDSForest cmdlet. Detailed descriptions of each parameter example,
and of additional parameters not mentioned here are found in "Install Active Directory Domain Services (Level 100)" referenced in the preceding note.

Table 13-3 Important Parameters of the Install-ADDSForest cmdlet

Parameter	Description
-SafeModeAdministratorPassword	Specifies the password used for the administrator password to be used when restarting the computer in Safe Mode or Directory Services Restore Mode. Use a secure value and keep a note of this password in a secure location for later use.
-CreateDNSDelegation	Specifies whether to create a DNS delegation that references the new DNS server being installed with the domain controller.
-DatabasePath	Specifies the local path to a folder on the fixed disk of the local computer for the AD DS database file. The default is %systemroot%\ntds.
-DomainMode	Specifies the domain functional level to be used.
-DomainNetBIOSName	Specifies a NetBIOS name to be associated with the new forest root domain.
-ForestMode	Specifies the forest functional level to be used.
-InstallDNS	Specifies whether the DNS Server service is to be installed and configured. By default, a DNS server is installed on the first domain controller in a new forest.
-SYSVOLPath	Specifies the local path to a folder on the fixed disk of the local computer for the SYSVOL shared folder. The default is %systemroot%\sysvol.
-Confirm	Prompts you for confirmation before installing the domain controller.

Use the following steps to install AD DS with a new forest with root domain name
`certguide.com`:

1. Type `Install-windowsfeature -name AD-Domain-Services
   -IncludeManagementTools` and press **Enter**.

2. Wait while Windows installs the AD DS server role. You are informed when
   installation is complete.

3. Type `Install-ADDSForest -domainname "certguide.com"` and press **Enter**.

4. Windows asks for `-safemodeadministratorpassword`. Type a secure password, which acts as the Directory Services Restore mode password and is also
   an administrative password to be used if you uninstall the domain later. Then
   press **Enter**.

5. Windows asks you to confirm this password. Retype the password you've
   entered, and press **Enter**.

6. The process of promoting the server to domain controller takes several minutes. Make a note of all messages displayed during this process. When the
   installation finishes, you are informed of the success or failure of the process,
   and the computer restarts automatically.

7. After the computer restarts, log on as the default administrator using the
   password utilized with the local administrator account that previously existed
   before the server was promoted.

TIP   If you are planning to install and promote several domain controllers, you
might consider creating a PowerShell script. Configure your settings using Notepad and save the file as a `.ps1` extension.

New Domains in Existing Forests

After you have installed the forest root domain, you can add child domains or
domain trees to the forest. Either procedure is similar to the procedure already outlined for creating a forest root domain, as follows:

1. Follow the procedure to install AD DS, and start the Active Directory Installation wizard as described in the previous section until you receive the Deployment Configuration page previously shown in Figure 13-9.

2. On this page, select **Add a new domain to an existing forest**. Specify the
   name of the forest root domain in the text box provided, and then click **Next**.

3. On the Domain Controller Options page (which is similar to that shown previously in Figure 13-10), specify the domain functional level and select the capabilities for DNS server and/or global catalog. Also specify a site name if different from the default of Default-First-Site-Name; type and confirm the Directory Services Restore Mode password. When finished, click **Next**.

4. Complete the installation of the domain controller according to steps 11–15 of the previous procedure.

To use PowerShell to create a child domain or new domain tree, utilize the following cmdlet:

```
Install-ADDSDomain -NewDomainName <string> -ParentDomainName <string>
```

where the `-NewDomainName` parameter specifies the name of the domain being created and `-ParentDomainName` specifies the name of the parent domain. You can also use any of the parameters previously included with the `-InstallADDSForest` cmdlet and already described.

> **NOTE**   For more information on creating child domains or new domain trees, refer to "Install a New Windows Server 2012 Active Directory Child or Tree Domain (Level 200)" at http://technet.microsoft.com/en-us/library/jj574105.aspx.

Existing Domains

Installing additional domain controllers in an existing domain is important for the following reasons:

- Doing so adds fault tolerance and load balancing to the domain. In other words, additional domain controllers help share the load and improve performance.

- Users logging on to the domain can connect to any available domain controller for authentication.

- Users at a remote location can connect to a domain controller at their site rather than making a slow connection across a WAN link.

- If a domain controller should become unavailable because of a network or hardware failure, users can still log on to the domain.

To install an additional domain controller in an existing domain, follow the same procedure as in the previous section, except select the **Add a domain controller to an existing domain** option previously shown in Figure 13-9. Then specify the domain to which you are adding the domain controller in the text box provided on this page. The remainder of the procedure is the same as that for creating a new domain in an existing forest, except that the Set Domain Functional Level page does not appear.

You can also use PowerShell to add another domain controller to an existing domain. Use the following cmdlet:

```
Install-ADDSDomainController -DomainName <string>
```

where the `DomainName` parameter specifies the name of the domain into which you are installing the domain controller. You can also use most of the parameters previously included with the `-InstallADDSForest` cmdlet described earlier in this section.

> **NOTE**   For more information on installing additional domain controllers in an existing domain, refer to "Install a Replica Windows Server 2012 Domain Controller in an Existing Domain (Level 200)" at http://technet.microsoft.com/en-us/library/jj574134.aspx.

Performing Unattended Installations of Active Directory

Windows Server 2012 R2 enables you to specify parameters for Active Directory installation in an answer file that you can use to facilitate the installation of multiple domain controllers. This file is formatted as a simple text file containing the statement [DCINSTALL] on the first line followed by statements in the form *option=value*.

To perform unattended installations of AD DS (or to script the installation of multiple domain controllers, you can use the `dcpromo` command, as follows:

```
dcpromo [/answer[:<filename>] | /unattend[:<filename>] | /unattend
| /adv] /uninstallBinaries [/CreateDCAccount | /UseExistingAccount:Attach]
/? /?[:{Promotion | CreateDCAccount | UseExistingAccount | Demotion}]
```

Where `/answer` or `/unattend` is used to specify the answer file named `<filename>`; `/adv` is used to perform an install from media (IFM) operation; `/UninstallBinaries` uninstalls AD DS binaries; `/CreateDCAccount` creates an RODC account; `/UseExistingAccount` attaches a server to an existing RODC account; and `/demotion` specifies demotion of an existing domain controller to a member server or standalone server.

Table 13-4 describes several of the more common options you can use in the answer file.

Table 13-4   Several Options Used for Unattended Domain Controller Installation

Option	Value	Meaning
UserName	Username of administrative user	Installs the domain controller in the context of this user.
Password	User's password | *	Specifies the password of user installing the domain controller. Use * to prompt for the password.
ReplicaOrNewDomain	Domain | Replica | ReadOnlyReplica	Specifies whether to install a new domain, an additional domain controller (replica) in an existing domain, or a RODC in an existing domain.
ReplicaDomainDNSName	Existing domain name	Specifies the fully qualified domain name (FQDN) of the domain in which you are installing an additional domain controller.
NewDomain	Forest | Tree | Child	Specifies whether to install a new forest, a new tree in an existing forest, or a child domain.
NewDomainDNSName	Domain name to be created	Specifies the FQDN for a new domain.
ParentDomainDNSName	Parent domain name	Specifies the FQDN of the parent domain when creating a child domain.
ChildName	Child domain name	Specifies the top level DNS name of the child domain. This name is prefixed to the parent name to create the FQDN of the child domain.
ForestLevel	3 | 4 | 5 | 6	Specifies the forest functional level of a new forest: 3 = Windows Server 2008 4 = Windows Server 2008 R2 5 = Windows Server 2012 6 = Windows Server 2012 R2
DomainLevel	3 | 4 | 5 | 6	Specifies the domain functional level of a new domain. Parameters have the same meaning as for ForestLevel.

Option	Value	Meaning
InstallDNS	Yes | No	Specifies whether a DNS server is installed.
ConfirmGC	Yes | No	Specifies whether the domain controller is installed as a global catalog server.
DatabasePath	Path to database folder	Default is `%systemroot%\NTDS`
LogPath	Path to log folder	Default is `%systemroot%\NTDS`
SysvolPath	Path to SYSVOL folder	Default is `%systemroot%\SYSVOL`
RebootOnCompletion	Yes | No	Specifies whether to restart the computer on completion, regardless of success.

The output to the `dcpromo` command will track the progress of promotion, and then the server will automatically reboot if the `RebootOnCompletion` parameter has been specified.

Many additional options are available, including options specific to the demotion of domain controllers. For additional information, consult "Dcpromo" at http://technet.microsoft.com/en-us/library/cc732887.aspx.

Adding, Removing, and Upgrading Domain Controllers

Many organizations have created Active Directory domains based on Windows Server 2003/2008/R2 domain controllers, and are now in a position to take advantage of the new features of Windows Server 2012 and Windows Server 2012 R2 Active Directory. You can add new Windows Server 2012 R2 domain controllers to an existing older Active Directory forest, or upgrade all domain controllers in the forest to Windows Server 2012 R2.

As summarized earlier in this chapter, Active Directory in Windows Server 2012 R2 introduces several additional features not supported by previous versions of Windows Server. Many of these features limit the interoperability of Windows Server 2012 R2 with previous versions, and Microsoft has extended the concept of domain and forest functional levels to define the actions that can be done on a network that includes older domain controllers.

This section takes a look at these functional levels and the tools used for upgrading an older Active Directory network to Windows Server 2012 R2.

Forest and Domain Functional Levels

As you noticed when installing your first domain controller (refer back to Figure 13-10), several domain and forest functional levels are available. Table 13-5 summarizes the forest and domain functional levels supported by Active Directory in Windows Server 2012 R2.

Table 13-5   Forest and Domain Functional Levels in Windows Server 2012 R2 Active Directory

Forest Functional Level	Domain Functional Levels Supported	Domain Controllers Supported
Windows Server 2008	Windows Server 2008	Windows Server 2008
	Windows Server 2008 R2	Windows Server 2008 R2
	Windows Server 2012	Windows Server 2012
	Windows Server 2012 R2	Windows Server 2012 R2
Windows Server 2008 R2	Windows Server 2008 R2	Windows Server 2008 R2
	Windows Server 2012 R2	Windows Server 2012 R2
Windows Server 2012	Windows Server 2012	Windows Server 2012
	Windows Server 2012 R2	Windows Server 2012 R2
Windows Server 2012 R2	Windows Server 2012 R2	Windows Server 2012 R2

To make use of the functionality provided by Windows Server 2012 R2 Active Directory, you must upgrade all domain controllers to Windows Server 2012 R2 and upgrade the functional levels accordingly. A domain running at the Windows Server 2012 R2 domain functional level located in a forest running at a lower functional level supports domain-based Windows Server 2012 R2 Active Directory features but not forest-based ones.

Furthermore, to make use of the newest Active Directory features in Windows Server 2012 R2, you must upgrade all domain controllers to Windows Server 2012 R2 and upgrade the domain and forest functional levels accordingly.

Windows Server 2012 R2 does not support the Windows 2000 or Windows Server 2003 mixed or native functional levels previously found in older Active Directory networks. If you still have any domain controllers running Windows 2003 or older, you must upgrade or remove these domain controllers before introducing a Windows Server 2012 R2 domain controller on your network.

To raise the forest functional level, you must first raise the functional level of all domains in the forest to the same or higher domain functional level. To raise the domain functional level, perform any of the following three actions:

- Open the Active Directory Administrative Center snap-in, right-click your domain, and then choose **Raise the domain functional level**.

- Open the Active Directory Users and Computers snap-in. Right-click **Active Directory Users and Computers** and choose **All Tasks > Raise domain functional level**.

- Open the Active Directory Domains and Trusts snap-in, right-click your domain, and choose **Raise domain functional level**.

In the dialog box shown in Figure 13-12, select the appropriate functional level and click **Raise**. Then click **OK** to accept the warning that is displayed.

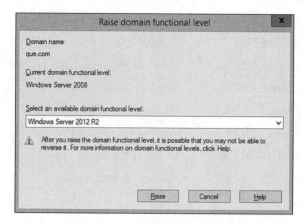

Figure 13-12   Raising the domain functional level.

To raise the forest functional level, access the Active Directory Domains and Trusts snap-in. Right-click **Active Directory Domains and Trusts** and select **Raise forest functional level**. Select the appropriate functional level, click **Raise**, and then click **OK** to accept the warning that is displayed. You can also right-click your domain name in the Active Directory Administrative Center, choose **Raise the forest functional level,** and then follow the same procedure described here.

WARNING   It is important to remember that raising forest and domain functional levels is a one-way operation. You cannot go back to a lower functional level. In addition, you cannot introduce an older domain controller after you have raised the domain functional level.

NOTE   For additional information on domain and forest functional level upgrades, refer to "Understanding Active Directory Domain Services (AD DS) Functional Levels" at http://technet.microsoft.com/library/understanding-active-directory-functional-levels%28WS.10%29.aspx.

The `Adprep` **Utility**

Windows Server 2012 R2 simplifies the forest and domain upgrade process by integrating the `Adprep` utility into the AD DS installation, whether you perform the installation from Server Manager or by using PowerShell as already described in this chapter. When you are upgrading an older forest or domain to Windows Server 2012 R2, the schema and infrastructure master roles in the domain are automatically targeted at the time the first Windows Server 2012 R2 is added, and then the required `Adprep` commands are run remotely to prepare these servers for the new Windows Server 2012 R2 domain controller.

You can still run `Adprep` as required on 64-bit domain controllers running Windows Server 2008 or later. You can run `Adprep` remotely, and you must run it remotely if the targeted operations master role is hosted on a Windows Server 2003 machine or a 32-bit Windows Server 2008 machine.

The `Adprep` utility has the following options:

- **`Adprep /forestprep`:** Prepares the forest for Windows Server 2012 R2 domain controllers. It is run on the schema master of the forest, and extends the schema to receive the new Windows Server 2012 R2 enhancements. After this command is run, its changes must be allowed to replicate across all domains of the forest.

- **`Adprep /domainprep`:** Prepares a domain for Windows Server 2012 R2 domain controllers. It is run on the infrastructure master of each domain in which Windows Server 2012 R2 domain controllers are to be installed or upgraded. It adjusts access control lists (ACLs) on Active Directory objects and on the `SYSVOL` shared folder for proper access by Windows Server 2012 R2 domain controllers.

- **`Adprep /rodcprep`:** Prepares a domain for adding RODCs by updating permissions on application directory partitions to enable replication of these partitions to RODCs. It contacts the infrastructure master in each domain to update these permissions.

NOTE   For more information on the `Adprep` command, refer to "Changes Made by `Adprep.exe`" at http://technet.microsoft.com/en-us/library/hh994609.aspx, and references cited therein.

> **TIP**   Remember that you must run `adprep /forestprep` on the schema master, and that you must run this command before you run `adprep /domainprep`. Also remember that you must run `adprep /domainprep` on the infrastructure master of each domain in which you want to introduce a Windows Server 2012 or Windows Server 2012 R2 domain controller and that you must complete these commands before promoting or upgrading an existing domain controller.

Upgrading a Windows Server 2008 Domain Controller

You can upgrade a server running Windows Server 2008 R2 or the original version of Windows Server 2012 to Windows Server 2012 R2. A server running Windows Server 2008 R2 must be running SP1 or higher to be upgraded. The available upgrade path depends on the edition of Windows Server 2008 that you are running, as follows:

- You can upgrade the Web Server edition of Windows Server 2008 R2 to the Standard edition of Windows Server 2012 R2.

- You can upgrade either the Standard or Enterprise edition of Windows Server 2008 R2 or the Standard edition of Windows Server 2012 to either the Standard or Datacenter edition of Windows Server 2012 R2.

- If you are running the Datacenter edition of Windows Server 2008 R2 or Windows Server 2012, you must upgrade to the Datacenter edition of Windows Server 2012 R2.

You cannot upgrade Windows 2000 or Windows Server 2003 servers to Windows Server 2012 R2 directly; you must perform a clean installation of Windows Server 2012 R2, or upgrade to Windows Server 2008 R2 and then upgrade to Windows Server 2012 R2.

Use the following procedure to upgrade a Windows Server 2008 R2 computer to Windows Server 2012 R2:

1. Ensure that the server to be upgraded meets system requirements. Refer to Chapter 1, "Introducing Windows Server 2012 R2," for more information.

2. Verify the compatibility of Active Directory-integrated applications such as Microsoft Configuration Manager, Microsoft SharePoint Server, Microsoft System Server, Exchange Server, and SQL Server.

3. Verify security settings.

4. Check the availability of required operations master roles. These relate to the ability of the installation wizard to run the `Adprep /domainprep` and `Adprep /forestprep` operations, and are as follows:

- To install the first Windows Server 2012 R2 in an existing domain or forest, you need connectivity to the schema master in order to run `adprep /forestprep` and the infrastructure master in order to run `adprep /domainprep`. The various operations master roles were introduced earlier in this chapter.

- To install the first domain controller in a domain in which the forest has been upgraded, you need connectivity to the infrastructure master.

- To install or remove a domain in an existing forest, you need connectivity to the domain naming master.

- To install a RODC in an existing forest, you need connectivity to the infrastructure master for each application directory partition.

- For any domain controller installation or upgrade, you also need connectivity to the RID master.

5. Ensure that you are logged on with the appropriate credentials to perform the installation or upgrade. To install a new domain in an existing forest or to run `adprep /rodcprep`, you must supply Enterprise Admins credentials. To install an additional domain controller in an existing domain or to run `adprep /domainprep`, you must be logged on as a member of the Domain Admins group. To run `adprep /forestprep` for upgrading an AD DS forest, you must be logged on with an account that is member of Schema Admins, Enterprise Admins, and Domain Admins. For more information on these and other groups in AD DS, refer to Chapter 15, "Active Directory Groups and Organizational Units (OUs)."

6. Insert the Windows Server 2012 R2 DVD and follow the instructions provided by the installation wizard. Refer to Chapter 2, "Installing and Configuring Windows Server 2012 R2," for detailed installation instructions.

NOTE   For more information on upgrading domain controllers (and servers in general) to Windows Server 2012 R2, refer to "Upgrade Options for Windows Server 2012 R2" at http://technet.microsoft.com/en-us/library/dn303416.aspx.

Removing Active Directory

Server Manager also enables you to remove Active Directory from a domain controller, thereby demoting it to a member server. Proceed as follows:

1. From Server Manager, click **Manage** > **Remove Roles and Features**.

2. The Remove Roles and Features Wizard starts with the Select destination server page. Ensure that the default option of **Select a server from the server pool** is selected, and then select the proper server from the list displayed. By default, this is the server on which you are performing this action. Select a different server to remotely remove Active Directory. Then click **Next**.

3. On the Remove Server Roles page, clear the check box labeled **Active Directory Domain Services**.

4. The message box shown in Figure 13-13 opens, which gives you the option of removing tools associated with AD DS or retain them to manage other domain controllers. If you want to retain these tools, clear the check box labeled **Remove management tools** (if applicable), which is selected by default; then click **Remove Features**.

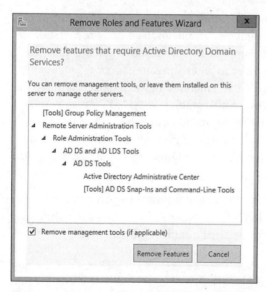

Figure 13-13   When you demote a domain controller, you are given the option to remove features and management tools associated with AD DS.

5. The message box shown in Figure 13-14 displays, warning you that you must demote the domain controller. Click **Demote this domain controller**.

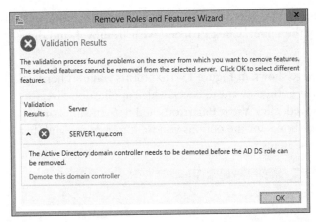

Figure 13-14   You are informed you must demote the domain controller to remove the AD DS server role.

6. On the Credentials page shown in Figure 13-15, verify that the user account specified is appropriate, or click **Change** to use an alternative user account. Note all the warnings displayed about the effects of removing a domain. Select the check box labeled **Force the removal of this domain controller** if previous attempts to uninstall AD DS have failed. Select the check box labeled **Last domain controller in this domain** only if you are removing the last domain controller from its domain. Then click **Next**.

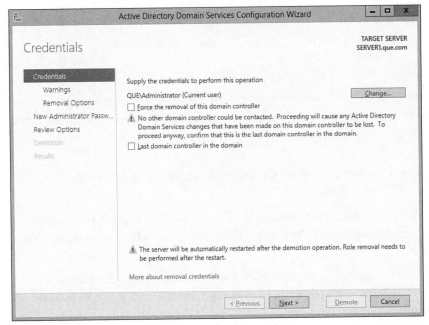

Figure 13-15   The Credentials page warns you of the effects of deleting the domain controller.

7. The Warnings page informs you of other roles, such as DNS Server and global catalog, hosted by the server. Click **Proceed with Removal**, and then click **Next** to continue.

8. The Removal Options page shown in Figure 13-16 informs you of other items that you might be removing. If you want to check which application directory partitions might be removed, click **View Partitions** and note the information supplied. Select the check boxes for the options you want to remove, and then click **Next** to remove these items.

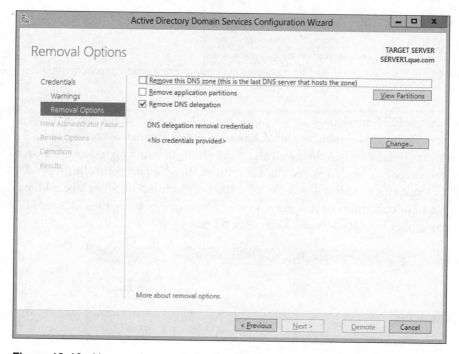

Figure 13-16 You are given several options to remove additional items from the domain controller.

9. Type and confirm a password for the local Administrator account on the server; then click **Next**.

10. Read the information provided on the Review Options page. If you need to make any changes, click **Previous**. When ready, click **Demote** to demote the server.

11. When the demotion is finished, click **Finish**, and then click **Restart** now to restart the server. To reboot the server automatically, select the **Reboot on Completion** check box.

After the server has restarted, you will need to run the Remove Roles and Features Wizard again to completely remove the AD DS server role unless you want to retain this role for managing other domain controllers or managing a directory-related server application such as Exchange Server or Active Directory Lightweight Directory Services (AD LDS).

NOTE You can also use the `Uninstall-WindowsFeature` cmdlet in Windows PowerShell to demote the domain controller. This cmdlet has similar options to those in the `Install-WindowsFeature` cmdlet used for installing AD DS. For more information on removing AD DS, refer to "Remove Active Directory Domain Services (Level 100)" at http://technet.microsoft.com/en-us/library/hh472163(v=ws.11).

Installing a Server Core Domain Controller

You cannot use Server Manager to promote a Server Core machine to a domain controller. You can use Windows PowerShell as already described to install the AD DS binaries and then promote the computer to domain controller. You can also use `dcpromo.exe` with an unattended installation answer file in a similar manner to that described earlier in this chapter. This file must include the information required to identify the domain being joined, including the username and password for a domain administrator account.

NOTE For further information on the use of Server Core, including its use as a domain controller, refer to "Install Server Roles and Features on a Server Core Server" at http://technet.microsoft.com/en-us/library/jj574158.aspx.

Using the Install from Media Option

Beginning with Windows Server 2008, Microsoft has provided the ability to install AD DS from media. The purpose of this function is to enable you to streamline deployments by minimizing replication traffic for Active Directory data over the network. This is especially helpful when installing multiple domain controllers or domain controllers at branch sites that might have low-speed/higher-latency links.

The `ntdsutil` command-line tool enables you to configure a deployment package to use for the installation from media (IFM) option. Using `ntdsutil`, you can create four types of installation packages as outlined in Table 13-6.

Table 13-6   Install from Media Options

Installation Media	Ntdsutil Parameter	Description
Full	Create Full [output path for media folder]	Creates installation media for a writable domain controller or AD Light Weight Directory Services.
RODC	Create RODC [output path for media folder]	Creates installation media to be used for a Read Only Domain Controller.

> **NOTE**   Installation media cannot be used between different versions of Windows Server. If you need to deploy a Windows Server 2012 R2 domain controller from media, you must create the IFM package from a Windows Server 2012 R2 (32- or 64-bit) domain controller.

> **NOTE**   For more information on installing a domain controller from media, refer to "Installing AD DS from Media" at http://technet.microsoft.com/en-us/library/cc770654%28v=WS.10%29.aspx.

Creating Installation Media

To create installation media for deploying domain controllers, perform the following steps:

1. Log on to a writable domain controller with a member of the Builtin Administrators, Server Operators, Domain Admins, or Enterprise Admins group.

2. Open a command prompt as an administrator.

3. Enter the **ntdsutil** command and then press **Enter**.

4. At the ntdsutil: prompt, type **activate instance ntds**; then press **Enter**. If successful, you will receive a message Active instance set to "ntds".

5. At the ntdsutil: prompt, type **ifm**. Then press **Enter**.

6. At the ifm prompt, type the **ntdsutil** command parameter as outlined in Table 13-6 and press **Enter**. For example, to create an ifm option for a writable 2012 R2 domain controller, type the parameter **create full c:\IFM**, where c:\IFM is the output location for the install from media files. This path can be a local folder, network share, or removable media such as a USB drive.

NOTE   If you forget the parameter syntax, type `help` at any point in `ntdsutil` to see the available parameters.

7.   The process can take a few moments depending on the size of the AD DS database. The Windows domain controller will create a temp database located under the `%TMP%` folder before writing to the target IFM folder specified. Once completed, `ntdsutil` will report the results as shown in Figure 13-17.

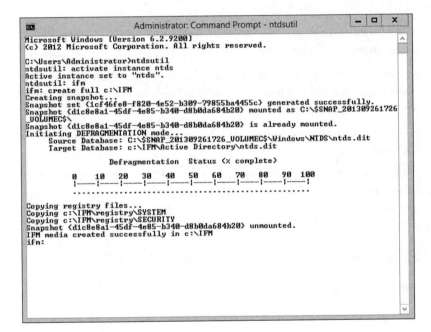

Figure 13-17   Creating IFM using `ntdsutil`.

NOTE   The IFM process requires available storage equal to 110% of the size of the AD DS database. If you do not have enough storage, you will need to move the `%TMP%` folder. Refer to "Move Temp and TMP Directories" at http://technet. microsoft.com/en-us/library/aa998306(v=exchg.80).aspx.

Deploying Domain Controllers Using the IFM Option

With a preconfigured IFM file set, you can quickly deploy domain controllers. Remember, depending on the type of domain controller you want to deploy, you will need to create the appropriate IFM file set as described in the previous section. To create a new domain controller using IFM, perform the following steps:

1. Log on to the server in which you will be deploying the AD DS role and promoting to a domain controller.

2. Ensure that you can access the IFM file set either from a network share or a copy saved on a removable drive.

3. Install the AD DS role and associated features as shown earlier in this chapter. After the AD DS role has been installed, click the **Promote this server to a domain controller** link (shown previously in Figure 13-8). This will launch the Active Directory Domain Services Configuration Wizard shown earlier in Figure 13-9.

4. On the Deployment Configuration screen, select **Add a domain controller to an existing domain** and click **Next**.

5. On the Domain Controller Options screen, select the appropriate domain controller capabilities and site name as done previously in Figure 13-10. Enter the Directory Services Restore Mode (DSRM) password, and click **Next**.

6. On the DNS Options screen, specify the DNS delegation options if necessary and click **Next**.

7. On the Additional Options screen (shown in Figure 13-18), check the box **for Install from media**. Under the Path field, specify or browse to the path of the folder containing the IFM data files. The wizard will verify the path and contents of the files. Click **Next** to continue.

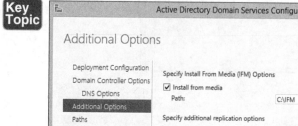

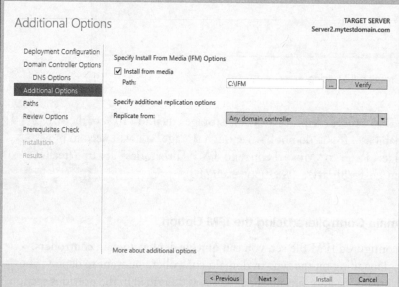

Figure 13-18   Specify the Install from Media (IFM) options.

8. On the Paths screen, confirm the paths for the **Database folder**, **Log files folder**, and **SYSVOL folder**. Click **Next** to continue.

9. Confirm your selections on the Review Options screen, and click **Next**.

10. After the wizard performs a prerequisites check, click **Install** to promote the server to a domain controller using the Install from Media option. Windows Server will promote the server using the offline IFM data to speed up the promotion process. After the promotion has completed, restart the server to complete the process.

Configuring Global Catalog Servers

Global catalog (GC) servers maintain a subset of information pertaining to all objects located in its domain, plus summary information pertaining to objects in other domains of its forest. In doing so, a GC server enables the following features:

- It validates universal group memberships at logon.

- It enables users to search the entire forest for resources they might need to access.

- It validates references to objects located in other domains in the forest.

- It validates user principal names (UPNs) across the entire forest, thereby enabling user logon in other domains.

> **NOTE**   For more information on the purposes of GC servers, refer to "Understanding the Global Catalog" at http://technet.microsoft.com/en-us/library/cc730749.aspx.

Planning the Placement of Global Catalog Servers

It is important to understand the need for GC servers and their functions, particularly on a multidomain network, when you are setting up your AD DS forest. In particular, you should have at least two GC servers in each domain for fault tolerance purposes. If you have just a single domain in your forest, the GC server plays a minor role, and it is unlikely that you would need to designate additional GC servers.

You should be concerned with the following two opposing issues when deciding how many GC servers to deploy and where to deploy them:

- As your forest increases in size, the size of the global catalog, and hence the amount of replication traffic among GC servers, increases. The GC servers replicate with each other in a loop that is separate from other AD DS replication. The more GC servers you deploy, the greater the amount of replication traffic generated.

- Alternatively, with increasing forest size, the forest will have more users with cross-domain queries. Consequently, the time required for users to reach resources in other domains will increase unless you add GC servers that users can easily reach. Adding such GC servers is especially important in multisite networks.

When a user logs on to a given domain controller for the first time in a large enterprise, it is important for this domain controller to connect to a GC server to obtain information about any universal groups to which the user might belong. This information includes access permissions assigned to these groups. If the user is located in a branch office that does not have a GC server locally present, the domain controller must cross the slow link to the location in which the GC server resides. This results in slow logon performance, particularly when several users are logging on at the same time.

Consider Figure 13-19, in which users in the head office and in Branch Office 1 have access to a GC server in their own sites; consequently, the logon and object search times are fast. However, users in Branch Office 2 must access a GC server in the head office across the slow intersite link. This can result in unacceptably slow logon and object search times, particularly if there is a lot of other intersite traffic. Furthermore, should the slow link go down and the GC server become unavailable as a result, users would be unable to log on at all.

If sufficiently high bandwidth exists between two sites, locating a GC server at the remote site might not be necessary. You should monitor the growth in network traffic and check with users to see whether performance suffers.

You should balance the need for additional GC servers against users' need for additional disk space and AD DS replication bandwidth. Windows Server 2012 R2 supports the feature of *universal group membership caching*, which enables users to log on without access to a GC server after they have logged on once to a given domain controller. This topic is discussed in Chapter 15.

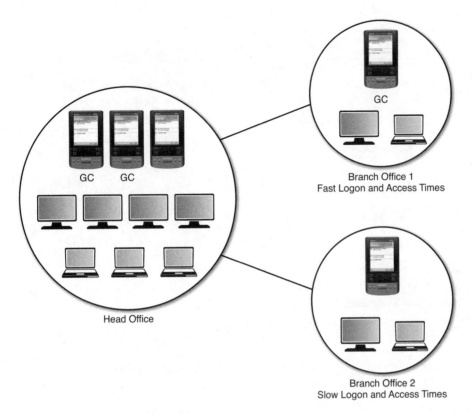

Figure 13-19 Logon and search times are much faster when a global catalog server is located onsite.

Promoting Domain Controllers to Global Catalog Servers

By default, the first domain controller in each domain is automatically designated as a GC server. You can designate additional GCs from the Active Directory Sites and Services snap-in by performing the following steps:

1. Expand the **Sites** container, and expand the site in which the domain controller is located.

2. Expand the **Servers** container, and expand the entry for the domain controller to be designated as a GC.

3. Right-click **NTDS Settings** and select **Properties**.

4. In the General tab of the NTDS Settings Properties dialog box, select the **Global Catalog** check box and click **OK** or **Apply,** as shown in Figure 13-20.

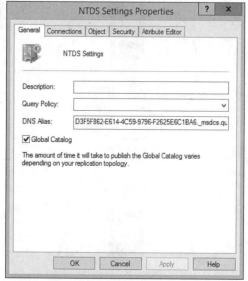

Figure 13-20 Designating an additional global catalog server.

You can also remove a GC server; simply clear the **Global Catalog** check box shown in Figure 13-20.

Deploying Active Directory Infrastructure as a Service in Windows Azure

Windows Azure is a cloud-based infrastructure service operated by Microsoft that enables enterprises to build a scalable server infrastructure that can easily be adapted to changing business requirements. It enables you to run Windows Server 2012 R2 virtual servers according to your company's usage needs. Microsoft provides pay-as-you-go solutions that are tailored to a company's needs, large or small. End-to-end support is available for a company's needs, including the infrastructure, server operating systems, and applications.

Virtual machines and networks running on Windows Azure are part of Microsoft's Infrastructure-as-a-Service (IaaS) offering for cloud computing for organizations. IaaS provides a pool of cloud-based computing, storage, and network connectivity resources that organizations can purchase and utilize on a per-usage billing basis. You can deploy AD DS as well as AD FS either completely in Windows Azure or split between physical servers and Windows Azure-based virtual servers. Included is the ability to deploy single sign-on to Software-as-a-Service (SaaS) applications such as Microsoft Office 365. Further, you can use AD DS in Windows Azure to enable user logon with identities from Facebook, Google, Microsoft, and other identity providers for accessing local or cloud-based applications.

Included with Windows Azure is server support for many Microsoft virtual machines, including servers running Windows Server 2008 R2, Windows Server 2012, and Windows Server 2012 R2. Most, but not all, server roles can be hosted on Windows Azure, as well as many specialized Microsoft servers.

NOTE   For summary information on server roles and specialized servers that are supported by Windows Azure, as well as server roles and features that cannot be supported, refer to "Microsoft server software support for Windows Azure virtual machines" at http://support.microsoft.com/kb/2721672.

You can host an entire Active Directory forest in Windows Azure or create child domains or additional domain controllers for existing physical AD DS forests. We shall look at each of these options in the following section.

Installing an AD DS Forest in Windows Azure

Installing an AD DS forest in Windows Azure involves creating a virtual network, adding a new virtual machine, and then installing AD DS. The following steps assume that you've signed up for Windows Azure and created your virtual network:

1. From the Windows Azure management portal, click **New > Computer > Virtual Machine > From Gallery**.

2. The Virtual machine image selection page displays. Select **Windows Server 2012 R2 Datacenter**.

3. On the Virtual machine configuration page, provide a name for the new virtual machine. Then type a username and password, and select a version release date and size.

4. On the next Virtual machine configuration page, provide networking information as required.

5. On the next Virtual machine configuration page, accept the default Remote Desktop and PowerShell endpoint options (or specify alternatives if required), and then click the check mark on this page to complete the wizard. The virtual machine you've created is added to the Windows Azure management portal page.

You next need to attach empty disks to the machine you've created. Proceed as follows:

1. From the Windows Azure management portal, select the name of your virtual machine, click **Attach**, and then click **Attach Empty Disk**.

2. On the Attach an empty disk to the virtual machine page, type the size of the disk in GB. Repeat as required to attach additional disks.

3. Click the name of the virtual machine, click **Connect**, and then click **Open**.

4. A Remote Desktop Connection page displays asking whether you want to connect. Select the check box labeled **Don't ask me again for connections to this computer**, and then click **Connect**.

5. In the Windows Security dialog box that appears, type your username and password as you've previously specified; then click **OK**.

6. If you receive a message box informing you that the identity of the remote computer cannot be verified, click **Yes** to complete the connection.

> **TIP** Note that Windows Azure provides two different disk types—operating system disks and data disks. This ensures that the integrity of an AD DS forest hosted entirely in Windows Azure is not compromised because of a loss of a single write, which could affect the entire system and not just a single machine. The AD DS database and SYSVOL share should be placed on Windows Azure data disks.

Having attached a disk and logged on to the virtual machine, you are ready to install AD DS. Proceed as follows:

1. From the left pane of Server Manager, click **File and Storage Services**.

2. Initialize the new disk and create a volume on which you will install AD DS. Refer to Chapter 3, "Configuring Windows Server 2012 R2 Local Storage," for more information.

3. In Server Manager, click **Manage > Add Roles and Features**. Follow the procedures given earlier in this chapter to install the AD DS server role and promote the virtual server to a domain controller. At Step 13 of this procedure, ensure that you place the database and SYSVOL folders on a Windows Azure data disk, not an operating system disk.

4. After you've completed installing AD DS and rebooted the virtual server, you should perform validation actions as described later in this chapter.

TIP   Note that Windows Azure virtual machines do not support static IP addresses. However, dynamic addresses created when installing virtual machines provide a lease lifetime that is essentially the lifetime of the Windows Azure cloud service. So, DNS servers and domain controllers can operate properly using the dynamic IP addresses leased by DHCP properly. Note that you cannot deploy a DHCP server in Windows Azure, however. This server must be hosted on your local physical network.

NOTE   For more information on installing an AD DS forest in Windows Azure, refer to "Install a new Active Directory forest on an Azure virtual network" at http://www.windowsazure.com/en-us/documentation/articles/active-directory-new-forest-virtual-machine/. This reference also provides information on using Windows PowerShell to complete the procedures described in this section.

Installing a Replica Domain Controller on Windows Azure

Windows Azure enables you to install additional domain controllers for an AD DS forest that is hosted on either a physical domain controller in your office or a Windows Azure virtual domain controller as described in the previous section. You can use the Windows Azure Management Portal to create and configure a virtual network in Windows Azure and set up site-to-site connectivity over IPsec virtual private networking (VPN) between the virtual network and your corporate LAN. After you've created a virtual network as described in Chapter 9, "Creating and Configuring Virtual Networks," you can follow the steps presented earlier in this chapter to install an additional domain controller for a domain that is hosted on either the virtual network or your corporate LAN.

NOTE   For information on installing replica domain controllers in Windows Azure, refer to "Install a Replica Active Directory Domain Controller in Azure Virtual Networks" at http://www.windowsazure.com/en-us/documentation/articles/virtual-networks-install-replica-active-directory-domain-controller/. Also refer to "Virtual Network Overview" at http://msdn.microsoft.com/en-us/library/windowsazure/jj156007.aspx for additional general information on Windows Azure virtual networks.

> **TIP**   Remember that Microsoft likes to ask questions on the latest Windows
> Server technologies. You can expect to find a question or two on installing and
> using domain controllers in Windows Azure on the 70-410 exam.

> **NOTE**   For more information on deploying AD DS on Windows Azure, refer to
> "Guidelines for Deploying Windows Server Active Directory on Windows Azure
> Virtual Machines" at http://msdn.microsoft.com/en-us/library/windowsazure/
> jj156090.aspx.

Troubleshooting Active Directory Installations

This section introduces the various troubleshooting tools that can be used to verify
that AD DS has been properly installed.

Verifying the Proper Installation of Active Directory

After you have installed Active Directory, there are several steps you should perform
to verify that the proper components have been installed. Open Server Manager
and click the **Tools** menu. On a Windows Server 2012 R2 computer, you should
see links to six Active Directory management tools: Active Directory Administrative
Center, Active Directory Domains and Trusts, Active Directory Module for Windows PowerShell, Active Directory Sites and Services, Active Directory Users and
Computers, and ADSI Edit. You should also see a link to the DNS snap-in, unless
you have specified another server as the DNS server for your domain.

Active Directory Users and Computers

Open Active Directory Users and Computers. You should see the default containers Builtin, Computers, ForeignSecurityPrincipals, Managed Service Accounts, and
Users under the domain you have created. You should also see a default Domain
Controllers OU. Select this OU and verify that computer accounts for all domain
controllers in the domain are present, as shown in Figure 13-21.

> **NOTE**   A successful installation of Active Directory includes the creation of the
> Active Directory database Ntds.dit located under `%Systemroot%\Ntds`.

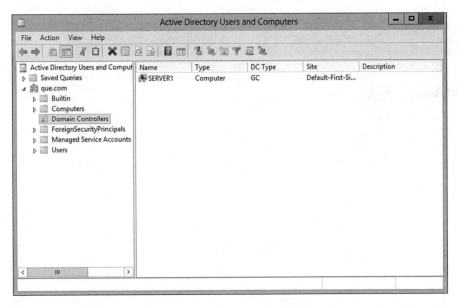

Figure 13-21   After installing Active Directory, you should see a default set of containers in the Active Directory Users and Computers, together with domain controller computer accounts in the Domain Controllers OU.

Active Directory Administrative Center

On a Windows Server 2012 R2 computer, open Active Directory Administrative Center. As shown in Figure 13-22 and discussed in Chapter 6, "Configuring Remote Management of Servers," the AD Administrative Center enables you to perform a large range of administrative tasks on your domain, including the following:

- Use AD Administrative Center to manage IT tasks. This can include creating and managing user, group, and computer accounts or creating and managing OUs and other Active Directory containers.

- Use AD module for Windows PowerShell.

- Find answers on AD forum.

- Deploy Dynamic Access Control.

- Get Microsoft Solution Accelerator to help configure Dynamic Access Control.

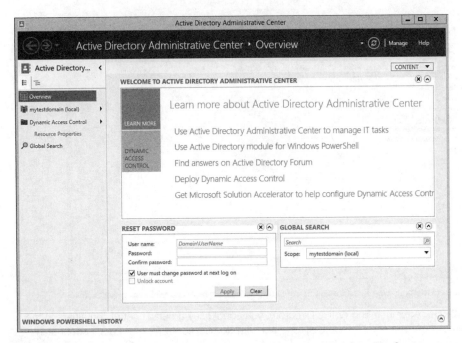

Figure 13-22   Windows Server 2012 R2's Active Directory Administrative Center.

The Active Directory Administrative Center is installed automatically when you install the AD DS server role in Windows Server 2012 R2. You can also install this tool on a Windows Server 2012 R2 member server or a Windows 8.1 computer by installing the Remote Server Administration Tools (RSAT) feature.

Active Directory Domains and Trusts

The Active Directory Domains and Trusts snap-in (see Figure 13-23) enables you to manage trust relationships between domains.

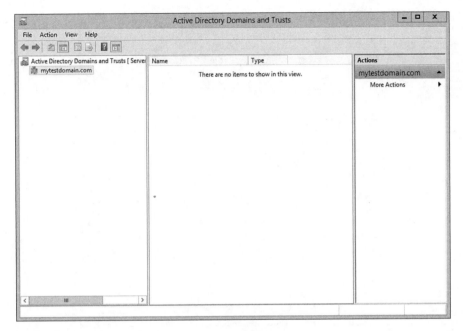

Figure 13-23 Active Directory domains and trusts.

Active Directory Sites and Services

If you have just created the first domain controller for the domain, the server will be created under a default AD site called *Default-First-Site-Name*. If you are adding another domain controller, verify that the server is listed under the appropriate site. In addition, the first domain controller in a domain will be configured as the global catalog. You can also verify this under the left pane of the AD Sites and Services snap-in by expanding the Default-First-Site-Name and viewing the properties of the domain controller (see Figure 13-24).

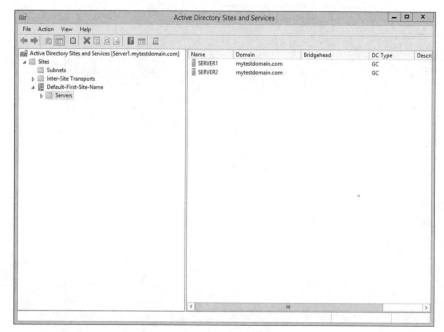

Figure 13-24 Active Directory Sites and Services.

Active Directory Module for Windows PowerShell

The Active Directory Module for Windows PowerShell is a collection of cmdlets used to manage Active Directory domains. Some useful commands to verify functionality include

- **Get-ADReplicationSite:** Retrieves information about AD sites

- **Get-ADTrust:** Retrieves information about configured trusts

- **Get-ADUser:** Retrieves information about a specific AD user

- **Test-ADServiceAccount:** Tests the functionality of a specified service account

> **NOTE** For a full list of commands and their uses, refer to "AD DS Administration Cmdlets in Windows PowerShell" at http://technet.microsoft.com/en-us/library/hh852274.aspx.

ADSI Edit

The Active Directory Services Interfaces Editor (ADSI Edit) is a low-level editor for AD DS or AD LDS. It enables you to view, modify, create, and delete any object in Active Directory. You can access the ADSI Edit tool via Administrative Tools or the Search charm. The first time you open ADSI Edit, you will need to configure a default connection by clicking Connect To under the Actions menu. You will be asked to specify the path to LDAP, as shown in Figure 13-25. On a new installation, the Path field will be populated with the path to LDAP based on the location of the SRV records for the domain controller. After you click OK, ADSI Edit will enable you to browse the contents of the AD Database (see Figure 13-26) and make any modifications.

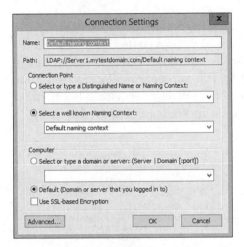

Figure 13-25   ADSI Edit Connection settings.

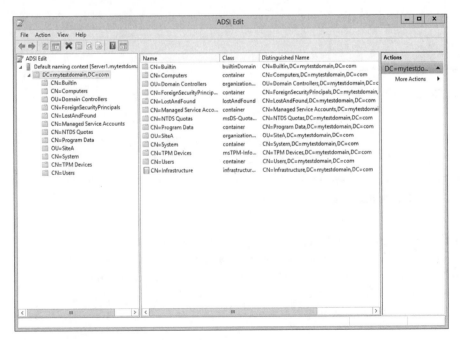

Figure 13-26   Browsing Active Directory using ADSI Edit.

NOTE   You should use ADSI Edit only when necessary and with extreme caution. Modifying data using a low-level editor might result in corruption or improper functionality of Active Directory. If any changes are required, you should back up any configurations or take note of any values changed.

Resolving SRV Record Registration Issues

For proper functionality, domain controllers register Service Locator (SRV) records. SRV records identify proper locations for domain controllers, AD sites, GC servers, Kerberos authentication parameters, and so on. Without these records, Active Directory would not function properly. You can confirm SRV records within DNS or via the `netlogon.dns` file. Because Active Directory requires a functional DNS server, you can review the DNS server for the presence of Active Directory SRV records, as shown in Figure 13-27.

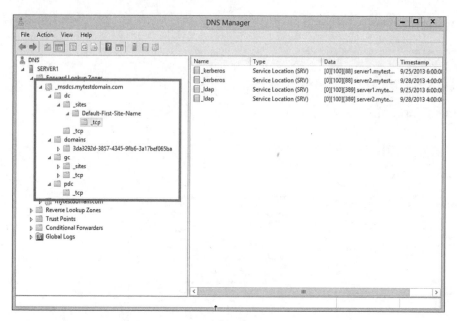

Figure 13-27   AD SRV resource records in DNS.

In addition to viewing SRV records in DNS, you can also view/edit the `netlogon.dns` file on a domain controller by opening the `netlogon.dns` file with Notepad (see Figure 13-28). The `netlogon.dns` file is located under `%windir%\system32\config\`.

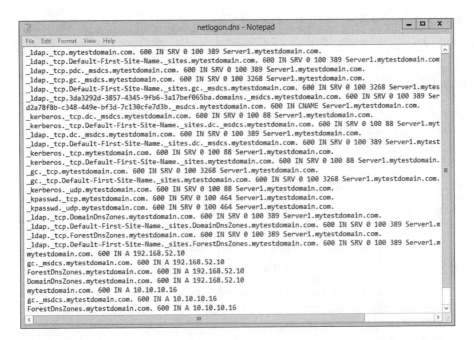

Figure 13-28 Viewing `netlogon.dns`.

> **NOTE** The `netlogon.dns` file can be helpful in situations where a domain controller fails. Using the information from the `netlogon.dns` file, you can identify the SRV records for which the failed server was responsible.

In the event that you do in fact notice strange issues with DNS or Active Directory–related activities, you should check the Event Viewer, specifically the System Event log. In most cases, the netlogon service will log events related to improper configurations. For more information, use the command-line tool `dcdiag` to test DNS and Active Directory functions. The basic syntax for `dcdiag` is `dcdiag /s:[domain controller]`. Review the output and follow the recommendations made.

> **NOTE** `dcdiag` offers a variety of switches and parameters. For a complete listing, refer to "Dcdiag" at http://technet.microsoft.com/en-us/library/cc731968.aspx.

Exam Preparation Tasks

Review All the Key Topics

Review the most important topics in the chapter, noted with the key topics icon in the outer margin of the page. Table 13-7 lists a reference of these key topics and the page numbers on which each is found.

Table 13-7   Key Topics for Chapter 13

Key Topic Element	Description	Page Number
List	Describes the partitions of Active Directory.	575
Paragraph	Introduces the logical building blocks of Active Directory.	578
List	Lists important guidelines you should follow in preparing to install AD DS.	593
List	Summarizes requirements for installing AD DS.	594
Figure 13-6	You use the Add Roles Wizard to begin the installation of AD DS.	597
Figure 13-10	Displays important options you must specify when installing AD DS.	600
List	Summarizes important reasons for installing multiple domain controllers in a domain.	605
Paragraph	Describes the methods of performing unattended installations of AD DS.	606
Table 13-5	Summarizes available forest and domain functional levels in Windows Server 2012 R2.	609
Paragraph	Describes the adprep utility used for preparing forests and domains for upgrade.	611
List	Provides instructions for creating Install From Media packages.	618
List	Provides instructions for installing a domain controller using the IFM option.	620
Figure 13-18	Shows the Install From Media Options screen under the AD DS Configuration Wizard.	620
Step list	Describes several benefits of deploying global catalog servers.	621
Figure 13-20	Deploying additional global catalog servers.	624

Key Topic Element	Description	Page Number
Figure 13-27	Shows SRV records as displayed in DNS.	634
Figure 13-28	Shows SRV records listed in the netlogon.dns file.	635

Complete the Tables and Lists from Memory

Print a copy of Appendix B, "Memory Tables" (found on the CD), or at least the section for this chapter, and complete the tables and lists from memory. Appendix C, "Memory Tables Answer Key," is also on the CD and includes completed tables and lists to check your work.

Definitions of Key Terms

Define the following key terms from this chapter, and check your answers in the glossary.

Active Directory Migration Tool (ADMT), Active Directory Administrative Center, Adprep, dcpromo, Domain controller (DC), Domain functional level, Forest functional level, Forest root, Install from Media (IFM), Read-only domain controller (RODC), Security identifier (SID), Windows Azure

This chapter covers the following subjects:

- **Creating User and Computer Accounts:** All users logging on to the domain must have user accounts, and these are combined into group accounts to facilitate resource access. This section introduces the various concepts of user and computer accounts and then shows you how to automate the creation of large numbers of accounts.

- **Managing and Maintaining Accounts:** You need to perform a large range of activities when managing user and group accounts. This section takes you through the various account maintenance tasks you should know how to perform. It also shows you how to provision a computer account for offline domain join and introduces the concept of user rights.

CHAPTER 14

Active Directory User and Computer Accounts

The heart and soul of any Active Directory implementation is the users who must access the network on a daily basis. A company must be able to ensure that its employees are able to access all the resources on the network that they require so they can perform the activities associated with their jobs, but not be able to access other resources that might contain confidential information.

This chapter turns its attention to the nuts and bolts of Active Directory that enable all these activities to take place in a controlled manner. It shows you how to create user accounts for all these various employees and manage them in terms of groups. It then takes you through all the account management tasks.

"Do I Know This Already?" Quiz

The "Do I Know This Already?" quiz enables you to assess whether you should read this entire chapter or simply jump to the "Exam Preparation Tasks" section for review. If you are in doubt, read the entire chapter. Table 14-1 outlines the major headings in this chapter and the corresponding "Do I Know This Already?" quiz questions. You can find the answers in Appendix A, "Answers to the 'Do I Know This Already?' Quizzes."

Table 14-1 "Do I Know This Already?" Foundation Topics Section-to-Question Mapping

Foundations Topics Section	Questions Covered in This Section
Creating User and Group Accounts	1–5
Managing and Maintaining Accounts	6–8

1. You are using the Active Directory Administrative Center to create several user accounts for new employees in your company. Which of the following are properties of these user accounts you can create directly using the Create User dialog box that you cannot create directly from the New Object – User dialog box in Active Directory Users and Computers? (Choose all that apply.)

   a. Whether the user must change the password at first logon

   b. Use of AES-based encryption

   c. Organizational information

   d. Whether the account is disabled

   e. Group membership

   f. Account expiry

2. Which of the following represents the most valid reason why you would want to create a template account in AD DS?

   a. Such an account enables an occasional user to log on to the domain and access a limited amount of resources.

   b. Such an account facilitates the creation of a large number of domain user accounts that have similar properties and need for resource access.

   c. Such an account provides a means of testing other domain user accounts to ensure that they have no more than the required resource access for users to do their jobs.

   d. Such an account enables you to group users with similar resource needs and add the appropriate permissions directly.

3. The Human Resources Department of your company has provided you with an Excel spreadsheet containing names and additional information pertaining to 75 student interns who will start work with the company next Monday. You need to create user accounts for these interns as soon as possible. Which tool should you use for this purpose?

   a. Csvde

   b. Ldifde

   c. Dsadd

   d. Active Directory Administrative Center

4. You would like to create a UPN suffix so users can log on directly to your company's domain using their email address. Which tool should you use?

   a. Active Directory Administrative Center

   b. Active Directory Users and Computers

   c. Active Directory Sites and Services

   d. Active Directory Domains and Trusts

5. You are a network administrator working for your state's environmental agency. You have been provided with a list of 50 individuals representing citizen groups and area companies who will be providing input on a proposed water diversion project. You need to ensure that these individuals receive email messages from the assessment committee that is studying this proposal regularly without receiving access to the agency's AD DS domain. What should you do?

   a. Create user accounts for each of these individuals, and add these contacts to a distribution group.

   b. Create contacts for each of these individuals, and add these contacts to a distribution group.

   c. Create user accounts for each of these individuals, and add these contacts to a security group.

   d. Create contacts for each of these individuals, and add these contacts to a security group.

6. Which of the following best describes the Protected Admin feature of Windows Server 2012 R2 Active Directory?

    a. A network administrator uses the default administrative account created when Windows Server 2012 R2 is installed. When she needs to perform an administrative task, User Account Control (UAC) asks her to confirm her intentions by clicking **Yes** in a message box.

    b. A network administrator uses an administrative user account that is a member of the Domain Admins group. When she needs to perform an administrative task, UAC asks her to confirm her intentions by clicking **Yes** in a message box.

    c. A network administrator uses an administrative user account that is a member of the Domain Admins group. When she needs to perform an administrative task, UAC asks her to confirm her intentions by retyping her username and password in a message box.

    d. A network administrator uses a standard (nonadministrative) user account that is a member of the Domain Admins group. When she needs to perform an administrative task, UAC asks her to confirm her intentions by clicking **Yes** in a message box.

7. Which of the following commands should you use to generate the necessary metadata to perform an offline join of a computer named Client1 to the certguide.com domain, storing the metadata in the `c:\client1.txt` file?

    a. `dsadd /RequestODJ /Domain certguide.com /Machine Client1 /SaveFile c:\Client1.txt`

    b. `dsadd /Provision /Domain certguide.com /Machine Client1 /SaveFile c:\Client1.txt`

    c. `djoin /RequestODJ /Domain certguide.com /Machine Client1 /SaveFile c:\Client1.txt`

    d. `djoin /Provision /Domain certguide.com /Machine Client1 /SaveFile c:\Client1.txt`

8. You are responsible for maintaining the user and group accounts in your company's AD DS domain. A user named Ryan whose job is vital to the company's business resigns to work for a competitor. You are afraid that Ryan might log back on to your network to steal corporate secrets. At the same time, your company must hire a replacement for Ryan to begin work as soon as possible. What should you do with Ryan's user account?

   a. Turn Ryan's account into a template that you can later copy it to create a user account for the new employee.

   b. Remove Ryan's account from the groups that grant him access to the resources he used in performance of his job. When the new employee is hired, rename the account and put it back into the groups for access to these resources.

   c. Disable Ryan's account, and then rename and reenable it when the new employee is hired.

   d. Delete Ryan's account, and then re-create a new user account when the new employee is hired.

Foundation Topics

Creating User and Computer Accounts

If a user is unable to log on to an Active Directory Domain Services (AD DS) network, he cannot gain access to the data and resources, such as files, folders, printers, and so on, that are stored on the network. Further, in most organizations numerous employees have similar work functions and requirements. Providing such employees access to resources individually would be a tedious and error-prone job were it not for the ability to group these users together. AD DS provides several types of group accounts for this purpose. In this chapter, you learn how to manage user accounts. You will learn how to manage group accounts in Chapter 15, "Active Directory Groups and Organizational Units."

Introducing User Accounts

Everyone who requires access to an AD DS network requires a user account. User accounts enable users to log on to computers and domains. They also authorize or deny access to specific resources within the domain. User accounts embody specific information pertinent to a user, such as username, password, and specific logon limitations. User accounts can either be built-in accounts or self-generated. Each user account has a comprehensive set of configurable properties associated with it. Among these are group memberships, logon scripts, logon hours, account expiration, user profile, and dial-in permission.

The following three types of user accounts are present in an AD DS network:

- **Domain user accounts:** This account is used to provide access to an AD DS domain and all its associated resources. It is the most common account type you will encounter on the network. You can give permission to an account from one AD DS domain to access resources in other domains.

- **Local user accounts:** This account exists on a standalone or member server, or on a Windows XP Professional; Vista Business, Enterprise, or Ultimate; Windows 7 Professional, Enterprise, or Ultimate; or Windows 8.1 Pro or Enterprise computer. It enables a user to log on to the computer with which it is associated and gain access to resources on that computer only. A local user account cannot gain access to domain-based resources.

- **Built-in user accounts:** These accounts exist for specific administrative tasks to ease the burdens of administration. Special accounts are defined up front that have permissions to various resources and components of the AD DS forest.

NOTE   For more information on user accounts and built-in accounts, refer to
"Understanding User Accounts" at http://technet.microsoft.com/en-us/library/
dd861325.aspx.

Manually Creating User Accounts

Before discussing the automation of AD DS account creation, this section takes a
quick look at manual creation of user accounts. You can perform this basic admin-
istrative task through the Active Directory Users and Computers console or the
Active Directory Administrative Center, both of which can be accessed from the
Tools menu in Server Manager or from the Start screen in the Full GUI mode of
Windows Server 2012 R2.

When you open either console, you can navigate through the list of containers in
the domain shown in the console tree. By default, user accounts are located in the
Users container, although you can create them in other folders as well.

Perform the following procedure to create a new user account:

1. Open either **Active Directory Users and Computers** or **Active Directory
   Administrative Center**, and expand the domain node in the console tree to
   reveal the OUs and other containers found within, as shown for the Active
   Directory Administrative Center in Figure 14-1.

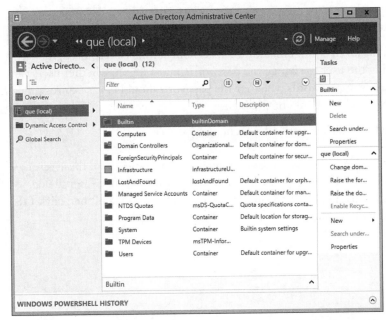

Figure 14-1   The Active Directory Administrative Center console enables you to perform many
administrative tasks, including the creation of user and computer accounts.

2. Right-click the desired container, and select **New** > **User**.

3. If you are using Active Directory Users and Computers, the New Object - User dialog box appears. Type the user's first and last names and assign a user logon name, as shown in Figure 14-2. When you type the user logon name, a pre-Windows 2000–compatible logon name is automatically created. This creates a NetBIOS-type name of the type used on older Windows NT networks.

Figure 14-2   Using Active Directory Users and Computers to create a new user account.

4. Click **Next**, enter a password for the user, and confirm this password.

5. Click **Next** again to configure additional account settings as required, including requiring the user to change the password at next logon, whether users can change their own passwords, whether the password should never expire, and whether the account should be disabled.

6. Click **Finish** to finish creating the account.

The Active Directory Administrative Center enables you to specify all these settings and additional ones, such as group membership from a single Create User dialog box, as shown in Figure 14-3. Supply all the needed information, and then click **OK** to create the new user account.

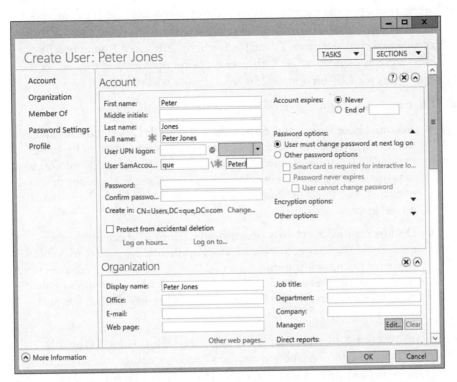

Figure 14-3   Using Active Directory Administrative Center to create a new user account.

You can specify the following additional information from the Create User dialog box (scroll through this dialog box to display available items):

- **Account expires:** Select **End of** to specify an expiry date after which the account is automatically disabled; otherwise, leave the default of **Never** selected. This option is useful for a temporary employee such as a student or contractor.

- **Password options:** By default, the user is required to change her password the first time she logs on, so that she can create a password that nobody else knows. If desired, select **Other options** and then select any of **Smart card required for interactive logon** (if you are using a system of smart cards with readers attached to client computers for secure logon), **Password never expires** (use only for service accounts accessed by applications that would fail if the password changes), or **User cannot change password** (not recommended except for accounts that you want to maintain control over, such as guest or temporary accounts).

- **Encryption options:** Enables several account encryption options. You should not select **Store password using reversible encryption** (this option actually decreases account security). To enable Kerberos Advanced Encryption System (AES) account security, select **Other encryption options** and then select the check boxes for **128-bit** and/or **256-bit** encryption as required.

- **Other options:** Enables you to select one or both of the following:

  - **Account is sensitive and cannot be delegated:** Delegated authentication occurs when a network service accepts a user request and assumes the user's identity to connect to a network service. Select this option to improve security when network services do not require account delegation, such as a guest or temporary account that should not be assigned for delegation.

  - **Do not require Kerberos preauthentication:** Kerberos authentication provides a secure, flexible means of authenticating users to AD DS. Kerberos preauthentication enables additional security and requires time synchronization between the client and server. Select this option only if users require access to pre-Windows 2000 computers, which are unable to use Kerberos.

- **Organization:** Enables you to add organizational information to the user account, such as addresses, phone numbers, manager names, and so on. Information in this section is stored in the Directory and can be searched on.

- **Member of:** Click **Add** to add the user to groups as required. You will learn more about this option in Chapter 15.

- **Directly Associated Password Settings:** Used when you have created Fine-Grained Password Policy (FGPP) objects, which specify user- or group-specific password policies that override domain password policies. You will learn more about password policies in the *Cert Guide* book for exam 70-411.

- **Profile:** Enables you to assign a profile path and logon script. You can also create a shared folder path to which the user will store her documents by default by typing a Universal Naming Convention (UNC) path such as `\\server2\documents\%username%`. Use the `%username%` variable to automatically create a subfolder named with the user's logon name.

NOTE   For more information on creating user accounts, refer to "Create a New User Account" at http://technet.microsoft.com/en-us/library/dd861308.aspx.

Creating Computer Accounts

Creating a computer account enables you to prepare for joining a client computer to the domain. Right-click the desired container and select **New > Computer**, as shown for Active Directory Administrative Center in Figure 14-4. In the Create Computer dialog box, type the computer name and, if necessary, click **Change** to assign the privilege of joining the computer to the domain to a different user or group. As for users, a NetBIOS-compatible computer name is automatically created. The procedure is similar when accessed from Active Directory Users and Computers; in this case, the dialog box is named New Object - Computer.

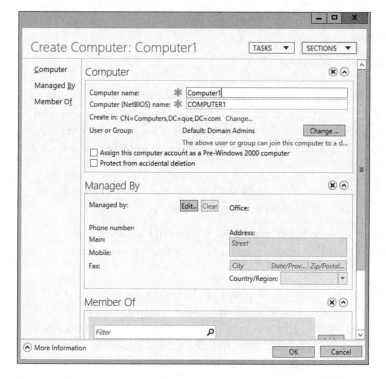

Figure 14-4   Using Active Directory Administrative Center to create a new computer account.

NOTE   For more information on creating computer accounts, refer to "Create a New Computer Account" at http://technet.microsoft.com/en-us/library/dd861319.aspx.

Using Template Accounts

A template account is a special account used only for copying as needed when you have to create a large number of user accounts. You should configure it to hold the various properties that are required for each and every user, so you need only enter individual information such as usernames.

Access the New Object - User or Create User dialog box in the appropriate AD DS container, and specify the following properties:

- Last name: `template`
- User logon name: `_TEMPLATE`
- Password: (blank)
- Account is disabled: (selected)

Note that using an underscore as the first character of the username causes this account to be listed at or very close to the top of the list of user accounts. You can also use a name that is descriptive of the type of user being created—for example, `_SALESPERSON`. By specifying that the account be disabled, it ensures that no one can log on using this account.

After completing this procedure, right-click the account and select **Properties** to configure common account properties such as the following:

- On the Account tab, specify any additional account options that might be required, such as requiring a smart card for interactive logon or the use of one of several types of encryption.

- On the Profile tab, specify a profile path to a share on a file server that will hold the user's documents and other settings—for example, `\\server1\docs\%username%`. By using the `%username%` variable, a subfolder for each employee is automatically created and given the same name as the employee's username. You can also specify a local path in the same location.

- On the Member Of tab, specify one or more groups that each user should be made a member of.

- Add any other common properties that apply to all users, such as address and organizational information, and Terminal Services and remote access settings.

TIP   When using the Active Directory Administrative Center to create the template account, you can add all the account properties described in the previous section at the time you create the account. Expand the Account section of the dialog box previously shown in Figure 14-3 to access additional user account options as discussed earlier in this section.

To use the template account, right-click it in the details pane of Active Directory Users and Computers and select **Copy**. The Copy Object - User dialog box displays, which is similar to the New Object - User dialog box shown previously in Figure 14-2 or the Create User dialog box shown in Figure 14-3. After you have provided name and password information, a user account is created with all the properties you have provided for the template account.

Using Bulk Import to Automate Account Creation

Although use of a template account can expedite the creation of a series of user accounts with similar properties, the creation of a large number of accounts in an enterprise environment can quickly become time consuming. If you need to create hundreds, or even thousands, of new user or group accounts, you can use one of several tools provided by Microsoft for automating the creation of new accounts, as follows:

- **Csvde:** The Comma Separated Value Data Exchange (`Csvde`) tool enables you to import data to AD DS from files containing information in the comma-separated (CSV) format. You can also export AD DS data to CSV-formatted files.

- **Ldifde:** The LDAP Data Interchange Format Data Exchange (`Ldifde`) tool enables you to create, modify, and delete directory objects. You can also extend the schema, export AD DS user and group information, and add data to AD DS from other directory sources.

- **Dsadd:** The `Dsadd` tool enables you to add object types such as computers, contacts, groups, users, organizational units (OUs), and quotas to AD DS.

- **Scripts:** You can use scripts and batch files with tools such as `Dsadd` to automate the creation of large numbers of accounts. You can also use Windows PowerShell to automate account creation.

Csvde

The `Csvde` tool works with comma-separated text files with a `.csv` extension—in other words, values are separated from one another by commas. This is a format supported by many other applications, such as Exchange Server and Microsoft Excel. Because Excel supports this format, it is a convenient tool for creating the `.csv` file.

The first line of the `.csv` file is known as the *attribute* line. It defines the format of the following lines according to attributes defined in the schema. The attributes are separated by commas and define the order in which the attributes will appear on each data line.

Following the attribute line, each line includes one set of user data to be included in the bulk import. The data must conform to the following rules:

- The sequence of the source values must be exactly the same as that specified in the attribute line.

- A value containing commas must be enclosed in quotation marks.

- If a user object does not have entries for all the values included in the attribute line, you can leave the field blank; however, you must include the commas.

The following are examples of code lines conforming to these rules:

```
Dn,cn,objectClass,sAMAccountName,userPrincipalName,telephoneNumber,
    userAccountControl

"cn=Peter Jones,OU=engineering,dc=que,dc=com", Peter Jones,user,
    PeterJ,PeterJ@que.com,555-678-9876,512
"cn=Catharine Smith,OU=sales,dc=que,dc=com", Catharine Smith,user,
    CatharineS,CatharineS@que.com,555-678-4321,514

"cn=Computer1,OU=engineering,dc=que,dc=com",Computer1,computer,
    Computer1,,,
```

The variable `userAccountControl` determines the account's Enabled status; a value of 512 enables the user account and a value of 514 disables it. The last entry is an example of a computer object (`objectClass=computer`), with no values defined for `userPrincipalName` or `telephoneNumber`. You would normally import this object to the default Computers container; however, you can import it to any desired container.

To import the `.csv` file to AD DS, run the following command from the command prompt:

```
Csvde -I -f filename.csv
```

In this command, `-I` specifies import mode (the default is export mode) and `-f filename.csv` specifies the name of the file to be imported. After you press **Enter**, the command provides status information including any errors that might occur. When the command has completed, you should check some of the user accounts to confirm its proper completion.

> **TIP**   `Csvde` is a convenient tool for importing user and group account information provided in an Excel spreadsheet file because Excel offers a convenient means for exporting data to a comma-separated text file.

Ldifde

The `Ldifde` tool works in a similar manner to `Csvde` except that it uses the LDIF file format, which is a line-separated format. In other words, each record is separated by a blank line. A record is a distinct collection of data to be added to AD DS or modify existing data—for example, a username or computer name.

Each line describes a singe attribute and specifies the name of the attribute (as defined by the schema) followed by its value. A line beginning with # is a comment line. The following example uses the text from one of the comma-separated values used in the previous section. This should enable you to compare the two formats:

```
# These are the attributes for Peter Jones.
DN—cn=Peter Jones,OU=engineering,dc=que,dc=com
CN—Peter Jones
DisplayName: Peter Jones
GivenName: Peter
Sn: Jones
ObjectClass: user
SAMAccountName: PeterJ
UserPrincipalName: PeterJ@que.com
TelephoneNumber: 555-678-4321
PhysicalDeliveryOfficeName: 7th Floor, SE Corner
```

To use `Ldifde`, run the following command from the command prompt:

```
Ldifde -I -f filename.ldf
```

The usage and parameters of Ldifde are identical to those used with `Csvde`. Table 14-2 describes several more common parameters used by these commands. You can also use `Ldifde` to modify or delete accounts, extend the schema, export AD DS data to other applications or services, and import information from other directory services to AD DS.

Table 14-2   Common Parameters Used by `Csvde` and `Ldifde`

Parameter	Description
`-I`	Specifies import mode. If not specified, the default is export mode.
`-f filename`	Specifies the import or export filename.
`-s servername`	Specifies the domain controller to be used during import or export.
`-c string1 string2`	Replaces occurrences of *string1* with *string2*. This is useful if you have to import data from one domain to another and need to modify the distinguished names accordingly.
`-j directory path`	Specifies the path to the log file. By default, this is the current directory path.
`-b username domain password`	Enables you to run the command using the credentials of another user account. Specify the username, domain, and password of the required account.

NOTE   For additional parameters used with `Csvde` and `Ldifde`, refer to the Windows Server 2012 R2 Help and Support Center or to "Csvde" at http://technet.microsoft.com/en-us/library/cc771621.aspx and "Ldifde" at http://technet.microsoft.com/en-us/library/cc730865.aspx.

Dsadd

The `dsadd` command-line tool enables you to add objects, including users, groups, computers, OUs, contacts, and quotas, to the AD DS database. To add a user, execute the following command:

Dsadd user UserDN **-fn** FirstName **-ln** LastName **-display** DisplayName
    -pwd {*password* | ***} **-samid** *SAMName* **-tel** *PhoneNumber*
    -disabled {yes | no}

In this command, *userDN* refers to the distinguished name of the user you are adding, *FirstName* and *LastName* are the user's first and last names, *DisplayName* is the display name, *password* is the password (if you specify ***, the user is prompted for the password), *SAMName* is the unique SAM account name, *PhoneNumber* is the user's telephone number, and `disabled` is the enabled/disabled status (if you specify `yes`, the account is disabled, and if you specify `no`, the account is enabled). An example follows:

```
Dsadd user "cn=Peter Jones,OU=accounting,dc=que,dc=com" -fn Peter
    -ln Jones -display "Peter Jones" -pwd P@ssw0rd =samid PeterJ
    -tel 555-678-1234 -disabled yes
```

Many additional parameters are available. For more information, execute this command followed by **/?** or consult the Windows Server 2012 R2 Help and Support Center.

Additional Command-Line Tools

AD DS provides the following command-line tools, the functionality of which is similar in nature to that of `dsadd`:

- **dsmod:** Modifies objects

- **dsrm:** Removes objects

- **dsmove:** Moves objects to another container within the domain

- **dsget:** Provides information about objects

- **dsquery:** Displays objects matching search criteria

> **NOTE**   For more information on all the command-line tools discussed in this section, refer to "11 Essential Tools for Managing Active Directory" at http://technet.microsoft.com/en-us/magazine/2007.09.adtools.aspx.

> **TIP**   You can use the commands in this section to script the creation, modification, or deletion of multiple AD DS objects. You can also use Windows PowerShell cmdlets in your scripts or for managing user accounts from a Server Core machine.

Using PowerShell to Configure User and Computer Accounts

Windows PowerShell is another powerful tool you can use to perform basic User/Computer tasks within AD DS. The following list contains a handful of the more common PowerShell cmdlets:

- **Add-Computer:** Adds a local computer or remote computer to the domain including adding it to a specific OU. The basic syntax is `Add-Computer -ComputerName Computer1`.

- **`Get-ADComputer`:** Useful to retrieve information about one or more AD computers, it has properties or attributes such as `LastLogonDate`, `LogonHours`, and so on. The basic syntax is `Get-ADComputer "Computer1" -Properties`.

- **`Remove-Computer`:** Removes a computer from the domain. The basic syntax is `Remove-Computer -ComputerName Computer1`.

- **`Rename-Computer`:** Renames a computer in the domain. The basic syntax is `Rename-Computer -ComputerName Computer1 -NewName Computer2`.

- **`Get-ADUser`:** Useful to retrieve information about one or more AD users, their properties, or even their attributes such as `LastLogonDate`, `LogonHours`, and so on. The basic syntax is `Get-ADUser BOB -Properties`.

- **`New-ADUser`:** Creates a new Active Directory user. The basic syntax is `New-ADUser -SamAccountName "firstlast" -UserPrincipalName "firstlast@mydomain.com" -GivenName "First" -Surname "Last" -DisplayName "First Last" -Name "First Last" -Enabled $true -path "ou=testou,DC=mydomain,DC=com"`.

> **NOTE**   For more information on all the command-line tools discussed in this section, refer to "Active Directory Cmdlets in Windows PowerShell" at http://technet.microsoft.com/en-us/library/ee617195.aspx.

> **NOTE**   Over the last several sections, we've discussed several tools used to join computers to a domain. If you recall, computers are automatically joined and placed in the default Computers container. If you plan on moving all computers to a specific OU, Microsoft has provided the ability to change the default path. Using the `Redircmp.exe` tool, you can redirect the default container for newly created computers to a specific OU. Computers joined will be created in the target OU instead of the default Computers container. To modify the default path, execute `Redircmp ou=newOU,dc=mydomain,dc=com`. For more information, refer to "Redircmp" at http://technet.microsoft.com/en-us/library/cc770619.aspx.

Configuring the UPN

A user principal name (UPN) is a logon name formatted in a manner similar to that of an email address, such as `user1@que.com`. The first part uniquely identifies the user, and the second part by default identifies the domain to which he belongs. It is especially convenient when logging on to a domain from a computer located in another domain in the forest or a trusted forest.

UPN Suffixes

Originally introduced in Windows Server 2003 and continued in each newer iteration of Windows Server is the concept of the UPN suffix. This is the portion of the UPN to the right of the at (@) character. By default, the UPN suffix is the DNS name of the domain to which the user belongs. You can provide an additional UPN suffix to simplify administrative and logon procedures. Doing so provides the following advantages:

- Using a common UPN suffix throughout a multidomain forest simplifies logon procedures for all users. This is especially true in the case of long child domain names. For example, a user with a default UPN of `James@east.marketing.que.com` could be provided with a simpler UPN such as `James@que`.

- Using a common UPN suffix also enables you to hide the true domain structure from users in external forests. It also simplifies configuring remote access servers for visitor access.

- You can use the UPN suffix to match the email domain name in cases where the company has more than one division with different email domain names but a common AD DS domain. Using the additional UPN suffix enables users to log on using their email addresses.

- A common UPN suffix is also useful in enabling users to log on to a domain in an existing forest. However, if more than one forest uses the same UPN suffix, you can log on to a domain in the same forest only; furthermore, if you are using explicit UPNs and external trusts, you can use the UPN to log on to a domain in the same forest only.

Adding or Removing UPN Suffixes

You can create alternative UPN suffixes by opening the Active Directory Domains and Trusts console. In the console tree, right-click **Active Directory Domains and Trusts** and select **Properties** to open the dialog box shown in Figure 14-5. Simply type the desired UPN suffix (for example, `certguide`), click **Add**, and then click **OK**.

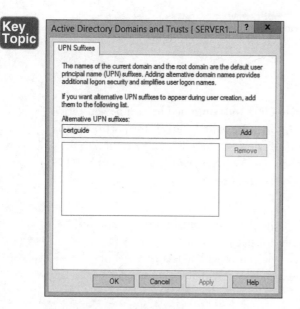

Figure 14-5 You can easily add or remove alternative UPN suffixes in Active Directory Domains and Trusts.

You can use the added UPN suffix in Active Directory Users and Computers to configure new or existing users. When adding a new user, the alternative UPN suffix is available from the drop-down list in the New Object - User dialog box (refer to Figures 14-2 and 14-3). You can also configure an existing user with the alternative UPN suffix from the Account tab of the user's Properties dialog box. As shown in Figure 14-6, the alternative UPN suffix is available in the drop-down list of the Account tab of the user's Properties dialog box.

To remove an alternative UPN suffix, access the same dialog box shown in Figure 14-5, select the UPN suffix, and click **Remove**. Then accept the warning that users who use this UPN suffix will no longer be able to log on to the network. You should then open **Active Directory Users and Computers** or **Active Directory Administrative Center**, select any user accounts that refer to this suffix, and change them to one that is still in use.

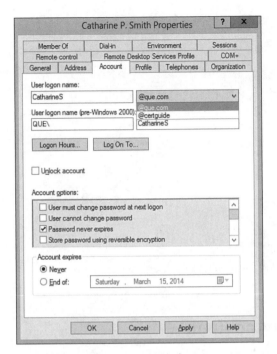

Figure 14-6   The Account tab of a user's Properties dialog box enables you to configure an alternative UPN suffix.

Configuring Contacts

A *contact* is simply a collection of information about an individual or organization. AD DS provides the Contacts folder, which you can use to store information such as the contact's name, email address, street address, and telephone number.

You can create a contact in the Users group or any OU in your domain's hierarchy. Right-click the container, and select **New > Contact**. This displays the dialog box shown in Figure 14-7.

The contact you have created appears in the details pane of Active Directory Users and Computers or Active Directory Administrative Center. Right-click the contact and select **Properties** to configure a limited set of properties, including items such as the address, telephone numbers, organization, and so on.

You can also automate the creation of contacts using any of the methods discussed earlier in this chapter and setting the `objectClass` value to `Contact`.

Figure 14-7   You can create contacts by using the New Object - Contact dialog box.

Managing and Maintaining Accounts

After you have created user and computer accounts that encompass all the employees and machines in your organization's AD DS structure, you must be able to work with and manage all these accounts. Account management is a large part of an administrator's everyday actions. The following aspects of account management are discussed in this section:

- Resetting passwords
- Protected Admin
- Offline domain join
- Configuring user rights
- Managing inactive and disabled accounts

The following sections briefly introduce each of these concepts.

Password Resets

A common task network administrators and desktop or help desk personnel must perform is the resetting of passwords for users who have forgotten them. Related to this is the task of unlocking user accounts that have been locked out because of too many attempts at entering an incorrect password.

To reset a password, open **Active Directory Users and Computers** or **Active Directory Administrative Center** and select the container or OU in which the account is located from the console tree listing. In the details pane, right-click the user account and select **Reset Password**. In the Reset Password dialog box shown in Figure 14-8, type and confirm a new password. By default, the user is required to change this password at next logon, thereby enabling the user to select a password of his choice. He must select a password that is within the limits of the password complexity policy, which is discussed in Chapter 17, "Configuring Security Policies." If the account is locked out, select the check box labeled **Unlock account**.

Figure 14-8   The Reset Password dialog box enables you to reset the password for a user who has forgotten his password.

NOTE   A Microsoft Gold Certified Partner, Lieberman Software, has produced an Account Reset Console that enables users to reset forgotten or expired passwords without the help of an administrator. Like other third-party add-on solutions, this product is beyond the scope of the 70-410 exam.

Protected Admin

Previous versions of Windows Server have limited the ability to perform tasks when using a nonadministrative user account, with the result that many users would always use an administrative account, whether they needed it or not. This practice often left the servers open to many types of attack by malware programs such as viruses, Trojan horses, spyware, and so on. Starting with Windows Vista and Windows Server 2008 and continued in Windows 7, Windows 8/8.1, and Windows Server 2012 R2, a feature called User Account Control (UAC) requires users performing administrative tasks to confirm that they actually initiated the task. This includes all administrative accounts except the default Administrator account created when you first install Windows Server 2012 R2 or the default account created when you create the first domain controller in a new forest.

Microsoft recommends that you not use this default administrative account and instead create a different administrative account for everyday domain administration activities. In doing so, you are working with what Microsoft calls a Protected Admin account. This account works with standard user privileges, thereby preventing many types of attack. When you need to perform an administrative task, Windows displays a UAC prompt as shown in Figure 14-9. You click **Yes** to perform the activity or **No** to quit. If a malicious program attempts to run, Windows displays the UAC prompt that includes the program name, alerting you to which program is asking for your permission. Thereby, you can cancel such an unexpected prompt and be protected from whatever damage could otherwise occur.

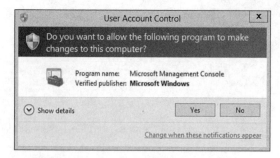

Figure 14-9   User Account Control displays this prompt to ask for approval of an administrative task.

If you are logged on as a user that is not a member of the Domain Admins group, you receive a slightly different UAC prompt, as shown in Figure 14-10. This prompt asks you to specify the username and password of an administrative account to proceed with your desired task.

Figure 14-10   User Account Control displays this prompt to ask for approval of an administrative task when logged on as a nonadministrative user.

> **WARNING**   When you receive a UAC prompt, always ensure that the action indicated is the one you want to perform. This is especially true if a UAC prompt appears unexpectedly, which could indicate a malware program attempting to run. Should this happen, click **No** and the program cannot run. You should then scan your computer with one or more malware detection programs.

Offline Domain Join

The concept of offline domain join enables you to configure a client computer running Windows 7/8//8.1/Server 2008 R2/2012/2012 R2 to join a domain without contacting a domain controller. Offline domain join facilitates the task of deploying large numbers of physical or virtual computers in a large office or datacenter.

The following are several benefits of using offline domain join:

- **Reduction of total cost of ownership (TCO):** The startup time for each computer being joined to the domain is reduced, and the reliability of domain join operations is improved. In addition, the potential for network connectivity problems when new computers attempt to access servers is reduced.

- **Improvement when using an RODC for domain joins:** Windows Server 2012 R2 provides a mechanism to perform offline domain join actions against an RODC. You can include the required information in a text file that is sent to the computer joining the domain; the domain join operation runs automatically when the computer is restarted.

- **Reduced network traffic:** You can join these computers to the domain on the initial restart following operating system installation, thereby reducing the overall time required for computer deployments. Further, network traffic is reduced, including traffic to the computers being joined as well as to the domain controllers.

- **Rapid enterprise deployments:** You can use deployment tools such as Windows System Image Manager to include the domain join within the operating system installation. You can include the required information in an `Unattend.xml` file with a special section that supports offline domain join.

To perform offline domain joins, you must be a member of the Domain Admins group or be granted the required user rights for creating computer accounts in the default Computers container or in the OU in which the computer accounts are to be located. It is possible to delegate the appropriate permissions in the access control list (ACL) of the Computers container or the appropriate OU. Configuration of user rights is discussed later in this chapter.

You use the Djoin.exe command-line tool from an administrative command account to enable the computer to join the domain offline. This command provisions the computer account metadata by creating a .txt file and inserts this information into the Windows directory of the computer being joined to the domain. You can also save the metadata into an Unattend.xml file for unattended operating system installation.

The syntax for the Djoin.exe commands for provisioning the computer account metadata for the computer to be joined to the domain and for inserting this metadata into the Windows directory of this computer, are as follows:

```
djoin /provision /domain <domain_name> /machine <destination
computer> /savefile <filename.txt> [/machineou <OU name>] [/dcname
<name of domain controller>] [/reuse] [/downlevel] [/defpwd]
[/nosearch] [/printblob] [/rootcacerts] [/certtemplate <name>]
[/policynames <name(s)>] [/policypaths <Path(s)>]
djoin /requestodj /loadfile <filename.txt> /windowspath <path to
the Windows directory of the offline image> /localos
```

The following are the most important parameters of the djoin.exe command:

- **/provision:** Creates a computer account in AD DS.

- **/domain** <domain_name >: Specifies the name of the domain being joined.

- **/machine** <destination computer>: Specifies the name of the computer to be joined to the domain.

- **/savefile** <filename.txt>: Specifies the name of a file to which provisioning data will be saved.

- **/machineou** <OU name>: Specifies the name of the OU where the computer account is created. If not used, the account is created in the Computers container.

- **/requestodj:** Requests an offline domain join at the next start.

- **/loadfile** <filename.txt>: Specifies the name of the previously created provisioning data file.

- **/localos:** Targets the local operating system installation rather than an offline image, with the domain join information.

- **/windowspath** *<path to the Windows directory of the offline image>*: Specifies the path to the Windows directory of the offline image. You can use `%systemroot%` or `%windir%` as the value of this parameter if you are using the `/localos` parameter.

For example, the following command creates the metadata required to join a computer named `Computer101` to the `que.com` domain:

```
djoin /Provision /Domain que.com /Machine Computer101 /SaveFile
c:\Computer101.txt
```

You would then use the following command to enable the `Computer101` computer to join the domain, after copying the `Computer101.txt` file to this computer:

```
djoin /requestODJ /loadfile Computer101.txt /windowspath %SystemRoot%
/localos
```

NOTE   For more information on offline domain join, including the definitions of parameters not mentioned here, refer to "Offline Domain Join (`Djoin.exe`) Step-by-Step Guide" at http://technet.microsoft.com/en-us/library/offline-domain-join-djoin-step-by-step(v=WS.10).aspx.

Configuring User Rights

User rights are defined as a default set of capabilities assigned to built-in domain local groups that define what members of these groups can and cannot do on the network. They consist of Privileges and Logon Rights.

You can manage these predefined user rights from the Computer Configuration \Policies\Windows Settings\Security Settings\Local Policies\User Rights Assignment node in the Group Policy Management Editor. When focused on the Default Domain Controllers Policy GPO, you can view the default rights assignments, as shown in Figure 14-11. To modify the assignment of any user right, right-click it and select **Properties**. In the Properties dialog box, click **Add User or Group**, and in the Add User or Group dialog box, type or browse to the required user or group. Then click **OK**.

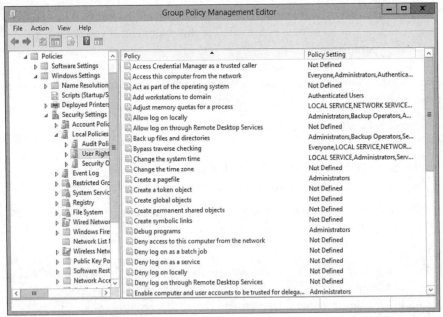

Figure 14-11   The Default Domain Controllers Policy GPO includes an extensive set of predefined user rights assignments.

You can also create a new GPO and configure a series of settings in this node to be applied to a specific group and then link the GPO to an appropriate OU and grant the required group the Read and Apply Group Policy permissions. This is an easy way to grant user rights over a subset of the domain to a junior group of employees such as help desk technicians.

Inactive and Disabled Accounts

What should you do if a user quits, is fired, or goes on some type of extended leave? You need to deprovision the user's account to prevent unauthorized access—in other words, prevent someone from logging on using this account. This section looks at two choices for deprovisioning an account: disabling or deleting the account.

When this happens, you have several choices. If a replacement has been hired, you can simply rename the user account for the replacement. Otherwise, you can simply delete it. However, if there is a possibility that a replacement will be hired in the future, you have an additional choice—disabling the account. Disabling an account rather than deleting it provides several advantages:

- When disabled, nobody can log on using this account. In this way, a disgruntled employee who has resigned or been fired cannot log on and delete or steal important data.

- Security is also improved in the case of an employee taking an extended sabbatical or disability leave.

- The disabled account retains all group memberships, rights, and permissions assigned to it. When you hire a replacement, you can reenable and rename the account and do not need to go through the procedure of creating everything from scratch.

To disable an account, right-click it in Active Directory Users and Computers or Active Directory Administrative Center and select **Disable Account**. You receive a message that the object has been disabled. To reenable the account, right-click it and select **Enable Account**. To delete an account, right-click it and select **Delete** or simply press the **Delete** key. You are asked whether you are sure you want to delete this account. Click **Yes** to confirm or **No** to cancel.

Exam Preparation Tasks

Review All the Key Topics

Review the most important topics in the chapter, noted with the key topics icon in the outer margin of the page. Table 14-3 lists a reference of these key topics and the page numbers on which each is found.

Table 14-3 Key Topics for Chapter 14

Key Topic Element	Description	Page Number
List	Describes the types of user accounts in AD DS.	644
Figure 14-1	The Active Directory Administrative Center enables you to perform most AD DS administrative actions.	645
Figure 14-3	When creating a user account from the Active Directory Administrative Center, you can configure a large range of user account properties.	647
Figure 14-4	Shows properties you can assign when creating a computer account.	649
Paragraph	Describes the use and purpose of template accounts.	650

Key Topic Element	Description	Page Number
List	Describes utilities available for automated creation of accounts in AD DS.	651
Table 14-2	Describes important parameters used with Csvde and Ldifde.	654
List	Lists the common PowerShell cmdlets used for managing users/computers.	655
Figure 14-5	Shows how to create alternative UPN suffixes.	658
Paragraph	Describes the Protected Admin capability.	662
List	Describes the benefits of configuring offline domain join for new computers.	663
Figure 14-11	Describes user rights policies available in Group Policy Management Editor.	666
List	Provides reasons for disabling, rather than deleting accounts.	667

Complete the Tables and Lists from Memory

Print a copy of Appendix B, "Memory Tables" (found on the CD), or at least the section for this chapter, and complete the tables and lists from memory. Appendix C, "Memory Tables Answer Key," is also on the CD and includes completed tables and lists to check your work.

Definitions of Key Terms

Define the following key terms from this chapter, and check your answers in the glossary.

Built-in account, Csvde, djoin.exe, Domain user account, Dsadd, Ldifde, Local user account, Offline domain join, Protected Admin, Template account, User Account Control (UAC), User principal name (UPN), User principal name (UPN) suffix, User logon name

This chapter covers the following subjects:

- **Creating and Managing Group Accounts:** Active Directory enables you to create groups that facilitate access to users with similar need for resources on the network. You can create these groups at various levels in the directory structure and nest them to facilitate resource access management. You can also convert various types and scopes of groups when changes become necessary.

- **Creating and Managing Organizational Units:** This section demonstrates the various methods to create and manage OUs within a domain. It provides instructions on how to create, rename, delete, and move OUs using the Active Directory Administrative Center.

- **Delegation of Active Directory Object Management:** This section introduces delegation of Active Directory object management and provides you with a framework for determining the appropriate delegation strategy for your organization.

Active Directory Groups and Organizational Units (OUs)

Chapter 14, "Active Directory User and Computer Accounts," introduced you to the management of user accounts and automated means for creating large numbers of accounts. This chapter continues the discussion of accounts by showing you how to group users in manners that facilitate access to resources on the network such as files, folders, and printers. It then turns its attention to the creation and management of organizational units (OUs). As introduced in Chapter 13, "Installing Domain Controllers," OUs enable you to organize your domain into logical subgroups that enable you to collect users, computers, and other resources for simplified local administration according to your company's organizational chart of departments, sections, work units, and so on. You can change this grouping of OUs easily if your company reorganizes; such a task is much easier than attempting to re-create child domains according to a new corporate structure.

"Do I Know This Already?" Quiz

The "Do I Know This Already?" quiz enables you to assess whether you should read this entire chapter or simply jump to the "Exam Preparation Tasks" section for review. If you are in doubt, read the entire chapter. Table 15-1 outlines the major headings in this chapter and the corresponding "Do I Know This Already?" quiz questions. You can find the answers in Appendix A, "Answers to the 'Do I Know This Already?' Quizzes."

Table 15-1 "Do I Know This Already?" Foundation Topics Section-to-Question Mapping

Foundations Topics Section	Questions Covered in This Section
Creating and Managing Group Accounts	1–6
Creating and Managing Organizational Units	7
Delegation of Active Directory Object Management	8–9

1. Sharon works for a company with an AD DS forest that consists of a forest root domain plus four child domains. She needs to create a group containing 55 users who require access to resources in all five domains. All the user accounts are located in the forest root domain. Which group scope should Sharon use?

   a. Local

   b. Domain local

   c. Global

   d. Universal

2. You are using Active Directory Administrative Center to create new groups in your company's AD DS domain. Which of the following are actions you can perform from the Create Group dialog box that you cannot perform directly from the Add Group dialog box in Active Directory Users and Computers? (Choose all that apply.)

   a. Define the type and scope for the group.

   b. Add users to the group.

   c. Nest this group into another group.

   d. Specify information of a user that is responsible for managing the group.

   e. Define permissions to resources for the group.

3. You are planning the group structure of your company's AD DS forest, which includes two domains in a single tree. You have created a domain local group in the child domain and want to add other groups to this domain. Which of the following can you add to this group? (Choose all that apply.)

   a. Universal groups from the parent domain

   b. Global groups from the parent domain

   c. Global groups from the child domain

   d. Domain local groups from the parent domain

   e. Domain local groups from the child domain

4. You are planning the group structure of your company's AD DS forest, which includes two domains in a single tree. You have created a global group in the child domain so that you can provide resource access throughout the forest. To which of the following can you add this group as a member? (Choose all that apply.)

   a. Universal groups from the parent domain

   b. Global groups from the parent domain

   c. Global groups from the child domain

   d. Domain local groups from the parent domain

   e. Domain local groups from the child domain

5. You are a network administrator working for your state's environmental agency. You have been provided with a list of 50 individuals representing citizen groups and area companies who will be providing input on a proposed water diversion project. You need to ensure that these individuals receive email messages from the assessment committee that is studying this proposal regularly without receiving access to the agency's AD DS domain. What should you do?

   a. Create user accounts for each of these individuals, and add these contacts to a distribution group.

   b. Create contacts for each of these individuals, and add these contacts to a distribution group.

   c. Create user accounts for each of these individuals, and add these contacts to a security group.

   d. Create contacts for each of these individuals, and add these contacts to a security group.

6. You are designing a group strategy for an AD DS forest consisting of seven domains in two trees. Twenty users, whose user accounts are located in various domains of the forest, require access to resources in three child domains, so you create a universal group to grant the required access to these users. Which of the following is the recommended strategy you should follow in granting the required access?

  a. Add the user accounts to the universal group, and then grant the universal group the required permissions for these resources.

  b. Add the user accounts to the universal group, and then add the universal group to three domain local groups, one located in each child domain to which the users need access. Finally, grant permissions to the domain local groups.

  c. Add the user accounts to global groups in their respective domains. Then add these global groups to the universal group, and grant the universal group the required permissions for these resources.

  d. Add the user accounts to global groups in their respective domains. Then add these global groups to the universal group, and add the universal group to three domain local groups, one located in each child domain to which the users need access. Finally, grant permissions to the domain local groups.

7. You are a consultant who has been given the responsibility of defining the OU structure for a new company just setting up its first domain. Which of the following types of information are helpful in designing an appropriate OU structure for this company? (Choose all that apply.)

  a. Corporate organizational charts

  b. Names and addresses of company executives

  c. Geographical distribution of company offices

  d. Requirements for delegation of administrative control

  e. AD DS information on partner companies and their need for resource access

8. You want to enable junior administrators to be able to create and manage a specific organizational unit for a branch site (Site1). Your solution should limit the amount of access these administrators have in the domain. What should you do?

   a. Add each junior admin to the Domain Admins group.

   b. Add each junior admin to a global security group. Add the security group to the Domain Admins group.

   c. Use the Active Directory Delegation of Control Wizard on the OU for Site1.

   d. Use the Administrative Delegation of Control Wizard on each user object.

9. You want to enable the help desk technicians to reset user passwords without permitting them to do other administrative tasks in your domain. The technicians have user accounts that are members of the HelpDesk global group. What should you do?

   a. Use the Delegation of Control Wizard to grant members of the HelpDesk global group the Reset user passwords and force password change at next logon task.

   b. Use the Delegation of Control Wizard to grant each help desk technician the Reset user passwords and force password change at next logon task.

   c. Add the HelpDesk group to the domain's Account Operators built-in group.

   d. Add each help desk technician's user account to the domain's Account Operators built-in group.

Foundation Topics

Creating and Managing Group Accounts

Common networks have hundreds to thousands of users and large numbers of network resources such as files, folders, and printers. Granting access to these resources based solely on user accounts would be time-consuming, error-prone, and highly repetitive. That's why there are groups. Simply put, you can create a group within Active Directory Domain Services (AD DS) and grant or deny access to this single entity. Then you can add user accounts as members of the group. Belonging to the group, the user accounts inherit the permissions assigned to the group. It is much simpler to modify the permissions once on a group object than many times on the users. Further, you can build a hierarchy of groups and assign different permissions to each level, an activity known as *nesting*. This refers to the act of making one group a member of a different group, thereby creating a hierarchy. Nesting groups further simplifies your security model.

Windows Server 2012 R2 provides two group types:

- **Security groups:** You can use these groups for assigning rights and permissions to users. They can also be used for distribution purposes. These group types have security information, such as unique security identifiers (SIDs), assigned to them.

- **Distribution groups:** You can use these groups for distribution purposes such as email lists. These groups do not possess SIDs and cannot be assigned permission to resources.

Within each group type, Windows Server 2012 R2 provides three group scopes:

- **Global:** These groups can include users, computers, and other global groups from the same domain. You can use them to organize users who have similar functions and therefore similar requirements on the network. For example, you might include all sales staff in one global group, all engineering staff in another global group, and so on.

- **Domain local:** These groups can include users, computers, and groups from any domain in the forest. They are most often utilized to grant permissions for resources and can be used to provide access to any resource in the domain in which they are located. It is thus logical for a domain local group to include global groups that contain all users with a common need for a given resource.

- **Universal:** These groups can include users and groups from any domain in the AD DS forest and can be employed to grant permissions to any resource in the forest. A universal group can include users, computers, and global groups from any domain in the forest.

When you install the first domain controller of a domain, a set of default security groups is created automatically. These built-in groups are placed within the Builtin and Users containers, as shown in Figure 15-1 for the Builtin container. The default security groups (see Table 15-2) are intended to be used as part of the security group strategy for a domain. You should consider using the default security groups in addition to the custom security groups that you create in your own strategy. Note that many of these groups are populated by default when certain actions occur, such as installing AD DS, promoting additional domain controllers, or adding computers to the domain.

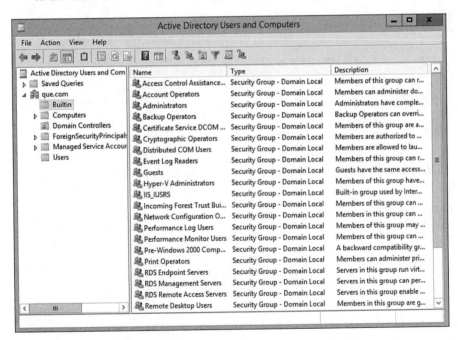

Figure 15-1   The Builtin container contains a large number of built-in security groups that are useful in configuring your domain.

Table 15-2 lists the default security groups.

Table 15-2   The Default Security Groups in Windows Server 2012 R2 Active Directory

Group Name	Where Found	Usage
Account Operators	Builtin container	This group has the rights to create, modify, and delete user, computer, and group objects. It is denied access to manage administrator accounts and domain controllers.
Access Control Assistance Operators	Builtin container	This group has the rights to remotely query authorization attributes and permissions for resources on the domain controllers.
Administrators	Builtin container	This group has full rights to manage the domain controllers.
Backup Operators	Builtin container	This group provides the rights to files and domain controller resources so the group can perform backups.
Certificate Service DCOM Access	Builtin container	Members are allowed to connect to Certification Authorities in the forest.
Cert Publishers	Users container	This group includes the rights to publish certificates.
Cloneable Domain Controllers	Users container	This group includes domain controllers that can be cloned.
Cryptographic Operators	Builtin container	This group is authorized to perform cryptographic operations.
Denied RODC Password Replicators	Users container	Members of this group cannot have their passwords replicated to any RODCs in the domain.
Distributed COM Users	Builtin container	Members are allowed to launch, activate, and use Distributed COM objects on this computer.
DnsAdmins	Users container	This group is available only when Domain Name System (DNS) is installed; it provides the rights required to manage DNS.
DnsUpdateProxy	Users container	This group is available only when DNS is installed, and it is used by Dynamic Host Configuration Protocol (DHCP) servers so they can perform dynamic DNS updates on behalf of other client computers.
Domain Admins	Users container	This group is granted full rights to manage the entire domain. It is automatically made a member of each member server's, member computer's, and domain controller's Administrators local groups.

Group Name	Where Found	Usage
Domain Computers	Users container	This group contains all member servers and computers in the domain.
Domain Controllers	Users container	This group contains all domain controllers in the domain.
Domain Guests	Users container	This group is automatically made a member of the Guests local group on each member server, member computer, and domain controller.
Domain Users	Users container	This group contains all users in the domain and is automatically made a member of the Users local group on each member server, member computer, and domain controller.
Enterprise Admins	Users container	This group is only in the root domain of the forest. It is granted full control of all the domains in the forest.
Enterprise Read-only Domain Controllers	Users container	This group contains all RODCs in the forest.
Event Log Readers	Builtin container	Members can read event logs from the local computer.
Guests	Builtin container	This group has no rights.
Hyper-V Administrators	Builtin container	Members have complete and unlimited access to all features of Hyper-V.
IIS_IUSRS	Builtin container	Built-in group used by Internet Information Services (IIS).
Incoming Forest Trust Builders	Builtin container	Members can create incoming, one-way trusts to this forest.
Network Configuration Operators	Builtin container	This group is granted the rights to manage the network configuration, such as TCP/IP, of domain controllers.
Performance Log Users	Builtin container	This group provides the rights to manage performance logs and alerts for Perfmon either locally or remotely.
Performance Monitor Users	Builtin container	This group provides the rights required to run Perfmon either locally or remotely.
Pre-Windows 2000 Compatible Access	Builtin container	This group provides backward compatibility to computers running Windows NT.
Print Operators	Builtin container	This group has the rights required for managing printers shared by domain controllers.

Group Name	Where Found	Usage
Protected Users	Users container	Members of this group receive additional protections against security threats, such as compromising of credentials, during the authentication process. This group is new to Windows Server 2012 R2.
RAS and IAS Servers	Users container	Servers in this group can access remote access properties of users.
RDS Endpoint Servers	Builtin container	Servers in this group run virtual machines and host sessions where users' RemoteApp programs and personal virtual desktops run.
RDS Management Servers	Builtin container	Servers in this group can perform routine administrative actions on servers running Remote Desktop Services.
RDS Remote Access Servers	Builtin container	Servers in this group enable users of RemoteApp programs and personal virtual desktops access to these resources.
Read-Only Domain Controllers	Users container	This group contains all RODCs in the domain.
Remote Desktop Users	Builtin container	This group allows users the right to log on remotely to domain controllers and member servers. Rights are granted locally on the servers and domain controllers.
Remote Management Users	Builtin container	Members can access Windows Management Instrumentation (WMI) resources over management protocols (such as WS-Management via the Windows Remote Management Service). This applies only to WMI namespaces that grant access to the user.
Replicator	Builtin container	Both the File Replication Service (FRS) and AD DS replication use this group. It is not intended for users.
Schema Admins	Users container	This group is found only in the forest root domain. It provides the rights to manage the schema of the forest.
Server Operators	Builtin container	This group provides the rights to manage domain controllers but not the rights to manage accounts.
Terminal Server License Servers	Builtin container	Servers in this group can update user accounts in AD DS with information about license issuance for the purpose of tracking and reporting TS Per User CAL usage.

Group Name	Where Found	Usage
Users	Builtin container	All user accounts are made members of this group.
Windows Authorization Access Group	Builtin container	This group has access to the computed `tokensGroupsGlobalAndUniversal` attribute on User objects.

> **NOTE**   For more information about the new Protected Users group, refer to "Protected Users Security Group" at http://technet.microsoft.com/en-us/library/dn466518.aspx.

Creating Group Accounts

As discussed in Chapter 14 with user and computer accounts, you can use either Active Directory Users and Computers or Active Directory Administrative Center to create a group account. Use the following procedure from Active Directory Users and Computers:

1. From the console tree of Active Directory Users and Computers, right-click the container in which you want to create the group (OU or Users container) and select **New > Group**.

2. In the New Object - Group dialog box shown in Figure 15-2, type the name of the group and choose the desired group type and scope, as already discussed. Accept the pre-Windows 2000 group name that's automatically supplied, or type another name if desired.

Figure 15-2   The New Object - Group dialog box enables you to create a group.

3. Click **OK**.

When using the Active Directory Administrative Center, the procedure is similar. The Create Group dialog box shown in Figure 15-3 (Managers is typed as a sample group name) enables you to create the following additional group properties:

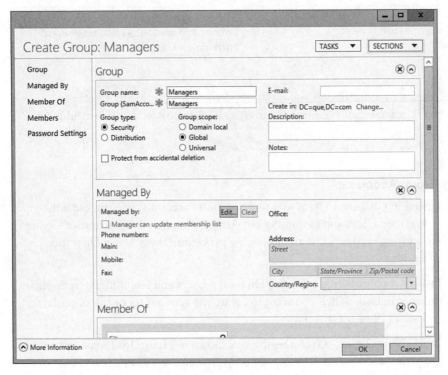

Figure 15-3   The Create Group dialog box in Active Directory Administrative Center enables you to specify several additional group properties.

- **E-mail:** Enables you to specify the email address of an individual responsible for managing the group.

- **Description and Notes:** Enables you to provide descriptive material that is searchable in the Directory.

- **Managed by:** Click **Edit** to add the name of a user or group that is responsible for managing the group. You can also add address and phone number information that is searchable in the Directory and is similar to that mentioned in Chapter 14 for users.

- **Member of:** Enables you to nest this group into another group. Click **Add** to do so.

- **Members:** Enables you to add users or groups to this group. Click **Add** to do so.

- **Directly Associated Password Settings:** Click **Assign** to display the Select Password Settings Object dialog box, which enables you to assign a Fine-Grained Password Policy (FGPP) object to members of the group. This specifies password policy settings that are specific to users to whom the policy has been assigned. You will learn more in the *Cert Guide* book for exam 70-411.

NOTE   For more information about creating groups in Windows Server 2012 R2, refer to "Create a New Group" at http://technet.microsoft.com/en-us/library/dd861305.aspx.

Configuring Group Membership

A group is of no use until you have added members to it. As already stated, groups are used to collect a set of users who need to share a particular set of permissions to a resource such as a file, folder, or printer. However, the available membership depends on the group scope. Table 15-3 outlines group membership and access considerations for the three group scopes.

Table 15-3   Comparison of Groups

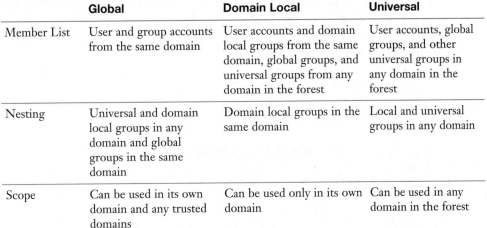

	Global	Domain Local	Universal
Member List	User and group accounts from the same domain	User accounts and domain local groups from the same domain, global groups, and universal groups from any domain in the forest	User accounts, global groups, and other universal groups in any domain in the forest
Nesting	Universal and domain local groups in any domain and global groups in the same domain	Domain local groups in the same domain	Local and universal groups in any domain
Scope	Can be used in its own domain and any trusted domains	Can be used only in its own domain	Can be used in any domain in the forest
Permissions	Resources in all domains in the forest	Resources in the domain in which the group exists only	Resources in any domain in the forest

Using Active Directory Users and Computers or Active Directory Administrative Center, you can configure group membership in any of the following ways:

- **Add a series of users or groups to the group:** Right-click the group and select **Properties**. On the Members tab, select **Add** and then enter the desired

account names in the Select Users, Contacts, Computers, Service Accounts, or
Groups dialog box, as shown in Figure 15-4.

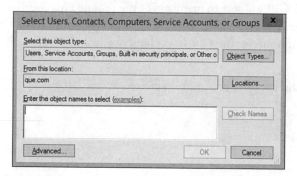

Figure 15-4   The Select Users, Contacts, Computers, Service Accounts, or Groups dialog box
enables you to add these types of objects to your distribution list.

- **Add a user to one or more groups:** In Active Directory Administrative
  Center, right-click the user and select **Add to group**. Then enter the desired
  groups in the Select Groups dialog box and click **OK**. Alternately, right-
  click the user account in Active Directory Users and Computers and select
  Properties. Select the **Member Of** tab of the user's Properties dialog box and
  click **Add**, as shown in Figure 15-5. You can also use this procedure to add one
  group to another within the limits described in Table 15-3.

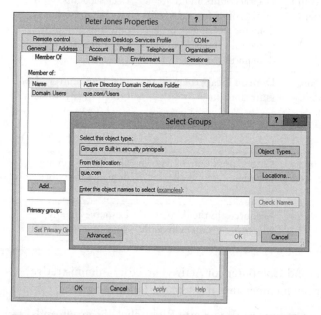

Figure 15-5   The Member Of tab of a user's Properties dialog box enables you to add the user
to a group.

- **Use the `dsadd` utility:** This utility enables you to add any allowable combinations of users and groups and enables you to script these actions.

To add a group, execute the following command:

```
Dsadd group GroupDN -fn FirstName -secgrp {yes | no} -scope {l |g |u}
    -samid SAMName -memberof Group ... -members member ...
```

In this command, `GroupDN` refers to the distinguished name of the group you are adding, `secgrp` specifies whether the group is a security group (`yes`) or distribution group (`no`), `scope` refers to the group scope (`l` for domain local, `g` for global, and `u` for universal), `memberof` specifies the groups to which the new group is to be added, and `members` specifies the members to add to the new group. By default, Windows creates a new group as a global security group.

You can also remove a user or group from another group if required. From the Members tab of the user or group's Properties dialog box, select the required entry and click **Remove** (or use the `dsrm` utility previously introduced in Chapter 14).

Creating Distribution Lists

Earlier in this chapter, the concept of distribution groups was introduced. The main purpose of a distribution group is to create a distribution list that is used with an email application, such as Microsoft Exchange Server, to send messages to a collection of users. By sending an email message to the group, it is automatically sent to all members of the group.

> **TIP**   You can also use a security group for distribution purposes. This is useful in cases where you need both the ability to send messages to a group and provide the same group access to resources in AD DS.

Windows Server 2012 R2 includes the Message Queuing feature, which provides guaranteed message delivery, efficient routing, security, and priority-based messaging between applications, including those that run on different operating systems. You can install Message Queuing from the Add Roles and Features Wizard in Server Manager.

Creating a distribution group is similar to creating other AD DS objects. Simply select the **Distribution** group type from the New Object - Group dialog box discussed earlier. Then right-click the new group and choose **Properties**. Select the **Members** tab; click **Add**; and add the required users and groups from the Select Users, Contacts, Computers, Service Accounts, or Groups dialog box previously shown in Figure 15-4. Use semicolons to separate multiple names from each other.

To add contacts or computers to the list, click **Object Types** to display the Object Types dialog box shown in Figure 15-6; then select either or both of these object types.

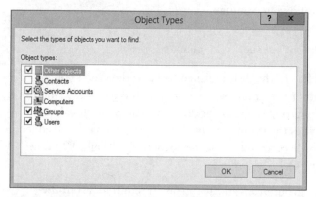

Figure 15-6   Select the appropriate object types from the Object Types dialog box to add these types of objects to your distribution list.

To send an email message to all members of a distribution list, simply right-click the list and select **Send Mail**. The default email application opens and displays a blank outgoing message with the email addresses of all members automatically filled in. You can do the same thing by selecting **New Message** from your email application and filling in the group name in the To field.

AGDLP/AGUDLP

Microsoft continues to recommend the same strategy for nesting groups that it has supported since Windows NT 4.0. The following list outlines the strategy:

1. Place accounts (A) into global groups (G).

2. Add the global groups to domain local groups (DL).

3. Finally, assign permissions (P) to the domain local groups.

In short, this strategy is known as AGDLP, or Accounts to Global groups to Domain Local groups to Permissions.

> **NOTE**   Simple nesting of groups is always best. Minimize levels of nesting as just stated (AGDLP). This strategy simplifies the process of keeping track of permissions and troubleshooting resource access. In addition, it is useful to base your global groups on job functions. When another person takes over a job, you need only change the person's group membership, and not all the associated permissions.

You can use the same strategy in multidomain environments. Add users from each child domain to a global group in the same domain. Then add these global groups to a domain local group in the parent domain and grant permissions to this group. Figure 15-7 shows this strategy in graphical form.

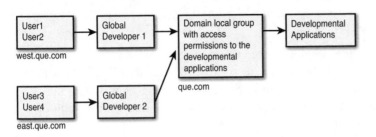

Figure 15-7   You can use the AGDLP strategy in multidomain situations.

You can extend this strategy by using universal groups, as shown schematically in Figure 15-8. Doing so changes the acronym from AGDLP to AGUDLP. The two child domains, `west.que.com` and `east.que.com`, both contain users that require access to developmental applications located in the `que.com` domain. By employing a universal group, you can grant access to these applications to users in both domains by employing just a single group (the universal group). Although you can grant access directly to the universal group, Microsoft recommends that you secure access to these resources by creating a domain local group in the domain in which they are located and adding the universal group to this domain local group. Then grant the appropriate permissions to the domain local group. If necessary, you can extend this strategy to domain local groups located in additional domains containing applications to which you must grant access.

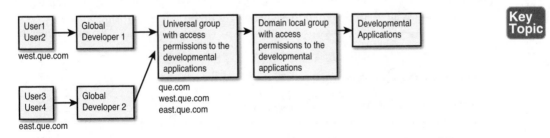

Figure 15-8   You can use the AGUDLP strategy to grant access to resources in more than one domain.

However, the use of universal groups results in a higher level of network traffic between domain controllers at replication time because any membership changes must be propagated to all global catalog servers in the forest.

The following are several suggestions for using universal groups:

- Use universal groups sparingly and use them only when their membership is relatively static. If universal group membership changes frequently, these changes result in a high level of network traffic between domain controllers in different domains because any membership changes must be propagated to all global catalog servers in the forest.

- Use universal groups when you need to assign permissions to resources located in several domains. Simply follow the strategy illustrated in Figure 15-8 and grant the appropriate permissions to the domain local groups. Use of this strategy simplifies the allocation of permissions and reduces the amount of interdomain replication traffic.

- In a single-domain forest, you do not need to use universal groups. Use the AGDLP strategy only.

Things Can Easily Go Wrong in Group Nesting

A few years ago, I heard of a situation in which student interns at a company where a friend worked were able to access confidential corporate documents and obtain information they could have passed on to a competitor. One network administrator at that company had assigned the interns to one global group. Another administrator then added this group to a second global group, which was included in a domain local group with permissions to confidential corporate documents. As a result, the interns had access to the confidential documents. Several of them used this confidential information in writing term papers at school the following semester.

In such an instance, the administrators should have created a global group specifically for the interns. Then they could have added this group to only the groups containing the required privileges or assigned these privileges directly to the group.

Local Versus Domain Groups

Similar to previous Windows versions, Windows 8.1 and Windows Server 2012 R2 enable you to create local groups on any computer that is not configured as a domain controller. Such machine-local groups are similar in usage and membership capabilities to a domain local groups. However, these types of local groups do not exist in AD DS and grant users access to resources on its computer only. For access to resources located on more than one computer in the domain, always use domain local groups.

To create a local group in Windows Server 2012 R2, proceed as follows:

1. Open **Server Manager** and then expand the **Configuration** node in the console tree to reveal the Local Users and Groups folder.

2. Expand this folder, right-click **Groups**, and select **New Group**.

3. In the New Group dialog box shown in Figure 15-9, type a name and optional description for the group; then click **Add** to add members to this group.

Figure 15-9 Creating a local group on a member server.

4. Type the usernames or group names in the Select Users, Computers, or Groups dialog box, and then click **OK**.

5. If a Windows Security dialog box displays, type the name and password of an appropriate domain account (member of Domain Admins, Account Operators, or another user that has been delegated this permission).

6. Click **Create** to create the group.

On a Windows XP, Windows Vista, or Windows 7 computer, click **Start**, right-click **My Computer** or **Computer**, and then select **Manage**. On a Windows 8 computer, access the **Search** charm, type `manage`, and then select **Computer Management**. On a Windows 8.1 computer, right-click **Start** and select **Computer Management** from the list that appears. If you see a UAC prompt in Windows Vista, 7, 8, or 8.1, click **Yes** or **Continue**. From the Computer Management console, expand the **Local Users and Groups** node, right-click **Groups**, select **New Group**, and then proceed from Step 3 in the previous list.

You can also use the `net localgroup` command from the command line to create and populate local groups. This command works on any member server or client computer, including Server Core machines. Type this command followed by `/?` to obtain information about its syntax.

Enumerating Group Membership

As you create groups within an organization, there might be a time when you need to review the users or nested groups contained within a particular group. Table 15-4 lists a handful of these tools used to review users or nested groups.

Table 15-4   Group Enumeration Tools

Tool	Syntax	Example	Reference
Dsget	Dsget group	`dsget group "CN=Test Users Group,OU=Test, DC=Mytestdomain,DC=Com" -members -expand` This command displays the list of members in the Test Users group in the mytestdomain. com domain. It expands all users in the group and also loops through and expands the users in any nested groups.	http://technet. microsoft.com/en-us/ library/cc755162.aspx
Dsquery	Dsquery group	`dsquery group domainroot -name MyGroup*` This command finds all groups in the current domain whose names begin with "MyGroup". This is helpful if you have a group naming convention per site. For example, if all groups in SiteA follow the format SiteA_GroupName, you can use this command to retrieve a list of groups. Then use the `Dsget` command to enumerate the group memberships. You can even pipe the results of `Dsquery` to `Dsget` using the command: `dsquery group -name "Group Name" | dsget group -members -expand`	http://technet. microsoft.com/en-us/ library/cc732952.aspx

Tool	Syntax	Example	Reference
Net	`Net group`	`Net group TestGroup` Displays users in the group "TestGroup".	http://technet.microsoft.com/en-us/library/cc754051.aspx
PowerShell	`Get-ADGroupMember`	`get-adgroupmember "Test Users Group" -recursive` This cmdlet gets all group members of the Test Users Group, including the members of any nested groups.	http://technet.microsoft.com/en-us/library/ee617193.aspx
VBScript	`GetObject`	Although PowerShell is typically used today, VBScripts are typically used with older versions of Windows Server. Nevertheless, you can still leverage the tool under Windows Server 2012 R2. It requires a basic understanding of VB Scripting and LDAP attributes.	http://msdn.microsoft.com/en-us/library/windows/desktop/aa772126(v=vs.85).aspx

Creating and Managing Organizational Units

If you recall from previous installations of Active Directory, an *organizational unit* is a logical subgroup within Active Directory that you can use to organize objects and resources within AD or control how they operate or are impacted by using Group Policies. Group Policies are covered in more detail in Chapter 16, "Creating and Applying Group Policy Objects."

Planning the OU Structure of Your Domain

An easily managed OU structure that reflects some aspects of your company's internal organization is highly important to the day-to-day functioning of your AD DS domain. Before you proceed to create new OUs in your domain, you should take some time to plan an appropriate OU structure. Your OUs must be meaningful to administrators for them to be able to navigate through the hierarchy and perform their functions. You can arrange OUs to be intuitive by using a model that combines the network administrative structure with the company's organizational chart. You can design an OU structure that is wide and shallow, as shown in Figure 15-10, or one that is slim and deep, as shown in Figure 15-11. You can have as many OUs as you want at any level, although a wide and shallow structure tends to be easier to manage, easier to navigate, and somewhat faster when performing LDAP queries than a slim and deep structure.

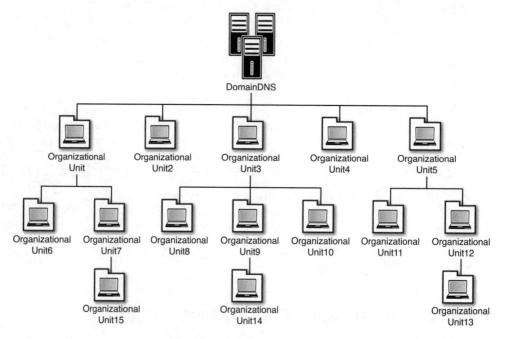

Figure 15-10   An OU structure can be wide and shallow.

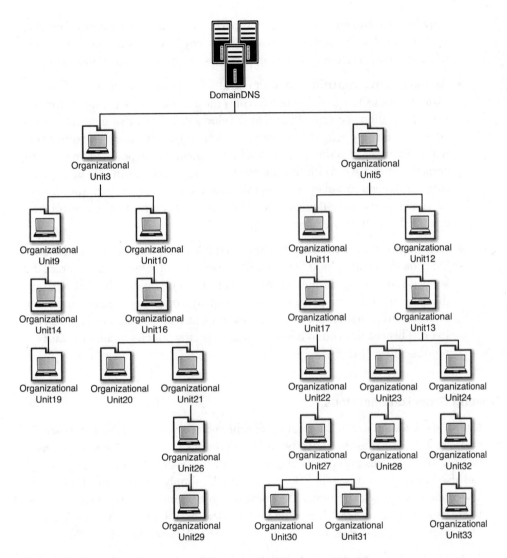

Figure 15-11   You can design an OU structure to be slim and deep.

Network designers often use OUs as a way of restructuring domains during an upgrade and migration project to provide an administrative boundary for delegated tasks. When planning an OU structure for an organization, your first task should be to gather the business requirements. The types of information you should collect include the following:

- **Corporate organizational charts:** Companies generally group persons within the same hierarchical structure when those persons must share the same physical location or production requirements. You can create an OU hierarchy that mirrors the company's organizational layout, including departments, branches, sections, work units, and so on. Such a hierarchy facilitates the administration of the network, including assigning permissions, group policies, and so on.

- **Administrative control:** The most useful information you will gather for planning your OUs to delegate control is the administrative configuration of the organization. You should find or develop a document that describes which administrators are assigned to manage which users, computers, and other network resources. In addition, you should document which powers of control the administrators have. With this information, you can create an OU hierarchy that enables you to assign junior administrators the ability to perform actions on certain parts of the domain only. Delegation of administrative control is discussed later in this chapter.

- **Geographical layout:** Many businesses establish administrative boundaries based on the geographical locations of the users, computers, and resources that are managed. Using this model, you can create an OU hierarchy that mirrors the geographical arrangement of your company's operations. This can include multiple levels that reflect countries, states or provinces, counties or cities, and so on. This enables you to design location-specific policies or administrative actions, and so on.

Creating Organizational Units

Creating OUs is similar to the creation of other object types in Active Directory. To create an OU, you must be a member of the Account Operators, Domain Admins, or Enterprise Admins groups by default. As you will see shortly, additional groups can also be delegated this ability. To create an OU, simply access Active Directory Users and Computers, right-click the domain or other container in which you want to create an OU, and then select **New > Organizational Unit**. In the New Object-Organizational Unit dialog box, type a name for the OU and then click **OK**.

You can also use the `dsadd` PowerShell cmdlet or from the Active Directory Module for Windows PowerShell available under Administrative Tools. For example, suppose you needed to create an OU called MyTestOU in the mytestdomain.com domain. Simply execute the following command:

```
dsadd ou ou=MyTestOU,dc=mytestdomain,dc=com
```

In addition to the traditional tools, Windows Server 2012 R2 enables you to perform this task from the Active Directory Administrative Center. To create a new OU using the AD Administrative Center, perform the following steps:

1. Open **Active Directory Administrative Center**.

2. Using the far left pane, right-click the domain, expand **New**, and select **Organizational Unit** as shown in Figure 15-12.

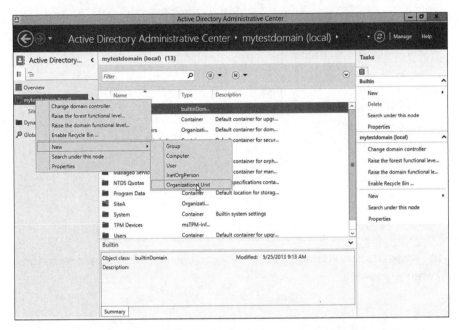

Figure 15-12   Active Directory Administrative Center New Organizational Unit.

3. The new OU dialog box will open, as shown in Figure 15-13. Type the name of the OU and add any optional information as desired in the available fields. Then click **OK**.

After you have created new OUs, it is easy to move objects such as users, computers, and groups to the new OU. Simply drag the required objects in Active Directory Users and Computers or Active Directory Administrative Center to the appropriate location. You can also right-click an object and select **Move**. Select the desired destination in the Move dialog box, and then click **OK**. Furthermore, you can use the dsmove utility to move a series of objects at the same time.

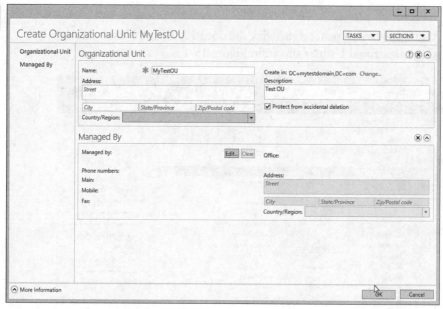

Figure 15-13   Active Directory Administrative Center enables you to specify several properties of a new OU when you create it.

TIP   Try to keep the OU hierarchy of your organization simple, with no more than two or three levels of OU nesting, if at all possible. Complex structures can result in unexpected application of Group Policy or difficulty locating and administering objects.

Managing Organizational Units

No matter how much planning is done up front, at some point you might be required to make changes to an OU or perform tasks such as moving or deleting an OU. As with previous installations of Windows Server and Active Directory, you have the ability to modify properties of an OU and perform other management tasks using Active Directory Users and Computers. Windows Server 2012 R2 makes routine tasks a bit easier using the Active Directory Administrative Center to configure OU properties and perform a series of management tasks as outlined in the next several sections.

Configuring OU Properties

Using the Active Directory Administrative Center, locate and select the OU you want to modify. Under the Tasks pane you will notice several options, including a Properties item. We will discuss some of these tasks shortly. Click **Properties** to open the OU Properties dialog box, as shown in Figure 15-14.

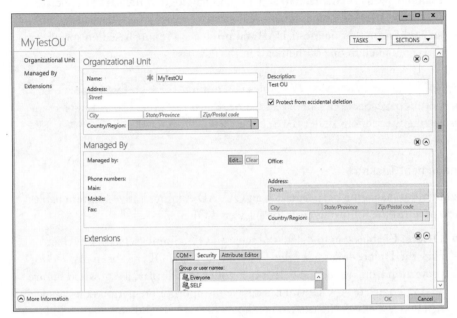

Figure 15-14   Active Directory Administrative Center enables you to manage the properties of an OU.

The OU properties dialog box enables you to specify or modify several properties. When complete, click **OK** to save your configuration. You can modify the following properties:

- **Organizational Unit:** This section enables you to change the name of the OU, description, and details with respect to the address if this OU represents a specific site. You also have the ability to protect the OU from accidental deletion. This also includes protection from accidental moves.

- **Managed By:** This section enables you to specify the account name and contact information for the individual responsible for managing the OU. This is particularly helpful when using a delegation model (discussed later).

- **Extensions:** This section enables you to associate the OU with a specific COM+ Partition set. This is helpful if you have applications that require isolation for different configurations. It can be helpful to control group policies for these applications or servers without impacting other resources under the OU.

The extensions section also enables you to modify security for the OU. This might be helpful when delegating management of specific objects contained under the OU. You can specify who is allowed to add/remove objects under the OU, rename, move, or even delete the OU. Lastly, the Attribute Editor function enables you to make changes to specific attributes for the OU. For example, perhaps you need to add a thumbnail logo to the OU to associate it with a specific site, brand, function, department, and so on. Perhaps you have an application that queries LDAP and produces a report based on specific criteria contained in one of the fields in the database.

NOTE   AD Administrative Center enables you to filter the sections visible under the properties page. Sections can be hidden or shown from the display by selecting or deselecting the sections under the Sections drop-down menu.

OU Management Tasks

In addition to managing properties for an OU, AD Administrative Center enables you to perform the following tasks for a selected OU:

- **Delete:** Enables you to delete the selected OU. Simply select the OU and click the **Delete** link under the Tasks menu. If the OU has been marked for protection from accidental deletion, a notice will display, as shown in Figure 15-15. To delete an OU, you must have the appropriate permissions as specified under the Security extensions shown previously, and you might need to clear the check box for accidental deletion protection.

- **Move:** Enables you to move a selected OU to another location. This can be helpful when transferring management of a particular OU or perhaps when you need to re-architect the layout of AD to help from an administrative or functional standpoint. Simply select the OU and click the **Move** link under the Tasks pane. This will open the Move dialog box shown in Figure 15-16.

- **Search under this node:** The search dialog box enables you to search for a particular object, such as a user, computer, or shared resource, contained under the OU. The search node can be invoked at the OU level or even at the domain level.

NOTE   If you recall from an earlier chapter, AD Administrative Center uses PowerShell as the underlying tool to complete tasks executed using the GUI. The Windows PowerShell History pane at the bottom of the screen displays the PowerShell cmdlets used to complete the actions initiated via the GUI. This is helpful if you need to create a script to automate some routine tasks.

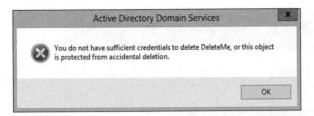

Figure 15-15 OU protected from accidental deletion.

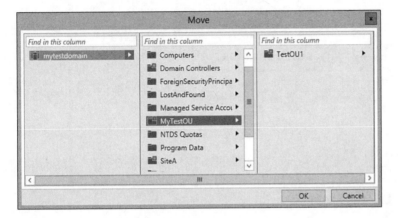

Figure 15-16 Moving OUs.

Active Directory Administrative Center Recycle Bin

AD Administrative Center for Server 2012 R2 now includes a GUI version of the Active Directory Recycle Bin feature introduced under Windows Server 2008 R2. By default, the Recycle Bin is disabled, but you can enable it from within AD Administrative Center. Click the **Enable Recycle Bin** option, as shown in Figure 15-17, under the Tasks pane for the domain. Once enabled, you have the ability to restore recently deleted items from Active Directory. To use this feature, your forest must be Windows Server 2008 R2 functional level or higher. It is also important to note that after the recycle bin is enabled, you cannot disable it.

Once enabled, deleted objects are placed in a deleted objects container and can be restored by right-clicking the object and selecting either **Restore** to restore it to its original location or **Restore To** to restore it to an alternative location.

For more information on the Active Directory Recycle Bin, refer to the *Cert Guide* for exam 40-411.

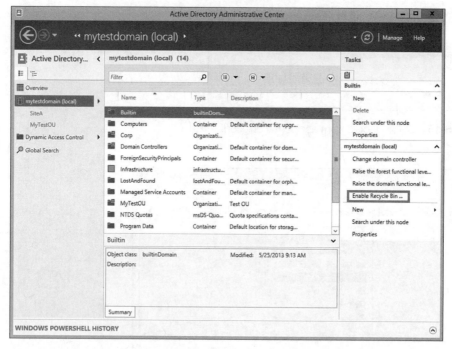

Figure 15-17   Active Directory Administrative Center Recycle Bin.

Delegating Active Directory Object Management

One of the major benefits of Active Directory is that you can split up administrative tasks among various individuals. You can assign different sets of administrative responsibility to different users, and these can include segments of the directory structure such as OUs or sites. The following are several benefits of delegating administrative control:

- You can assign subsets of administrative tasks to users and groups.

- You can assign responsibility of a limited portion of the domain, such as OUs or sites, to users or groups.

- You can use a nested hierarchy of OUs for even more granular control over which users can perform certain administrative tasks.

- You can enhance network security by placing more restrictive limits on the membership of powerful groups such as Domain Admins, Enterprise Admins, and Schema Admins.

When designing your AD DS forest structure, you should keep in mind the administrative requirements of each domain. Each domain has the capability to contain a different OU hierarchy. The forest administrators, who are members of the Enterprise Admins group, are automatically granted the ability to create an OU hierarchy in any domain within the entire forest. Domain administrators, who are members of the Domain Admins group in each separate domain, by default are granted the right to create an OU hierarchy within their own domain.

When you initially create your OU design, you should do so to enable administration. After that, you should create any additional OUs required for the application of Group Policy. You might also need to create OUs to limit the visibility of some objects. For example, if you have a business requirement from a security standpoint that restricts access to user accounts created for use solely with applications, such as a SQL Administrator account, you could create an OU that is outside the main OU hierarchy and limit access to that OU and its contents.

You have the capability to assign a single user or group full control of the entire domain, of a single OU, or limited rights to a set of OUs. When you delegate control, keep in mind that the default behavior of AD DS is to make such permissions inheritable. For example, if your top-level OU is named Corp and it contains OUs named Users and Computers, as shown in Figure 15-18, and if you delegate full control of Corp to a user named Joe, he is able to make changes throughout all the Users and Computers child OUs, as well as the parent OU named Corp. However, if you delegate to another user named Jean the Reset Password right in Users, she will not be able to reset passwords for users in the Corp or Computer OUs.

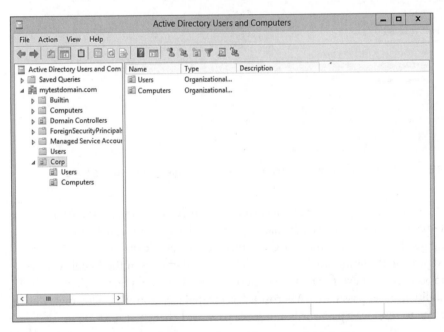

Figure 15-18   Organizational Units configured for ease of delegation.

Windows Server 2012 R2 provides the Delegation of Control Wizard to facilitate the task of delegating administrative control. Proceed as follows:

1. In Active Directory Users and Computers or Active Directory Administrative Center, right-click the desired OU and select **Delegate Control**. To delegate control over a site, right-click the desired site in Active Directory Sites and Services and select **Delegate Control**.

2. Click **Next** to bypass the introductory page of the Delegation of Control Wizard.

3. On the Users or Groups page, click **Add** and type the name of the required user or group in the Select Users, Computers, or Groups dialog box. Click **OK**, and then click **Next**.

4. On the Tasks to Delegate page shown in Figure 15-19, select the task(s) you want to delegate. If you want to delegate a task that is not shown in the list provided, select the **Create a custom task to delegate** option. Then click **Next**.

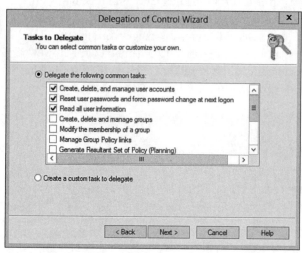

Figure 15-19   Using the Delegation of Control Wizard to delegate administrative tasks.

5. If you have chosen the Create a custom task to delegate option, the Active Directory Object Type page enables you to delegate control over a large range of subfolders in the AD DS namespace. Click **Next** to choose whether to provide the ability to create or delete selected objects in the folder; you can choose from an extensive range of permissions. For example, to delegate the ability to reset passwords, Microsoft has created a custom task allowing a delegate to reset user passwords and force password change at next logon.

6. When finished, click **Next**.

7. Review the information presented on the completion page. If you need to make any changes, click **Back**. When done, click **Finish**.

> **NOTE** AD DS provides several built-in security groups that enable members to perform limited administrative capabilities within the domain in which they are located. These include Account Operators, Server Operators, Print Operators, and Backup Operators. You can add members to these groups when their defined rights match the administrative capabilities you want to confer to these users. Note that these groups are defined on a domain-wide basis.

> **TIP** You should know when and how to use the Delegation of Control Wizard. The exam might present a scenario requiring a limited set of control over a given list of objects. You should also be aware that if you run the Delegation of Control Wizard multiple times, permissions granted are cumulative rather than having the wizard replace prior permissions each time you run it.

To view, modify, or delete permissions granted using this wizard, open the Active Directory Administrative Center in Windows Server. From the console tree, right-click the OU or site and select **Properties**. Scroll through this dialog box to the Extensions section, select the **Security** tab of the dialog box found here, and then click **Advanced** to display the Advanced Security Settings for the (container) dialog box shown in Figure 15-20.

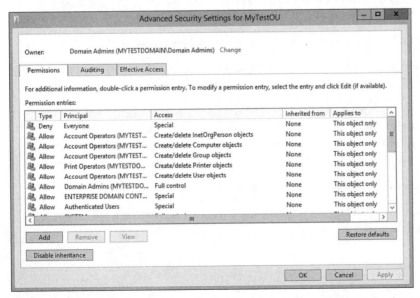

Figure 15-20 The Advanced Security Settings dialog box enables you to view and modify granular permissions.

If you are using Active Directory Users and Computers and do not see the Security tab, make sure that **Advanced Features** are displayed under the view menu of the console as shown in Figure 15-21. Then right-click the OU and select **Properties**. Select the **Security** tab and then click **Advanced**.

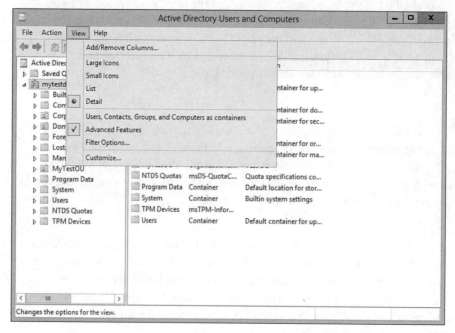

Figure 15-21   Display Advanced Features using Active Directory Users and Computers.

Regardless of the tool you use, the Security tab enables you to do the following:

- To add another user or group with permission to perform a listed task, select the task and click **Add**. Then type the required user or group in the Select Users, Computers, or Groups dialog box.

- To modify the scope of a permissions entry, select it and click **Edit**. From the Permission Entry dialog box that appears, select the appropriate permissions. You can also explicitly deny permissions from this dialog box.

- To remove a delegated permission, select it and click **Remove**.

- To remove all delegated permissions from the container, click **Restore defaults**.

TIP   To view the effective permissions granted to a user or group, click the **Effective Permissions** tab and then select the required user or group. This tab displays a long list of permissions, with check marks beside the granted permissions. This includes all permissions inherited through membership in other groups.

Exam Preparation Tasks

Review All the Key Topics

Review the most important topics in the chapter, noted with the key topics icon in the outer margin of the page. Table 15-5 lists a reference of these key topics and the page numbers on which each is found.

Table 15-5   Key Topics for Chapter 15

Key Topic Element	Description	Page Number
List	Describes group scopes available in AD DS	676
Table 15-2	Describes built-in groups available in AD DS	678
Table 15-3	Compares group scopes and their nesting capabilities in AD DS	683
Figure 15-7	Describes the AGDLP strategy	687
Figure 15-8	Describes the AGUDLP strategy	687
Table 15-4	Shows you the tools used to enumerate groups	690
Figure 15-13	Shows how to create an OU using Active Directory Administrative Center	696
List	Shows how to delegate tasks in Active Directory	702
Figure 15-19	Shows how to use the Delegation of Control Wizard to delegate administrative tasks	702

Complete the Tables and Lists from Memory

Print a copy of Appendix B, "Memory Tables" (found on the CD), or at least the section for this chapter, and complete the tables and lists from memory. Appendix C, "Memory Tables Answer Key," is also on the CD and includes completed tables and lists to check your work.

Definitions of Key Terms

Define the following key terms from this chapter, and check your answers in the glossary.

AGDLP, AGUDLP, Built-in group, Domain local group, Global group, Nesting, Universal group

This chapter covers the following subjects:

- **Overview of Group Policy:** This section provides a foundation for the remainder of your studies on Group Policy by introducing its components and summarizing the major updates to Group Policy included with Windows Server 2012 R2.

- **Creating and Applying GPOs:** This section shows you how to use the Group Policy Management Console to create and work with Group Policy objects. You also learn how to configure Starter GPOs, which are sets of preconfigured Administrative Template policy settings, including comments, which you can use for ease of creating new GPOs. This section shows you how to work with Starter GPOs and use them to create customized policies.

- **Managing GPOs and Their Links:** This section shows you how to perform several important GPO management tasks, including creating and managing links, disabling and deleting GPOs, and using Windows PowerShell to manage GPOs.

- **Configuring Multiple Local Group Policies:** This section discusses the types of Local Group Policies. It shows you how to use MMC to manage local policies and how they are incorporated into domain-based policies. This section also provides an overview of how to manage groups using Group Policy under Active Directory.

- **Configuring Security Filtering:** This section discusses the Administrative Templates feature of Group Policy and shows you how to configure the more important settings.

CHAPTER 16

Creating and Applying Group Policy Objects

Users are naturally curious beings. It is human nature to explore your computer and see what you can do, what Control Panel is all about, and so on. Invariably, problems result, users make changes, cannot back out of them, and call the help desk for assistance. For a business network to function properly, it is mandatory that a secure means of limiting what users can do is in place, and Microsoft has recognized this fact ever since the days of Windows NT and its system policies.

Beginning with Windows 2000, Group Policy enabled administrators to exert more control over users' environments and reduce the extent of user-originated problems. Each successive iteration of Windows has added components to the list of available policies, and Windows Server 2012 R2 is no exception.

"Do I Know This Already?" Quiz

The "Do I Know This Already?" quiz enables you to assess whether you should read this entire chapter or simply jump to the "Exam Preparation Tasks" section for review. If you are in doubt, read the entire chapter. Table 16-1 outlines the major headings in this chapter and the corresponding "Do I Know This Already?" quiz questions. You can find the answers in Appendix A, "Answers to the 'Do I Know This Already?' Quizzes."

Table 16-1 "Do I Know This Already?" Foundation Topics Section-to-Question Mapping

Foundations Topics Section	Questions Covered in This Section
Overview of Group Policy	1
Creating and Applying GPOs	2–4
Managing GPOs and Their Links	5–6
Configuring Multiple Local Group Policies	7–8
Configuring Security Filtering	9–10

1. Which of the following best describes how Active Directory stores the various components of Group Policy?

   a. Group Policy containers (GPCs) are stored in the SYSVOL shared folder, and Group Policy templates (GPTs) are stored in the domain partition of AD DS.

   b. GPCs are stored in the domain partition of AD DS, and GPTs are stored in the SYSVOL shared folder.

   c. Both GPCs and GPTs are stored in the domain partition of AD DS.

   d. Both GPCs and GPTs are stored in the SYSVOL shared folder.

2. Which tool do you use in Windows Server 2012 R2 for creating GPOs and performing various management activities on them?

   a. Group Policy Management Console

   b. Group Policy Management Editor

   c. Active Directory Users and Computers

   d. Active Directory Administrative Center

3. Which of the following components of GPOs enables you to configure the settings that influence the appearance of the desktop environment including many of the actions users are permitted to perform?

   a. Preferences

   b. Software settings

   c. Windows settings

   d. Administrative templates

4. You are responsible for configuring Group Policy in a child domain of your company's AD DS forest. One of your colleagues, who is responsible for the forest root domain, has created a Starter GPO that contains settings you want to apply to computers in your domain. What should you do?

   a. Link the Starter GPO to the child domain.

   b. Copy the settings in the Starter GPO to the Default Domain Policy GPO in the child domain.

   c. Create a new GPO linked to the child domain, and copy the settings in the Starter GPO to this GPO.

   d. Create a new GPO linked to the child domain, and specify the name of the Starter GPO in the New GPO dialog box.

5. You have configured a GPO with user-specific settings for sales staff in your company and linked the GPO to the Sales OU in your company's AD DS domain. You want to ensure that settings in this GPO are applied to sales staff as rapidly as possible with minimal delay in the logon experience. Which of the following should you do?

   a. From the Details tab of the GPO's Properties, as displayed in the details pane of GPMC, disable the user configuration settings.

   b. From the Details tab of the GPO's Properties, as displayed in the details pane of GPMC, disable the computer configuration settings.

   c. From the Settings tab of the GPO's Properties, as displayed in the details pane of GPMC, disable the user configuration settings.

   d. From the Settings tab of the GPO's Properties, as displayed in the details pane of GPMC, disable the computer configuration settings.

6. You have configured a GPO whose settings were needed for a special project and are no longer needed. You expect that the settings in this GPO might be needed for a similar project next year. Which of the following should you not do with the GPO?

   a. Delete the links of the GPO to various AD DS containers.

   b. Disable the links of the GPO to various AD DS containers.

   c. Delete the GPO.

   d. Disable the GPO.

   e. Disable the User Configuration and Computer Configuration branches of the GPO.

7. Which of the following is the correct order in which Local Group Policies are applied?

   a. Administrator & Non-Administrator, Computer, User

   b. User, Computer, Administrator & Non-Administrator

   c. Computer, User, Administrator & Non-Administrator

   d. Computer, Administrator & Non-Administrator, User

8. You need to create a new local group on all your member servers in the domain. You need the Group Policy to apply to only Servers in the Servers OU. What should you do?

   a. Configure Local Users and Groups preferences settings to create the group. Link the policy to the Servers OU.

   b. Use the Restricted Groups security setting, and link the policy to the domain level.

   c. Add the group to the domain controller.

   d. Add a domain group and store it under the Servers OU.

9. You have configured a domain-based GPO that locks down the desktop settings of all computers in the domain. You realize that this will limit the actions administrators can perform, so you want to ensure that members of the Domain Admins group are not affected by this GPO. Members of this group might need access to users' computers to correct problems from time to time. What should you do?

   a. Use a WMI filter that exempts members of the Domain Admins group from applying the GPO.

   b. Write a Windows PowerShell script that disables application of the policies in the GPO from applying to computers used by members of the Domain Admins group.

   c. Disable the GPO's link for computers used by members of the Domain Admins group.

   d. Deny the Apply Group Policy permission to the Domain Admins group from the Delegation tab of the GPO's Properties in the GPMC.

10. You would like to configure a GPO with settings that should be applied to all laptop computers in your company's AD DS domain. Users of these computers are located in various departments of the company, each of which is configured with its own OU. What should you do to accomplish this task with the least amount of administrative effort?

   a. Use a WMI filter that specifies that only laptop computers should receive the policy's settings.

   b. Create a new OU. Move all laptop computers' accounts to this OU, and link the GPO to this OU.

   c. Create a new global group, and place all desktop computers' accounts in this group. Then deny the Apply Group Policy permission to this group.

   d. Disable the GPO's link for desktop computers.

Foundation Topics

Overview of Group Policy

Group Policy lies at the heart of every Active Directory implementation. It does far more than just define what users can and cannot do with their computers. It is a series of configuration settings you can apply to an object or a series of objects in Active Directory to control a user's environment in numerous contexts, including the following:

- **Network access:** Enables you to control access to network devices, including terminal servers, wireless access, and so on.

- **Folder redirection:** Enables you to use Group Policy settings to redirect users' local folders to network shares.

- **Logon/logoff/startup/shutdown scripts:** Enable you to assign scripts on a user or computer basis for such events as logon, logoff, startup, and shutdown.

- **Application deployment:** Enables you to administer applications on your network, including their assignment, publication, updating, repair, and removal.

- **Security options of all types:** Enable you to use Group Policy security settings to enforce restrictions and control access on user or computer properties.

Group Policy can be applied to server and client computers running all recent versions of Windows and includes both computer and user settings. As the names suggest, computer policies are computer-specific and are applied when the computer starts up, and user policies are user-specific and are applied with the user logs on to the computer.

Components of Group Policy

As its name implies, a group policy is a group of policies that are applied together. It is a set of configuration settings that can be applied to one or more Active Directory Domain Services (AD DS) objects to define the behavior of the object and its child objects.

Group Policy has a structure that provides a high degree of flexibility in managing users and computers. The policies are contained in sets known as *Group Policy objects (GPOs)*. In turn, the content of GPOs is stored in two locations:

- **Group Policy containers (GPCs):** Directory Services objects that include subcontainers for machine and user Group Policy information

- **Group Policy templates (GPTs):** Folder structures including a GPT folder and its subfolders that together contain all the Group Policy information, including the actual policy settings for any particular GPO

All GPOs are identified by their Globally Unique Identifier (GUID), which is a unique 128-bit number assigned when the GPO is first created. This number is stored as an attribute of the object and is used to identify it within the AD DS hierarchy.

Group Policy Containers

GPCs are objects defined within AD DS that are used to store the properties of GPOs, including attributes and version information. They contain subcontainers for user and computer Group Policy data. Information as to whether the GPO is enabled or disabled is also stored here.

Being stored in AD DS, computers can access GPCs to locate GPTs, and domain controllers can access them to obtain version information that verifies that they have the most recent edition of GPOs. If not, they can use AD DS replication to obtain the latest version of the GPO from another domain controller.

You can view GPCs in Active Directory Users and Computers by using the following procedure:

1. From Server Manager, click **Tools** > **Active Directory Users and Computers**.

2. In the View menu of Active Directory Users and Computers, select **Advanced Features**.

3. Expand your domain name and then expand the **System** folder.

4. Select the **Policies** node. The GUIDs of existing GPCs appear in the details pane, as shown in Figure 16-1.

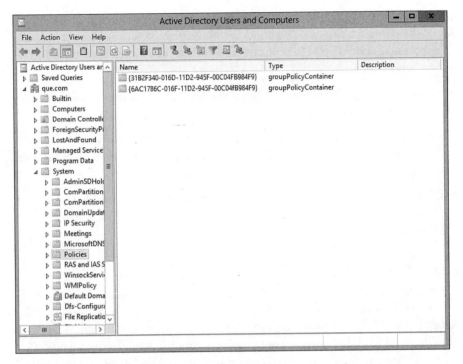

Figure 16-1   You can view GPCs in Active Directory Users and Computers.

Group Policy Templates

The GPT is a folder hierarchy composed of the GPT folder at the top and sub-folders under it. This structure holds all the information for a given GPO.

Every domain has associated with it a folder hierarchy found in the domain controllers at the shared folder `%systemroot%\SYSVOL\sysvol\<domain_name>\Policies`. For example, consider the following shared folder:

```
C:\WINDOWS\SYSVOL\Sysvol\Que.com\Policies\{31B2F340-016D-11D2-945F-
00C04FB984F9}
```

This container object holds policy settings for the various GPOs that have been created for that domain at any level. Subfolders are defined within this shared folder and named by the GUID of the GPO, as mentioned previously. Inside each GPT is a series of subfolders related to user and machine settings and administrative template files, and there are additional subfolders under them. Within the subfolders are text files named `Registry.pol`; these files are processed by Windows Server 2012 R2 to apply changes to the Registry as a computer is started up and a user logs on. As with other components of SYSVOL, Windows Server 2012 R2 uses

Distributed File System (DFS) to replicate changes in GPT to other domain controllers if the domain functional level is Windows Server 2008 or higher, or it uses File Replication Service (FRS) to replicate SYSVOL if the domain functional level is Windows Server 2003.

The root of each GPT also contains a file called Gpt.ini. This file contains entries for the following parameters:

- **Version:** The version number is a variable that starts at 0 when the GPO is first created and increments by 1 each time it is modified. This number is used for replication purposes.

- **Disabled:** This parameter indicates whether a local GPO is enabled or disabled. Information for nonlocal GPOs is contained in a GPC within Active Directory.

NOTE   Besides the GPOs stored in AD DS, every computer has its own local GPO, which is stored on the local hard drive in the `%systemroot%\sysWOW64\GroupPolicy` folder on a 64-bit server. Settings in this GPO apply only to the computer on which it is configured and are always overridden by any policy settings applied in AD DS. It is recommended that you not use these settings within a domain environment, except for standalone machines that do not belong to a domain, or specific settings that are required by one or two machines only.

New Features of Group Policy in Windows Server 2012 and Windows Server 2012 R2

Group Policy in Windows Server 2012/R2 provides several new features, as described in Table 16-2.

Table 16-2   New/Updated Features for Group Policy in Windows Server 2012 and Windows Server 2012 R2

Feature/ Functionality	Description	Windows Server 2012	Windows Server 2012 R2
Remote Group Policy update	Group Policy Management Console (GPMC) now enables you to refresh policy settings for remote computers from the context menu for an organizational unit. You can use GPMC to schedule the execution of gpupdate.exe on remote computers. You can also use the new Invoke-GPUpdate cmdlet in Windows PowerShell.	X	X

Feature/ Functionality	Description	Windows Server 2012	Windows Server 2012 R2
Group Policy Results report improvements	More information is provided to help you determine whether a Group Policy setting was applied to a computer or user, including why policies were not applied as intended.	X	X
Group Policy infrastructure status	You can view the status of AD DS and SYSVOL replication as it relates to all GPOs or a single GPO.	X	X
Local Group Policy support for Windows RT 8.1	This enables you to configure Group Policy for devices running Windows RT 8.1. You need to turn on the Group Policy client service on each device for which you want to enable Group Policy.	X	X
Sign-in optimizations	Detection and processing of slow-link network connections has been improved, enabling users to log on faster. On a connection that uses DirectAccess, Group Policy processing defaults to slow-link mode when the network connection speed cannot be determined. A new policy enables you to specify that all 3G connections are treated as a slow link. You can disable this policy if desired.	X	X
New Starter GPOs	Several new Starter GPOs are available by default, including the ability to allow remote reporting of Resultant Set of Policy (RSoP) queries and updating of Group Policy. It is also easier to configure firewall port requirements using a Starter GPO.	X	X
New PowerShell Group Policy cmdlets	Several new cmdlets provide additional functionality when using Windows PowerShell to configure and apply Group Policy. This is especially helpful when managing Server Core computers.	X	X
New Group Policy settings and preferences for Internet Explorer 11	The Administrative Templates folder includes new policy settings that support new features included in Internet Explorer 11. Group Policy Preferences support is also added for Internet Explorer 11 running on Windows 8/8.1 and Windows Server 2012/R2 computers.	X	X

Feature/ Functionality	Description	Windows Server 2012	Windows Server 2012 R2
Improved support for IPv6	Windows Server 2012 R2 improves IPv6 support for Group Policy, including new policy settings for printers, item-level targeting, and virtual private networks (VPNs).		X
Policy caching	New for Windows Server 2012 R2, servers receiving the latest version of a policy from the domain controller caches the policy to a local store. On the next reboot, if Group Policy is running in synchronous mode, the server obtains the policy from the local store rather than downloading it again. This improves server startup times.		X
Improved event logging capabilities	Windows Server 2012 R2 improves the details provided for events logged to the operational event log. Additional information includes the time taken to download and process policies, as well as details about WMI processing.		X

Several features have been removed from Windows Server 2012 and Windows Server 2012 R2 Group Policy, including the Immediate Task preference item, which no longer supports sending an email or displaying a message. NetMeeting Administrative Template files have also been removed.

NOTE   For additional details on new Group Policy features in Windows Server 2012 R2, refer to"What's New in Group Policy in Windows Server" at http://technet.microsoft.com/en-us/library/dn265973.aspx. Further information on Group Policy as a whole and up-to-date team blogs and forums are available from "Group Policy in Windows Server 2012: Overview" at http://blogs.technet.com/b/grouppolicy/archive/2012/11/26/group-policy-in-windows-server-2012-overview.aspx and "Group Policy Overview" at http://technet.microsoft.com/library/hh831791.

Creating and Applying GPOs

You perform all Group Policy administrative activities, including creating, editing, and applying GPOs, from the GPMC. First available for download with Windows Server 2003 R2, GPMC is the sole location for managing all aspects of Group Policy in Windows Server 2012 R2. GPMC provides a simplified user interface for managing Group Policy in multisite, multidomain environments. It enables an administrator to back up, restore, copy, and import GPOs in these environments. You can create scripts to simplify the various management tasks. Key features of GPMC include the following:

- An advanced GUI that facilitates the use and management of Group Policy

- The ability to back up and restore GPOs

- The ability to copy, paste, import, and export GPOs and Windows Management Instrumentation (WMI) filters

- Enhanced management of security within Group Policy

- Enhanced reporting by means of HTML for policy settings and Resultant Set of Policy (RSoP) data

- The ability to script Group Policy–related tasks

Let's take a look at the GPMC and go through a sample procedure showing how you would create and link a new GPO:

1. From the Start screen, click **Administrative Tools** and then select **Group Policy Management** from the list of tools that appears. You can also open the GPMC by typing `Group Policy Management` in the Search charm. Either method opens the GPMC, which shows a node for your forest in the console tree that you can expand to reveal subnodes for every domain with entries for each OU as well as a Group Policy Objects node.

2. In the console tree, expand your forest to display your domain, and then expand your domain. You will notice several default folders, including one for Group Policy Objects.

3. Expand the **Group Policy Objects** node. You will notice two default GPOs: the Default Domain Policy and the Default Domain Controllers Policy. These are installed automatically when you create your domain. Policy settings you define here are automatically applied to the entire domain and to the domain controllers, respectively.

4. Select one of these policies. As shown in Figure 16-2, the details pane displays GPO properties and configuration options. Included are the following tabs:

- **Scope:** Enables you to display GPO link information and configure security group filtering and WMI filtering.

- **Details:** Displays information on the owner, dates created and modified, version numbers, GUID value, and enabled status. The enabled status is the only configurable option on this tab.

- **Settings:** Enables you to display policy settings, as shown in Figure 16-3. You can expand and collapse nodes to locate information on any policy setting. Note that the account settings shown in this figure are configured for the Default Domain Policy GPO by default when you install AD DS.

- **Delegation:** Enables you to view and modify GPO permissions.

- **Status:** Displays the status of AD DS and SYSVOL replication for the domain as related to Group Policy.

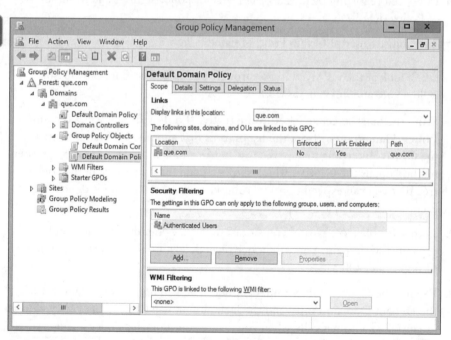

Figure 16-2   You perform all Group Policy management activities from the GPMC.

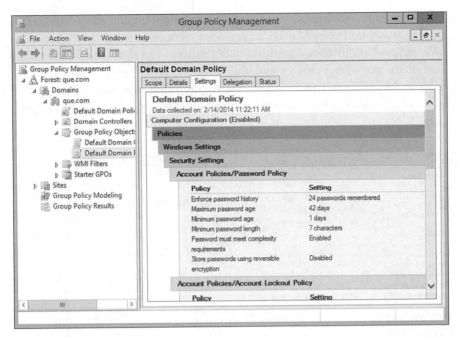

Figure 16-3   The Settings tab of a GPO enables you to view configured policy settings.

5. To create and link a GPO to a domain or OU, right-click the desired domain or OU and select **Create a GPO in this domain, and Link it here**. This displays the New GPO dialog box, as shown in Figure 16-4.

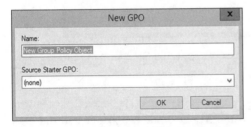

Figure 16-4   The New GPO dialog box enables you to create and name a new GPO.

6. Type a suitable name for the GPO. If you have a Starter GPO that includes settings you want to include in the new GPO, type its name in the **Source Starter GPO** field and then click **OK**. The new GPO is added to the list in the console tree under the Group Policy Objects node.

7. To define policy settings for the new GPO, right-click it and select **Edit**. This opens the Group Policy Management Editor console, as shown in Figure 16-5. We will discuss the more significant policy settings you should be familiar with in the rest of this chapter and in Chapter 17, "Configuring Security Policies," and Chapter 18, "Configuring Application Restriction Policies." We also discuss additional policy settings in the *Cert Guide* books for exams 70-411 and 70-412.

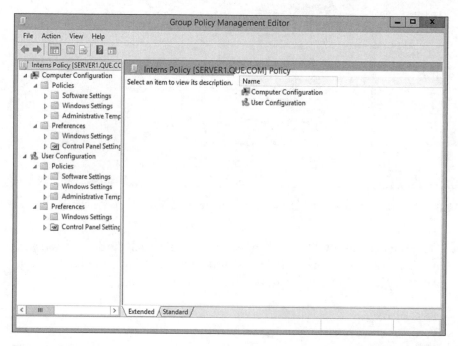

Figure 16-5   You can configure all policy settings associated with a GPO from the Group Policy Management Editor snap-in.

NOTE   The GPMC is installed when you install AD DS. You can also install the GPMC on a member server by accessing the Add Roles and Features Wizard in Server Manager. GPMC is also included in the Remote Server Administration Tools package, which you can install on a client computer running Windows 8.1 Pro or higher.

TIP   You can also access the GPMC directly from Server Manager, where it can be found under the Features node. In this case, it opens as a component snap-in within the Server Manager console.

The Group Policy Management Editor (formerly known as the Group Policy Object Editor) is where you perform all policy configuration actions for your GPO. Let's take a brief look at this tool here; we will cover many of the configuration activities later in this chapter and in Chapters 17 and 18. Table 16-3 describes its container structure.

Table 16-3 Group Policy Management Editor Container Structure

Component	Description
Root container	Defines the focus of the Group Policy Management Editor by showing the GPO being edited plus the fully qualified domain name (FQDN) of the domain controller from which you are working.
Computer Configuration	Contains all computer-specific policy settings. Remember that these settings are processed first when the computer starts up and before the user logs on.
User Configuration	Contains all user-specific policy settings. Remember that these settings are processed after the user logs on.
Policies	Includes classic and new Group Policy settings for Software Settings, Windows Settings, and Administrative Templates.
Preferences	Includes new Group Policy extensions that expand the range of configurable policy settings. Included are items such as folder options, mapped drives, printers, local users and groups, scheduled tasks, services, and Start menu settings. You can manage these items without using scripts.
Software Settings	A subcontainer found under both the Computer and User Configuration Policies containers that holds software installation settings for computers and users.
Windows Settings	A subcontainer found under the Computer and User Configuration Policies and Preferences containers that holds script and security settings, plus other policy settings that affect the behavior of the Windows environment.
Administrative Templates	A subcontainer found under both the Computer and User Configuration Policies containers that holds most of the settings that control the appearance of the desktop environment. Also included is an All Settings subnode that provides a comprehensive list of all policy settings you can sort according to name, state, comment, path, or filter according to several criteria.
Control Panel Settings	A subcontainer found under both the Computer and User Configuration Preferences containers that holds most of the preferences settings related to Control Panel applets.

NOTE   When you create a new GPO or edit an existing one, users affected by the GPO must log off and log back on again to receive the new settings in the User Configuration node. If you have configured new settings in the Computer Configuration node, users must reboot their computers to receive the new settings.

TIP   Consider using Loopback processing to configure user settings. This option keeps the configuration of the computer the same regardless of who logs on, where they are located in AD, and what settings apply to them. This configuration can be helpful with Remote Desktop Services, kiosks, or other shared computers. The location for this policy setting is `Computer Configuration\Policies\Administrative Templates\System\Group Policy`. The policy can be configured to merge or replace. For more information, refer to "Windows Server 2012 GPO Loopback Processing" at http://social.technet.microsoft.com/Forums/windowsserver/en-US/1a6252c7-4e2d-483d-984a-4521a01b16fd/windows-server-2012-gpo-loopback-processing?forum=winserverGP.

Using Starter GPOs

Group Policy in Windows Server 2012 R2 provides the ability to create *Starter GPOs*. These are sets of preconfigured Administrative Template policy settings, including comments, which you can use for ease of creating new GPOs. When you use a Starter GPO to create a new GPO, the new GPO includes all settings—their values, comments, and delegation—as defined in the Starter GPO. They also enable you to import and export them to other environments such as additional domains in the forest or a trusted forest.

To create a Starter GPO, perform the following steps:

1. In GPMC, right-click the **Starter GPOs** folder and select **New**.

2. In the New Starter GPO dialog box, type a name and optional comment and then click **OK**. This adds the Starter GPO to this folder, as shown in Figure 16-6.

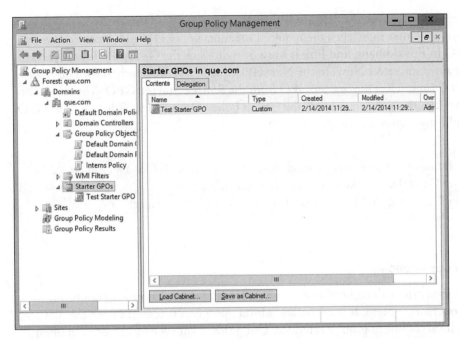

Figure 16-6 Starter GPOs are stored in the Starter GPOs folder and available for use in creating new GPOs.

3. To configure settings in this Starter GPO, right-click it and select **Edit** to open the Group Policy Starter GPO Editor snap-in.

4. Configure the required settings. This tool works the same way as the Group Policy Management Editor, except that only the Administrative Templates folder is available under both Computer Configuration and User Configuration.

The settings and their comments that you configure here are incorporated into all GPOs you create later from this Starter GPO.

You can also perform the following tasks with Starter GPOs:

- **Delegate the action of creating Starter GPOs:** Select the **Delegation** tab. Then click **Add** to add a user or group with ability to create additional Starter GPOs in the domain.

- **Export for use elsewhere in the forest or another forest:** Click **Save as Cabinet** and specify a location to save the set of Starter GPOs.

- **Import GPOs from another forest:** Click **Load Cabinet**; then in the Load Starter GPO dialog box that appears, click **Browse for CAB** to locate and import the desired file.

After you have created a Starter GPO, you can use this GPO to create new GPOs. To do so, either right-click the required site, domain, or OU and select **Create a GPO in this domain, and link it here** or right-click the **Group Policy Objects** container and select **New**. In the New GPO dialog box previously shown in Figure 16-4, select the Starter GPO from the **Source Starter GPO** drop-down list and click **OK**. You can now use the Group Policy Management Editor on this GPO to add any required settings.

> **TIP**   Remember the proper method of applying a Starter GPO. You can create another GPO that is linked to an AD DS object, but you cannot directly link a Starter GPO to an AD DS object, as an exam answer choice might suggest.

Shell Access Policies

The shell can be thought of as the command interpreter that passes commands to the operating system. It is a separate software program that works from the non-graphical command prompt interface. Using this, a knowledgeable user can often circumvent restrictive policy settings by entering the corresponding command from the command prompt.

To prevent users from accessing the command prompt, open an appropriate GPO in the Group Policy Management Editor and navigate to the **User Configuration\Policies\Administrative Templates\System** node. In the details pane of GPMC, scroll down to right-click the **Prevent access to the command prompt** policy setting and select **Edit**. From the dialog box shown in Figure 16-7, enable this setting and select an appropriate option for the **Disable the command prompt script processing also?** setting, as follows:

- If you select **Yes**, no scripts can be run. This prevents the user from running batch files, but also prevents any logon, logoff, startup, or shutdown scripts from running even if these have been configured in Group Policy to run.

- If you select **No**, logon, logoff, startup, or shutdown scripts can run but the user might be able to execute script files from within a program window.

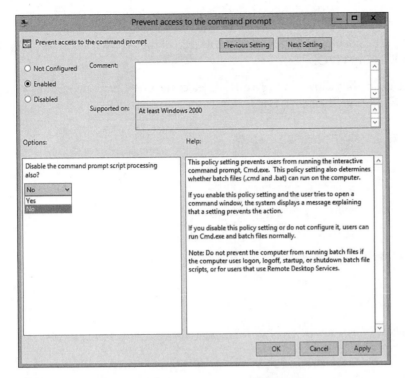

Figure 16-7 Disabling access to the command prompt.

Managing GPOs and Their Links

You have seen how to create a GPO. Now it's time to turn your attention to several additional activities that you should be aware of, including the following:

- Linking GPOs

- Managing GPO links

- Disabling and deleting GPOs

- Specifying a domain controller

- Using Windows PowerShell to manage GPOs

Linking GPOs

The GPMC also enables you to create unlinked GPOs and link any GPO to other Active Directory containers. To create an unlinked GPO, right-click **Group Policy Objects** and select **New**. The same dialog box previously shown in Figure 16-4 displays. The resulting GPO is not linked to any container.

To link this (or any other) GPO to a domain or OU, use the following steps:

1. Right-click the domain or OU in the console tree of the GPMC, and select **Link an Existing GPO**.

2. From the dialog box shown in Figure 16-8, select the GPO that you want to link in this location; then click **OK**.

Figure 16-8   Selecting a GPO for linking to a domain.

Linking a GPO to a site is similar. However, the Sites node in the GPMC does not show any sites by default. To include the available sites, right-click **Sites** and select **Show Sites**. Then select the desired site (or click **Select All** to display all sites) and click **OK**. After you have done this, you can right-click the desired site and select **Link an Existing GPO** to display the same dialog box previously shown in Figure 16-8.

> **TIP**   When linking GPOs to sites, you might need to consider the bandwidth connecting the sites. Consider using the Group Policy Slow Link Detection policy under `Computer Configuration\Administrative Templates\System\ Group Policy`. For more information, refer to "Group Policy slow link detection" at http://technet.microsoft.com/en-us/library/cc978717.aspx.

Managing GPO Links

When you perform the procedure outlined in the previous section, you can link GPOs to multiple AD DS containers. This is perfectly acceptable; however, you might need to view the existing GPO links to keep track of them. You can do so by selecting the desired GPO under the Group Policy Objects node of the GPMC. As shown in Figure 16-9, the Links section of the GPO's properties shows the available links. In a multiple-domain environment, simply select the required domain from the drop-down list. To view links to sites, select **All Sites** from the drop-down list, and to view links to all sites and domains in the forest, select **Entire forest** from this list.

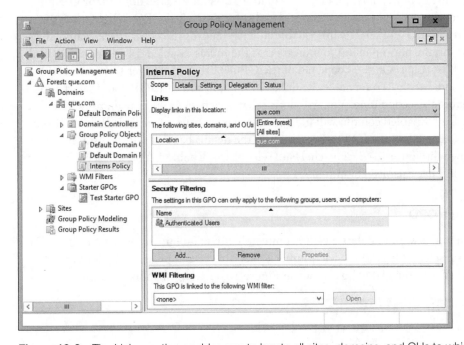

Figure 16-9 The Links section enables you to locate all sites, domains, and OUs to which a GPO is linked.

If you need to delete a GPO link to test its effects or because the GPO is linked to the wrong AD DS container, you can delete the link. Expand the container from which you want to delete the link, right-click the desired GPO, and then select **Delete** (or press the **Delete** key). Click **OK** in the dialog box shown in Figure 16-10 to confirm its deletion.

Figure 16-10   Deleting a GPO link.

You can also disable a GPO link if you want to temporarily stop the GPO from applying to a site, domain, or OU. To do so, expand the site, domain, or OU in Group Policy Management Console to display the linked GPOs. Right-click the desired GPO and select **Link Enabled**. This removes the check mark against this entry in the pop-up menu to indicate that the link is disabled. In addition, the Link Enabled column in the Scope tab of the GPO's Properties (refer to Figure 16-9) will indicate No. To reenable the link, simply right-click the GPO and select **Link Enabled** a second time. You will notice that the check mark is again present and the Link Enabled column will indicate Yes. You can also disable a GPO link from the Scope tab of the GPO's Properties in the details pane of GPMC as previously shown in Figure 16-9; right-click and select **Link Enabled**. You will see a No entry in the Link Enabled column here.

Deleting a GPO

You might want to delete a GPO completely if you no longer need its settings. To do so, select it from the Group Policy Objects node and press the **Delete** key. Then click **Yes** in the dialog box shown in Figure 16-11 to confirm its deletion.

Figure 16-11   Deleting a GPO.

CAUTION   Be sure you never need the GPO again before you delete it! There is no way to recover a deleted GPO. If you need it back, you must re-create it and all the policy settings contained within it. If you might want the GPO back, it is better to disable it or remove the links.

Disabling GPOs or Portions of GPOs

When troubleshooting Group Policy problems, you might want to disable portions of a GPO. The Details tab of the GPO's properties in the details pane of the GPMC lets you disable the entire GPO or the computer or user configuration settings. Select the desired option from the GPO Status drop-down list, as shown in Figure 16-12. The option you have applied is then indicated with a check mark. After you have completed policy troubleshooting, you can reenable the GPO from the same location.

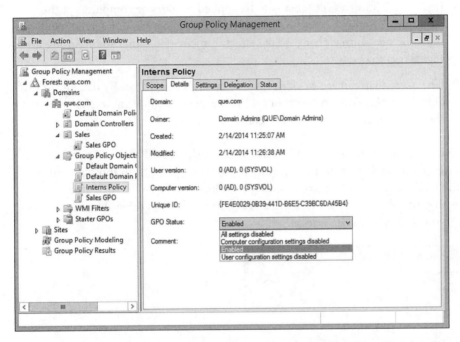

Figure 16-12   From the GPO's Details tab, you can disable either the computer or user configuration portion of a GPO or the entire GPO.

TIP   If a given GPO has no settings configured in one of the Computer Configuration or User Configuration branches, you can speed up policy processing by disabling that branch from this location.

Specifying a Domain Controller

You can edit a GPO from any writable domain controller, or even connect to a writable domain controller from a client computer running Windows 8.1 Pro or

Enterprise. You might want to specify which domain controller you are working against for any of the following reasons:

- If multiple administrators are working on the same GPO from multiple machines, conflicting changes will be overwritten and lost.

- If you are working against a domain controller at a remote site, you might encounter slow performance, which can become frustrating. You can select a local domain controller to avoid this problem.

- If you are editing a GPO that is to be applied to users or computers at the remote site, it might be advantageous to work against the domain controller in the same site, so that changes take effect immediately rather than waiting for replication to occur.

- To ensure that you are working against the PDC emulator. By default, AD DS defaults to this domain controller. However, you might want to change this if the PDC emulator is not readily available.

To select a domain controller, right-click your domain in GPMC and select **Change Domain Controller**. Select an appropriate option from those provided by the Change Domain Controller dialog box shown in Figure 16-13. The selected domain controller saves your changes and replicates them to other domain controllers in the next AD DS replication.

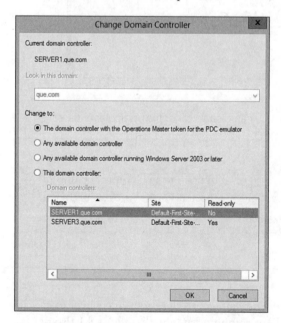

Figure 16-13   You can specify which domain controller you are working against when editing a GPO.

Using Windows PowerShell

You've already seen many examples of using Windows PowerShell to perform many server administrative tasks. As might be expected, you can also use Windows PowerShell cmdlets to automate many of the tasks already described for managing GPOs from GPMC. These include such tasks as creating GPOs and managing their links, setting permissions on GPOs, and modifying their processing and inheritance hierarchy. You can also back up, restore, and import GPOs using PowerShell. You can also write Windows PowerShell scripts and configure these scripts to run during startup, logon, logoff, or shutdown.

To create a new GPO using PowerShell, issue the cmdlet `New-GPO -Name MyGPO -comment "This is my GPO"`. Use the `-StarterGPOName` switch to create a new GPO from a Starter GPO. Windows Server 2012 R2 provides more than 20 Group Policy cmdlets to assist you in performing these actions. You must be working from either a computer running either Windows Server 2012 R2 or a Windows 8.1 Pro or Enterprise computer on which you have installed the Remote Server Administration Tools (RSAT). Before working with these cmdlets, you must import the Group Policy module. To do so, open Windows PowerShell and type `Import-Module GroupPolicy -verbose` at the Windows PowerShell command prompt. As shown in Figure 16-14, you see a series of messages informing you that the cmdlets have been imported. You can now use them to perform most Group Policy management tasks.

Figure 16-14 Importing Group Policy management cmdlets in Windows PowerShell.

To learn how to use any cmdlet, type `Get-Help` *<cmdlet>* at the PowerShell command prompt. Use the `-detailed` or `-full` keywords to obtain additional information on the specified cmdlet.

NOTE   For more information on using PowerShell to manage Group Policy, refer to "Using Windows PowerShell to Manage Group Policy" at http://technet.microsoft.com/en-us/library/dd759177.aspx. For a complete list of cmdlets for Group Policy in Windows Server 2012 R2, refer to "Group Policy Cmdlets in Windows PowerShell" at http://technet.microsoft.com/library/hh967461.aspx.

TIP   In addition to the `import-module` cmdlet, you might also use the `Import-GPO` cmdlet to perform the same function. The basic syntax is `Import-GPO -BackupGPOName TestGPO -TargetName MyImportGPO -path c:\backups`. For more information, refer to "Import-GPO" at http://technet.microsoft.com/en-us/library/ee461044.aspx.

To apply PowerShell scripts, open the Group Policy Management Editor focused on the desired GPO. For startup or shutdown scripts, expand the `Computer Configuration\Policies\Windows Settings\Scripts` node, and for logon or logoff scripts, expand the `User Configuration\Policies\Windows Settings\ Scripts` node. In the details pane, right-click the desired script type and select **Properties**. From the dialog box shown in Figure 16-15, you can perform the following actions:

- **Add or remove scripts:** Click **Add** to add a script, or select a script and click **Remove** to remove it.

- **Replace a script:** Select a script and click **Edit**. From the dialog box that appears, you can type the name of a different script to be used.

- **Change the sequence of script processing:** Scripts are processed in the sequence displayed in the dialog box. Select a script and use the **Up** and **Down** buttons to change the sequence.

- **Change the processing order of PowerShell and other scripts:** The drop-down list enables you to run Windows PowerShell scripts either first or last.

Figure 16-15 Configuring the use of PowerShell scripts.

Configuring Multiple Local Group Policies

Up to this point, we have been discussing Group Policy as it applies to the domain. At the local computer level, Microsoft has provided the ability to apply a series of policies using a collection of Local Group Policy Objects often referred to as Multiple Local Group Policy Objects (MLGPO). As its name indicates, Multiple Local Group Policy is broken into multiple parts or layers. Each layer applies configurations based on specific criteria. Combined, these configured policies make up a complete Local Group Policy configuration that is applied to a user or computer. The following layers exist:

- **Local Group Policy:** Local Group Policy or Local Computer Policy is the top layer of the policy stack. Settings configured here apply to the local computer. As a result, any user that logs on, including the administrator, receives the policy settings.

- **Administrators and Non-Administrators:** When an operating system is installed, a set of built-in users and groups are created. These users/groups are categorized by accounts with administrative access and accounts without administrative access. This policy layer allows configurations to be applied to either local administrative accounts or those accounts without administrative access.

- **User-Specific Group Policy:** This policy layer is used to configure user-specific policies for any new local users created on the computer.

MMC and Multiple Local Group Policies

To configure Multiple Local Group Policies, perform the following steps:

1. Open the **Microsoft Management Console**.

2. From the File menu, select **Add/Remove Snap-in**.

3. Select **Group Policy Object Editor**, and then click **Add**.

4. Click the **Browse** button to select the computer you for which want to manage the Local Computer policies. Click **OK** to continue.

5. Click **Finish** to add the Local Computer Group Policy Object to the Snap-in.

6. Before you commit the Snap-ins to the MMC console, add more Snap-ins for Administrator and Non-Administrator local group policies. Select **Group Policy Object Editor** again, and click **Add**.

7. Click the **Browse** button as you have done previously, but this time click the **Users** tab.

8. You will be presented with a list of Local Users and Groups compatible with Local Group Policy as shown in Figure 16-16. Select **Administrator** and then click **OK**.

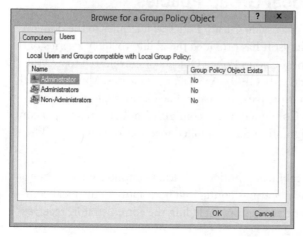

Figure 16-16   Local Computer Policy: Administrator & Non-Administrator Policies.

9. Click **Finish** to add the Local Computer\Administrator policy.

10. Repeat steps 6–9 to add the remaining Local Users and Groups compatible with Local Computer Policy.

11. Click **OK** to add the Snap-ins to the MMC console. Once completed, you will be able to use the MMC as shown in Figure 16-17 to configure various settings for the Multiple Local Group Policies added.

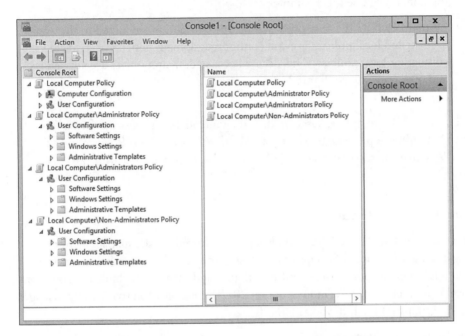

Figure 16-17   Using MMC to manage multiple local group policies.

NOTE   For more information, refer to "Edit Multiple Local Group Policy" at http://technet.microsoft.com/en-us/library/cc731758.aspx.

Using Multiple Local Group Policies

Because there are multiple layers of Local Group Policy, Microsoft has created a series of rules to help with the configuration and management of using multiple local group policies. To keep things from getting out of control, Microsoft has included the following mechanisms:

- **Local Group Policy Processing Order:** One of the important pieces of group policy is the order in which policies are applied. Local Group Policy objects containing computer settings are applied first. After these policies are applied, any settings configured under the Administrators and Non-Administrators Local Group Policy Objects are applied. Lastly, any user-specific settings (also applying to the local administrator) specified under Local Group Policy are applied.

- **Conflict Resolution:** In some cases, you can configure policy settings under more than one Local Group Policy object. When this occurs, it is important to keep in mind that the last policy applied wins. If you understand this, managing policies will be much simpler.

- **Domain Policy:** If at any point standalone computers are joined to the domain and local policies are still configured, domain policies override any conflicting local policies. This occurs because domain policies are applied last and overwrite any configured local policies.

> **NOTE**   MLGPOs are not available on domain controllers. For more information, refer to "Step-by-Step Guide to Managing Multiple Local Group Policy Objects" at http://technet.microsoft.com/en-us/library/cc766291(v=ws.10).aspx.

Managing Restricted Groups

With the release of Active Directory, Microsoft allowed for the management of groups using a Restricted Groups policy. Using this function, an Administrator could apply a group policy to centrally configure and manage the built-in groups on a local computer. Today, Windows Server 2012 R2 enables you to centrally manage built-in groups via the following methods:

- Restricted Groups
- Group Policy Preferences

Suppose you have a group of IT analysts who need local administrator access to workstations. Using the principle of least privilege, you are looking to grant local administrator access to workstations in the domain. You might have a domain group called WorkstationAdmins containing user accounts for all IT analysts. You could go around to each workstation and add the WorkstationAdmins group to the built-in Administrators group on all workstations, but depending on the number of workstations this might not be a viable option. In the past, you might have resorted to using startup scripts to manipulate groups. Although this might have been useful, management or modification of these scripts often became a challenge.

Group Policy enables you to create a Restricted Group policy that you can apply to workstations via OU or even based on a group membership. By configuring a Restricted Group policy, you can tell Active Directory to nest the domain WorkstationAdmins group in the local Administrators group on all workstations to which the policy is applied. Restricted Groups can be modified centrally by adding and removing groups or users to the built-in groups.

To create a Restricted Group Policy, perform the following steps:

1. Using Group Policy Management Editor, create and link a new GPO. Depending on your need, this can be linked to various levels and can be filtered to apply to specific groups.

2. Under Computer Configuration, browse to **Policies>Windows Settings>Restricted Groups**. Right-click **Restricted Groups** and select **Add Group** as shown in Figure 16-18.

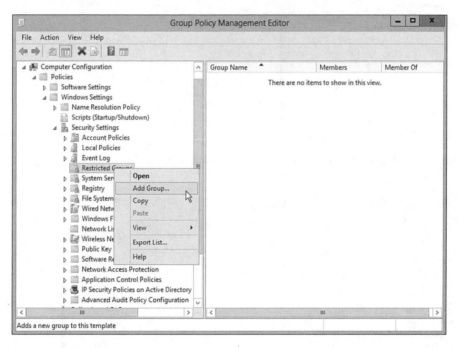

Figure 16-18   Add a Restricted Group.

3. In the Add Group dialog box, browse to the local server and type the case-sensitive name of the appropriate local group you want to manage via group policy; then click **OK**. If you type a group name that does not exist locally, the policy will not apply. In this example, type `Administrators` and click **OK**.

4. As shown in Figure 16-19, the dialog box for the Administrators Group will enable you to add and remove individual user accounts or groups under the Members of this group section. These accounts can be local or domain based. If you need to add or remove a group of which the built-in group is a member, use the **Add** and **Remove** buttons under the **This group is a member of** section. When complete, click **Apply** followed by **OK**. The restricted group will be established within Group Policy as shown in Figure 16-20.

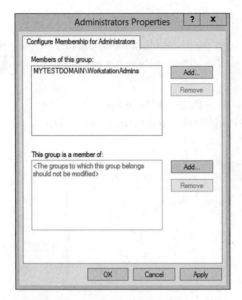

Figure 16-19   Adding and removing members of a Restricted Group.

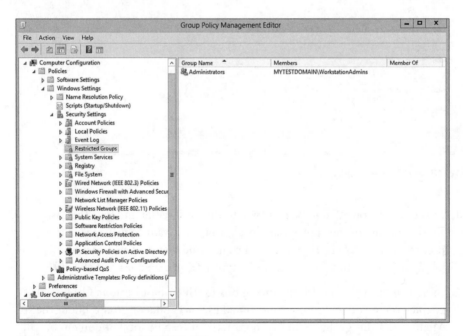

Figure 16-20   Modifying Restricted Groups.

5. After the computer reboots or the Group Policy refresh interval is met, the Restricted Groups policy will take effect. If at any point you decide to modify the members of the group, simply use the Group Policy Management Editor and edit the members of the restricted group you created. Similarly, if you want to remove the policy and built-in group configuration, simply delete the group under Restricted Groups. After the policy is deleted, built-in group members are removed because the policy no longer applies.

Local Users and Groups Extension

With the release of Windows 8.1 and Server 2012 R2, Group Policy enables local users and groups to be managed centrally using the Local Users and Groups Extension located under Computer/User Configuration>Preferences>Control Panel Settings>Local Users and Groups. Unlike Restricted Groups, this Group Policy feature enables you to not only manage built-in groups, but also perform the following tasks:

- Create local users and groups

- Delete local users and groups

- Rename local users and groups

- Modify local group memberships

- Change local user passwords

Configuring Local Groups Using Local Users and Groups Extension

To configure a local group using the Local Users and Groups Extension, perform the following steps:

1. From the Group Policy Management Console, navigate to **Computer/User Configuration** > **Preferences** > **Control Panel Settings**.

2. Right-click **Local Users and Groups**, point to **New**, and select **Local Group** as shown in Figure 16-21. This will open the New Local Group Properties dialog box (shown in Figure 16-22).

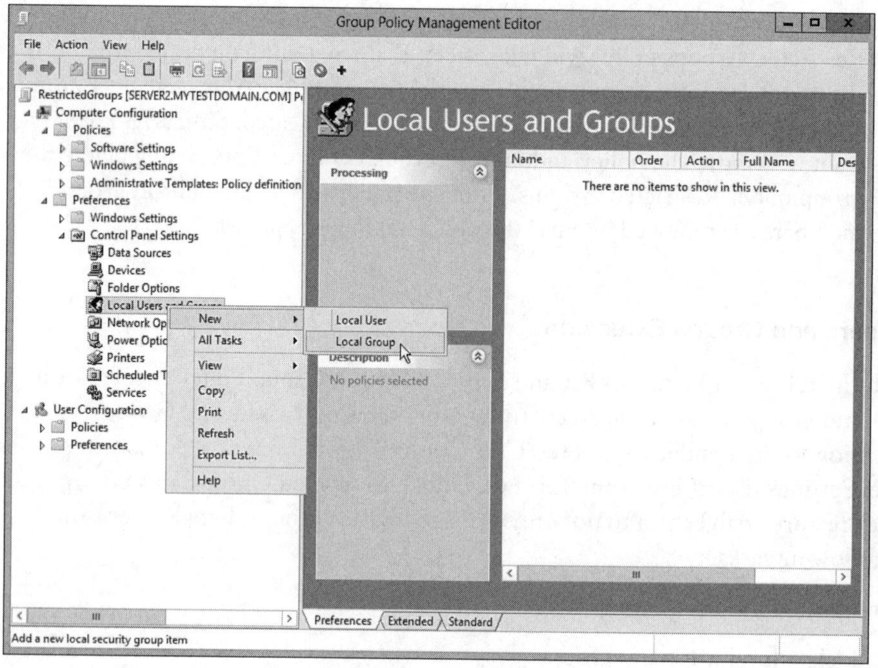

Figure 16-21   Create New Local Group using Local Users and Groups Extension.

Figure 16-22   New Local Group properties.

3. In the New Local Group Properties dialog box (refer to Figure 16-22), specify the following:

- **Action:** Select **Create** to create a new group matching the name specified, select **Replace** to replace any existing group by first deleting then re-creating it based on the group specified, select **Update** to update the group with the settings specified in the policy, or select **Delete** to delete the group altogether.

- **Group Name:** Type a group name or select one of the built-in groups available in the drop-down list. You also can choose to browse to a specific group.

- **Rename to:** If you plan on renaming a local group, enter the new name for the group.

- **Description:** Type a description to help identify the group.

- **Delete all member users:** Select this check box to delete any members of the local group.

- **Delete all member groups:** Select this check box to delete any groups of which the local group is a member.

- **Members:** You can add, remove, or change any members of the group. You can specify multiple operations and actions for each. For example, if you need to add User1 as a member, select **Add** as the action. You might decide that when the policy is applied, you want to remove User2. If any changes need to be made, use the **Remove** or **Change** button accordingly.

4. When complete, click **Apply** followed by **OK**.

Configuring Local Users Using Local Users and Groups Extension

To configure a local user using the Local Users and Groups Extension, perform the following steps:

1. From the Group Policy Management Console, navigate to **Computer/User Configuration** > **Preferences** > **Control Panel Settings**.

2. Right-click **Local Users and Groups**, point to **New**, and select **Local User** as shown previously in Figure 16-21. This will open the New Local User Properties dialog box shown in Figure 16-23.

Figure 16-23   New Local User properties.

3. In the New Local User Properties dialog box, specify the following:

 - **Action:** Select **Create** to create a new local user matching the name specified, select **Replace** to replace any existing user by first deleting then re-creating it based on the information specified, select **Update** to update an existing user with the settings specified in the policy, or select **Delete** to delete the user altogether.

 - **User details:** Several fields are available for configuration, many of which you might be familiar with. The benefit of using Group Policy to manage local user accounts is that you have the ability to alter passwords, disable the account, set expiration dates, and so on, all from a central location.

4. Select or specify a username and configure the appropriate settings. When complete, click **Apply** followed by **OK** to save the policy.

Configuring Group Policy Common Options

In addition to configuring group policy preferences, Microsoft has allowed administrators to configure Group Policy Common Options. Common Options provide granular control over how the policy is applied and which actions should be taken if specific criteria is met. You can specify Common Options by clicking the **Common** tab shown in Figure 16-24.

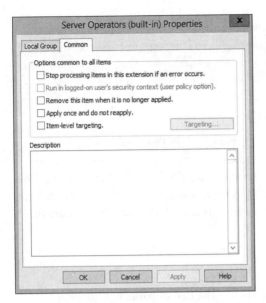

Figure 16-24 Group Policy Common Options.

The Common Options tab provides the ability to select and apply the following:

- **Stop processing items in this extension if an error occurs:** Group Policy will skip processing of items in the extension if any conflicts occur.

- **Run in logged-on user's security context (user policy option):** This setting applies only to user policy options. When enabled, the policy applies using the user's context as opposed to the Local System account, which is the default.

- **Remove this item when it is no longer applied:** If a specific computer is targeted to receive this setting but is later removed from the targeted list, the current applied settings are no longer applied via Group Policy.

- **Apply once and do not reapply:** By default, Group Policies are applied during startup, logon, or periodic refresh intervals. Each time one of these events occurs, Group Policy will reapply any configured settings. If you choose to improve processing performance, you might decide to apply the policy only once.

- **Item-level targeting:** Item-level targeting enables you to apply policies based on specific criteria such as Computer Name, CPU Speed, Disk Space, IP Address Range, Operating System, Site, the existence of executable files, and so on. This function leverages WMI queries to provide complete control over targeting specific items.

> **NOTE** For more information on configuring users and groups via Group Policy, refer to "Local Users and Groups Extension" at http://technet.microsoft.com/en-us/library/cc731972.aspx.

Configuring Security Filtering

The Security Filtering section of the Scope tab of a GPO's Properties (refer to Figure 16-9) displays the users, groups, and computers to which the GPO settings apply. These users, groups, and computers automatically have the Apply Group Policy permission granted to them. You can add users and groups to this list by clicking the **Add** button provided. To remove a user or group, select it and click **Remove**.

Denying the Application of a GPO

To filter the application of a GPO, select it in the console tree of GPMC and select the **Delegation** tab from its properties in the details pane. As shown in Figure 16-25, this tab lists all users and groups with specified permissions on the GPO. You can add or remove users or groups by using the Add and Remove buttons in the same way as described for the Scope tab.

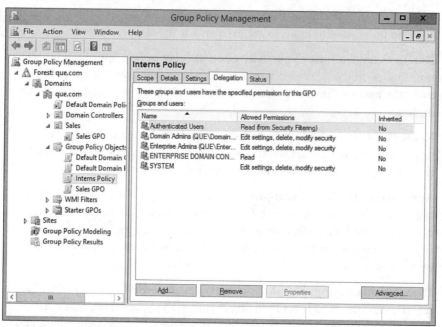

Figure 16-25   The Delegation tab lists all users and groups with specified permissions on its GPO.

This location enables you to explicitly deny application of a GPO to certain groups. For example, you might want to lock down the desktops of all users except members of the Domain Admins group. To do this, you would deny the Apply Group Policy permission to this group. Use the following procedure:

1. From the Delegation tab, select the **Domain Admins** group and click **Advanced**.

2. On the Security Settings dialog box that appears, select the required group and deny the Apply group policy permission, as shown in Figure 16-26.

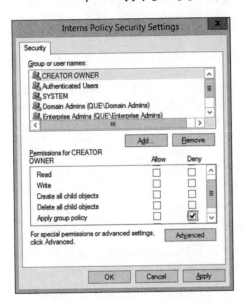

Figure 16-26   You can deny the application of a GPO to a given group by selecting the Deny entry for the Apply group policy permission.

3. Click **OK**. You are reminded that the Deny entry takes precedence over Allow entries, as shown in Figure 16-27.

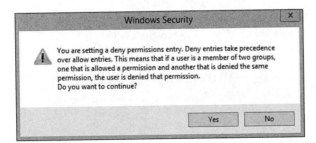

Figure 16-27   You are warned that the Deny entry takes precedence over Allow.

4. Click **Yes** to accept this warning. The entry for this group under Allowed Permissions in the Delegation tab now states Custom to inform you that you have set a customized permission.

NOTE   The Properties button at the bottom of the Delegation tab takes you to the same Properties dialog box for the user or group we discussed in Chapter 14, "Active Directory User and Computer Accounts," enabling you to modify the membership of the group. For a user, you see the dialog box previously shown in Figure 14-6.

Windows Management Instrumentation

First introduced with Windows XP and Windows Server 2003 and continued with Windows Vista/7/8/8.1 and Windows Server 2008/R2/2012/R2, WMI filters enable an administrator to modify the scope of a GPO according to the attributes of destination computers.

WMI in Windows Server 2012 R2 provides several new features, including the following:

- **Improved tracing and logging:** WMI uses Event Tracing for Windows, which enables the logging of WMI events available in Event Viewer.

- **Connection with User Account Control:** UAC now affects what WMI data is returned, remote access to WMI, and how WMI runs scripts.

- **Enhanced WMI namespace security and auditing:** You can now secure WMI namespace security in the Managed Object Format file. Further, WMI audits system access control lists (SACLs) and reports events to the Security event log.

The WMI Filters node in GPMC enables you to configure WMI filters. You can create new WMI filters and import filters from external locations at this location. These WMI filters are then available to any GPO in your forest. Use the Scope tab of a GPO's Properties in GPMC to apply a WMI filter to the GPO.

TIP   You do not need to know how to write WMI filter queries for the 70-410 exam. However, you do need to know that WMI filters can query destination computers for hardware and other attributes.

NOTE   For more information on creating and applying WMI filters, refer to "Work with WMI Filters" at http://technet.microsoft.com/en-us/library/cc732796.aspx.

Exam Preparation Tasks

Review All the Key Topics

Review the most important topics in the chapter, noted with the key topics icon in the outer margin of the page. Table 16-4 lists a reference of these key topics and the page numbers on which each is found.

Table 16-4   Key Topics for Chapter 16

Key Topic Element	Description	Page Number
Paragraph	Describes the components of Group Policy	713
Step list	Describes how to create a GPO	719
Figure 16-2	Introduces the Group Policy Management Console and shows its main features	720
Table 16-3	Describes the components of the Group Policy Management Editor snap-in	723
Step list	Describes how to create and configure a Starter GPO	724
Figure 16-9	Shows how to manage GPO links	729
List	Lists the various types of Local Group Policies	735
Step list	Lists the steps used to configure Restricted Groups	739
Paragraph	Describes the benefits of using Local Users and Groups Extension to configure Local Users and Groups	741
Figure 16-25	Shows the process of delegating control of GPOs to users or groups	746
Figure 16-26	Shows how to deny processing of a GPO to a security group	747

Complete the Tables and Lists from Memory

Print a copy of Appendix B, "Memory Tables" (found on the CD), or at least the section for this chapter, and complete the tables and lists from memory. Appendix C, "Memory Tables Answer Key," is also on the CD and includes completed tables and lists to check your work.

Definitions of Key Terms

Define the following key terms from this chapter, and check your answers in the glossary.

Administrative Templates, Filtering, Group Policy, Group Policy object (GPO), Group Policy Management Editor, Group Policy Management Console (GPMC), Linked policy, Starter GPOs, Windows Management Instrumentation (WMI)

This chapter covers the following subjects:

- **Configuring User Rights Assignment:** User rights are defined as a default set of capabilities for performing administrative tasks on the network that are assigned to built-in domain global and local groups by default. This section shows you how to use Group Policy for modifying the assignment of these rights to suit the particular requirements of your network.

- **Configuring Security Options Settings:** Group Policy in Windows Server 2012 R2 contains a comprehensive set of policy settings that enable you to configure the security of servers on your AD DS network. This section describes the more important security settings you can configure and introduces several tools that assist you in configuring server security.

- **Auditing of Active Directory Services:** Auditing lets you record actions that take place across your domain, including attempts to access user accounts and resources. This section shows you how to use Group Policy to set up policies that effectively track these types of activities on your network.

- **Configuring User Account Control (UAC):** UAC is designed to enable all users, even administrators, to run with a standard access token. When a user requires administrative privileges for a task that can affect system properties, such as installing a program, the user receives a prompt that requests administrative credentials. UAC helps prevent unauthorized program installation and system modification. Group Policy enables you to modify the settings that determine when these prompts appear; you learn how to work with these settings in this section.

CHAPTER 17

Configuring Security Policies

Chapter 16, "Creating and Applying Group Policy Objects," showed you how Group Policy works and how to set up Group Policy objects (GPOs) to configure various aspects of the Windows computing environment. Now we turn our attention to the use of Group Policy to help provide your network with a safe and secure computing environment. Malicious individuals are forever devising new means of invading your network to steal and corrupt data, prevent your network from functioning, and disrupt business activities. Group Policy enables you to configure security policy settings that help to ensure that uninvited users are kept away from sensitive parts of your network, and if they do gain access, you can use auditing tools to determine which resources they've managed to access or unsuccessfully attempted to access. This chapter focuses on the use of Group Policy to create and enforce a secure computing environment that protects your computers and data from whatever the bad guys might attempt to throw at you.

Group Policy contains an entire series of policy settings found under the Security Settings subnode in both the Computer Configuration and User Configuration sections. This chapter looks primarily at the policy settings contained under the Local Policies sub-subnode beneath Security Settings. Found here are audit policies, which enable you to track access to and use of resources on the network; user rights assignments, which determine which users and groups can perform various system-based activities; and security options, which include a long list of security-related policies. We also take a look at policies that govern the use of User Account Control (UAC), which prompts users for administrative credentials before permitting potentially harmful actions such as installing software at the local computer.

"Do I Know This Already?" Quiz

The "Do I Know This Already?" quiz enables you to assess whether you should read this entire chapter or simply jump to the "Exam Preparation Tasks" section for review. If you are in doubt, read the entire chapter. Table 17-1 outlines the major headings in this chapter and the corresponding "Do I Know This Already?" quiz questions. You can find the answers in Appendix A, "Answers to the 'Do I Know This Already?' Quizzes."

Table 17-1 "Do I Know This Already?" Foundation Topics Section-to-Question Mapping

Foundations Topics Section	Questions Covered in This Section
Configuring User Rights Assignment	1
Configuring Security Options Settings	2–3
Auditing of Active Directory Services	4–8
Configuring User Account Control (UAC)	9

1. You would like to review the default user rights for administering your AD DS domain granted to the various built-in groups in Windows Server 2012 R2, so you open the Group Policy Management Console. What should you do?

   a. Right-click the **Default Domain Policy** GPO and select **Edit**. In the Group Policy Management Editor, navigate to the **Computer Configuration\Policies\Windows Settings\Security Settings\Local Policies\User Rights Assignment** node and select this node. View the default user rights in the details pane.

   b. Right-click the **Default Domain Controllers Policy** GPO and select **Edit**. In the Group Policy Management Editor, navigate to the **Computer Configuration\Policies\Windows Settings\Security Settings\Local Policies\User Rights Assignment** node and select this node. View the default user rights in the details pane.

   c. Right-click the **Default Domain Policy** GPO and select **Edit**. In the Group Policy Management Editor, navigate to the **User Configuration\Policies\Windows Settings\Security Settings\Local Policies\User Rights Assignment node** and select this node. View the default user rights in the details pane.

   d. Right-click the **Default Domain Controllers Policy** GPO and select **Edit**. In the Group Policy Management Editor, navigate to the **User Configuration\Policies\Windows Settings\Security Settings\Local Policies\User Rights Assignment** node and select this node. View the default user rights in the details pane.

2. You are using the Security Configuration Wizard to configure a security policy to be applied in a GPO linked to your company's AD DS domain. Which of the following security categories can you configure using this tool? (Choose all that apply.)

   a. Server roles, features, and administrative options

   b. Background services running on the server, including their startup modes

   c. Network security, including rules for the Windows Server Firewall with Advanced Security snap-in.

   d. Registry-based settings for configuring protocols used to communicate on the network

   e. Users that are permitted to be members of specified groups

   f. Audit policy settings

3. You are responsible for configuring the security policy for all computers on your company's network, which is configured as an AD DS domain. The network also includes a standalone server that is not configured as a domain member. How should you configure security policy settings to apply to this server using the least amount of administrative effort?

   a. Use the Security Configuration and Analysis tool to analyze the security settings on a member server, and apply these security settings to the standalone server.

   b. Use the Security Templates tool to save a custom security policy template on a member server on the domain; then use the Security Configuration and Analysis tool to create a database containing settings in the policy template, and apply them to the standalone server.

   c. Use the Security Configuration Wizard to copy the required settings from a member server, and paste them into the standalone server.

   d. Manually specify all the required settings using the Local Security Policy snap-in at the standalone server.

4. You are responsible for the auditing of directory-based actions occurring within your company's AD DS domain. You need to track replication events occurring within the domain, including the establishment, removal, or modification of AD DS replica source naming contexts; replication of attributes for an AD DS object; and removal of lingering objects from a replica. Which of the following audit subcategories should you configure for auditing?

   a. Directory Service Access

   b. Directory Service Changes

   c. Directory Service Replication

   d. Detailed Directory Service Replication

5. You are responsible for the auditing of activities taking place within your company's AD DS domain. Your boss has requested that you implement auditing of the following:

   ■ Attempts to log on to any local computer

   ■ Creation of a user account or group or changing of a user account password

   Which auditing components should you configure? (Each answer represents part of the solution. Choose two.)

   a. Audit account management, success

   b. Audit account logon events, success and failure

   c. Audit object access, success

   d. Audit logon events, success and failure

6. You have enabled the auditing of object access in a GPO linked to the Default Domain Policy GPO in your company's AD DS domain. All departments in your company are represented by organizational units within the domain structure. The manager of the Legal department reports that someone has improperly modified many of the legal documents stored on the department's member server, which runs Windows Server 2012 R2. Checking Event Viewer, you cannot find any evidence of who performed these actions. What do you need to do so that future actions of this type are properly documented?

   a. You also need to enable auditing of logon events in the Local Security Policy snap-in at the member server.

   b. You should have enabled auditing of object access in a GPO linked to the Legal OU.

   c. You also need to access File Explorer at the member server. From this location, ensure that the appropriate auditing entries have been enabled for the folder in which the legal documents are located.

   d. You should have enabled auditing of directory service access.

7. Users in your company's AD DS domain have been complaining about frequent account lockouts at their client computers in recent days. Domain servers run Windows Server 2012 R2, and client computers run Windows 8.1. You decide to implement a stronger audit policy that is designed to specifically track account lockouts without generating audit trails for other user account-related events. How should you proceed?

   a. From the Group Policy Management Editor focused on the appropriate GPO, navigate to the **Computer Configuration\Policies\Windows Settings\Security Settings\Local Policies\Audit Policy** subnode. Then enable the Audit account logon events policy.

   b. From the Group Policy Management Editor focused on the appropriate GPO, navigate to the **Computer Configuration\Policies\Windows Settings\Security Settings\Local Policies\Audit Policy** subnode. Then enable the Audit logon events policy.

   c. From the Group Policy Management Editor focused on the appropriate GPO, navigate to the **Computer Configuration\Policies\Windows Settings\Security Settings\Advanced Audit Policy Configuration\Audit Policies\Account Logon** subnode. Then enable the Audit Account Lockout policy setting.

   d. From the Group Policy Management Editor focused on the appropriate GPO, navigate to the **Computer Configuration\Policies\Windows Settings\Security Settings\Advanced Audit Policy Configuration\Audit Policies\Logon/Logoff** subnode. Then enable the Audit Account Lockout policy setting.

8. You are working from a computer running the Server Core version of Windows Server 2012 R2. You need to enable auditing of object access for computers in your company's AD DS domain. Which tool should you use for this purpose?

   a. Adsiedit.msc

   b. Auditpol.exe

   c. Gpedit.msc

   d. Scwcmd.exe

9. You need to ensure that users receive a prompt when trying to perform administrative commands. Which security setting should you modify from local security policy?

    a. Local Policies

    b. Account Policies

    c. Public Key Policies

    d. Software Restriction Policies

Configuring User Rights Assignment

You can use Group Policy to manage security settings quite effectively on a Windows Server 2012 R2 network. An enhanced range of security options is available, with settings designed for both user and computer configuration. Microsoft continues to expand the available range of security policies, compared to those included with previous versions of Windows Server.

User rights are defined as a default set of capabilities assigned to built-in domain local groups that define what members of these groups can and cannot do on the network. They consist of privileges and logon rights.

You can manage these predefined user rights from the Computer Configuration\Policies\Windows Settings\Security Settings\Local Policies\User Rights Assignment node in the Group Policy Management Editor. Use the following procedure.

1. Open the Group Policy Management Editor focused on an appropriate Group Policy object.

2. Navigate to the **Computer Configuration\Policies\Windows Settings\ Security Settings\Local Policies\User Rights Assignment** node and select this node. The details pane shows a series of predefined user rights. When focused on the Default Domain Controllers Policy GPO, you see a default set of user rights assignments, as shown in Figure 17-1.

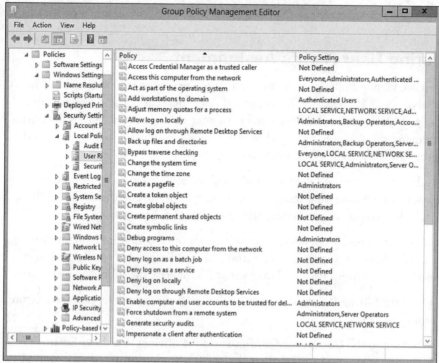

Figure 17-1 The Default Domain Controllers Policy GPO includes an extensive set of predefined user rights assignments.

3. To modify the assignment of any right, right-click it and select **Properties**. As shown for the Back up files and directories user right in Figure 17-2, the Properties dialog box displays the built-in groups that are granted this right by default.

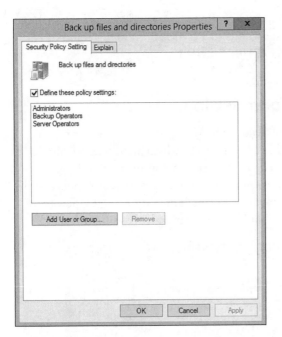

Figure 17-2   The Back up files and directories Properties dialog box displays the groups that are granted this right by default, and it enables you to modify this assignment if required.

4. To grant this right to another user or group, click **Add User or Group**. In the Add User or Group dialog box that appears, type or browse to the required user or group. Then click **OK**. To remove a user or group, select it and click **Remove**.

5. When finished, click **OK** to close the Properties dialog box. You are returned to the Group Policy Management Editor, where you can continue to configure additional user rights as needed.

Note that each user rights Properties dialog box has an Explain tab, which provides additional information about what each user right involves. Consult this tab before modifying any of the default user rights.

You can also create a new GPO and configure a series of settings in this node to be applied to a specific group, and then link the GPO to an appropriate OU and grant the required group the Read and Apply Group Policy permissions. This is an easy way to grant user rights over a subset of the domain to a junior group of employees, such as help desk technicians.

> **NOTE**   For more information on granting user rights in Active Directory Domain Services (AD DS), refer to "Assign User Rights to a Group in AD DS" at http://technet.microsoft.com/en-us/library/cc754142.aspx.

Configuring Security Options Settings

Within the Local Policies subnode of Security Settings, you have the user rights assignment already discussed, as well as audit policies, which are discussed later in this chapter. This section introduces you to the Security Options subnode, which includes a large set of policy options, as shown in Figure 17-3, that are important in controlling security aspects of the computers to which the GPO applies. Several of the more important options that you should be familiar with are as follows:

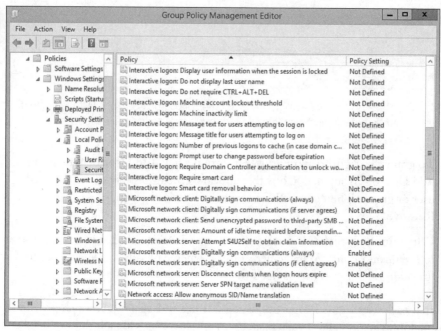

Figure 17-3   You can configure numerous local security policy settings with Group Policy in Windows Server 2012 R2.

- **Accounts: Block Microsoft accounts:** Prevents users from using Microsoft accounts to access the computer or creating new Microsoft accounts on the computer. This setting was new to Windows 8 and Windows Server 2012 and is continued in Windows 8.1 and Windows Server 2012 R2.

- **Accounts: Rename administrator account:** This option renames the default administrator account to a value you specify. Intruders cannot simply look for "Administrator" when attempting to crack your network.

- **Interactive logon: Do not display last user name:** Enable this option to prevent the username of the last logged-on user from appearing in the logon dialog box, thus preventing another individual from seeing a username. This can also help to reduce lockouts.

- **Interactive logon: Do not require CTRL+ALT+DEL:** When enabled, a user is not required to press **Ctrl+Alt+Delete** to obtain the logon dialog box. Disable this policy in a secure environment to require the use of this key combination. Its use prevents rogue programs such as Trojan horses from capturing usernames and passwords.

- **Interactive logon: Require smart card:** When enabled, users must employ a smart card to log on to the computer.

- **User Account Control:** Several policy settings determine the behavior of the UAC prompt for administrative and nonadministrative users, including behavior by applications that are located in secure locations on the computer such as `%ProgramFiles%` or `%Windir%`.

> **NOTE** For more information on the policy settings in the Security Options subnode, refer to "Security Policy Settings Technical Overview" at http://technet.microsoft.com/en-us/library/jj966251.aspx and "Security Options" at http://technet.microsoft.com/en-us/library/jj852268.aspx.

The Security Options node also contains the following additional sets of security-related policies:

- **Event Log:** Configuration options for the Event Viewer logs, including log sizes and action taken when an event log is full.

- **Restricted Groups:** Determines who can belong to certain groups. We discussed group accounts in Chapter 15, "Active Directory Groups and Organizational Units (OUs)."

- **System Services:** Enables you to configure system services properties, such as startup type, and restrict users from modifying these settings.

- **Registry:** Enables you to control the permissions that govern who can access and edit portions of the Registry.

- **File System:** Enables you to configure permissions on folders and files and prevent their modification.

- **Wired Network (IEEE 802.3) Policies:** Enables you to specify the use of IEEE 802.1X authentication for network access by Windows Vista, Windows 7, Windows 8, or Windows 8.1 computers and includes the protocol to be used for network authentication.

- **Windows Firewall with Advanced Security:** Enables you to configure properties of Windows Firewall for domain, private, and public profiles. You can specify inbound and outbound connection rules as well as monitoring settings.

- **Network List Manager Policies:** Enables you to control the networks that computers can access and their location types such as public and private (which automatically specifies the appropriate firewall settings according to location type). You can also specify to which networks a user is allowed to connect.

- **Wireless Network (IEEE 802.11) Policies:** Enables you to specify wireless settings, such as enabling 802.1X authentication and the preferred wireless networks that users can access.

- **Public Key Policies:** Enables you to configure public key infrastructure (PKI) settings. Certificate Services and PKI are discussed in the *Cert Guide* book for exam 70-412.

- **Software Restriction Policies:** Enables you to specify which software programs users can run on network computers, which programs users on multiuser computers can run, and the execution of email attachments. You can also specify whether software restriction policies apply to certain groups such as administrators. We discuss software restriction policies in Chapter 18, "Configuring Application Restriction Policies."

- **Network Access Protection:** Network Access Protection (NAP) is a feature first introduced in Windows Server 2008. It enables you to define client health policies that restrict access to your network by computers that lack appropriate security configurations. The NAP policies enable you to specify settings for client user interface items, trusted servers, and servers used for enforcement of client computer security health status. We discuss NAP in the *Cert Guide* book for exam 70-411.

- **Application Control Policies:** These are a set of software control policies first introduced with Windows 7 and Windows Server 2008 R2 that introduces the AppLocker feature. AppLocker provides new enhancements that enable you to specify exactly what users are permitted to run on their desktops according to unique file identities. We discuss application control policies in Chapter 18.

- **IP Security Policies on Active Directory:** Controls the implementation of IP Security (IPsec) as used by the computer for encrypting communications over the network.

- **Advanced Audit Policy Configuration:** First introduced in Windows Server 2008 R2 and continued in Windows Server 2012 R2, this node contains 53 new policy settings that enable you to select explicitly the actions you want to monitor and exclude actions that are of less concern. More information is provided later in this chapter.

You can obtain additional information on many of these policy settings in the Windows Server 2012 R2 Help and Support.

Using Additional Security Configuration Tools

Windows Server 2012 R2 includes the following additional tools that are useful in configuring and maintaining the security of your AD DS network:

- **Security Configuration Wizard:** This wizard assists you in maintaining the security of your servers and checks for vulnerabilities that might appear as server configurations change over time. You can access this wizard from the Search charm or the Administrative Tools tile on the Start screen. As shown in Figure 17-4, you can create a new security policy or perform actions on an existing security policy, including editing, applying, or rolling back the policy. This wizard is particularly useful in maintaining the security of servers hosting roles that are not installed using Server Manager, such as SQL Server and Exchange Server, as well as servers that host non-Microsoft applications. Microsoft also includes a command-line version, `scwcmd.exe`, which is useful in configuring Server Core computers. Using this wizard, you can configure security for the following items:

    - Server roles, features, and administrative options

    - Background services running on the server, including their startup modes

    - Network security, including rules for the Windows Server Firewall with Advanced Security snap-in

    - Registry-based settings for configuring protocols used to communicate on the network

    - Audit policy settings

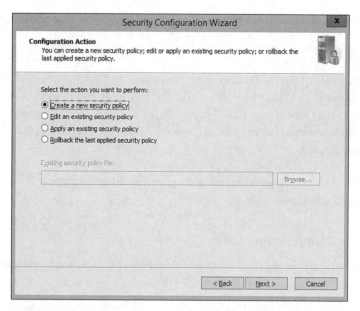

Figure 17-4 The Security Configuration Wizard assists you in working with security policies.

- **Security Templates snap-in:** From this snap-in, you can save a custom security policy that includes settings from the various subnodes of the Security Settings node of Computer Configuration that we discussed in the preceding sections. It is most useful in defining a security configuration for standalone servers that are not members of a domain.

- **Security Configuration and Analysis:** This snap-in enables you to analyze and configure local computer security. You can compare security settings on the computer to those in a database created from the Security Templates snap-in and view any differences that are found. You can then use this database to configure the computer's security so that it matches the database settings.

These two snap-ins are not contained in any MMC console by default; to use them you must open a blank console (type **mmc** from the Run dialog box or the Search charm) and add them using the Add or Remove Snap-ins dialog box shown in Figure 17-5.

NOTE For more information on these tools, refer to "Security Configuration Wizard" at http://technet.microsoft.com/en-us/library/cc754997.aspx, "Security Tools to Administer Windows Server 2012" at http://technet.microsoft.com/en-us/library/jj730960.aspx, and "Security Configuration Wizard Documentation" at http://www.microsoft.com/en-us/download/details.aspx?id=6334.

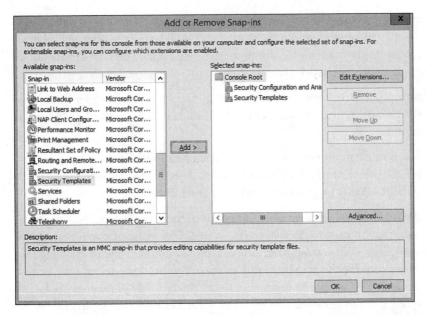

Figure 17-5   You can use the Add or Remove Snap-ins dialog box to create a Security console containing the Security Templates and Security Configuration and Analysis tools.

Password and Account Lockout Policies

As an administrator, one of your goals is to secure your network. While security is a broad area to cover, one of the tasks you have is to define a password policy and account lockout policy, both of which are configured using Group Policy Management console.

Password Policy Settings

Password Policy settings are located and can be configured under Computer Configuration\Windows Settings\Security Settings\Account Policies\Password Policy. When configuring a password policy, you should consider configuring the following settings:

- **Enforce password history:** Determines the number of unique new passwords the user must use before an old password can be reused. The default is 24 passwords remembered.

- **Minimum password age:** Defines the minimum period of time in days that a password can be used before the system requires the user to change it. The default value is 1 day.

- **Maximum password age:** Defines the maximum period of time in days that a password can be used before the system requires the user to change it. This value must be greater than the minimum password age. The default value is 42 days. If set to 0, the password never expires.

- **Minimum password length:** Defines the minimum number of characters (up to 14) a password must contain. The default value is 0, indicating no password is required.

- **Password must meet complexity requirements:** Indicates whether passwords must meet complexity requirements as described in the next section. The default value is Enabled in Windows Server 2012 R2.

- **Store password using reversible encryption:** Stores encrypted passwords with information used to decrypt the password. This policy setting is typically associated with custom or in-house applications that require knowing the user's password for the authentication process. Applications decrypt the stored password and process logon requests. Due to the fact that passwords can be decrypted, it is recommended to keep the default setting of Disabled unless there is a specific need that outweighs the security risk.

Password Complexity

Previous editions of Windows Server introduced the concept of *strong passwords*. A strong password is a password comprised of at least eight characters including a combination of letters, numbers, and symbols. Strong passwords help protect accounts, especially administrative accounts, from being compromised by unauthorized users.

In legacy versions of Windows Server, strong passwords could be enforced throughout the organization through a password policy that was applied to the entire domain. A password policy could be applied to the domain using a domain-based GPO that specified password requirements for the domain. To configure strong passwords, Microsoft created the Passwords must meet complexity requirements Group Policy setting. The password complexity setting prevents users from employing simple, easy-to-guess passwords by enforcing the following requirements with respect to creating passwords:

- Passwords may not contain user account name or display name.

- Passwords must contain characters from three of the following categories:

  - Uppercase letters A–Z

  - Lowercase letters a–z

  - Base 10 digits 0–9

  - Non-alphanumeric characters, also known as special characters such as !,@,#,$

Account Lockout Policy

As with previous versions of Windows Server, domain controllers keep track of logon attempts. By configuring Account Lockout Policy settings, you can control what happens when unauthorized access attempts occur. Account Lockout Policy settings are configured under Computer Configuration\Windows Settings\Security Settings\Account Policies\Account Lockout Policy. You can configure the following settings for the entire domain:

- **Account lockout duration:** Specifies the number of minutes an account is locked before automatically being unlocked by the system. A value of 0 specifies that the account will be locked until an administrator intervenes and unlocks the account. By default, account lockout durations are undefined.

- **Account lockout threshold:** Defines the number of failed logon attempts that causes the user account to be locked out.

- **Reset account lockout counter after:** Specifies the number of minutes that must pass after the account is locked before the account logon counter is reset to 0. This setting is not defined by default.

Fine-Grained Password Policy

With the release of more recent editions of Windows Server, Microsoft has created a concept known as a *fine-grained password policy*. Also included in Windows Server 2012 R2, fine-grained password policies enable you to configure *different* password policies and lockout settings (as discussed previously) that can be applied to specific users or groups within a domain. If you recall, previously these were applied to the entire domain. Fine-grained password policies are particularly helpful in the following scenarios:

- A group of users, such as administrators, require a different, perhaps more complex password policy than the rest of the users.

- Different departments, such as Legal or Human Resources, require stronger password policies than the rest of the organization.

- Your company has merged or acquired a new company with different password policy requirements.

Fine-grained password policies use an object class defined in the AD DS schema known as a Password Settings object (PSO). The PSO holds attributes for the fine-grained password and account lockout policy settings. Password settings are stored in a Password Settings Container (PSC) located under the default System container in the domain.

NOTE   For more information, refer to "Password Policy" at http:// technet.microsoft.com/en-us/library/hh994572.aspx, "Account Lockout Policy" at http://technet.microsoft.com/en-us/library/hh994563.aspx, and "AD DS: Fine-Grained Password Policies" at http://technet.microsoft.com/en-us/ library/056a73ef-5c9e-44d7-acc1-4f0bade6cd75.aspx.

Auditing of Active Directory Services

Auditing enables you to track actions performed by users across the domain such as logging on and off or accessing files and folders. When you create and apply an auditing policy, auditable events are recorded in the Security log of the computer at which they happen. You can then use Event Viewer to view any computer's Security log by connecting to the required computer.

New Audit Functionality

Windows Server 2012 introduces new expression-based audit policies, which are continued in Windows Server 2012 R2. Dynamic Access Control in Windows Server 2012/R2 allows you to create audit policies by using expressions based on user, computer, or resource request. Expression-based audit policies are helpful in situations where you need to minimize audit logs but still track the necessary data. You can apply expression policies centrally through Group Policy using Global Object Access Auditing. Global Object Access Auditing enables administrators to define computer system access control lists (SACLs) per object type for the file system or registry. The SACL is then applied to every object for that type.

Active Directory Auditing

Windows Server 2008 introduced the command-line tool `auditpol.exe` as well as subcategories in the Audit Directory Service Access category. In addition, Windows Server 2008 R2 introduced an Advanced Audit Policy subnode in the Group Policy Management Editor. In previous versions of Windows Server, a single Directory Service Access category controlled the auditing of all directory service events. Windows Server 2012 expanded on this. Windows Server 2012 R2 continues to leverage four subcategories for auditing directory service access:

- **Directory Service Access:** Tracks all attempts at accessing AD DS objects whose SACLs have been configured for auditing. This includes deletion of objects.

- **Directory Service Changes:** Tracks modifications to AD DS objects whose SACLs have been configured for auditing. The following actions are included:

  - When an attribute of an object has been modified, the old and new values of the attribute are recorded in the Security log.

  - When a new object is created, values of their attributes, including new attribute values, are recorded in the Security log. This includes objects moved from another domain.

  - When objects are moved from one container to another, the distinguished names of the old and new locations are recorded in the Security log.

  - When objects are undeleted, the location in which they are placed is recorded in the Security log. Any added, modified, or deleted attributes are also recorded.

- **Directory Service Replication:** Tracks the beginning and end of the synchronization of a replica of an Active Directory naming context.

- **Detailed Directory Service Replication:** Tracks additional AD DS replication events, including the establishment, removal, or modification of an Active Directory replica source naming context; replication of attributes for an AD DS object; or removal of a lingering object from a replica.

Using GPOs to Configure Auditing

Group Policy enables you to configure success or failure for several types of actions. In other words, you can choose to record successful actions, failed attempts at performing these actions, or both. For example, if you are concerned about intruders that might be attempting to access your network, you can log failed logon events. You can also track successful logon events, which is useful in case the intruders succeed in accessing your network.

You can use Group Policy to enable auditing at domain controllers, member servers, and client computers. Be aware that all auditing takes place at the local computer on which the events take place only and that these events are recorded on that computer's Security log. To enable auditing on all domain controllers, configure the auditing settings in the Default Domain Controllers Policy GPO; to enable auditing on other domain computers, configure the auditing settings in the Default Domain Policy GPO or in another GPO as required.

Available Auditing Categories

Windows Server 2012 R2 enables you to audit the following types of events:

- **Account logon:** Logon or logoff by a domain user account at a domain controller. You should track both success and failure.

- **Account management:** Creation, modification, or deletion of computer, user, or group accounts. Also included are enabling and disabling of accounts and changing or resetting passwords. You should track both success and failure.

- **Directory service access:** Access to an AD DS object as specified by the object's SACL. This category includes the four subcategories mentioned earlier in this section; enabling directory service access from the Group Policy Management Editor enables all four subcategories. Enable this category for failures (if you record success, a large number of events will be logged).

- **Logon events:** Logon or logoff by a user at a member server or client computer. You should track both success and failure (success logging can record an unauthorized access that succeeded).

- **Object access:** Access by a user to an object such as a file, folder, or printer. You need to configure auditing in each object's SACL to track access to that object. Track success and failure to access important resources on your network.

- **Policy change:** Modification of policies, including user rights assignment, trust, and audit policies. This category is not normally needed unless unusual events are occurring.

- **Privilege use:** Use of a user right, such as changing the system time. Track failure events for this category.

- **Process tracking:** Actions performed by an application. This category is primarily for application developers and does not need to be enabled in most cases.

- **System events:** Events taking place on a computer such as an improper shutdown or a disk with very little free space remaining. Track success and failure events.

NOTE   Note the difference between Logon and Account Logon events. *Logon* events refer to authentication of a local user at a workstation or member server, while *Account Logon* events refer to the authentication of a domain user account at a domain controller.

> **TIP** Know which types of actions to audit for different scenarios. For example, the exam might present a drag-and-drop interface in which you must select success and failure actions to achieve a given objective.

Configuring Basic Auditing Policies

Use the following procedure to specify basic audit policy settings:

1. Access the Group Policy Management Editor snap-in for the appropriate GPO linked to a site, a domain, or an organizational unit (OU).

2. Navigate to the **Computer Configuration\Policies\Windows Settings\ Security Settings\Local Policies\Audit Policy** node.

3. Click this node to display the available policies in the details pane.

4. Right-click the appropriate policy and select **Properties**.

5. In the Properties dialog box for the policy, select **Define these policy settings**; then select **Success**, **Failure**, or both, as desired (see Figure 17-6). Then click **OK**. Refer to the Explain tab of each policy's Properties dialog box for more information on what the setting does.

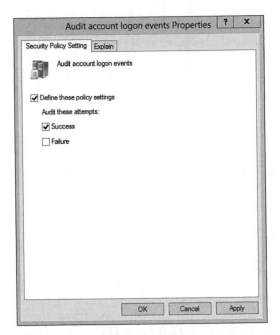

Figure 17-6 Enabling auditing of account logon events.

To track object access or directory service access, you must configure the SACL for each required object. Perform the following procedure:

1. In File Explorer, right-click the required file, folder, or printer and select **Properties**.

2. Select the **Security** tab of the object's Properties dialog box.

3. Click **Advanced** to open the Advanced Security Settings dialog box, and then select the **Auditing** tab.

4. To add users or groups, click **Add**.

5. In the Auditing Entry dialog box, click the **Select a principal** link. Type the required user or group in the **Select User, Computer, Service Account or Group** dialog box; then click **OK**.

6. On the Auditing Entry dialog box for the Principal (see Figure 17-7), select the types of actions you want to track. As an optional task under Windows Server 2012 R2, you might choose to add a condition to limit the scope of the auditing entry. Click **OK** when complete.

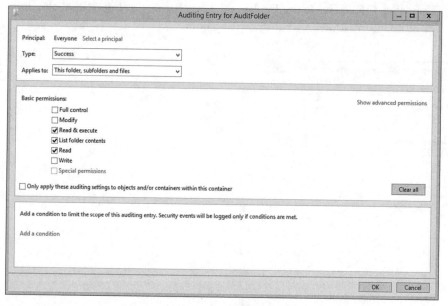

Figure 17-7   Configuring the SACL for an AD DS object.

7. The completed auditing entries appear in the Auditing tab of the Advanced Security Settings dialog box, as shown in Figure 17-8. Click **OK** twice to close these dialog boxes. To modify any existing audit entries, select the entry and click the **Edit** button.

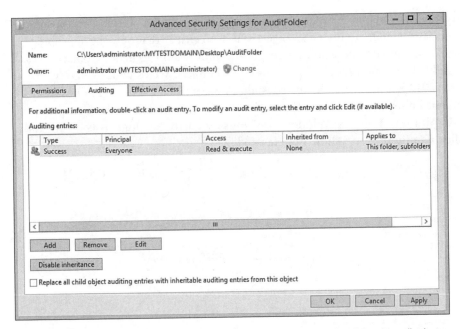

Figure 17-8   The Auditing tab of the Advanced Security Settings dialog box displays
information on the types of object auditing actions that have been specified.

After you have configured object access auditing, attempts to access audited objects
appear in the Security Log, which you can view from the Event Viewer—either in
Server Manager or in its own snap-in from the Administrative Tools folder. For
more information on any audited event, right-click the event and select **Event
Properties**.

> **TIP**   Ensure that the security log has adequate space to audit the events you con-
> figure for auditing because the log can fill rapidly. The recommended size is at
> least 128 MB. You should also periodically save the existing log to a file and clear
> all past events. If the log becomes full, the default behavior is that the oldest events
> will be overwritten (and therefore lost). You can also configure the log to archive
> when full and not to overwrite events, but new events will not be recorded. Loss of
> recorded events could be serious in the case of high-security installations.

Configuring Advanced Audit Policies

The Advanced Audit Policy Configuration node in Windows Server 2012 R2
enables you to configure granular auditing policies for the 10 subcategories shown
in Figure 17-9. Using these policies, you can even determine which access control

entry (ACE) in an object's ACL allowed access to an audited object. This capability can assist you in modifying an object's ACL to ensure that only the appropriate access is permitted. These policies enable an administrator to manage object access centrally. This concept is also known as Global Object Access under Windows Server 2012 R2. To access Advanced Audit Policies, open the Group Policy Management Editor snap-in for the appropriate GPO and navigate to the **Computer Configuration\Policies\Windows Settings\Security Settings\Advanced Audit Policy Configuration\Audit Policies** node.

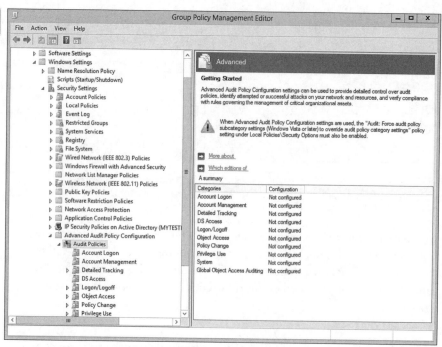

Figure 17-9 The Advanced Audit Policy node in Windows Server 2012 R2 enables you to configure auditing policies in 10 subcategories.

To configure any of these policies, simply right-click the desired policy and select **Properties.** You can define auditing for success and/or failure of each policy setting in a manner similar to that shown previously in Figure 17-6. Consult the Explain tab of each policy setting's Properties dialog box for further information.

NOTE   For more information on the available advanced policy settings, refer to "Advanced Security Audit Policy Settings" and references cited therein at http://technet.microsoft.com/en-us/library/dd772712(WS.10).aspx.

TIP   You should ensure that advanced audit policy settings are not overwritten by basic audit policy settings. To do so, navigate to the **Computer Configuration\Policies\Windows Settings\Security Settings\Local Policies\Security Options** node and enable the **Audit: Force audit policy subcategory settings (Windows Vista or later) to override audit policy category settings** policy setting.

NOTE   For additional information on configuring audit policies, including a comprehensive guide for setting up a series of policies on a test network, refer to "Advanced Security Audit Policy Step-by-Step Guide" at http://technet.microsoft.com/en-us/library/dd408940(WS.10).aspx.

Using `Auditpol.exe` to Configure Auditing

The `Auditpol.exe` tool performs audit policy configuration actions from the command line. This is the only tool you can use to configure auditing on a Server Core computer or to configure directory service auditing subcategories.

To use this tool, type the following in a command line:

```
Auditpol command [sub-command options]
```

Table 17-2 describes the available commands, and Table 17-3 describes several of the more important subcommands and options you should be aware of.

Table 17-2   `Auditpol` Commands

Command	Meaning
/get	Displays the current auditing policy.
/set	Sets the audit policy.
/list	Displays audit policy categories and subcategories or lists users for whom a per-user audit policy is defined.
/backup	Saves the audit policy to a specified file.
/restore	Retrieves the audit policy from a specified file.
/clear	Clears the audit policy.
/remove	Removes per-user audit policy settings and disables system audit policy settings.

Table 17-3   `Auditpol` Subcommands and Options

Option	Meaning
`/user:<username>`	Specifies the security principal for a per-user audit. Specifies the username by security identifier (SID) or by name. It requires either the `/category` or `/subcategory` subcommand when used with the `/set` command.
`/category:<name>`	Specifies one or more auditing categories separated by | and specified by name or globally unique identifier (GUID).
`/subcategory:<name>`	Specifies one or more auditing subcategories separated by | and specified by name or GUID.
`/success:enable`	Enables success auditing when using the `/set` command.
`/success:disable`	Disables success auditing when using the `/set` command.
`/failure:enable`	Enables failure auditing when using the `/set` command.
`/failure:disable`	Disables failure auditing when using the `/set` command.
`/file`	Specifies the file to which an audit policy is to be backed up or from which an audit policy is to be restored.

For example, to configure auditing for directory service changes, you would type the following:

```
Auditpol /set /subcategory:"directory service changes"
/success:enable
```

Additional subcommands and options are available with most of the `auditpol` commands discussed here. For information on the available subcommands and options available for a specified command, type **auditpol** `/command` **/?**.

Configuring User Account Control

User Account Control (UAC) is a feature that was designed to protect your computer from unauthorized changes. It is designed to enable all users, even administrators, to run with a standard access token. When a user requires administrative privileges for a task that can affect system properties, such as installing a program, modifying data under `%ProgramFiles%` or `%Windir%`, or starting up an application, the user might receive a prompt requesting administrative credentials.

By default, UAC is enabled under Windows Server 2012 R2. Because many applications are considered trusted in your organization, there might come a time when you decide to disable UAC (not recommended), or modify notification settings. You can modify UAC via the Control Panel, Local Security Policy, or Group Policy.

Using Control Panel to Configure UAC

You can configure UAC from the Control Panel on a local server or workstation using the following process:

1. From the settings tile, open **Control Panel** and click **User Accounts**.

2. When the User Accounts panel opens, click **User Accounts** to change user account settings.

3. Click **Change User Account Control settings** to open the User Account Control Settings dialog box shown in Figure 17-10. You can also access this link via **System and Security>Action Center** under Control Panel.

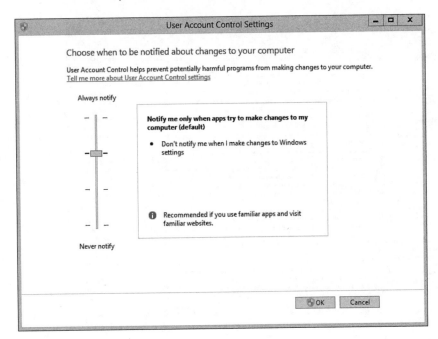

Figure 17-10   Change User Account Control settings.

4. Use the slider to change how Windows Server notifies you for any changes. Select the setting that best meets your needs, and click **OK** to commit the changes.

Configuring UAC via Policy

You can configure User Account Control using the Local Security Policy Snap-in for MMC. You can manage UAC settings under Security Settings\Local Policies\ Security Options. For larger networks, it might be more appropriate to configure

UAC through Group Policy. To configure UAC using Group Policy, perform the following steps:

1. Open **Group Policy Management**, and either create a new GPO or modify an existing one.

2. Under Computer Configuration, expand **Policies\Windows Settings\ Security Settings\Local Policies\Security Options**.

3. Scroll to the bottom of the Policy setting list to view all the available settings for User Account Control (see Figure 17-11). Enable the appropriate settings to suit your needs. Save the policy and link it accordingly.

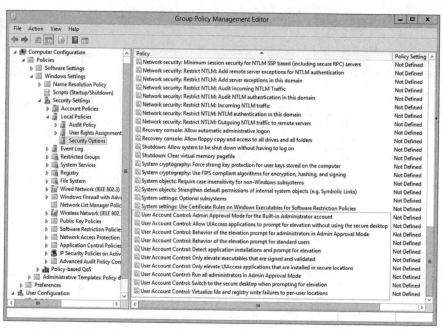

Figure 17-11 User Account Control Policy settings.

NOTE For more information on UAC, refer to "What is User Account Control?" at http://windows.microsoft.com/en-us/windows7/what-is-user-account-control.

Exam Preparation Tasks

Review All the Key Topics

Review the most important topics in the chapter, noted with the key topics icon in the outer margin of the page. Table 17-4 lists a reference of these key topics and the page numbers on which each is found.

Table 17-4   Key Topics for Chapter 17

Key Topic Element	Description	Page Number
Figure 17-1	The Default Domain Controllers Policy contains a series of predefined user rights that specify what members of built-in groups can do on the network in an AD DS domain.	760
Figure 17-2	You can add or remove users or groups that are entitled to perform any of the predefined user rights.	761
Figure 17-3	Displays policy settings available from the Security Options node of Group Policy.	762
List	Describes the available categories of audit policies.	772
Figure 17-6	Shows you how to enable basic auditing of object access.	773
Figure 17-9	Shows you how to configure advanced audit policies in Windows Server 2012 R2.	776
Figure 17-10	Displays the User Account Control dialog under Control Panel.	779
Figure 17-11	Displays the User Account Control settings configurable via Group Policy.	780

Complete the Tables and Lists from Memory

Print a copy of Appendix B, "Memory Tables" (found on the CD), or at least the section for this chapter, and complete the tables and lists from memory. Appendix C, "Memory Tables Answer Key," is also on the CD and includes completed tables and lists to check your work.

Definitions of Key Terms

Define the following key terms from this chapter, and check your answers in the glossary.

Account lockout, Account policies, Auditing, `auditpol.exe`, Fine-grained password policies, Password Settings object (PSO), Password complexity, Password policy, Security Configuration Wizard, User rights, User Account Control

This chapter covers the following subjects:

- **Introducing Rule Enforcement:** This section introduces the benefits of using Group Policy to deploy software and describes the methods you can use for software deployment. It provides an introduction of the solutions Microsoft has in place for defining policies and enforcing software deployment and application usage rules.

- **Configuring Software Restriction Policies:** A lot of time can be lost over users running inappropriate applications or malicious websites downloading and installing inappropriate software. Software restriction policies enable you to limit the programs users are permitted to run, both at the local computer and at the domain level.

- **Configuring AppLocker Rules:** Microsoft added application control policies to Windows 7 and Windows Server 2008 R2 and continued these policies in Windows 8.1 and Windows Server 2012 R2 to enhance available software limitations according to file identities and user groups. This section shows you how to create and modify software-specific rules.

CHAPTER 18

Configuring Application Restriction Policies

In Chapter 16, "Creating and Applying Group Policy Objects," you learned the nuts and bolts of Group Policy and how you can use Group Policy to control the working environment applied to users and computers in your Active Directory Domain Services (AD DS) network. In Chapter 17, "Configuring Security Policies," you continued exploring Group Policy and its uses to improve network security. Now you learn about how you can use Group Policy to ensure that users have the software they need to perform their job tasks efficiently and properly. You also learn how to ensure that users have the most up-to-date versions of their software and that old software no longer required for their job functions is promptly removed from their computers. Now we turn our attention to securing the software environment of your network.

Users often like to download software from the Internet. Such programs can bring malware such as viruses, Trojan horses, and spyware with them, thereby resulting in downtime and support calls. Other software (such as games) can result in users being distracted from important work objectives. Microsoft provides tools that limit user access to software programs that can either damage computers and network access or distract users from important work objectives; it is important that you are able to configure these tools to maximize user productivity.

"Do I Know This Already?" Quiz

The "Do I Know This Already?" quiz enables you to assess whether you should read this entire chapter or simply jump to the "Exam Preparation Tasks" section for review. If you are in doubt, read the entire chapter. Table 18-1 outlines the major headings in this chapter and the corresponding "Do I Know This Already?" quiz questions. You can find the answers in Appendix A, "Answers to the 'Do I Know This Already?' Quizzes."

Table 18-1   "Do I Know This Already?" Foundation Topics Section-to-Question Mapping

Foundations Topics Section	Questions Covered in This Section
Introducing Rule Enforcement	1
Configuring Software Restriction Policies	2–3
Configuring AppLocker Rules	4–6

1. As an administrator for your organization, you have been tasked with controlling unauthorized applications on your network. Which mechanisms can you leverage using Group Policy to enforce these requirements? (Choose all that apply.)

   a. Software Assurance

   b. Software Restriction Policies

   c. Software Locker Rules

   d. AppLocker Policies

2. Which of the following are types of rules you might configure in Software Restriction Policies? (Choose all that apply.)

   a. Certificate rule

   b. Operating system version rule

   c. Hash rule

   d. Internet zone rule

   e. Path rule

3. You are the systems administrator for a company that operates an AD DS domain with client computers running a mix of Windows XP Professional, Windows 7 Enterprise, and Windows 8.1 Enterprise. You are responsible for ensuring that applications used by employees do not result in corporate downtime because of inappropriate software being downloaded from various websites. But users occasionally need to download programs or updates from several trusted sites that you have specified in the Internet Options dialog box. You open a GPO focused on your company's domain and access the Software Restriction Policies subnode. What should you do?

   a. Ensure that all websites from which users are allowed to download software possess a valid certificate, and download these certificates to a file server on your network. Create a new certificate rule, specify the path to these certificates, and select the **Unrestricted** option.

   b. Download all software programs users might need to a file server on your network. Create a new path rule, specify the path to the download folder, and select the **Unrestricted** option.

   c. Create a new network zone rule. Set the Internet zone to **Disallowed** and the Trusted Sites zone to **Unrestricted**.

   d. Create a new network zone rule. Set the Restricted Sites zone to **Disallowed** and the Internet zone to **Unrestricted**.

4. Which of the following represent improvements that can be obtained through the use of AppLocker rather than Software Restriction Policies? (Choose two.)

   a. You can specify any of Disallowed, Basic User, and Unrestricted rule settings.

   b. You can gather advanced data on software usage by implementing audit-only mode.

   c. You can lock down applications on a domain basis using Group Policy.

   d. You can create multiple rules at the same time with the help of a wizard.

5. You would like to obtain information on the programs in use on your network with a view of setting limits on app use at a later date. All computers on the network are members of your company's AD DS domain. The information should enable you to make a positive decision on all programs currently in use. What should you do?

a. From a GPO linked to the domain, run AppLocker. Click **Configure rule enforcement**; then on the AppLocker Properties dialog box, select the **Configured** check box against the Executable rules option. In the drop-down list that appears, select the **Audit only** option. Repeat this action for the Packaged app Rules option.

b. From a GPO linked to the domain, run AppLocker. Click **Configure rule enforcement**; then on the AppLocker Properties dialog box, select the **Configured** check box against the Executable rules option. In the drop-down list that appears, select the **Enforce rules** option. Repeat this action for the Packaged app Rules option.

c. From a GPO linked to the domain, run AppLocker. Select the **Executable rules** option to display the default rules. Right-click the first rule and select **Properties**. Then select the **Audit only** option in the dialog box that appears. Repeat this action for the other two rules.

d. From a GPO linked to the domain, run AppLocker. Select the **Executable rules** option to display the default rules. Right-click the first rule and select **Properties**. Then select the **Enforce rules** option in the dialog box that appears. Repeat this action for the other two rules.

6. You are the systems administrator for a company that operates an AD DS domain. The CIO has requested that only members of the Graphic Artists global group be allowed to run Adobe Photoshop CS6; all others should not receive this permission. What should you do?

a. Move the Photoshop CS6 files to a path location not included in any of the default AppLocker rules. Create a new AppLocker rule. On the Permissions page, select **Deny** and specify the **Everyone** group. Then on the Exceptions page, specify the Graphic Artists group and select the **Allow** option.

b. Move the Photoshop CS6 files to a path location not included in any of the default AppLocker rules. Create a new AppLocker rule. On the Permissions page, select **Allow** and specify the **Graphic Artists** group. Then on the Conditions page, select **Publisher** and specify the path to the Photoshop CS6 files.

c. Create a new AppLocker rule. On the Permissions page, select **Deny** and specify the **Everyone** group. Then on the Conditions page, select **Publisher**, specify the path to the Photoshop CS6 files, and click **Next** to access the Exceptions page. On this page, specify the **Graphic Artists** group and select the **Allow** option.

d. Create a new AppLocker rule. On the Permissions page, select **Deny** and specify the **Everyone** group. Then on the Conditions page, select **Publisher** and specify the path to the Photoshop CS6 files. Create a second AppLocker rule. On the Permissions page, select **Allow** and specify the **Graphic Artists** group. Also specify the same path to the Photoshop CS6 files on the Conditions page of this rule.

Foundation Topics

Introducing Rule Enforcement

An important aspect of network security in today's computing environments is the assurance that users have available all software programs they need to do their jobs but are prevented from installing software that can be harmful to the network or the computers and other devices contained within, or other software that creates distraction and wastes employees' time on trivial activities such as playing games on the corporate network.

For these reasons, Microsoft has developed the following two systems of controlling what software users can install and execute on their systems, both of which you can configure using Group Policy:

- **Software restriction policies:** Originally introduced with Windows XP and Windows Server 2003 and also supported on all the more recent versions of Windows, you can create rules for files that should not be allowed on the network, while remaining files can be allowed to run by default. You can control executables, DLL files, scripts, and Windows Installer files. However, you cannot control each file type separately; all software restriction policy rules are contained within a single rule collection.

- **AppLocker policies:** First introduced with Windows 7 and Windows Server 2008 R2 and continued in Windows 8/8.1 and Windows Server 2012/R2, you can create separate rules for Windows Installer files, executable files, and script files. You can restrict applications according to *publisher rules*, which limit application execution according to the application's digital signature. This even allows you to specify which versions are permitted; for example, you could allow Microsoft Office 2010 or later, while preventing use of older versions of Office.

Software Restriction policies and AppLocker policies enable you to put controls in place that are defined by a set of rules. These policies can then be enforced so that all member servers and workstation in the domain adhere to the policies. The next several sections provide a more in-depth look at each of these mechanisms and how to enforce them in your organization.

Configuring Software Restriction Policies

Application restrictions enable you to limit the types of software that run on computers to which the policy applies. For individual computers running Windows 7 Professional, Enterprise, or Ultimate or Windows 8 or 8.1 Pro or Enterprise or those that belong to a homegroup or workgroup, you can set these policies by using the Local Group Policy or the Local Security Policy tool. On an Active Directory Domain Services (AD DS) domain, you can use Group Policy to configure these policies at a site, a domain, or an organizational unit (OU) level.

Configuring application restrictions provides you with the following benefits:

- **Control which programs can run on computers on your network:** You can allow only those programs that users require to do their jobs properly, and you can restrict the use of other programs such as games. You can also limit the downloading of ActiveX controls and ensure that only digitally signed scripts can be run. This also helps to prevent viruses, Trojan horses, and other malware programs from executing.

- **Control which programs users on multiuser computers can run:** When more than one user can access a computer, you can set user-specific policies that prevent users from accessing programs only needed by other users of the same computer.

- **Control whether software restriction policies apply to all users:** You can specify whether software restriction policies apply to administrators.

- **Prevent email attachments from executing:** If you are concerned about users receiving viruses through email, you can apply policies that restrict files with certain extensions from executing.

NOTE For more information on software restriction policies in Windows Server 2012 R2, refer to "Software Restriction Policies" at http://technet.microsoft.com/en-us/library/hh831534.aspx.

Local Security Policy and Group Policy both enable you to set software restriction policies (SRP) and application control policies. You can choose to set policies according to security levels, and you can configure additional rules. Security-level rules enable you to set a default policy and create exceptions. You can select from the following security levels:

- **Disallowed:** Does not allow any software to run, regardless of a user's access rights. Four Registry path rules that allow system software to run are specified in the Additional Rules folder, preventing users from being completely locked out of the computer.

- **Basic User:** Enables the user to run applications as a normal user only. This privilege level was introduced in Windows Vista and is not supported on Windows 7/8/8.1 or Windows Server 2008 R2/2012/2012 R2 computers.

- **Unrestricted:** Allows software to run according to a user's access rights. This is the default policy level.

Use the following steps to configure SRP in AD DS at the domain or OU level. Configuration of SRP at the local computer level is similar, except that you use the Local Security Policy snap-in to perform the procedure:

1. From the Group Policy Management Editor, select an appropriate GPO (or create and link a new GPO), right-click it, and select **Edit** to open the Group Policy Object Editor.

2. Navigate to **Computer Configuration\Policies\Windows Settings \Security Settings\Software Restriction Policies**. When first accessed, this node informs you that no software restriction policies are defined.

3. Right-click the **Software Restriction Policies** node, and select **New Software Restriction Policies**. This creates a default set of SRP, which are displayed in the details pane shown in Figure 18-1.

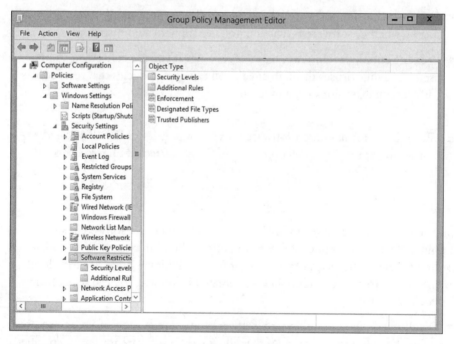

Figure 18-1   Windows provides a default set of SRP.

4. In the console tree, click **Security Levels** to show the three default security levels already described in the details pane.

5. To specify either the Basic User or Disallowed security level, right-click the desired level and select **Set as default**. You are warned that the default level you selected is more restricted than the current security level (see Figure 18-2). Click **Yes** to continue. The selected security level is marked with a small black check mark in the details pane.

Figure 18-2   This message warns you that the chosen security level is more restricted than the current security level.

6. To specify rules that govern exceptions to the security level you specified, right-click **Additional Rules** and select one of the following four rules, as shown in Figure 18-3.

   - **New Certificate Rule:** This type of rule identifies software according to its signing certificate. You can use a certificate rule to specify the source of trusted software that should be allowed to run without prompting a user.

   - **New Hash Rule:** A hash is a fixed-length series of bytes that uniquely identifies an application or file. The policy uses a hash algorithm to calculate the hash of a specified program and compares this to the hash of a program that a user attempts to run to determine whether the application or file should run.

   - **New Network Zone Rule:** This type of rule identifies software according to an Internet Explorer network zone, including the Internet, Local Intranet, Trusted sites, and Restricted sites zones. You can specify zone rules only for Windows Installer software packages.

   - **New Path Rule:** This type of rule identifies software according to its local or Universal Naming Convention (UNC) file path. This rule enables you to grant access to software located in a specific folder for each user.

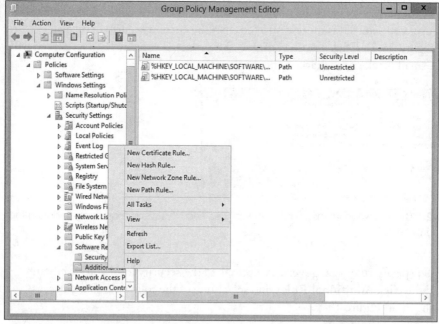

Figure 18-3   You can configure four types of new rules in the Additional Rules folder.

7. For example, to specify a path rule, select **New Path Rule** to display the New Path Rule dialog box, as shown in Figure 18-4. To create an exception to the Disallowed security level, type the path to the applications that are allowed, select **Basic User** or **Unrestricted** from the drop-down list, and then click **OK**. If you have retained the default Unrestricted security level, select **Disallowed** from the drop-down list to disallow the specified software. You also can type an optional description. You can follow a similar procedure to designate any of the other rule types.

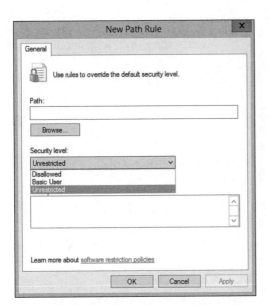

Figure 18-4   The New Path Rule dialog box enables you to specify the path to software defined by an additional rule.

8. If required, specify rules for enforcement, designated file types, and trusted publishers by clicking **Software Restriction Policies** in the console tree to display these items in the details pane, as shown previously in Figure 18-1. Right-click the desired rule category, and select **Properties** to configure any of these rules. The following describes the functions of these items:

   - **Enforcement:** You can determine the scope of SRP policies, as shown in Figure 18-5. This capability is useful for exempting local administrators from SRP policies or for ignoring certificate rules.

   - **Designated File Types:** This option determines which file types, in addition to standard file types such as .exe, are considered as executable code and subject to SRP policies.

   - **Trusted Publishers:** This option enables you to determine which users can select trusted publishers and to check for revoked certificates.

Figure 18-5   You can modify the scope of SRP policies from the Enforcement Properties dialog box.

NOTE   For more information on configuring SRP policies in Windows Server 2012 R2, refer to "Administer Software Restriction Policies" at http://technet.microsoft.com/en-us/library/hh994606.aspx.

TIP   Software restriction policies are applied in the sequence hash rules, certificate rules, path rules, Internet zone rules, and default rules. If rules do not apply as expected, evaluate the rules you have applied; then, if necessary, remove all but the default rule. For further suggestions regarding problems applying SRP policies, refer to "Troubleshoot Software Restriction Policies" at http://technet.microsoft.com/en-us/library/hh994599.aspx.

CAUTION   Use caution when selecting the **Disallowed** security level. This security level prevents all applications from running except those you have specified using additional rules.

Configuring AppLocker Rules

First introduced with Windows 7 and Windows Server 2008 R2 and continued in Windows 8/8.1 and Windows Server 2012/2012 R2 is the concept of *Application Control Policies*, which includes the AppLocker feature. AppLocker provides new enhancements that enable you to specify exactly what users are permitted to run on their desktops according to unique file identities. You can also specify the users or groups permitted to execute these applications. Users are allowed to run the applications and scripts required for them to be productive while still providing the operational, security, and compliance benefits provided by application standardization.

NOTE   You can use AppLocker on computers running Windows 7 Enterprise or Ultimate, Windows 8 or 8.1 Enterprise, or any edition of Windows Server 2008 R2 or Windows Server 2012 or 2012 R2. You can also use a computer running Windows 7 Professional to create AppLocker rules, but you cannot enforce these rules on a Windows 7 Professional computer. Rules configured for packaged apps are enforced only on Windows 8/8.1 and Windows Server 2012/2012 R2 computers.

NOTE   For detailed information on AppLocker, refer to "AppLocker Technical Overview" at http://msdn.microsoft.com/en-us/subscriptions/downloads/hh831440.aspx and "AppLocker Step-by-Step Guide" at http://technet.microsoft.com/library/dd723686(WS.10).aspx.

Capabilities of AppLocker

AppLocker provides enhanced options for managing the configuration of desktop computers, either local or domain-based. It enables you to perform actions such as the following:

- Specify the types of applications users can run, including executables, scripts, Windows Installer files, and DLL files.

- Define rules according to file attributes specified in the digital signature, such as the publisher, product name, filename, and file version. For example, you can allow Adobe Reader 11 and later to run while forbidding the use of an older version.

- Prevent the execution of unlicensed, unapproved applications or those that destabilize machines and increase help desk support calls.

- Prevent the execution of outdated versions of programs or of programs that are no longer supported by your organization.

- Prevent unauthorized applications, such as malware, from executing.

- Prevent users from running programs that needlessly affect the corporate computing environment by consuming network bandwidth.

- Enable users to run approved applications and software updates while maintaining the requirement that only administrative users are permitted to install applications and software updates.

- Specify rules that apply to a given user or security group.

- Ensure that your computers are in compliance with licensing and corporate requirements.

Table 18-2 provides a comparison of AppLocker with SRP.

Table 18-2   Comparing AppLocker to SRP

Feature	AppLocker	SRP
Rule scope	Specific users or groups	All users
Rule conditions	File hash, path, and publisher	File hash, path, certificate, registry path, and Internet zone
Rule types	Allow and deny	Disallowed, Basic User, and Unrestricted
Default rule action	Implicit denial	Unrestricted
Audit-only mode	Yes	No
Wizard for creating multiple rules at the same time	Yes	No
Policy import or export	Yes	No
Rule collection	Yes	No
Support for Windows PowerShell	Yes	No
Custom error messages	Yes	No

AppLocker enables you to configure rules that govern the use of executable files (*.exe and *.com), Windows Installer files (*.msi and *.msp), scripts (*.js, *.ps1, *.vbs, *.cmd, and *.bat), DLL files (*.dll and *.ocx), and Windows 8/8.1 packaged applications. It comes with the default rules described in Table 18-3.

Table 18-3 Default AppLocker Rules

Default Group	Executable Rule	Windows Installer Rule	Script Rule	Packaged app rule
Everyone	All files located in the Program Files folder	All digitally signed Windows Installer files	All scripts located in the Program Files folder	All signed packaged apps
Everyone	All files located in the Windows folder	All Windows Installer files in `%systemdrive%\Windows\Installer`	All scripts located in the Windows folder	
BUILTIN\Administrators	All files	All Windows Installer files	All scripts	

Basic Configuration of AppLocker Policies

As with Software Restriction Policies, you can configure policies for an AD DS domain or OU from the Group Policy Object Editor. You can also configure AppLocker policies for the local computer in the Local Group Policy or Local Security Policy snap-in. Use the following procedure to configure default AppLocker rules at the domain or OU level:

1. In the Group Policy Management Editor, right-click a GPO linked to the appropriate AD DS container and select **Edit** to open the Group Policy Object Editor.

2. Expand the **Computer Configuration\Policies\Windows Settings\ Security Settings\Application Control Policies** node to reveal AppLocker. AppLocker displays information and configurable links in the details pane shown in Figure 18-6.

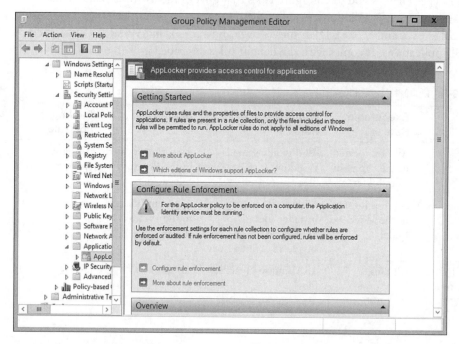

Figure 18-6 You can configure AppLocker from the Application Control Policies node of the Group Policy Management Editor.

3. To obtain more information about AppLocker and the editions of Windows it supports, click the links provided in the **Getting Started** section. This opens Microsoft Management Console Help files. Read this information, and then close the console when finished.

4. In the Configure Rule Enforcement section, click **Configure rule enforcement**. In the AppLocker Properties dialog box shown in Figure 18-7, select the check boxes against the four rule types you want to configure. From the drop-down lists, select **Enforce rules** to create rules you want to enforce or **Audit only** to test rules for future use. Then click **OK**.

> **TIP** The Audit only option enables you to determine who is using which applications in your company without enforcing the rules you have specified. When a user executes an application specified in the rule, information about that use is written into the AppLocker event log.

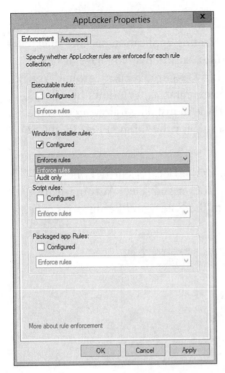

Figure 18-7   You can choose to enforce AppLocker rules or select **Audit only** to gather information.

5. In the console tree, expand **AppLocker** to reveal subnodes for each of these four rule types.

6. For each of the rule types you want to configure, create a default set of rules by right-clicking the rule type and selecting **Create Default Rules**. This adds the rules (all set to Allow) previously described in Table 18-3 to each specified rule type.

7. If you want to delete any of these default rules, right-click the desired rule and select **Delete**. Then click **Yes** in the confirmation dialog box that appears.

TIP   You can also use Windows PowerShell to configure AppLocker on computers running the Server Core version of Windows Server 2012 R2. For more information, refer to "Use the AppLocker Windows PowerShell Cmdlets" at http://technet.microsoft.com/en-us/library/hh994594.aspx.

Creating Additional AppLocker Rules

AppLocker provides wizards that assist you in creating application-specific rules and policies. Before you begin creating these rules, ensure that you have installed the required applications or scripts and created any required security groups. You can automatically generate AppLocker rules for executables, Windows Installer, or scripts; the procedure is similar for each of these items. The following example describes a procedure that applies to creating a rule for the Adobe Photoshop CS6 executable:

1. In the Group Policy Management Editor or the Local Security Policy snap-in, right-click the desired subnode of AppLocker and select **Automatically Generate Rules**. This starts a wizard with the Folder and Permissions page, as shown in Figure 18-8.

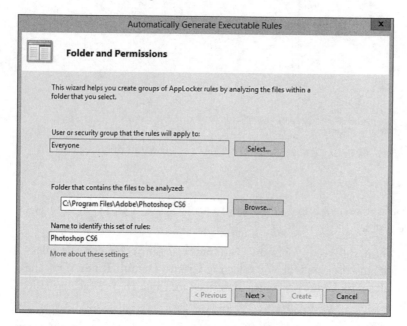

Figure 18-8   Creating AppLocker rules to be applied to Adobe Photoshop CS6.

2. Type or browse to the folder containing the executable files.

3. Specify the user or security group to which the rule will apply. Click **Select** to display the Select User or Group dialog box, from which you can select the desired user or group. The wizard supplies a default name based on the folder containing the executable. If you want to change this name, do so.

4. Click **Next** to display the Rule Preferences page shown in Figure 18-9; then specify the following options:

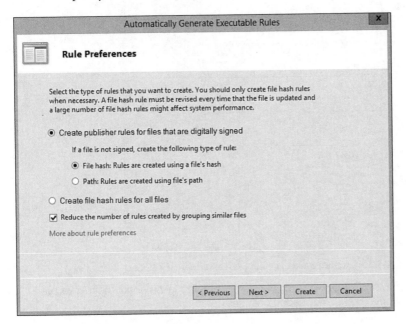

Figure 18-9   Specifying the types of rules to be created.

- **Create publisher rules for files that are digitally signed:** Specifies that rules are created according to the publisher for digitally signed files. If the file is not digitally signed, you can specify that the rule is created according to either a file hash or a path.

- **Create file hash rules for all files:** Specifies the file hash will be used for all files, regardless of whether the files are digitally signed.

- **Reduce the number of rules created by grouping similar files:** Selected by default, this option helps you to organize AppLocker rules by creating a single publisher, path, or file hash condition according to files that have the same publisher, product name, subfolder of the specified folder, or file hash.

5. Click **Next** and review the information provided on the Review Rules page shown in Figure 18-10.

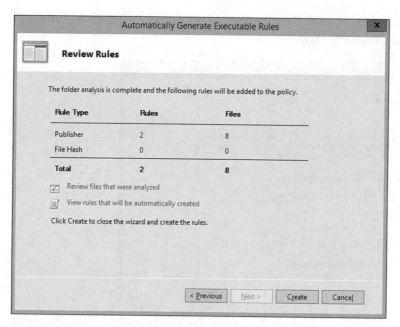

Figure 18-10   The Review Rules page provides summary information about the rule you've created and enables you to make any needed changes.

6. If you need to change any rule types, click **Previous**. When finished, click **Create** to create the rules and close the wizard.

AppLocker also includes a wizard you can use to create granular rules according to any of the available options. To use this wizard, proceed as follows:

1. In the Group Policy Management Editor snap-in, right-click the desired sub-node of AppLocker and select **Create New Rule**. This starts the wizard with a Before You Begin page that describes preliminary steps you should take.

2. Click **Next** to display the Permissions page. On this page, specify the **Allow** or **Deny** action; then click the **Select** button to display the Select User or Group dialog box, which enables you to select the desired user or group.

3. Click **Next** to display the Conditions page shown in Figure 18-11, from which you can select **Publisher**, **Path**, or **File hash**.

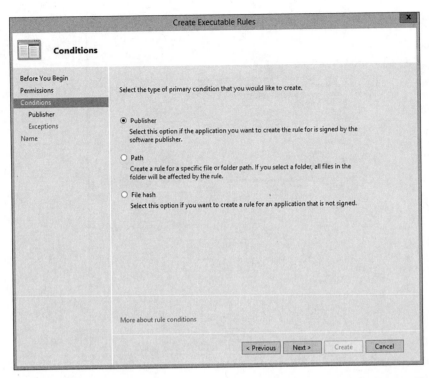

Figure 18-11   The Create Executable Rules Wizard enables you to create any of publisher, path, or file hash rules.

4. If you select **Publisher**, the page shown in Figure 18-12 displays. Click **Browse** to browse to the desired publisher, as shown for Adobe Photoshop CS6. This page also enables you to choose how specific you want the rule to become by moving the slider provided. For example, to create a rule that applies to all Adobe products, you would move the slider up to the Publisher line.

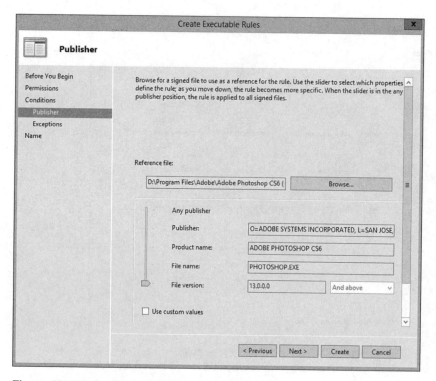

Figure 18-12   Creating a publisher-based executable file rule.

5. Click **Create** to create your rule, or click **Next** to specify exceptions. These include any publisher, path, or file hash you want to exclude from the rule.

6. The wizard creates a name for the rule automatically. Click **Next** to modify this name and add an optional description. When finished, click **Create** to create the rule. This creates the rule and adds it to the list in the details pane of the Local Security Policy or Group Policy Object Editor snap-in.

At Step 3 of this procedure, you can also select **Path** and then browse to or type a local or UNC path to the executable file(s) the rule is to cover. Or you can select **File hash** and then browse to the folder or file containing the file hash. You can specify any number of folders containing hashes to be covered by this rule.

You can also edit the properties of any rule you've created by any of the methods described here. To do so, right-click the rule in the details pane and click **Properties**. This displays the dialog box shown in Figure 18-13, which enables you to modify the properties described in Table 18-4. Note that not all tabs listed will appear; the type of rule being configured determines whether you see the Path, Publisher, or File Hash tab.

Table 18-4 Configurable AppLocker Properties

Tab	Description
General	Enables you to modify the action (allow or deny) and select a different group to which to apply the rule.
Path	Enables you to change the path to the files or folders to which the rule should apply. This tab appears only for rules that have path conditions. (It is not shown in Figure 18-13.)
Publisher	Enables you to change the publisher, product name, filename, and file version. This tab appears only for rules that have publisher conditions.
File Hash	Enables you to add or remove files to be included in a file hash rule. This tab appears only for this type of rule. (It is not shown in Figure 18-13.)
Exceptions	Enables you to add, edit, or remove exceptions to the rule, according to publisher, file path, or hash.

Figure 18-13 You can modify the properties of any AppLocker rule from the rule's Properties dialog box.

NOTE If you have used both SRP and AppLocker policies in the same domain or OU, AppLocker policies will take precedence over SRP on computers running Windows 7, Windows Server 2012, and later. For more information, refer to "Using Software Restriction Policies and AppLocker Policies" at http://technet.microsoft.com/en-us/library/ee791851(v=ws.10).aspx.

Exam Preparation Tasks

Review All the Key Topics

Review the most important topics in the chapter, noted with the key topics icon in the outer margin of the page. Table 18-5 lists a reference of these key topics and the page numbers on which each is found.

Table 18-5   Key Topics for Chapter 18

Key Topic Element	Description	Page Number
Figure 18-3	Shows the types of rules you can configure when using SRP	794
Figure 18-4	Shows the three available security level options when configuring a new path rule	795
List	Describes capabilities of AppLocker	797
Table 18-3	Describes default AppLocker rules	799
List	Shows how to configure AppLocker policies	799
List	Shows you how to configure AppLocker rules	802
Table 18-4	Describes available AppLocker rule properties	807

Complete the Tables and Lists from Memory

Print a copy of Appendix B, "Memory Tables" (found on the CD), or at least the section for this chapter, and complete the tables and lists from memory. Appendix C, "Memory Tables Answer Key," is also on the CD and includes completed tables and lists to check your work.

Definitions of Key Terms

Define the following key terms from this chapter, and check your answers in the glossary.

AppLocker, Application control policies, Certificate rule, Executable rule, Hash rule, Network zone rule, Packaged apps rule, Path rule, Script rule, Software restriction policies, Windows Installer rule

This chapter covers the following subjects:

- **Configuring Windows Firewall:** All Windows computers come with an easily configurable firewall tool that can block undesired communications, including those that attempt to install malicious software. This section shows you how to configure the most important options that come with Windows Firewall.

- **Using the Windows Firewall with Advanced Security Snap-in:** This section introduces the capabilities of Windows Firewall with Advanced Security, which comes with a large set of inbound and outbound firewall rules and enables you to configure rules for domain, private, and public firewall profiles.

- **Configuring Security Rules:** This section builds on the first two sections by showing you how to configure the various types of security rules available with the Windows Firewall with Advanced Security snap-in.

- **Configuring Firewall Properties and Authenticated Exceptions:** This section shows you how to use Group Policy so that Windows Firewall with Advanced Security rules can apply to all computers to which the policy applies. It also shows you how to enable all authenticated traffic from approved computers to bypass firewall settings designed to restrict unauthorized traffic from access to your network.

- **Exporting and Importing Firewall Settings:** Windows Firewall with Advanced Security places all its rules and settings in a policy file you can export so you can use this file on another network or restore the settings later in the event of a problem or failure of some kind.

CHAPTER 19

Configuring Windows Firewall

The Internet is truly a twenty-first–century version of the Wild West out there. All sorts of villains lurk behind seemingly innocuous web pages, looking to steal your money and even your identity. They want to install their various malicious software programs such as adware, spyware, rootkits, Trojan horses, worms, and other nasty bits of malware. Companies have utilized hardware devices called firewalls for many years that block undesired network communications from accessing their networks and servers. Starting with Windows Server 2003 and Windows XP prior to SP2, Microsoft introduced a software firewall known as the Internet Connection Firewall. This was upgraded and renamed Windows Firewall in Windows XP SP2. Microsoft has further improved and refined Windows Firewall in each iteration of the client and server Windows versions; Windows Server 2012 R2 is no exception.

Windows Firewall works together with Internet Protocol Security (IPsec) to provide complex static filtering based on IP addresses and Windows Firewall and provide stateful filtering for all addresses across network interfaces.

"Do I Know This Already?" Quiz

The "Do I Know This Already?" quiz enables you to assess whether you should read this entire chapter or simply jump to the "Exam Preparation Tasks" section for review. If you are in doubt, read the entire chapter. Table 19-1 outlines the major headings in this chapter and the corresponding "Do I Know This Already?" quiz questions. You can find the answers in Appendix A, "Answers to the 'Do I Know This Already?' Quizzes."

Table 19-1 "Do I Know This Already?" Foundation Topics Section-to-Question Mapping

Foundations Topics Section	Questions Covered in This Section
Configuring Windows Firewall	1–2
Using the Windows Firewall with Advanced Security Snap-in	3–4
Configuring Security Rules	5–7

Foundations Topics Section	Questions Covered in This Section
Configuring Firewall Properties and Authenticated Exceptions	8–9
Exporting and Importing Firewall Settings	10

1. Your company's web server, which is located on a perimeter network but is a member of the Active Directory Domain Services (AD DS) domain, has been hacked and all pages replaced by messages of an undesirable nature. You want to temporarily prevent outsiders from accessing this server while you restore the proper pages and check the server for malicious software. What should you do?

   a. In Window Firewall, select the **Turn off Windows Firewall** option under the Home or work (private) network location settings section of the Customize Settings dialog box.

   b. In Window Firewall, select the **Block all incoming connections, including those in the list of allowed programs** option, under the Home or work (private) network location settings section of the Customize Settings dialog box.

   c. In Window Firewall, select the **Turn off Windows Firewall** option under the Public network location settings section of the Customize Settings dialog box.

   d. In Window Firewall, select the **Block all incoming connections, including those in the list of allowed programs** option, under the Public network location settings section of the Customize Settings dialog box.

2. Which of the following actions can you perform from the Windows Firewall Control Panel applet on your Windows Server 2012 R2 computer? (Choose three.)

   a. Specify ports that are allowed to communicate across the Windows Firewall.

   b. Specify programs that are allowed to communicate across the Windows Firewall.

   c. Configure logging settings for programs that are blocked by the firewall.

   d. Set the firewall to block all incoming connections, including those in the list of allowed programs.

   e. Specify a series of firewall settings according to the type of network to which you are connected.

3. You open the Windows Firewall with Advanced Security snap-in and notice that a large number of firewall rules have already been preconfigured. Which of the following rule settings types does not include any preconfigured firewall rules?

    a. Inbound rules

    b. Outbound rules

    c. Connection security rules

    d. Monitoring rules

4. Which of the following profiles are available for configuration from the Windows Firewall with Advanced Security snap-in? (Choose three.)

    a. User

    b. Computer

    c. Private

    d. Domain

    e. Public

5. You are using the New Rule Wizard to create an incoming rule in the Windows Firewall with Advanced Security snap-in. You want to ensure that authentication, integrity, and privacy are all enabled on communications permitted by this rule. What should you do?

    a. From the Action page of the wizard, select the **Allow the connection if it is secure** option. Then select the **Require the connections to be encrypted** option on the Customize Allow if Secure Settings dialog box that appears.

    b. From the Action page of the wizard, select the **Allow the connection if it is secure** option. Then select the **Allow the connection if it is authenticated and integrity-protected option** on the Customize Allow if Secure Settings dialog box that appears.

    c. From the Action page of the wizard, select the **Allow the connection** option. Then select the **Require the connections to be encrypted** option on the Customize Allow if Secure Settings dialog box that appears.

    d. From the Rule Type page of the wizard, select the **Authentication exemption** option. Then select the **Allow the connection if it is authenticated and integrity-protected** option on the Customize Allow if Secure Settings dialog box that appears.

6. You are in charge of configuring Windows Firewall with Advanced Security on a Windows Server 2012 R2 computer on which confidential research files are stored. You are using the New Rule Wizard to create an inbound rule that is designed to allow members of the Research global security group in your company's AD DS domain to access this server. How should you proceed?

    a. From the Action page of the wizard, select the **Allow the connection if it is secure** option. Then from the Users page of the wizard that appears, select **Only allow connections from these users** and add the Research group.

    b. From the Action page of the wizard, select the **Allow the connection if it is secure** option. Then from the Users page of the wizard that appears, select **Skip this rule for connections from these users** and add the Research group.

    c. From the Action page of the wizard, select the **Allow the connection** option and complete the rest of the steps in the wizard. Then in the details pane of the Windows Firewall with Advanced Security snap-in, right-click the new rule and select **Properties**. From the Users tab of the dialog box that appears, select **Only allow connections from these users** and add the Research group.

    d. From the Action page of the wizard, select the **Allow the connection** option and complete the rest of the steps in the wizard. Then in the details pane of the Windows Firewall with Advanced Security snap-in, right-click the new rule and select **Properties**. Then from the Users tab of the dialog box that appears, select **Skip this rule for connections from these users** and add the Research group.

7. You have configured a new inbound rule that limits connections by a specific application on your computer to only those connections that have been authenticated using IPsec. The next day when you start your application, you realize that you should have configured this rule as an outbound rule. What should you do to correct this error with the least amount of effort?

> **a.** Access the Scope tab of the Properties dialog box for your rule, and change the scope from Inbound to Outbound.
>
> **b.** Access the Advanced tab of the Properties dialog box for your rule, and change the interface type from Inbound to Outbound.
>
> **c.** Select the rule from the list of inbound rules in the details pane of Windows Firewall with Advanced Security, and drag the rule to the Outbound Rules node in the console tree.
>
> **d.** Deactivate or delete the inbound rule you configured, and then use the New Outbound Rule Wizard to set up a new rule that is specific to your application.

8. You are responsible for maintaining your company's network including security of network transmissions. Computers on the network run Windows 7, Windows 8, Windows 8.1, or Windows Server 2012 R2. You have implemented policies requiring IPsec-secured transmissions. However, while troubleshooting possible network connectivity problems, a junior desktop support technician informs you that when he attempts to ping computers on the network, he always receives the Request timed out message. Even when he pings between two computers that he knows are able to communicate, he still receives this message. What should you do to enable the desktop support technician to use the ping tool properly?

> **a.** Use Group Policy to apply the Client (Respond Only) policy setting to domain computers.
>
> **b.** Use Group Policy to create a new connection security rule that includes an authorization exemption.
>
> **c.** Configure an IPsec tunnel authorization.
>
> **d.** Configure an IPsec exemption.

9. You want to allow all authenticated IP traffic from computers in your intranet web server farm to bypass Windows Firewall for communications with computers on your company's AD DS domain. What should you do to enable this bypass? (Each correct answer represents a complete solution. Choose two answers.)

a. In a GPO linked to the domain, navigate to **Computer Configuration\ Policies\Security Settings\Local Policies\Security Options**. Scroll down to right-click the **Windows Firewall: Allow authenticated IPsec bypass** policy and select **Edit**. Enable this policy and specify the Security Descriptor Definition Language (SDDL) strings corresponding to the web servers; then click **OK**.

b. In a GPO linked to the domain, navigate to **Computer Configuration\ Policies\Administrative Templates\Network\Network Connections\Windows Firewall**. Right-click the **Windows Firewall: Allow authenticated IPsec bypass** policy, and select **Edit**. Enable this policy and specify the Security Descriptor Definition Language (SDDL) strings corresponding to the web servers; then click **OK**.

c. In Windows Firewall with Advanced Security, create a new inbound rule that specifies the **Allow the connection if it is secure** option. Then on the Customize Allow if Secure Settings dialog box, select the **Override block rules** option. Also, on the Computers page of the wizard, select **Only allow connections from these computers**, click **Add**, and then type the names of the web servers or a group into which you've placed the web servers. Click **OK**, and complete the remaining steps of the wizard.

d. In Windows Firewall with Advanced Security, create a new outbound rule that specifies the Allow the connection if it is secure option. Then on the Customize Allow if Secure Settings dialog box, select the **Override block rules** option. Also, on the Computers page of the wizard, select **Only allow connections from these computers**, click **Add**, and then type the names of the web servers or a group into which you've placed the web servers. Click **OK**, and complete the remaining steps of the wizard.

e. In Windows Firewall with Advanced Security, create a new connection security rule that specifies the **Allow the connection if it is secure** option. On the Rule Type page, select the **Authentication exemption** option. Then specify the names of the web servers or a group into which you've placed the web servers, click **OK**, and complete the remaining steps of the wizard.

10. You have configured Windows Firewall with Advanced Security on a member server on your AD DS network with settings that are specific to your company's written security policy. The network also has a standalone server that is not a member of the domain and requires the same firewall settings as the domain computers. What should you do?

- **a.** At the standalone server, right-click **Windows Firewall with Advanced Security** and select **Export Policy**. Save the policy settings to a shared folder on the network. Then at a member server, right-click **Windows Firewall with Advanced Security** and select **Import Policy**. Click **Yes** to accept the warning provided, select the policy file you just created, and then click **Open**.

- **b.** At a member server, right-click **Windows Firewall with Advanced Security** and select **Export Policy**. Save the policy settings to a shared folder on the network. Then at the standalone server, right-click **Windows Firewall with Advanced Security and** select **Import Policy**. Click **Yes** to accept the warning provided, select the policy file you just created, and then click **Open**.

- **c.** At the standalone server, run Windows Server Backup and select the folder containing the firewall policy. Back up this file to a shared folder accessible by both servers. Then at a member server, run Windows Server Backup to restore the folder containing the firewall policy.

- **d.** At a member server, run Windows Server Backup and select the folder containing the firewall policy. Back up this file to a shared folder accessible by both servers. Then at the standalone server, run Windows Server Backup to restore the folder containing the firewall policy.

Foundation Topics

Configuring Windows Firewall

Windows Firewall is a stateful host-based firewall that you can configure to allow or block specific network traffic. It includes a packet filter that uses an Access Control List (ACL) specifying parameters (such as IP address, port number, and protocol) that are allowed to pass through. When a user communicates with an external computer, the stateful firewall remembers this conversation and allows the appropriate reply packets to reach the user. Packets from an outside computer that attempts to communicate with a computer on which a stateful firewall is running are dropped unless the ACL contains rules permitting them. Using Windows Firewall reduces the chance that an attacker will compromise your server, resulting in actions such as crashing your computer, modifying or deleting data, copying unwanted files or information to your computer, creating user accounts with elevated privileges, and using these accounts to access other computers or devices on your network.

Each successive version of Windows Server has introduced considerable improvements to its original implementation in Windows Server 2003 SP1, including outbound traffic protection, support for IPsec and IP version 6 (IPv6), improved configuration of exceptions, support for command-line configuration, support for multiple active profiles, the ability to specify port numbers or protocols, and the ability to specify that outbound Allow rules can override block rules, among many other improvements. Microsoft has introduced the following additional enhancements to Windows Firewall with Advanced Security in Windows Server 2012 and Windows Server 2012 R2:

- **Internet Key Exchange version 2 (IKEv2) for IPsec transport mode:** Additional scenarios that include IPsec end-to-end transport mode connections have been added, thereby improving the interoperability with other operating systems that use IKEv2 for end-to-end security. You can use IKEv2 as a virtual private network (VPN) tunneling protocol that supports automatic reestablishment of VPN connections.

- **Windows Store app network isolation:** This enables you to control the use of Windows Store apps on your network by enforcing network boundaries and ensuring that compromised apps can only access networks to which they have been explicitly granted access. The impact of compromised apps on the network is consequently reduced.

- **Windows PowerShell cmdlets for Windows Firewall:** This enables you to use Windows PowerShell to configure and manage Windows Firewall, IPsec, and related features on the network and at Server Core machines. This improves considerably on the older `Netsh` command-line management capabilities.

Windows Firewall enables you to specify multiple profiles, each of which is a series of firewall settings customized according to the environment in which the computer is located. The following firewall profiles are available:

- **Domain Profile:** Specifies firewall settings for use when connected directly to an Active Directory Domain Services (AD DS) domain; more specifically, this profile is applied when a computer is able to access a domain controller in its domain. If the network is protected from unauthorized external access, you can specify additional exceptions that facilitate communication across the LAN to network servers and client computers.

- **Private Profile:** Specifies firewall settings for use when connected to a private network location, such as a home or small office. You can open up connections to network computers and lock down external communications as required. Settings in this profile should be more restrictive than those in the domain profile.

- **Guest or Public Profile:** Specifies firewall settings for use when connected to an insecure public network, such as a Wi-Fi access point at a hotel, a restaurant, an airport, or another location where unknown individuals might attempt to connect to your computer. This profile should contain the most restrictive settings of all three profiles. By default, network discovery and file and printer sharing are turned off, inbound connections are blocked, and outbound connections are allowed. Although mentioned for completeness purposes, it is extremely unlikely that you would ever use this profile on a server computer.

Basic Windows Firewall Configuration

The Windows Firewall Control Panel applet, found in the System and Security category and shown in Figure 19-1, enables you to set up firewall rules for each of the same network types introduced earlier in this chapter for configuring network settings.

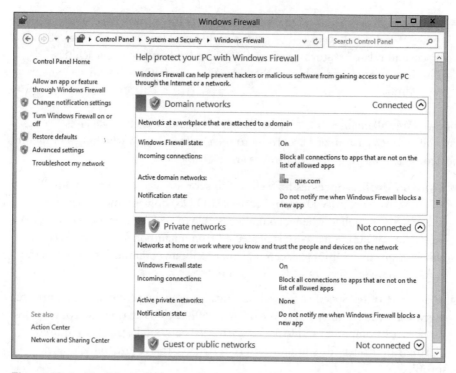

Figure 19-1   The Windows Firewall Control Panel applet enables you to configure basic firewall settings for different network locations.

You can enable or disable the Windows Firewall separately for each connection. In doing so, you are able to use Windows Firewall to protect a computer connected to the Internet via one adapter and not use Windows Firewall for the adapter connected to the private network. Use the following instructions to perform basic firewall configuration:

1. Open the Windows Firewall applet by using any of the following methods:

   ■ From Control Panel, click **System and Security** > **Windows Firewall**.

   ■ From the Search charm, type `firewall` in the Search field. From the list of programs displayed, click **Windows Firewall**.

   ■ From the Network and Sharing Center, select **Windows Firewall** from the link at the bottom-left corner of this applet.

2. From the left pane, select **Turn Windows Firewall on or off**. If a User Account Control (UAC) prompt displays, click **Yes**. This displays the Customize settings for each type of network page shown in Figure 19-2.

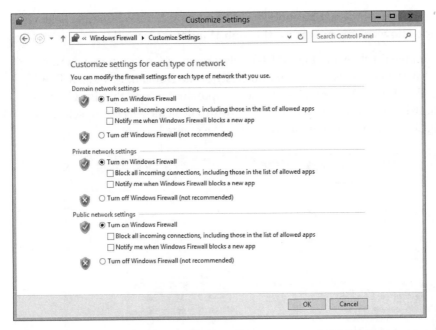

Figure 19-2   The Customize settings for each type of network dialog box enables you to turn the firewall on or off and to block incoming connections.

3. If you are connected to a corporate network with a comprehensive hardware firewall, you might need to select **Turn off Windows Firewall** (not recommended) under the Domain or Private Network Location Settings section. This is true because some hardware firewalls might conflict with Windows Firewall or turn it off automatically. However, from a defense-in-depth perspective, it's best to keep both enabled if at all possible.

NOTE   If you connect at any time to an insecure network, such as an airport or restaurant Wi-Fi hot spot, select the **Block all incoming connections, including those in the list of allowed apps** option under Public network location settings. This option disables all exceptions you've configured on the Exceptions tab.

WARNING   Don't disable the firewall unless absolutely necessary, even on the Domain or Private Network Location Settings section. Never select the **Turn off Windows Firewall** option in Figure 19-2 unless you're absolutely certain that your network is well protected with a good firewall. The only exception should be temporarily to troubleshoot a connectivity problem; after you've solved the problem, be sure to reenable the firewall immediately.

4. To configure program exceptions, return to the Windows Firewall applet and click **Allow an app or feature through Windows Firewall**.

5. From the list shown in Figure 19-3, select the programs or ports you want to have access to your computer on either of the Domain, Private, or Public profile. Table 19-2 describes the more important items in this list. Clear the check boxes next to any programs or ports to be denied access, or select the check boxes next to programs or ports to be granted access.

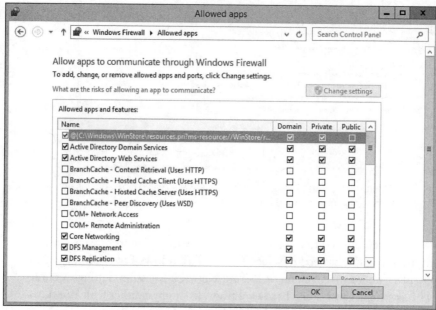

Figure 19-3 The Allow apps to communicate through Windows Firewall page enables you to specify which programs are allowed to communicate through the firewall.

Table 19-2 Windows Firewall Configurable Exceptions

Exception	Description	Enabled by Default?
Active Directory Domain Services	Found on domain controllers only, enables your computer to connect to other domain computers and perform AD DS tasks	Yes
Core Networking	Enables your computer to connect to other network computers or the Internet	No
DFS Management	Enables you to manage Distributed File System (DFS) shares on a file server	Yes

Exception	Description	Enabled by Default?
DHCP Relay Agent, DHCP Server, DHCP Server Management, and DHCPv6 Relay Agent	Enables your computer to act as a DHCP server and relay agent; also enables you to manage your DHCP server remotely	Yes
Distributed Transaction Coordinator	Coordinates the update of transaction-protected resources such as databases, message queues, and file systems	No
File and Printer Sharing	Enables your computer to share resources such as files and printers with other computers on your network	Yes (not on public networks)
iSCSI Service	Used for connecting to iSCSI target servers and devices	No
Key Management Service	Used for machine counting and license compliance in enterprise environments	No
Netlogon Service	Maintains a secure channel between domain clients and a domain controller for authenticating users and services	Only on a computer joined to an Active Directory domain
Network Discovery	Allows computers to locate other resources on the local network	Yes, for home or work only
Performance Logs and Alerts	Allows remote management of the Performance Logs and Alerts service	No
Remote Administration	Enables an administrator to connect with and administer a remote server	No
Remote Desktop	Enables a user to connect with and work on a remote computer	No
Remote (item) Management	Enables an administrator to manage items on a remote computer, including event logs, scheduled tasks, services, and disk volumes	No for all these tasks
Routing and Remote Access (RRAS)	Enables remote users to connect to a server to access the corporate network (used on RRAS server computers only)	Yes
Windows Remote Management	Enables you to manage a remote Windows computer	No

6. To add a program not shown in the list, click **Allow another app**. From the Add an app dialog box shown in Figure 19-4, select the program to be added; then click **Add**. If necessary, click **Browse** to locate the desired program. You can also click **Network types** to choose which network type is allowed by the selected program.

Figure 19-4 The Add an app dialog box enables you to allow specific programs access through the Windows Firewall.

7. In the Allow apps to communicate through Windows Firewall dialog box (refer to Figure 19-3), to view properties of any program or port on the list, select it and click **Details**.

8. To remove a program from the list, select it and click **Remove**. You can do this only for programs you have added using Step 6.

9. If you need to restore default settings, return to the Windows Firewall applet previously shown in Figure 19-1 and click **Restore defaults**. Then confirm your intention in the Restore default settings dialog box that appears.

10. If you are experiencing networking problems, click **Troubleshoot my network** to access a network troubleshooter window.

11. When you are finished, click **OK**.

> **TIP** When allowing additional programs to communicate through the Windows Firewall, by default these programs are allowed to communicate through the Domain or Private network profiles only. You should retain this default unless you need a program to communicate through the Internet from a public location, which is sometimes true for a client computer but almost never the case for a server.

Configuring Windows Firewall Using PowerShell

Many PowerShell cmdlets are available for configuring Windows Firewall. Table 19-3 outlines a listing of the more common cmdlets used for configuring basic firewall settings.

Table 19-3 PowerShell Cmdlets for Configuring Windows Firewall

Cmdlet	Description
`Copy-NetFirewallRule`	Copies a firewall rule and filters. `Copy-NetFirewallRule -DisplayName "Rule1" -NewName "Rule2"` This cmdlet can also be used to copy rules to different policy stores.
`Disable-NetFirewallRule`	Disables a specific firewall rule. `Disable-NetFirewallRule -DisplayName "Rule1"`
`Enable-NetFirewallRule`	Enables a disabled or inactive firewall rule. `Enable-NetFirewallRule -DisplayName "Rule1"`
`Get-NetFirewallProfile`	Retrieves a listing of firewall profiles and their associated settings. Can be filtered by using the `-Name [profile name]`. To view all settings configured for the Public firewall profile: `Get-NetFirewallProfile -Name Public`
`Get-NetFirewallRule`	Retrieves a listing of firewall rules in a firewall store. `Get-NetFirewallRule -PolicyStore ActiveStore`
`Get-NetFirewallSetting`	Retrieves a listing of global firewall settings on the computer. For example, to retrieve global firewall settings from a GPO policy store named DomainSecurity in the que.com domain, execute the following command: `Get-NetFirewallSetting -PolicyStore que.com/ DomainSecurity`
`New-NetFirewallRule`	Creates a new firewall rule. For example, to create a new inbound rule to allow RDP using a rule named "TestRDPRule," execute the following command: `New-NetFirewallRule -DisplayName "TestRDPRule" -Direction Inbound -LocalPort 3389 -Protocol TCP -Action Allow`
`Remove-NetFirewallRule`	Removes a specified rule. `Remove-NetfirewallRule -DisplayName "TestRDPRule"`
`Rename-NetFirewallRule`	Renames a specified rule. `Rename-NetFirewallRule -Name "oldrulename" -NewName "newrulename"`

Cmdlet	Description
`Set-NetFirewallProfile`	Configures settings for a specific firewall profile.
	To enable or disable a specific profile: `Set-NetFirewallProfile -Name Domain -Enabled True`
	Use the `-Enabled False` switch to disable.
`Set-NetFirewallRule`	Changes options for a firewall rule or a group of rules. For example, to enable all rules for Remote Desktop settings, execute this command: `Set-NetfirewallRule -DisplayGroup "Remote Desktop" -Enabled True`
	To change options for a specific rule, use the `-DisplayName` flag. `Set-NetfirewallRule -DisplayName "TestRDPRule" -Enabled True`
`Set-NetFirewallSetting`	Configures a specific global firewall setting.
	To change the global firewall settings of a GPO policy store named PolicyStore to exempt protocols from IPsec requirements, use this command: `Set-NetFirewallSetting -InputObject "PolicyStore" -exemptions RouterDiscovery`

TIP When preparing for the 70-410 exam, you should be familiar with the common cmdlets as outlined in Table 19-3. For a full listing of Windows Firewall cmdlets, refer to "Network Security Cmdlets in Windows PowerShell" at http://technet.microsoft.com/en-us/library/jj554906.aspx. For more advanced PowerShell support refer to "Windows Firewall with Advanced Security Administration with Windows PowerShell" at http://technet.microsoft.com/en-us/library/hh831755.aspx.

Using the Windows Firewall with Advanced Security Snap-in

The Windows Firewall with Advanced Security snap-in enables you to perform a comprehensive set of configuration actions. You can configure rules that affect inbound and outbound communication, and you can configure connection security rules and the monitoring of firewall actions. Inbound rules help prevent actions such as unknown access or configuration of your computer, installation of undesired software, and so on. Outbound rules help prevent utilities on your computer from performing certain actions, such as accessing network resources or software without your knowledge. They can also help prevent other users of your computer from downloading software or inappropriate files without your knowledge.

When you install a server role, role service, or feature that utilizes incoming or outgoing connections, Windows Server 2012 R2 automatically configures the appropriate firewall rules. For example, Figure 19-3 shows DHCP firewall rules that were automatically added to Windows Firewall when this role was installed, thereby enabling the DHCP server to function properly on the network. However, third-party applications you install on your server might not necessarily create the firewall rules needed for proper communication on the network. In this case, you need to use the Windows Firewall with Advanced Security snap-in to create the required rules.

To access this snap-in, type **firewall** in the Search charm and then select **Windows Firewall with Advanced Security** from the Programs list. You can also click **Advanced settings** from the task list in the Windows Firewall applet or select **Windows Firewall with Advanced Security** from the list of Administrative Tools displayed by selecting the **Administrative Tools** tile from the Start screen. After accepting the UAC prompt (if you receive one), the snap-in shown in Figure 19-5 displays.

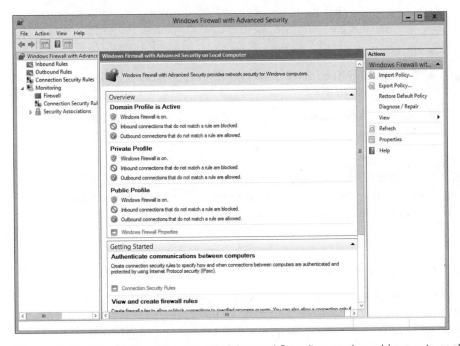

Figure 19-5   The Windows Firewall with Advanced Security snap-in enables you to configure firewall settings for each of the domain, private, and public firewall profiles.

Overview of Default Windows Firewall with Advanced Security Rules

When the snap-in first opens, it displays a summary of configured firewall settings. From the left pane, you can configure any of the following types of properties:

- **Inbound Rules:** Displays a series of defined inbound rules. Enabled rules are shown with a green check mark icon. If the icon is dark in appearance, the rule is not enabled. To enable a rule, right-click it and select **Enable Rule**; to disable an enabled rule, right-click it and select **Disable Rule**. You can also create a new rule by right-clicking **Inbound Rules** and selecting **New Rule**. We discuss creation of new rules later in this chapter.

- **Outbound Rules:** Displays a series of defined outbound rules, also with a green check mark icon for enabled rules. You can enable or disable rules and create new rules in the same manner as with inbound rules.

- **Connection Security Rules:** By default, this branch does not contain any rules. Right-click it and select **New Rule** to create rules that are used to determine limits applied to connections with remote computers.

- **Monitoring:** Displays a summary of enabled firewall settings and provides links to active rules and security associations. This includes a domain profile for computers that are members of an AD DS domain. The following three links are available from the bottom of the details pane:

  - **Firewall:** Displays enabled inbound and outbound rules

  - **Connection Security Rules:** Displays enabled connection security rules you have created

  - **Security Associations:** Displays IPsec main mode and quick mode associations

NOTE   For additional introductory information on the Windows Firewall with Advanced Security snap-in, refer to "Windows Firewall with Advanced Security Overview" at http://technet.microsoft.com/en-us/library/hh831365.aspx.

Configuring Multiple Firewall Profiles

A *profile* is simply a means of grouping firewall rules so that they apply to the affected computers dependent on where the computer is connected. The Windows Firewall with Advanced Security snap-in enables you to define different firewall behavior for each of the domain, private, and public profiles introduced earlier in this chapter.

To configure settings for these profiles from the Windows Firewall with Advanced Security snap-in, right-click **Windows Firewall with Advanced Security** at the upper-left corner and select **Properties**. This opens the dialog box shown in Figure 19-6.

Figure 19-6 The Windows Firewall with Advanced Security on Local Computer Properties dialog box enables you to configure several properties that are specific for domain, private, and public profiles.

You can configure the following properties for each of the three profiles individually from this dialog box:

- **State:** Enables you to turn the firewall on or off for the selected profile and block or allow inbound and outbound connections. For inbound connections, you can either block connections with the configured exceptions or block all connections. Click **Customize** to specify which connections you want Windows Firewall to help protect.

- **Settings:** Enables you to customize firewall settings for the selected profile. Click **Customize** to specify whether to display notifications to users when programs are blocked from receiving inbound connections or allow unicast responses. You can also view, but not modify, how rules created by local administrators are merged with Group Policy-based rules.

- **Logging:** Enables you to configure logging settings. Click **Customize** to specify the location and size of the log file and whether dropped packets or successful connections are logged (see Figure 19-7).

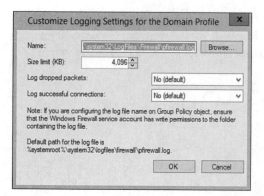

Figure 19-7   You can customize logging settings for each of the Windows Firewall profiles.

In addition, you can configure IPsec settings from the IPsec Settings tab, including defaults and exemptions. IPsec authentication rules enable you to configure bypass rules for specific computers that enable these computers to bypass other Windows Firewall rules. Doing so enables you to block certain types of traffic while enabling authenticated computers to receive these types of traffic. The IPsec Settings tab is discussed later in this chapter.

Configuring Security Rules

The Windows Firewall with Advanced Security snap-in enables you to create inbound, outbound, and connection security rules, as described earlier in this section.

Configuring Inbound Rules or Outbound Rules

By clicking **New Rule** under Inbound Rules or Outbound Rules in the Windows Firewall with Advanced Security snap-in, you can create rules that determine programs or ports that are allowed to pass through the firewall. There are a total of 65,535 TCP/UDP ports, so knowing all of them is probably going to be quite an undertaking. The following list describes the more commonly used ports for which you might need to create Windows Firewall rules:

- **BOOTP/DHCP:** Communicates through UDP port 67.

- **DNS:** DNS lookups on UDP port 53 and DNS Zone transfers on TCP port 53.

- **Echo/Echo Request:** Echo/Echo Request are often allowed through a firewall for troubleshooting with ping. It uses TCP/UDP on port 7.

- **FTP:** File Transfer Protocol operates on TCP ports 20 and 21.

- **HTTP:** Hyper Text Transport Protocol, also called Web, uses TCP port 80.

- **HTTPS:** Hypertext Transport Protocol over SSL—also known as Secure Web—uses TCP port 443.

- **NTP:** Network Time Protocol, used to synchronize system clocks, uses TCP port 123.

- **POP3:** Post Office Protocol v3 is used for incoming mail on TCP port 110.

- **RDP:** Remote Desktop Protocol is used for Terminal Services connections on TCP port 3389.

- **SSH:** Secure Shell, used to securely transmit data, uses TCP port 22.

- **SMTP:** Simple Mail Transfer Protocol is used to send email on TCP port 25.

- **SNMP:** Simple Network Management Protocol is used to send network alerts and traps on UDP port 161.

- **Telnet:** Insecure transfer protocol that uses TCP port 23.

- **TFTP:** Trivial File Transfer Protocol, typically seen with the PXE process to transfer boot images, uses UDP port 69.

- **VPN:** Two of the common Virtual Private Network protocols are PPTP and L2TP. Point to Point Tunneling Protocol (PPTP) uses TCP port 1723, and Layer 2 Tunneling Protocol (L2TP) uses UDP port 1701. Windows Server 2012 R2 VPN connections might also require the use of Generic Routing Encapsulation (GRE), which uses TCP port 47.

Use the following procedure to create a new rule:

1. Right-click the desired rule type in the Windows Firewall with Advanced Security snap-in (refer to Figure 19-5), and select **New Rule**. This starts the New (Inbound or Outbound) Rule Wizard, as shown in Figure 19-8. (We chose a new inbound rule, so our example shows the New Inbound Rule Wizard.)

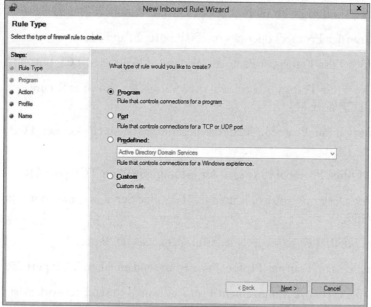

Figure 19-8 The New (Inbound or Outbound) Rule Wizard starts with a Rule Type page, which enables you to define the type of rule you want to create.

2. Select the type of rule you want to create:

■ **Program:** Enables you to define a rule that includes all programs or a specified program path.

■ **Port:** Enables you to define rules for specific remote ports using either the TCP or UDP protocol.

■ **Predefined:** Enables you to select from a large quantity of predefined rules covering the same exceptions described previously in Table 19-2 and shown in Figure 19-3. Select the desired exception from the drop-down list.

■ **Custom:** Enables you to create rules that apply to combinations of programs and ports. This option combines settings provided by the other rule-type options.

3. After you've selected your rule type, click **Next**.

4. The content of the next page of the wizard varies according to which option you've selected. For example, the following steps show you how to define a port rule with port 3389 used on a terminal server with Remote Desktop Protocol (RDP).

5. On the Protocol and Ports page shown in Figure 19-9, select the **TCP and the Specific local ports** option. Type 3389 in the text box provided, and then click **Next**.

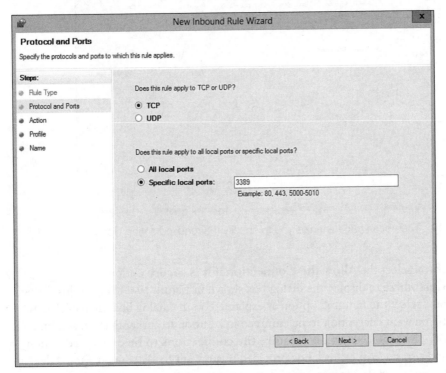

Figure 19-9   The Protocol and Ports page enables you to specify whether the rule applies to TCP or UDP and specify the port or ports to which the rule will apply.

6. On the Action page, specify the action to be taken when a connection matches the specified conditions, as shown in Figure 19-10.

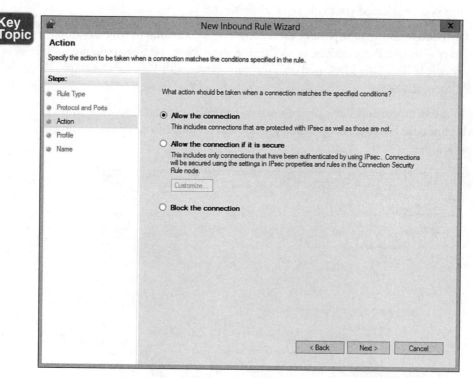

Figure 19-10   The Action page enables you to specify the required action type.

7. If you select the **Allow the Connection if it is secure** option, click
   Customize to display the dialog box shown in Figure 19-11. From this dialog
   box, select the required option as explained on the dialog box; then click **OK**.
   If you want encryption to be enforced in addition to authentication and integrity protection, select the **Require the connections to be encrypted** option
   and also select the check box provided if you want to allow unencrypted data
   to be sent while encryption is being negotiated.

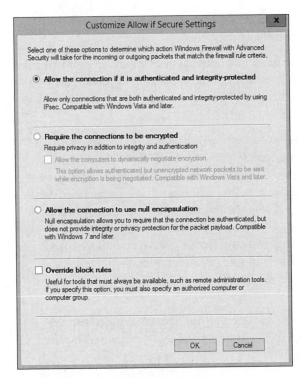

Figure 19-11 The Customize Allow if Secure Settings dialog box enables you to select additional actions to be taken for packets that match the rule conditions being configured.

8. Click **Next** to display the Users page. By default, connections from all users are authorized to make a connection specified by the rule. To limit connections to authorized users or groups, select **Only allow connections from these users** and click the **Add** button. In the Select Users, Computers, or Groups dialog box that appears, type the name of the authorized user or group and then click **OK**. Repeat as desired to add users or groups. When finished, click **Next**.

9. The Computers page enables you to limit the computers that are allowed to use the rule. By default, connections from all computers are authorized to make a connection. To limit connections to authorized computers, select **Only allow connections from these computers** and click the **Add** button. In the Select Computers or Groups dialog box that appears, type the name of the authorized computer or group and then click **OK**. Repeat as desired to add computers. When finished, click **Next**.

10. On the Profile page, select the profiles (**Domain, Private,** and **Public**) to which the rule is to be applied. Then click **Next**.

11. On the Name page, specify a name and optional description for your new rule. Click **Finish** to create the rule, which will then appear in the details pane of the Windows Firewall with Advanced Security snap-in.

NOTE   In general, you do not need to create rules for filtering outbound traffic. Windows Server 2012 and Windows Server 2012 R2 include outbound filters for basic networking services such as DHCP or DNS requests, Group Policy communications, and networking protocols such as IPv6 and Internet Group Management Protocol (IGMP). Blocking outbound communications can prevent many default Windows features, such as Windows Update, from communicating properly. However, you can block malware such as worms, viruses, and Trojan horses from spreading to other computers by using appropriate outbound traffic filters.

TIP   If you create outbound filters to help secure your network against malware propagation, be sure to test third-party applications running on your network to ensure that they communicate properly.

NOTE   For more information on creating inbound and outbound rules, refer to "Creating New Rules" at http://technet.microsoft.com/en-us/library/cc771477(WS.10).aspx. Though written for Windows Server 2008, the procedures are unchanged for Windows Server 2012 R2.

Configuring Connection Security Rules

Creating a new connection security rule is similar to that for inbound or outbound rules, but the options are slightly different. Windows Firewall with Advanced Security provides the following types of connection security rules:

- **Isolation:** Enables you to limit connections according to authentication criteria you define. For example, you can use this rule to isolate domain-based computers from external computers such as those located across the Internet. Such a rule enables you to implement server or domain isolation strategies, which are discussed later in this chapter. You can request or require authentication and specify the authentication method that must be used.

- **Authentication exemption:** Enables specified computers, such as DHCP and DNS servers, to be exempted from the need for authentication. Computers listed here do not require authentication to communicate with computers in an isolated domain. You can specify computers by IP address ranges or subnets, or you can include a predefined set of computers.

- **Server-to-server:** Enables you to protect communications between two specified groups of computers (known as *endpoints*). Specify the endpoints by IP address range or those that are accessible through a specified connection type, such as a wireless connection.

- **Tunnel:** Enables you to secure communications between two computers by means of IPsec tunnel mode. This encapsulates network packets that are routed between the tunnel endpoints. You would typically use this rule type to secure connections across the Internet between security gateways. You can choose from several types of tunnels; you can also exempt IPsec-protected computers from the defined tunnel.

- **Custom:** Enables you to create a rule that requires special settings not covered explicitly in the other options. All wizard pages except those used to create only tunnel rules are available.

Use the following procedure to create a connection security rule:

1. From the Windows Firewall with Advanced Security dialog box previously shown in Figure 19-5, right-click **Connection Security Rules** and select **New Rule** to display the New Connection Security Rule Wizard, as shown in Figure 19-12. Connection security rules manage authentication of two machines on the network and the encryption of network traffic sent between them using IPsec. Security is also achieved with the use of key exchange and data integrity checks.

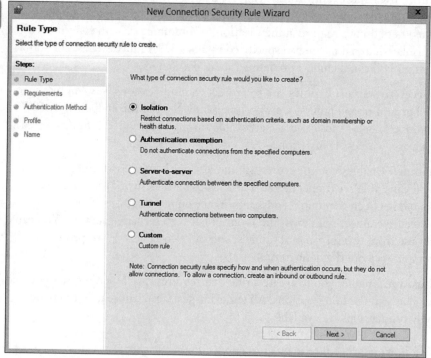

Figure 19-12   The New Connection Security Rule Wizard enables you to create five types of connection security rules.

2. Choose from one of the five types of connection security rules already described, and then click **Next**.

3. The remaining pages of the wizard depend on the type of rule you are configuring. The following steps take you through creating a server-to-server rule. Select **Server-to-Server** and then click **Next**.

4. On the Endpoints page shown in Figure 19-13, select the range of IP addresses to be included in endpoints 1 and 2. By default, computers from any IP addresses are included. To limit the rule's application, select **These IP addresses** under each endpoint and click **Add**. On the IP Address dialog

box that appears, select an option for an IP address or subnet, a range of IP addresses, or a predefined set of computers as required. When finished, click **OK**; then repeat for the other endpoint if needed. You can also select the interface types to which the rule applies by clicking **Customize**. In the Customize Interface Types dialog box that appears, select any or all of **Local area network**, **Remote access**, or **Wireless**; then click **OK**. When finished, click **Next**.

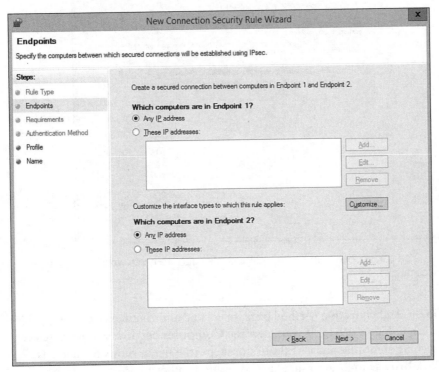

Figure 19-13   The Endpoints page enables you to define the computers at the endpoints of the connection.

5. On the Requirements page, select one of the authentication options shown in Figure 19-14, and then click **Next**.

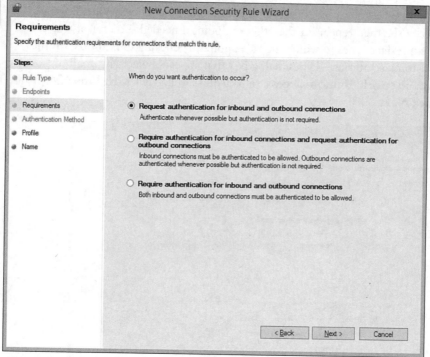

Figure 19-14   You can choose from several authentication requirements when configuring a connection security rule.

6. On the Authentication Method page, select one of the authentication methods shown in Figure 19-15. If you select the **Computer certificate** option, select a signing algorithm and certificate store type (the figure shows the defaults). Click **Browse** to locate a suitable certification authority. If you select the **Advanced** option, click **Customize** and provide information for the first and second authentication settings in the dialog box that appears. When finished, click **Next**.

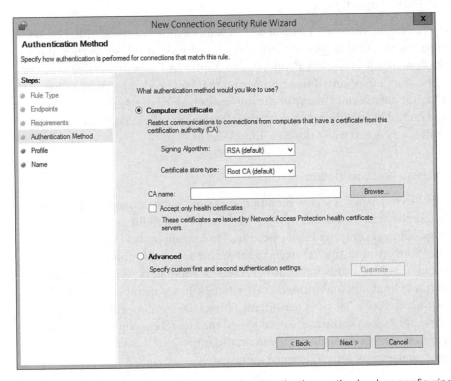

Figure 19-15 You can choose from several authentication methods when configuring a connection security rule.

7. All rule types enable you to select any or all of the domain, private, or public profiles described earlier in this chapter. Make the appropriate choice and click **Next**.

8. Specify a name and optional description for the rule on the last page of the wizard, and then click **Finish**. The rule appears in the details pane of the Windows Firewall with Advanced Security snap-in.

NOTE For more information on creating connection security rules, refer to "Creating Connection Security Rules" at http://technet.microsoft.com/en-us/library/cc725940(WS.10).aspx. Though written for Windows Server 2008, procedures described here are unchanged in Windows Server 2012 R2.

Configuring Rule Properties

All firewall rules in Windows Firewall with Advanced Security come with a Properties dialog box that enables you to modify an extensive set of rule properties. Right-click the desired rule and select **Properties** to display its Properties dialog box. We discuss the more important of these properties that you need to be aware of here. Note that, for default rules, many of the options contained in this dialog box are fixed and cannot be modified; however, these options are available for any new rules you might have created using the New Rule Wizard.

Authorizing Users and Computers

Windows Firewall enables you to require that remote users or computers be authorized before they can connect to your server. This can be useful in some situations; for example, if your company has a customized billing application that uses a specific TCP port, any user that connects to the server across this port can access data that should be available only to authorized users or computers. Windows Firewall enables you to limit inbound connections to users who are members of a specific group for which access has been permitted. This enables you to add access control to custom applications without the need to add specific access-control code to the application. If users or computers are not on the authorized lists you've specified, attempted connections will be dropped immediately.

Use the following procedure to authorize users and computers in Windows Firewall:

1. On the General tab of the rule's Properties dialog box, select **Allow the connection if it is secure**, as shown in Figure 19-16. If necessary, click **Customize** to specify one of the options previously shown in Figure 19-11. Then click **Apply**. This enables you to designate authorized or excepted users or computers.

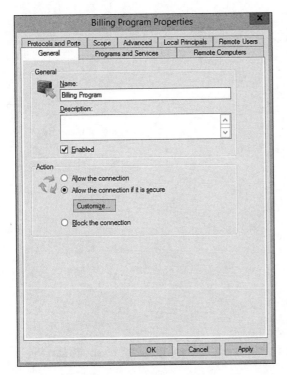

Figure 19-16   The General tab of a rule's Properties dialog box enables you to modify the action taken by the rule.

2. To limit the users that are enabled to connect using the rule, select the **Remote Users** tab. Select the check box labeled **Only allow connections from these users**, and then click **Add**.

3. Type the name of the user or group allowed to use this connection in the Select Users or Groups dialog box, and then click **OK**. The user or group is added to the Authorized users group, as shown in Figure 19-17.

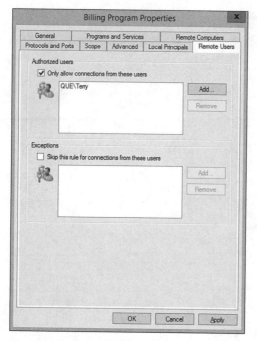

Figure 19-17   The Remote Users tab of a rule's Properties dialog box enables you to limit the users authorized to use the connection covered by the rule.

4. To designate users or groups whose traffic is to be blocked by Windows Firewall despite being included in the Allowed list, select the check box labeled **Skip this rule for connections from these users** and click **Add**. Type the required user or group name in the Select Users or Groups dialog box, and click **OK**.

5. To limit the computers that are allowed to access the server through this connection, first add the names of the computers to an appropriate security group. From the Remote Computers tab, select the check box labeled **Only allow connections from these computers**. Click **Add** and add the group name in the Select Computers or Groups dialog box that appears; then click **OK**.

6. You can also designate computers whose traffic is to be blocked by Windows Firewall despite being included in the Allowed list in a similar manner. Select the check box labeled **Skip this rule for connections from these computers**, click **Add**, and add the group name in the Select Computers or Groups dialog box. Then click **OK**.

NOTE   The Remote Users tab is provided for inbound rules only; it is not available for outbound rules.

TIP   The purpose of the Skip this rule for connections from these (users or computers) option is to block traffic from users or computers that would otherwise be allowed by virtue of their group membership. For example, if user1 is a member of a group that has been authorized on the Remote Users tab but you want to block this user's communications, include user1 in the Skip this rule section.

Modifying Rule Scope

The Scope tab of a rule's Properties dialog box enables you to limit the scope of connections from your internal network and also block connections from undesired network segments—internal or external. This helps you to limit access to a specific server to users or computers that have the need to access resources on this server, blocking those with no need to access the server. This can include web servers such as those configured for intranet websites only.

Use the following procedure to modify the scope of a rule:

1. On the Scope tab of the rule's Properties dialog box, select the option labeled **These IP addresses** under Remote IP address.

2. Click **Add**. As shown in Figure 19-18, specify the IP address or subnet either as a single IPv4 or IPv6 address or network number, or an IPv4 or IPv6 address range limited by the addresses you specify in the From and To fields. Then click **OK**.

Figure 19-18   The Scope tab of a rule's Properties dialog box enables you to limit the IP addresses that are allowed to access your server.

3. The IP address or range you specify is displayed on the Scope tab. Click **Add** again to add another IP address range, or click **OK** to finish configuring IP addresses.

Additional Rule Properties

The other tabs of a rule's Properties dialog box enable you to configure the following additional functions related to each firewall rule:

- **Programs and Services tab:** Enables you to specify the program or service that is permitted to communicate using this rule. By default, all programs that meet conditions specified elsewhere in the rule's properties are allowed to communicate. To limit the programs being used, select the **This program** option and either type the complete path to the program's executable file or click **Browse** to locate the required program. To configure customized application settings that can communicate using this rule, click the **Settings** command button under Application Packages and select the programs and application packages to which the rule should apply. To limit the services that can communicate using the rule, click the **Settings** command button under Services and select the appropriate services in the Customize Service Settings dialog box.

- **Protocols and Ports tab:** Enables you to specify the protocol type and the local and remote ports covered by the rule. A comprehensive list of available protocols and ports is included in the drop-down lists on this tab. You can add a custom protocol by selecting the **Custom** option and typing any protocol number designated by the Internet Assigned Numbers Authority (IANA). Note that the local port is the port on the computer for which you are configuring the rule and the remote port is the port on any computer that is sending or receiving communications from the local port.

NOTE For a list of the most often-used protocols and their numbers, refer to "Firewall Rule Properties Page: Protocols and Ports Tab" at http://technet. microsoft.com/en-us/library/dd421720(WS.10).aspx.

- **Advanced tab:** Enables you to specify the profiles (domain, private, or public) to which the rule applies. You can also specify the interface types (local area network, remote access, and/or wireless) and whether edge traversal (traffic routed through a Network Address Translation [NAT] device) is allowed or blocked for incoming rules. The following edge traversal options are available:

  - **Block edge traversal:** Blocks the reception of unsolicited Internet traffic through a NAT device

  - **Allow edge traversal:** Enables applications to receive unsolicited Internet traffic through a NAT device

  - **Defer to user:** Enables the user to decide whether traffic from the Internet will be allowed through a NAT device when requested by an application

  - **Defer to application:** Enables each application to determine whether Internet traffic will be allowed through a NAT device

NOTE   For additional information on the various tabs of the firewall rule's Properties dialog box, refer to references cited at "Firewall Rule Properties Page" at http://technet.microsoft.com/en-us/library/dd421727(WS.10).aspx. Though written for Windows Server 2008, information provided here is largely unchanged for Windows Server 2012 R2.

Configuring Notifications

You can configure Windows Firewall with Advanced Security to display notifications when a program is blocked from receiving inbound connections according to the default behavior of Windows Firewall. When you have selected this option and no existing block or allow rule applies to this program, a user is notified when a program is blocked from receiving inbound connections.

To configure this option, right-click **Windows Firewall with Advanced Security** at the top of the left pane in the Windows Firewall with Advanced Security snap-in and then select **Properties**. This opens the dialog box previously shown in Figure 19-6. Select the tab that corresponds to the profile you want to configure, and then click the **Customize** command button in the Settings section. From the Customize Settings for the (selected) Profile dialog box, select **Yes** under Display a notification (as shown in Figure 19-19) and then click **OK** twice.

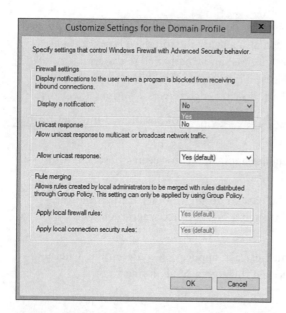

Figure 19-19 Configuring Windows Firewall to display notifications.

Configuring Firewall Properties and Authenticated Exceptions

Group Policy enables you to define IPsec policies that apply to all computers in your AD DS domain, site, or OU. You can also define policies that provide authenticated exceptions for IPsec traffic from authorized computers that crosses the server's firewall. As with other Group Policy settings, you can define these policies in a GPO linked to a site, a domain, or an OU as required.

Creating Windows Firewall with Advanced Security Policies

Group Policy enables you to configure Windows Firewall with Advanced Security so that the configured options apply to all computers affected by the GPO in the AD DS object to which it is linked. Use the following procedure:

1. From the Group Policy Management Editor focused on the appropriate GPO, navigate to **Computer Configuration\Policies\Windows Settings\ Security Settings\Windows Firewall with Advanced Security\Windows Firewall with Advanced Security**.

2. Expand this node. You will notice subnodes for Inbound Rules, Outbound Rules, and Connection Security Rules, as shown in Figure 19-20.

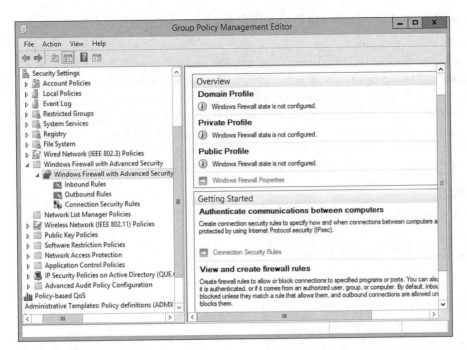

Figure 19-20   Using Group Policy to configure Windows Firewall with Advanced Security options.

3. To configure a Group Policy-based IPsec policy, right-click **Connection Security Rules** and select **New Rule**.

4. The New Rule Wizard starts with the Rule Type page, which provides you with the same five rule types previously shown in Figure 19-12. Select the desired rule type, and then click **Next**.

5. Complete the New Rule Wizard as described earlier in this chapter; the same pages previously shown in Figures 19-13 to 19-15 display. After clicking **Finish**, your rule will appear in the details pane of the Group Policy Management Editor snap-in.

If you need to modify any policy rules, right-click the required rule in the details pane and select **Properties**. You can modify all the same options that the New Rule Wizard initially configures. You can also disable a policy rule if required by right-clicking the rule and selecting **Disable Rule**. This option then changes to **Enable Rule** so that you can reenable it later.

Windows Firewall Group Policy Property Settings

Group Policy also enables you to define several properties that apply to all policies configured in a given GPO. In the Group Policy Management Editor, right-click the second **Windows Firewall with Advanced Security** node and select **Properties**. For each of the domain, private, and public profiles, you can specify the behavior of the firewall state (on, off, or not configured), plus several settings that control Windows Firewall behavior and logging options. Available settings are similar to those previously shown in Figure 19-6 for local computer firewall properties. The IPsec Settings tab shown in Figure 19-21 provides the following options:

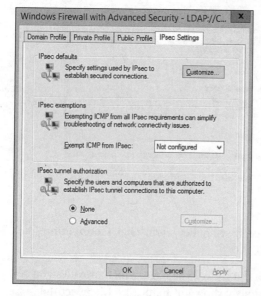

Figure 19-21   You can choose from three authentication methods when configuring a connection security rule.

- **IPsec defaults:** Click **Customize** to specify settings used by IPsec to establish secured connections when there are active connection security rules. The Customize IPsec Settings dialog box that appears enables you to specify settings for key exchange, data protection, and authentication method.

- **IPsec exemptions:** You can chose whether to exempt ICMP from IPsec requirements. Select the **Yes** option to enable ICMP packets, such as ping or tracert, to pass without being examined by IPsec rules. This can assist in troubleshooting network connectivity problems.

- **IPsec tunnel authorization:** By clicking **Advanced**, you can customize the computers and/or users that are authorized to use the IPsec tunnel or deny connections. This dialog box works in a similar fashion to that shown previously in Figure 19-17.

Configuring Authenticated Bypass

You can allow all authenticated IP traffic from approved computers to bypass Windows Firewall by configuring the Allow authenticated IPsec bypass Group Policy setting or using a Security Descriptor Definition Language (SDDL) string to describe the computers enabled to bypass Windows Firewall. The SDDL string includes the security identifiers (SIDs) of computer or group accounts for which you want to enable IPsec bypass. This string is formatted similar to the following example:

```
O:DAG:DAD:(A;;CC;;;SID1) (A;;CC;;;SID2) (A;;CC;;;SID3) ...
```

In this string, *SID1*, *SID2*, and so on are the SIDs of the computer or group accounts you want to authorize. Include as many of the SID specifications as required. You can use the Getsid.exe command-line tool to obtain the SIDs of the required accounts.

Use the following procedure to enable authenticated IPsec bypass:

1. Open the Group Policy Management Editor focused on a GPO linked to the site, domain, or OU for which you want to configure authenticated bypass.

2. Navigate to **Computer Configuration\Policies\Administrative Templates\Network\Network Connections\Windows Firewall**. The policy settings shown in Figure 19-22 display.

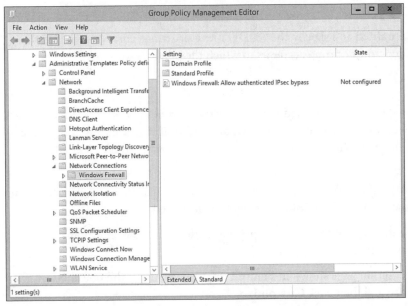

Figure 19-22   Group Policy enables you to configure authenticated IPsec bypass.

3. Right-click the **Windows Firewall: Allow authenticated IPsec bypass** policy, and select **Edit**. The dialog box shown in Figure 19-23 opens.

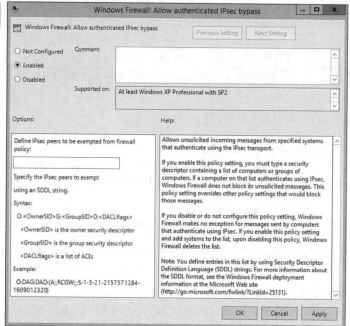

Figure 19-23   Configuring authenticated IPsec bypass settings.

4. Click **Enabled** and specify the SDDL string or strings corresponding to the computer and/or group accounts to which the policy is to apply.

5. Click **OK**.

You can also enable authenticated bypass directly from Windows Firewall with Advanced Security by selecting the **Allow connection if it is secure** option while performing the New Rule Wizard described earlier in this chapter. Proceed as follows:

1. In the Windows Firewall with Advanced Security snap-in, right-click **Inbound Rules** and select **New Rule**, as previously described.

2. Follow the steps of the wizard as previously described and shown in Figures 19-8 to 19-10.

3. On the Action page shown in Figure 19-10, select **Allow the connection if it is secure** and then click **Customize**.

4. On the Customize Allow if Secure Settings dialog box previously shown in Figure 19-11, select **Override block rules** and then click **OK**.

5. Click **Next** twice to display the Computers page. To specify the computers authorized to bypass the firewall rule, select **Only allow connections from these computers** and then click **Add**.

6. In the Select Computers or Groups dialog box that appears (see Figure 19-24), type the names of the computers or computer groups to be authorized for bypass; then click **OK**.

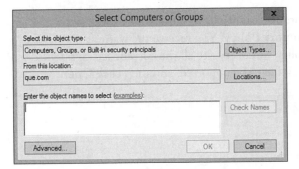

Figure 19-24 Selecting computers or groups for authorized IPsec bypass.

7. Complete the remaining steps of the wizard, as previously described.

> **NOTE**   For more information on enabling authenticated bypass, refer to "How to Enable Authenticated Firewall Bypass" at http://technet.microsoft.com/en-us/library/cc753463(v=WS.10).aspx. This reference also tells you how to use the Getsid.exe command to obtain the SID of a computer group if you're using the Allow authenticated IPsec bypass policy shown in Figure 19-23.

> **NOTE**   For a comprehensive guide on using Windows PowerShell to administer Windows Firewall with Advanced Security, refer to "Windows Firewall with Advanced Security Administration with Windows PowerShell" at http://technet.microsoft.com/en-us/library/hh831755.aspx.

Exporting and Importing Firewall Settings

All the Windows Firewall with Advanced Security settings that have been discussed in this section, including the domain, private, and public profiles, are included in a policy file with the .wfw extension. You can export a configured policy and import it to a new location.

These actions are helpful if you decide to restore Windows Firewall with Advanced Security defaults, which you might want to do should problems arise with firewall settings. Doing so deletes all firewall settings, firewall rules, and IPsec connection security rules that have been configured on the computer. Exporting the firewall policy enables you to restore your settings later if desired. To export your policy, right-click **Windows Firewall with Advanced Security** and select **Export Policy**. Provide a name and path for the export file, and then click **Save**.

To import a saved policy configuration, right-click **Windows Firewall with Advanced Security** and select **Import Policy**. You receive the warning shown in Figure 19-25 that importing a policy will overwrite all the current settings. Click **Yes**, specify the name of the policy file to be imported, and then click **Open**.

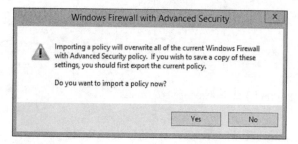

Figure 19-25   You are warned that importing a policy will overwrite all current firewall policy settings.

Exam Preparation Tasks

Review All the Key Topics

Review the most important topics in the chapter, noted with the key topics icon in the outer margin of the page. Table 19-4 lists a reference of these key topics and the page numbers on which each is found.

Table 19-4   Key Topics for Chapter 19

Key Topic Element	Description	Page Number
List	Describes the available Windows Firewall profiles.	819
Step list	Shows you how to use the Windows Firewall Control Panel applet.	820

Key Topic Element	Description	Page Number
Figure 19-3	You can choose to allow individual apps through the Windows Firewall Control Panel applet for either the Domain, Private, or Public profiles.	822
Table 19-3	Lists the commonly used PowerShell cmdlets for configuring Windows Firewall.	825
Figure 19-5	Windows Firewall with Advanced Security enables you to configure settings for each of the Domain, Private, and Public profiles.	827
List	Describes the purposes of each of the three firewall profiles and when you would use them.	829
Figure 19-8	Shows the types of rules you can create using the New Rule Wizard.	832
Figure 19-10	You can choose from three actions when a connection matches rule criteria.	834
Figure 19-12	Shows the custom rule types you can create using the New Connection Security Rule Wizard.	838
Figure 19-14	Choosing an authentication requirement for a New Connection Security Rule.	840
Figure 19-15	Choosing an authentication method for a New Connection Security Rule.	841
Step list	Describes how to authorize users and computers in Windows Firewall.	842
Figure 19-18	Modifying a rule's scope to define which computers are affected by the rule.	845
Figure 19-20	Shows you how to use Group Policy to create an IPsec policy.	849
Figure 19-23	Shows how to configure authenticated IPsec bypass settings.	852
Paragraph	Shows how to import firewall policy configurations.	854

Definitions of Key Terms

Define the following key terms from this chapter, and check your answers in the glossary.

Authentication, Authenticated bypass, Connection security rule, Filter action, Firewall, Firewall profile, Firewall rule, IP Security (IPsec), Stateful firewall, Windows Firewall, Windows Firewall with Advanced Security

Practice Exam 1

1. Your network contains an Active Directory domain named mydomain.com. The domain contains three domain controllers named DC1, DC2, and DC3. You install a new server named DC4 and need to configure it as a domain controller. Which tool should you use?

    a. dcpromo.exe

    b. Server Manager

    c. Active Directory Users and Computers

    d. Active Directory Domains and Trusts

2. Your network consists of a single Active Directory domain named mydomain.com. The domain contains 50 Windows 8.1 workstations and 5 Windows Server 2012 R2 member servers. You need to install a new server that will provide mobile support and the ability for users to connect to applications from anywhere. You install Windows Server 2012 R2 on a new server that you name Server6. Which server role should you install to meet this need?

    a. Terminal Server

    b. File and Storage Services

    c. Web Server (IIS)

    d. Remote Desktop Services

3. You are a consultant charged with the responsibility of deploying a computer network to a new accounting firm. The owner would like you to install a Windows Server 2012 R2 computer to store data for the office network, which is not expected to grow beyond a maximum of 10 computers including the server. The owner wants to keep deployment costs as low as possible. Which edition of Windows Server 2012 R2 should you recommend?

   a. Windows Server 2012 R2 Essentials

   b. Windows Server 2012 R2 Standard

   c. Windows Server 2012 R2 Foundation

   d. Windows Server 2012 R2 Datacenter

4. Which of the following are valid charms available under the Windows Server 2012 R2 user interface? (Choose all that apply.)

   a. Search

   b. Find

   c. Share

   d. Delegate

   e. Configuration

   f. Settings

5. You have recently installed Windows Server 2012 R2 Core and need to change Windows Update settings using a command-line tool. Which command can you use to manage the new Server Core instance?

   a. Server Manager

   b. RemoteConfig

   c. sconfig

   d. Mstsc

6. Server1 is a full GUI installation of Windows Server 2012 R2. You decide that you want to minimize the attack footprint and reduce to Server Core. You need to uninstall all GUIs on Server1. How can you accomplish this? (Each answer represents a complete solution. Choose two).

   a. Start Server1 with the installation media, and reinstall using the Server Core option.

   b. From a Windows 8.1 workstation or another server, access Server Manager for Server1 remotely and uninstall the User Interfaces and Infrastructure features.

   c. From a PowerShell session, execute the `Uninstall-WindowsFeature Server-Gui-Mgmt-Infra,Server-Gui-Shell` cmdlet.

   d. From PowerShell, execute the `Install-WindowsFeature Server Core` cmdlet.

7. You receive reports that performance is poor while transferring files from your file server. You review the LAN switching infrastructure and do not see any issues. You begin to look at your file server and notice that your NIC is over-utilized. You decide to increase throughput by configuring a NIC team. You add two additional NICs and need to configure all three in a team. Which tool should you use?

   a. Server Manager

   b. Routing and Remote Access

   c. NLB Manager

   d. File Server Resource Manager

8. You are the systems administrator for mycompany.com. Mycompany.com contains four servers as outlined in the following table:

Server	CPU Support	Memory	Operating System
Server1	x86	4 GB	Windows Server 2008 32-bit
Server2	x86/x64	2 GB	Windows Server 2008 32-bit
Server3	x64	4 GB	Windows Server 2008 R2 64-bit
Server4	x64	2 GB	Windows Server 2008 R2 64-bit

You need to ensure that mycompany.com contains only Windows Server 2012 R2 installations. You need to minimize cost and upgrade whenever possible. What should you do? (Each answer represents part of the solution. Choose all that apply.)

    a. Replace Server1 and perform a clean installation of Windows Server 2012 R2.

    b. Replace both Server1 and Server2 and perform a clean installation of Windows Server 2012 R2.

    c. Perform an in place upgrade on Server3 and Server4 to Windows Server 2012 R2.

    d. Perform a clean install of Windows Server 2012 R2 on Server2.

    e. Replace Server2 and perform a new installation of Windows Server 2012.

    f. Replace all servers and perform clean installations of Windows Server 2012.

    g. Install an additional 2 GB of RAM in Server4 and perform an in-place upgrade to Server 2012.

9. Server1 is a Windows Server 2012 R2 WDS server. `C:\testimages\testimage.wim` contains the following image details:

You need to update the image to include an additional feature. First, you pre-pare to mount the image to a staging location in `c:\mountedimage`. Which command can you issue to mount the image?

   a. `Dism.exe /Mount-Image /ImageFile:c:\testimages\testimage.wim /Index:1 /MountDir:c:\mountedimage`

   b. `Dism.exe /Mount c:\testimages\testimage.wim /Index:1 /MountDir:c:\mountedimage`

   c. `Dism.exe /Mount-Image c:\testimages\testimage.wim /Name:"Windows Server 2012 SERVERDATACENTER" c:\mountedimage`

   d. `Dism.exe /Mount c:\testimages\testimage.wim /Name:"Windows Server 2012 SERVERDATACENTER" /MountDir:c:\mountedimage`

10. Using the principle of least privilege, which local built-in group can you use to delegate the ability to read performance counter data?

   a. Administrators

   b. Event Log Readers

   c. Performance Log Users

   d. Performance Monitor Users

11. Server1 is a new file server that stores user data for your small business. You have noticed that Server1 is running low on disk space. To remediate the issue, you decide to add a new 3-TB disk, Disk 2. How should you configure Disk 2 so that you can create a new 3-TB volume on Server1?

   a. Format it as FAT.

   b. Use DiskPart and convert the disk to a GPT disk.

   c. Use the MBR partition table when creating the volume.

   d. Attach the volume as a VHD.

12. You are planning to design a new storage space on Server1, a Windows Server 2012 R2 server with four 2-TB locally attached hard disks. Your goal is to maximize the amount of storage but also provide fault tolerance should a single disk fail. Which kind of storage space should you create?

   a. Parity storage space

   b. Mirror storage space

   c. Simple storage space

   d. Spanned volume

13. You have been asked to design a local storage solution that offers fast read and write access for your files. Data protection is not a concern. Which RAID level should you use?

   a. RAID-0

   b. RAID-1

   c. RAID-2

   d. RAID-5

14. Several months after installing a new Windows Server 2012 R2 file server and configuring quotas for users in her company's AD DS domain, Kelly notices that the hard disk on which users' shared folders are located is over three-quarters full. On checking through the contents of the shared folders, Kelly notices a large number of audio and video files.

   Kelly would like to prevent users from storing audio and video files on the shared folder. What should she do?

   a. Use File Server Resource Manager (FSRM) to block audio/video file types.

   b. Use File Server Resource Manager (FSRM) to generate an alert when users save audio/video file types.

   c. Modify the quota to reduce the amount of disk space available to each user.

   d. Modify the quota to disallow the saving of audio and video files.

15. You need to create a shared folder on your Windows Server 2012 R2 computer to which users on a UNIX server require access. You want to configure access-denied assistance and quotas on this share. So you start the New Share Wizard from Server Manager. Which of the following options should you choose?

   a. SMB Share–Quick

   b. NFS Share–Advanced

   c. SMB Share–Advanced

   d. NFS Share–Quick

   e. SMB Share–Applications

16. You have granted a user named Megan the Read NTFS permission on a folder named Sales. Megan is also a member of the Finance group, which has been explicitly denied the Full Control NTFS permission on the Sales folder. What is Megan's effective permission on this folder?

    a. Full Control.

    b. Megan does not have access to the folder.

    c. Modify.

    d. Read.

17. Which NTFS Quota configuration should you enable to actively notify users that they are nearing their quota limit?

    a. Set warning level

    b. Deny disk space to users exceeding quota limit

    c. Limit disk space

    d. Log event when user exceeds their warning level

18. Tyrone is the network administrator for a company named All Roads Engineering Consultants, which operates an AD DS network configured as a single domain. The Designing Department has recently acquired a high-speed laser printer to handle printing requirements of the various staff.

Tyrone has created three domain local groups on the print server for purposes of managing the printer, as follows: Designers have Print permission, Supervisors have Manage Documents permission, and Managers have Manage Printer permission.

Tyrone needs to give a staff member in the Designing Department named Yolanda the ability to pause, resume, and cancel documents printed by all staff, but not control the permissions assigned to other staff members on the printer.

To which group should Tyrone add Yolanda's user account?

    a. Supervisors.

    b. Designers.

    c. Managers.

    d. Tyrone does not need to add Yolanda to any of these groups; she can perform these tasks by default.

19. You have recently configured a new Windows Server 2012 R2 print server. You install a new high-capacity printer in one of your satellite offices. For ease of administration, the printer is shared on the print server located in the corporate office. All satellite users are configured to use the shared printer `\\Server1\Printer1`. Users in one of the branch sites print to this printer over the corporate WAN link. You need to ensure that users are able to print to the printer in the event of a WAN link failure. What can you do to meet this requirement?

    a. Disable Printer Pooling.

    b. Install a second printer and share it as `\\Server1\Printer2` as a backup.

    c. Enable Printer Pooling.

    d. Enable Branch Office Direct Printing

20. Your network consists of a single Active Directory domain. Server1 is a Windows Server 2012 R2 server with the Print and Document server role installed. Only one print device exists for the company. Sales, Finance, and Marketing users all share the same print device. You need to ensure that all users can print to this print device, but that Finance documents print before any other department. What should you do?

    a. Add three printers. Modify the priorities of each printer and security settings for each printer so that each department has its own printer to which to submit jobs.

    b. Purchase another print device and configure a printer pool.

    c. Add one printer. Establish a priority on the printer, and require all departments to submit jobs to this printer.

    d. Add one printer. Configure the printer security settings to allow Finance users to print. Deny all other users the ability to print.

21. You are responsible for printers connected to Windows Server 2012 R2 print servers in your company's AD DS domain. These servers are configured as member servers in the domain. You have installed a printer that should be accessible to computers in the Graphics Department but not to computers in other departments of the company. All resources in this department are located in the Graphics organizational unit (OU). What should you do?

   a. Right-click this printer in the details pane of the Print Management snap-in and select **Deploy with Group Policy**. Choose a GPO that is linked to the Graphics OU, and select the option labeled **The computers that this GPO applies to (per machine)**.

   b. From the Sharing tab of the printer's Properties dialog box, select the **List in the directory** option.

   c. Right-click this printer in the details pane of the Print Management snap-in, and select **List in Directory**.

   d. Right-click this printer in the details pane of the Print Management snap-in, and select **Deploy with Group Policy**. Choose a GPO that is linked to the Graphics OU, and select the option labeled **The users that this GPO applies to (per user)**.

22. Your network consists of two servers. Server 1 is a Windows Server 2012 application server, and Server 2 is a Windows Server 2008 R2 SP1 file server. You need to ensure that you can manage Server 2 from Server 1 using Server Manager. What do you need to do to ensure that you can manage Server 2? (Choose two.)

   a. Install WMF 4.0 on Server 2.

   b. Install .NET Framework 4.5 on Server 2.

   c. Install WMF 4.0 on Server 1.

   d. Install .NET Framework 4.5 on Server 1.

   e. Remove SP1 on Server 2.

   f. Upgrade Server 1 to Windows Server 2012 R2.

23. You are the systems administrator for mydomain.com. Your network consists of a single Active Directory domain containing 650 Windows 8.1 workstations and 30 Windows Server 2012 R2 member servers. You just finished configuring a new remote server named RemoteServer1. You have taken the necessary steps to configure the WS Management listener service on the new server. You would like to confirm functionality before releasing the server to production. Which command can you execute to confirm WinRM functionality?

   a. `Winrs -r:RemoteServer1 Test`

   b. `Psremote -exec RemoteServer1 Test`

   c. `Test-WsMan RemoteServer1`

   d. `WinRM -Test RemoteServer1`

24. Bob has recently installed a Hyper-V host with 64 GB of RAM and two quad-core processors. He plans to install four virtual guest servers. He would like each guest to be able to use up to 16 GB of memory. In the event of a host shutdown, Bob needs to be able to reserve a portion for startup memory to allow him to bring up the host and all guest servers simultaneously. What should he configure on each virtual machine?

   a. Windows Paging

   b. Static Memory

   c. Dynamic Memory

   d. Fast Cache

25. Server1 is a Windows Server 2012 R2 Hyper-V host. Server1 contains a virtual machine named VM1. You must configure VM1 to boot from PXE in the event of a restart. Which virtual machine setting should you configure for VM1 to accomplish this?

   a. Configure the standard Network Adapter setting to boot from PXE.

   b. Configure the Legacy Network Adapter to boot from PXE.

   c. Configure the BIOS startup order.

   d. Disable Diskette Drive.

26. You are the administrator for a two-node Windows Server 2012 R2 Hyper-V cluster. You configure two new virtual machines: VM1 and VM2. You need to ensure that all virtual machines are able to be backed up via the host using a third-party backup application. What should you configure?

    a. Network adapter

    b. Router Guard

    c. Guest Integration Services

    d. Windows Backup

27. You are the administrator for Server1, a Windows Server 2012 R2 Hyper-V host. You configure two new virtual machines: VM1 and VM2. You need to ensure that you can track CPU, memory, disk space, and network usage. Which command do you configure?

    a. `Enable-GstIntSvc`

    b. `Enable-VMResourceMetering`

    c. `Enable-VMResource Management`

    d. `Enable-VMPerfMon`

28. You are preparing to deploy Hyper-V to your infrastructure. Server1 is a Windows Server 2012 development server with the Hyper-V server role installed. You need to test the ability to use pass-through disks for a new VM. Your local disk configuration is configured as shown in the following figure:

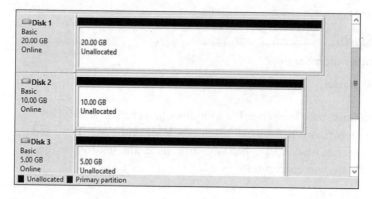

You are unable to configure a pass-through disk using Disk 1 for your virtual machine VM1. What should you do?

   a. Take Disk 1 offline.

   b. Create a 20-GB volume on Disk 1.

   c. Create a new striped volume using the space in Disks 1 and 2.

   d. Upgrade Server1 to Windows Server 2012 R2.

29. You need to share the contents of a virtual hard disk between multiple guest virtual machines. What can you do?

   a. Establish a parent/child relationship, and configure the virtual hard disk containing the files as the parent disk.

   b. Convert the virtual hard disk to a fixed sized disk.

   c. Establish a dynamically expanding disk relationship between the virtual machines.

   d. Add a second virtual hard disk and configure a virtual mirror.

30. Dave is the network administrator for pearson.com. He plans to configure a server as a Hyper-V host. To reduce cost, Dave has decided to repurpose an existing server. The server has 32 GB of RAM, two quad-core CPUs, 4 TB of local storage, and four network adapters configured as a single NIC Team. Dave upgrades the server to 256 GB of RAM and installs the Hyper-V server role. Dave needs to create two virtual network switches. Half the virtual machines will be configured as development servers connected to Virtual-Switch1, while the other half will be configured as production servers connected to VirtualSwitch2. During the configuration, Dave realizes that he is unable to split the VMs between two virtual switches. What is the first thing Dave must do to accomplish this?

   a. Upgrade the Hyper-V Integration Services.

   b. Execute the `Remove-NetLbfo Team` cmdlet.

   c. Execute the `Set-NetAdapter` cmdlets to configure VLAN IDs.

   d. Add an available interface to the NIC Team using the `Add-NetLbfoTeamNic` cmdlet.

31. Server1 is a Windows Server 2012 R2 server with the Hyper-V role installed. You configure VM1 to support an in-house application. You configure a legacy network adapter for VM1. You need to ensure that VM1 uses only 50% of the available bandwidth. How should you do this?

   a. Add a second legacy network adapter to increase throughput.

   b. Remove the legacy network adapter and add an up-to-date network adapter.

   c. Configure a NIC Team.

   d. Reinstall Hyper-V Integration Services.

32. You are the administrator for Server1, a two-node Windows Server 2012 R2 Hyper-V cluster. You configure two new virtual machines: VM1 and VM2. You need to ensure that these virtual machines are not able to communicate with rogue DHCP servers. What should you configure?

   a. MAC Address Spoofing

   b. Router Guard

   c. Port mirroring

   d. DHCP Guard

33. You are the Hyper-V administrator for mycompany.com. You manage a Hyper-V host named HyperV1. HyperV1 contains three Windows Server 2008 virtual machines and six Windows Server 2012 R2 virtual machines. You have configured a virtual switch configured using the external switch type. You need to ensure that the virtual machines are only able to talk to each other. What should you do?

    a. Upgrade all 2008 virtual machines to Windows Server 2012 R2.

    b. Add a second virtual switch. Move all Windows Server 2008 VMs to virtual switch 1 and all Windows Server 2012 R2 VMs to virtual switch 2.

    c. Remove the virtual switch and re-create it using the private switch type.

    d. Remove the virtual switch and re-create it using the public switch type.

34. You are designing a multitenant Hyper-V infrastructure. You need to ensure that tenants are unable to see each other's resources. What should you configure?

    a. Hyper-V virtual grid

    b. Virtual Cloud Partitions (VCP)

    c. Port Virtual Local Area Network (PVLAN)

    d. MAC Address Isolation

35. Amanda is configuring IP addressing for a company that has a head office in midtown Manhattan and 11 branch offices in various locations throughout the New York metropolitan area. She has decided that each office will correspond to a single subnet on the company's wide area network (WAN). The company itself can use a single Class C network for this purpose. Which of the following subnet masks would provide the most host addresses for each office?

    a. 255.255.255.192

    b. 255.255.255.224

    c. 255.255.255.240

    d. 255.255.255.248

36. Neil administers a network that is configured as a single AD DS domain for his firm. He is assigned the task of maintaining his company's DNS and DHCP servers. He decides that DHCP clients running Windows 8.1 should be configured to automatically select their primary DNS server.

Neil configures a Windows Server 2012 R2 computer named Server4 as a DNS server. In the DHCP server's scope options for a subnet containing 25 client computers, Neil configures Server4's IP address in the 006 DNS Servers option. He also ensures that a DHCP reservation exists for Server4. Next, he restarts all the client computers on the subnet. He makes his way to a client computer and is disappointed to discover that it is still configured to use as its DNS server a computer that was taken offline just before Neil began making changes to the network. How can Neil correct this problem?

a. Execute the `ipconfig /release` and `ipconfig /renew` commands on each computer.

b. Configure both the 006 and the 015 options for the DNS server in the DHCP scope.

c. Use `ipconfig /setclassid` at each client computer to set DHCP class ID information.

d. Manually edit the TCP/IP properties on each client computer.

e. Isolate the subnet to eliminate the possibility that clients are receiving scope information from a remote subnet.

37. Your company uses Class B network ranges. You plan to configure the subnet mask for a branch site containing 450 Windows 8.1 client computers. Your company policy requires you to use 1 subnet per branch site. You plan to add another 150 computers in the next year. You need to select a subnet mask that satisfies the requirements for today and also the future growth. You want to limit the amount of wasted addresses. Which subnet mask should you select?

a. 255.255.254.0

b. 255.255.252.0

c. 255.255.255.240

d. 255.255.255.0

38. You need to plan an IPv6 addressing scheme. The following table lists each class of IPv6 address. Complete the table with the appropriate address prefix.

IPv6 Class	IPv6 Address Prefix
Global unicast	
Link-Local unicast	
Unique local IPv6 unicast	
Multicast	

    a. `Fe::`

    b. `2000::/3`

    c. `fc00::/7`

    d. `Ff`

    e. `fe80::/64`

39. Your company consists of a main site and two branch sites. Each branch site is connected to the main via a WAN link. You need to configure a new server for the main site. You need to configure an IPv6 address for the new server. You plan to use an IPv6 address class that is private to the organization but unique across all the organization's sites. Which address meets this requirement?

    a. f00:3fff:64df:155c:dca7::81a4

    b. fe80::cc33:456a:3719:1234

    c. 2003:414:ab86:731f::230:1:45ab

    d. fd12:cde6:1208:9::f92b

40. You are the network engineer for a consulting firm. You have been tasked with designing a subnet mask for a network that will support up to 20,046 client computers. You must minimize the number of wasted addresses. Which subnet mask should you select?

    a. 255.255.252.0

    b. 255.255.248.0

    c. 255.255.240.0

    d. 255.255.128.0

41. Ruby is the systems administrator for a company that operates an AD DS network with a single domain called que.com. All servers run either the original or R2 version of Windows Server 2012. One Monday, she notices that the hard disk on DHCP server named Server6 has failed. She installs a new hard disk and performs a bare metal restore from a recent backup.

    Ruby must ensure that DHCP clients do not receive IP addresses that have already been leased to other DHCP clients. What should she do?

    a. Set the DHCP server option 47 value to 0.

    b. Set the DHCP server option 47 value to 1.

    c. Set the Conflict Detection value to 0.

    d. Set the Conflict Detection value to 1.

42. Your network consists of two subnets. Users on Subnet1 complain that they are unable to access any resources outside of their subnet. No other users from any other subnet are experiencing the issue. You review the DHCP configuration for Subnet1 and notice that the Router option does not exist. Which option allows you to specify the IP address of the router or default gateway?

    a. 044 WINS/NBNS Servers

    b. 003 Router

    c. 066 Boot Server Host Name

    d. 030 Router

43. The Mydomain.com network contains a single Active Directory forest. Sales.mydomain.com and Marketing.mydomain.com are child domains. Bob is the administrator of Sales.mydomain.com, and Mike is the administrator of marketing.mydomain.com. Mike needs to authorize a new DHCP server for his domain. What does Mike need to do to authorize his server?

    a. Authorize the server in the mydomain.com parent domain.

    b. Authorize the server in marketing.mydomain.com.

    c. Authorize the server in all domains in the forest.

    d. Authorize the server in sales.mydomain.com.

44. Which of the following messages are exchanged between an IPv6 client computer and DHCPv6 server when requesting configuration information? (Choose all that apply; arrange your answers in the proper sequence in which the messages are exchanged.)

   a. Discover

   b. Offer

   c. Advertise

   d. Request

   e. Solicit

   f. Confirm

   g. Reply

45. You are the administrator for mycompany.com. You are installing a new development server named Server1. You need to make sure Server1 does not receive any IP addresses from the DHCP server, Server2. What should you configure to accommodate this?

   a. DHCP Exclusion

   b. DHCP Reservation

   c. DHCP Filter

   d. DHCP Block Service

46. Ellen is the systems administrator for a company that operates an AD DS network consisting of a single domain. The company has been using a Windows 2000 Server computer running WINS for single-name resolution of computer names on the network.

   As part of a move to decommission all older servers and convert the network to using Windows Server 2012 R2 servers exclusively, Ellen needs to configure DNS to provide forest-wide single name resolution. What should she do?

   a. Create a secondary zone named GlobalNames. Add host (A) resource records for all computers that require single name resolution. Then create corresponding secondary zones on all other DNS servers on the network.

   b. Create an Active Directory–integrated zone named GlobalNames. Add host (A) resource records for all computers that require single name resolution.

   c. Create SRV resource records for all computers that require single name resolution.

   d. Create CNAME resource records for all computers that require single name resolution.

47. Server1 is a Windows Server 2012 R2 server with the DNS role installed. You need to review the root hints for Server1. How can you accomplish this? (Each answer represents a complete solution. Choose two.)

   a. Open the `%systemroot%\system32\dns\cache.dns` file on Server1 using `notepad.exe`.

   b. Open the `%systemroot%\system\dns\cache.dns` file on Server1 using `notepad.exe`.

   c. Use the Root Hints tab of the DNS Server Properties dialog box.

   d. Use the HLKM\DNS registry hive.

48. Your network consists of a single Active Directory domain named mydomain.com. The domain contains a domain controller named DC1 that hosts the primary DNS zone for the company. All 100 Windows 8.1 client workstations are configured to use DC1 as the primary DNS server. You need to configure DC1 to use your Internet service provider's DNS server to resolve all requests for name resolutions outside of mydomain.com. What should you configure?

   a. An AAAA Record containing your ISP's DNS server

   b. A forwarder containing your ISP's DNS server

   c. A forward lookup zone for your ISP

   d. A reverse lookup zone for your ISP

49. You are the Enterprise administrator for Pearson. You have just installed your first domain controller to create Pearson.com. You need to replace the configuration for DNS to send any unresolved DNS client queries and all external queries to your ISP's DNS server. Which PowerShell cmdlet must you execute to accomplish this objective?

   a. `Add-DNSServerForwarder`

   b. `Add-DNSServerPrimaryZone`

   c. `Set-DNSServerForwarder`

   d. `Set-DNSServerPrimaryZone`

50. Complete the following table:

DNS Record	Description
A	
CNAME	
AAAA	
PTR	
MX	
SRV	

Choices:

a. Alias record.

b. Enables reverse lookups for a host record.

c. A host resource record maps the FQDN of any computer (host) in the domain to its IPv4 address.

d. Identifies the exchange mail server responsible for managing mail flow in your organization.

e. Used by services such as Active Directory Domain Services or applications like Office Communicator use specific protocols that enable communication.

f. This record maps the FQDN of any computer (host) in the domain to its IPv6 address.

51. Your network contains a single Active Directory domain mydomain.com. DC1 exists in your main office and contains all FSMO roles. DC2 is located in a branch site connected via a 10-Mbps WAN link. DC2 does not contain any FSMO roles. After a storm, your WAN link goes down and no users can log on. Which FSMO role must you bring online at a minimum?

a. Infrastructure master

b. Domain naming master

c. PDC emulator

d. RID master

52. You are the administrator for mycompany.com. Mycompany.com consists of 3 domain controllers and 23 Windows Server 2012 R2 member servers. You plan to remove DC3. You need to identify which SRV records are registered by DC3. How can you retrieve this information?

- **a.** Run `ntdsutil.exe /SRV`.
- **b.** Open `SRV.dns` in `%windir%\system32\config`.
- **c.** Open `netlogon.dns` in `%windir%\system32\config`.
- **d.** Run `nslookup /SRV/Server:DC3`.

53. Your network consists of a single Active Directory domain—pearson.com. Currently, two domain controllers exist. DC2 is a Windows Server 2012 domain controller holding the PDC Emulator role. DC1 is a Windows Server 2008 R2 domain controller holding all remaining FSMO roles. You need to install a new Windows Server 2012 R2 file and print server named Server1. You need to perform an offline domain join of Server1. How can you accomplish this?

- **a.** Run `dsadd.exe` to join Server1.
- **b.** Upgrade DC1 to Windows Server 2012.
- **c.** Transfer all FSMO roles to DC2.
- **d.** Run `Djoin.exe` to join Server1.

54. Your network consists of a single Active Directory domain pearson.com. You need to retrieve a list of all servers along with the last time they authenticated with AD DS. Which cmdlet can you use to accomplish this?

- **a.** `Get-ADComputer` and specify the last logon property
- **b.** `Get-ADServer` and specify the last logon property
- **c.** `Get-ADLastLogon`
- **d.** `DSquery ADServers`

55. You are the administrator for pearson.com. You have recently created a new share, Share1, located in the Sales.pearson.com child domain. You grant access to Share1 using a Global Group named SalesUsers. A Domain Local distribution group, Group1, is located in the parent domain person.com. You need to allow members in Group1 to access Share1. What must you do first?

- **a.** Convert Group1 to a universal security group.
- **b.** Convert Group1 to a domain local security group.
- **c.** Convert Group1 to a global distribution group.
- **d.** Convert Group1 to a universal distribution group.

56. As the only network administrator for a pharmaceutical company, Mike is feeling overwhelmed with the increased administrative overhead of supporting the business. The company has recently expanded so Mike decides to bring on a junior administrator. He wants to ensure that the new junior administrator is only able to link and unlink Group Policy objects that he creates to the computers located under the Warehouse OU. Mike uses the Delegation of Control Wizard on the Warehouse OU. Shortly after, Mike needs to make a change to what he has previously delegated. How can Mike view the existing authority for the junior admin and make the necessary changes?

  a. Modify the permissions in the security tab of the Warehouse OU.

  b. Add the junior admin's user account to the domain Admins group.

  c. Add the junior admin's user account to the local Administrators group on all warehouse workstations.

  d. Add the junior admin's user account to the Enterprise Admins group.

57. You work for a company that contains a single Active Directory forest. The forest contains two domains: mydomain.com and sales.mydomain.com. You are the senior systems engineer for mydomain.com. You have recently acquired three new branch sites, each containing a domain controller, file server, and application server. One of the tasks on your plate is to standardize backups across the domain. Part of the solution requires you to ensure that members of the domain group BackupAdmins are added to the local Backup Operators group on all servers in the domain. How can you do this with the least administrative effort?

  a. Log in to each server and add the domain BackupAdmins group to the local Backup Operators group.

  b. Configure a restricted group for mydomain\BackupAdmins.

  c. Configure a restricted group for the local Backup Operators group on each server.

  d. Nest the local Backup Operators group in the mydomain\BackupAdmins group.

58. You work for a company that contains an Active Directory domain named passthetest.com. All domain controllers run Windows Server 2012 with the exception of one legacy Windows Server 2008 domain controller. Your domain consists of 20 Windows Server 2012 member servers located in the Servers OU and 150 Windows 8.1 client workstations located in the Workstations OU. You need to create a group named Group1 on all servers in the domain. No other computer should receive this group. What should you configure?

   a. A Local Users and Groups preferences setting linked to the Servers OU

   b. A Local Users and Groups preferences setting linked to the Domain

   c. A Restricted Groups setting linked to the Domain

   d. A Restricted Groups setting linked to the Servers OU

59. Which PowerShell cmdlet can you use to create a new GPO?

   a. Add-GPO

   b. New-GPO

   c. Set-GPO

   d. DSAdd.exe /NewGPO

60. Your company has hired a new chief security officer. One of her requirements is to ensure that all local administrator accounts receive User Account Control prompts when any elevated tasks are performed. You plan to implement this via a group policy. What is the appropriate location for configuring these policies?

   a. Security Settings\Local Policies

   b. Security Settings\Account Policies

   c. Security Settings\Windows Firewall with Advanced Security

   d. Security Settings\Application control policies

61. You would like to review the default user rights for administering your AD DS domain granted to the various built-in groups in Windows Server 2012, so you open the Group Policy Management Console. What should you do?

   a. Right-click the **Default Domain Policy** GPO and select **Edit**. In the Group Policy Management Editor, navigate to the **Computer Configuration\Policies\Windows Settings\Security Settings\Local Policies\User Rights Assignment node**, and select this node. View the default user rights in the details pane.

   b. Right-click the **Default Domain Policy** GPO and select **Edit**. In the Group Policy Management Editor, navigate to the **User Configuration\Policies\ Windows Settings\Security Settings\ Local Policies\User Rights Assignment** node, and select this node. View the default user rights in the details pane.

   c. Right-click the **Default Domain Controllers Policy** GPO and select **Edit**. In the Group Policy Management Editor, navigate to the **Computer Configuration\Policies\Windows Settings\Security Settings\Local Policies\User Rights Assignment** node, and select this node. View the default user rights in the details pane.

   d. Right-click the Default **Domain Controllers Policy** GPO and select **Edit**. In the Group Policy Management Editor, navigate to the **User Configuration\ Policies\Windows Settings\Security Settings\ Local Policies\User Rights Assignment** node, and select this node. View the default user rights in the details pane.

62. Your domain contains 6 Windows Server 2012 R2 member servers and 80 Windows 8.1workstations. Users perform their work using an in-house application App1.exe. App1 is updated on a monthly basis. Corporate policy mandates that all users must use the latest version of App1.exe. How can you enforce this rule? (Choose two.)

   a. Create a software restriction policy using and application executable rule.

   b. Create a Windows installer rule.

   c. Create an AppLocker rule to restrict older versions of the application.

   d. Use group policy to publish all instances of the application.

63. David has used Windows Firewall with Advanced Security on a Windows Server 2012 R2 computer named Server3 to configure several custom outbound and inbound rules. He would like to copy these rules to another computer named Server4, which also runs Windows Server 2012 R2. What should he do to accomplish this task with the least amount of administrative effort?

    a. Use the `netsh advfirewall dump` command at Server3 to copy the Windows Firewall with Advanced Security rules. Then use the `netsh advfirewall reset` command on Server4 to restore the rules on this computer.

    b. Use the `wbadmin` utility on Server3 to back up the Windows Firewall with Advanced Security rules. Then restore these rules at Server4.

    c. In the Windows Firewall with Advanced Security snap-in on Server3, right-click **Inbound Rules** and select **Export Policy**. After saving the export file, go to Server4, right-click **Inbound Rules**, and select **Import Policy**. Click **Yes**, specify the name of the policy file to be imported, and then click **Open**. Then repeat this procedure with the Outbound Rules node.

    d. In the Windows Firewall with Advanced Security snap-in on Server3, right-click **Windows Firewall with Advanced Security** and select **Export Policy**. After saving the export file, go to Server4, right-click **Windows Firewall with Advanced Security** and select **Import Policy**. Click **Yes**, specify the name of the policy file to be imported, and then click **Open**.

64. You have recently installed a new Windows Server 2012 R2 file server, Server1. You decide to test access from a Windows 8.1 client. You attempt to ping Server1 but receive a Request timed out message. You log on locally to Server1 and confirm that all IP address information is correct. You can successfully ping your default gateway from Server1. You also verify that you can access the Internet and other resources on your network. What should you check?

    a. Verify that the latest service pack is enabled on Server1.

    b. Verify that the Windows Remote Access Service is started.

    c. Verify that the appropriate inbound firewall rule is enabled for Echo Request ICMP.

    d. Verify that the appropriate inbound firewall is enabled for Remote Access.

65. You are the administrator for mycompany.com. Your network consists of 150 Windows 8.1 client computers and 5 Windows Server 2012 R2 member servers. Your development team creates a new application that you need to host on AppServer1, one of the Windows Server 2012 R2 member servers. The application installs a new service that listens on TCP port 5432. Client computers use this service to interact with the application. AppServer1 also sends regular alerts to a monitoring server using TCP port 4567. You notice that clients are unable to access the application hosted on AppServer1. The alerting function appears to be working properly. You realize that you forgot to configure the Windows Firewall rule on AppServer1. What do you need to configure?

   a. An inbound rule to allow connection to TCP port 5432

   b. An inbound rule to allow connections to TCP port 4567

   c. An outbound rule to allow connections to TCP port 4567

   d. An outbound rule to allow connection to TCP port 5432

66. You are a systems administrator for pearson.com. You configure a new Windows Server 2012 R2 member server named Server1. You need to configure a Windows Firewall rule to allow inbound access for a PPTP VPN? Which ports should you enable? (Each answer represents part of the solution. Choose two.)

   a. 1701

   b. 1723

   c. 47

   d. 80

Answers to Practice Exam 1

1. **B.** Server Manager is a Microsoft Management Console (MMC) utility that replaces the Computer Management console found in previous Windows Server versions and adds considerable new management functionality. In particular, it includes the management tools formerly part of the Manage Your Server, Configure Your Server, and Add or Remove Windows Components applications in previous versions of Windows Server. Answer A is incorrect because Microsoft has removed `dcpromo.exe` in Windows Server 2012/2012 R2. Answers C and D are not used to configure the server as a domain controller. These tools are available after the server has been promoted to a domain controller. For more information, refer to "Server Manager" in Chapter 1.

2. **D.** The Remote Desktop Services role provides mobile support and the ability for users to connect to desktops and applications from virtually anywhere. Terminal Server is a legacy term and is not a valid role under Windows Server 2012 R2. File and Storage Services does not meet the needs for this scenario. The Web Server (IIS) role will provide web services and can be used in larger Remote Desktop deployments, but it is not the most correct answer for this scenario. For more information, refer to "Server Roles and Role Migration" in Chapter 1.

3. **C.** Windows Server 2012 R2 Foundation is capable of supporting up to 15 computers and is entirely suitable for this type of installation. The other versions of Windows Server 2012 R2 are designed for more client computers and are more expensive and not required here. For more information, refer to "Windows Server 2012 R2 Editions" in Chapter 1.

4. **A, C, F.** All of these are valid charms available under Windows Server 2012 R2. The Devices and Start charms are also available. All other answers are invalid here. For more information, refer to "The Windows Server 2012 R2 Start Screen and Charms" in Chapter 1.

5. **C.** The `sconfig` command (see figure) enables you to perform basic Server Core configurations such as managing the Domain/Workgroup settings, Computer Name, Local Administrators, Remote Management Settings, Windows Updates, and so on. Although Server Manager will allow you to configure servers remotely, it is more often used to configure roles/features. For basic command-line management `sconfig` is the more appropriate tool to be used in this case. The other choices are invalid. For more information, refer to "Useful Server Core Commands" in Chapter 2.

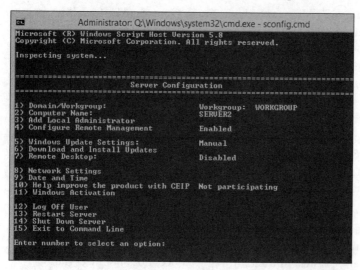

6. **B, C.** To remove the User interfaces on a Full GUI installation, you can remove the feature from another workstation or server using a remote Server Manager session. The removal can also be completed using PowerShell. Answer A might work, but it is not necessary to wipe all data. Windows Server 2012 and 2012 R2 enable you to remove the Feature for the GUI. Answer D is an invalid option. For more information, refer to "Converting Between Core and GUI" in Chapter 2.

7. **A.** The NIC Teaming configuration interface can be accessed from the Server Manager local screen. All other choices are incorrect. For more information, refer to "Configuring NIC Teaming" in Chapter 2.

8. **A, C, D.** The objective here is to minimize cost and to ensure that all servers are Windows Server 2012 R2 in the end state. Server1 contains an x86 processor driving a 32-bit installation of Windows Server 2008. Windows Server 2012 R2 supports only 64-bit installations, so Server1 cannot be upgraded. It must be replaced, so Answer A is correct. Server2 does support both 32- and 64-bit operating systems so no hardware replacement is required, thus Answers B and E are incorrect from a cost standpoint. Currently, Server2

contains Windows Server 2008 32-bit so a clean install is required. As a result, Answer D is correct. Server3 and Server4 can be upgraded directly to Server 2012 R2 without any hardware replacements so Answer C is correct. Answer F will not minimize cost so it is incorrect. Answer G will require some cost but is not necessary per the Microsoft recommended requirements. As a result, Answer G is not a good choice. For more information, refer to "Windows Server 2012 R2 Hardware Requirements" in Chapter 2.

9. **A.** To mount `testimage.wim` to `c:\mountedimages`, issue the command `Dism.exe /Mount-Image /ImageFile:c:\testimages\testimage.wim /Index:1 /MountDir:c:\mountedimage`. All other answers are invalid. The `/Mount` option in Answer B is an invalid option. Answer C is missing the `/ImageFile` option that specifies the location of the image. Answer D uses an invalid option of `/Mount` and is also missing the `/Imagefile` option. For more information, refer to "Deployment Image Servicing and Management" in Chapter 2.

10. **D.** The Performance Monitor Users group provides the ability to monitor performance counters and read performance counter data. Answer A will provide more access than required, so this is not a viable option. Answer B is incorrect as this is an invalid built-in group. Answer C provides the ability to manage and schedule performance counters logs, and alerts on the computer. For more information, refer to "Establishing Delegate Access" in Chapter 2.

11. **B.** The GPT partition style is recommended for disks larger than 2 TB in size and for disks used on Itanium-based computers. Not all previous Windows versions can recognize this disk style, however. When you add a new disk of less than 2 TB size, it is added as an MBR disk. You can convert an MBR disk to a GPT one using either Disk Management or the DiskPart tool, provided there are no partitions or volumes on the disk. Answer A is incorrect because a 3-TB volume cannot be formatted with FAT. Answer C is incorrect because MBR supports only up to 2-TB volumes. Answer D would not help in this situation. For more information, refer to "Configuring MBR and GPT Disks" in Chapter 3.

12. **A.** A parity storage space will be able to take advantage of all four disks to maximize overall storage. Data and parity information is striped across physical disks to protect the storage space from a single disk failure. Answer B will provide the necessary fault tolerance; however, it does not maximize the overall space. Simple storage spaces will maximize storage but not provide any fault tolerance, so Answer C is incorrect. Answer D is incorrect because a spanned volume does not provide fault tolerance. For more information, refer to "Designing Storage Spaces" in Chapter 3.

13. **A.** RAID-0 (striped) volumes contain space on 2–32 separate hard disks. Data is written in 64-KB blocks (stripes) to each disk in the volume, in turn. A striped volume offers considerable improvement in read/write efficiency because the read/write heads on each disk are working together during each I/O operation. A striped volume offers a maximum amount of space equal to the size of the smallest disk multiplied by the number of disks in the volume. However, the striped volume does not offer fault tolerance; if any one disk is lost, the entire volume is lost. Answer B (Mirroring) would be required if you wanted to protect data and were not concerned with slower write performance. Answer C is not a RAID type commonly used today. RAID-5 offers fast read/write performance but also protects data. It is not the best choice to meet the requirements in this scenario. For more information, refer to "RAID Volumes" in Chapter 3.

14. **A.** Kelly should use FSRM to block audio and video files. Alerting will not resolve the issue, so Answer B is incorrect. Reducing the amount of disk space available to each user might prevent them from saving important business data; further, it would not stop them from saving audio or video files, so Answer C is incorrect. It is not possible to modify the quota to disallow the saving of audio or video files, so Answer D is incorrect. For more information, refer to "Understanding the File and Storage Services Role in Windows Server 2012 R2" in Chapter 4.

15. **B.** You should choose the NFS Share–Advanced option. This option enables you to share files with UNIX servers. It also includes configuration of folder owners for access-denied assistance, default classification of data, and the enabling of quotas. You would use SMB sharing options only when sharing data with Windows computers and not UNIX computers so Answers A, C, and E are incorrect. Answer D is incorrect as the Quick option includes basic sharing permissions but not access-denied assistance or quota enabling. For more information, refer to "Creating a Shared Folder" in Chapter 4.

16. **B.** Although NTFS permissions are cumulative such that a user receives the least restrictive permission, an explicit denial of permission overrides all allowed permissions. Therefore, in this scenario, Megan does not have access to the Sales folder. For more information, refer to "NTFS Permissions" in Chapter 4.

17. **A.** To actively notify users that they are reaching their quota limit, you should configure the Set warning level to a specific threshold below the hard quota limit. Answers B and C will take a more active approach to restricting the disk writes. In this scenario, you are asked to enable notifications when users are nearing the limit. Answer D is incorrect because logging an event will log an event log entry but not actively notify users. For more information, refer to "Configuring NTFS Quotas" in Chapter 4.

18. A. To perform the stated tasks on documents produced by all staff members at this printer, Yolanda needs the Manage Documents permission. This permission also allows her to modify document priorities and scheduling, as well as set notifications for users. It does not allow her to control the permissions of other staff or take ownership of print jobs; these tasks require the Manage Printer permission. The Print permission granted to the Designers group does not enable Yolanda to perform the required tasks, so Answer B is incorrect. The Manage Printer permission would enable Yolanda to control the permissions assigned to other task members. Because this is not desired, Answer C is incorrect. The default permission is Print, which does not enable her to perform these tasks, so Answer D is incorrect. For more information, refer to "Security Tab and Printer Permissions" in Chapter 5.

19. D. Branch Office Direct Printing is a new technology included in Windows Server 2012/2012 R2. It was designed to help reduce bandwidth costs, lower server load, and provide resilience for branch site printing. In the event of a WAN link failure, Branch Office Direct Printing allows clients to continue to print directly to the print device through the use of cached printer information. Answer A will have no impact. Answers B and C can be used to support load balancing and backup printing; however, if the WAN link fails, the users will not be able to access the print share. For more information, refer to "Branch Office Direct Printing" in Chapter 5.

20. A. To allow all users to print but ensure that Finance jobs print first, you should create three printers and configure each department to use its respective printer. Each printer will need to be assigned a priority from 1 to 99. The higher the number, the higher the priority, so you must configure the Finance printer with a higher priority than the others. Answer B will ensure that all users can print, but it won't guarantee that Finance jobs are printed first. Answer C will not work as all users will receive the same priority. Answer D will prevent all users except those in Finance from printing. For more information, refer to "Using the Printer Properties Dialog Box" in Chapter 5.

21. A. By using Group Policy to deploy the printer and choosing the option labeled **The computers that this GPO applies to (per machine)**, you can ensure that the printer is available to all computers in the Graphics OU. If you use the **List in the directory** option from either source, the printer will be available everywhere in the domain. If you select the option labeled **The users that this GPO applies to (per user)**, users in the Graphics OU will be able to access the printer from computers in other departments of the company and users in other OUs will not be able to access it when printing from a computer in the Graphics OU. For more information, refer to "Using Group Policy to Deploy Printer Connections" in Chapter 5.

22. **A, B.** Down-level installations can be managed using Server Manager or Remote Server Administration Tools. On each down-level server you want to manage, install the Windows Management Framework 4.0 available from the Microsoft Download Center. Ensure that the latest service pack has been installed for the Windows Server 2008 installations. Lastly, ensure .NET Framework 4.5 has been installed on each down-level server. Answers C and D are incorrect because you do not need to install these on the source management server. Answer E is incorrect because no instance exists where you would want to remove a service pack from a server, and Answer F would not make a difference in this scenario For more information, refer to "Configuring Down-Level Server Management" in Chapter 6.

23. **C.** To confirm WinRM functionality, use the `Test-WsMan [remote computer]` command. Answer A is incorrect because the `Winrs` command is used to remotely execute commands on a remote server. The syntax is `Winrs -r:Servername [command]`. Answer B is invalid. The `Enable-PSremoting -Force` command is used to enable remote management on down-level servers. Answer D contains an invalid switch, `-Test`, for the `WinRM` command. For more information, refer to "Windows Remote Shell (WinRS)" in Chapter 6.

24. **C.** By enabling Dynamic Memory on each virtual machine, Hyper-V will redistribute available memory depending on which virtual machine is requesting it. Bob can modify the settings of each virtual machine to the enable Dynamic Memory. All other answers are incorrect. For more information, refer to "Configuring Dynamic Memory" in Chapter 7.

25. **C.** To ensure that your virtual machine boots to PXE, you should modify the startup order under the BIOS setting. Much like a physical computer, Hyper-V enables you to specific the startup or boot order for drives, removable media, and whether the VM should boot using PXE. Answers A and B are incorrect. Answer D might work if all other boot devices are also disabled, leaving only PXE as the viable option. Because we can't assume this, Answer D is not correct. For more information, refer to "Virtual Machine Settings" in Chapter 7.

26. **C.** Guest Integration Services is a suite of tools that can be installed after the guest operating system has been configured. Integration Services are designed to optimize the performance of a virtual machine. Upon installation, generic operating system drivers for keyboard, video, mouse, network, disk controllers, and so on are replaced with versions optimized for Hyper-V. Guest Integration Services allows for host-based snapshot backups through the use of the Shadow Copy service. For more information, refer to "Configuring Guest Integration Services" in Chapter 7.

27. **B.** Hyper-V Resource Metering provides a simple, streamlined solution for gathering this type of data. Windows Server 2012 R2 allows Hyper-V administrators to retrieve historical data on the usage of virtual machine resources. To enable resource metering, issue the cmdlet `Enable-VMResourceMetering`. For more information, refer to "Configuring Resource Metering" in Chapter 7.

28. **A.** To create a pass-through disk, the local storage must be offline for the virtual machine to access it. None of the other answers are correct. For more information, refer to "Configuring Pass-Through Disks" in Chapter 8.

29. **A.** Differencing disks are helpful if you need to share the same data set, rather contents of a specific virtual hard disk file with multiple virtual machines. The shared data can be stored on the parent disk that is then available to all virtual machines configured with a differencing disk. None of the other answers will meet the requirement of sharing the contents of a virtual hard disk between multiple virtual machines. For more information, refer to "Differencing Disks" in Chapter 8.

30. **B.** In this case, Dave is reusing an existing server. The server is upgraded to meet the needs of the new project. To successfully split virtual machines between two virtual switches, Dave must first break the existing NIC Team and reconfigure it. Without this, Hyper-V will recognize one logical NIC to be used to connect virtual machines to a virtual switch. If a choice existed to install a new network interface card, this can present a viable solution. Answer A is incorrect. Answer C might be required down the road, but it will not help the situation here. Answer D is incorrect because all existing adapters are already joined to a NIC Team. For more information, refer to "Configuring Virtual Network Switches" in Chapter 9.

31. **B.** The legacy network adapter uses a legacy driver to support legacy operating systems. It offers the most compatibility but is limited in functionality. These adapters perform much slower and are unable to take advantage of bandwidth throttling or hardware acceleration capabilities. To implement bandwidth throttling, it is necessary to remove the legacy network adapter and install an up-to-date network adapter. None of the other choices will accomplish this. For more information, refer to "Configuring Virtual Network Adapters" in Chapter 9.

32. **D.** DHCP Guard is used to block rogue DHCP servers. This setting drops DHCP server messages from unauthorized virtual machines. Answer A is incorrect because MAC Address Spoofing is used when you need to specify a specific MAC address for a virtual machine. It is not used to block rogue DHCP servers. Answer B is used to block rogue routers from sending advertisements to the virtual machine. Answer C is used to monitor network traffic sent to/from virtual machines. For more information, refer to "Advanced Adapter Features" in Chapter 9.

33. C. The requirement here is to ensure that virtual machines are only able to talk to each other. This indicates that you do not want them to be able to talk to the host HyperV1. By removing and re-creating the virtual switch as a private switch type, you enable connectivity between one virtual machine and others on the same physical server. This configuration does not allow communication between the virtual machine and the host operating system. Answer A would not have an impact in this scenario. Answer B would isolate the Windows Server 2008 virtual machines from the Windows Server 2012 R2 virtual machines, thus not meeting the requirement for enabling all of the VMs to be able to communicate with each other. Answer D would allow the virtual machines to communicate, but the public switch type would also enable communication with other virtual machines and devices external to the virtual switch. For this reason, Answer D is incorrect. For more information, refer to "Network Virtualization Components" in Chapter 9.

34. C. In the case of a shared cloud-based solution, Hyper-V Network Virtualization enables you to further isolate virtual machines at the port level on the virtual switch. This allows you to isolate specific customer traffic, isolate specific customer virtual machines, and allow customers to use the same IP Address ranges without overlapping or impacting other customers or virtual machines. The mechanism responsible for this is known as Port Virtual Local Area Network (PVLAN). All other answers are invalid options. For more information, refer to "Using PVLANs for Isolation" in Chapter 9.

35. C. The purpose of subnetting is always to make more networks available by altering the subnet mask applied to a network ID. This is done by borrowing bits from the host ID and assigning them to the network ID. After this is done there are more networks available with fewer hosts on each network. Of the choices available the subnet mask 255.255.255.240 borrows the fewest number of bits, while still providing for 14 networks. Hence, it provides the most hosts. Valid subnet masks for a Class C address that can create appropriate combinations of subnets and hosts include the following:

Subnet Mask	Networks	Hosts
255.255.255.192	2	62
255.255.255.224	6	30
255.255.255.240	14	14
255.255.255.248	30	6

Subnet masks ending in 192 or 224 do not provide enough networks to fit this scenario, so Answers A and B are incorrect. A subnet mask ending in 248 provides enough networks but does not provide the maximum possible hosts within a single network, so Answer D is incorrect. For more information, refer to "Subnetting and Supernetting in IPv4" in Chapter 10.

36. **D.** Neil should manually edit the TCP/IP properties on each client computer. More specifically, he needs to select the **Obtain DNS server address automatically** option on the General tab of the Internet Protocol version 4 (TCP/IPv4) Properties dialog box. The most likely reason that clients remain configured to use a DNS server other that the one specified in the scope for their subnet is that they have been previously configured manually with DNS information. Scope information will not override information that has been manually configured for a client computer, even when that computer has been configured as a DHCP client and has been restarted properly. The `ipconfig /release` and `ipconfig /renew` commands are designed to reset any TCP/IP configurations that have been applied to DHCP client computers, but these commands won't reset manual configurations, so Answer A is incorrect. Typically, the options 006 for DNS Servers and 015 for Domain Name need to be specified in a scope designed to configure DNS options for such clients. If Neil needed to enable certain computers on the subnet to use a different DNS server from what all other computers use, he might consider configuring an advanced user class option. He can apply those types of options using the command `ipconfig /setclassid` at each client computer to set DHCP class ID information for those computers. Nothing in the question suggests that this requirement exists in this instance, so Answers B and C are incorrect. Isolating the subnet does not make sense because the problem would not be solved when he eventually reconnects the subnet to the rest of the network, so Answer E is incorrect. For more information, refer to "Configuring IPv4 Address Options" and "Using TCP/IP Utilities to Troubleshoot TCP/IP" in Chapter 10.

37. **B.** The subnet mask required must support 600 hosts, 450 today and another 150 in the future. A 255.255.252.0 or /22 subnet mask will allow you assign IP addresses to 1,022 hosts. Answer A is incorrect because a /23 subnet mask will accommodate only 510 hosts. Although it might work today, you would not have enough addresses to accommodate future growth. Answer C will not meet the requirement of limiting the amount of wasted addresses. Answer D will accommodate only 254 hosts on the subnet.

Dotted Decimal Subnet Mask	CIDR Notation	Number of Subnets	Number of Hosts per Subnet
255.255.128.0	/17	2	32766
255.255.192.0	/18	4	16382
255.255.224.0	/19	8	8190
255.255.240.0	/20	16	4094
255.255.248.0	/21	32	2046
255.255.252.0	/22	64	1022
255.255.254.0	/23	128	510
255.255.255.0	/24	256	254

For more information, refer to "Subnetting and Supernetting in IPv4" in Chapter 10.

38. Answer:

IPv6 Class	IPv6 Address Prefix
Global unicast	b. 2000::/3
Link-Local unicast	e. fe80::/64
Unique local IPv6 unicast	c. fc00::/7
Multicast	d. Ff

For more information, refer to "IPv6 Addressing" in Chapter 10.

39. **D.** Answer D is a unique local IPv6 unicast address class. This can be identified by a few things. First, the first 7 bits are all 1s; the eighth bit is also a 1, which is the local (L) flag. The next 40 bits are 02:cde6:1208 and represent a global network ID, which is a randomly generated site-specific value. The 16-bit subnet ID has a value of 0009; its use is for further subnetting the internal network in an analogous manner to the IPv4 subnetting. Finally, the last 64 bits are 0:0:0:f92b, which specifies the unique host interface ID. Again, the 0s are represented by the double-colon. For more information, refer to "Types of IPv6 Addresses" in Chapter 10.

40. **D.** 255.255.128.0 meets this requirement. None of the other answers provide enough hosts to meet this requirement.

Dotted Decimal Subnet Mask	CIDR Notation	Number of Subnets	Number of Hosts per Subnet
255.255.128.0	/17	2	32766
255.255.192.0	/18	4	16382
255.255.224.0	/19	8	8190
255.255.240.0	/20	16	4094
255.255.248.0	/21	32	2046
255.255.252.0	/22	64	1022
255.255.254.0	/23	128	510
255.255.255.0	/24	256	254

For more information, refer to "Subnetting and Supernetting in IPv4" in Chapter 10.

41. **D.** Ruby should set the Conflict Detection value to 1. When this parameter is set to a nonzero value, the DHCP server uses the `ping` utility to test an IP address before leasing it to a client; the value represents the number of times the server performs this test. The value can range from 0 to 6; higher values perform a more thorough test at the expense of server resources. The DHCP option 47 refers to the NetBIOS scope ID. Hosts can communicate only with other hosts configured with the same scope ID. This value is irrelevant to the situation here, so Answers A and B are incorrect. If the Conflict Detection value is set to 0 (which is the default), the DHCP server does not check for IP address conflicts. This would allow DHCP clients to receive IP addresses that have already been leased to other clients, so answer C is incorrect. For more information, refer to "Monitoring and Troubleshooting a DHCP Server" in Chapter 11.

42. **B.** DHCP Option 003 Router is used to specify the IP address of the default gateway. The default gateway allows users to reach destinations outside of their local subnet. None of the other options would resolve this issue. For more information, refer to "Configuring DHCP Options" in Chapter 11.

43. **B.** In an AD DS domain, you must authorize the DHCP server in Active Directory before it can lease IP addresses. This is to prevent rogue DHCP servers from leasing improper IP addresses that would result in communication problems. When a domain controller or member server running DHCP starts up, it queries AD DS for the list of authorized servers as identified by their IP addresses. If its IP address is not present on this list, the DHCP Server service does not complete its startup sequence. For more information, refer to "Authorizing a DHCP Server in Active Directory" in Chapter 11.

44. **C, D, E, G.** The messages sent are Advertise, Request, Solicit, and Reply. These correspond to the DHCPDISCOVER, DHCPOFFER, DHCPRE-QUEST, and DHCPACK messages sent when requesting an IPv4 address lease. The Confirm message is sent by a client to all servers to determine the validity of a client's configuration, so Answer F is incorrect. The other options mentioned do not exist with DHCPv6. For more information, refer to "The Four-Phase DHCP IPv4 Leasing Process" and "How DHCPv6 Works" in Chapter 11.

45. **C.** With the release of Windows Server 2008 R2, Microsoft included a DHCP Filter function. Today, administrators can continue to take advantage of this function under Windows Server 2012 R2. Using the filter, you can specify a MAC address or range and allow or deny IP address assignment on the network. For more information, refer to "DHCP Filters" in Chapter 11.

46. **B.** Ellen should create an Active Directory-integrated zone named Global-Names. Add host (A) resource records for all computers that require single name resolution. This action is suitable in a situation such as this one where WINS is being retired. This zone must be Active Directory-integrated; a secondary zone will not suffice, so Answer A is incorrect. SRV resource records enable Ellen to specify parameters such as Service, Protocol, Weight, and Port Number for a service running on the network. CNAME resource records enable Ellen to define aliases for servers on the network. Neither of these record types enables single-name resolution, so Answers C and D are incorrect. For more information, refer to "GlobalNames Zone for Single-Label Resolution" in Chapter 12.

47. **A, C.** The DNS Root hints configuration can be viewed by opening the cache. dns file with `notepad.exe`. They can also be viewed via the Properties dialog box using the DNS Server console. All other choices are incorrect. For more information, refer to "Root Hints Tab" in Chapter 12.

48. **B.** Forwarding refers to the relaying of a DNS request from one server to another one when the first server is unable to process the request. This is especially useful in resolving Internet names to their associated IP addresses. By using an external forwarder, the internal DNS server passes off the act of locating an external resource. For more information, refer to "Forwarders Tab" in Chapter 12.

49. **C.** To clear and set a DNS server forwarder, issue the cmdlet `Set-DNSServerForwarder`. Answer A will add a new forwarder but not replace the configuration. Answer B is the command used to add a new Primary DNS Zone, so it will not help in this situation. Answer D will modify an existing setting on a Primary DNS Zone, so it will not accomplish this objective. For more information, refer to "Using PowerShell for DNS Server Administration" in Chapter 12.

50. Answer:

DNS Record	Description
A	C. A host resource record maps the FQDN of any computer (host) in the domain to its IPv4 address.
CNAME	A. Alias record.
AAAA	F. This record maps the FQDN of any computer (host) in the domain to its IPv6 address.
PTR	B. Enables reverse lookups for a host record.
MX	D. Identifies the exchange mail server responsible for managing mail flow in your organization.
SRV	E. Used by services such as Active Directory Domain Services or applications like Office Communicator use specific protocols that enable communication.

For more information, refer to "Configuring Common Resource Records" in Chapter 12.

51. **C.** The PDC emulator is probably one of the more critical roles. It serves as a primary domain controller (PDC) for legacy servers such as Windows NT 4.0 client computers authenticating to the domain. Today, the PDC emulator functions to handle daily operations such as logons, directory maintenance such as object changes, or even password changes. This server also acts as a time synchronization master to synchronize the time on the remaining domain controllers in the domain. The infrastructure master role is used to ensure that domain objects are able to be referenced between domains. For this reason, Answer A is incorrect. The domain naming master ensures that any newly created domains are uniquely identified and adhere to proper naming conventions so Answer B is incorrect. Lastly, Answer C is incorrect as the RID master role is responsible for assigning security identifiers (SIDs) to objects created in the domain. For more information, refer to "Physical Components of Active Directory" in Chapter 13.

52. **C.** For proper functionality, domain controllers register Service Locator (SRV) records. SRV records identify proper locations for domain controllers, AD sites, global catalog servers, Kerberos authentication parameters, and so on. Without these records, Active Directory would not function properly. You can confirm SRV records within DNS or via the `netlogon.dns` file. The `netlogon.dns` file is located under `%windir%\system32\config\`. All other answers are invalid. For more information, refer to "Verifying the Proper Installation of Active Directory" in Chapter 13.

53. D. You can use the `Djoin.exe` command-line tool from an administrative command account to enable the computer to join the domain offline. This command provisions the computer account metadata by creating a `.txt` file and inserts this information into the Windows directory of the computer being joined to the domain. You can also save the metadata into an `Unattend.xml` file for unattended operating system installation. Answer A is incorrect as `dsadd.exe` cannot perform an offline join. None of the other answers will accomplish this task. For more information, refer to "Offline Domain Join" in Chapter 14.

54. A. You can use the `Get-ADComputer` cmdlet to retrieve information about one or more AD computers, its properties, or even its attributes. It can be used with a filter to retrieve a list of specific attributes such as `LastLogonDate`, `LogonHours`, and so on. The basic syntax is `Get-ADComputer "Computer1" -Properties`. All other answers are invalid. For more information, refer to "Using Bulk Import to Automate Account Creation" in Chapter 14.

55. A. Because of the rules of group nesting, you must first convert Group1 to a universal security group. Group1 is currently a distribution group used for distribution lists. It needs to be a security group type, thus Answers C and D are incorrect. It should be converted to either a global or universal type because domain local groups are not added to global groups. Global groups can be added to domain local, but not vice versa. For this reason, Answer B is incorrect. For more information, refer to "Creating and Managing Group Accounts" in Chapter 15.

56. A. To modify what was previously delegated, Mike can modify the assigned permissions under the security tab of the Warehouse OU. For more information, refer to "Delegation of Active Directory Object Management" in Chapter 15.

57. B. To ensure that the domain group BackupAdmins is added to all local Backup Operators groups, you can use a group policy and configure a restricted group. Answer A would work, but it does not meet the requirement of least administrative effort. Answers C and D are incorrect. For more information, refer to "Configure Restricted Groups via Group Policy" in Chapter 16.

58. A. Released under Windows 8/ Server 2008 R2 and still used today under Windows 8.1 and Server 2012 R2, Group Policy allows local users and groups to be managed centrally using the Local Users and Groups Extension located under Computer/User Configuration>Preferences>Control Panel Settings>Local Users and Groups. Administrators can create, delete, rename, modify membership, and change passwords for local users and groups. Restricted groups will not create new local groups so Answers C and D are incorrect. The requirement is to add the group to only servers. Answer B would create the group; however, it will be applied to all workstations and servers in the domain. For this reason, Answer B is incorrect. For more information, refer to "Local Users and Groups Extension" in Chapter 16.

59. **B.** To create a new GPO using PowerShell, issue the cmdlet `New-GPO –Name MyGPO -comment "This is my GPO"`. Use the `-StarterGPOName` switch to create a new GPO from a Starter GPO. All other answers are incorrect. For more information, refer to "Using Windows PowerShell" in Chapter 16.

60. **A.** You can modify User Account Control settings using Group Policy under Security Settings\Local Policies\Security Options. You can also configure these settings via Control Panel under User Accounts and System and Security\Action Center. Although the other answers allow you to configure different security settings, UAC is available only under the Local Policies section. For more information, refer to "Configuring User Account Control" in Chapter 17.

61. **C.** You should right-click the **Default Domain Controllers Policy GPO** and select **Edit**. In the Group Policy Management Editor, navigate to the **Computer Configuration\Policies\Windows Settings\Security Settings\ Local Policies\User Rights Assignment** node and select this node. View the default user rights in the details pane. The Default Domain Policy GPO does not include any default user rights. User rights are defined according to the computers at which the users will be performing these actions, and not to users themselves; consequently, no user rights are defined in the User Configuration branch of the Group Policy Management Editor. For more information, refer to "Configuring User Rights Assignment" in Chapter 17.

62. **A, C.** You can control applications by using Software Restriction Policies or AppLocker Rules. For more information, refer to "Configuring Software Restriction Policies" and "Configuring AppLocker Rules" in Chapter 18.

63. **D.** David can export Windows Firewall with Advanced Security rules for use on another computer by using the Export Policy command, which is available by right-clicking **Windows Firewall with Advanced Security** and selecting **Export Policy**. He can then import the rules to another computer by using the **Import Policy** command in a similar fashion. The `netsh advfirewall dump` command does not produce the required output, so Answer A is incorrect. (Note, however, that David could use the `netsh advfirewall export` and `netsh advfirewall import` commands to export the rules from Server3 and import them to Server4; these perform the same tasks as the right-click commands mentioned here). It might be possible to back up the rules using `wbadmin`, but this would be more complex and difficult to perform than using the Export Policy and Import Policy commands, so Answer B is incorrect.

The right-click menus available for the Inbound Rules and Outbound Rules nodes in the Windows Firewall with Advanced Security snap-in do not contain **Export Policy** and **Import Policy** options, so Answer C is incorrect. For more information, refer to "Exporting and Importing Firewall Settings" in Chapter 19.

64. **C.** In this scenario, you have confirmed the appropriate IP address, subnet mask, and default gateway. By default, Windows Server 2012 R2 blocks Echo Request ICMP (ping). To fix this, you must ensure that the proper inbound firewall rule has been established. For more information, refer to "Using the Windows Firewall with Advanced Security Snap-in" in Chapter 19.

65. **A.** The Windows Firewall rule set for AppServer1 is missing the inbound rule for client connections destined for TCP port 5432. Answer B is incorrect as AppServer1 does not host any services that listen on port TCP 4567. There are no connection attempts being made to this port, so an inbound rule is not needed. Answer C is incorrect because the alerting function is working properly. Alerts are generated from AppServer1 and are sent outbound to a monitoring server. This function is working properly, so there isn't an issue with the outbound firewall rule. Answer D is incorrect as TCP 5432 is a listening service on AppServer1. Clients communicate to this port so this would require an inbound rule from AppServer1's perspective. For more information, refer to "Configuring Windows Firewall Using PowerShell" and "Configuring Security Rules" in Chapter 19.

66. **B, C.** Two of the common Virtual Private Network protocols are PPTP and L2TP. Answer B is correct because Point-to-Point Tunneling Protocol (PPTP) uses TCP 1723. Although Answer A is the correct port for Layer 2 Tunneling Protocol (L2TP), this scenario stated that PPTP is being used. For this reason, Answer A is incorrect. Answer C is also correct as Windows Server 2012 R2 VPN connections also might require the use of Generic Routing Encapsulation (GRE), which uses TCP 47. Answer D is incorrect because TCP 80 is used for HTTP. For more information, refer to "Configuring Inbound Rules our Outbound Rules" in Chapter 19.

Answers to the "Do I Know This Already?" Quizzes

Chapter 1

1. **A.** Windows Server 2012 R2 Foundation is capable of supporting up to 15 computers and is entirely suitable for this type of installation. The other versions of Windows Server 2012 R2 are designed for more client computers and are more expensive and not needed here.

2. **D.** The complete Windows 8.1 shell with access to the Windows Store requires the Desktop Experience installation option in Windows Server 2012 R2. None of the other installation options provide this facility.

3. **C, D.** The charms are available in either the Server with a GUI or the Desktop Experience installation option in Windows Server 2012 R2. The other options do not provide the charms.

4. **A, B, C, D, E.** You can perform all of these tasks and many others from Server Manager in Windows Server 2012 R2.

5. **B.** Clean install is the best option in this scenario. A clean installation followed by data migration will reduce the administration overhead. Answer A is incorrect as there are no direct upgrade paths from Server 2003 to 2012 R2. Answer C is not the best option here. You would need to perform several upgrades for each server to step it up to 2012 R2. Answer D is not a valid option.

6. **E.** Windows Deployment Services is the role that allows for the creation, management, and deployment of images.

7. **B.** Hyper-V is the role responsible for server virtualization and management.

8. **D.** Active Directory Domain Services is the role responsible for installing and managing Active Directory.

9. **B, C.** Windows features can be removed through the manage menu available within Server Manager as well as via PowerShell cmdlets.

10. **B.** The syntax for the cmdlet to remove an installed feature is `Uninstall-WindowsFeature <feature name> -Remove`. To remove the graphical interface and infrastructure management features, issue the command `Uninstall-WindowsFeature Server-Gui-Mgmt-Infra -Remove`.

Chapter 2

1. **A.** You require at least a 1.4 GHz processor on your computer to install Windows Server 2012 R2. The computer meets the other minimum hardware requirements. Note that in a production server, you should have much higher hardware capabilities than the minima so that users have no difficulty in accessing files, folders, and applications on your server.

2. **A, C, D, E, F.** You do not need to disconnect USB devices. However, you should perform all other tasks listed here before installing Windows Server 2012 R2.

3. **B.** The `Get-WindowsFeature PowerShell` cmdlet enables you to obtain a list of server roles and features installed on a Windows Server 2012 R2 Server Core computer. `sconfig.cmd` enables you to configure and manage several aspects of a Server Core computer but not server roles or features. The other commands given here were all used in Windows Server 2008 but are no longer supported.

4. **D.** You should run the `Uninstall-WindowsFeature Server-Gui-Shell` command to convert the server to the minimal server interface mode. The `Uninstall-WindowsFeature Desktop-Experience` command converts the server to Server Core mode, which does not enable the Server Manager interface. The other two commands listed are invalid.

5. **C.** Delegating administrative responsibilities will help divide up the administrative and support workload for an organization. Answer A would enable administrators to manage servers remotely; however, it would further increase the overhead to support servers in the organization. Answers B and D would not help in this situation.

6. **B.** Adding the technicians' user account to the Performance Monitors Users group will satisfy this requirement. It will provide him with the ability to read and monitor performance data but not enable him to make any changes to configurations of the Performance Logging levels or any other administrative function.

7. **C.** Creating a custom configuration using PowerShell Desired State Configuration will provide a configuration baseline used to deploy standard configurations using PowerShell across all the servers specified. Answer A would be a repeatable process, but it would increase administrative overhead and might not guarantee accuracy. Answer B would create identical images and would simplify deployments, but any existing configurations, applications, or data would be replaced with the contents of the image. Answer D would be inefficient and would result in lost data.

8. **A, C, D, E.** Remote Install Services is an invalid service so it is not possible to perform this function during an offline services. Scanning and removing virus threats is not possible with offline servicing of an image.

9. **A, B, C.** These are the only three valid methods for actively adding servers to Server Manager. Server Manager does not provide the ability to add servers by scanning a subnet so Answer D is incorrect. MMC and RDP are not related to the process of adding servers to Server Manager, so Answers E and F are incorrect.

10. **B, D.** These are the only two methods listed that allow you to manage services on local or remote computers. Services Manager for Windows is not a valid tool in Windows Server 2012 R2, so Answer A is incorrect. Remote Desktop Services is not used to manage services on local or remote servers, so Answer C is incorrect.

11. **C.** The `New-NetLbfoTeam` command is the proper syntax for creating a new NIC Team. Reinstalling the operating system is not required to create a NIC team, so Answer A is incorrect. Answer B will remove the NIC team. Answer D is an invalid command.

Chapter 3

1. **B.** Storage spaces configured to use parity will provide fault tolerance for a three-drive configuration.

2. **A, D.** Dynamic disks are used to create a mirrored volume as well as other RAID configurations. Choices B and C are used with basic disks.

3. **B.** The GPT partition type must be used with partitions over 2 TB.

4. **D.** RAID 5 offers both fast read access and protection against a single drive failure.

5. **B.** .VHDX will enable you to create virtual hard disks over 2 TB in size.

6. **C.** .VHD formatting enables backward compatibility with Windows Server 2008.

7. **B.** `DiskPart` is the command-line tool used to mount and dismount virtual disks.

8. **C.** File and Storage Services is used to create and manage storage pools.

9. **A.** The name of the default storage pool containing a listing of physical disks installed on your server is the primordial pool.

10. **B, D.** To satisfy this requirement, you must first create a storage pool using File and Storage Services. Because you require 700 GB total storage, you will need to use all four 200-GB drives to pool enough storage. To ensure that

both applications have enough storage and that neither application interferes with the other, you will need to create two virtual disks. Each virtual disk should be configured with fixed provisioning. This will prevent either application from overconsuming storage from the pool.

Chapter 4

1. **E.** You should choose the **NFS Share–Advanced** option. This option enables you to share files with UNIX servers. It also includes configuration of folder owners for access-denied assistance, default classification of data, and the enabling of quotas. You would use SMB sharing options only when sharing data with Windows computers and not UNIX computers. The **Quick** option includes basic sharing permissions but not access-denied assistance or quota enabling.

2. **A, C, E.** You can specify any of Read, Change, or Full Control shared folder permissions. The Modify and Read and Execute permissions are NTFS security permissions; they are not shared folder permissions.

3. **B.** You would use the `net share` command to create a shared folder from the Server Core version of Windows Server 2012 R2. There is no such command as `share`. The `net user` command enables you to create or modify user accounts but not share folders. The `netsh` command provides a variety of subcommands useful for networking configuration but not folder sharing.

4. **E.** You should assign the Read and Execute permission to enable users to view files and run programs in the folder. The Full Control permission and Modify permission would enable users to edit or delete files in the folder. The Read permission does not enable them to run programs. The Change permission is a shared folder permission only.

5. **C.** The **All files and programs that users open from the shared folder are automatically available offline** option makes every file in the share available for caching by a remote user. When a user opens a file from the share, the file is downloaded to the client's cache and replaces any older versions of the file. The **Only the files and programs that users specify will be available offline** option requires that users specifically indicate which files are to be available. The **Enable BranchCache** option enables a branch office computer to serve files to other branch office client computers. The **Optimize for performance** option improves performance, but only on computers running Windows XP or older versions of Windows.

6. **C, D, G.** The new Work Folders role service in Windows Server 2012 R2 enables users to access work-related documents across the Internet without need for a VPN connection. Neither Offline Files nor BranchCache enable

this connectivity, so answers A and B are incorrect. For Work Folders to function properly, a server certificate is required for the file server. However, client certificates are not required, so answer E is incorrect. To make the proper connection, users must configure their work email address or file server URL in the Work Folders Control Panel applet; because this applet is present on Windows 8.1 computers, it is not necessary to install client software, so answer F is incorrect.

7. **D.** Although NTFS permissions are cumulative such that a user receives the least restrictive permission, an explicit denial of permission overrides all allowed permissions. Therefore, in this scenario, Alice does not have access to the Documents folder.

8. **B, C, D, F.** The Read NTFS permission consists of the List folder/read data attributes, Read attributes, Read extended attributes, and Read special access permissions. The Traverse folder/execute file permission is included in the Read and Execute or higher basic NTFS permission; the Delete permission is included in the Modify or higher basic NTFS permission; and the Take ownership permission is included in the Full Control basic NTFS permission only.

9. **A.** Because all NTFS permissions are inherited, permissions granted to the Documents folder are by default inherited by the Specifications folder. So that members of the Interns group do not receive the permission to modify contents of this folder, you must remove the inherited permission by selecting the **Remove all inherited permissions from this object** option. If you select the **Convert inherited permissions into explicit permissions on this object** option, members of the Interns group receive the inherited permissions and members of the Interns group can modify this folder. If you deny the Full Control permission to members of the Interns group, they will be unable to access the contents of this folder. If you don't do anything, members of the Interns group can modify the contents of the folder by way of the inherited permission.

10. **C.** If a shared folder has both shared folder and NTFS permissions assigned to it and a user accesses this folder across the network, the most restrictive permission is the effective permission. Therefore, in this scenario, Peter has Read permission on the Documents folder.

11. **A.** When a user accesses a shared folder on the same computer on which it is located, the shared folder permission does not apply and the user receives only the NTFS permission that has been assigned to the folder. Therefore, in this scenario, Fred has Full Control permission on the Documents folder.

12. **C.** To configure a share to be hidden from network browsing, append $ at the end of the share name.

13. **B.** If your server has a higher disk I/O load, enabling VSS can further degrade performance due to a higher I/O load. To help with this, you can configure shadow copies to occur less frequently or even after hours if necessary.

14. **D.** To control storage on your file server, you can introduce NTFS Quotas. To do this, you can use File Server Resource Manager or File Explorer to enable NTFS Quotas. All other answers will not satisfy this requirement.

15. **C.** To actively notify users who are reaching their quota limits, you should configure the Set warning level to a specific threshold below the hard quota limit. Logging an event will log an event log entry but not actively notify users.

Chapter 5

1. **D.** It is important to remember that in Microsoft terminology, the printer is the software (logical) interface between the operating system and the physical print device. Microsoft refers to the physical (hardware) device that produces the printed output as the print device. The program that converts graphics commands into instructions is called the print driver, and the computer that controls the printing process on the network is referred to as the print server.

2. **B.** The act of copying a print job to a reserved area within the system root folder of the computer before being sent to the print device is known as spooling. Doing so can improve performance by eliminating the print device as a bottleneck that ties up the operating system or an application until the entire print job is output by the print device. There is no such an action as preprinting. An EMF is the rendering of the print job by the graphics device interface (GDI) and the print driver before spooling takes place. The print router (not to be confused with a network router) is a program that routes a print job to the appropriate print processor component of the local provider or to a remote print server for processing on a network printer.

3. **A, E.** You can use either the Print Management snap-in or Control Panel Devices and Printers to install a printer on the network. None of the other tools mentioned here enable you to install a printer, either on the local computer or across the network.

4. **B.** When print jobs come out with unintelligible characters, this means that the print driver is incorrect. Computers running different versions of Windows, such as Windows XP, 7, 8, or 8.1 might use different drivers. The Additional Drivers dialog box lets you install a driver that enables Windows XP users to print their documents properly. The Render print jobs on client computers option transfers the processing load of rendering print jobs to the client computers (rather than the print server); however, this does not fix the

problem encountered here. Granting users the Manage Documents permission or adding a new printer also will not solve this problem.

5. **D.** By using Group Policy to deploy the printer and choosing the option labeled **The computers that this GPO applies to (per machine)**, you can ensure that the printer is available to all computers in the Graphics OU. If you use the **List in the directory** option from either source, the printer will be available everywhere in the domain. If you select the option labeled **The users that this GPO applies to (per user)**, users in the Graphics OU will be able to access the printer from computers in other departments of the company and users in other OUs will not be able to access it when printing from a computer in the Graphics OU.

6. **B.** A benefit of Branch Office Direct Printing is that it allows clients to continue to print if the print server is offline.

7. **C.** By configuring the option to Use Terminal Services Easy Print, printer driver first allows your servers to use the Easy Print driver whenever possible. If a driver is not present, the server will attempt to locate a more suitable driver.

8. **D.** The Ports tab of the printer's Properties dialog box enables you to redirect a printer if a problem occurs with its print device and you need to take it offline for maintenance. By specifying the UNC path to the other printer as described in the option, all print jobs are automatically redirected to the other printer. You would use printer pooling to enable multiple print devices with a single printer but not to redirect print jobs. Renaming shared printers will not cause existing print jobs to be redirected.

9. **C.** By configuring a second printer with a priority of 99 and granting only the boss permission to print documents to this printer, she can ensure that her documents are printed promptly. Consequently, it is not necessary to ask her secretary to come in at 7 a.m. to print the documents. She could print her documents more promptly by clicking **Cancel All Documents** before printing the document, provided she is granted the Manage Documents permission; however, this would make her very unpopular with all the other users who would need to resubmit their print jobs. There is no such permission as Prioritize Documents.

10. **A.** The Printer Migration Wizard enables you to migrate all printer settings for each printer from one server to another. This includes print queues, printer settings, printer ports, and language monitors and enables you to consolidate multiple print servers as being done in this scenario. You might be able to accomplish this task using Windows Server Backup, but this is less convenient and takes more administrative effort. Simply moving the spooler file from each old print server to the new server will not accomplish the objective

of this task. You could reinstall each printer at the new print server, but this would take far more effort and in itself would not copy over any customized printer-specific settings that you might have configured in the past.

11. **D.** Printer driver isolation enables you to configure printer driver components to run in an isolated process that improves the reliability of the Windows print service by preventing a faulty printer driver from stopping all print operations on the print server. You can enable driver isolation by selecting the **Set Driver Isolation > Isolated** option. It would be possible to restore the laser printers by installing them to a different print server, but that would take more administrative effort. Because the print drivers run in the same process as the spooler, rolling back the drivers in Device Manager would not restore the laser printers. The **None** option disables driver isolation and does not solve this problem.

12. **A.** You should access the Security tab of the Print Server Properties dialog box and add Evelyn to list of usernames or group names. Then select the **View Server, Print, Manage Documents**, and **Manage Printer** permissions under the Allow column. By granting Evelyn these permissions, you delegate to her the ability to manage print queues without granting her excess administrative capabilities. Granting her the Manage Server permission would provide her with excess administrative capabilities. The Print Operators group exists only in a domain environment; so you would need to create a similar group in a workgroup environment. The Power Users group exists only to provide backward compatibility with earlier Windows operating systems; its use would not provide Evelyn with the required capabilities.

Chapter 6

1. **C.** `Winrm quickconfig` performs a default configuration for the `WS-Management` listener service. All other answers are invalid.

2. **A.** `Winrs -r:ServerB ipconfig` will remotely execute `ipconfig` on the remote server, `ServerB`. IP address information will be retrieved from the `ipconfig` command. All other answers are invalid.

3. **D.** To enable remote management using PowerShell on down-level servers, the command `Enable-PSremoting -Force` can be used. All other answers are invalid.

4. **D.** Windows Server 2003 servers only update online/offline status under Server Manager. No other remote management ability for Server 2003 is supported under Server Manager. All other answers are valid options and are fully supported by Server Manager.

5. **B.** To save a copy of Server Manager Settings, you can use the Export Server Manager Settings function within Server Manager. This will save configuration files to disk, which can be copied and imported for the purpose of restoring settings or creating additional management stations. Answer A would enable you to restore settings but is not the choice of least administrative effort. All other answers are incorrect.

6. **C.** To connect to a server using RDP, you must ensure that the **Allow remote connections to this computer** option is selected under system properties. Answer A will install the Remote Desktop Services Role that will enable users to access virtual desktops, session-based desktops, and RemoteApp programs. The indicator here is that the client is failing to connect. This option is required in either scenario, so Answer C is a better choice. All other answers are incorrect.

7. **B.** Remote Server Administration Tools is the downloadable package that can be installed on Windows 8.1 to manage a Server Core Installation. RSAT includes several Active Directory tools, snap-ins, and PowerShell cmdlets used for remote administration. All other answers are invalid.

8. **A.** When using MMC to remotely manage a server, you must ensure that the Windows Firewall has the appropriate rule group enabled for the snap-in. All other answers are incorrect.

9. **A.** The Get cmdlets enables you to retrieve information about a specific function. Answer B is invalid. Answers C and D are typically used with Set cmdlets or as parameters to actively change a function. For this reason, Answers C and D are incorrect.

10. **B, D, E.** These are all tools that can be used to simplify daily management tasks. Task Scheduler can schedule custom scripts or applications to execute on a specific time schedule, AD Administrative Center enables you to automate some Active Directory tasks such as granting resource access based on specific criteria. PowerShell is used to create custom scripts for virtually any task. It is also the underlying technology used to perform the tasks created under the AD Administrative Center GUI.

Chapter 7

1. **B.** The Hypervisor is the underlying mechanism that is responsible for managing virtual machines. All other answers are invalid.

2. **A, C.** This question asks you to introduce virtualization into your organization. To do this, you must first install the Hyper-V role. Hyper-V can be installed by adding the Hyper-V role using Server Manager or by downloading the standalone version of Hyper-V Server 2012. Answers B and D are invalid.

3. **C, E.** To move the checkpoint folder for a virtual machine, you must first ensure that no checkpoints exist. Delete any existing checkpoints, and then modify the path for the Checkpoint File Location. Answer A will not address this request. Answer B will not impact the checkpoint location. Answer D will not satisfy the request.

4. **A.** The Remote Desktop Virtualization role must be installed to take advantage of the RemoteFX 3D Video Adapter Driver for a virtual machine. If this role is not installed, the option to add the RemoteFX 3D driver will be grayed out. All other answers are invalid.

5. **D.** To delegate administrative control over Hyper-V, add the users to the Hyper-V Administrators group. Answer A would work but would give the junior admins more access than required. Answers B and C would not provide the required access to administer Hyper-V.

6. **C.** Virtual machines might experience poor network performance when the legacy network adapter is used. Windows Server 2012 R2 introduces us to virtual machine generations. Windows Server 2012 R2 provides the capability to configure either generation 1 or generation 2 virtual machines. One of the key differences between these virtual machine types is that generation 2 virtual machines do not include the option to configure a legacy network adapter. This option has been removed and we are forced to use the **standard network adapter** option. In this scenario, you are told that the newly created virtual machine is a generation 1 virtual machine configured with a legacy network adapter. To take advantage of advanced features and to improve network throughput, remove the legacy network adapter and install a standard network adapter. Legacy network adapters are used to support virtualization of legacy operating systems such as Windows NT. Removing Guest Integration Services would not resolve the issue and can create additional issues, so Answer A is incorrect. Adding a secondary legacy adapter would not resolve the issue, so Answer B is incorrect. Increasing the memory for the virtual machine can help with other aspects, but the key point here is that after installing a legacy adapter, you notice poor performance. The issue is not with memory, but with the adapter used. Answer D is incorrect.

7. **A.** To ensure that a particular virtual machine is given priority to the host's processor, modify the resource control options for the VM. From here you can specify the processor weight and set reservations on processor usage. Adding virtual processors would not guarantee that VM1 receives higher priority, so Answer B is incorrect. Reducing the processors on all VMs except for VM1 would not guarantee that VM1 will receive priority. All other VMs, however, will be impacted by this change but still be able to use all resources. Answer C is incorrect. Answer D will not help in this case.

8. **D.** Enabling Dynamic Memory will enable virtual machines to use available memory from idle or underutilized virtual machines. Answers A and B are invalid. Smart Paging ensures that the difference between minimum and startup memory is available using a temporary page file stored on the disk, so Answer C is incorrect.

9. **B.** Resource metering enables you to gather statistics on memory, CPU, and network usage. Answers A and D are incorrect. Answer C is invalid.

10. **A.** Integration Services improves input peripheral response time by replacing generic drivers with those optimized for virtual machines. All other answers are incorrect.

Chapter 8

1. **D.** Fixed-size VHDs are best used when you need optimal performance and to eliminate the risk of overcommitting storage on virtual machines. As an administrator, there is an increased risk of storage overcommit when using dynamically expanding disks. As a result, choice A is incorrect. Choice B is a disk format, but not a disk type. Although Fixed-size disks can be created as a .VHD, this answer is not the best choice. Choice C is incorrect.

2. **C, E.** When data is removed from a dynamically expanding disk, host storage fragmentation occurs. To fix this, you must compact the VHD file to reclaim space and defragment the host storage. Choices A, B, and D would not address the situation. Choice F would further impact the situation, and choice G is incorrect.

3. **A.** To share the contents of a VHD between guests, you can establish a parent/child relationship between VHDs. Use the original VHD and link differencing disks to it on different virtual machines. All other choices are incorrect.

4. **A, C, D, G.** Compact, Inspect, Shrink, and Reconnect are all valid management tasks for VHDs. Although they are not listed here, Convert, Expand, and Merge are the other available management tasks.

5. **C.** To properly configure pass-through disks, you must install and initialize the disk on the host. Typically a newly initialized drive will be left in an online state that does not allow the pass-through function to work. Take the host disk offline and ensure that no drive letters are established on it. Then configure the virtual machine to use the physical disk.

6. **B.** If your virtual machine contains many checkpoints, it can degrade performance of the virtual machine due to an increase in I/O load. In extreme scenarios, checkpoints fill up all available storage, which suspends a virtual machine. To remediate these issues, delete unnecessary checkpoints. None of the other choices are correct.

7. **C.** To connect a virtual machine to a specific SAN, create a virtual fibre channel SAN and associate it with the specific HBAs on the host server.

8. **D.** To restore a virtual machine to a previous configuration with little downtime, use an existing checkpoint and the revert action to restore it to the previous state. All other choices would require a significant amount of downtime and would result in increased data loss.

Chapter 9

1. **A, B, E, F.** All these options are considered benefits of Hyper-V network virtualization. HNV provides the ability to create public, private, and hybrid clouds. It also enables you to deploy resources on demand.

2. **A.** The `New-NetSwitchTeam` cmdlet enables you to create NIC teams using PowerShell.

3. **B.** Port mirroring is a feature that enables you to send a copy of inbound or outbound traffic to a destination virtual machine.

4. **D.** To allow virtual machines to communicate with physical servers or resources outside of your network, create and configure an external Hyper-V virtual switch.

5. **B.** In the event that you have a NIC team enabled on a Hyper-V host, you might need to remove the team so you can dedicate specific adapters to different virtual switch types. The reason for this is that the host operating system will present the logical adapter representing the team to Hyper-V. As a result, you will be able to add the team adapter to only one virtual switch type. Adding more physical adapters to the host would also be a viable option, but of the available options here, executing the `Remove-NetLbfoTeam` cmdlet is the only available option.

6. **A, C, D.** These are three potential strategies to improve virtual machine performance.

7. **C.** By configuring a static MAC address, the virtual machine's network adapter will retain the same MAC address even if it is moved between different hosts. If an application uses a MAC address for licensing purposes, you should configure a static MAC address to avoid licensing issues.

8. **B.** MAC address spoofing should be enabled when using network load balancing between virtual machines.

9. **A, D, E.** Isolated, Promiscuous, and Community are the only three PVLAN modes available.

10. **B.** DHCP Guard can be enabled for a virtual machine's network adapter so that the virtual machine does not accept DHCP packets from unauthorized servers.

11. **C.** The correct syntax for retrieving VLAN configuration for a virtual machine is to execute the `Get-VMNetworkAdapterVlan` PowerShell cmdlet on the Hyper-V host.

Chapter 10

1. **D.** The TCP protocol operates at the Transport layer of the TCP/IP reference model layer stack, while the IP protocol operates at the Internet layer. The Application layer holds application-related protocols such as HTTP, FTP, SNMP, and SMTP. The Network Interface layer provides an interface for the layer above it to the network media and holds only media-related protocols such as Ethernet and Frame Relay. The Presentation layer does not exist in the TCP/IP reference model, only in the seven-layer OSI model.

2. **C.** The default gateway is the IP address of the router that connects your computer's subnet to other subnets on your company's network, as well as the Internet. Though important for your computer's TCP/IP configuration, the other items given here do not address this objective.

3. **B.** Any IP address in the range 128.0.0.0–191.255.255.255 belongs to Class B. Class A addresses are in the range 1.0.0.0– 126.255.255.255; Class C addresses are in the range 192.0.0.0– 223.255.255.255; Class D addresses are in the range 224.0.0.0– 239.255.255.255; and Class E addresses are in the range 240.0.0.0– 254.255.255.255.

4. **A, C.** To configure your computer to use DHCP, you should ensure that the **Obtain an IP address automatically** and **Obtain DNS server address automatically** options are selected. You would specify the other two options if you were configuring your computer to use static IP addressing.

5. **A.** If your computer is using an IPv4 address on the 169.254.0.0/16 network, it is configured to use APIPA. An address on this network is assigned when the computer is configured to receive an IP address automatically but is unable to reach a DHCP server. An alternative IP configuration is a separate static IP address you can configure on a computer that is using DHCP; it would not be using this address. Private IPv4 addressing is in use if the IP address is on any of the 10.0.0.0/8, 172.16.0.0/16, or 192.168.0.0/24 networks.

6. **A.** A global unicast address is a globally routable Internet address that is equivalent to a public IPv4 address. A link-local unicast address is used for communication between neighboring nodes on the same link; a site-local unicast

address is used for communication between nodes located in the same site; a multicast address provides multiple interfaces to which packets are delivered; and an anycast address is utilized only as destination addresses assigned to routers. None of these address types are suitable for direct Internet contact. Note that site-local addresses have been deprecated.

7. **C.** A link-local IPv6 address has an address prefix of fe80::/64. This address is equivalent to an APIPA-configured IPv4 address. The other address types have different network prefixes.

8. **A.** The two IPv6 addresses are link-local addresses that include the ISATAP identifier, 5efe. An ISATAP address utilizes the locally administrative interface identifier ::0:5efe:*w.x.y.z*, where *w.x.y.z* is any private unicast IPv4 address, or ::200:5efe:*w.x.y.z*, where *w.x.y.z* is a public IPv4 unicast address. Teredo uses a 2001::/32 prefix, and 6to4 uses a 2002::/16 prefix. An IPv4-mapped address would contain an ffff prefix.

9. **D.** A 6to4 relay forwards 6to4 addressed traffic between 6to4 routers and 6to4 host/routers on the IPv4 Internet and hosts on the IPv6 Internet. Such computers utilize ICS to enable IPv6 forwarding on both the 6to4 tunneling and private interfaces. The other 6to4 components mentioned do not utilize ICS in forwarding network traffic.

10. **C.** 2001::ce49:7601:2cad:dfff:7c94:fffe represents a Teredo address because the first 16 bits (2001 hex) contain the Teredo prefix used in Windows Server 2012 R2. 2003:414:ab86:731f::230:1:45ab represents a global unicast address that is globally routable on the Internet and is equivalent to a public IPv4 address. 3ffe:831f::ab86:731f:230:1:45ab contains the prefix 3ffe:831f:—which was originally used by computers running Windows XP and Windows Server 2003 but is no longer used with Teredo. 2002::ce49:7601:2cad:dfff:7c94:fffe represents a 6to4 address because the 16-bit prefix (2002 hex) represents the 6to4 prefix.

11. **B.** You should use the `ipconfig /renew` command. This command forces the computer to try again to connect to the DHCP server and obtain an IP address lease. In this case, the computer was unable to access the DHCP server and configured itself with an APIPA address. The `/release` parameter releases the current IP address configuration but does not contact the DHCP server. The `/flushdns` parameter flushes the contents of the DNS cache. You would use this parameter when the computer has connected to an incorrect network because of incorrect information in the DNS resource records. The `/displaydns` parameter displays the contents of the DNS cache. This is also useful if the computer connects to an incorrect network.

12. **A.** If two computers on the network are configured with the same IP address, the first one will connect properly but the second one that attempts to connect

will fail to do so, and this problem will result. If your computer is configured for static IP addressing, it will never use APIPA. If the subnet mask is incorrect, your computer would not connect to machines on another subnet at any time. If your computer is configured with static IP addressing, the alternate IP address option will be unavailable.

13. **B, D, E.** When verifying IPv6 network connectivity, you might need to specify a zone ID for the sending interface with the `ping` command. You can obtain this zone ID by running either the `netsh interface ipv6 show interface` command or the `ipconfig /all` command (but not the `ipconfig /displaydns` command). Before using `ping` to check IPv6 network connectivity, clear the neighbor cache on your computer by running the `netsh interface ipv6 delete neighbors` command. You can optionally run the `netsh interface ipv6 show neighbors` command to view the neighbor cache; however, you are not required to run this command. After you've performed these steps, you can run the `ping` command, suffixing it with the `%<ID>` parameter to include the zone ID.

Chapter 11

1. **F, B, A, D.** When an IPv4 client is requesting an address from the DHCP server, it first sends a DHCPDISCOVER message to locate a server. The server sends a DHCPOFFER message to offer an IP address lease. The client sends a DHCPREQUEST message to indicate it is requesting this lease, and finally the server sends a DHCPACK message to acknowledge acceptance of the lease. DHCPINFORM is used by workgroup DHCP servers for locating other DHCP servers on the network. There is no such message as DHCPADVERTISE; however, DHCPv6 servers use an Advertise message to offer a lease to a client computer. Note that on the exam, you must sequence your answers in the proper order; otherwise, the answer will be considered incorrect.

2. **A.** A client will first attempt to renew its lease with the DHCP server that provided its lease and configuration information after 50 percent of the lease time has elapsed. If a client still does not have a renewed lease after 87.5 percent of the active lease period has gone by, it will attempt to communicate with any DHCP server on the network to secure IP addressing and configuration information. No specific action occurs after either 80 or 95 percent of the lease time.

3. **B.** An IPv6 client can use the process of stateless address configuration to automatically configure itself without the use of DHCPv6 using a link-local address and router discovery. This process uses Router Solicitation and Router Advertisement messages that are exchanged with neighboring routers. Stateful

address configuration uses DHCPv6 to obtain non–link-local addresses and other IPv6 configuration parameters. Managed address configuration is not a configuration procedure; it is a flag that determines when DHCPv6 is used to obtain IPv6 stateful addresses. Automatic Private IP addressing is used to auto-assign IPv4 addresses in the absence of a DHCP server; it is not used with IPv6.

4. **E, C, D, G.** The messages sent are Solicit, Advertise, Request, and Reply. These correspond to the DHCPDISCOVER, DHCPOFFER, DHCPREQUEST, and DHCPACK messages sent when requesting an IPv4 address lease. The Confirm message is sent by a client to all servers to determine the validity of a client's configuration. The other options mentioned do not exist with DHCPv6.

5. **B, D.** To install DHCP on a server, you must be logged on as an administrator and the server must be configured with a static IP address. It does not matter whether the server is configured with IPv4, IPv6, or both; it also does not matter whether the server is a domain controller.

6. **B, D.** Microsoft recommends that you use the PowerShell cmdlet `Install-WindowsFeature DHCPServerCore` to install DHCP on a Windows Server 2012 R2 Server Core computer. You can also use the `Dism /online /enable-feature /featurename:DHCPServerCore` command to install DHCP on a Server Core computer. The `Start /w ocsetup DHCPServerCore` command would install DHCP on a Server Core computer running the original version of Windows Server 2008 but not Windows Server 2012 R2. The `servermanagercmd -install` command installs certain roles and role features with Server Core, but not DHCP.

7. **B.** DHCP options are always applied in the sequence: server, scope, class, client. This is important to know because options applied at a later stage of this sequence always overwrite options applied earlier in the sequence. For example, server options are overwritten by any conflicting option applied at any of the other levels and client options always overwrite other options.

8. **A.** You should specify a user class option that sets the lease interval to 12 hours for all laptop computers. This type of class is used to differentiate clients according to their type, such as desktop, laptop, or server computer. A vendor class option might be applicable if all laptops are obtained from one vendor, but this is not normally the case. Specifying client options for each laptop would take more work than specifying a user class option and would be open to error. It might be possible to use a separate scope, but this would also take more effort and be error-prone.

9. **A, C.** To ensure that these servers retain their IP addresses but receive other IP configuration information from the DHCP server, you should create an

exclusion range within the scope plus reservations for each of the servers. The exclusion range prevents the server from assigning these IP addresses to other computers and the reservation ensures that these computers always receive their proper IP address. If you create two scopes as described in Answer B, the file servers would not receive other IP configuration information from the DHCP server. This is also true if you assign these servers static IP addresses.

10. **B, D.** To deploy images using PXE boot, you will need to configure DHCP options 66 and 67. Answers A, C, and E are all options used for services or functions outside of the scope of this book and the 70-410 exam.

11. **D.** You need to authorize the DHCP server in Active Directory. This requirement is necessary to prevent rogue DHCP servers from coming online and assigning improper IP addresses to clients, which would disrupt network communications. Reactivating the scope in this situation does not help. There is no such option in DHCP that would prevent the use of APIPA. A DHCP server on an AD DS domain does not need to be a domain controller.

12. **B.** The DHCP relay agent is a server configured with RRAS that listens for DHCP broadcast messages from client computers on its own subnet and forwards these messages to the DHCP server. The relay agent must be configured on the subnet away from the DHCP server and not on the subnet (A in this case) where the DHCP server is located. There is no scope option that specifies the IP address of a remote DHCP server. There is also no option within a client's TCP/IP Properties dialog box from which you can specify the IP address of a DHCP server.

13. **A.** The message stating `The specified DHCP client is not a reserved client` indicates that you have attempted to reserve an IP address that is outside the range of the DHCP server's scope. To correct the problem, modify the scope so that the desired IP address is within the scope or select a different IP address. There is no such scope option to specify a reserved IP address. If a duplicate IP address were configured on another computer, you would still be able to create a reservation but connectivity problems would occur afterward. You could specify a static IP address at the server in question, but then this server would not receive other IP options from the DHCP server.

Chapter 12

1. **A, B, C, D.** The DNS namespace includes root domains, top-level domains, second-level domains, and hostnames. You can even have additional subdomains at levels beneath the second level. However, NetBIOS names are not a component of the DNS namespace.

2. **C, D, F.** These three computer names qualify as FQDNs, which generally consist of a hostname, second-level domain name, and top-level domain name separated by periods. `SERVER1` is a NetBIOS name, not an FQDN. `http://www` is an incomplete name; further, an FQDN does not start with `http:`, so answer B is incorrect. `webserver.anydomain.` is an incomplete name, so answer E is incorrect.

3. **C.** In an iterative query, the name is resolved in the sequence root domain, top-level domain, second-level domain, and then hostname. If the ISP's DNS server can resolve the query, this is a recursive query and not an iterative query. Beginners might think that a query is resolved from the front of the name to the back (parallel to a filename plus extension), but this sequence as described in Answer B is backwards. A client does not communicate directly with a root server, as Answer D suggests.

4. **A, D.** You can install DNS on a Windows Server 2012 R2 computer by using the Add Roles and Features Wizard or the PowerShell `Add-WindowsFeature` cmdlet. In addition, if you promote your server to domain controller, the Active Directory Installation Wizard automatically installs DNS if another DNS server is not available on the network. Because DNS is a server role and not a feature, you cannot use the Add Features Wizard. The Control Panel Add or Remove Programs applet was used to install DNS on servers running Windows 2000 Server or Windows Server 2003, but it is no longer used for this purpose. DNS Manager is used to configure DNS after installation; it is installed when you install DNS.

5. **B.** When installing a DNS server, you should ensure that it has a static IP address. If it is configured to use DHCP to obtain an IP address automatically, then its IP address could change and client computers would be unable to locate the DNS server. The server does not need to be configured as a domain controller or an application server; further, it can function properly with only a single network adapter.

6. **B.** An Active Directory-integrated zone is required when you require secure dynamic updates.

7. **A.** By specifying the DNS server of the partner company as a conditional forwarder, requests for resources in this company are automatically forwarded to this DNS server. If you specified the IP address and FQDN of the partner company DNS server on the Forwarders tab of your DNS server, the partner company DNS server could receive requests from your company's users for Internet resources. Specifying your DNS server's IP address and FQDN on the partner company's DNS server would forward requests in the opposite direction. Specifying the partner DNS server on the Root Hints tab would cause requests for Internet resources to go to the partner DNS server.

8. **B.** You should check the root hints on the DNS server. These specify the IP addresses of the Internet root servers that contain information for all the top-level Internet domains. If they are incorrect or missing, users will be unable to access external websites. A conditional forwarder is a DNS server that handles name resolution for specific domains. If the conditional forwarder were incorrect, errors would occur for the domain name specified in the New Conditional Forwarder dialog box only and not for other domains. Round robin randomizes access to multiple DNS servers that resolve names on the same zone. None of these provide Internet name resolution. SRV records would not come into play here.

9. **D.** Debug logging records information on packets sent to and from the DNS server and stores this information in a text file named `dns.log`. DNS monitoring enables you to run test queries that check your server's configuration but does not create this log file. Event logging determines what type of events are recorded in the Event Viewer log. DNS Notify enables a master server to notify secondary servers of changes to its zone but does not perform logging.

10. **B.** CNAME records are used to create an alias for a particular resource record.

Chapter 13

1. **A, B, D, E.** The logical components of AD DS include forests, trees, domains, and OUs. Sites and global catalogs are physical components.

2. **A, B, C, D.** You can install AD DS on any edition of Windows Server 2012 R2.

3. **A, B, C, D, E, F.** All of these are best practices that you should follow and be completely aware of at an early stage of planning your domain structure. You should also ensure that you know everything there is to know about the network.

4. **A, D, E.** You can use either the Add Roles and Features Wizard in Server Manager, Windows PowerShell, or the `dcpromo.exe` command with an answer file to install AD DS on a Windows Server 2012 R2 computer. Microsoft has depreciated the `dcpromo.exe` command in Windows Server 2012 R2 and no longer supports it for use without an answer file. The Configure Your Server tool was used in Windows Server 2003 but is no longer supported.

5. **C.** The Active Directory Domain Services Configuration Wizard automatically installs the DNS Server role if it cannot find this role elsewhere on the network because DNS is required for AD DS to function. None of the other server roles listed here are required by AD DS; consequently, the wizard does not install them.

6. **A, B, C.** The Windows 2000 and Windows Server 2003 mixed and native functional levels are no longer supported by Windows Server 2012 R2; consequently, you must remove or upgrade any Windows 2000 or 2003 servers before installing a Windows Server 2012 R2 domain controller. All the other functional levels listed are supported in Windows Server 2012 R2.

7. **C.** When you run the Active Directory Domain Services Configuration Wizard on a server that is already a domain controller, the domain controller is demoted to a member server. The wizard will not install a new or second copy of AD DS in these circumstances, nor will an error message appear.

8. **C, E.** You can use the `Install-ADDSDomainController` cmdlet in Windows PowerShell to install AD DS on a Server Core computer. You can also use `dcpromo.exe` together with an answer file that provides the required parameters to install a domain controller on a Server Core machine, though Microsoft recommends that you use PowerShell. Server Core does not contain any GUI tools or wizards, and it also does not permit you to specify parameters during the installation. Because you can use `dcpromo.exe` with an answer file, you do not have to reinstall Windows Server 2012 R2 as a full edition server (note, however, that in Windows Server 2012 R2, you can convert between Server Core and a full GUI server using PowerShell, as you learned in Chapter 2).

9. **C.** To use the IFM option for a Windows Server 2012 R2 domain controller, you must use a package created from a Windows Server 2012 R2 domain controller. In this scenario, you must first upgrade the 2008 DC to Windows Server 2012 R2.

10. **A, C.** Global catalog servers validate universal group memberships at logon and UPNs across the entire forest. They also validate references to objects located in other domains in the forest.

11. **A, B, C.** Windows Azure enables you to deploy a forest root domain controller, a child domain controller, or an additional domain controller for a domain hosted on your corporate network. It also enables you to deploy a DNS server that supports AD DS (as on a physical network, this can be on the same server as the domain controller). However, you cannot deploy a DHCP server in Azure; this server must be located on your corporate network. Also, you need to deploy AD DS on an operating system disk and the database and SYSVOL folders on a data disk in Windows Azure.

12. **D.** The file used to identify SRV records for a domain controller is the `netlogon.dns` file. This file is located on domain controllers under the `%windir%\system32\config\` folder.

Chapter 14

1. **B, C, E, F.** The Create User dialog box in the Active Directory Administrative Center enables you to configure the use of AES-based encryption, organizational information, group membership, and account expiry. When creating a user account in Active Directory Users and Computers, you can configure whether the user must change the password at first logon and whether the account is disabled, but you must right-click the account and select **Properties** after the fact to configure the other properties mentioned here.

2. **B.** You would use a template account in creating a large number of domain user accounts that have similar properties and need for resource access. Copying this account and supplying a username and password for each user that requires access is easy.

3. **A.** The `Csvde` tool enables you to import data to AD DS from files containing information in the comma-separated (CSV) format. Exporting Excel data to a file in this format is easy. It is not as simple to convert this data to a format that would be supported by either `Ldifde` or `Dsadd`. Using the Active Directory Administrative Center would take much more time to create these user accounts.

4. **D.** Active Directory Domains and Trusts provides you with the capability of creating a UPN suffix. You would use either Active Directory Administrative Center or Active Directory Users and Computers to specify the UPN suffix that each user will use during logon; however, these tools do not allow you to add a new UPN suffix. Active Directory Sites and Services does not enable any facet of UPN suffix administration.

5. **B.** You should create contacts for each of these individuals and add these contacts to a distribution group. A contact is simply a collection of information about an individual or organization. It can be included in a distribution list created for the purpose of sending email messages. User accounts provide them with access to the domain, which is not desired here. Security groups enable permissions to be granted to their members; you cannot include contacts as members of security groups.

6. **B.** A Protected Admin user account is an administrative user account other than the default account created when Windows Server 2012 R2 is installed or the first domain administrator account created when AD DS is installed. When using this account to perform an administrative task, you will be prompted by UAC to confirm your intentions by clicking **Yes** or **Continue** in a message box. When using either of the default administrative accounts mentioned here, you will not receive a UAC prompt. When using an administrative account other than the default accounts, you will not be asked to

type your username and password. When using a standard user account, you will be required to type an administrative password, not merely click **Yes** or **Continue** in a message box.

7. **D.** You should use the `djoin /Provision /Domain certguide.com / Machine Client1 /SaveFile c:\Client1.txt` command to create the metadata that will enable offline domain join for this target computer. The `dsadd` command would let you add objects including users and computers to the AD DS database but does not enable offline domain join. The `djoin /requestODJ` command enables the target computer to join the domain, but this takes place after you've used the `djoin /Provision` command to create the required metadata for the offline domain join.

8. **C.** You should disable Ryan's account and then rename and reenable it when the new employee is hired. This is the most secure means of deprovisioning an account so that it cannot be used in the interim and so that all its rights and privileges are maintained for later use. It does not make sense to turn the account into a template. You could remove the account from the groups that grant him access to the resources he used in performance of his job. However, Ryan could still log on until you rename the account, and this entire method is more complex and error-prone. If you delete Ryan's account, you will need to re-create all the privileges associated with it when you re-create the account; disabling the account instead leaves these privileges intact but prevents use of the account in the interim.

Chapter 15

1. **C.** Sharon should use a global group. All 55 users belong to a single domain, so a global group is most appropriate in this situation. A local group on a member server or client computer provides access to resources on that computer only. A domain local group provides access to resources within its domain only (note, however, that Sharon can, and should, add the global group to domain local groups in each domain for access to the resources). Sharon does not need a universal group because all users are located in a single domain.

2. **B, C, D.** The Create Group dialog box in Active Directory Administrative Center enables you to add users to the group, nest this group into another group, and specify information of a user that is responsible for managing the group, among other actions that are possible from this dialog box but not from the New Group dialog box in Active Directory Users and Computers. You can specify the group scope in either the New Group or Create Group dialog box. Neither of these dialog boxes enables you to assign permissions to the group being created; you must perform this action later.

3. **A, B, C, E.** You can add user accounts and domain local groups from the same domain, global groups, and universal groups from any domain in the forest to this domain local group. However, you cannot add domain local groups from other domains to this group.

4. **A, C, D, E.** You can nest the global group into universal and domain local groups in any domain and global groups in the same domain. However, you cannot nest the group into a global group in a different domain (in this case, the parent domain).

5. **B.** You should create contacts for each of these individuals and add these contacts to a distribution group. A contact is simply a collection of information about an individual or organization. It can be included in a distribution list created for the purpose of sending email messages. User accounts provide them with access to the domain, which is not desired here. Security groups enable permissions to be granted to their members; you cannot include contacts as members of security groups.

6. **D.** You should add the user accounts to global groups in their respective domains. Then add these global groups to the universal group, and add the universal group to three domain local groups—one located in each child domain to which the users need access. Finally, grant permissions to the domain local groups. This strategy follows Microsoft's AGDLP recommended group nesting strategy. Even though the other strategies might seem simpler, they can all introduce problems at some time in the future. For example, adding the user accounts to the universal group increases replication traffic at any time the membership in this group changes. Granting permissions to the universal group might expose this group to unnecessary resources and can increase replication traffic if these permissions change.

7. **A, C, D.** Of the types of information listed here, these are the most helpful ones. They will enable you to design an OU structure that will best suit the company's needs. Although you will need to consult with company executives throughout the design process, you do not need this information for inclusion in the OU design. Information on partner companies is needed for planning trust relationships but is not needed for designing the company's OU structure.

8. **C.** The Delegation of Control Wizard enables you to grant the ability to manage OUs. Answers A and B will allow this ability but will also give junior admins more access than required. You would not use the Delegation of Control Wizard on each user object. This would not satisfy the requirement here. For this reason, Answer D is incorrect.

9. **A.** The Delegation of Control Wizard enables you to grant the ability to perform various administrative tasks to users or groups. This includes the Reset user passwords and force password change at next logon task. You can (and should) use a group account rather than individual user accounts when running this wizard. The Account Operators group would grant the help desk technicians more administrative privileges than required in this scenario.

Chapter 16

1. **B.** GPCs are stored in the domain partition of AD DS, and GPTs are stored in the SYSVOL shared folder. Group Policy is specific to each domain in the forest so the domain partition is used for GPCs. In addition, each domain has a folder hierarchy found in the domain controllers at the shared folder `%systemroot%\SYSVOL\sysvol\<domain_name>\Policies`.

2. **A.** First introduced in Windows Server 2003 R2, Group Policy Management Console is the tool that enables you to perform all management activities on GPOs including such functions as creating and linking GPOs, modifying their inheritance, disabling or deleting them, and so on. You use the Group Policy Management Editor to edit policy settings within GPOs but not to manage them. Active Directory Users and Computers contained Group Policy management tools in Windows 2000 and Windows Server 2003 before R2, but it no longer does so. Active Directory Administrative Center performs many administrative activities in Windows Server 2008 R2/2012/R2, but not with Group Policy.

3. **D.** The Administrative Templates folder enables you to configure these types of settings on computers and users to which the GPO is applied. The Preferences container includes new Group Policy extensions that control items such as folder options, mapped drives, printers, scheduled tasks, and so on. Software Settings enable you to specify which software is deployed to users and computers. Windows Settings include scripts and security settings as well as other settings that affect the behavior of the Windows environment.

4. **D.** You should create a new GPO linked to the child domain and specify the name of the Starter GPO in the New GPO dialog box. The Starter GPO contains settings that can be used for creating new GPOs in this fashion. Note that you cannot link a Starter GPO to any AD DS container. It would be possible to copy settings in the Starter GPO to the Default Domain Policy GPO or another GPO, but this would defeat the purpose of using a Starter GPO in the first place.

5. **B.** You should disable the computer settings for this GPO. Doing so speeds up the processing of the GPO and enables users to log on faster. If you were

to disable the user settings, users would not receive the policy settings you've configured. The ability to disable user or computer settings in a GPO is found in the Details tab of the GPO's properties in GPMC and not in the Settings tab.

6. **C.** You should not delete the GPO. There is no way to recover a deleted GPO if you need its settings in the future (though you could recover it from a backup if one exists). Performing any of the other actions listed retains the GPO together with its settings but renders it incapable of applying its settings to any container in your domain.

7. **D.** Local Computer policies are applied first, followed by Administrator & Non-Administrator policies. User-specific policies are applied last.

8. **A.** To create local groups on all member servers in the domain, an administrator can implement Restricted Groups security setting or use the Local Users and Groups preferences setting under Group Policy. The policy can then be linked to the Servers OU to apply to those individual member servers. One of the requirements was to ensure that the Group Policy applies to only Servers in the Servers OU. Although Answer B would apply the policy, it would also be applied to all servers in the domain; consequently, Answer B is incorrect.

9. **D.** By denying the Apply Group Policy permission to the Domain Admins group, you prevent the settings in the GPO from applying to any member of this group regardless of the computer to which they log on. It might be possible to use a WMI filter or a Windows PowerShell script to perform this action, but either of these would be far more complex and error-prone than denying the Apply Group Policy permission. Disabling the link for computers used by members of this group would prevent the GPO from applying to these computers, but it would still be applied elsewhere; further, you would need to place these computers into their own OUs to do so.

10. **A.** You should create and use a WMI filter that specifies that only laptop computers should receive the policy's settings. The hardware configuration of a computer is a property that you can specify in a WMI filter against which the computers will be evaluated in determining whether the GPO should be applied. It would also be possible to create a new OU and place the laptop computer accounts in this OU, but you would have to carefully look at each computer account and decide whether it applies to a desktop or laptop computer, a process that takes more administrative effort and is error-prone. Creating a global group and denying the Apply Group Policy permission would also present similar problems. It is not possible to disable a GPO's link for a certain type of computers.

Chapter 17

1. **B.** You should right-click the **Default Domain Controllers Policy** GPO and select **Edit**. In the Group Policy Management Editor, navigate to the **Computer Configuration\Policies\Windows Settings\Security Settings\ Local Policies\User Rights Assignment** node and select this node. View the default user rights in the details pane. The Default Domain Policy GPO does not include any default user rights. User rights are defined according to the computers at which the users will be performing these actions, and not to users themselves; consequently, no user rights are defined in the User Configuration branch of the Group Policy Management Editor.

2. **A, B, C, D, F.** The Security Configuration Wizard does not contain an option to configure users who are permitted to be members of specified groups. All other actions specified here can be configured using the Security Configuration Wizard, but you must use the Restricted Groups policy setting to configure group membership restrictions.

3. **B.** The Security Templates tool enables you to save a custom security policy template on a member server. You can then use the Security Configuration and Analysis tool to create a database containing settings in the policy template and apply them to the standalone server. You cannot apply these settings directly to the standalone server by means of Security Configuration and Analysis. The Security Configuration Wizard enables you to check the security settings applied to your servers but not to copy settings from one server to another. You could manually specify all the required settings using the Local Security Policy snap-in at the standalone server; however, this procedure is more tedious and error-prone than using the Security Configuration and Analysis and Security Templates tools.

4. **D.** You should audit the Detailed Directory Service Replication subcategory of directory service auditing. This subcategory tracks all the actions specified here. To enable this auditing subcategory, use the Advanced Audit Policy Configuration node in the Windows Server 2012 R2 Group Policy Management Console.

5. **A, D.** The audit account management event includes creation, modification, or deletion of user accounts or groups; renaming or disabling of user accounts; and configuring and changing passwords. Also, the audit logon events tracks logon or logoff by a user at a member server or client computer. Audit account logon events tracks logon or logoff by a domain user account at a domain controller and not at local computers. Audit object access tracks when a user accesses an object such as a file, folder, Registry key, or printer that has its own system access control list (SACL) specified. This action is not required in this scenario.

6. **C.** Auditing of object access is a two-step process. First, you must enable auditing of object access in the appropriate GPO, as you have done. Second, you must also configure the SACL for each required object. This involves specifying auditing entries for the folder containing the documents to be audited. It is not necessary to enable auditing of logon events to track modifications to documents. Auditing of object access can be enabled at any GPO applicable to the server containing the documents; it is not necessary to enable this in a GPO linked to the Legal OU. Directory service access tracks access to AD DS objects such as user or group accounts or OUs; it does not track access to document files or folders.

7. **D.** The Audit Account Lockout policy enables you to configure auditing of this specific action. It is found only under **Logon/Logoff** within **Advanced Audit Policy Configuration\Audit Policies**. The granular auditing policies found in Windows Server 2012 R2 enable this level of auditing, which is not found in the **Computer Configuration\Policies\Windows Settings\Security Settings\Local Policies\Audit Policy** subnode and is not available on older Windows Server computers. Further, this setting is not found under Account Logon (which deals with logons and logoffs at domain controllers and not at member servers or client computers).

8. **B.** The `Auditpol.exe` tool enables you to configure auditing from the command line, as is necessary when working at a Server Core computer.

9. **A.** This question is asking you about User Account Control and where to configure the settings. UAC can be configured from the Control Panel, or it can be applied through policy under the Local Policies section.

Chapter 18

1. **B, D.** Software Restriction Policies and AppLocker Policies can be implemented and enforced via Group Policy to control software and execution of applications on the domain.

2. **A, C, D, E.** You can configure any of these rule types in Software Restriction Policies. There is no such thing as an operating system version rule.

3. **C.** The network zone rule option enables you to configure a software restriction policy that limits downloads and installs from Internet zones you specify. By setting the trusted sites zone to **Unrestricted**, you enable users to download and install any software from sites you've personally places in this zone. If you were to set the Internet zone to **Unrestricted**, users would be able to download software from any website except those you've placed into the restricted sites zone, which is not desirable. It would be far more cumbersome and error-prone to attempt to use the path rule or the certificate rule for this purpose.

4. **B, D.** AppLocker enables you to gather advanced data on software usage by implementing audit-only mode and to create multiple rules at the same time with the help of a wizard. Disallowed, Basic User, and Unrestricted are the rule settings available with Software Restriction Policies; AppLocker uses Allow and Deny. You can use either Software Restriction Policies or App-Locker with Group Policy.

5. **A.** By selecting the **Audit only** option, you can obtain information about which software packages currently in use are actually being used by users. If you were to select the **Enforce rules** option, software restrictions would be enforced immediately and users of specified applications would be unable to access them. The Properties dialog box for the default AppLocker rules does not contain an option to select **Audit only** or **Enforce rules**.

6. **B.** Executable file locations not covered by AppLocker default rules are implicitly denied access. By moving the Photoshop CS6 files to a path location not included in any of the default AppLocker rules and creating a new AppLocker rule that allows members of the Graphic Artists group to access this location, you limit the execution of Photoshop to only members of this group. If you deny the Everyone group access, nobody would be able to access the Photoshop files. The Exceptions page does not enable you to specify a user or group allowed to execute an application. Because explicit denial overrides explicitly granted access, creation of two AppLocker rules including a denial to the Everyone group would not provide access to members of the Graphic Artists group.

Chapter 19

1. **B.** By selecting the **Block all incoming connections, including those in the list of allowed programs** option, you stop all attempts by outsiders to reach your server. This enables you to perform whatever detective and remedial measures you need to perform before putting the server back online. You need to do this within the Home or work (private) network location settings because your computer is connected to the work network. Public network location settings are used with mobile computers connecting from an insecure location such as a public Wi-Fi hotspot; although present on the server interface, you should never use this option on a server. You would use the **Turn off Windows Firewall** option only when troubleshooting a connectivity problem and not when troubleshooting improper access to your computer.

2. **B, D, E.** You can configure Windows Firewall to specify programs that are allowed to communicate, or you can configure Windows Firewall to block all incoming connections, from the Windows Firewall Control Panel applet. You can also specify firewall settings for home, work, and public networks from

this location. However, you must use the Windows Firewall with Advanced Security snap-in to configure ports and logging (the Windows Firewall applet in the original version of Windows Server 2008 allowed specifying allowed ports, but this function was removed from this location in Windows Server 2008 R2).

3. **C.** Windows Firewall with Advanced Security does not include any connection security rules by default. You can use the New Rules Wizard to set up connection security rules as well as additional rules for the other rule types.

4. **C, D, E.** Windows Firewall with Advanced Security enables you to configure settings for the domain, private, and public profiles. There are no user or computer profiles in this tool.

5. **A.** To enable privacy, you must ensure that accepted communications are encrypted. To do so, you need to select the **Allow the connection if it is secure** option from the Action page of the wizard. Then select the **Require the connections to be encrypted** option on the Customize Allow if Secure Settings dialog box that appears. If you select the **Allow the connection if it is authenticated and integrity-protected** option, it does not ensure that all accepted communications will be encrypted. If you select the **Allow the connection** option from the Action page, you do not receive the Customize Allow if Secure Settings dialog box and therefore do not have a chance to select the **Require the connections to be encrypted** option. The **Authentication exemption** option enables specified computers to be exempted from authentication and does not meet the requirements of this scenario; furthermore, it is found in the New Connection Security Rule Wizard and not in the New Incoming Rule Wizard.

6. **A.** When you select the **Allow the connection if it is secure** option in the New Rule Wizard, you are provided with a Users page that enables you to select the users or groups that are permitted access using the firewall rule you're creating. To grant access to the Research group, you must select the check box labeled **Only allow connections from these users**, click **Add**, and then add the Research group. If you select the **Skip this rule for connections from these users** option, you would designate the Research group as being blocked from access, which is not the desired result. You could complete the wizard after selecting the **Allow the connection if it is secure** option and then access the rule's Properties dialog box; however, this would take more administrative effort. Further, you would have to change the rule action to **Allow the connection if it is secure** to make changes at the Users tab.

7. **D.** It is not possible to change a rule from Inbound to Outbound from any setting that is available in the rule's Properties dialog box. It is also not possible to drag a rule from one node to another in Windows Firewall with Advanced Security. You must create a new outbound rule to perform this action.

8. **D.** An IPsec exemption enables you to choose whether to exempt ICMP from IPsec requirements. Selecting the **Yes** option enables ICMP packets such as `ping` or `tracert` to pass without being examined by IPsec rules, thereby enabling the desktop support technician to use these tools. The Client (Respond Only) setting formerly used with older computers is no longer available to Windows 7, Windows Server 2008 R2, or more recent computers; anyway, it would not enable ICMP packets to pass. An authorization exemption is used to designate computers that do not require authentication. IPsec tunnel authorization is used in conjunction with tunnel mode IPsec, which is not used here; it would not permit ICMP packets to pass anyway.

9. **B, C.** You can use either the Windows Firewall: Allow authenticated IPsec bypass policy in Group Policy or the Allow connection if it is secure and Only Allow connections from these computers settings in an inbound rule created from Windows Firewall with Advanced Security tool. The required policy is found in the **Administrative Templates\Network\Network Connections** branch of Group Policy and not in the **Windows Settings\Security Settings\Local Policies\Security Options** section of Group Policy. In Windows Firewall with Advanced Security, you must create an inbound rule, not an outbound or connection security rule.

10. **B.** Windows Firewall with Advanced Security enables you to create a backup file containing all the settings you have configured. This process, known as *exporting firewall settings*, enables you to recover settings if they've been corrupted or deleted. It also enables you to import the settings to another server, as required in this scenario. Exporting at the standalone server and importing to a member server is backward to what this scenario requires. It is not necessary to use Windows Server Backup to perform this task.

Glossary

6to4 A tunneling protocol that enables two nodes running both IPv4 and IPv6 across an IPv4 routing infrastructure to use a special address obtained by combining the prefix 2002::/16 with the 32-bit public IPv4 address to form a 48-bit prefix of the form 2002:wwxx:yyzz::/48 in the case of a public IPv4 address w.x.y.z. These nodes use this address type when communicating with each other.

Access control list (ACL) A list of users and groups that can access an object such as a file, folder, or printer and the type of access granted.

Account lockout A series of policy settings that locks a user out of an account after a predetermined number of incorrect attempts at entering a password has occurred. This increases security by foiling random dictionary-based or brute-force password hack attempts.

Account policies A series of settings in Group Policy that determine the characteristics of an acceptable password as well as account lockout settings and Kerberos settings.

Active Directory Administrative Center An Active Directory snap-in in Windows Server 2012 R2 that enables the administration of most Active Directory functions from a single console.

Active Directory Domain Services (AD DS) The Windows Server 2012 R2 hierarchical directory service that enables the management of all objects on Windows Server 2012 R2 networks, including users, groups, computers, shared resources, and so on. It was originally developed by Microsoft in Windows 2000 to replace the antiquated, flat directory structure of Windows NT.

Active Directory Migration Tool (ADMT) A utility that enables you to move objects such as users, groups, and computers between Active Directory domains in the same or different forests.

Address Resolution Protocol (ARP) A TCP/IP protocol that is used to resolve the IP address of the destination computer to the physical or MAC address. Also the command-line utility that displays the MAC address of a computer.

Administrative Templates   The section of Group Policy from which administrators can configure settings that are applied to users' desktops, specify programs that users can run, and so on. They apply changes to client computer Registry settings.

`Adprep`   A utility that prepares a Windows 2003 or Windows Server 2008 forest or domain for receiving domain controllers running Windows Server 2012 R2. It has several parameters, the most important of which are `forestprep`, which prepares the forest, and `domainprep`, which prepares the domain.

AGDLP   An acronym that stands for Microsoft's recommendation of placing Accounts into Global groups, then placing these groups into Domain local groups, and finally granting Permissions to the domain local groups.

AGUDLP   An acronym that stands for Microsoft's recommendation of placing Accounts into Global groups, then placing these groups into Universal groups, then placing these groups into Domain local groups, and finally granting Permissions to the domain local groups.

Always offline mode   A new Offline Files mode in Windows Server 2012 R2 that enables faster access to cached files and redirected folders in an AD DS environment.

Anycast IPv6 address   A type of IPv6 address that is utilized only for a destination address assigned to a router.

Application control policies   An update to the older Software Restriction Policies, providing new enhancements that enable you to specify exactly what users are permitted to run on their desktops according to unique file identities. You can also specify users or groups permitted to execute these applications. These policies use the AppLocker feature and can be enforced on computers running Windows 7, Windows Server 2008 R2, and later.

AppLocker   A Windows Server 2012 R2 tool that enables you to control which files and applications users can run, including executable files, scripts, Windows Installer files, DLLs, packaged apps, and packaged app installers.

Auditing   A security process that tracks the usage of selected network resources, typically storing the results in a log file.

`auditpol.exe`   A command-line tool that enables you to configure audit policy settings and directory service auditing subcategories.

Authenticated bypass   A procedure in which you can enable all communications from approved computers to bypass the firewall when communicating with the server using IPsec-secured messages.

Authentication   A process whereby an individual or a computer on a network proves he is who he says he is. The authentication process validates the source and identity of information and includes such tasks as confirming the identity of a user, computer, or digital signature.

Automatic Private IP Addressing (APIPA) The dynamic IPv4 addressing system used when DHCP is unavailable. It uses the IP address range of 169.254.y.z.

Basic Disk The default type for new disks installed. Basic disks support the creation of simple volumes and up to four primary partitions.

Bootstrap Protocol (BOOTP) A UDP network protocol used by a network client to obtain its IP address automatically. This is usually done during the bootstrap process when a computer is starting up.

Branch Office Direct Printing A printer setting that is designed to conserve bandwidth and allow client printing if a print server failure occurs.

Broadcast A routing technology that transmits data to all possible destinations on the local subnet. This permits the sender to send the data only once and all receivers can copy it.

Built-in account A user account created by default when Windows is installed on a computer. An example is the local Administrator account.

Built-in group A group account created by default when Windows or Active Directory is installed on a computer. An example is the Domain Admins group. You can use these groups to set up a system of assistant administrators within your company.

Certificate rule A software restriction policy rule that identifies software to be allowed or prohibited according to an application's signing certificate.

Checkpoint A technology used to create a point-in-time backup of the virtual machine configuration and data.

Classless Inter-Domain Routing (CIDR) A flexible method of stating IP addresses and masks without needing to classify the addresses. An example of the CIDR format is 192.168.1.0/24.

Client reservation A DHCP mechanism that ensures that a client always gets the same reserved IP address.

Conditional forwarding The relaying of a DNS request for zone information for specific domains from one server to another one, when the first server is unable to process the request.

Connection security rule A type of firewall rule that requires two computers to authenticate with each other to establish a connection and secure their communications. Windows Firewall uses IPsec to enforce these rules and secure the communication channel.

Csvde A utility that imports comma-separated text files into the AD DS database. You can use this utility to automate the bulk creation of user or group accounts.

Customer Address Space In a cloud computing environment, the customer address space are the dedicated servers and network assigned to a specific customer.

dcpromo The command-line utility used to promote a Windows Server 2012 R2 system to a domain controller. In Windows Server 2012 R2, dcpromo can be used only in conjunction with an answer file that supplies parameters required for domain controller promotion.

Default gateway The term applied to the router that leads to other networks.

Desired State Configuration (DSC) DSC is a PowerShell extension designed to enhance the levels of automation using PowerShell 4.0. It helps administrators cut down on repetitive tasks by defining prebuilt configurations that accompany a PowerShell cmdlet.

DHCP options Options that a DHCP server configures for clients on the network, such as the addresses of the DNS and WINS servers.

DHCP relay agent A server configured to relay DHCP broadcast messages from one subnet to another. In Windows Server 2012/R2, the DHCP relay agent service is a component of RRAS.

DHCP scope A range of IP addresses on a DHCP server that is available for the server to lease to client computers. A scope generally defines a single physical subnet on a network.

Differencing disk The child disk in a parent/child relationship. Differencing disks are linked to a parent disk. Together both disks enable access to the operating system and/or data. The parent disk becomes read only once linked, and all changes are written to the differencing disk.

DiskPart The command-line tool used to manage partitions for both physical and virtual disks. It can be used attach, expand, shrink, or detach drives.

Djoin.exe A utility that enables you to configure a client computer running Windows 7/8/8.1/Server 2008/R2/2012/2012 R2 to join a domain without contacting a domain controller.

DNS Manager The Microsoft Management Console (MMC) snap-in from which you can manage most of the activities associated with operating a DNS server.

DNSSEC (Domain Name System Security Extensions) A suite of DNS extensions that adds security to the DNS protocol by providing origin authority, data integrity, and authenticated denial of existence. It enables DNS servers to use digital signatures to validate responses from other servers and resolvers.

Domain controller (DC) A server capable of performing authentication. In Windows Server 2012 R2, a domain controller holds a copy of the Active Directory database.

Domain functional level Windows Server 2012 R2 domains can operate at one of four functional levels: Windows Server 2008, Windows Server 2008 R2, Windows Server 2012, or the Windows Server 2012 R2 functional level. Each functional level has different tradeoffs between features and limitations.

Domain local group A domain local group can contain other domain local groups from its own domain, as well as global groups from any domain in the forest. A domain local group can be used to assign permissions for resources located in the same domain as the group.

Domain Name System (DNS) A hierarchical name-resolution system that resolves hostnames into IP addresses, and vice versa. DNS also allows the distributed Active Directory database to function by enabling clients to query the locations of services in the forest and domain.

Domain user account A user account that is stored in the AD DS database. It permits a user to log on to any computer in the domain in which it is located or a trusted domain.

Dsadd A command-line tool that enables you to add objects such as users, groups, contacts, or computers to the AD DS database.

Dynamic Host Configuration Protocol (DHCP) A service that enables an administrator to specify a range of valid IP addresses to be used on a network, as well as exclusion IP addresses that should not be assigned (for example, if they were already statically assigned elsewhere). These addresses are automatically given out to computers configured to use DHCP as they boot up on the network, thus saving the administrator from having to configure static IP addresses on each individual network device.

Dynamic IP address An IP address that is provided to a computer by a Dynamic Host Configuration Protocol (DHCP) server when it needs to be connected to the network.

Dynamic Memory A Hyper-V function that allows for memory to be pooled within a host. As VMs require more memory, Hyper-V allocates additional memory by taking it from an underutilized or overcommitted VM.

Dynamically expanding disk A VHD type that starts small and expands automatically to accommodate data growth. Useful for testing and development.

Easy Print Driver A universal cross platform compatible used to simplify driver management when using Remote Desktop Services.

Enhanced Session Mode   A Hyper-V feature that supports redirecting of local resources such as keyboard, video, mouse, audio, printers, clipboard, USB devices, drives, plug-and-play devices, and so on to a VM session.

Exclusion   A range of IP addresses within a scope that is configured to not be leased by DHCP to clients. Typically, these are IP addresses of computers such as servers configured with static or reserved IP addresses.

Executable rule   A default AppLocker rule that enables you to control classic executable programs (as opposed to the newer Windows 8 packaged apps) that are typically located in the Program Files default folder.

Failover   Failover refers to the NIC Teaming concept of using multiple links in an Active/Passive configuration. If the active link fails, the passive link is promoted to an active state allowing data to continue to flow.

Feature   An optional component that adds a specific function such as Network Load Balancing.

Features on Demand   A new ability of Windows Server 2012 and Windows Server 2012 R2 that enables you to preserve space by completely removing roles and features along with source files from the operating system.

File and Storage Services role   A server role that provides utilities that enable you to manage files, folders, and other shared resources. It's installed by default when you install Windows Server 2012 R2.

Filter action   A configured set of actions within a firewall rule that determines whether the firewall will permit or block traffic attempting to cross it. You can also select an option to negotiate security based on several IPsec criteria, including whether encryption is used.

Filtering   A Group Policy option that enables you to limit the effect of a GPO according to definitions such as security group membership or Windows Management Instrumentation (WMI).

Fine-grained password policies   A feature of Windows Server 2012 R2 that enables you to configure password policies which apply only to specific users or groups within a domain.

Firewall   A system designed to prevent unauthorized access to or from a private network. This can be either a dedicated hardware device or a software program installed on a server or client computer.

Firewall profile   A means of grouping firewall rules so they apply to the affected computers dependent on where the computer is connected.

Firewall rule A set of conditions used by Windows Firewall to determine whether a particular type of communication is permitted. You can configure inbound rules, outbound rules, and connection security rules from the Windows Firewall with Advanced Security snap-in or from Group Policy.

Fixed Provisioning An option configured while creating a virtual hard disk. The size specified for the virtual disk is allocated and committed at the time of creation.

Fixed-size disk A VHD type that uses a preconfigured disk size that allocates physical storage matching the size of the configured virtual disk from the point at which the disk is created.

Forest functional level The four forest functional levels are Windows Server 2008, Windows Server 2008 R2, Windows Server 2012, and Windows Server 2012 R2. The default forest functional level is Windows Server 2008. When the forest functional level is raised to Windows Server 2008 R2, Windows Server 2012, or Windows Server 2012 R2, advanced forest-wide Active Directory features are available according to the level chosen.

Forest root The first domain created in a forest.

Forward lookup query A DNS name-resolution process by which a hostname is resolved to an IP address.

Forwarding The relaying of a DNS request from one server to another one when the first server is unable to process the request.

Fully qualified domain name (FQDN) A DNS domain name that unambiguously describes the location of the host within a domain tree. An example of an FQDN would be the computer www.certguide.com.

Global group A global group can contain users from the same domain in which the global group is located, and global groups can be added to domain local groups to control access to network resources.

Global unicast IPv6 address An IPv6 address that uses a global routing prefix of 45 bits to identify a specific organization's network, a 16-bit subnet ID, and a 64-bit interface ID. These addresses are globally routable on the Internet and are equivalent to public IPv4 addresses.

GPT GUID partition table is a newer partition type that is used to create drives larger than 2 TB.

Group Policy The Windows Server 2012 R2 feature that allows for policy creation, which affects domain users and computers. Policies can be anything from desktop settings to application assignments to security settings and more.

Group Policy Management Console (GPMC)   The MMC snap-in from which you can perform all management activities on GPOs, including such functions as creating and linking GPOs, modifying their inheritance, disabling or deleting them, and so on.

Group Policy Management Editor   The Microsoft Management Console (MMC) snap-in used to modify the settings of a Group Policy object.

Group Policy object (GPO)   A collection of policies that apply to a specific target, such as the domain itself (Default Domain Policy) or an OU. GPOs are modified through the Group Policy Management Editor to define policy settings.

Guest   Refers to the virtual machine that runs on a specific physical host.

Guest Integration Services   A suite of services available for installation after a virtual machine has been created. Guest Integration Services improve virtual machine performance to provide a more "physical-like" feel.

Hash rule   A software restriction policy rule that identifies software to be allowed or prohibited according to a hash, which is a fixed-length series of bytes that uniquely identifies the application.

Host (Hyper-V)   Refers to the physical server that provides physical resources such as CPU and memory to virtual machines.

Host (Network)   Any computing device that has been assigned an IP address.

Host bus adapter (HBA)   The interface card that enables Hyper-V hosts to connect to and communicate with storage area networks.

Hostname   In DNS, the first or most specific name assigned to an individual computer.

Hyper-V   Microsoft's version of a hypervisor or Virtual Machine Manager. Hyper-V can be installed as a role under Windows Server 2012/R2, or it can be installed as a standalone server.

Hyper-V Network Virtualization   Hyper-V Network Virtualization (HNV) is the infrastructure responsible for creating shared computing environments using Hyper-V.

Hypervisor   The mechanism that is responsible for managing virtual machines.

Install from Media (IFM)   An option that enables you to install a domain controller from a series of files created from an existing domain controller in the domain. This option is helpful when deploying domain controllers at branch sites because it minimizes the amount of data that must be replicated from an existing domain controller.

Internet Protocol (IP)   A TCP/IP protocol that handles, addresses, and routes packets between hosts on a network. It performs this service for all other protocols in the TCP/IP protocol suite.

Intra-Site Automatic Tunnel Addressing Protocol (ISATAP)   A tunneling technology that enables unicast IPv6 connectivity between IPv6/IPv4 hosts over an IPv4 intranet.

IP address   A logical address that is used to identify both a host and a network segment. Each network adapter on an IP network requires a unique IP address.

IP Security (IPsec)   A suite of protocols that provide a mechanism for data integrity, authentication, and privacy for the Internet Protocol. IPsec can provide message authentication and/or encryption.

IP version 4 (IPv4)   The version of the Internet Protocol that has been in use for many years and provides a 32-bit address space formatted as four octets separated by periods.

IP version 6 (IPv6)   A newer version of the Internet Protocol that provides a 128-bit address space formatted as eight 16-bit blocks, each of which is portrayed as a 4-digit hexadecimal number and is separated from other blocks by colons.

ipconfig   The command-line utility that provides detailed information about the IP configuration of a Windows computer's network adapters.

IPv4-compatible address   An IPv6 address represented in the form 0:0:0:0:0:0:w.x.y.z, where w.x.y.z is the IPv4 address in dotted-decimal. This enables communication between IPv4 and IPv6 networks.

IPv4-mapped address   An IPv4-only node is represented as ::ffff:.w.x.y.z to an IPv6 node. Used only for internal representation.

ISATAP   A tunneling technology that enables unicast IPv6 connectivity between IPv6/IPv4 hosts over an IPv4 intranet. You do not need to perform any manual configuration actions on an ISATAP host.

Iterative query   A DNS query that gives the best answer it currently has back as a response. The best answer is the address being sought or an address of a server that would have a better idea of its address.

Ldifde   A utility that enables you to import data formatted in the LDAP Data Interchange Format (LDIF) format to the AD DS database. You can use this tool to automate the creation of user, computer, or group accounts.

Lease   A predefined interval of time for which an IP address obtained from a DHCP server is valid. The lease must be renewed before this time interval expires for the client to continue using it.

Link local IPv6 address   A type of IPv6 address used for communication between neighboring nodes on the same link. Equivalent to IPv4 addresses configured using APIPA.

Linked policy   A Group Policy that exists in one object and is linked to another object. Linked policies are used to reduce administrative duplication in applying the same policies to multiple OUs.

Load Balancing   Load balancing is a function of NIC Teaming and also a concept in which network traffic is split across multiple links to provide increased throughput.

Local printer   A printer that is connected directly to a computer.

Local user account   A user account stored in the Security Accounts Manager (SAM) of a member server or client computer. Such an account can be used to log on to that computer only and does not possess any domain privileges.

Location-aware printing   A printer setting that enables a user with a portable computer to print to a printer physically located close to her computer; for example, to the home printer when at the home location or to the office printer when in the office.

MAC Address   Media Access Control (MAC) Address refers to the layer 2 address assigned to a network adapter.

Managed Address Configuration (M) flag   A parameter that determines when DHCPv6 is used to obtain IPv6 stateful addresses. When set to 0, DHCPv6 is not used and stateless addresses are obtained. When set to 1, DHCPv6 is used to assign stateful addresses to IPv6 clients.

MBR   Master Boot Record is an older partition type that is used to create drives up to 2 TB.

MMC   Microsoft Management Console is a collection of management tools known as snap-ins that are organized under a single management tool. The tool is used for both local and remote administration.

Mount   Refers to the task of attaching a drive to the operating system so that its contents can be accessed.

Multicast   The technology that enables the sender to send a single transmission to the multicast address and the routers take care of making copies and sending them to all receivers that have registered their interest in data from that sender.

Multicast IPv6 address   An IPv6 address that enables the delivery of packets to each of multiple interfaces.

Multipath I/O (MPIO)   An advanced feature that enables guests to take advantage of redundant links to access storage area networks.

Nesting   The act of creating a hierarchy of groups to provide users from different containers (domains, OUs, and so on) access to the resources they require for their jobs.

Network File System (NFS)   Technology that enables UNIX to share files and applications across the network.

Network Interface layer   The bottom layer of the TCP/IP protocol stack, it provides an interface for the Internet layer to the network media. This layer controls the way frames are ultimately built and sent out on to the network media or received from the network media and sent to the upper layers.

Network printer   A printer that is equipped with its own network adapter card and connected to the network.

Network zone rule   A software restriction policy rule that identifies software to be allowed or prohibited according to a network zone as described by Microsoft Internet Explorer.

New Technology File System (NTFS)   The file system originally provided with Windows NT and present in modern server versions that supports volume mounting, compression, encryption, and security.

NIC Team (virtual)   In addition to physical NIC Teams, Windows Server 2012/2012 R2 allow you to create a *virtual* NIC team using up to two virtual network adapters up to two virtual network switches.

NTFS permissions   The security feature available in NTFS that allows you to grant or deny various levels of access to files and folders on NTFS-formatted volumes.

Offline domain join   An action in which you use the `djoin.exe` command to create metadata that will enable a new computer to automatically join a domain and then add this metadata to the installation files to enable the domain join to take place on installation of the operating system.

Offline files   A feature built in to Windows Server 2012 R2/Windows 8/8.1 that enables you to cache locally stored copies of shared files and folders, so that you can work with them while offline and resynchronize your changes when you go back online.

Other Stateful Configuration (O) flag   A parameter that determines how additional IPv6 configuration parameters are obtained. This includes such settings as the IPv6 addresses of DNS servers.

Packaged app rule   A default AppLocker rule that enables you to control the use of packaged apps (which are apps that include all the required files within an app package) on computers running Windows 8 or Windows Server 2012 R2.

Pass-through disk   A virtual disk method used to enable the virtual operating system to access a physical disk on the host directly. The guest is granted exclusive access to the physical disk.

Password complexity   A rule that can be applied using Group Policy to prevent users from employing simple, easy-to-guess passwords. The default password complexity requires at least three of the following four groups: lowercase letters, uppercase letters, numerals, and special characters.

Password policy   Policy settings in a domain-based GPO that specify the requirements for passwords in the domain.

Password Settings object (PSO)   An object class defined in the AD DS schema that holds attributes for the fine-grained password and account lockout policy settings.

Path rule   A software restriction policy rule that identifies software to be allowed or prohibited according to the local or UNC path to the application's executable files. The path rule enables you to grant or deny access to software located in a specific folder for each user.

Preboot Execution Environment (PXE)   A bootable ROM chip contained on compatible network interface cards that enables client computers without an operating system to boot and connect to the network for locating a WDS server.

Print device   The hardware device that produces the printed output.

Print driver   The program that converts graphics commands into instructions a given type of print device can understand.

Print driver isolation   The capability of the print service in Windows Server 2012 R2 that improves the reliability of the print service by enabling print drivers to run in separate processes from the print spooler process.

Print pooling   The act of setting up two or more physical printers (print devices), each associated with a single printer.

Print queue   The series of documents that have been scheduled to print to a specific printer.

Print server   Any computer on which printers have been configured. This can include a client computer such as Windows 8.1, as well as a Windows Server 2012 R2 or older server computer.

Print spooler   An area on a computer's hard drive where documents to be printed are stored while awaiting printing. The spooler software formats the documents so that the associated printer can print them properly.

Printer   The software interface between the operating system and the print device that determines various aspects of the printing process.

Printer pool   A set of two or more identical print devices associated with a single printer.

Printer priority   A number from one to 99 that determines which document is printed first. Printers with a higher priority print their documents first.

Private IPv4 network   An IPv4 network that can be accessed only within a corporation and cannot be accessed from the public Internet. Private IPv4 networks can be configured with one of the following network addresses—10.0.0.0/8, 172.16.0.0/16, or 192.168.0.0/24.

Protected Admin   An administrative user account other than the default domain administrator, which operates normally with ordinary user rights and asks for confirmation of any administrative task by displaying a User Account Control (UAC) prompt.

Provider Address Space   Refers to the hardware and shared computing environment that the hosting company or IT department within a company owns.

PVLAN   Port Virtual Local Area Network (PVLAN) is a concept similar to VLANs that allows you isolate specific virtual machines on a port basis on the virtual switch.

Quota   A specific limit configured. Disk quotas are used to limit user data stored on servers with the use of NTFS quotas.

RAID   Redundant Array of Independent (or Inexpensive) Disks. Provides advanced storage capabilities to increase performance and/or hardware resiliency.

Read-only domain controller (RODC)   A Windows Server 2012 R2 feature in which the domain controller is installed with a read-only directory database. You cannot perform any directory updates directly from the RODC. It is especially suitable in reduced security environments such as branch offices.

Recursion   The name-resolution technique wherein a DNS server queries other DNS servers on behalf of the requesting client to obtain the required FQDN, which it returns to the client.

Remote Server Administration Tools (RSAT)   A series of Windows Server 2012 R2 administrative utilities that you can download from Microsoft and install on a Windows 8.1 computer. RSAT enables you to perform most server administrative actions from your desktop computer, including some of the management actions on older Windows Server computers.

Reservation An IP address configured so that DHCP always assigns it to a specific DHCP client.

Resource Metering A process that tracks virtual machine resource usage for reporting purposes.

Reverse lookup query A DNS name-resolution process by which an IP address is resolved to a hostname.

Role A specific function that a server performs on the network such as a file server or terminal server.

Role Service A role service is a component of a role that focuses on providing a specific function to support the specific role.

Root hints A list of the names and IP addresses of DNS servers that are authoritative for the Internet root domains. Used by a DNS server to forward queries for Internet domains that it is unable to resolve from its own database.

RSAT Remote Server Administration Tools are a collection of tools used to administer and manage servers, especially Server Core installations, remotely.

Sconfig.cmd A text-based Windows Server 2012 R2 Server Core utility that enables you to configure a series of common Server Core properties.

Script rule A default AppLocker rule that enables you to control who is able to run scripts such as `*.js`, `*.ps1`, `*.vbs`, `*.cmd`, and `*.bat` files.

Security Configuration Wizard A Windows Server 2012 R2 tool that enables you to create or modify security policies applied to servers in your AD DS domain or OU.

Security identifier (SID) A number that uniquely identifies a user, group, or computer account. Every account is issued one when created, and if the account is later deleted and re-created with the same name, it will have a different SID. Once an SID is used in a domain, it can never be used again.

Server Core A feature of Windows Server 2012 R2 that enables you to install a minimal version of the server without a GUI, Start screen, taskbar, or many ancillary components. A Server Core computer can hold most of the roles that an ordinary Windows Server 2012 R2 computer holds, but with a smaller network footprint and fewer points of attack.

Server Manager A Windows Server 2012 R2 management utility that enables you to perform a large range of management tools on your server or other servers on the network.

Server Message Block (SMB)   A network file sharing protocol that enables applications to read and write data and request information from programs on network servers.

Shared folder permissions   The security feature available when sharing files and folders across a network that allows you to grant or deny access rights to network users.

Shared folders   Folders that are made available for access by users who are working at another computer on the network.

Smart Paging   A Hyper-V function that allows for temporary paging of virtual machine memory to a disk.

Snapshot   Refers to the concept of creating a point-in-time copy of a file or virtual machine.

Software restriction policies   A series of settings included in Group Policy that you can use to limit the types of software that can be run on any computer running Windows XP or later. You can limit users to running only those applications they need to do their jobs, and you can prevent malicious applications from installing or running.

Starter GPOs   Sets of preconfigured Administrative Template policy settings, including comments, which you can use for ease of creating new GPOs. When you use a Starter GPO to create a new GPO, the new GPO includes all settings, their values, comments, and delegation as defined in the Starter GPO.

Stateful address configuration   A type of IPv6 address autoconfiguration that uses a stateful address configuration protocol such as DHCPv6 to obtain non–link-local addresses and other IPv6 configuration parameters.

Stateful firewall   A firewall that monitors the state of active connections and uses the information gained to determine which network packets are allowed through the firewall. Packets sent by an outside computer attempting to communicate with a computer protected by a stateful firewall are dropped unless the packet or protocol was granted access by an access control list (ACL).

Stateless address configuration   A type of IPv6 address autoconfiguration that uses Router Advertisement messages to configure link-local addresses and additional addresses by exchanging Router Solicitation and Router Advertisement messages with neighboring routers.

Static IP address   An IP address that is permanently assigned to a computer on the network.

Storage Pool   Grouping of physical disks for the purpose of combining or pooling available storage.

Storage Quality of Service (QoS)   A new feature for Server 2012 R2 that enables administrators to monitor and control virtual disk performance.

storage space   A portion of an overall storage pool that is defined by the size of a virtual disk.

Subnet mask   A set of numbers, 32 bits in length, that begins with 1s and ends with 0s in binary notation. The number of 1s represents the number of bits that are considered the subnet address. The bits that are 0s are the host address. Using a subnet mask, you can create more subnets with a smaller number of computers per subnet. All computers on a given subnet must have the same subnet mask. Using dotted decimal notation, a subnet mask is written as 255.255.0.0 (which is the default mask for a Class B address).

Subnetting   A process that enables you to reconfigure which portion of the subnet mask constitutes the network portion and which portion constitutes the computer portion.

Synchronizing files   The act of copying files from a shared folder on the network to an offline files cache on a computer, or copying the same files back to the shared folder after a user has modified them.

Task Scheduler   A tool used to schedule and automate tasks to perform a specific function at a specific time.

Template account   A special account created for the sole purpose of copying as needed when creating a large number of user accounts with similar privileges.

Tenant   Refers to a specific customer that owns or rents resources from the shared computing environment.

Teredo   A tunneling communication protocol that enables IPv6 connectivity between IPv6/IPv4 nodes across network address translation (NAT) interfaces, thereby improving connectivity for newer IPv6-enabled applications on IPv4 networks.

Thin Provisioning   An option configured while creating a virtual hard disk. The virtual hard disk starts small and grows as data is written. The virtual hard disk file grows up to the size of the physical disk containing it.

Transmission Control Protocol (TCP)   A TCP/IP protocol that provides connection-oriented, reliable communication between two hosts, typically involving large amounts of data.

Universal group   An Active Directory security group that can be used anywhere within a domain tree or forest.

User Account Control (UAC)   Starting with Windows Vista and continued in Windows 7/8/8.1 and Windows Server 2008/R2/2012/R2, UAC is a security feature designed to protect your computer from unauthorized changes by alerting you of pending administrative actions. UAC displays a prompt that requests approval when you want to perform an administrative task. If malicious software attempts to install itself or perform undesirable actions, you will receive a prompt that you can use to prevent such actions from occurring.

User class   An options class used to differentiate clients according to their type, such as desktop, laptop, or server computer.

User Datagram Protocol (UDP)   A TCP/IP protocol that provides fast, non–connection-oriented communications with no guarantee of delivery and no error checking.

User logon name   The name employed by a user to log on to a domain. AD DS uses this name and its associated password to authenticate the user.

User principal name (UPN)   An alternative username formatted in a manner similar to that of an email address (for example, user@domain.com). Its use enables a user to more easily log on to a domain in the forest other than the domain to which the user belongs.

User principal name (UPN) suffix   The portion of the UPN following the "@" character. By default, this is the DNS domain name of the domain in which the user account is located. However, you can define an alternative UPN suffix that enables you to conceal the actual domain structure of the forest or match the user's email address domain name.

User rights   A default set of capabilities assigned to built-in groups in AD DS that define what members of these groups can and cannot do on the network.

Vendor class   An options class used to identify a client's vendor type and configuration when obtaining a DHCP lease. You can use the vendor class ID option (code 60) to specify vendor classes.

VHD   Virtual hard disk refers to the formatting of a virtual hard drive. VHDs are available in legacy VHD format or the newer Server 2012 R2 VHDX format, which provides support for larger drives.

Virtual fibre channel adapter   The virtual interface that enables communication between the guest, Hyper-V host, and storage area networks.

Virtual SAN   The mechanism used to identify a specific physical SAN by name and associate the connection to it with one or more Host Bus Adapters installed on the Hyper-V host.

VSS Volume Shadow Services refers to the infrastructure required to create copies of files on your server for the purpose of quick restores of previous versions.

Windows Azure A cloud-based computing infrastructure that enables you to build, deploy, and manage services and applications including Active Directory throughout a global network.

Windows Firewall The personal firewall software incorporated in Windows Vista/7/8/8.1/Server 2008/R2/2012/R2 that filters incoming TCP/IP traffic. Windows Firewall was first introduced in Windows XP SP2.

Windows Firewall with Advanced Security A Microsoft Management Console (MMC) snap-in that provides enhanced firewall management capabilities, including the ability to create firewall rules that are specifically configured to protect a specific type or source/destination path of network traffic.

Windows Installer rule A default AppLocker rule that enables you to control the installation of applications packaged into Windows Installer `.msi` files, as well as their transforms (`*.mst`) and patch (`*.msp`) files.

Windows Management Instrumentation (WMI) A Windows Server 2012 R2 management infrastructure for monitoring and controlling system resources.

Windows PowerShell An enhanced task-based command-line scripting interface that enables you to perform a large number of server management tasks. You can create scripts that enable automated management of large numbers of servers at the same time.

WinRM Windows Remote Management is Microsoft's version of the WS-Management protocol.

WinRS Windows Remote Shell is the client component used to executed commands against a server running the Windows Remote Management service.

Work Folders A new role service in the Windows Server 2012 R2 File and Storage Services server role that enables users to access data on a file server from any remote location without the need for a VPN connection.

Index

Numbers

A

G

N

P

Z